MW01065504

NSTRUCTOR'S SOLUTIONS MANUAL

M&N Toscano

APPLIED STATISTICS

FOR ENGINEERS AND SCIENTISTS

Using Microsoft Excel® and MINITAB®

David M. Levine | Patricia P. Ramsey | Robert K. Smidt

Prentice Hall

Upper Saddle River, NJ 07458

Executive Editor: Kathy Boothby Sestak
Supplement Editor: Joanne Wendelken
Special Projects Manager: Barbara A. Murray
Production Editor: Benjamin St. Jacques
Supplement Cover Manager: Paul Gourhan
Supplement Cover Designer: PM Workshop Inc.
Manufacturing Buyer: Lisa McDowell

Printed in the United States of America

10 9 8 7 6 5 4 3 2 1

ISBN 0-13-027423-2

Prentice-Hall International (UK) Limited, London
Prentice-Hall of Australia Pty. Limited, Sydney
Prentice-Hall Canada, Inc., Toronto
Prentice-Hall Hispanoamericana, S.A., Mexico
Prentice-Hall of India Private Limited, New Delhi
Pearson Education Asia Pte. Ltd., Singapore
Prentice-Hall of Japan, Inc., Tokyo
Editora Prentice-Hall do Brazil, Ltda., Rio de Janeiro

Contents

chapter 1

Introduction to Statistics and Quality Improvement

1. (a) discrete; however, if the question were the time it takes to read a page in this text; the answer would be continuous
   (b) discrete (c) continuous (d) discrete
   (e) discrete (f) continuous

2. From weakest to strongest, the correct order is: nominal, ordinal, interval, ratio levels of measurement. The answers will vary.

3. (a) Place of residence: Morristown, New Jersey—is not a continuous variable; nominal scale.
   (b) Type of residence: Single family home—is not a continuous variable; nominal scale.
   (c) Date of birth: August 13, 1966—is not a continuous variable; interval scale.
   (d) Projected monthly payments: $2,479—is a continuous variable (although, in practice, the exactness of measurements is limited by conventions of rounding monetary amounts to the nearest cent); ratio scale.
   (e) Occupation: Director of Food Chemistry— is not a continuous variable; nominal scale.
   (f) Employer: Venus Candy Company—is not a continuous variable; nominal scale.
   (g) Number of years at jobs: 10—is not a continuous variable; ratio scale.
   (h) Annual income: $140,000—is a continuous variable (see comment in part d); ratio scale.
   (i) Amount of mortgage requested: $220,000—is a continuous variable (see comment in part d); ratio scale.
   (j) Term of mortgage: 15 years—is a continuous variable; ratio scale. Note: If we were to assume that mortgages can be given only on a *whole* number of months or years, then it would not be a continuous variable.

4. (a) attribute measure (b) variables measure (c) variables measure
   (d) attribute measure (e) attribute measure (f) variables measure

5. (a) variables measure (b) variables measure (c) attribute measure
   (d) attribute measure (e) variables measure (f) attribute measure

6. Answers will vary.

7. Answers will vary.

8. (a) systematic random sample (b) convenience sample (c) simple random sample

9. (a) Sample without replacement: You need to select a two-digit number inside the range of 01 to 97 each time. Starting at row 12, column 1 the first ten 2 digit numbers obtained from Row 12 are:
   39 08 77 19 38 40 35 55 43 24.
   All two-digit numbers obtained from row 12 fall inside the range of 01 to 97 and are thus selected.
   (b) Sample with replacement: Because none of the numbers selected in Part A occur twice within the sample, this sample: 39, 08, 77, 19, 38, 40, 35, 55, 43, 24 is the answer to both (a) and (b).
   (c) The results are the same, because, in this series of numbers, no two digit numbers occurred more than once. Note: if you were asked to draw a sample of $n = 11$, then you would see a difference between the two results. The eleventh two-digit number is 08, which would be selected in (b) and would not be selected in (a) because 08 was the second selection.

10. (a) Sample without replacement: Starting in column 1, row 5, you need to select a four-digit number inside the range 0001 to 5000 each time.
The numbers are:
3385 3781 3908 1475 3216 2323 4579 0989
1110 3684 2391 0687 1247 2758 1669
(Numbers 7054 and 8938 were discarded as they were outside the range).
(b) Same with replacement: The sample obtained in Part A is the answer to both (a) and (b) because none of the selected numbers in Part B occur twice within the sample.
(c) There is no difference between the results in (a) and (b) because none of the 15 selected numbers occur twice within the sample.

11. (a) quality of design (b) quality of conformance (c) quality of design
(d) quality of conformance (e) quality of performance (f) quality of performance
(g) quality of design
Note that (b) and (d) could also result in poor quality performance: the cake is burned—cannot be used or the bearings are too small or too large to fit into a wheel—cannot be used.

12. *Descriptive statistics* consists of methods dealing with the collection, tabulation, summarization, and presentation of data. *Inferential statistics* consists of methods that permit one to reach conclusions and make estimates about a population based on information from a sample.

13. A *population* consists of *all* members of a class or category of interest. A *sample* is some portion or subset of a population.

14. A *parameter* is a summary measure of the individual observations made in a census of an entire *population.* A *statistic* is a summary measure of the individual observations made by evaluation of a sample.

15. *Discrete variables* are countable as there is a gap between each possible value.
Continuous variables can take any numerical value within a continuum or an interval.

16. In order from the weakest to the strongest, the four levels of measurement are nominal, ordinal, interval and ratio scales.

17. *Attribute measures* either are nominal variables based on counts or involve proportions calculated from discrete data.
Variables measures are any continuous variables measured on an interval or ratio scale.

18. An operational definition defines a characteristic of an object or event by the active process or by a set of operations by which the characteristic is evaluated. An operational definition is important because its meaning conveys precisely the same information to different individuals and it remains static over time.

19. A probability sampling is one in which the probability of selecting an element from a population for inclusion in the sample is known. In nonprobability sampling, this probability is not known.

20. *Quality of design* refers to the intentional differences between products or services that are included in the design by an engineer or planner.
Quality of conformance refers to the degree to which a product or service conforms to, meets, or exceeds the standards set forth by the design specifications.
Quality of performance refers to the long-term consistent functioning of the product and the related product characteristics of reliability, safety, serviceability, and maintainability.

21. Quality management views the management's role as managing the process; traditional managerial approach views management's role as the managing of people (i.e., motivating, disciplining and rewarding).

22. The first step is *planning*. Planning is based on data collected to determine customer needs and the characteristics of quality that customers deem important. The second step is *doing*. This involves the implementation of the plan set forth in step 1. During implementation, careful attention must be given to operational definitions and specifications described in the plan. The third step is *studying*. This step involves evaluating the process and the output of the process. The fourth step is acting. In this step, examination of the data collected in step three will suggest an action to be taken to improve quality.

23. (a) It is a continuous numerical variable and represents a ratio scale. The distance between a supporting leg of one desk to the closest supporting leg of another desk measured in feet.
(b) It is a categorical variable and represents an ordinal scale. Desks are categorized as small, medium, large and extra large as evaluated by the office supply catalog. Alternatively, if the size is understood to be, for example, the volume of the desk in square inches, then it is a continuous numerical variable and represents a ratio scale.
(c) It is a categorical variable and represents a nominal scale. Gender is male or female, as self-reported by the office worker.
(d) It is a continuous numerical variable and represents a ratio scale. Time in minutes measured from the time the worker leaves home to the time he/she enters the office.
(e) It is a categorical variable and represents a nominal scale. Job classification, as defined in the office management bulletin.
(f) It is a continuous numerical variable and represents an interval scale if the temperature is measured on either the Celsius or Fahrenheit scale or a ratio scale if the temperature is measured on the Kelvin scale.
The answers will vary for all of the operational definitions.

24. (a) It is a continuous numerical variable and represents a ratio scale. The weight of an automobile measured in kilograms.
(b) It is a categorical variable and represents a nominal scale. Color as defined by the dealer's manual.
(c) It is a categorical variable and represents an ordinal scale. Automobiles are categorized as sub-compact, compact, midsize, and luxury as listed by the dealer. Alternatively, if the size is understood to be, for example, the volume of the car in square feet, then it is a continuous numerical variable and represents a ratio scale.
(d) It is a discrete numerical variable and represents a ratio scale. The cost of the car, as defined by the factory that produced it.
(e) It is a categorical variable and represents an ordinal scale. One star, two star, three star, four star or five star, as listed by the consumer organization.
(f) It is a categorical variable and represents an ordinal scale. Trunks are categorized as small, medium, large and extra large as evaluated by the consumer reports publication. Alternatively, if the size is understood to be, for example, the volume of the trunk in square inches, then it is a continuous numerical variable and represents a ratio scale
The answers will vary for all of the operational definitions.

25. (a) It is a continuous numerical variable and represents a ratio scale. Time in minutes measured from the time the student enters the bookstore until he/she passes through the exit door.
(b) It is a categorical variable and represents a nominal scale. Gender is male or female, as self-reported by the student.
(c) It is a categorical variable and represents an ordinal scale. Freshman, Sophomore, Junior, or Senior as defined in the school bulletin.
(d) It is a categorical variable and represents a nominal scale. Academic major, as defined in the school bulletin.
(e) It is a continuous numerical variable and represents an interval scale. Grade-point average as calculated by the registrar.
(f) It is a categorical variable and represents a nominal scale. Payment; defined as currency, personal check, or credit card.

(g) It is a discrete numerical variable and represents a ratio scale. Number of books, either paperback or hard-cover , as defined by the bookstore.
The answers will vary for all of the operational definitions.

26. Answers will vary. **27.** Answers will vary. **28.** Answers will vary.

chapter 2

Tables and Charts

1. Both the cause-and-effect diagram (fishbone) and the process flow diagram help to provide a clearer understanding of a process or a problem. The process diagram is used to show the flow of steps in a process from its beginning to its termination, whereas the cause and effect diagram can help to organize ideas and identify cause-and-effect relationships. In other words, a cause-and-effect diagram helps to identify factors that may be causing variability in the process output, whereas a process flow diagram serves as a road map for locating and solving problems and improving quality.

2. Answers will vary. **3.** Answers will vary. **4.** Answers will vary. **5.** Answers will vary.

6. Answers will vary.

7. (a) Time order plot using NOISE data table.

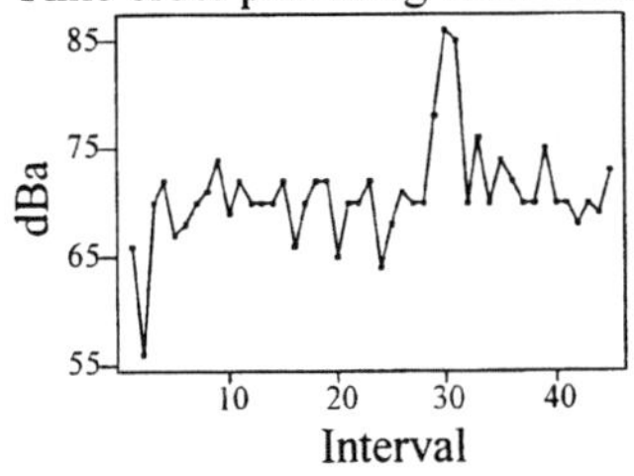

(b) The data appear to be relatively stable with no evidence of a pattern over time.

8. (a) Time order plot using TRANSDRM data table.

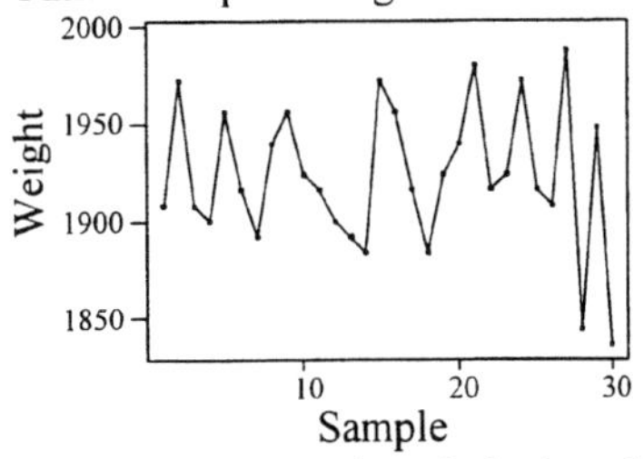

(b) The data appear to be relatively stable with no evidence of a pattern over time.

9. (a) Time order plot using RECWATER data table.

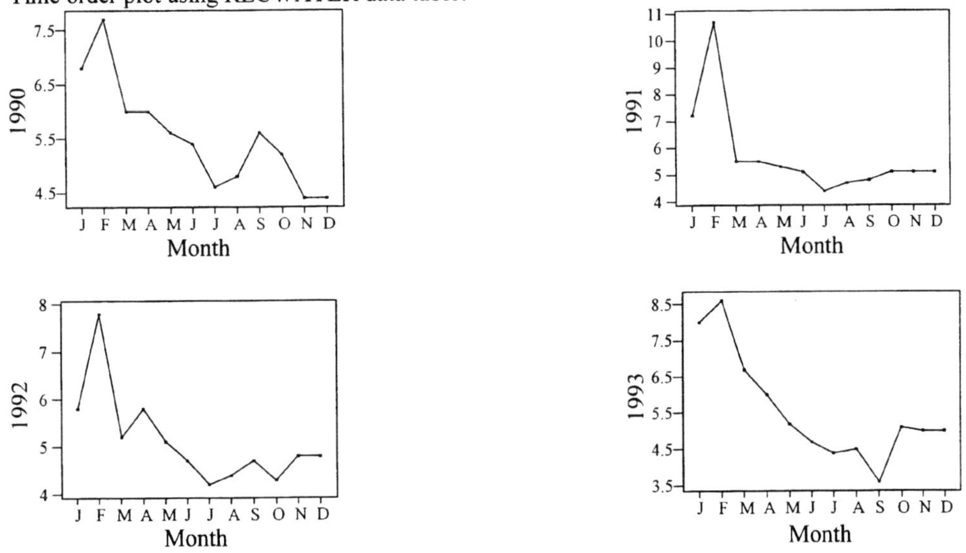

(b) The data are not relatively stable during the year. From these time-order plots a downward trend is evident in the monthly mean for the reclaimed water discharge.

10. (a) Time order plot using TRAFFIC data table.

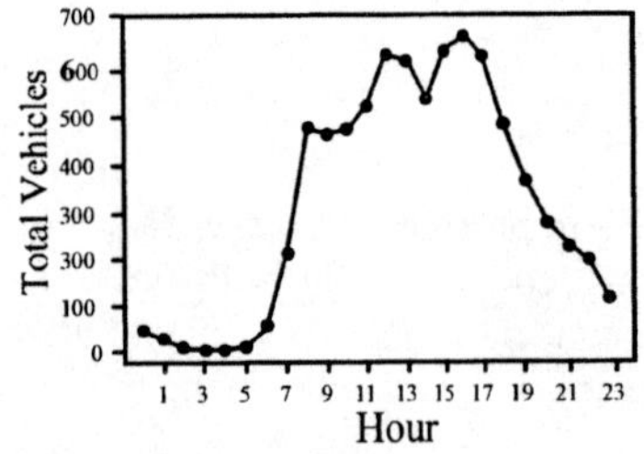

(b) The data are not relatively stable with the evident maximum during the working hours.

(c) It appears that one will encounter a problem when using this data set, because these data are not relatively stable.

11. Stem-and-leaf of C1, $N = 7$
Leaf Unit = 1.0

5	34
6	9
7	4
8	0
9	38

12. (a) 91, 94, 97, 100, 102, 102, 103, 108, 111, 113, 115, 115, 116, 116, 117, 117, 117, 122, 122, 123, 124, 128, 129, 130, 132

(b) 117 gallons of gasoline is most likely to be purchased.

(c)

Gallons	Frequency	Percentage
91–95	2	8.00
96–100	2	8.00
101–105	3	12.00
106–110	1	4.00
111–115	4	16.00
116–120	5	20.00
121–125	4	16.00
126–130	3	12.00
131–135	1	4.00

(d)

Gallons	Cumulative Frequency	Cumulative %
91–95	2	8.00
96–100	4	16.00
101–105	7	28.00
106–110	8	32.00
111–115	12	48.00
116–120	17	68.00
121–125	21	84.00
126–130	24	96.00
131–135	25	100.00

(e)

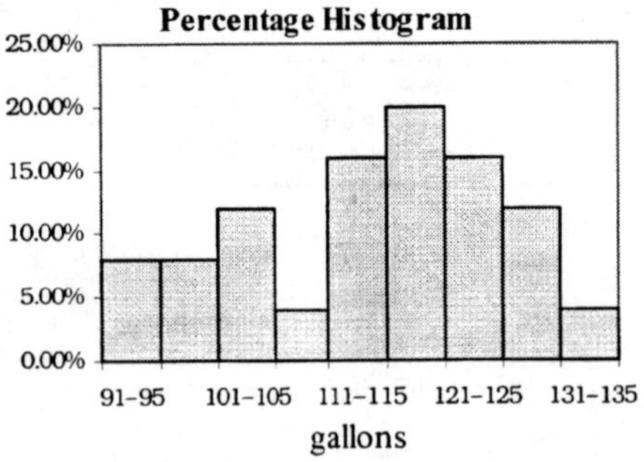

(f)

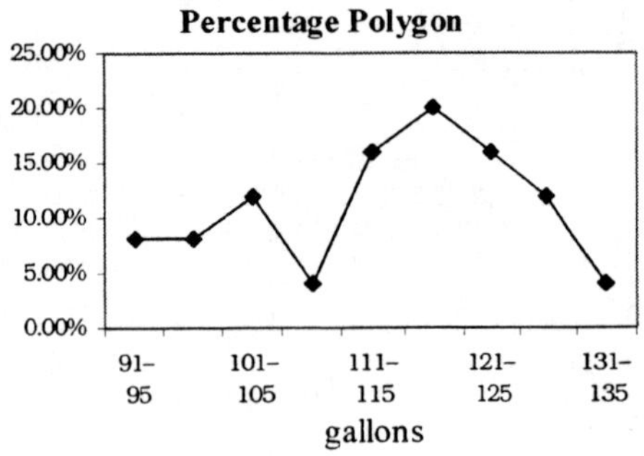

(g)

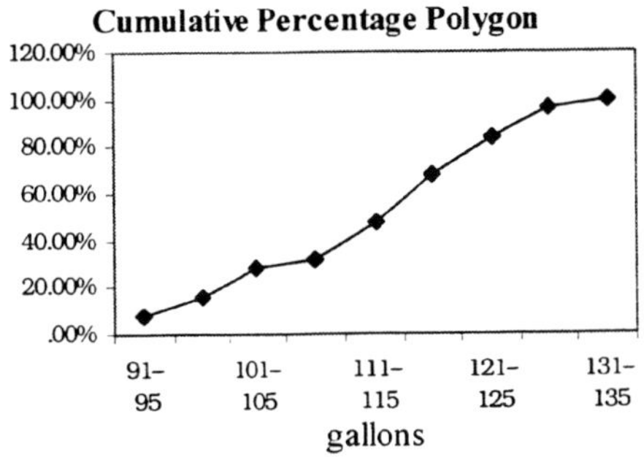

(h) Yes, there is some concentration between 115 and 125 gallons.

13. (a) and (b)

Manufacturer A:

Lengths of Life	Frequency
650–749	3
750–849	5
850–949	20
950–1049	9
1050–1149	3
1150–1249	0

Manufacturer B:

Lengths of Life	Frequency
650–749	0
750–849	2
850–949	8
950–1049	16
1050–1149	9
1150–1249	5

(c) Manufacturer A:

Lengths of Life	Frequency
650–699	2
700–749	1
750–799	1
800–849	4
850–899	9
900–949	11
950–999	5
1000–1049	4
1050–1099	3
1100–1149	0
1150–1199	0
1200–1249	0

Manufacturer B:

Lengths of Life	Frequency
650–699	0
700–749	0
750–799	0
800–849	2
850–899	2
900–949	6
950–999	6
1000–1049	10
1050–1099	6
1100–1149	3
1150–1199	4
1200–1249	1

(d) Manufacturer A:

Lengths of Life	Percentage
650–749	7.50%
750–849	12.50%
850–949	50.00%
950–1049	22.50%
1050–1149	7.50%
1150–1249	0.00%

Manufacturer B:

Lengths of Life	Percentage
650–749	0.00%
750–849	5.00%
850–949	20.00%
950–1049	40.00%
1050–1149	22.50%
1150–1249	12.50%

(e) Manufacturer A:

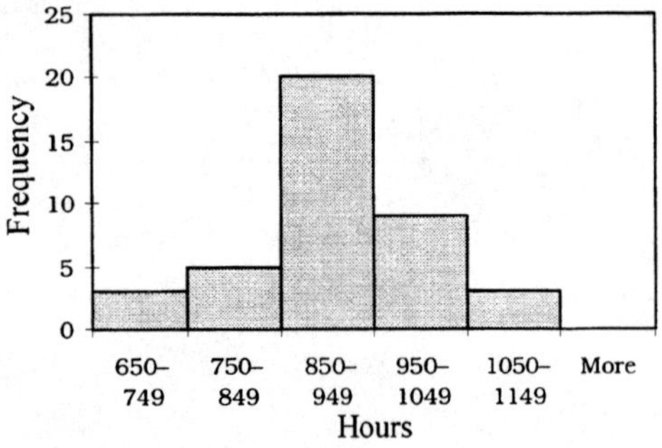

Manufacturer B:

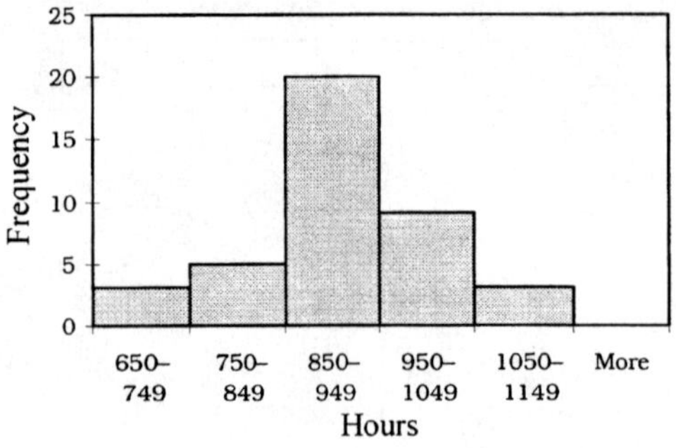

(f)

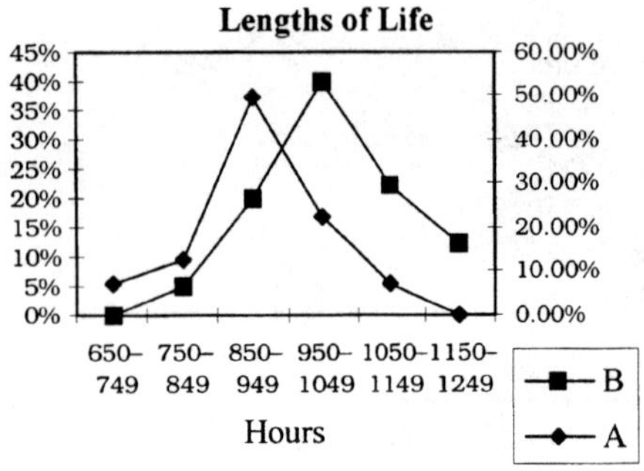

(g) Manufacturer A:

Lengths of Life	Cumulative Frequency
650–749	3
750–849	8
850–949	28
950–1049	37
1050–1149	40
1150–1249	40

Manufacturer B:

Lengths of Life	Cumulative Frequency
650–749	0
750–849	2
850–949	10
950–1049	26
1050–1149	35
1150–1249	40

(h) Manufacturer A:

Lengths of Life	Cumulative %
650–749	7.50
750–849	20.00
850–949	70.00
950–1049	92.50
1050–1149	100.00
1150–1249	0.00

Manufacturer B:

Lengths of Life	Cumulative %
650–749	0.00
750–849	5.00
850–949	25.00
950–1049	65.00
1050–1149	87.50
1150–1249	100.00

(i)

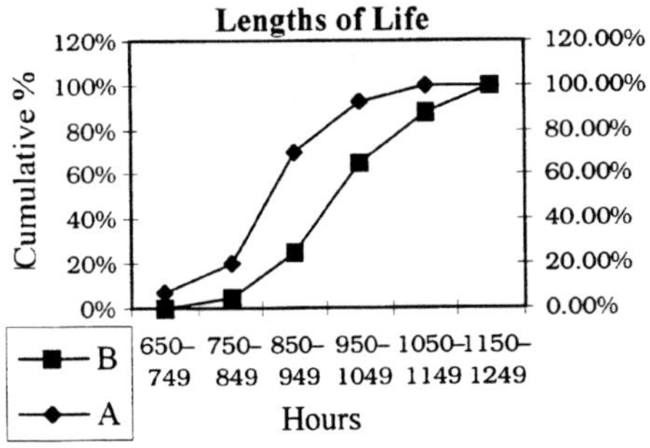

(j) Manufacturer B bulbs have a longer life. From part (d) A-lamps are concentrated in the 950 hr to 1050 hr range. B-lamps are concentrated between the 1050 hr and 1150 hr range. There are no B-lamps with shorter life than 750 hr, whereas 7.5% of A-lamps live less than 750 hr. In addition, one can see from (I), that A-lamp ogive is drawn to the left of the B-lamp ogive.

14. (a) Carnes 3-Way Diffusers: Stem-and-Leaf Display

Stem unit: 10

16	0
17	
18	0 0
19	0 0 5 5
20	0 0 5
21	0 5 5
22	0 5 5
23	0 5 5
24	0 0 0 5
25	0 0 0 0 0 5 5
26	5
27	0 0 0 5
28	0 0 5 5 5
29	0 0 5 5 5 5
30	0 0
31	0 0

Krueger 4-Way Diffusers Stem-and-Leaf Display

Stem unit: 10

19	0 5
20	0 0 5 5 5
21	
22	5 5 5 5 5 5
23	0 0 0 0 0 0 0
24	0 0 0 0 5 5 5
25	0 0 0 0 0 0 5 5
26	0 5 5 5
27	0 5 5 5 5 5 5
28	5
29	0
30	0 0

(b) Carnes 3-Way Diffusers:

cfm	Frequency
151–175	1
176–200	8
201–225	7
226–250	12
251–275	7
276–300	13
301–325	2
More	0

Krueger 4-Way Diffusers:

cfm	Frequency
151–175	0
176–200	4
201–225	9
226–250	20
251–275	13
276–300	4
301–325	0
More	0

(c) Carnes 3-Way Diffusers:

cfm	Percentage
151–175	2.00
176–200	16.00
201–225	14.00
226–250	24.00
251–275	14.00
276–300	26.00
301–325	4.00
More	0.00

Krueger 4-Way Diffusers:

cfm	Percentage
151–175	0.00
176–200	8.00
201–225	18.00
226–250	40.00
251–275	26.00
276–300	8.00
301–325	0.00
More	0.00

(d) Carnes 3-Way Diffusers:

cfm	Cumulative %
151–175	2.00
176–200	18.00
201–225	32.00
226–250	56.00
251–275	70.00
276–300	96.00
301–325	100.00
More	100.00

Krueger 4-Way Diffusers:

cfm	Cumulative %
151–175	.00
176–200	8.00
201–225	26.00
226–250	66.00
251–275	92.00
276–300	100.00
301–325	100.00
More	100.00

(e) Carnes 3-Way Diffusers:

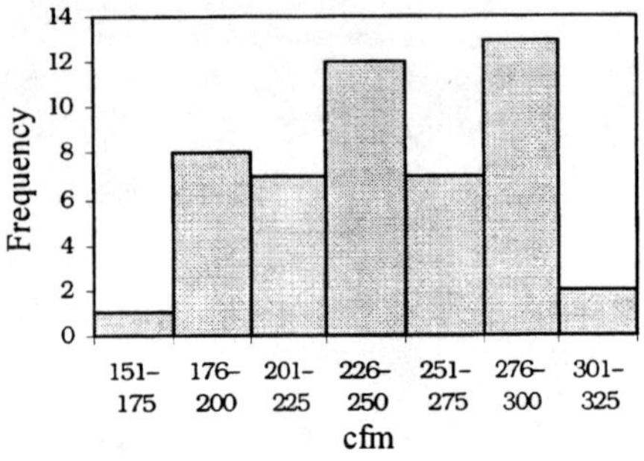

Krueger 4-Way Diffusers:

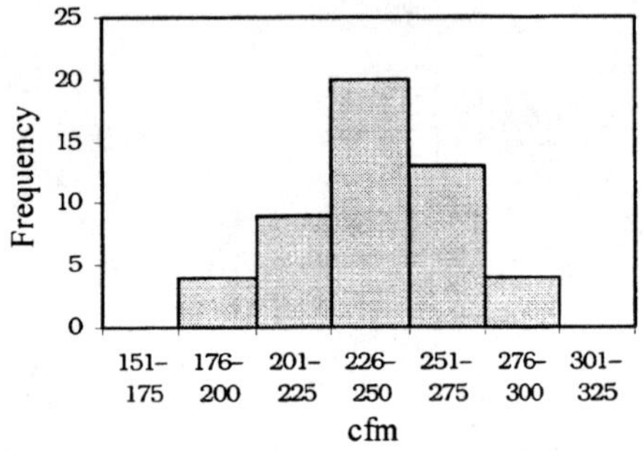

(f) Carnes 3-Way Diffusers:

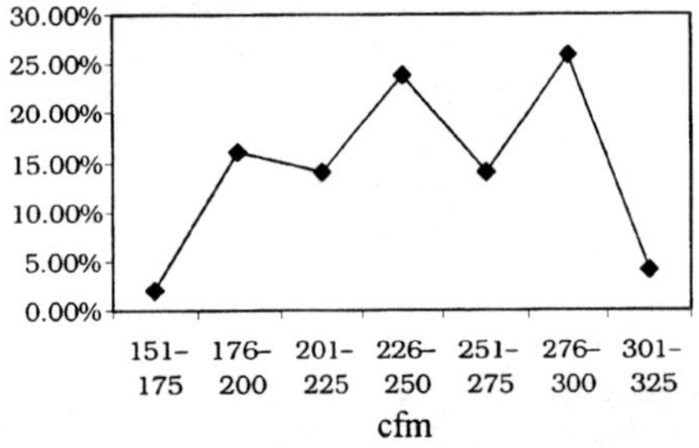

Krueger 4-Way Diffusers:

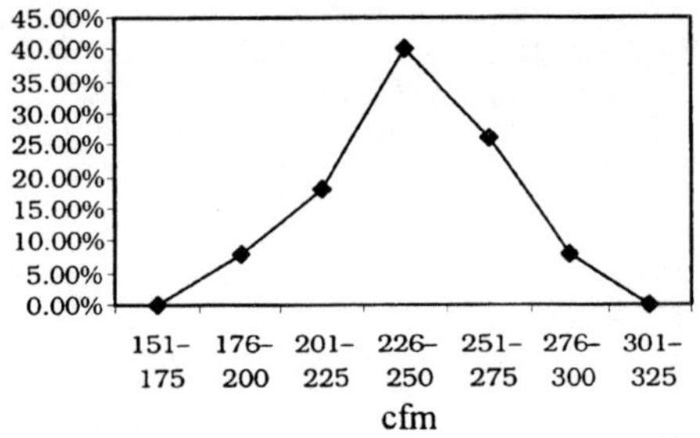

(g) Carnes 3-Way Diffusers:

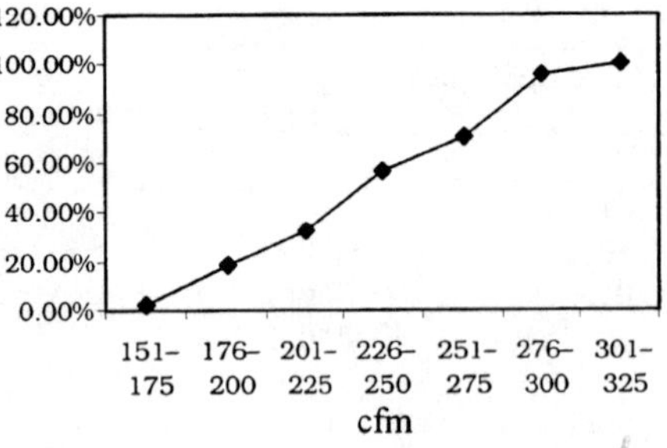

Krueger 4-Way Diffusers:

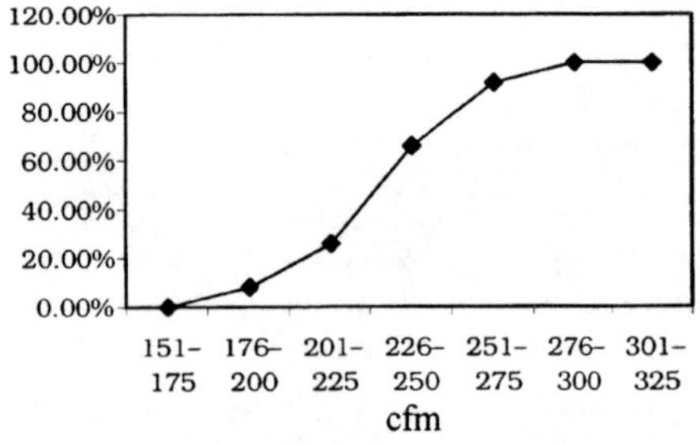

(h) Carnes 3-Way airflow has a larger distribution range. There are no diffusers in Krueger data with cfm less than 175 or more than 300, whereas 2% of Carnes' data have less cfm than 175 and 4% of them have more than 300. Krueger 4-Way Diffusers have only one extreme in the distribution, whereas Carnes' data have three extremes.

15. (a)

dB	Frequency
66.0–67.9	2
68.0–69.9	0
70.0–71.9	1
72.0–73.9	4
74.0–75.9	10
76.0–77.9	10
78.0–79.9	8
80.0–81.9	4
82.0–83.9	1

(b)

dB	Frequency
66.0–67.9	5.00
68.0–69.9	0.00
70.0–71.9	2.50
72.0–73.9	10.00
74.0–75.9	25.00
76.0–77.9	25.00
78.0–79.9	20.00
80.0–81.9	10.00
82.0–83.9	2.50

(c)

dB	Cumulative %
66.0–67.9	5.00
68.0–69.9	5.00
70.0–71.9	7.50
72.0–73.9	17.50
74.0–75.9	42.50
76.0–77.9	67.50
78.0–79.9	87.50
80.0–81.9	97.50
82.0–83.9	100.00

(d)

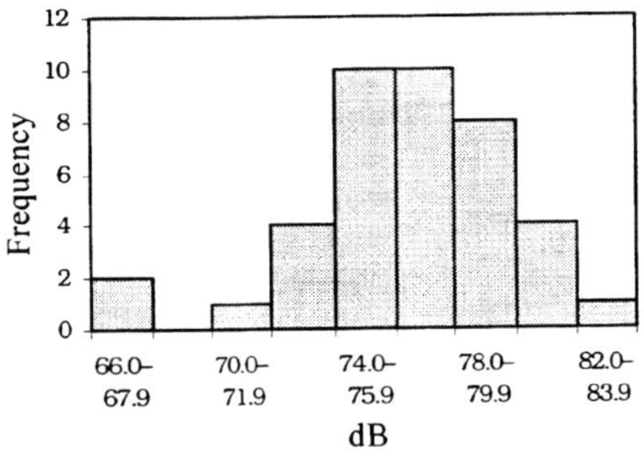

(e)

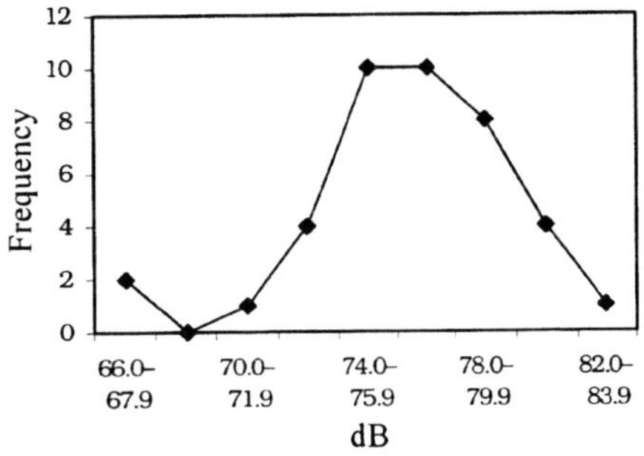

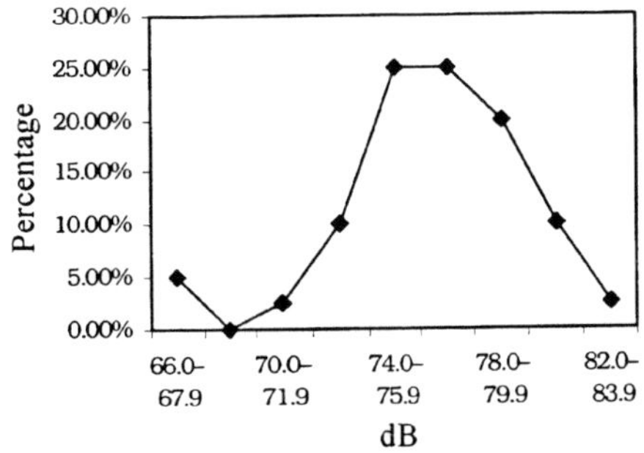

(f)

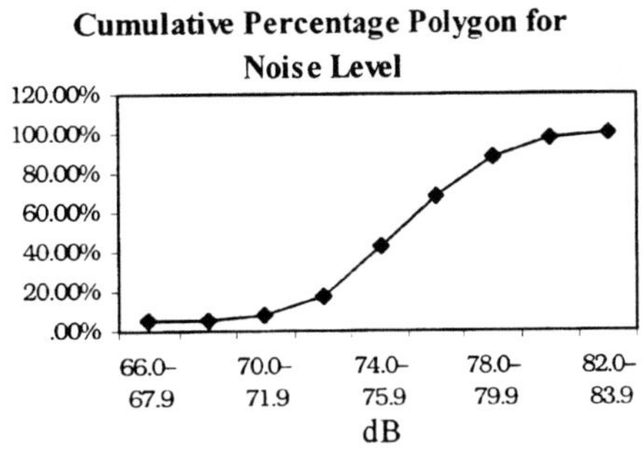

(g) The noise level data are concentrated in the 74 dB and 80 dB range. There is no sound level lower than 66 dB or higher than 84 dB.

16. (a) Males:

Cholesterol	Frequency
125–149	2
150–174	2
175–199	3
200–224	2
225–249	1
250–274	2
275–299	2
300–324	0
325–374	2
More	0

Females:

Cholesterol	Frequency
100–124	1
125–149	5
150–174	4
175–199	7
200–224	5
225–249	1
250–274	1
275–299	0
More	0

(b) Males:

Cholesterol	Percentage
125–149	12.50
150–174	12.50
175–199	18.75
200–224	12.50
225–249	6.25
250–274	12.50
275–299	12.50
300–324	0.00
325–374	12.50
More	0.00

Females:

Cholesterol	Percentage
100–124	4.17
125–149	20.83
150–174	16.67
175–199	29.17
200–224	20.83
225–249	4.17
250–274	4.17
275–299	0.00
More	0.00

(c) Males:

Cholesterol	Cumulative %
125–149	12.50
150–174	25.00
175–199	43.75
200–224	56.25
225–249	62.50
250–274	75.00
275–299	87.50
300–324	87.50
325–374	100.00
More	100.00

Females:

Cholesterol	Cumulative %
100–124	4.17
125–149	25.00
150–174	41.67
175–199	70.83
200–224	91.67
225–249	95.83
250–274	100.00
275–299	100.00
More	100.00

(d) Males:

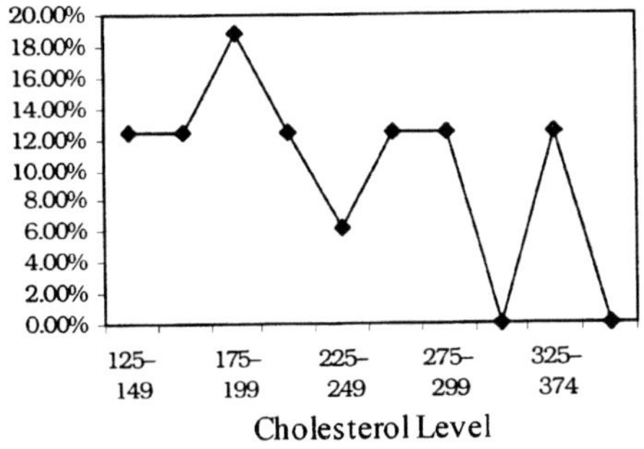

Females:

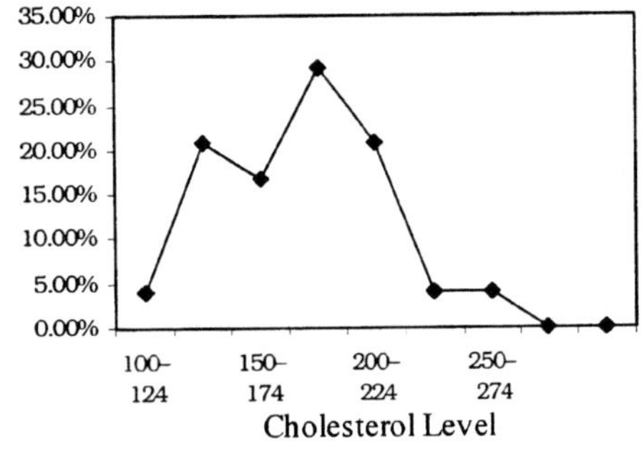

(e) Males:

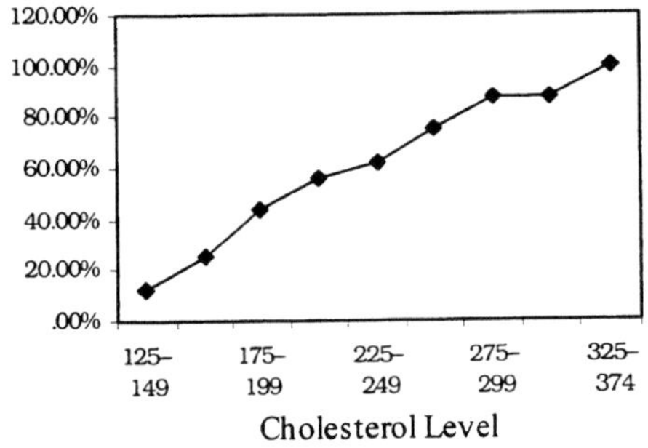

Females:

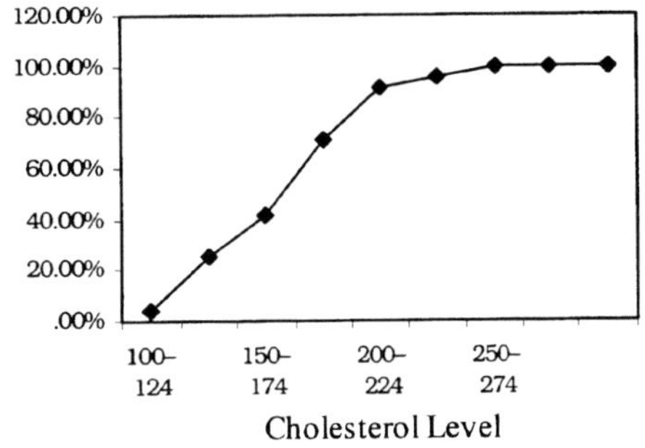

(f) Males:

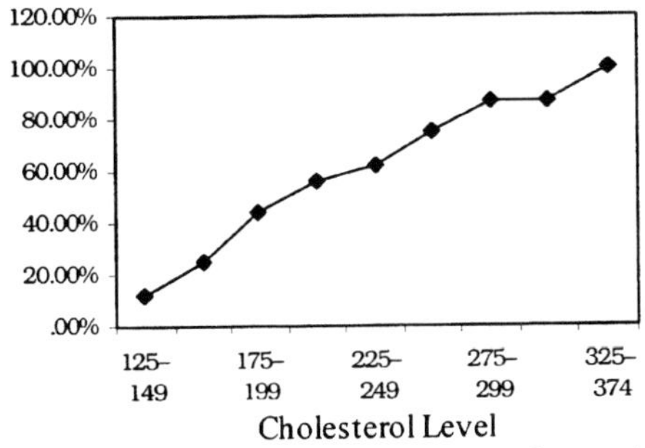

Females:

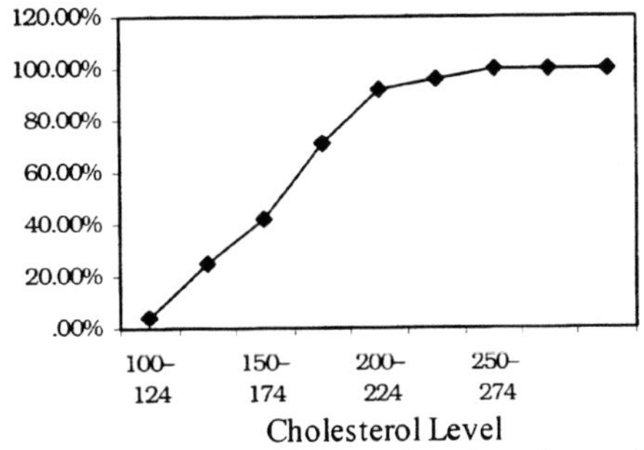

(g) Cholesterol levels for the male patients have a larger range of distribution. There are no female patients with a cholesterol level of more than 275, whereas 4% of male patients have cholesterol levels of more than 275. Both distributions are concentrated in the range between 175 and 199.

17. (a) The numbers of daily calls are stable over the 30 days.

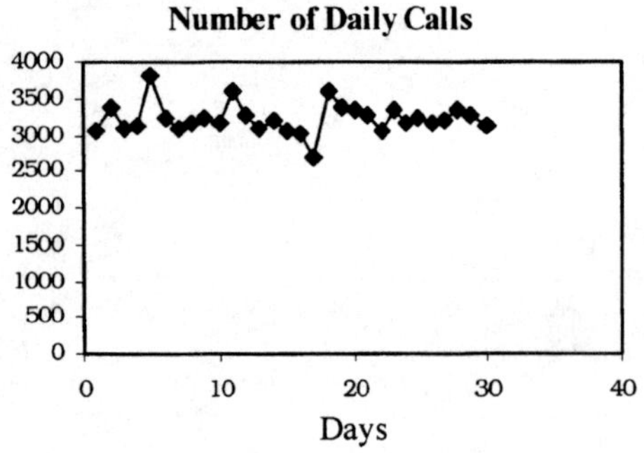

(b) Stem-and-Leaf Display for Number of Calls

Stem unit:	100
26	9
27	
28	
29	
30	0 6 6 7 8 9
31	1 3 4 6 7 7 8 9 9
32	3 4 5 6 8 8
33	4 5 5 7 7
34	
35	
36	0 2
37	
38	1

(c)

Number	Frequency	Percentage
2500–2749	1	3.33
2750–2999	0	0.00
3000–3249	17	56.67
3250–3499	9	30.00
3500–3749	2	6.67
3750–3999	1	3.33
More	0	0.00

(d)

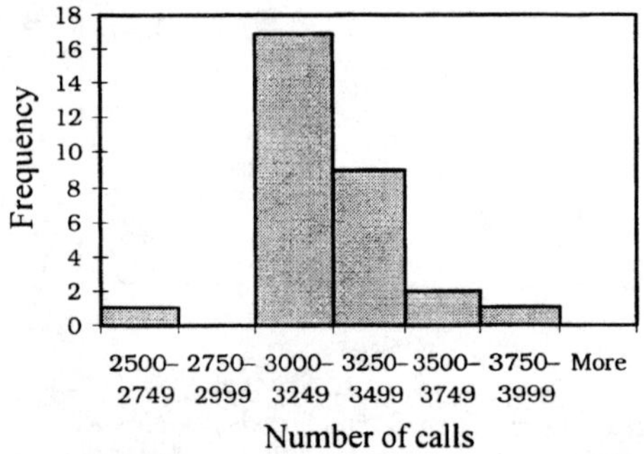

(e)

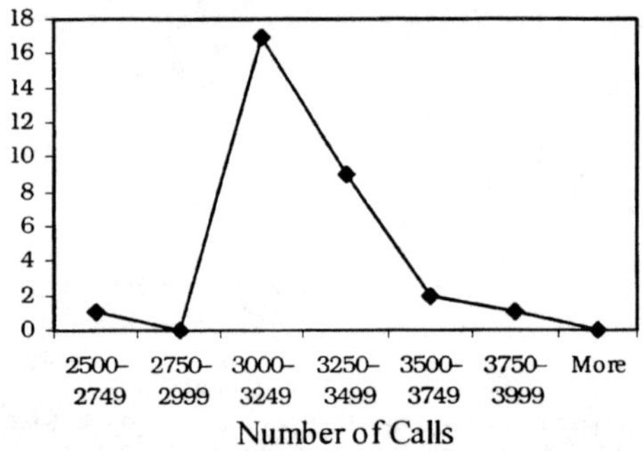

(f)

Number	Cumulative %
2500–2749	3.33
2750–2999	3.33
3000–3249	60.00
3250–3499	90.00
3500–3749	96.67
3750–3999	100.00
More	100.00

(g)

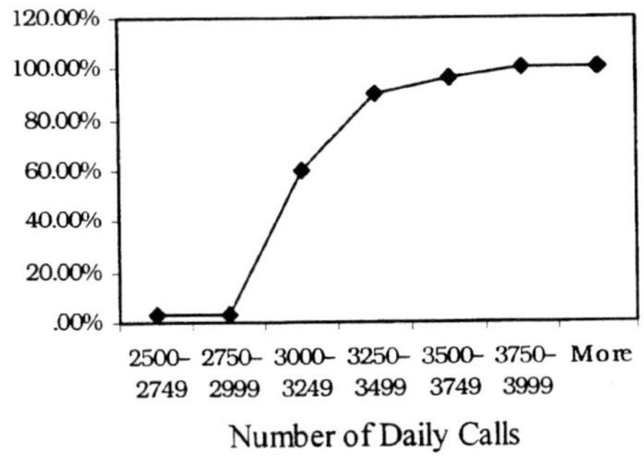

(h) The number of daily calls is concentrated between 3000 and 3249 calls per day. Only 3.33% of daily calls are less than 3000 or more than 3250 calls per day.

18. (a) HC Stem-and-Leaf Display

Stem unit:	0.1
3	4 6 7 8 8 9
4	1 1 1 1 1 3 4 6 6 7 7 8 8
5	0 0 1 1 1 2 2 2 5 5 6 7 7 8
6	0 1 4 5 5
7	0 2 3
8	3 3 7
9	
10	2
11	0

CO Stem-and-Leaf Display

Stem unit:	1
1	9
2	0 3
3	4 5 8
4	0 0 1 1 1 3 4 6 7
5	0 0 0 2 2 4 7 8
6	0 0 3 8
7	2 5 5
8	0 4 6
9	6
10	
11	2 5
12	1 3
13	
14	7 8
15	0 0 1
16	
17	
18	
19	0
20	
21	
22	9
23	5

(b) HC

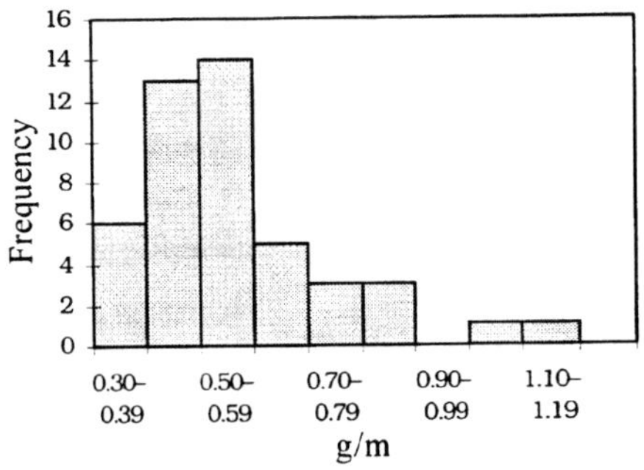

CO

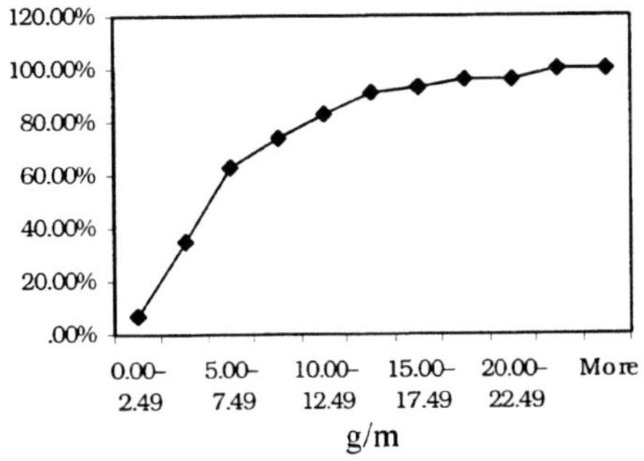

(c) HC

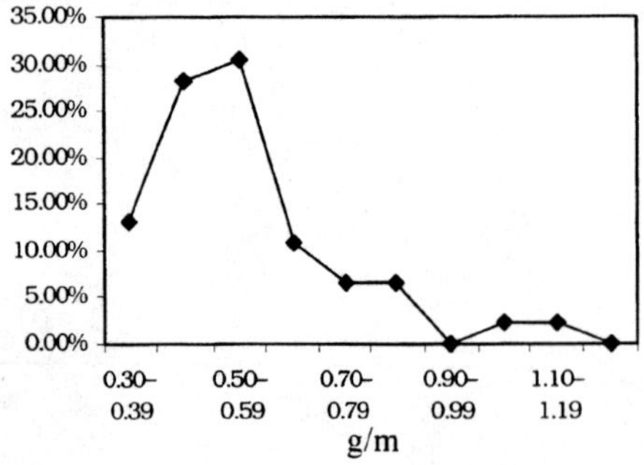

CO

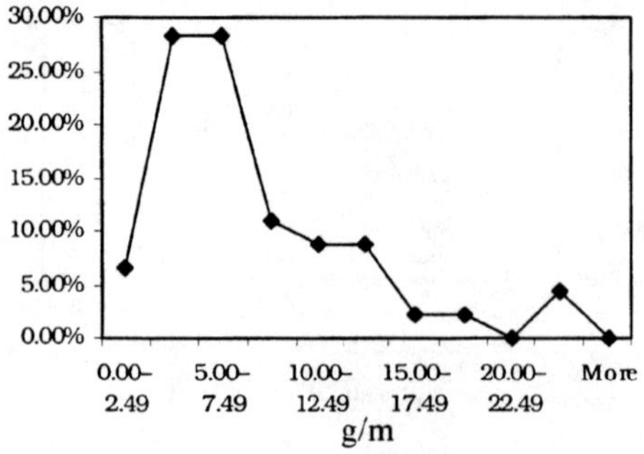

(d) HC

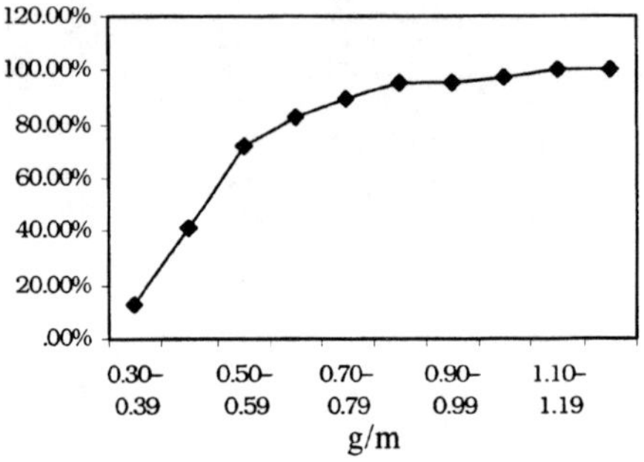

CO

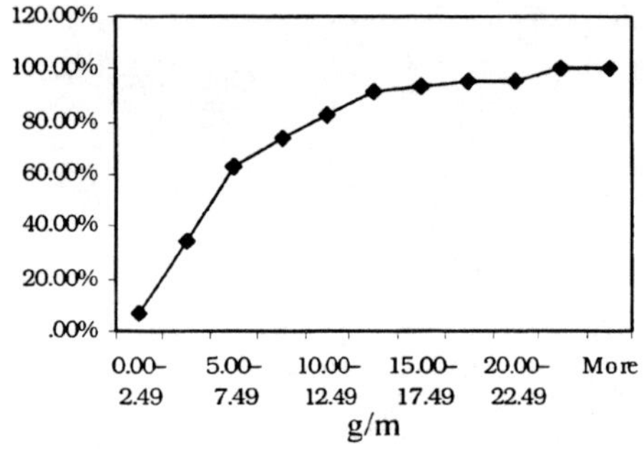

(e) Carbon monoxide and hydrocarbon emissions data have similar distribution concentrated near the left side.

19. (a) DMY Stem-and-Leaf Display

Stem unit:	1
11	6 9
12	7
13	0 5 7
14	6 6 8
15	6 8
16	
17	1 2 9
18	2 6 8
19	5
20	6 7 7
21	1
22	2

NC Stem-and-Leaf Display

Stem unit:	1
11	8
12	2 7 7 7 8 9
13	1 1 3 4 4 6 6 7
14	0 1 7 8 8
15	1 3
16	0

(b) DMY

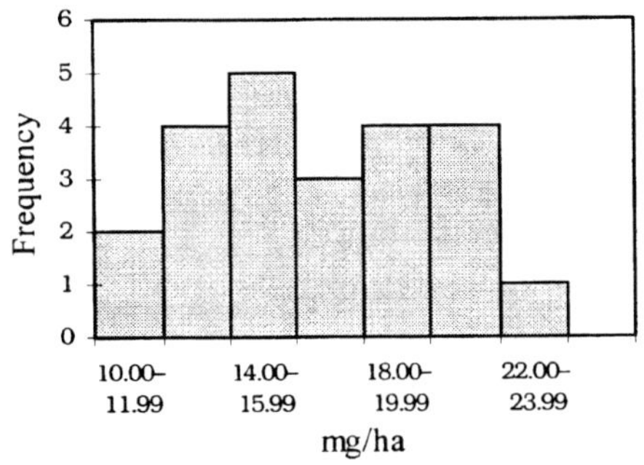

NC

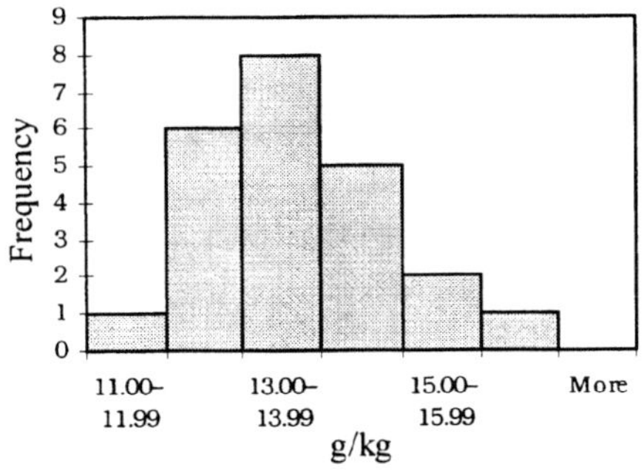

(c) DMY

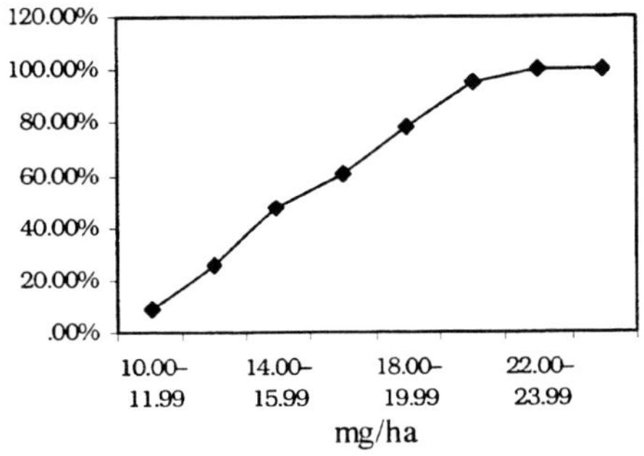

NC

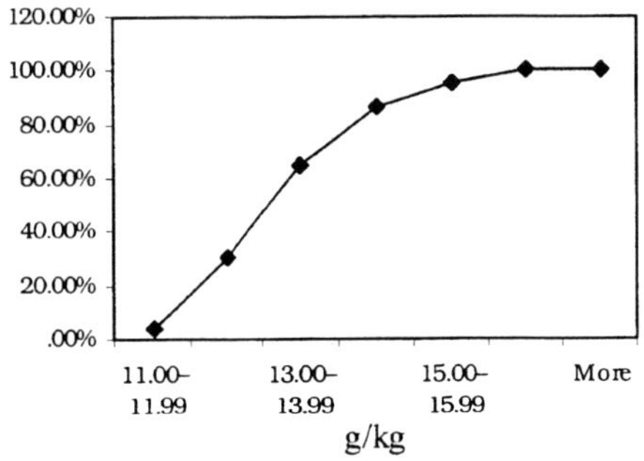

(d) DMY

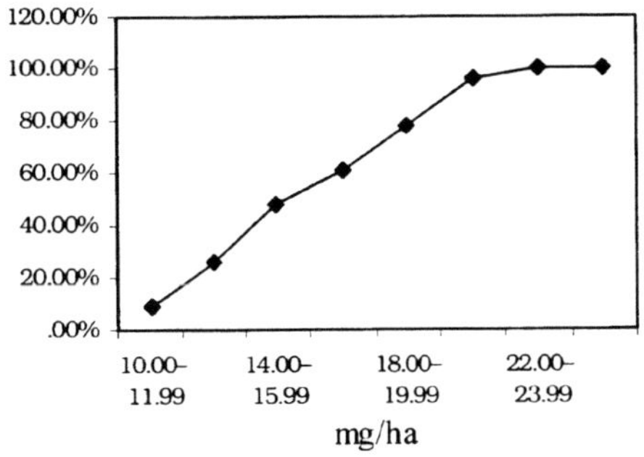

NC

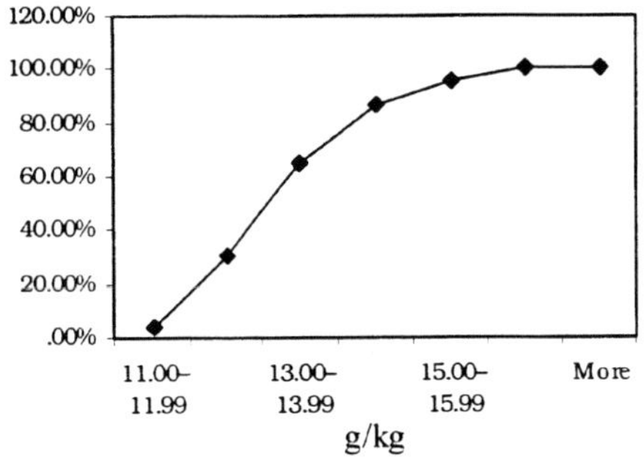

(e) The dry matter yield data have two high points whereas the nitrogen concentration data have only one. DMY data are distributed over a wider range than NC data.

20. Answers will vary. **21.** Answers will vary. **22.** Answers will vary. **23.** Answers will vary.

24. Answers will vary. **25.** Answers will vary.

26. (a)

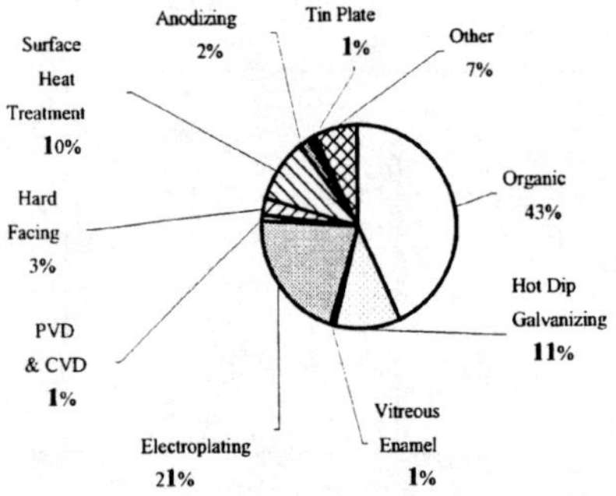

(b)

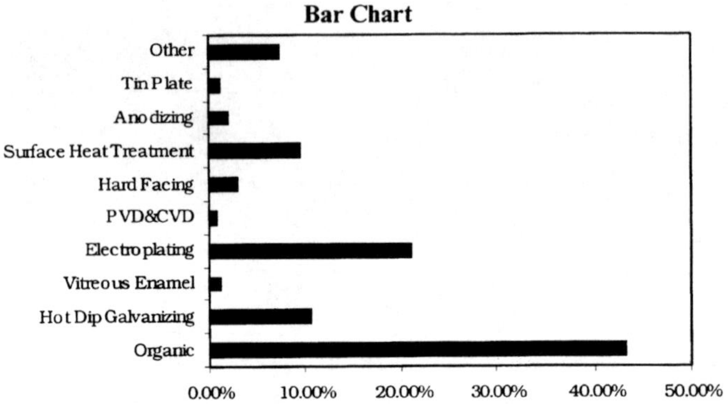

(c)

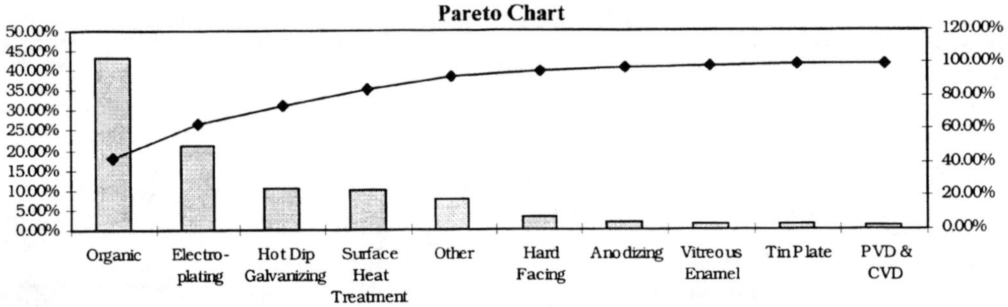

(d) Organic coating is the most widespread engineering coating and PVS & CVD, vitreous enamel and tip plate are the least spread.

27. (a)

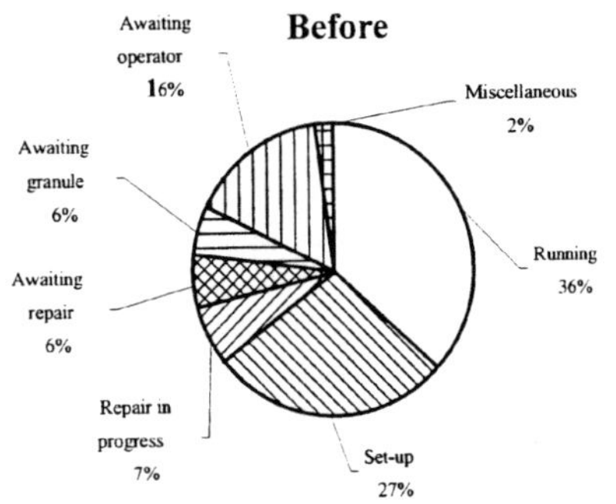

(b)

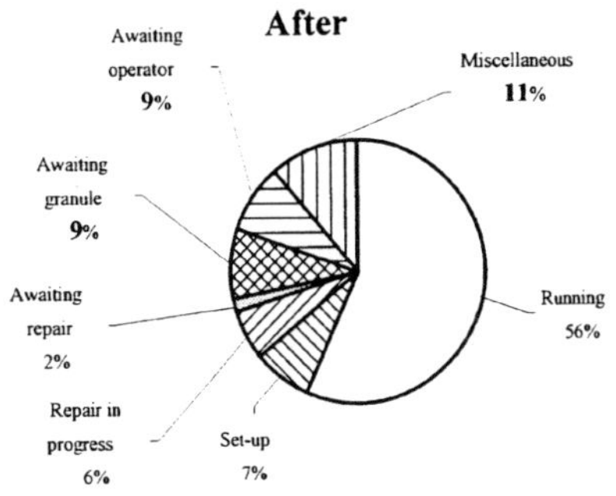

(c) The percent of running time after a quality improvement study increases and the percent of set-up time decreases.

(d)

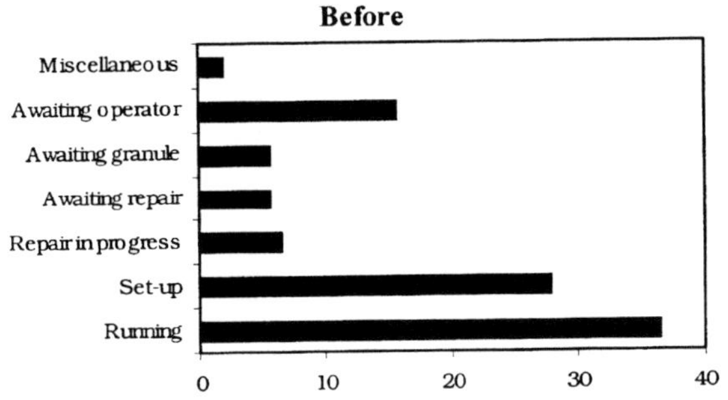

(e)

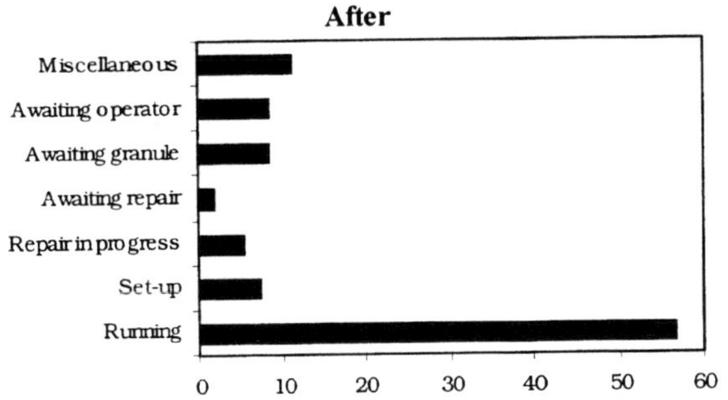

(f) The percent of running time after a quality improvement study greatly exceeds the percent of time the machine expends on other activities, whereas before the improvement study it was comparable with set-up time percent.

(g)

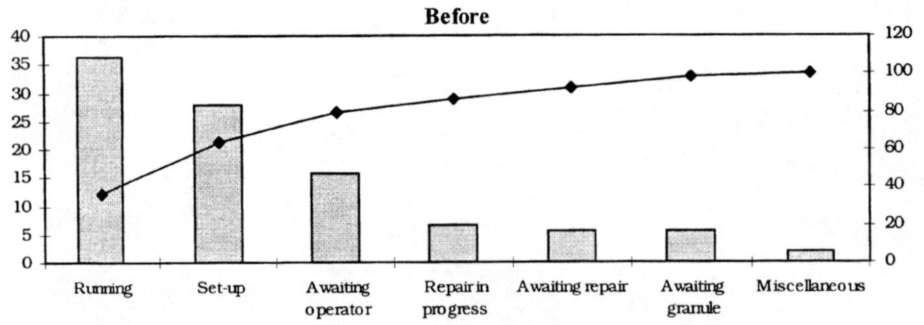

(h)

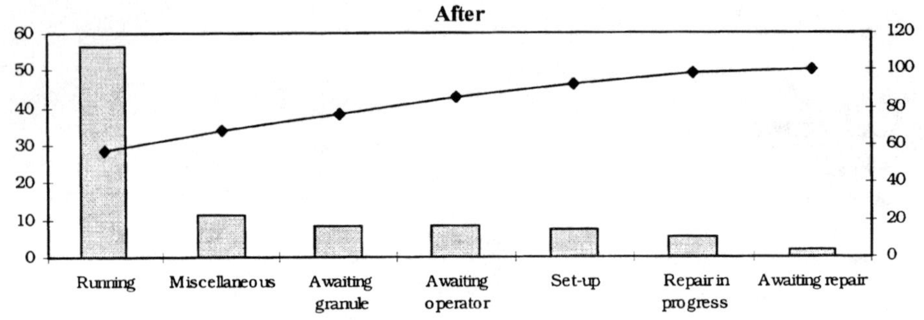

(i) After the quality improvement study the amount of running time greatly exceeds the amount of time the machine spent on other activities, while before the improvement study it was comparable with the amount of time spent for set-up. Pareto chart shows that before the improvement had been made the first two categories accounted for about 60% of all the time, while after the improvement the first category alone takes about 60% of the time.

28. (a)

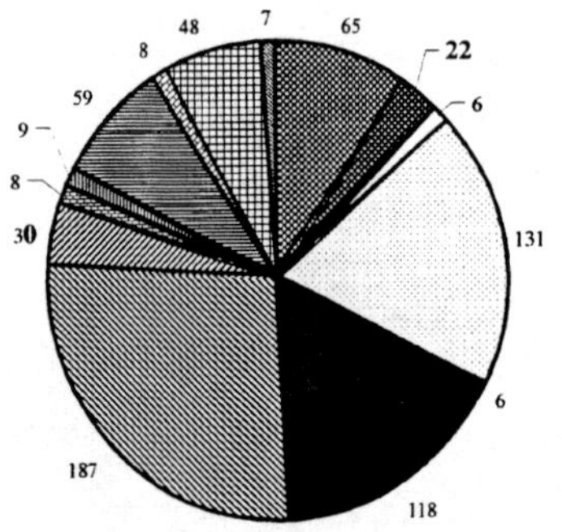

(b)

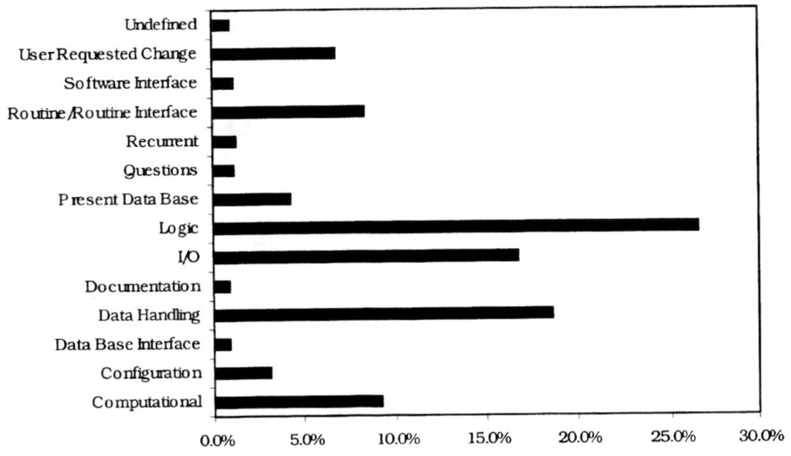

(c)

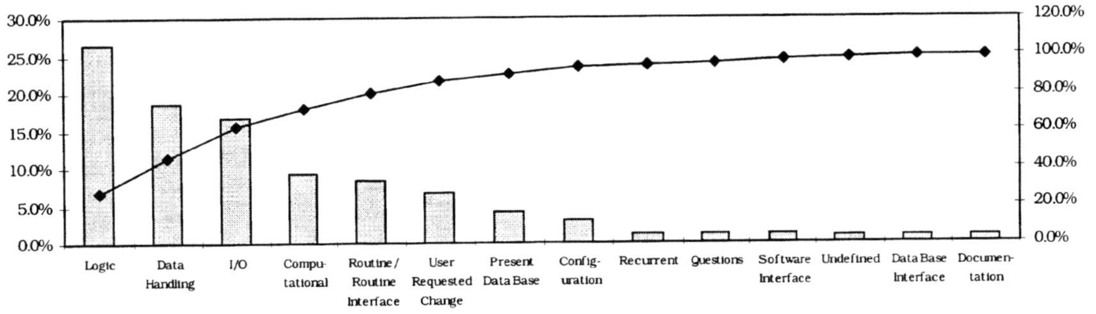

(d) The software development companies should focus on logic (26.6% of errors), data handling (18.6%) and I/O (16.8%) as these categories combined account for about 60% of all the errors.

29. (a) One-Way Summary Table

Count of Variable

Variable	Total
C	2
D	9
G	4
H	1
I	2
P	1
R	3
S	16
U	12
Grand Total	50

Variable	Frequency	Percentage	Cumulative Pct.
H	1	2.00	2.00
P	1	2.00	4.00
C	2	4.00	8.00
I	2	4.00	12.00
R	3	6.00	18.00
G	4	8.00	26.00
D	9	18.00	44.00
U	12	24.00	68.00
S	16	32.00	100.00

(b)

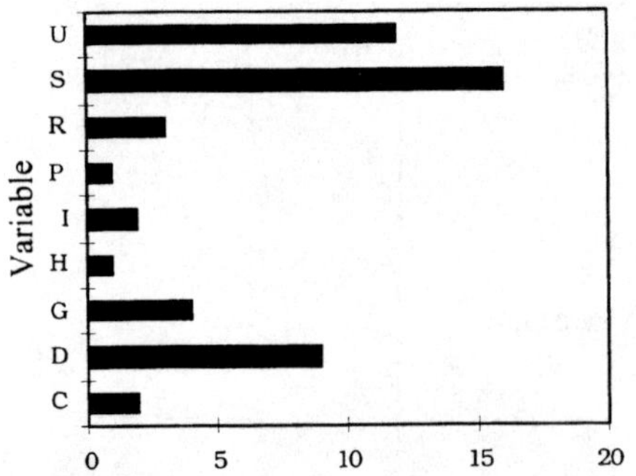

(c)

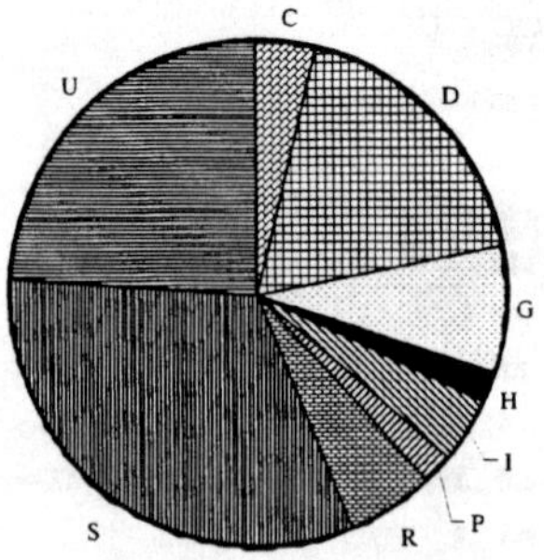

(d)

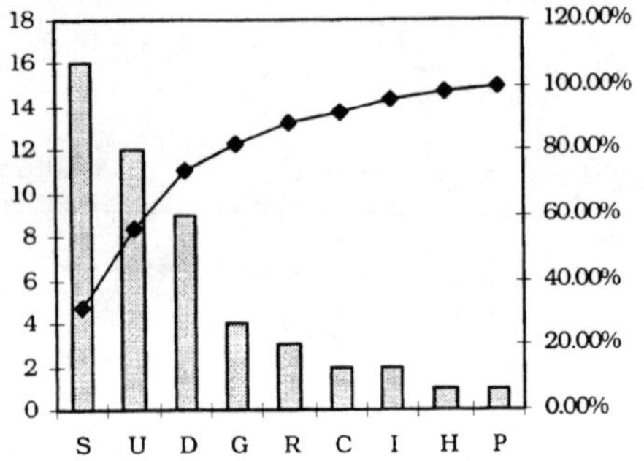

(e) The operator manager should focus on unsealed box top (32%), unreadable label (24%) and dirty carton (18%) as these categories combined account for about 70% of all the errors.

30. (a)

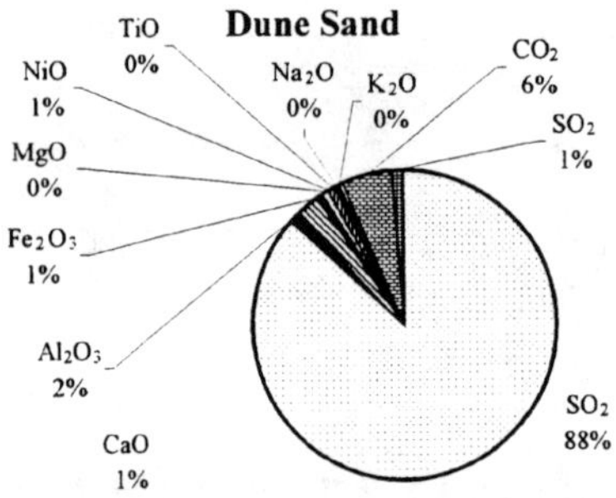

(b)

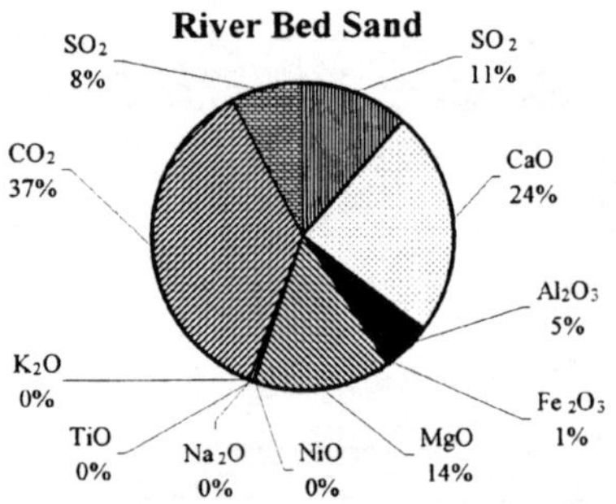

(c) Ninety percent of the Dune Sand sample is represented by SO_2; therefore the pie chart is not the best method for displaying Dune Sand data. The majority of the River Bed sample is represented by CO_2 and CO.

(d)

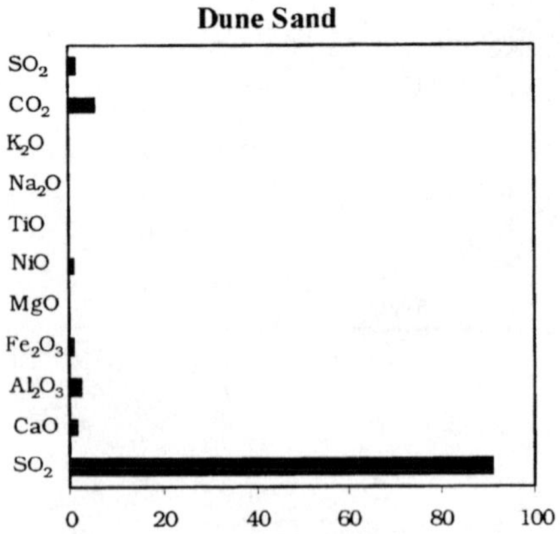

(e)

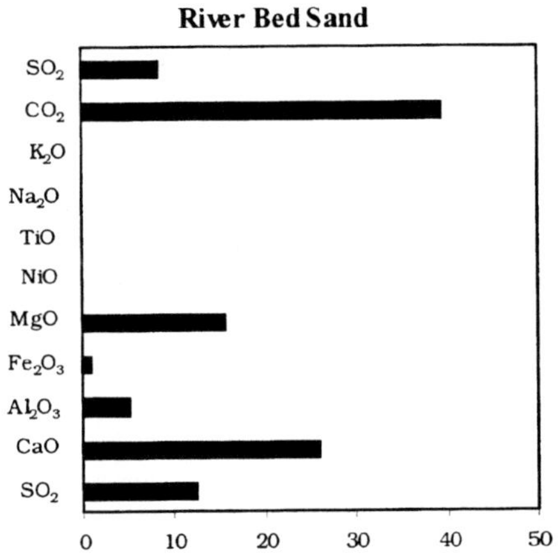

(f) The bar chart for River Bed Sand has four main categories, whereas the bar chart for Dune Sand has one dominant category. SiO_2 makes up about 90% of Dune Sand, but only about 15% of River Bed Sand.

(g)

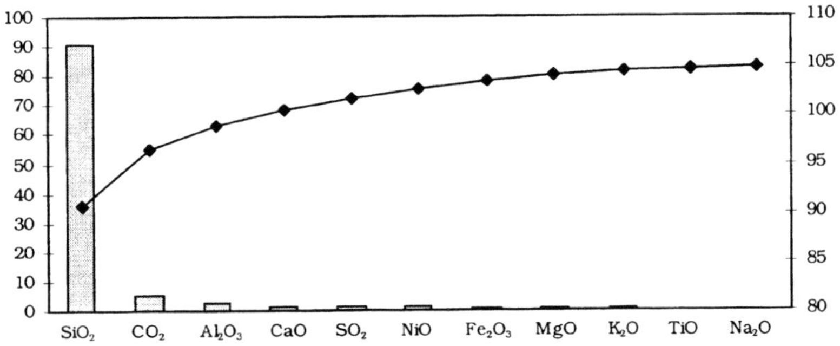

(h)

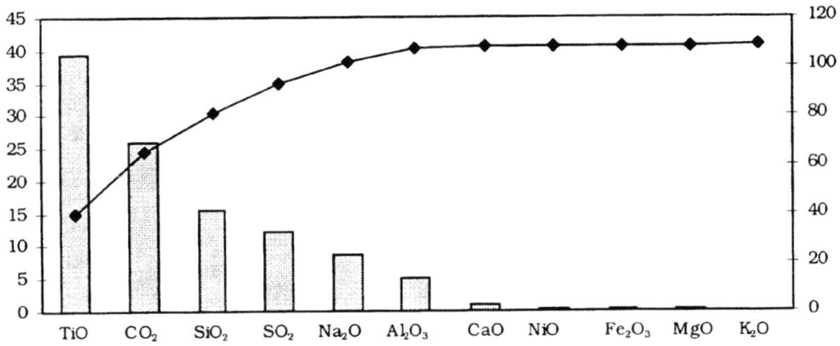

(i) The Pareto chart for Dune Sand shows the dominant role of SiO_2, whereas the Pareto chart for River Bed sand indicates that this sample has a more complex structure. The Pareto chart for River Bed Sand shows that the first five categories make up about 90% of all components, whereas the Pareto chart for Dune Sand shows that the first category alone comprises about 90%.

31. (a)

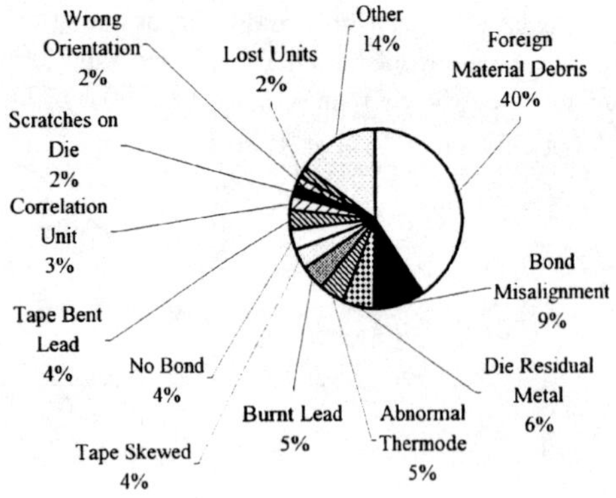

(b)

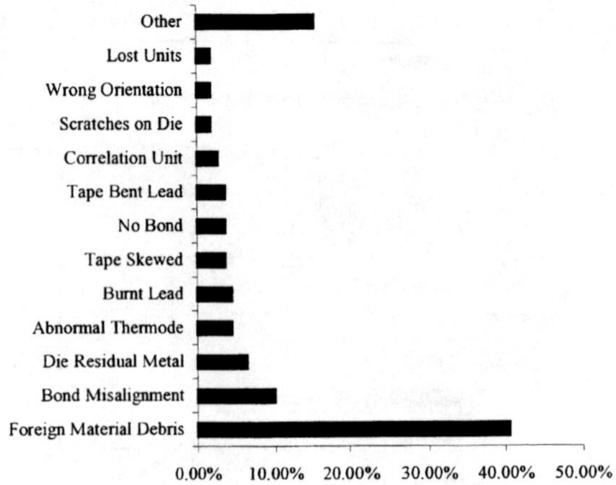

(c)

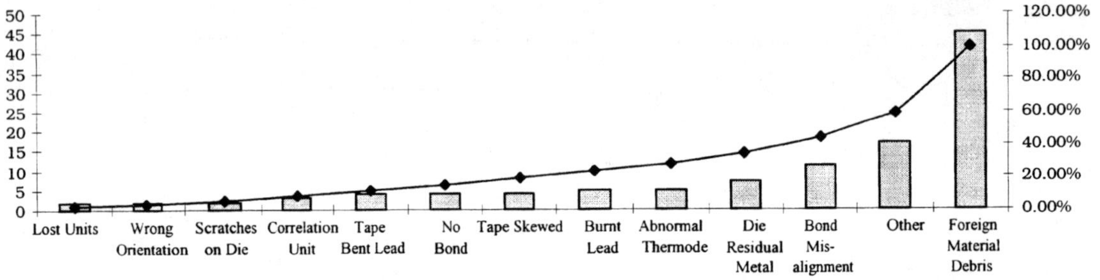

(d) The pie chart is not the best method to display these data because there are too many categories. It can be seen from the Pareto chart that foreign material debris comprises about 40% of the rejects. The Pareto diagram represents the categories in the descending rank order of their frequencies and makes it easier to determine which types of rejects are more important.

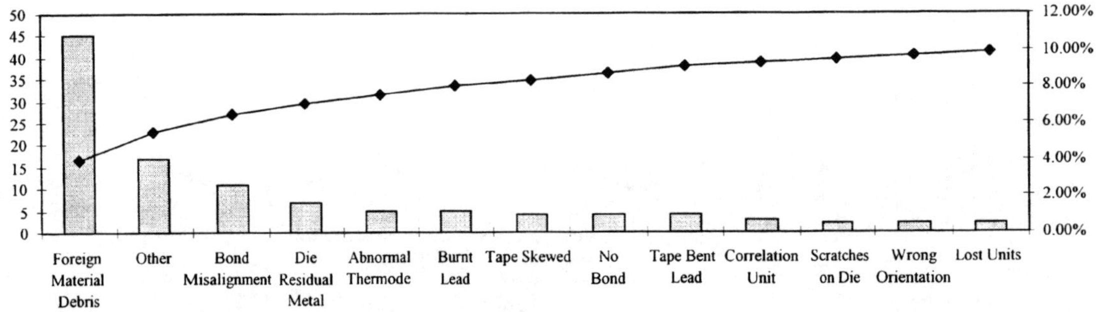

32. (a) Rows: Gender Columns: Major

	C	E	O	All
F	6	6	3	15
M	9	14	2	25
All	15	20	5	40

(b)

	C	E	O	All
F	15.00	15.00	7.50	37.50
M	22.50	35.00	5.00	62.50
All	37.50	50.00	12.50	100.00

(c)

	C	E	O	All
F	40.00	40.00	20.00	100.00
M	36.00	56.00	8.00	100.00
All	37.50	50.00	12.50	100.00

(d)

	C	E	O	All
F	40.00	30.00	60.00	37.50
M	60.00	70.00	40.00	62.50
All	100.00	100.00	100.00	100.00

(e)

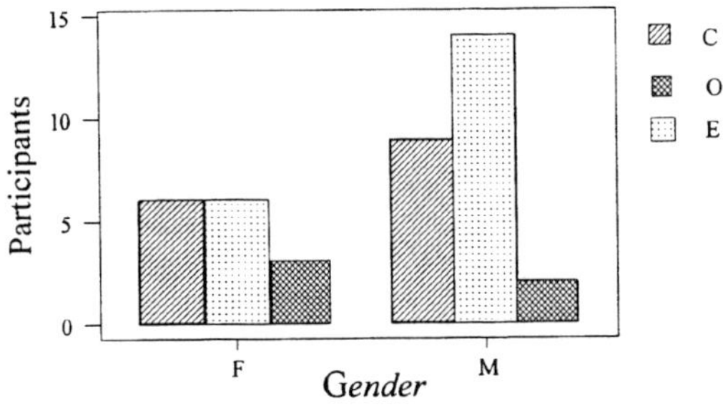

33. (a) Rows: Gender Columns: Major

	No	Yes	All
Ns	28	16	44
S	10	22	32
All	38	38	76

(b)

	No	Yes	All
Ns	36.84	21.05	57.89
S	13.16	28.95	42.11
All	50.00	50.00	100.00

(c)

	No	Yes	All
Ns	63.64	36.36	100.00
S	31.25	68.75	100.00
All	50.00	50.00	100.00

(d)

	No	Yes	All
Ns	73.68	42.11	57.89
S	26.32	57.89	42.11
All	100.00	100.00	100.00

(e)

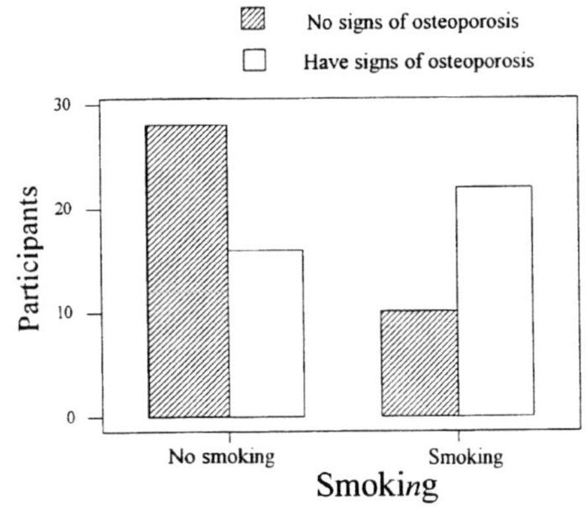

(f) Women who smoked displayed signs of osteoporosis more often compared to women who did not smoke.

34. (a) Rows: Quality Columns: Conditions

	No Particles	Particle	All
Bad	80	36	116
Good	320	14	334
All	400	50	450

(b)

	No Particles	Particle	All
Bad	17.78	8.00	25.78
Good	71.11	3.11	74.22
All	88.89	11.11	100.00

(c)

	No Particles	Particle	All
Bad	68.97	31.03	100.00
Good	95.81	4.19	100.00
All	88.89	11.11	100.00

(d)

	No Particles	Particle	All
Bad	20.00	72.00	25.78
Good	80.00	28.00	74.22
All	100.00	100.00	100.00

(e)

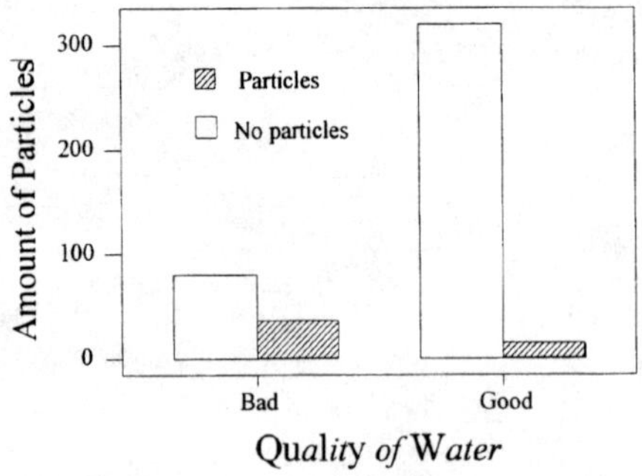

(f) Fewer particles were found in the good water than in bad water.

35. (a) Rows: Age Columns: Side

	Left	Right	Symmetrical	All
Adult	86	82	108	276
Juvenile	61	14	21	96
Pup	11	3	1	15
All	158	99	130	387

(b)

	Left	Right	Symmetrical	All
Adult	22.22	21.19	27.91	71.32
Juvenile	15.76	3.62	5.43	24.81
Pup	2.84	0.78	0.26	3.88
All	40.83	25.58	33.59	100.00

(c)

	Left	Right	Symmetrical	All
Adult	31.16	29.71	39.13	100.00
Juvenile	63.54	14.58	21.88	100.00
Pup	73.33	20.00	6.67	100.00
All	40.83	25.58	33.59	100.00

(d)

	Left	Right	Symmetrical	All
Adult	54.43	82.83	83.08	71.32
Juvenile	38.61	14.14	16.15	24.81
Pup	6.96	3.03	0.77	3.88
All	100.00	100.00	100.00	100.00

(e)

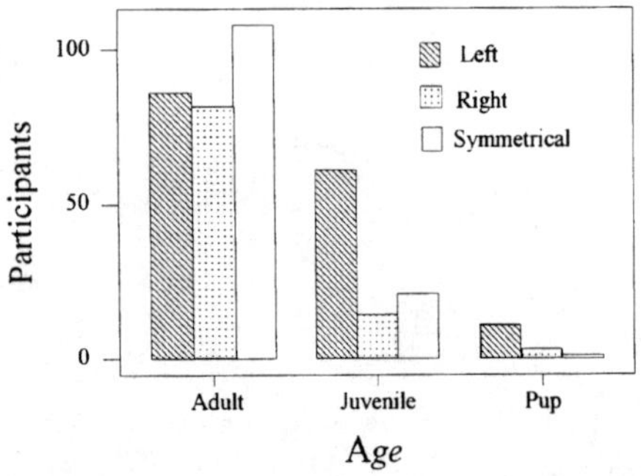

(f) Most of the juvenile and pups displayed saggital crest defects on the left side, whereas most adults had it symmetrically.

36. (a) Rows: Type Columns: References

	Immediate	Indirect	Register	All
Optimized	29	47	88	164
Unoptimized	45	88	186	319
All	74	135	274	483

(b)

	Immediate	Indirect	Register	All
Optimized	6.00	9.73	18.22	33.95
Unoptimized	9.32	18.22	38.51	66.05
All	15.32	27.95	56.73	100.00

(c)

	Immediate	Indirect	Register	All
Optimized	17.68	28.66	53.66	100.00
Unoptimized	14.11	27.59	58.31	100.00
All	15.32	27.95	56.73	100.00

(d)

	Immediate	Indirect	Register	All
Optimized	39.19	34.81	32.12	33.95
Unoptimized	60.81	65.19	67.88	66.05
All	100.00	100.00	100.00	100.00

(e)

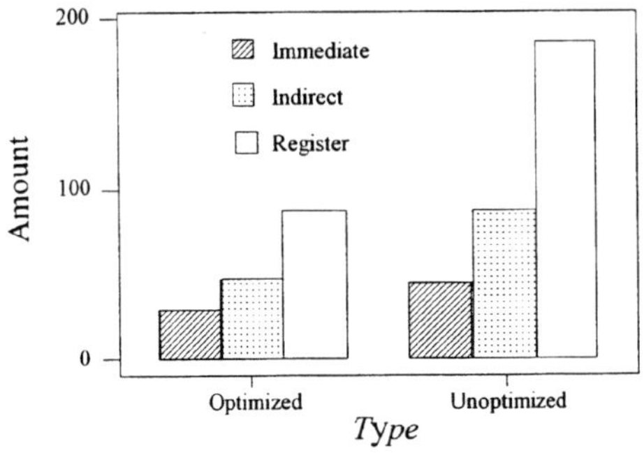

(f) There is little difference between the optimized and unoptimized programs. The optimized programs had a slightly lower percentage of registered references and a slightly higher percentage of immediate and indirect references than did the unoptimized programs.

37. (a) Rows: Lab test Performed Columns: Shift

	Day	Evening	All
Conforming	68.13	31.88	100.00
Nonconforming	40.00	60.00	100.00
All	67.00	33.00	100.00

(b)

	Day	Evening	All
Conforming	97.61	92.73	96.00
Nonconforming	2.39	7.27	4.00
All	100.00	100.00	100.00

(c)

	Day	Evening	All
Conforming	65.40	30.60	96.00
Nonconforming	1.60	2.40	4.00
All	67.00	33.00	100.00

(d) A table of row percentages is more informative because it shows the percentage of conforming and nonconforming tests that correspond to the morning or evening shift. The row percentages allow us to block the effect of disproportionate group size and show us that the pattern for day and evening tests among the nonconforming group is very different from the pattern for day and evening tests among the conforming group. Where 40% of the nonconforming group was tested during the day, 68% of the conforming group was tested during the day.

(e)

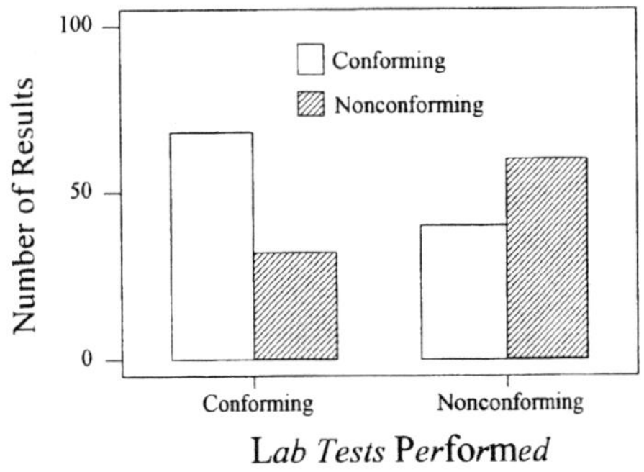

(f) Evening shift performed more nonconforming tests than the day shift did.

38. Answers will vary. **39.** Answers will vary. **40.** Answers will vary.

41. The process flow diagram is useful because it serves as a pictorial representation of a system and allows one to see the flow of steps in a process from its beginning to its termination.

42. The Fishbone diagram is useful in process improvement because it helps organize the ideas and identify cause-and-effect relationships, thereby helping to identify factors that may be causing variability in the process output.

43. A time-order plot helps to see whether the data are stable over the time periods involved. Until one can be reasonably certain that no patterns in the data exist over time, the use of any other method of analysis is premature and conclusions drawn from it may be misleading.

44. A Pareto diagram is preferable when the categorical variable of interest contains many categories. A pie chart may be preferable if there are few categories and one wants to visualize the portion of the entire pie that is in each category.

45. In a histogram the rectangular bars are constructed at the boundaries of each class whereas a polygon is formed by having the midpoint of each class represent the data in that class and then connecting the sequence of midpoints at their respective class percentages. Histograms cannot be constructed for more than one set of data, whereas polygons allow for such representations.

46. A concentration diagram is useful because it allows one to visualize the location of the studied items and to determine their concentrations.

47. A bar chart should be used to directly compare the data variables.

48. A pie chart may be preferable if there are few categories and one wants to visualize the portion of the entire pie that is in each category.

49. A Pareto diagram is preferable when the categorical variables of interest are many.

50. The total percentages, the row percentages and the column percentages.

51. A side-by-side bar chart is used for examination of the responses to two categorical variables simultaneously, whereas the bar chart is used for one categorical variable. A side-by-side bar chart is best suited to demonstrate the differences in magnitude rather than the percentage differences.

52. (a) With magnets

Grams	Frequency	Percentage
13.00–18.99	1	3.33
19.00–19.19	1	3.33
19.20–19.39	3	10.00
19.40–19.59	3	10.00
19.60–19.79	5	16.67
19.80–19.99	2	6.67
20.00–20.19	5	16.67
20.20–20.39	2	6.67
20.40–20.59	4	13.33
20.60–20.79	3	10.00
20.80–20.99	1	3.33
21.00–21.19	0	0.00
21.20–21.39	0	0.00
21.40–21.59	0	0.00
More	0	0.00

(b) Without magnets

Grams	Frequency	Percentage
13.00–18.99	0	0.00
19.00–19.19	0	0.00
19.20–19.39	0	0.00
19.40–19.59	1	2.22
19.60–19.79	2	4.44
19.80–19.99	4	8.89
20.00–20.19	6	13.33
20.20–20.39	6	13.33
20.40–20.59	10	22.22
20.60–20.79	9	20.00
20.80–20.99	2	4.44
21.00–21.19	1	2.22
21.20–21.39	2	4.44
21.40–21.59	2	4.44
More	0	0.00

(b) Data obtained for a group with magnets are distributed in the range between 13.00 and 20.99; data for the groups without magnets are distributed in the range between 19.40 and 21.59.

(c) These two distributions are equivalent. In this case, percentage distribution is preferred because two groups are compared that have different numbers of observations in each set.

(d) With magnets

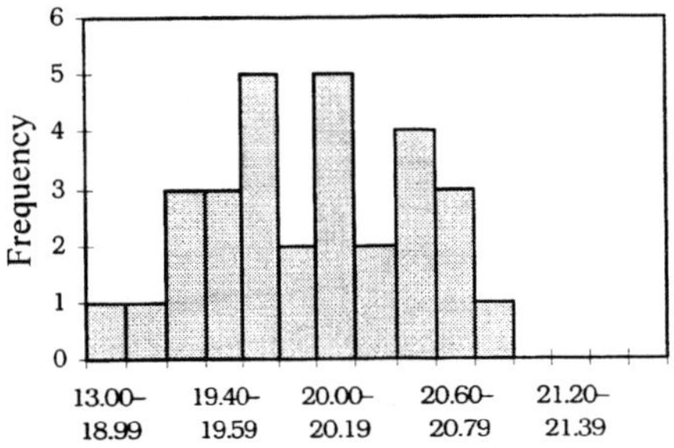

Without magnets

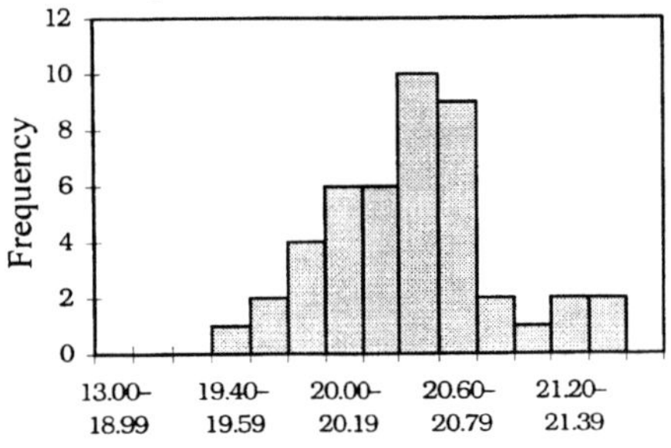

(e) Data obtained for the group with magnets have three higher points whereas data for the group without magnets have only one maximum.

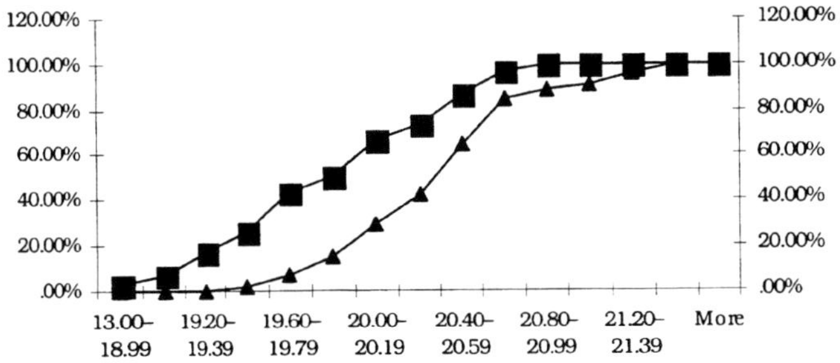

(f) From the cumulative percentage polygons one can see that ogive for data with magnets are drawn to the left of the ogive for data without magnets. It can, therefore be concluded that the group with magnets is preferred.

53. (a)

Liters	Frequency	Percentage
1.870–1.909	2	4.0
1.910–1.949	4	8.0
1.950–1.989	13	26.0
1.990–2.029	20	40.0
2.030–2.069	8	16.0
2.070–2.109	3	6.0
More	0	0.0

(b)

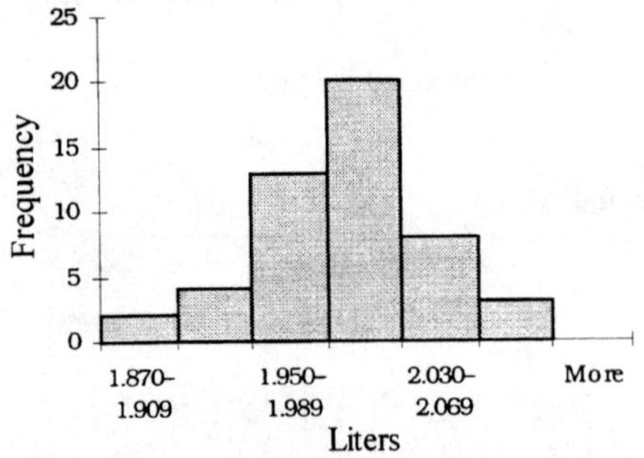

(c)

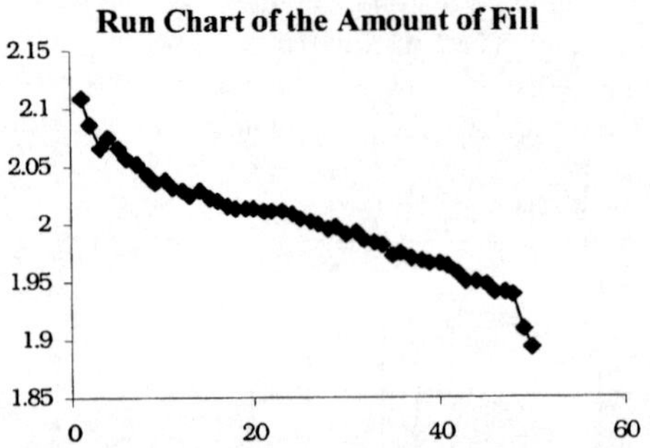

(d) From the run chart a downward trend appears evident in the process of filling two-liter bottles of soft drink.

(e) Using this histogram is premature and any conclusions drawn from it may be misleading.

54. (a) Stem-and-Leaf Display for Calories

Stem unit:	10
9	8 8 9
10	
11	0 2 6
12	
13	
14	
15	7
16	
17	5
18	1 2 3 4
19	0 1 9
20	8
21	5 7
22	
23	9
24	0 4
25	0
26	3
27	
28	7
29–38	
39	7

Stem-and-Leaf Display for Cholesterol

Stem unit:	10
3	9
4	8
5	3 4 6
6	9
7	1 4
8	2 2 7 8 9 9 9
9	0 1 3 4
10	0
11	
12	1 7
13	1
14	
15	6
16–47	
48	2

(b) Calories

	Frequency	Cumulative %
50–99	3	12.0
100–149	3	12.0
150–199	9	36.0
200–249	6	24.0
250–299	3	12.0
300–349	0	0.0
350–399	1	4.0
More	0	0.0

Cholesterol

mg	Frequency	Cumulative %
0–49	2	8.0
50–99	17	68.0
100–149	4	16.0
150–199	1	4.0
200–249	0	0.0
250–299	0	0.0
300–349	0	0.0
350–399	0	0.0
400–449	0	0.0
450–499	1	4.0
More	0	0.0

(c) Calories

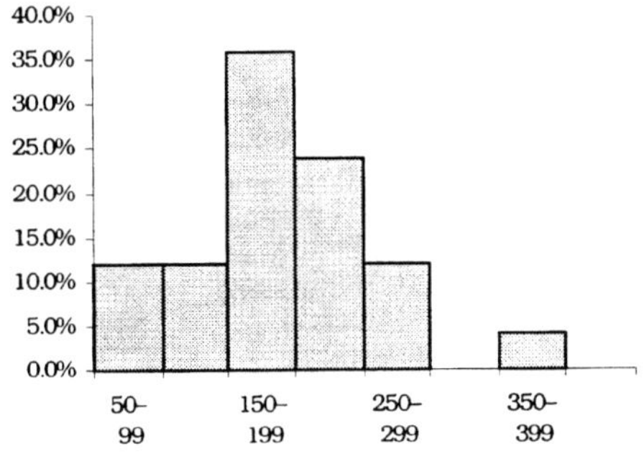

Cholesterol

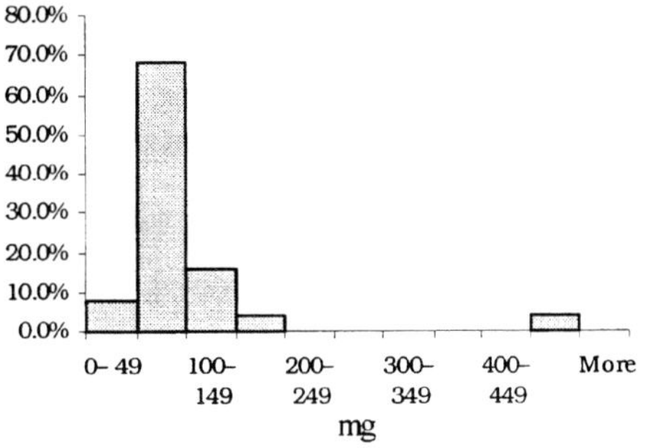

(d) Calories

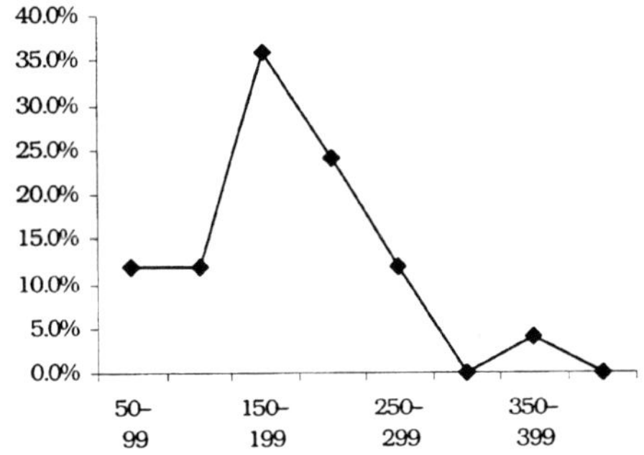

Cholesterol

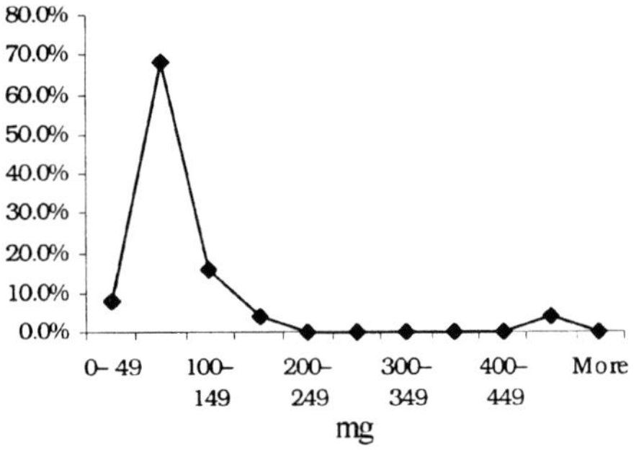

(e) Calories

	Frequency	Cumulative %
50–99	3	12.00
100–149	3	24.00
150–199	9	60.00
200–249	6	84.00
250–299	3	96.00
300–349	0	96.00
350–399	1	100.00
More	0	100.00

Cholesterol

mg	Frequency	Cumulative %
0–49	2	8.00
50–99	17	76.00
100–149	4	92.00
150–199	1	96.00
200–249	0	96.00
250–299	0	96.00
300–349	0	96.00
350–399	0	96.00
400–449	0	96.00
450–499	1	100.00
More	0	100.00

(f) Calories

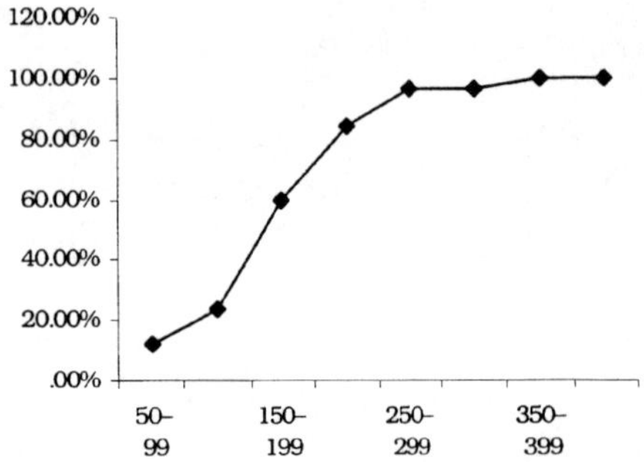

Cholesterol

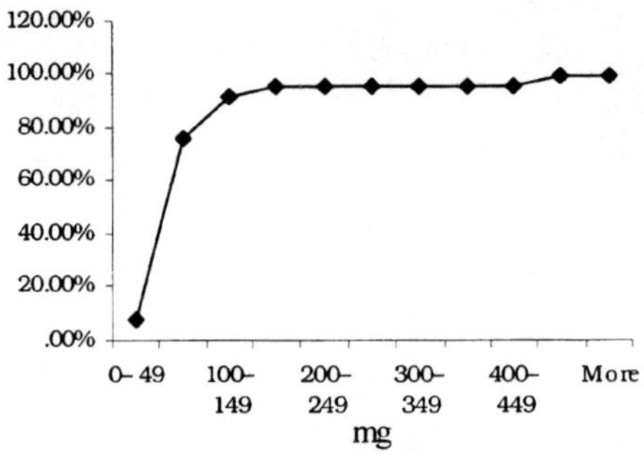

(g) The data relating to the amount of calories are distributed between 50 and 399 with concentration from 150 to 199 (36%). The data related to the amount of cholesterol are concentrated between 50 and 99 (76%). Most foods have cholesterol levels in the range between 0 and 199 mg.

55. (a)

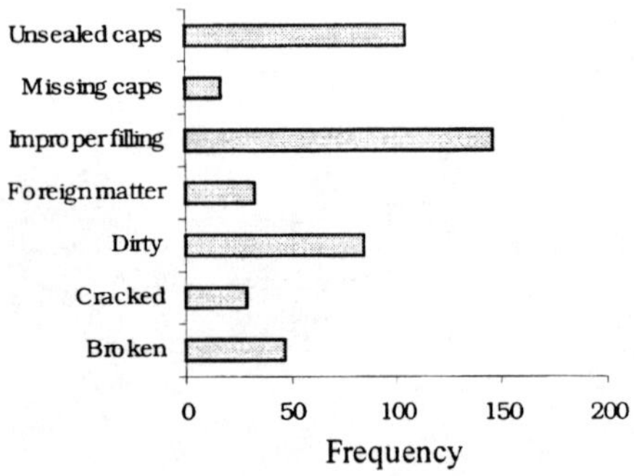

(b)

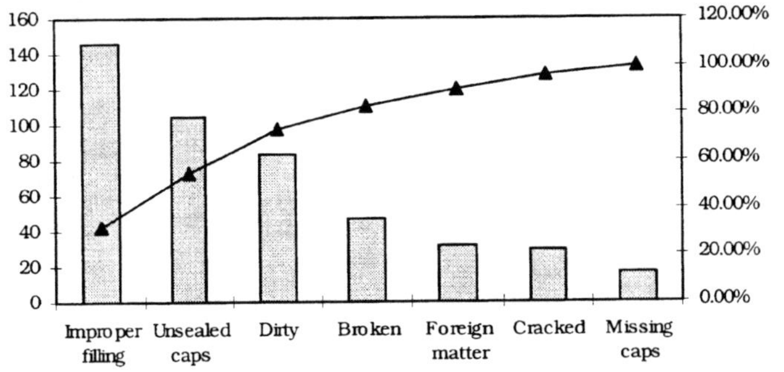

(c)

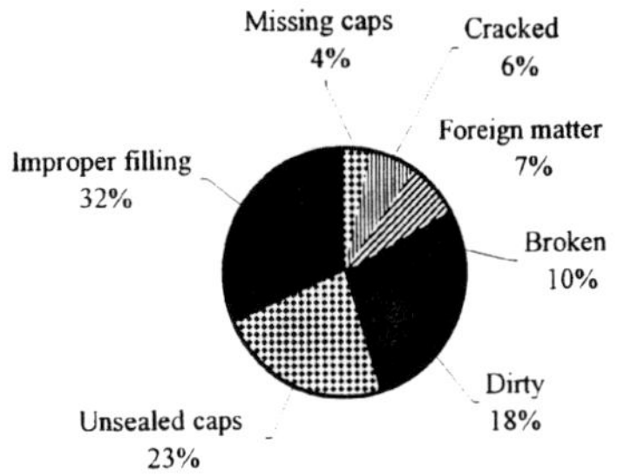

(d) It might be useful when determining which filling and capping machines give the most nonconforming bottles.

(e) The Pareto diagram is more clear and straightforward in showing the relationship between different types of nonconforming bottles. As this is a subjective issue, different opinions are possible.

56. (a)

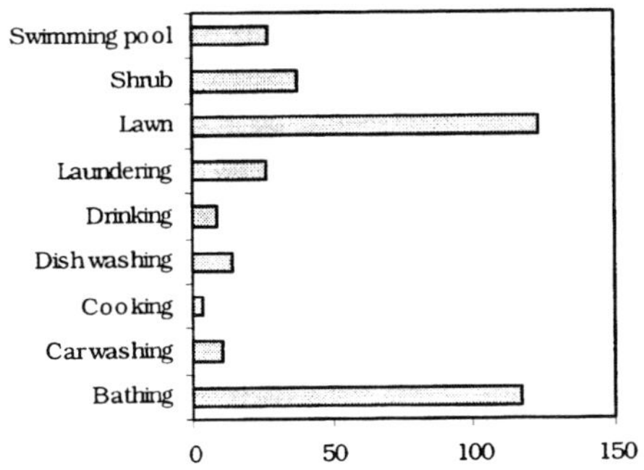

(b)

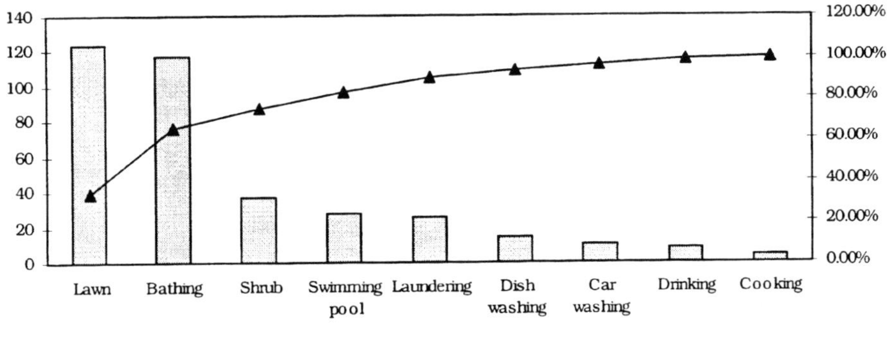

(c)

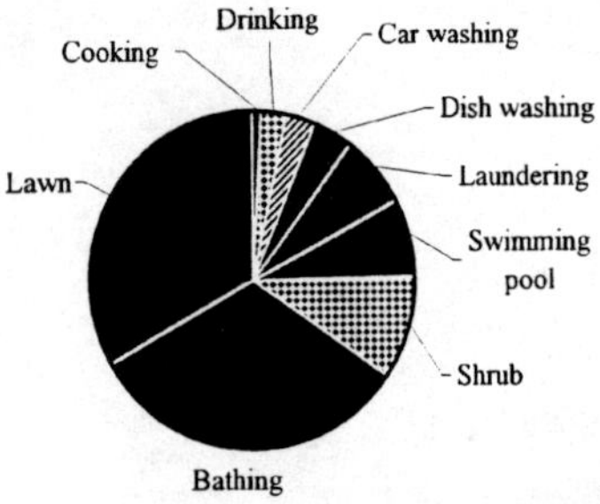

(d) A Pareto diagram is more preferable because the variable of interest contains many categories.

(e) Answers will vary.

(f) They should focus on lawn watering and bathing.

57. (a)

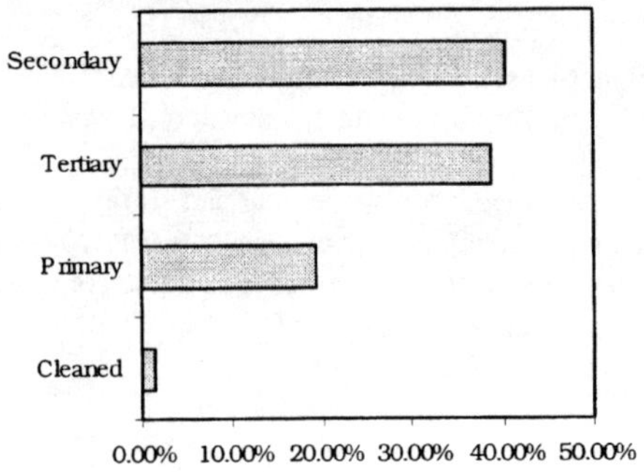

(b)

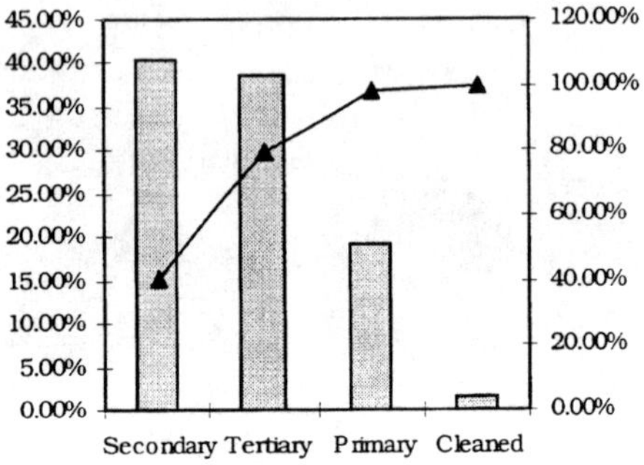

(c)

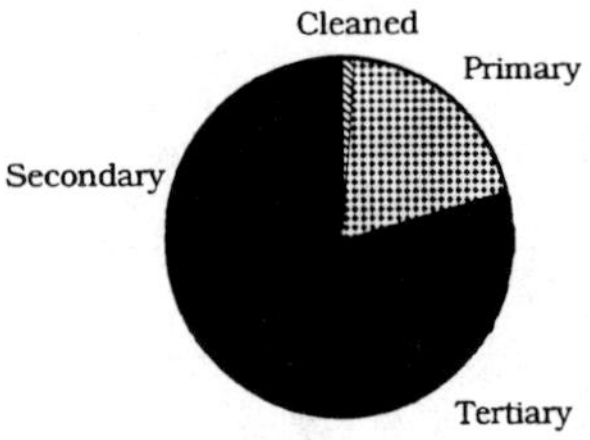

(d) The Pareto chart, because it shows that the secondary treatment has a higher percentage than the tertiary treatment, whereas it is not evident from the pie or bar charts.

(e) Secondary and tertiary treatments have almost the same percentage of waste, whereas the cleaned treatment has the smallest.

58. (a)

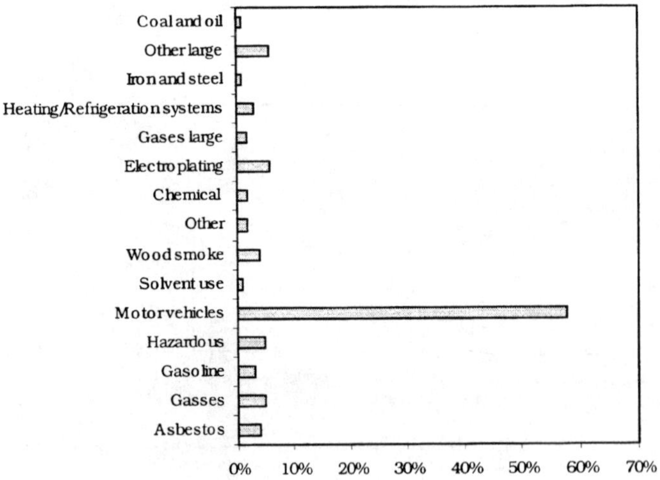

(b)

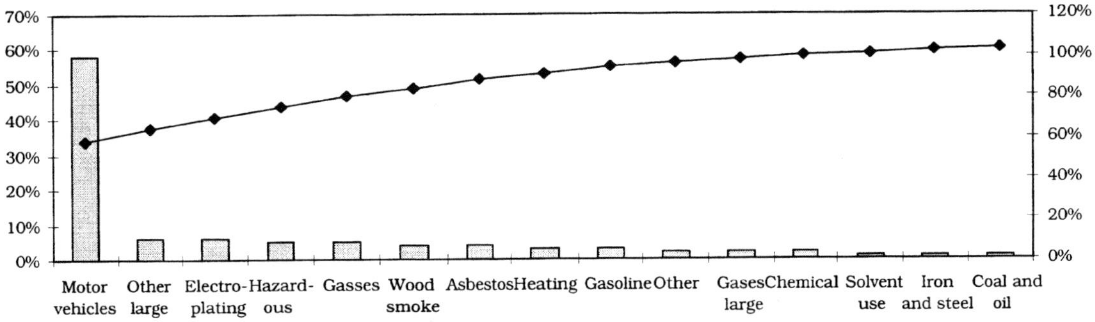

(c)

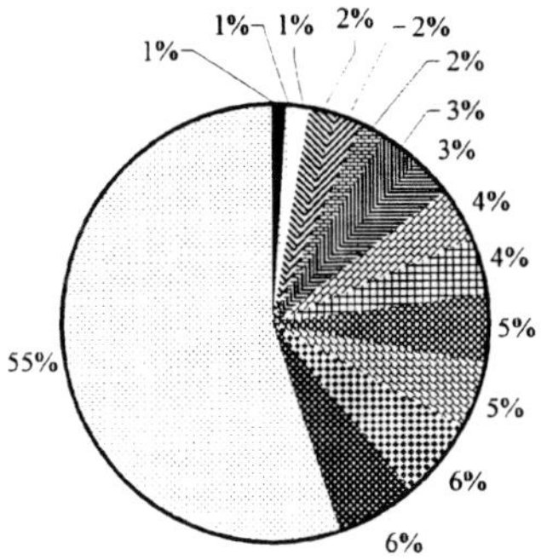

(d) A Pareto diagram is more preferable because the variables of interest contains many categories.

(e) Motor vehicles are a major source of release of toxic materials into the air.

59. (a)

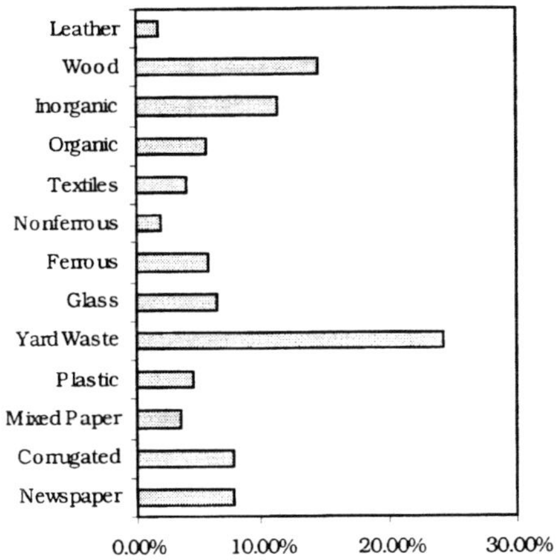

(b)

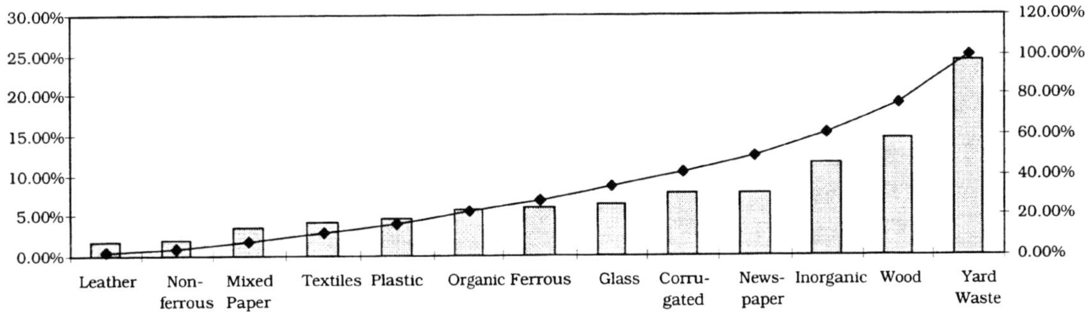

(c)

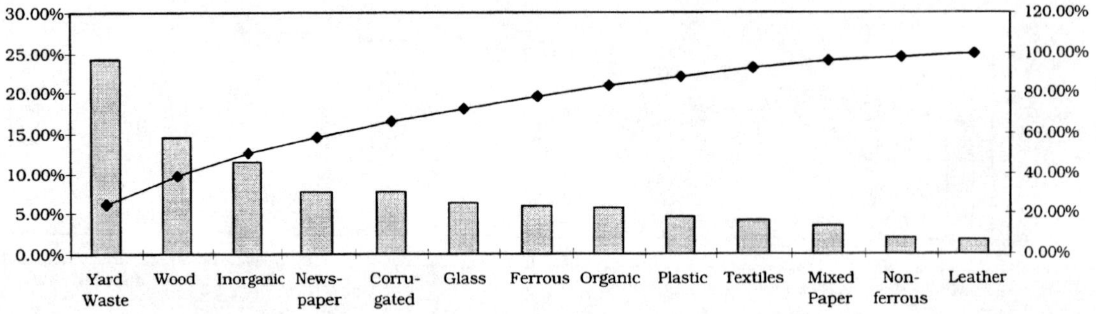

(d) A Pareto diagram is more preferable because the variable of interest contains many categories.

(e) Yard waste has the largest percent (about a quarter of all the waste profiled) whereas leather and nonferrous are the least.

60. (a)

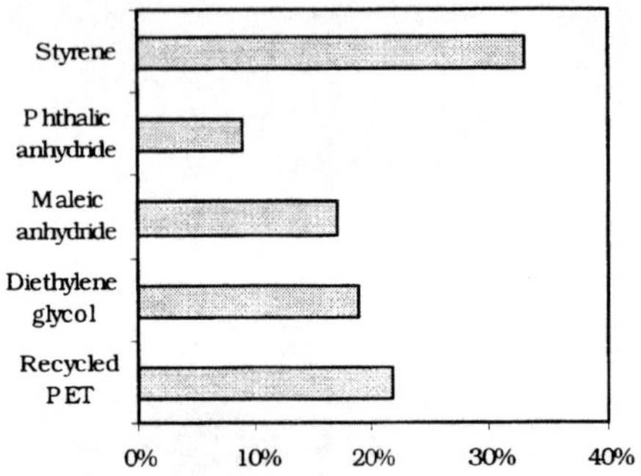

(b)

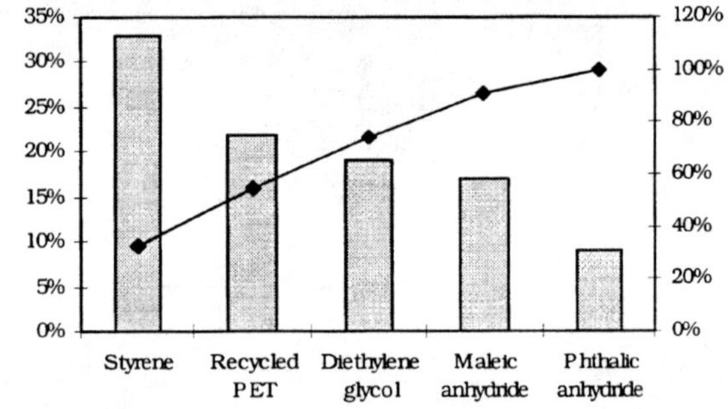

(c)

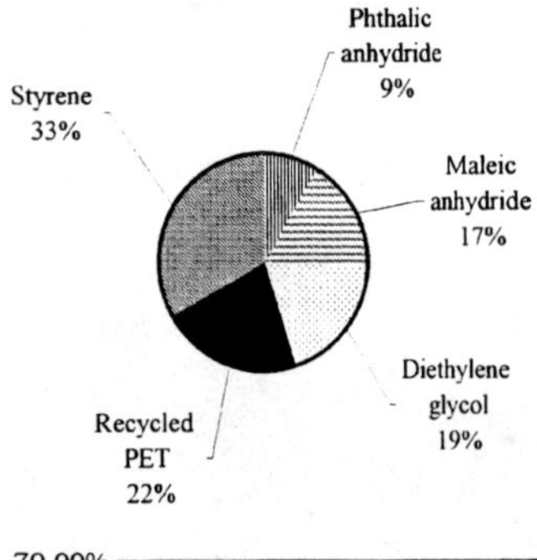

(d) The bar chart.

(e)

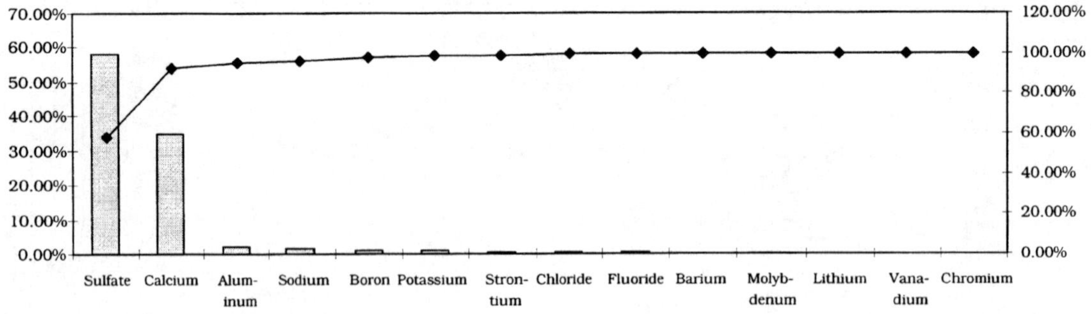

(f)

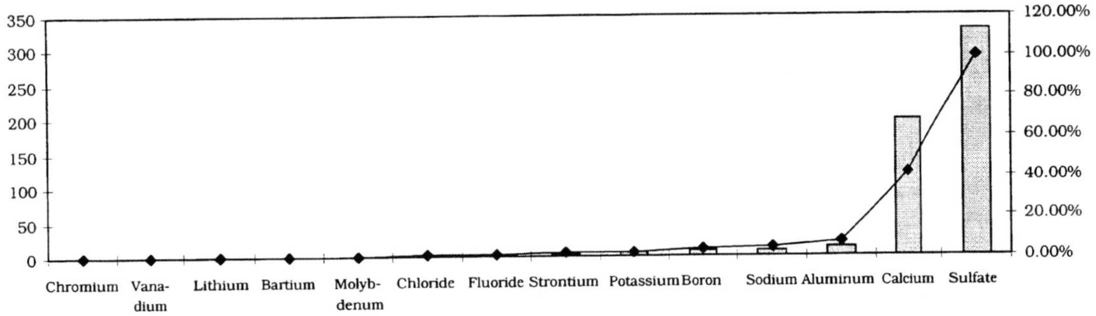

(g)

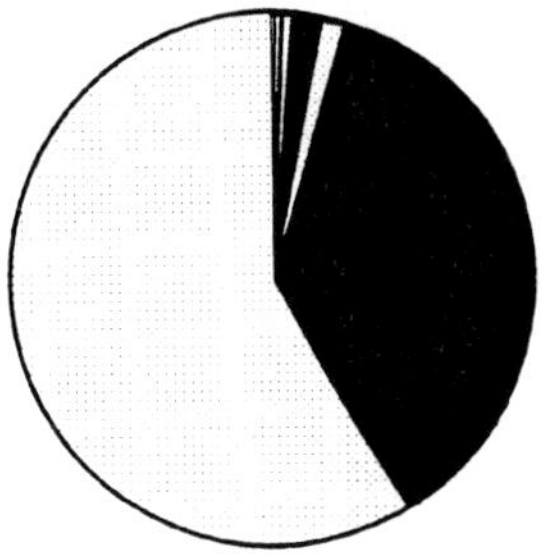

(h) The Pareto chart is more preferable because categorical variable of interest contains many categories.

61. (a) County A

	Cast Iron Pipe Break	Cast Iron Joint Break	Corroded Steel	Other	All
1989	43.44	1.56	41.56	13.44	100.00
1990	22.46	1.07	64.17	12.30	100.00
1991	20.75	0.47	68.87	9.91	100.00
All	31.29	1.11	55.49	12.10	100.00

County B

	Cast Iron Pipe Break	Cast Iron Joint Break	Corroded Steel	Other	All
1989	84.98	1.10	3.05	10.87	100.00
1990	79.81	1.24	1.86	17.08	100.00
1991	77.48	—	—	22.52	100.00
All	82.54	0.95	2.27	14.23	100.00

County C

	Cast Iron Pipe Break	Cast Iron Joint Break	Corroded Steel	Other	All
1989	72.53	8.58	8.15	10.73	100.00
1990	86.79	1.89	4.91	6.42	100.00
1991	77.55	2.86	3.67	15.92	100.00
All	79.27	4.31	5.52	10.90	100.00

County D

	Cast Iron Pipe Break	Cast Iron Joint Break	Corroded Steel	Other	All
1989	29.85	1.49	50.75	17.91	100.00
1990	22.46	0.72	51.45	25.36	100.00
1991	30.41	1.03	39.69	28.87	100.00
All	8.14	1.13	46.90	23.83	100.00

(b) County A

	Cast Iron Pipe Break	Cast Iron Joint Break	Corroded Steel	Other	All
1989	61.78	62.50	33.33	49.43	44.51
1990	18.67	25.00	30.08	26.44	26.01
1991	19.56	12.50	36.59	24.14	29.49
All	100.00	100.00	100.00	100.00	100.00

County B

	Cast Iron Pipe Break	Cast Iron Joint Break	Corroded Steel	Other	All
1989	61.87	69.23	80.65	45.88	60.09
1990	22.84	30.77	19.35	28.35	23.62
1991	15.29	—	—	25.77	16.29
All	100.00	100.00	100.00	100.00	100.00

County C

	Cast Iron Pipe Break	Cast Iron Joint Break	Corroded Steel	Other	All
1989	28.69	62.50	46.34	30.86	31.36
1990	39.05	15.63	31.71	20.99	35.67
1991	32.26	21.88	21.95	48.15	32.97
All	100.00	100.00	100.00	100.00	100.00

County D

	Cast Iron Pipe Break	Cast Iron Joint Break	Corroded Steel	Other	All
1989	40.00	50.00	40.80	28.35	37.71
1990	20.67	16.67	28.40	27.56	25.89
1991	39.33	33.33	30.80	44.09	36.40
All	100.00	100.00	100.00	100.00	100.00

(c) County A

	Cast Iron Pipe Break	Cast Iron Joint Break	Corroded Steel	Other	All
1989	19.33	0.70	18.50	5.98	44.51
1990	5.84	0.28	16.69	3.20	26.01
1991	6.12	0.14	20.31	2.92	29.49
All	31.29	1.11	55.49	12.10	100.00

County B

	Cast Iron Pipe Break	Cast Iron Joint Break	Corroded Steel	Other	All
1989	51.06	0.66	1.83	6.53	60.09
1990	18.86	0.29	0.44	4.04	23.62
1991	12.62	—	—	3.67	16.29
All	82.54	0.95	2.27	14.23	100.00

County C

	Cast Iron Pipe Break	Cast Iron Joint Break	Corroded Steel	Other	All
1989	22.75	2.69	2.56	3.36	31.36
1990	30.96	0.67	1.75	2.29	35.67
1991	25.57	0.94	1.21	5.25	32.97
All	79.27	4.31	5.52	10.90	100.00

County D

	Cast Iron Pipe Break	Cast Iron Joint Break	Corroded Steel	Other	All
1989	11.26	0.56	19.14	6.75	37.71
1990	5.82	0.19	13.32	6.57	25.89
1991	11.07	0.38	14.45	10.51	36.40
All	28.14	1.13	46.90	23.83	100.00

(d) A table of row percentages is more useful for determining the nature of the accidents, whereas a table of column percentages is more useful for showing the dynamics of change; causes of accidents for a range of years.

(e) County A
There were two almost equally frequent causes for leaks in 1989, but during the following years corroded steel became the main reason of the leak.
County B
The main reason of leaks was the cast iron joint break, but the percentage of leaks caused by the cast iron joint break decreased in the period from 1989 to 1991.
County C
The main reason of leaks was the cast iron joint break, and the percentage of leaks caused by the cast iron joint break was almost the same in the period from 1989 to 1991.
County D
The main reason of leaks was the corroded steel during 1989–1990, but the percentage of leaks caused by the corroded steel decreased while the percentage of leaks caused by the cast iron joint break and other reasons increased in 1991.

62. (a)

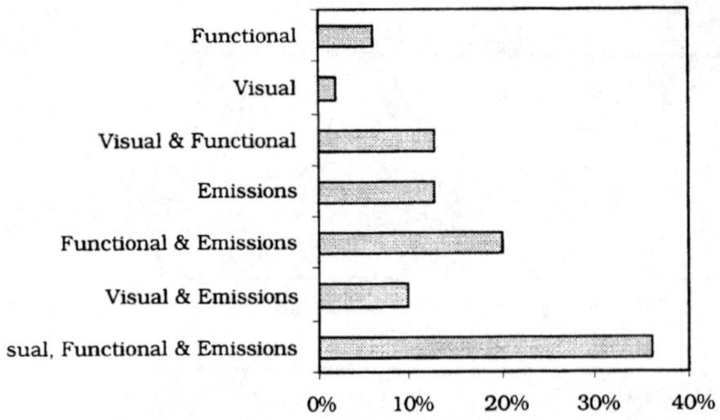

(b)

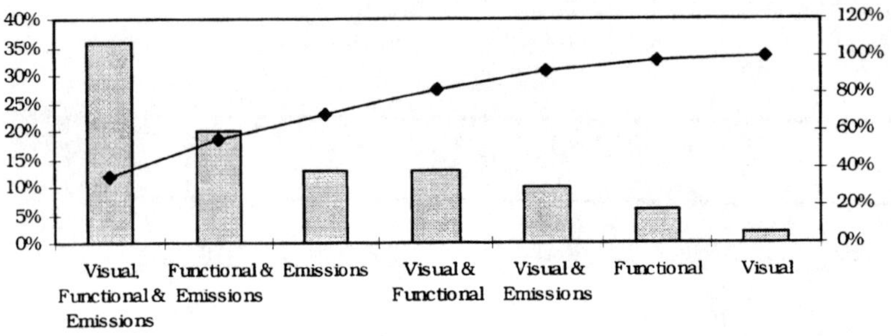

(c)

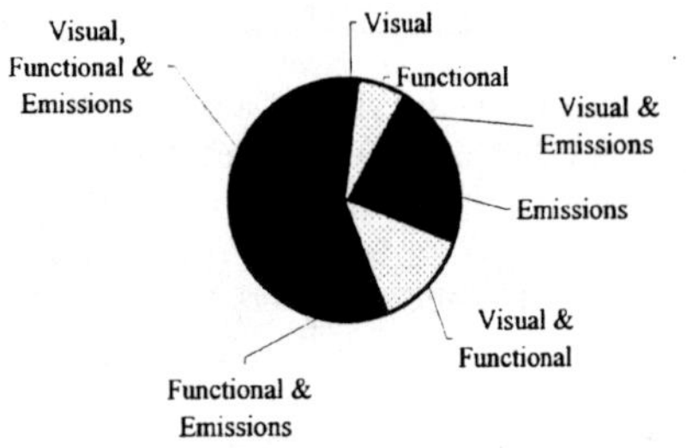

(d) A bar chart is more preferable because it clearly shows the percentage of vehicle failures by emissions and that visual and functional failures are the same, whereas on the Pareto chart the visual and functional failures appear smaller than the emissions percentage.

(e) Visual, functional and emissions are the most frequent types of failure.

63. (a) Stem-and-Leaf Display for MPG

```
Stem unit: |10
         1 |5 7 7 7 7 7 7 8 8 8 9 9 9 9 9 9
         2 |0 0 0 0 0 0 0 0 0 0 0 0 1 1 1 1 1 1 1 1 1 2 2 2 2 2 2 2 2 2 2 2 3 3 3 3 3 3 4 4 4 4 4 4 5 5 6 6 6 6 6 6 6 7
           | 8 8 8 8 9 9 9 9 9 9
         3 |0 0 0 1 2 3 4 4 6
```

Stem-and-Leaf Display for Fuel Capacity

```
Stem unit:   1
        10 | 0 6 6
        11 | 9 9 9 9
        12 | 5 5 8 8
        13 | 2 2 2 2 2 2 2 3 5
        14 | 5 5 5 5
        15 | 2 2 4 5 5 5 5 5 6 9 9 9 9 9 9
        16 | 0 0 0 0 4 5 5 5 5 5 9
        17 | 0 0 1 1 2 2 4
        18 | 0 0 0 0 0 0 0 0 0 0 5 5 5 5 5 5 5
        19 | 0 0 3
        20 | 0 0 0 0 0 0 0 6 8
        21 | 1
        22 | 5
        23 | 0
```

Stem-and-Leaf Display for Length

```
Stem unit:   10
        14 | 9
        15 | 6
        16 | 0 2 2 4 5
        17 | 0 1 1 2 2 2 2 3 3 4 4 5 5 5 5 5 6 7 7 8 8
        18 | 0 0 1 2 2 2 2 3 4 4 4 4 4 5 6 6 7 7 7 7 8 8 8
           |  8 8 9 9
        19 | 0 0 0 0 1 1 2 2 3 4 5 5 5 7 8
        20 | 0 0 0 0 0 1 1 1 2 2 2 2 4 5 7 7
        21 | 2 2 4
```

Stem-and-Leaf Display for Width

```
Stem unit:   1
        63 | 0 0
        64 | 0
        65 | 0
        66 | 0 0 0 0 0
        67 | 0 0 0 0 0 0 0 0 0 0 0 0 0 0 0 0 0
        68 | 0 0 0 0 0 0 0
        69 | 0 0 0 0 0 0 0 0 0 0 0
        70 | 0 0 0 0 0 0 0 0 0 0 0 0 0 0
        71 | 0 0 0 0 0 0
        72 | 0 0 0
        73 | 0 0 0 0 0 0
        74 | 0 0 0 0 0 0 0
        75 | 0 0 0 0
        76 | 0
        77 |
        78 | 0 0 0 0
```

Stem-and-Leaf Display for Weight

Stem unit: 100

18	5
19	
20	7
21	4 7
22	9 9
23	9 9
24	1 2 4
25	0 1 4 4 7
26	0 0 3 4 7
27	2 7 7 9
28	6 7 7 7
29	0 1 1 6
30	3 5 7 9 10
31	0 0 1 5 5 8 8 8 10
32	3 5 6 8 8 9
33	2 5 7 10
34	0 1 2 2 4 5 5 5 6 9
35	2 4 4 5 5 5 6
36	7
37	1 1 1 3 7 7
38	1 4
39	4 10
40	1 1
41	

Stem-and-Leaf Display for Wheelbase

Stem unit: 10

9	3 3 4 4 5 7 7 7 7 8 8 8 8 8 9
10	0 0 0 0 0 1 1 1 2 2 3 3 3 3 3 3 3 3 3 3 3 3 4 4 4 4 4 4 4 5 5 5 6 6 6 6 6 6 6 7 7 7 7 7 8 8 8 8 8 8 8 8 8 9
	9 9 9 9
11	1 1 1 2 3 3 3 3 3 3 3 4 4 4 4 6

Stem-and-Leaf Display for Turning Circle

Stem unit: 1

34	0
35	0 0 0 0 0 0 0 0 0 0
36	0 0 0 0 0
37	0 0 0 0
38	0 0 0 0 0 0 0 0 0 0 0 0 0 0
39	0 0 0 0 0 0 0 0 0 0 0 0 0 0 0 0 0 0 0
40	0 0 0 0 0 0 0 0 0 0
41	0 0 0 0
42	0 0 0 0 0 0 0
43	0 0 0 0 0 0 0 0 0 0 0 0 0
44	0
45	0

Stem-and-Leaf Display for Luggage Capacity

Stem unit: 1

8	0
9	0 0
10	0 0 0 0 0 0
11	0 0 0 0
12	0 0 0 0 0 0 0 0 0 0 0 0 0
13	0 0 0 0 0 0 0 0 0 0 0
14	0 0 0 0 0 0 0 0 0 0 0 0 0 0 0 0 0
15	0 0 0 0 0 0 0 0
16	0 0 0 0 0 0 0 0 0 0 0 0
17	0 0 0 0 0
18	0
19	0 0 0 0
20	0
21	0 0
22	
23	
24	0 0

Stem-and-Leaf Display for Front Leg Room

Stem unit: 1

Stem	Leaves
40	0 0 0 5 5 5 5 5
41	0 0 0 0 0 0 0 0 0 0 0 0 0 0 5 5 5 5
	5 5 5 5 5 5 5 5 5 5 5 5 5
42	0 0 0 0 0 0 0 0 0 0 0 0 0 0 0 0 0 0
	0 0 0 0 0 5 5 5 5 5 5 5 5 5 5 5 5
43	0 0 0 0 0 0 0 0 0 0 0 5 5
44	0 5

Stem-and-Leaf Display for Front Head Room

Stem unit: 1

Stem	Leaves
1	0 5 5 5
2	0 0 0 0 0 0 5 5 5 5 5 5 5
3	0 0 0 0 0 0 0 0 0 0 0 0 0 0 0 0 0 5 5 5 5 5 5
	5 5 5 5 5 5 5 5 5 5
4	0 0 0 0 0 0 0 0 0 0 0 0 5 5 5 5 5 5 5 5 5 5 5
	5
5	0 0 0 0 0 0 0 0 0 5 5 5 5
6	0 5

(b)

mpg	Frequency	Percentage
10.0–14.0	0	0.00
15–19	16	17.98
20–24	44	49.44
25–29	20	22.47
30–34	8	8.99
35–39	1	1.12
More	0	0.00

Fuel Capacity	Frequency	Percentage
9.01–11.00	3	3.37
11.01–13.00	8	8.99
13.01–15.00	13	14.61
15.01–17.00	28	31.46
17.01–19.00	24	26.97
19.01–21.00	10	11.24
21.01–23.00	3	3.37
More	0	0.00

Length	Frequency	Percentage
151–160	3	3.37
161–170	5	5.62
171–180	22	24.72
181–190	29	32.58
191–200	16	17.98
201–210	11	12.36
211–220	3	3.37
More	0	0.00

Width	Frequency	Percentage
62.1–64.0	3	3.37
64.1–66.0	6	6.74
66.1–68.0	24	26.97
68.1–70.0	25	28.09
70.1–72.0	9	10.11
72.1–74.0	13	14.61
74.1–76.0	5	5.62
76.1–78.0	4	4.49
More	0	0.00

Weight	Frequency	Percentage
1499–2000	1	1.12
2001–2500	11	12.36
2501–3000	21	23.60
3001–3500	34	38.20
3501–4000	18	20.22
4001–4500	4	4.49
More	0	0.00

Wheel Base	Frequency	Percentage
91–95	5	5.62
96–100	15	16.85
101–105	27	30.34
106–110	26	29.21
111–115	15	16.85
116–120	1	1.12
More	0	0.00

Turning Circle	Frequency	Percentage
33.1–35.0	11	12.36
35.1–37.0	9	10.11
37.1–39.0	33	37.08
39.1–41.0	14	15.73
41.1–43.0	20	22.47
43.1–45.0	2	2.25
More	0	0.00

Luggage Capacity	Frequency	Percentage
7.1–10.0	9	10.11
10.1–13.0	28	31.46
13.1–16.0	37	41.57
16.1–19.0	10	11.24
19.1–22.0	3	3.37
22.1–25.0	2	2.25
More	0	0.00

Front Leg Room	Frequency	Percentage
39.9–40.0	3	3.37
40.1–41.0	19	21.35
41.1–42.0	40	44.94
42.1–43.0	23	25.84
43.1–44.0	3	3.37
44.1–45.0	1	1.12
More	0	0.00

Front Head Room	Frequency	Percentage
0.1–1.0	1	1.12
1.1–2.0	9	10.11
2.1–3.0	24	26.97
3.1–4.0	28	31.46
4.1–5.0	21	23.60
5.1–6.0	5	5.62
6.1–7.0	1	1.12
More	0	0.00

(c)

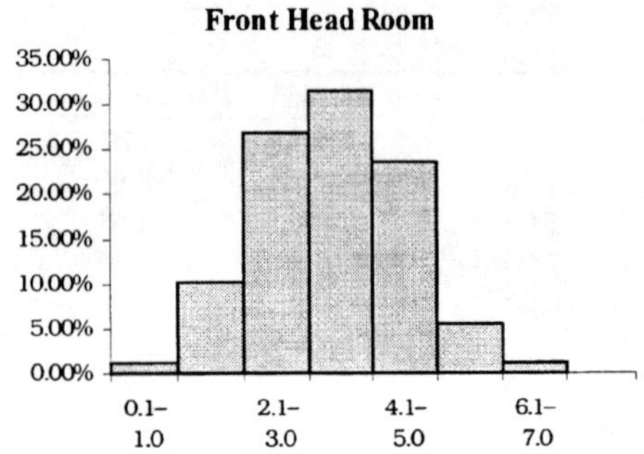

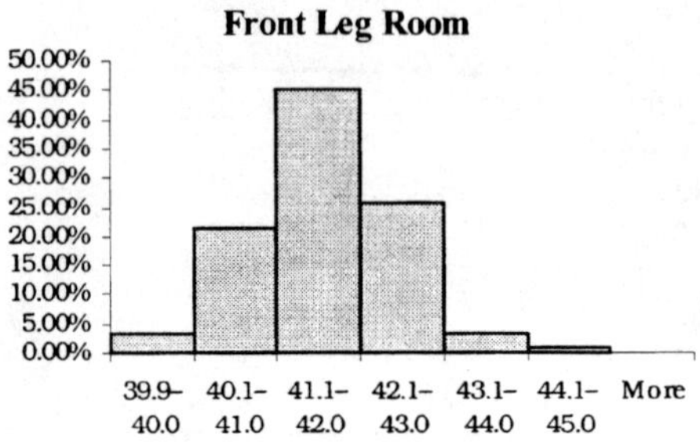

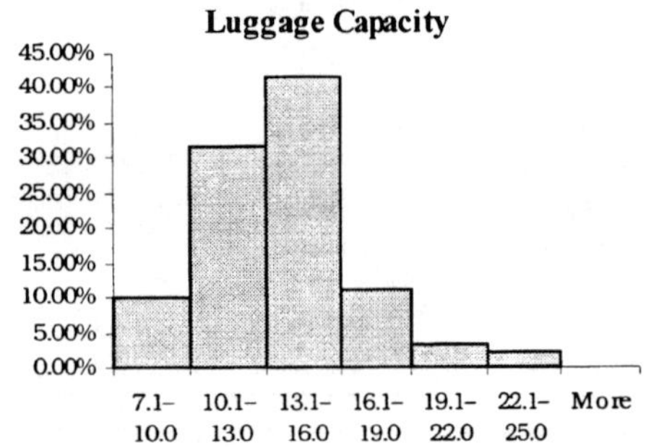

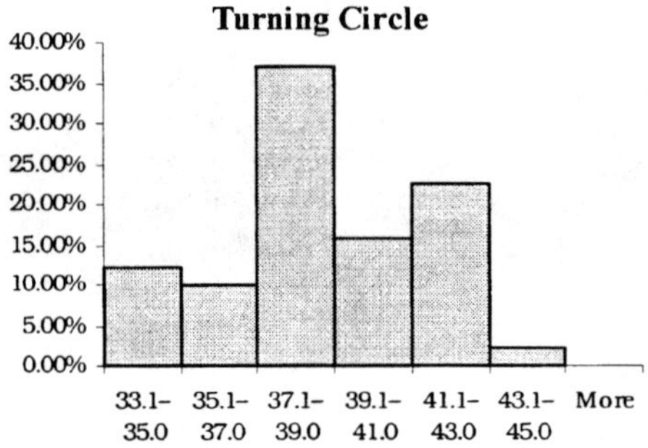

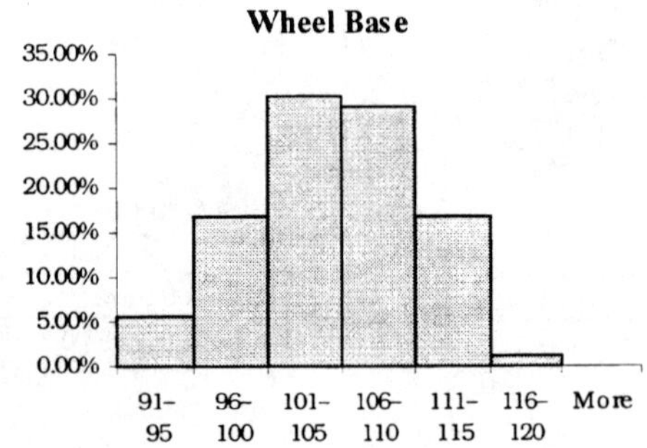

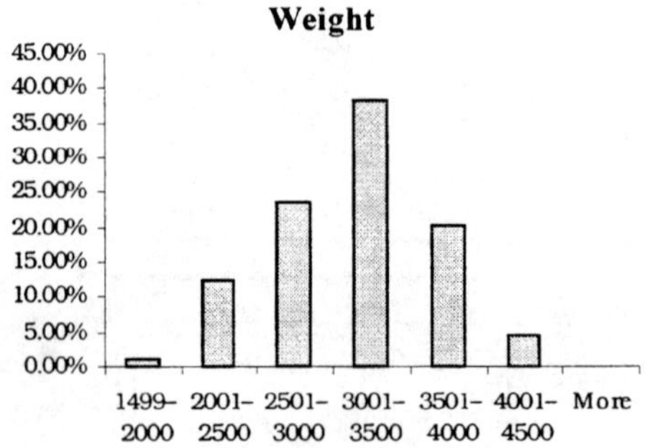

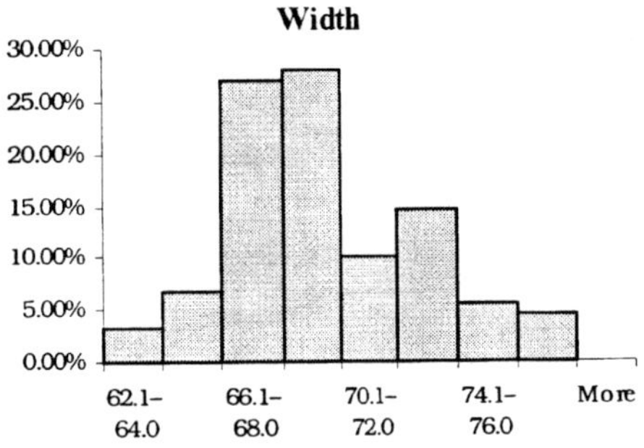
Width
30.00%
25.00%
20.00%
15.00%
10.00%
5.00%
0.00%
62.1– 64.0
66.1– 68.0
70.1– 72.0
74.1– 76.0
More

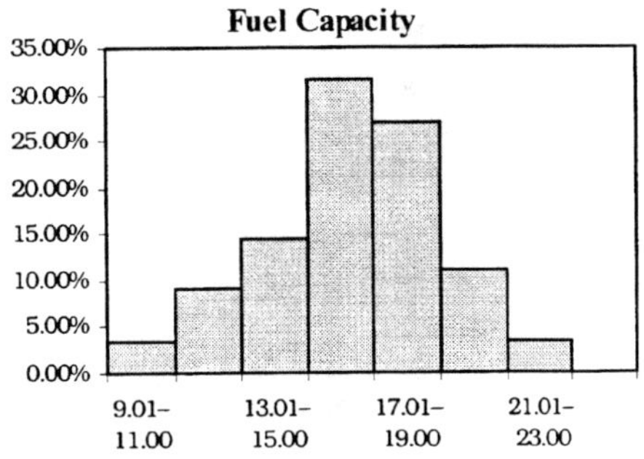
Fuel Capacity
35.00%
30.00%
25.00%
20.00%
15.00%
10.00%
5.00%
0.00%
9.01– 11.00
13.01– 15.00
17.01– 19.00
21.01– 23.00

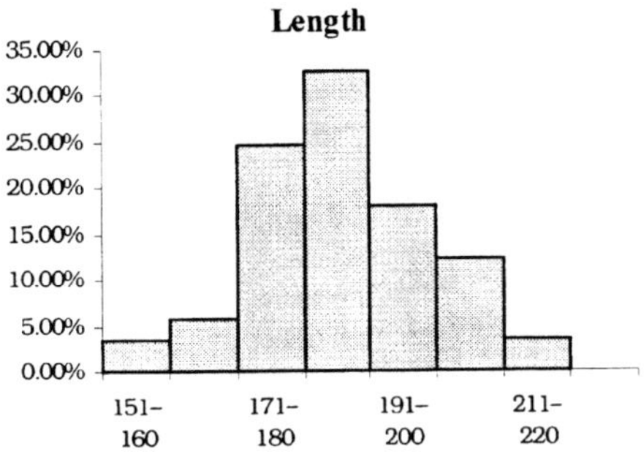
Length
35.00%
30.00%
25.00%
20.00%
15.00%
10.00%
5.00%
0.00%
151– 160
171– 180
191– 200
211– 220

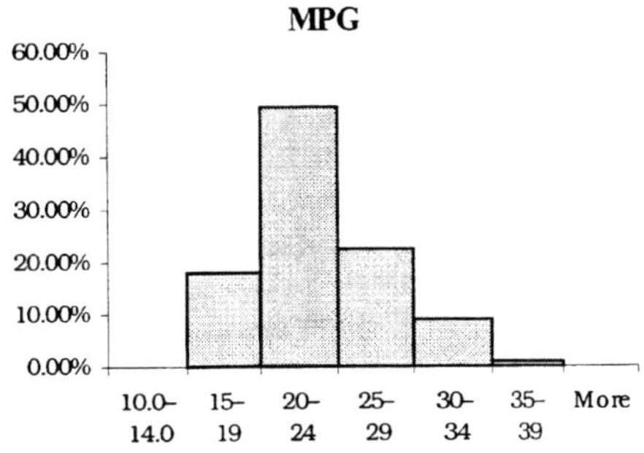
MPG
60.00%
50.00%
40.00%
30.00%
20.00%
10.00%
0.00%
10.0– 14.0
15– 19
20– 24
25– 29
30– 34
35– 39
More

(d)

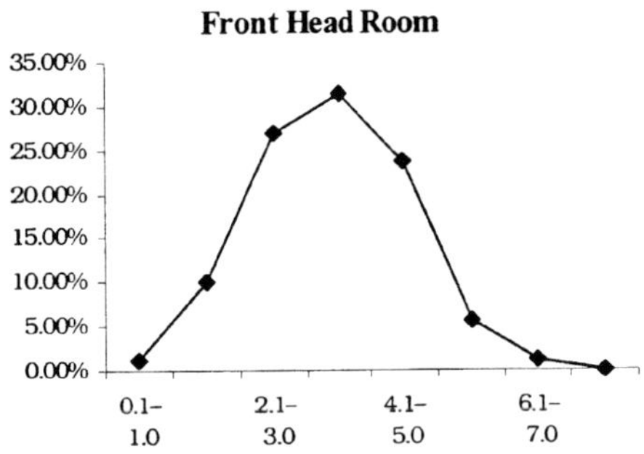
Front Head Room
35.00%
30.00%
25.00%
20.00%
15.00%
10.00%
5.00%
0.00%
0.1– 1.0
2.1– 3.0
4.1– 5.0
6.1– 7.0

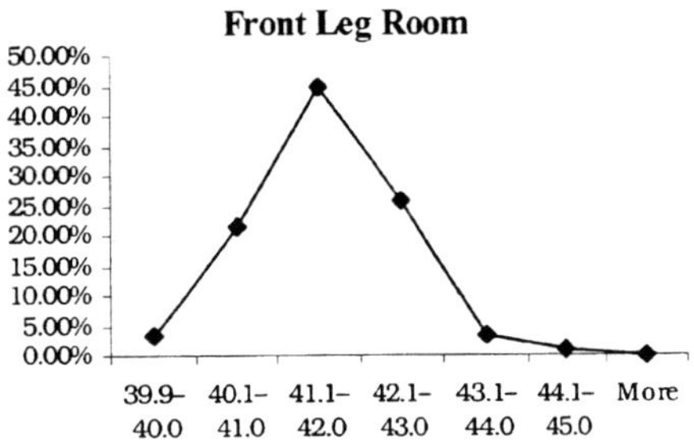
Front Leg Room
50.00%
45.00%
40.00%
35.00%
30.00%
25.00%
20.00%
15.00%
10.00%
5.00%
0.00%
39.9– 40.0
40.1– 41.0
41.1– 42.0
42.1– 43.0
43.1– 44.0
44.1– 45.0
More

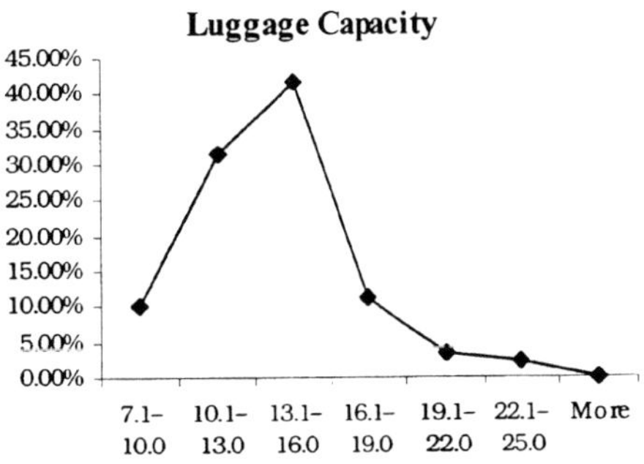
Luggage Capacity
45.00%
40.00%
35.00%
30.00%
25.00%
20.00%
15.00%
10.00%
5.00%
0.00%
7.1– 10.0
10.1– 13.0
13.1– 16.0
16.1– 19.0
19.1– 22.0
22.1– 25.0
More

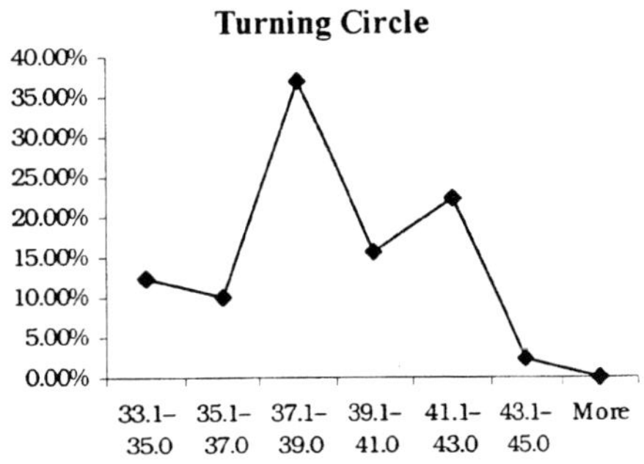
Turning Circle
40.00%
35.00%
30.00%
25.00%
20.00%
15.00%
10.00%
5.00%
0.00%
33.1– 35.0
35.1– 37.0
37.1– 39.0
39.1– 41.0
41.1– 43.0
43.1– 45.0
More

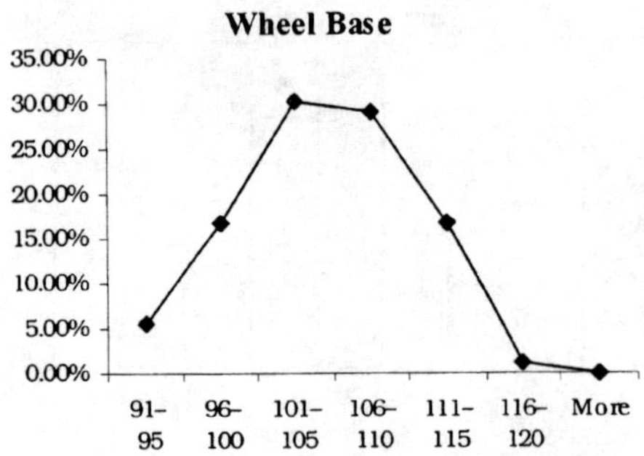

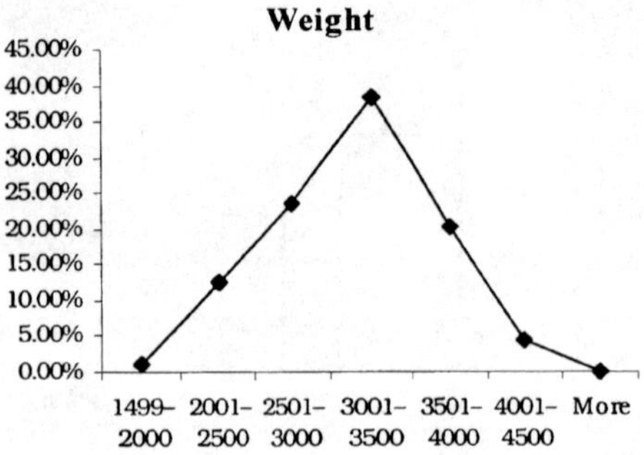

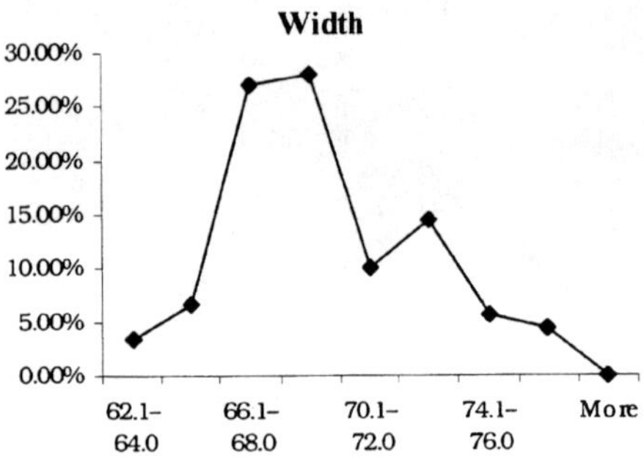

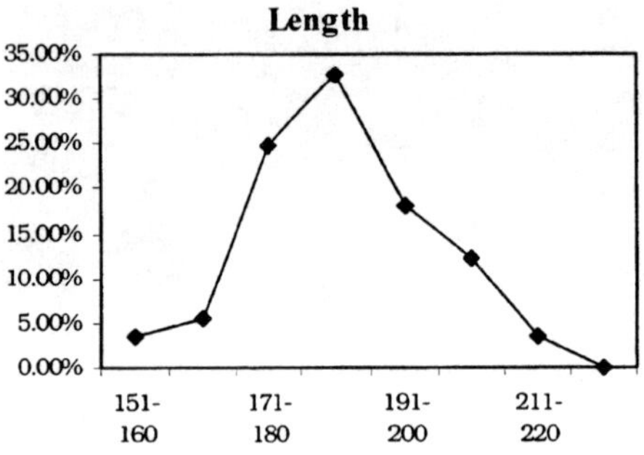

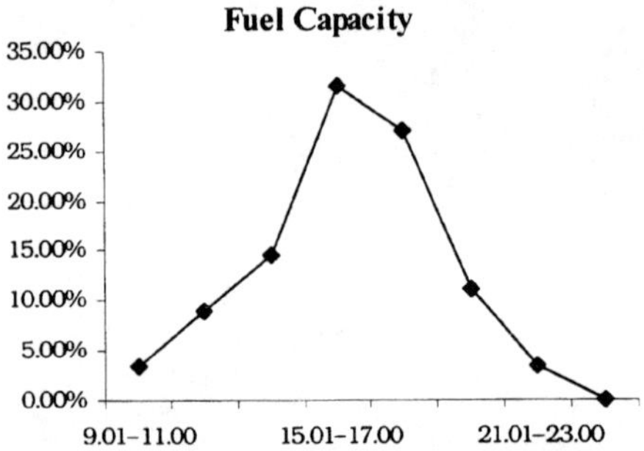

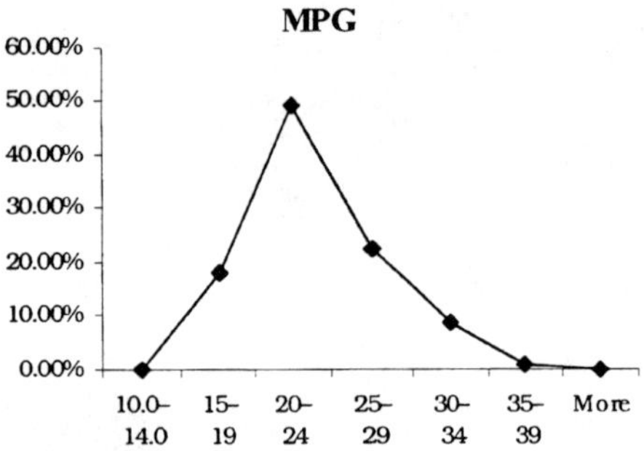

(e)

mpg	Frequency	Cumulative %
10.0–14.0	0	.00
15 –19	16	17.98
20–24	44	67.42
25–29	20	89.89
30–34	8	98.88
35–39	1	100.00
More	0	100.00

Fuel Capacity	Frequency	Cumulative %
9.01–11.00	3	3.37
11.01–13.00	8	12.36
13.01–15.00	13	26.97
15.01–17.00	28	58.43
17.01–19.00	24	85.39
19.01–21.00	10	96.63
21.01–23.00	3	100.00
More	0	100.00

Length	Frequency	Cumulative %
151–160	3	3.37
161–170	5	8.99
171–180	22	33.71
181–190	29	66.29
191–200	16	84.27
201–210	11	96.63
211–220	3	100.00
More	0	100.00

Width	Frequency	Cumulative %
62.1–64.0	3	3.37
64.1–66.0	6	10.11
66.1–68.0	24	37.08
68.1–70.0	25	65.17
70.1–72.0	9	75.28
72.1–74.0	13	89.89
74.1–76.0	5	95.51
76.1–78.0	4	100.00
More	0	100.00

Weight	Frequency	Cumulative %
1499–2000	1	1.12
2001–2500	11	13.48
2501–3000	21	37.08
3001–3500	34	75.28
3501–4000	18	95.51
4001–4500	4	100.00
More	0	100.00

Wheel Base	Frequency	Cumulative %
91–95	5	5.62
96–100	15	22.47
101–105	27	52.81
106–110	26	82.02
111–115	15	98.88
116–120	1	100.00
More	0	100.00

Turning Circle	Frequency	Cumulative %
33.1–35.0	11	12.36
35.1–37.0	9	22.47
37.1–39.0	33	59.55
39.1–41.0	14	75.28
41.1–43.0	20	97.75
43.1–45.0	2	100.00
More	0	100.00

Luggage Capacity	Frequency	Cumulative %
7.1–10.0	9	10.11
10.1–13.0	28	41.57
13.1–16.0	37	83.15
16.1–19.0	10	94.38
19.1–22.0	3	97.75
22.1–25.0	2	100.00
More	0	100.00

Front Leg Room	Frequency	Cumulative %
39.9–40.0	3	3.37
40.1–41.0	19	24.72
41.1–42.0	40	69.66
42.1–43.0	23	95.51
43.1–44.0	3	98.88
44.1–45.0	1	100.00
More	0	100.00

Front Head Room	Frequency	Cumulative %
0.1–1.0	1	1.12
1.1–2.0	9	11.24
2.1–3.0	24	38.20
3.1–4.0	28	69.66
4.1–5.0	21	93.26
5.1–6.0	5	98.88
6.1–7.0	1	100.00
More	0	100.00

(f)

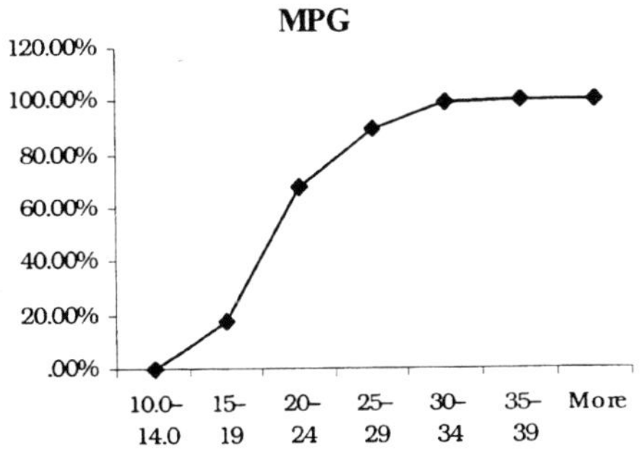

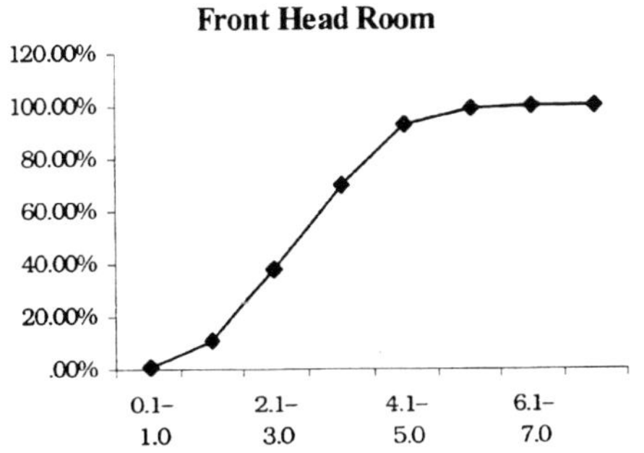

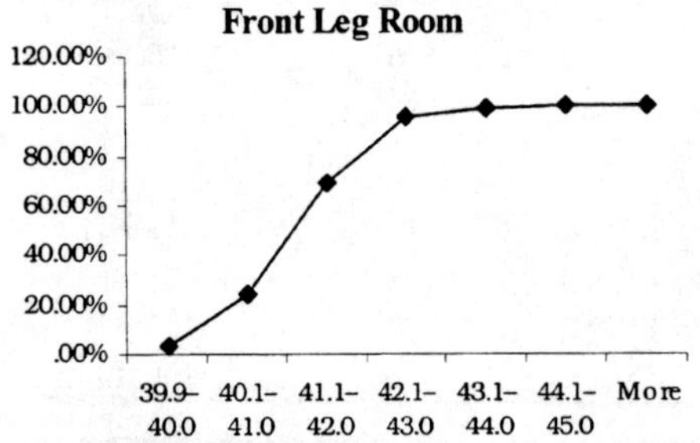

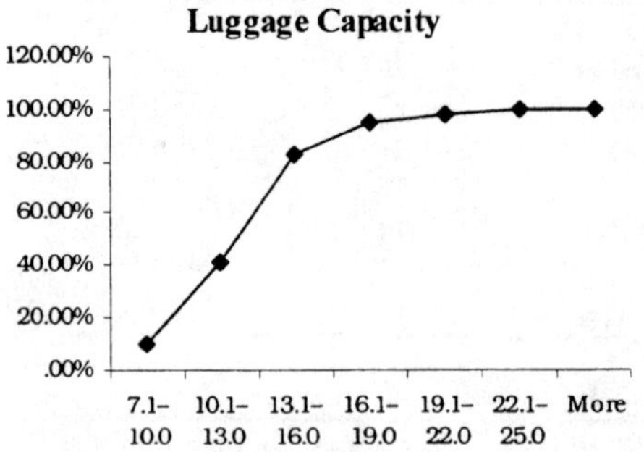

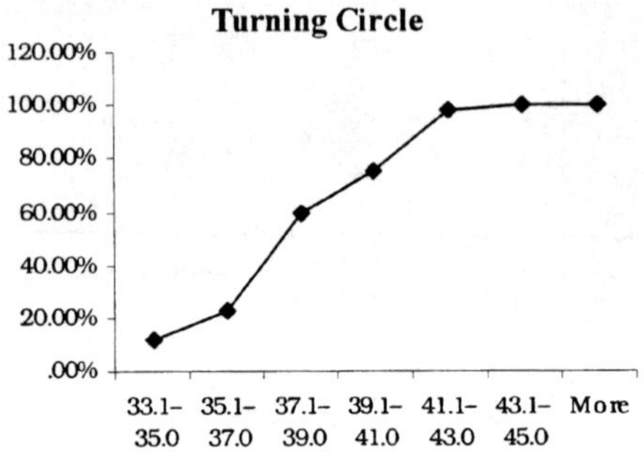

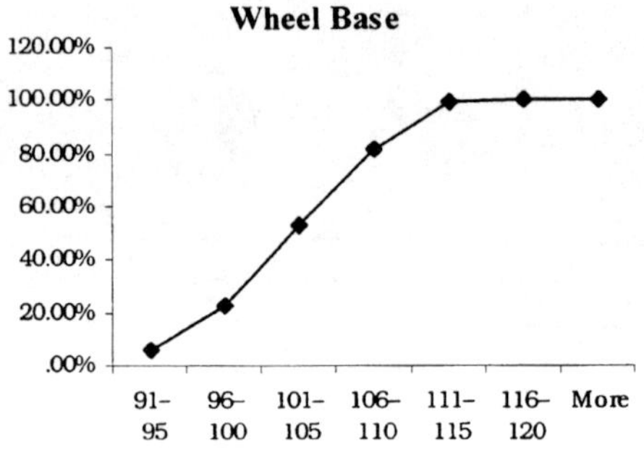

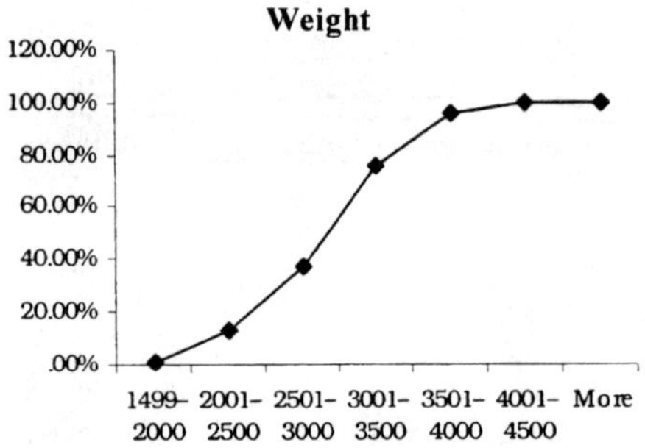

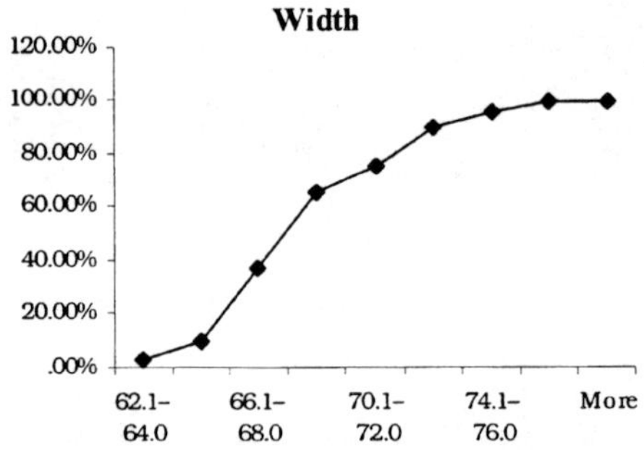

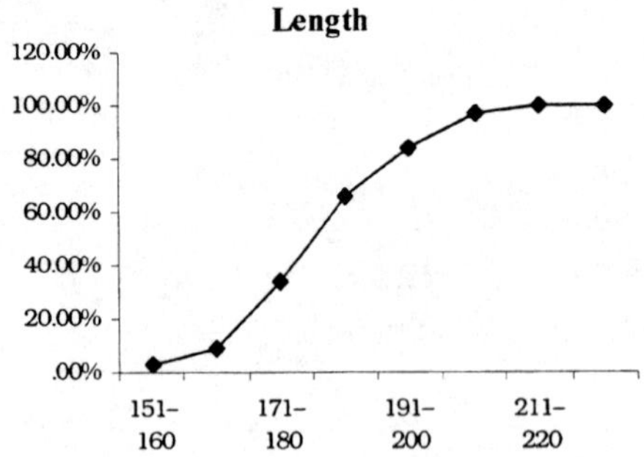

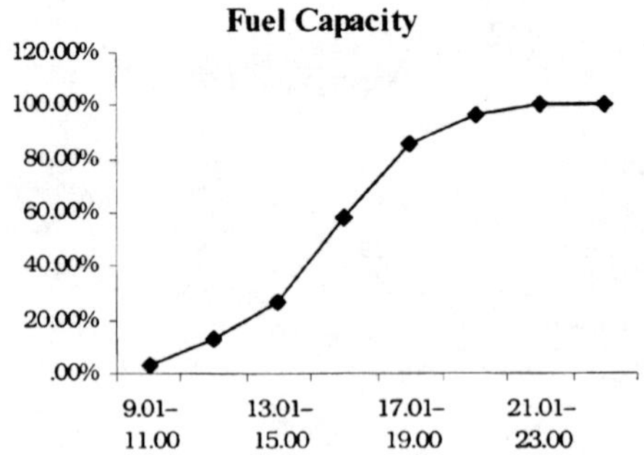

(g) Answers will vary.

(h)

mpg	Frequency	Percentage	Cumulative %
10.0–14.0	0	0.00	.00
15 –19	9	52.94	52.94
20–24	8	47.06	100.00
25–29	0	0.00	100.00
30–34	0	0.00	100.00
35–39	0	0.00	100.00
More	0	0.00	100.00

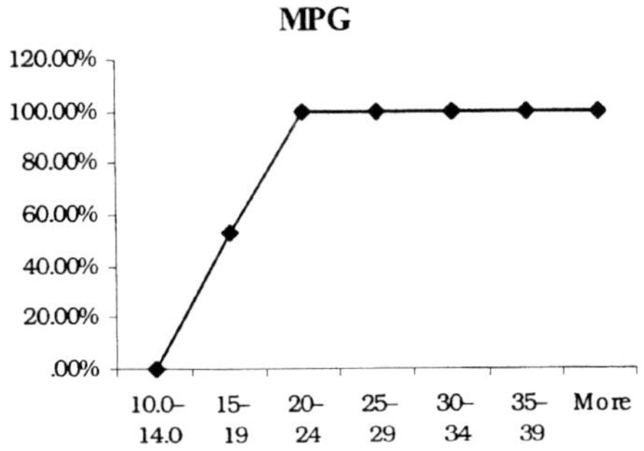

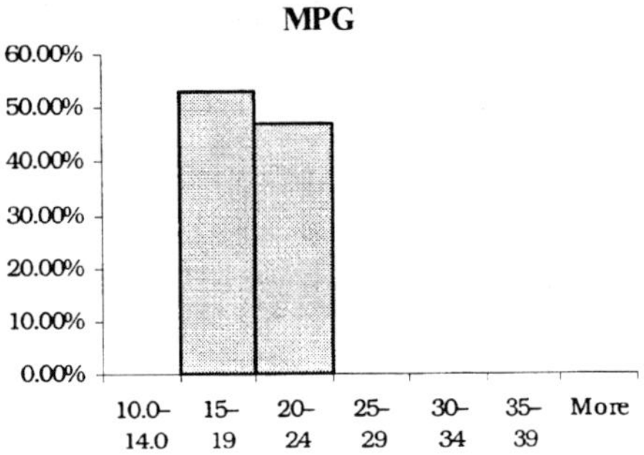

mpg	Frequency	Percentage	Cumulative %
10.0–14.0	0	0.00	.00
15–19	7	9.72	9.72
20–24	36	50.00	59.72
25–29	20	27.78	87.50
30–34	8	11.11	98.61
35–39	1	1.39	100.00
More	0	0.00	100.00

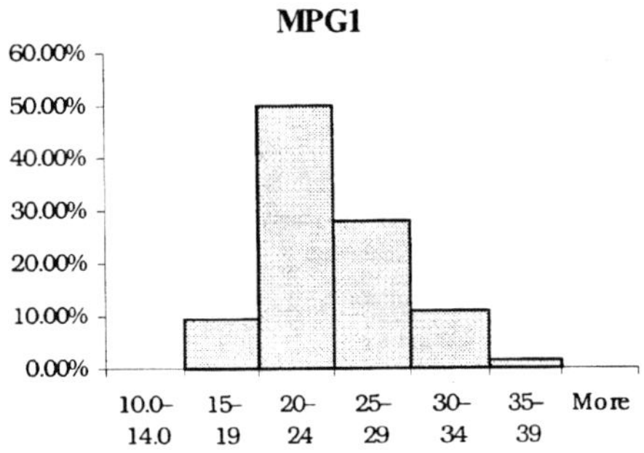

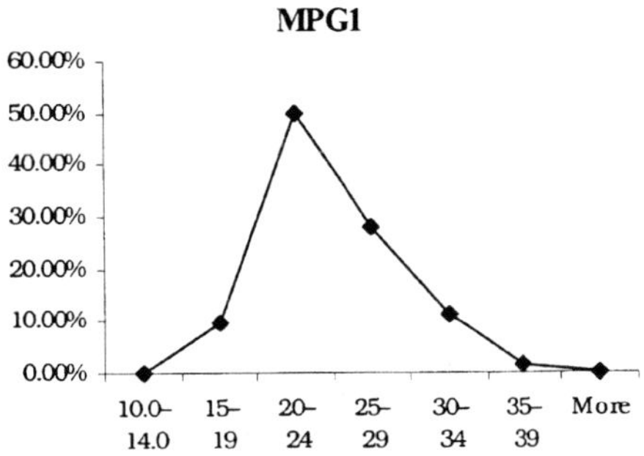

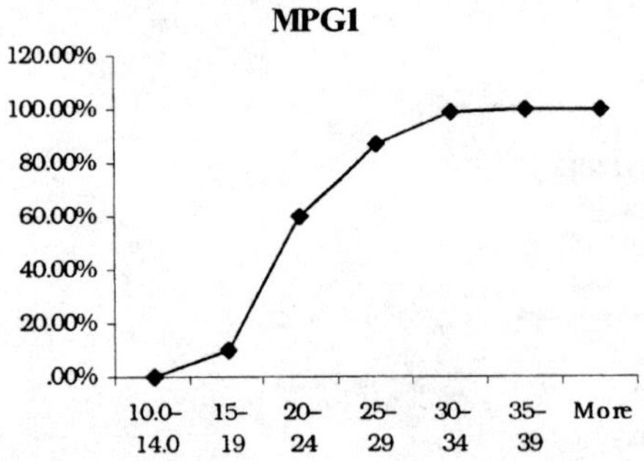

Fuel Capacity	Frequency	Percentage	Cumulative %
9.01–11.00	0	0.00	.00
11.01–13.00	0	0.00	.00
13.01–15.00	0	0.00	.00
15.01–17.00	5	29.41	29.41
17.01–19.00	5	29.41	58.82
19.01–21.00	4	23.53	82.35
21.01–23.00	3	17.65	100.00
More	0	0.00	100.00

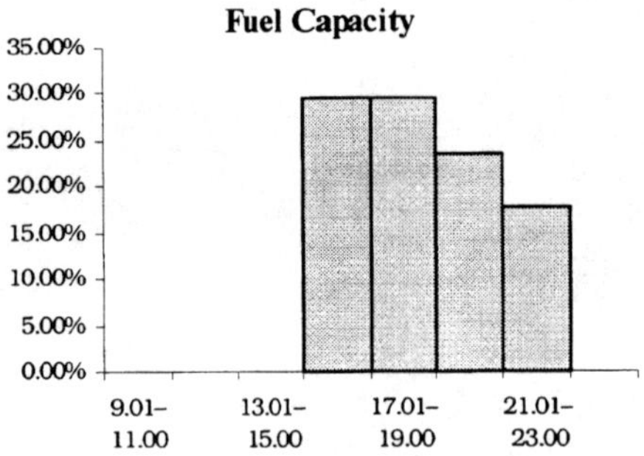

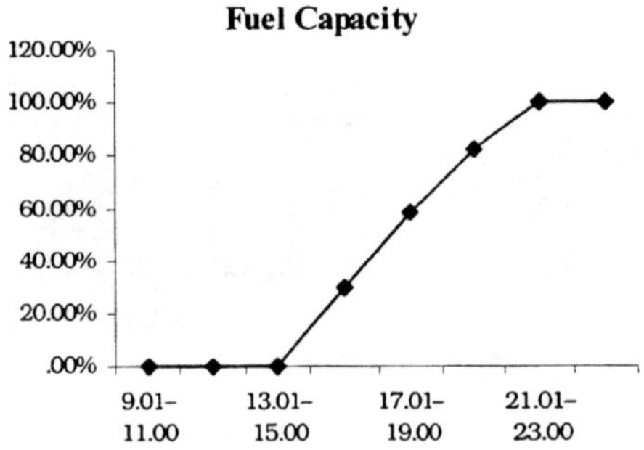

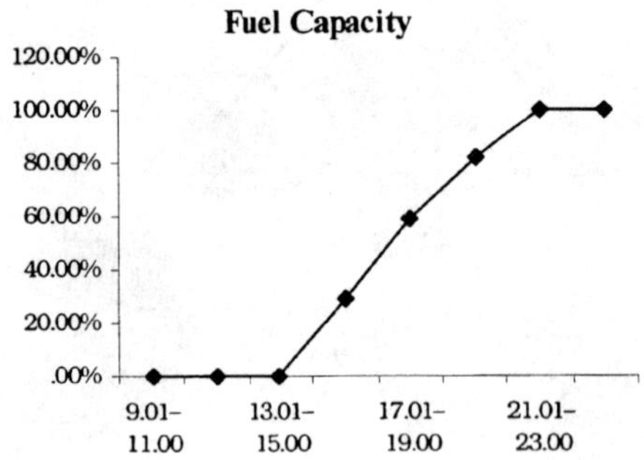

Fuel Capacity	Frequency	Percentage	Cumulative %
9.01–11.00	3	4.17	4.17
11.01–13.00	8	11.11	15.28
13.01–15.00	13	18.06	33.33
15.01–17.00	23	31.94	65.28
17.01–19.00	19	26.39	91.67
19.01–21.00	6	8.33	100.00
21.01–23.00	0	0.00	100.00
More	0	0.00	100.00

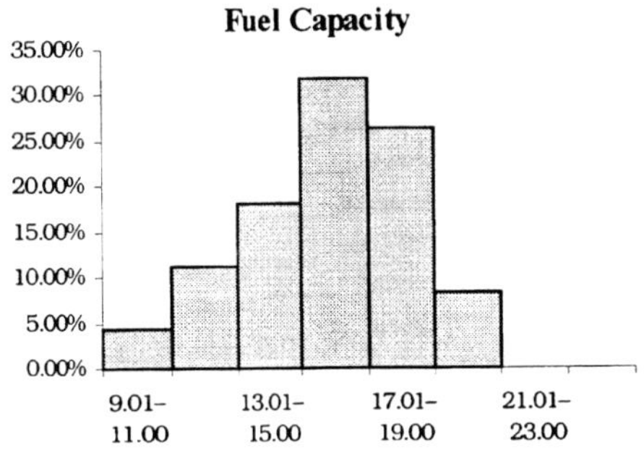

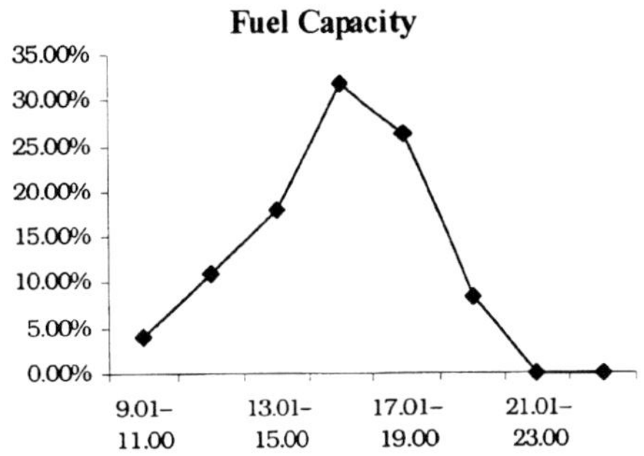

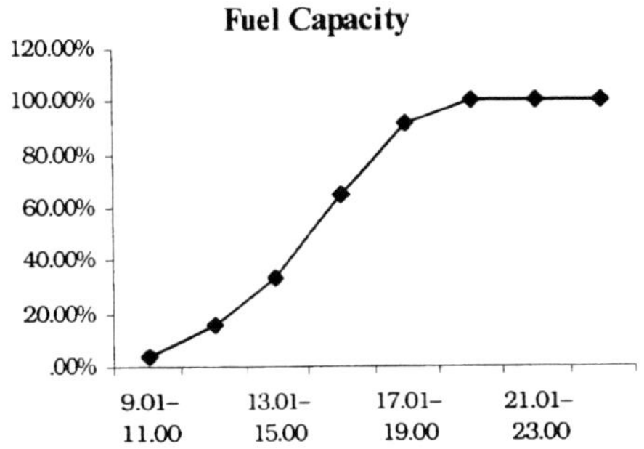

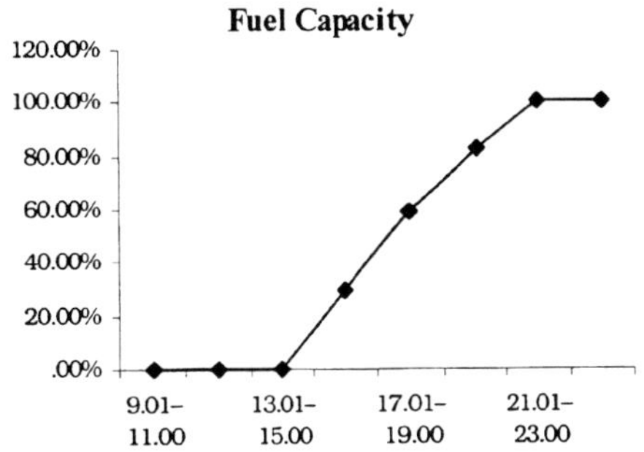

Length	Frequency	Percentage	Cumulative %
151–160	0	0.00	.00
161–170	0	0.00	.00
171–180	3	17.65	17.65
181–190	1	5.88	23.53
191–200	9	52.94	76.47
201–210	1	5.88	82.35
211–220	3	17.65	100.00
More	0	0.00	100.00

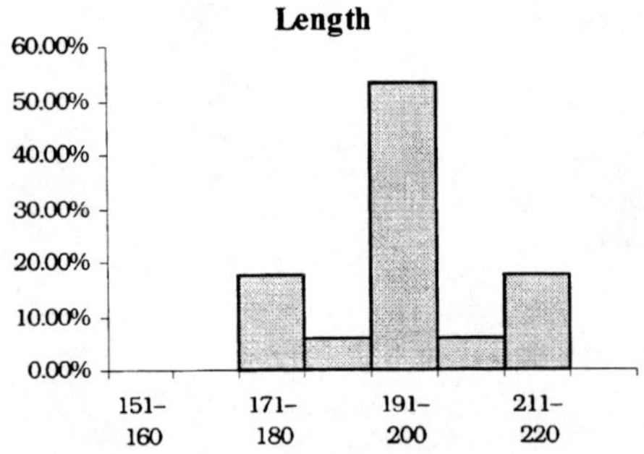

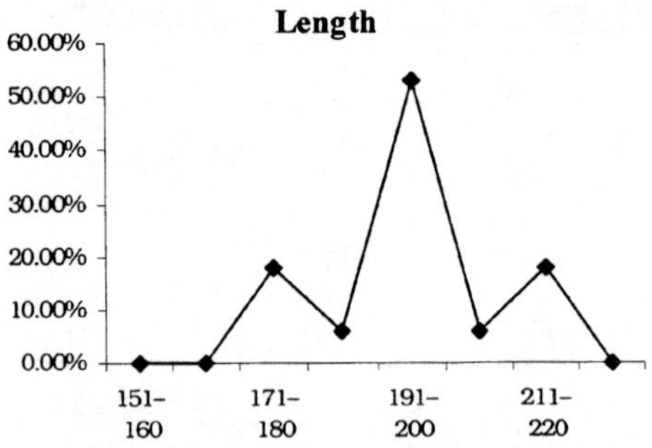

Length	Frequency	Percentage	Cumulative %
151–160	3	4.17	4.17
161–170	5	6.94	11.11
171–180	19	26.39	37.50
181–190	28	38.89	76.39
191–200	7	9.72	86.11
201–210	10	13.89	100.00
211–220	0	0.00	100.00
More	0	0.00	100.00

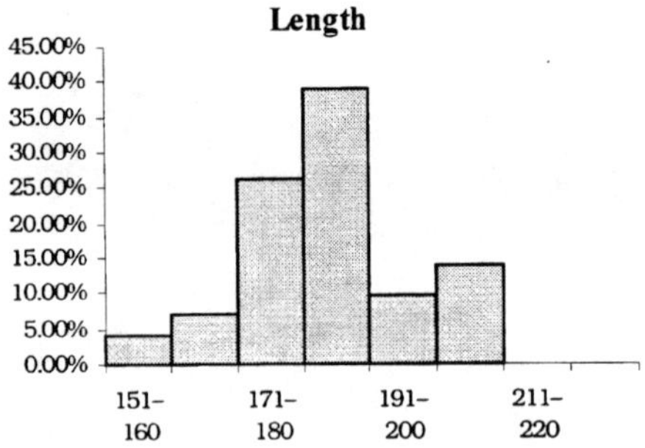

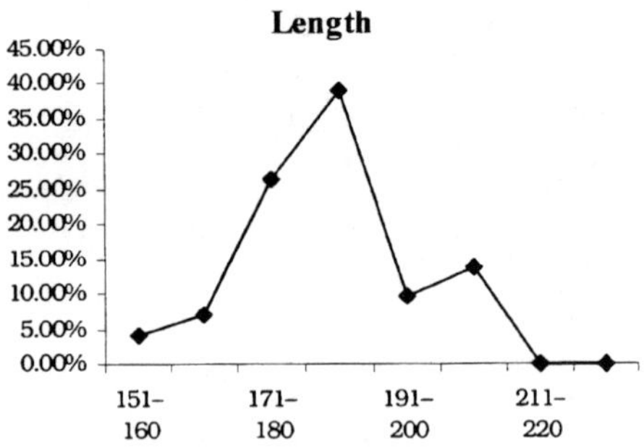

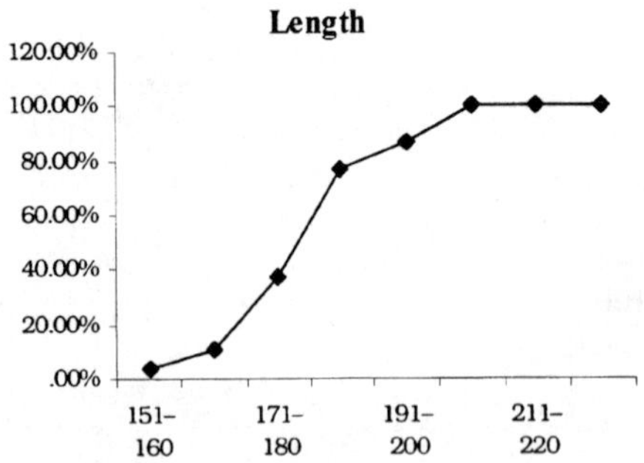

Width	Frequency	Percentage	Cumulative %
62.1–64.0	0	0.00	.00
64.1–66.0	0	0.00	.00
66.1–68.0	2	11.76	11.76
68.1–70.0	2	11.76	23.53
70.1–72.0	4	23.53	47.06
72.1–74.0	3	17.65	64.71
74.1–76.0	2	11.76	76.47
76.1–78.0	4	23.53	100.00
More	0	0.00	100.00

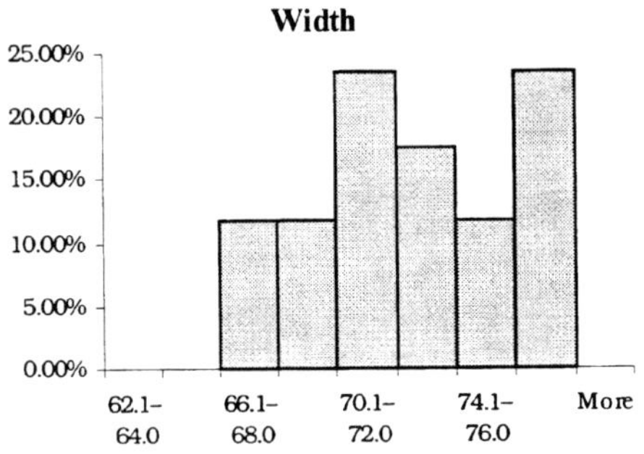

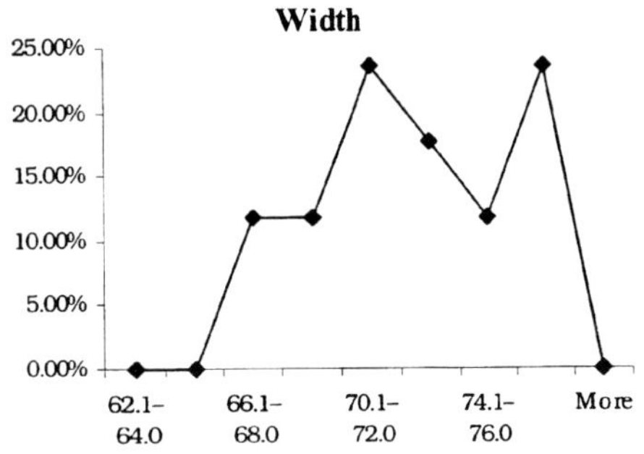

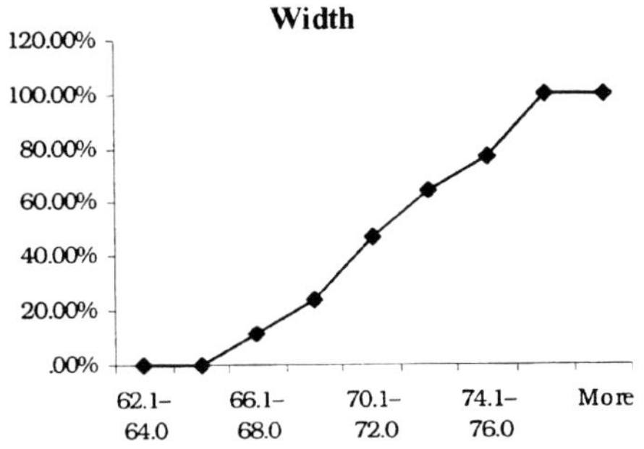

Width	Frequency	Percentage	Cumulative %
62.1–64.0	3	4.17	4.17
64.1–66.0	6	8.33	12.50
66.1–68.0	22	30.56	43.06
68.1–70.0	23	31.94	75.00
70.1–72.0	5	6.94	81.94
72.1–74.0	10	13.89	95.83
74.1–76.0	3	4.17	100.00
76.1–78.0	0	0.00	100.00
More	0	0.00	100.00

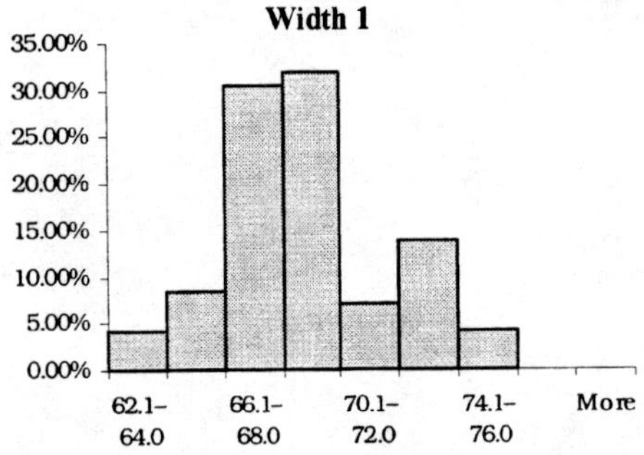

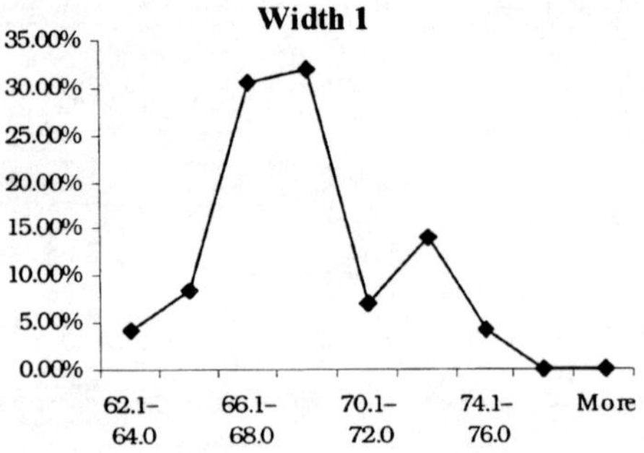

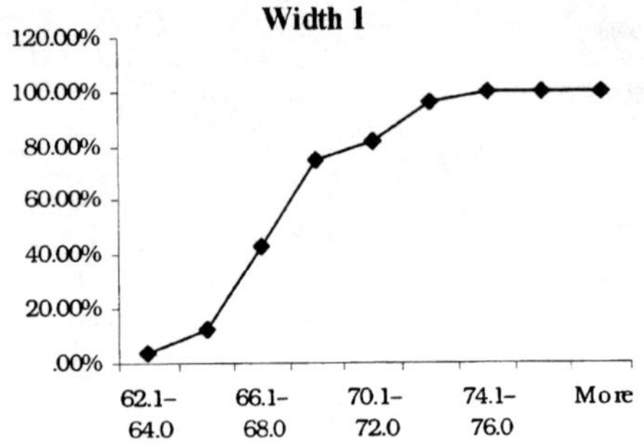

Weight	Frequency	Percentage	Cumulative %
1499–2000	0	0.00	.00
2001–2500	0	0.00	.00
2501–3000	0	0.00	.00
3001–3500	5	29.41	29.41
3501–4000	8	47.06	76.47
4001–4500	4	23.53	100.00
More	0	0.00	100.00

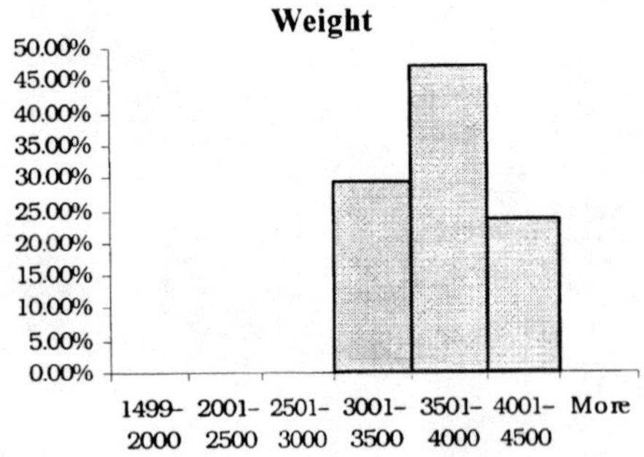

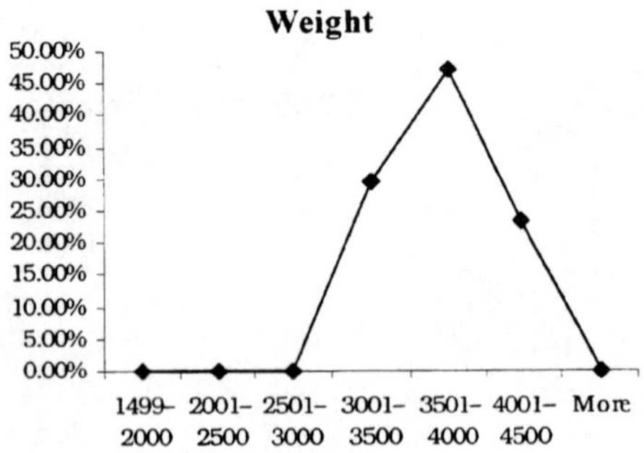

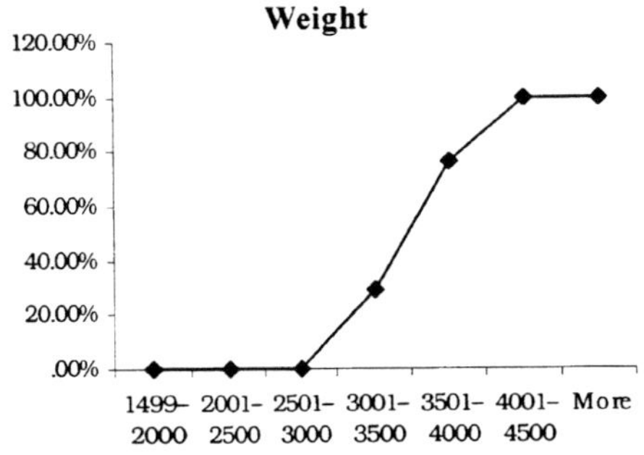

Weight	Frequency	Percentage	Cumulative %
1499–2000	1	1.39	1.39
2001–2500	11	15.28	16.67
2501–3000	21	29.17	45.83
3001–3500	29	40.28	86.11
3501–4000	10	13.89	100.00
4001–4500	0	0.00	100.00
More	0	0.00	100.00

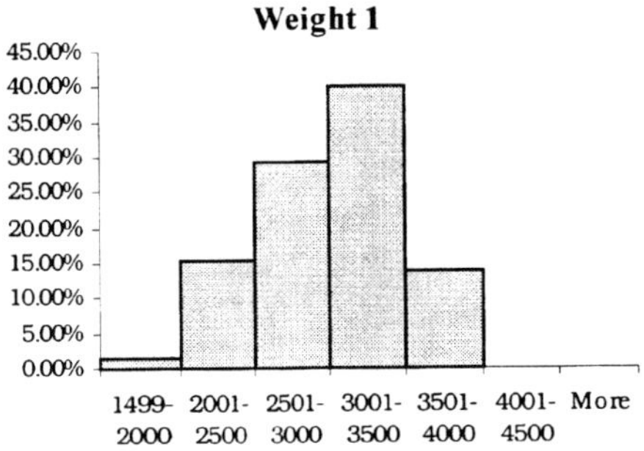

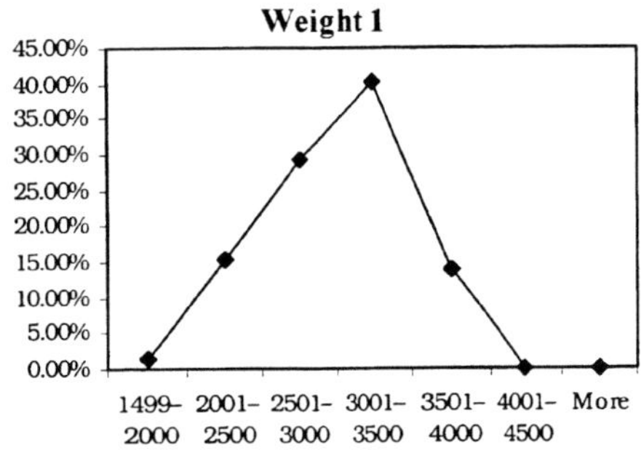

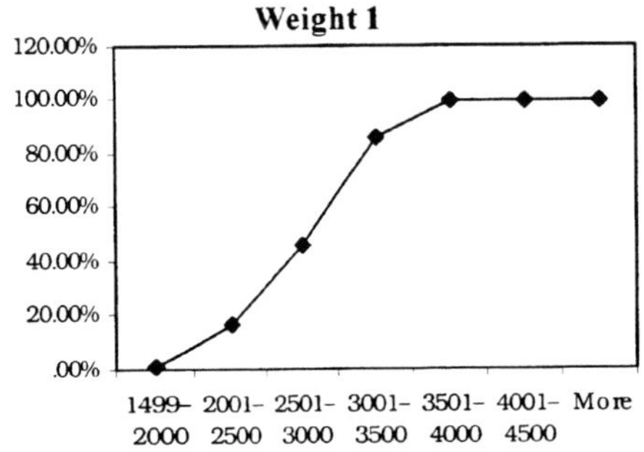

Wheel Base	Frequency	Percentage	Cumulative %
91–95	0	0.00	.00
96–100	1	5.88	5.88
101–105	3	17.65	23.53
106–110	6	35.29	58.82
111–115	6	35.29	94.12
116–120	1	5.88	100.00
More	0	0.00	100.00

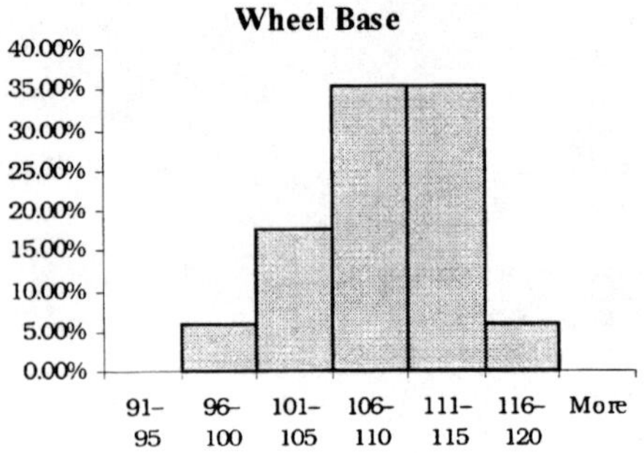

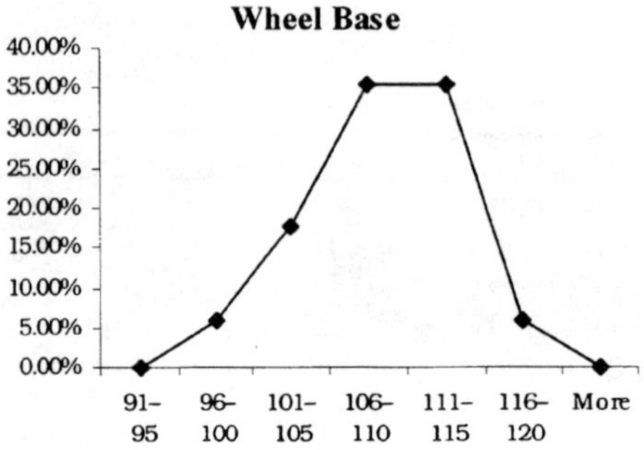

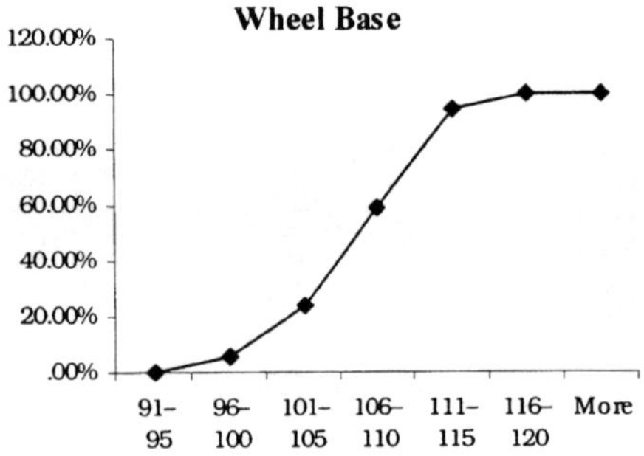

Wheel Base	Frequency	Percentage	Cumulative %
91–95	5	6.94	6.94
96–100	14	19.44	26.39
101–105	24	33.33	59.72
106–110	20	27.78	87.50
111–115	9	12.50	100.00
116–120	0	0.00	100.00
More	0	0.00	100.00

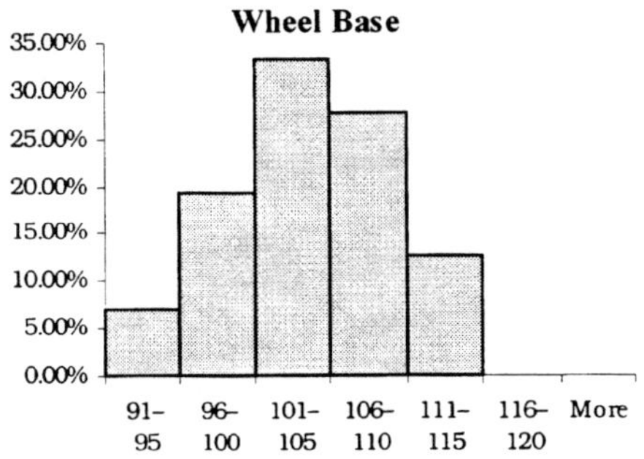

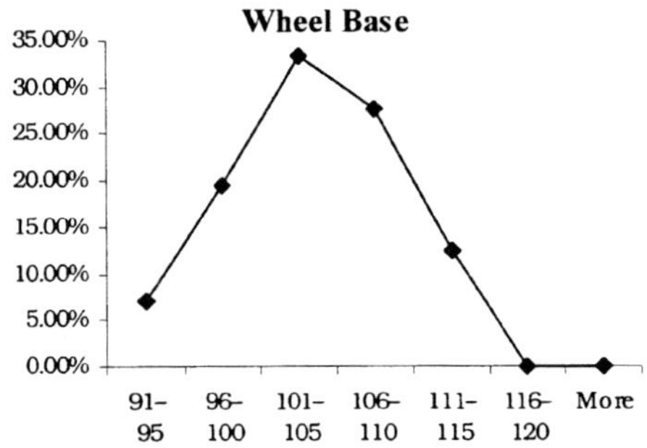

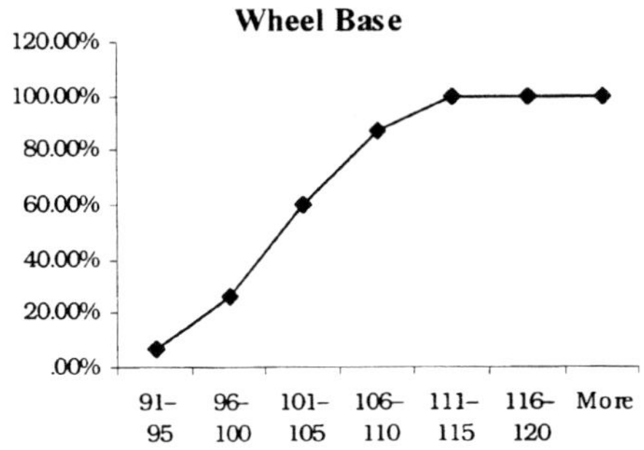

Turning Circle	Frequency	Percentage	Cumulative %
33.1–35.0	1	5.88	5.88
35.1–37.0	2	11.76	17.65
37.1–39.0	5	29.41	47.06
39.1–41.0	3	17.65	64.71
41.1–43.0	5	29.41	94.12
43.1–45.0	1	5.88	100.00
More	0	0.00	100.00

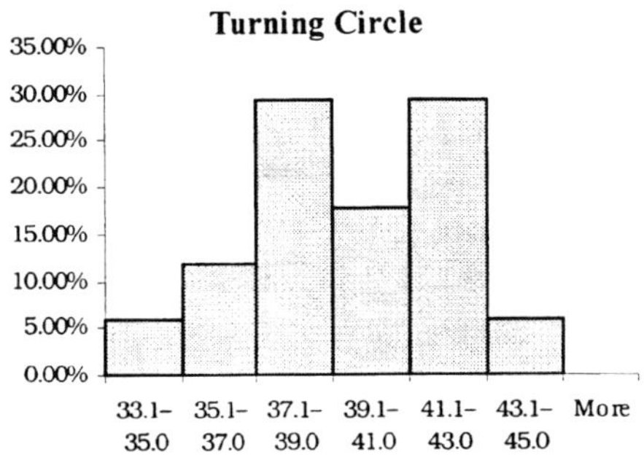

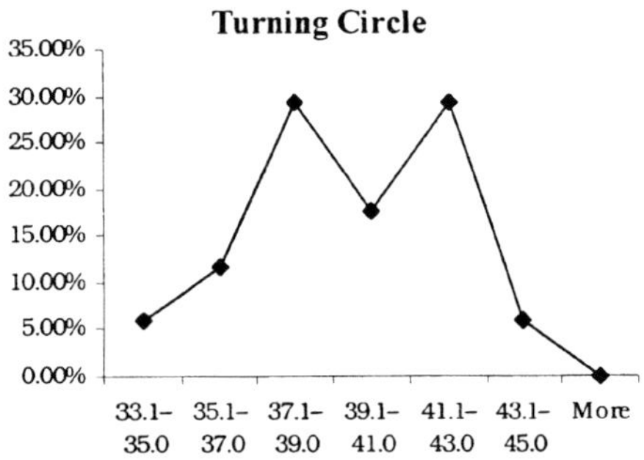

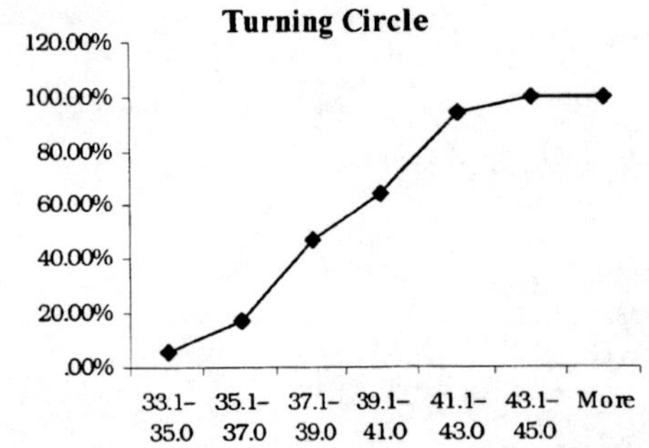

Turning Circle	Frequency	Percentage	Cumulative %
33.1–35.0	10	13.89	13.89
35.1–37.0	7	9.72	23.61
37.1–39.0	28	38.89	62.50
39.1–41.0	11	15.28	77.78
41.1–43.0	15	20.83	98.61
43.1–45.0	1	1.39	100.00
More	0	0.00	100.00

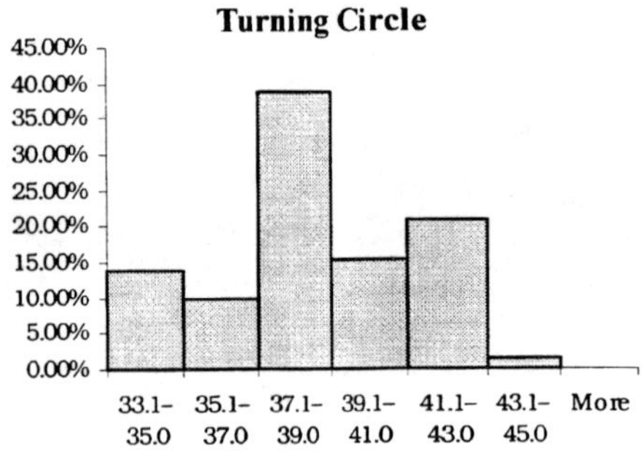

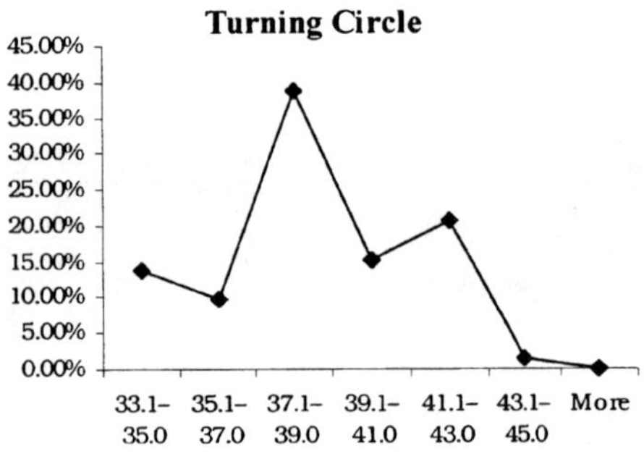

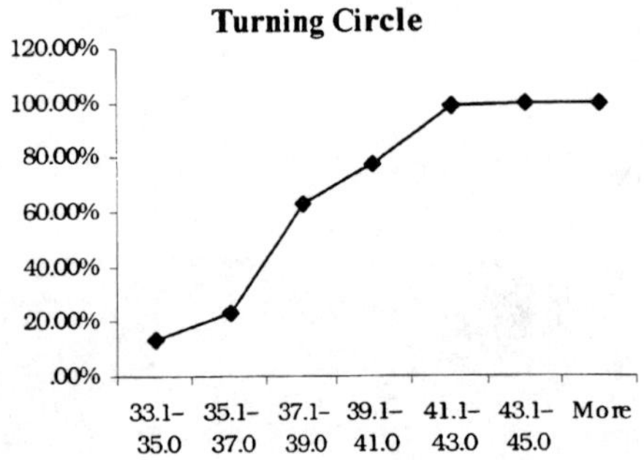

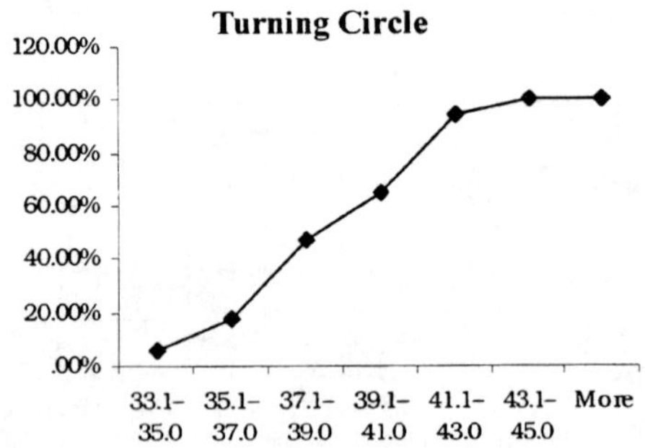

Luggage Capacity	Frequency	Percentage	Cumulative %
7.1–10.0	5	29.41	29.41
10.1–13.0	4	23.53	52.94
13.1–16.0	5	29.41	82.35
16.1–19.0	0	0.00	82.35
19.1–22.0	3	17.65	100.00
22.1–25.0	0	0.00	100.00
More	0	0.00	100.00

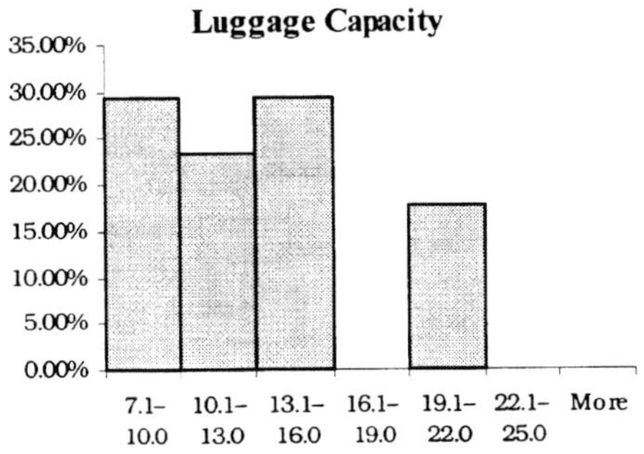

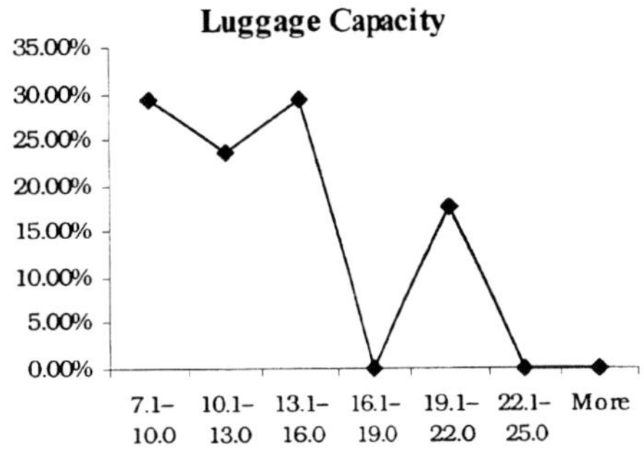

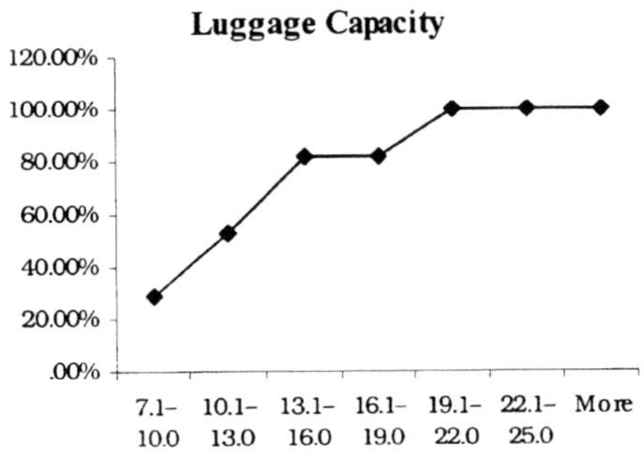

Luggage Capacity	Frequency	Percentage	Cumulative %
7.1–10.0	4	5.56	5.56
10.1–13.0	24	33.33	38.89
13.1–16.0	32	44.44	83.33
16.1–19.0	10	13.89	97.22
19.1–22.0	0	0.00	97.22
22.1–25.0	2	2.78	100.00
More	0	0.00	100.00

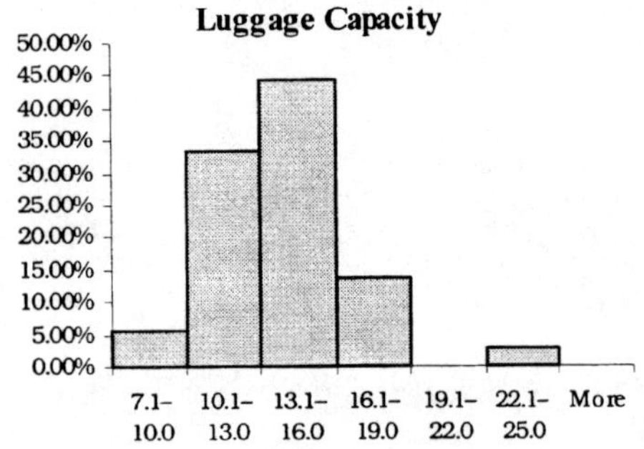

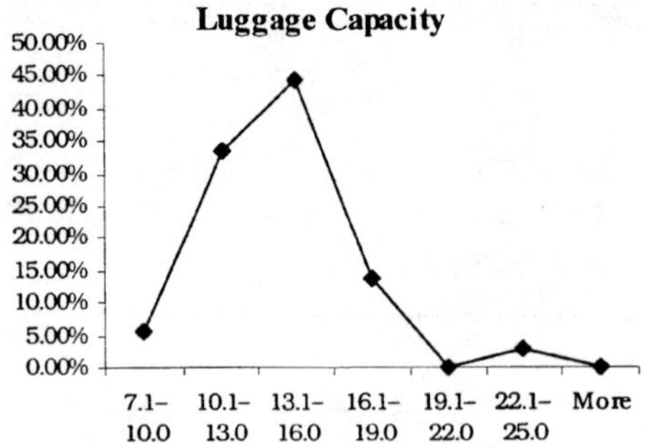

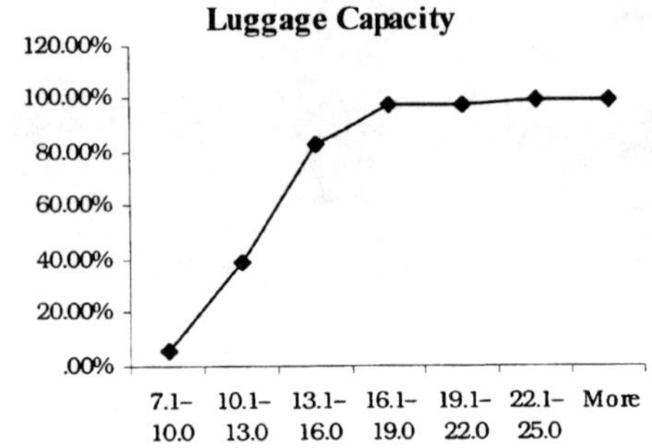

Front Leg Room	Frequency	Percentage	Cumulative %
39.9–40.0	0	0.00	.00
40.1–41.0	1	5.88	5.88
41.1–42.0	6	35.29	41.18
42.1–43.0	8	47.06	88.24
43.1–44.0	2	11.76	100.00
44.1–45.0	0	0.00	100.00
More	0	0.00	100.00

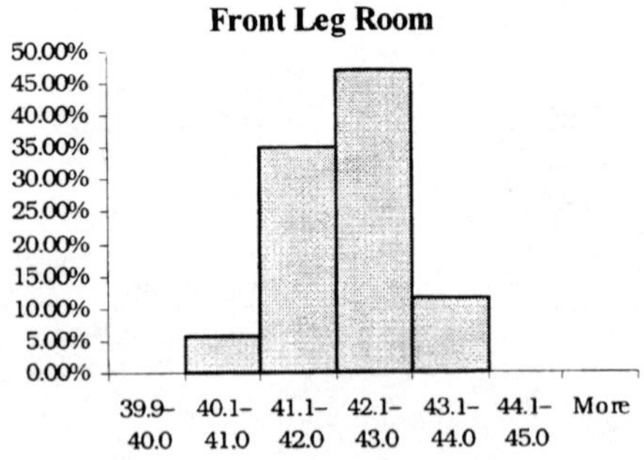

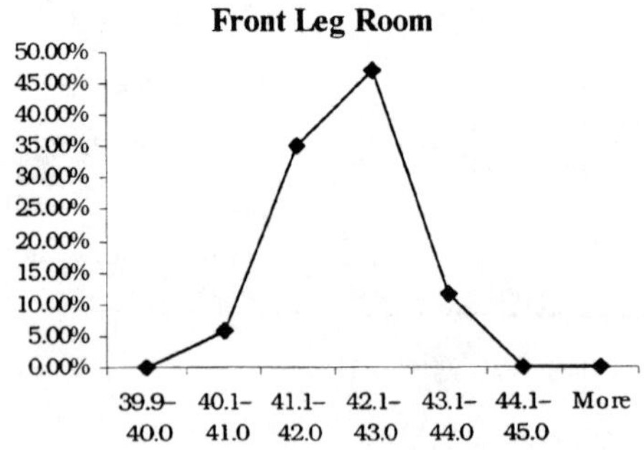

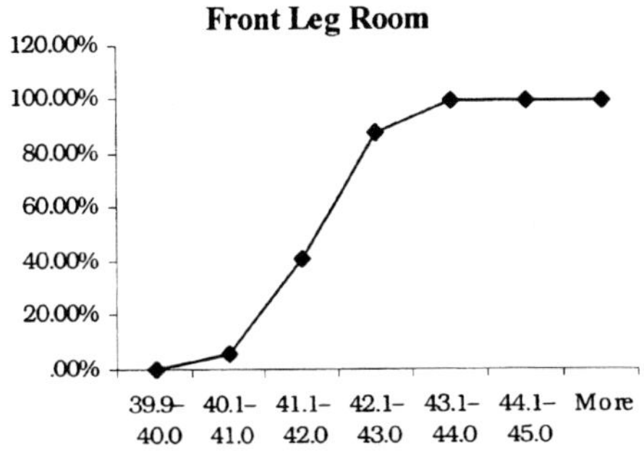

Front Leg Room 1	Frequency	Percentage	Cumulative %
39.9–40.0	3	4.17	4.17
40.1–41.0	18	25.00	29.17
41.1–42.0	34	47.22	76.39
42.1–43.0	15	20.83	97.22
43.1–44.0	1	1.39	98.61
44.1–45.0	1	1.39	100.00
More	0	0.00	100.00

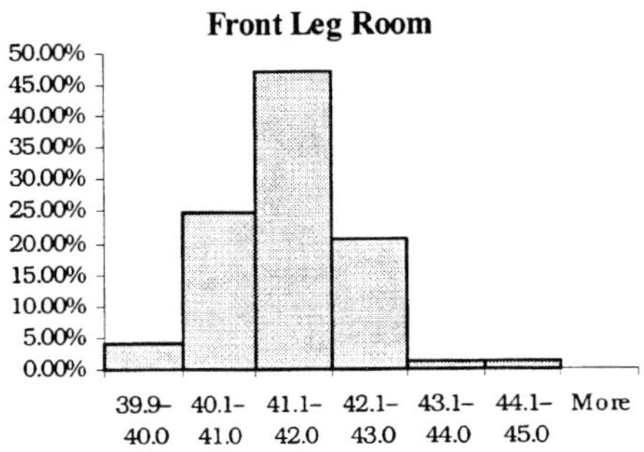

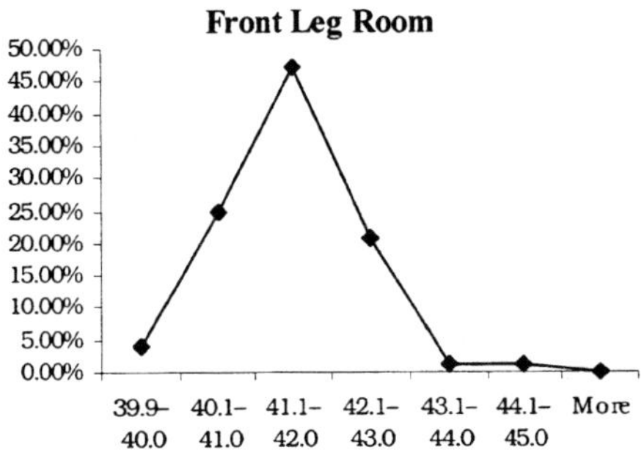

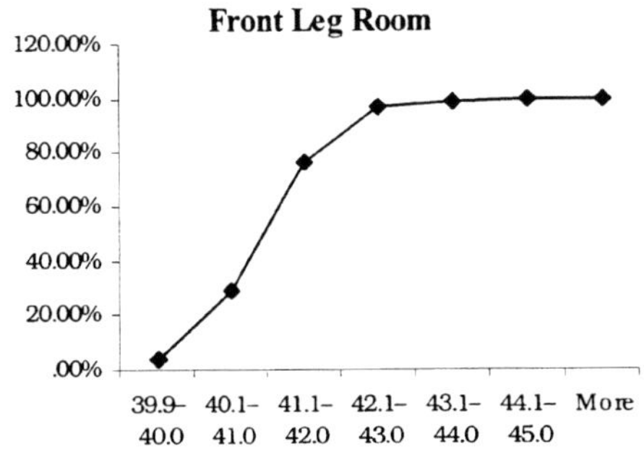

Front Head Room	Frequency	Percentage	Cumulative %
0.1–1.0	0	0.00	.00
1.1–2.0	2	11.76	11.76
2.1–3.0	6	35.29	47.06
3.1–4.0	5	29.41	76.47
4.1–5.0	4	23.53	100.00
5.1–6.0	0	0.00	100.00
6.1–7.0	0	0.00	100.00
More	0	0.00	100.00

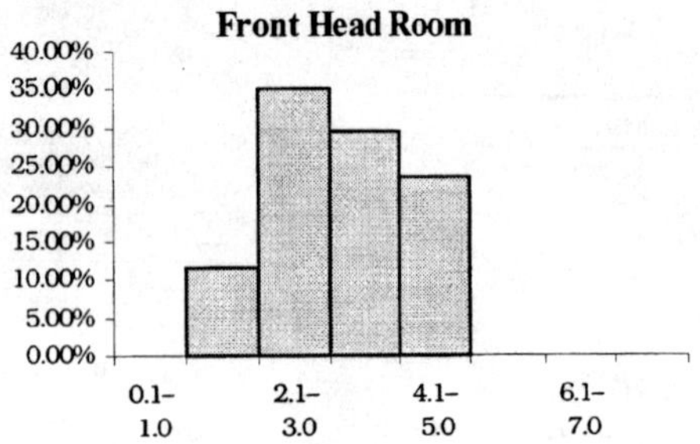

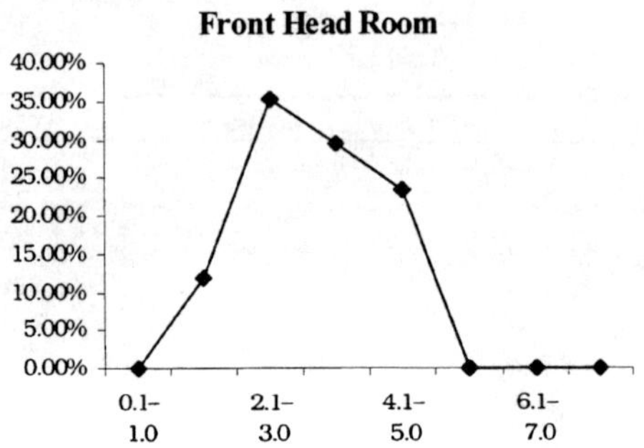

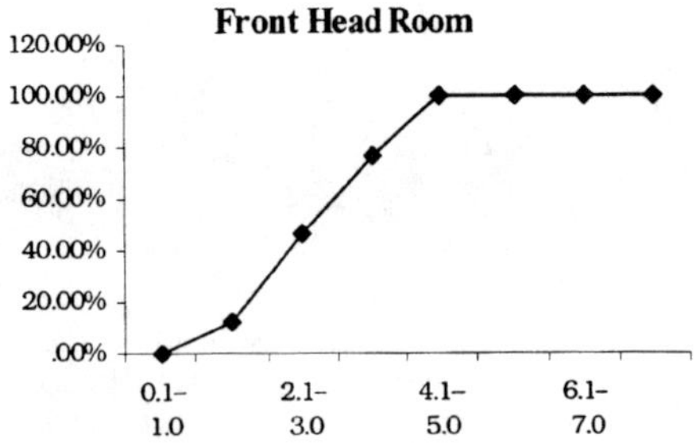

Front Head Room 1	Frequency	Percentage	Cumulative %
0.1–1.0	1	1.39	1.39
1.1–2.0	7	9.72	11.11
2.1–3.0	18	25.00	36.11
3.1–4.0	23	31.94	68.06
4.1–5.0	17	23.61	91.67
5.1–6.0	5	6.94	98.61
6.1–7.0	1	1.39	100.00
More	0	0.00	100.00

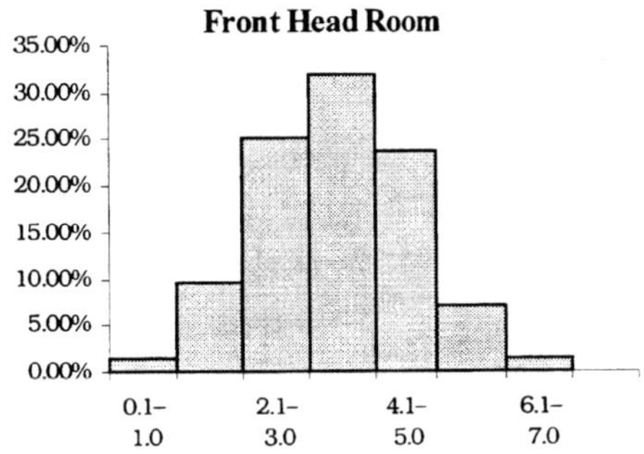

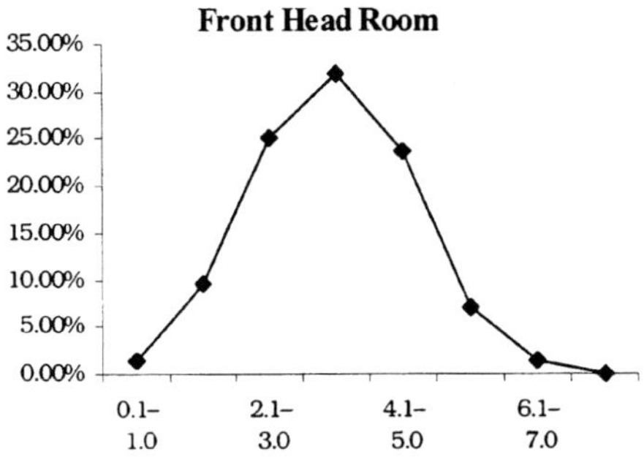

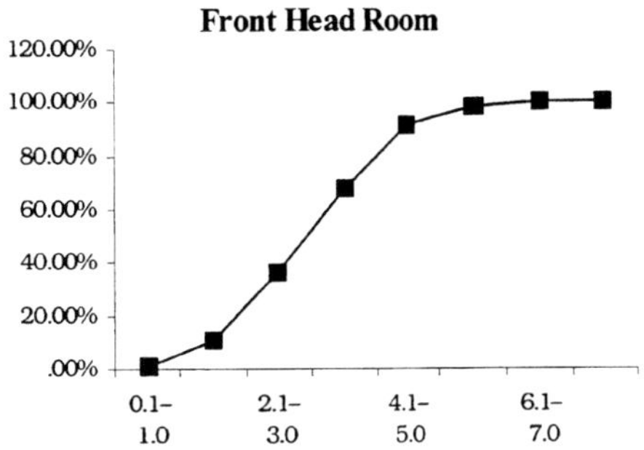

The front-wheel-drive cars have greater mpg and smaller fuel capacity, length, width, weight, wheel base, slightly more luggage capacity and front leg room, and almost the same front head room as the rear-wheel-drive cars.

(i) Rows: Drive Columns: Fuel

	0	1	All
0	9	8	17
1	16	56	72
All	25	64	89

(j)

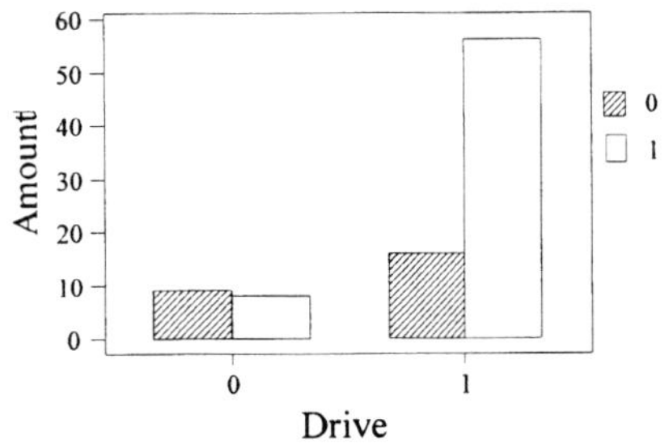

(k) It does not matter what type of gasoline is used for rear-wheel cars, but it seems that most of front-wheel cars used the first type of gasoline.

64. FSH

(a) Male Dover sole
Stem-and-Leaf Display for Body Depth

Stem unit: 10

8	3 9
9	1 2 7 8 10
10	3 3 3 4 4 6 7 7 9 9 10
11	0 0 1 2 2 2 2 3 3 3 4 4 7 9 9
12	0 1 1 3 5 6 6
13	6
14	
15	
16	7

Female Dover sole
Stem-and-Leaf Display for Body Depth

Stem unit: 10

9	4 7
10	2 3 5 9
11	1 1 2 4 5 5 5 9
12	0 1 1 1 2 3 4 4 5 7 8
13	0 0 0 1 1 1 2 2 3 3 3 4 4 7 8 8 9 9 9 9 9
14	1 2 2 3 3 3 5 6 7 7
15	2 5

(b) Male Dover sole

Bin	Frequency	Percentage
80.00–89.99	0	0.00
90.00–99.99	2	3.45
100.00–109.99	4	6.90
110.00–119.99	8	13.79
120.00–129.99	11	18.97
130.00–139.99	21	36.21
140.00–149.99	10	17.24
150.00–159.99	2	3.45
160.00–169.99	0	0.00
More	0	0.00

Female Dover sole

Bin	Frequency	Percentage
80.00–89.99	2	4.76
90.00–99.99	5	11.90
100.00–109.99	11	26.19
110.00–119.99	15	35.71
120.00–129.99	7	16.67
130.00–139.99	1	2.38
140.00–149.99	0	0.00
150.00–159.99	0	0.00
160.00–169.99	1	2.38
More	0	0.00

(c)

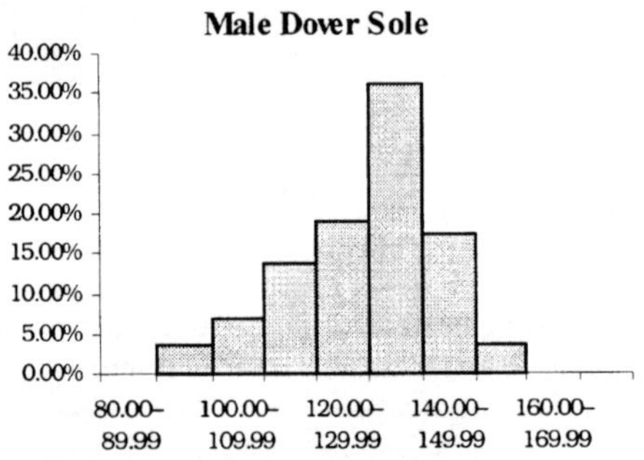

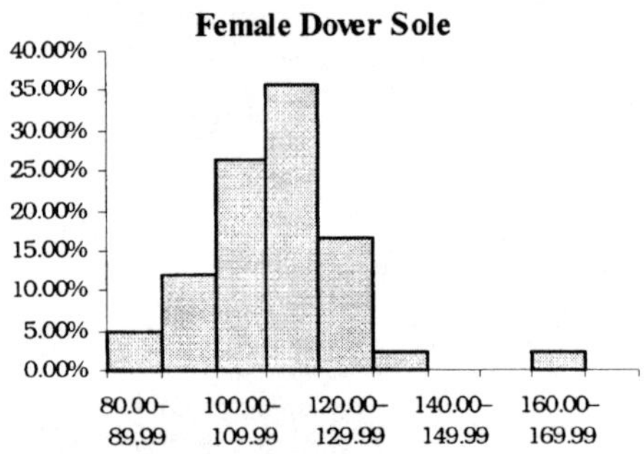

(d)

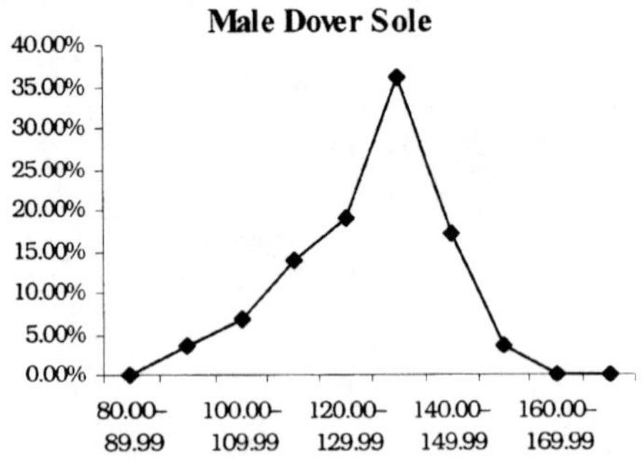

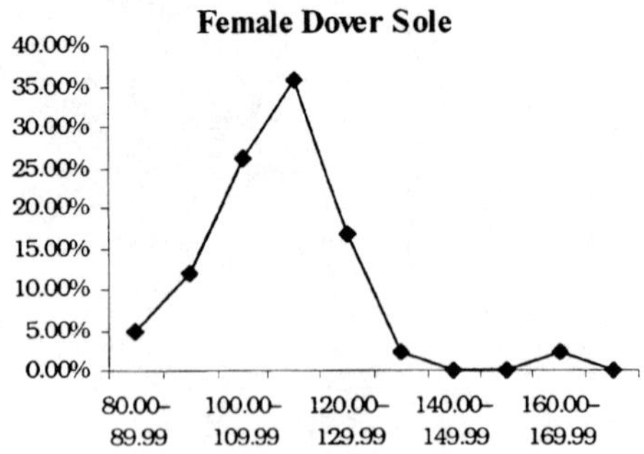

(e) Male Dover sole

Bin	Cumulative %
80.00–89.99	.00
90.00–99.99	3.45
100.00–109.99	10.34
110.00–119.99	24.14
120.00–129.99	43.10
130.00–139.99	79.31
140.00–149.99	96.55
150.00–159.99	100.00
160.00–169.99	100.00
More	100.00

Female Dover sole

Bin	Cumulative %
80.00–89.99	4.76
90.00–99.99	16.67
100.00–109.99	42.86
110.00–119.99	78.57
120.00–129.99	95.24
130.00–139.99	97.62
140.00–149.99	97.62
150.00–159.99	97.62
160.00–169.99	100.00
More	100.00

(f)

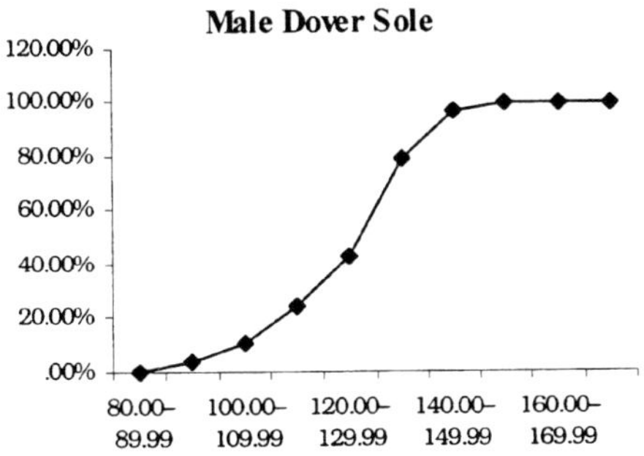

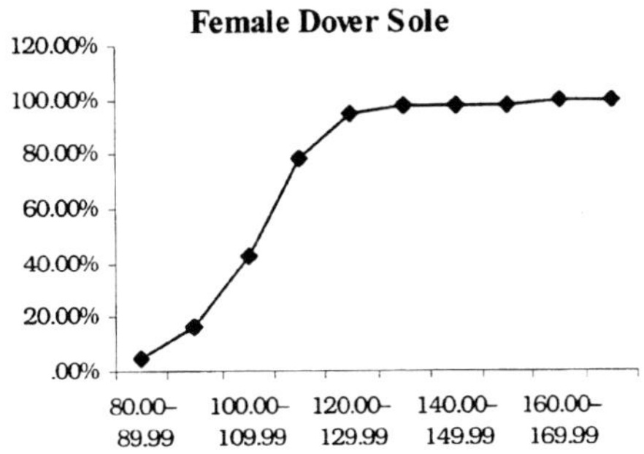

Body width

(a) Male Dover sole
Stem-and-Leaf Display for Width

Stem unit: 1

18	0 8
19	4 8
20	
21	0 4 4 7
22	0 2 6 6 6 8
23	0 2 2 6 6 8 8
24	2 6 6 8 8
25	0 0 2 4 8
26	0 2 2 4 4 6 8
27	0 8
28	4
29	
30	
31	
32	
33	
34	0

Female Dover sole
Stem-and-Leaf Display for Width

Stem unit: 1

19	4 4
20	2 4
21	4 9
22	4
23	4 6 6 7 8
24	2 4 4 6 6 6 8 8 8
25	0 0 1 4 4 6 6 6 8 8 8 8
26	0 0 1 2 2 6 8
27	2 2 6 8
28	2 2 4 4 9
29	2 4 4 4 4 8
30	4 8
31	
32	
33	6

(b) Male Dover Sole

Bin	Frequency	Percentage
18.00–19.99	2	3.45
20.00–21.99	4	6.90
22.00–23.99	6	10.34
24.00–25.99	21	36.21
26.00–27.99	11	18.97
28.00–29.99	11	18.97
30.00–31.99	2	3.45
32.00–33.99	1	1.72
34.00–35.99	0	0.00
More	0	0.00

Female Dover Sole

Bin	Frequency	Percentage
18.00–19.99	4	9.52
20.00–21.99	4	9.52
22.00–23.99	13	30.95
24.00–25.99	10	23.81
26.00–27.99	9	21.43
28.00–29.99	1	2.38
30.00–31.99	0	0.00
32.00–33.99	0	0.00
34.00–35.99	1	2.38
More	0	0.00

(c)

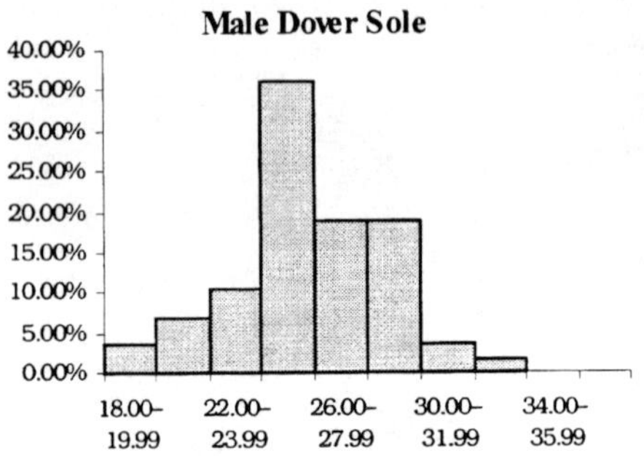

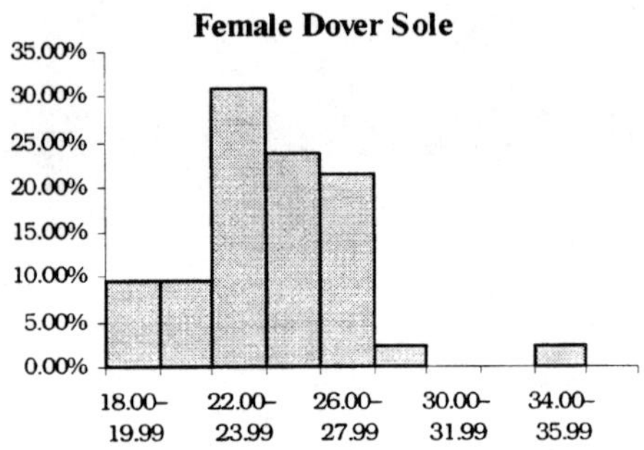

(d)

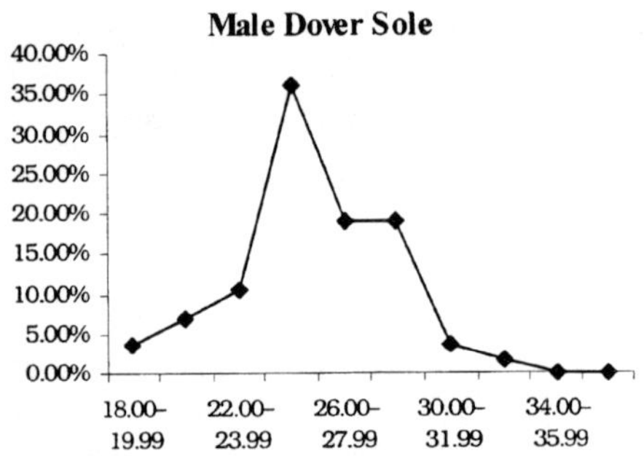

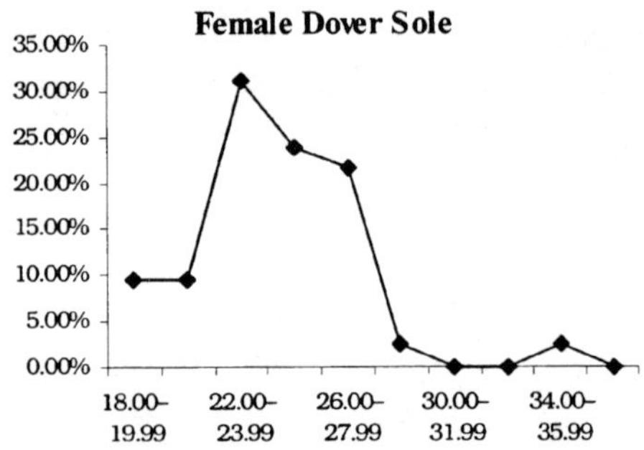

(e) Male Dover Sole

Bin	Cumulative
18.00–19.99	3.45
20.00–21.99	10.34
22.00–23.99	20.69
24.00–25.99	56.90
26.00–27.99	75.86
28.00–29.99	94.83
30.00–31.99	98.28
32.00–33.99	100.00
34.00–35.99	100.00
More	100.00

Female Dover Sole

Bin	Cumulative
18.00–19.99	9.52
20.00–21.99	19.05
22.00–23.99	50.00
24.00–25.99	73.81
26.00–27.99	95.24
28.00–29.99	97.62
30.00–31.99	97.62
32.00–33.99	97.62
34.00–35.99	100.00
More	100.00

(f)

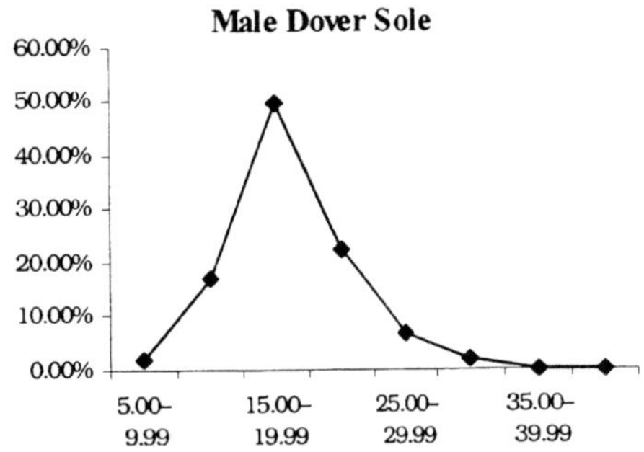

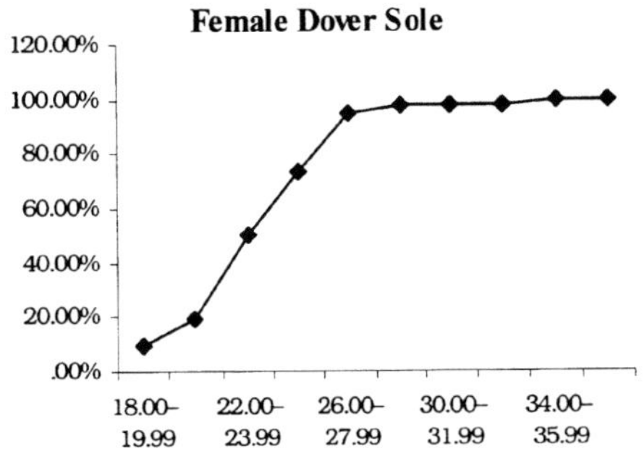

Body weight

(a) Male Dover Sole
Stem-and-Leaf Display for Weight

Stem unit: 1

9	0
10	0 0 0
11	0
12	0
13	0 0 0 0
14	0
15	0 0 0
16	0 0 0 0 0 0 0 0 0
17	0 0 0 0 0 0
18	0 0 0 0 0
19	0 0 0 0 0 0 0
20	
21	0 0 0 0 0 0
22	0 0
23	0 0 0 0
24	0
25	0
26	
27	0
28	0
29	0
30	
31	
32	0

Female Dover Sole
Stem-and-Leaf Display for Weight

Stem unit: 10

0	6 8
1	0 0 0 0 1 1 1 1 2 2 2 2 2 2 3 3 3 4 4 5 5 5 5
	5 6 6 6 6 6 6 6 7 8 9 9
2	0 0 3 5
3	5

(b) Male Dover Sole

Bin	Frequency	Percentage
5.00–9.99	1	1.72
10.00–14.99	10	17.24
15.00–19.99	29	50.00
20.00–24.99	13	22.41
25.00–29.99	4	6.90
30.00–34.99	1	1.72
35.00–39.99	0	0.00
More	0	0.00

Female Dover Sole

Bin	Frequency	Percentage
5.00–9.99	2	4.76
10.00–14.99	19	45.24
15.00–19.99	16	38.10
20.00–24.99	3	7.14
25.00–29.99	1	2.38
30.00–34.99	0	0.00
35.00–39.99	1	2.38
More	0	0.00

(c)

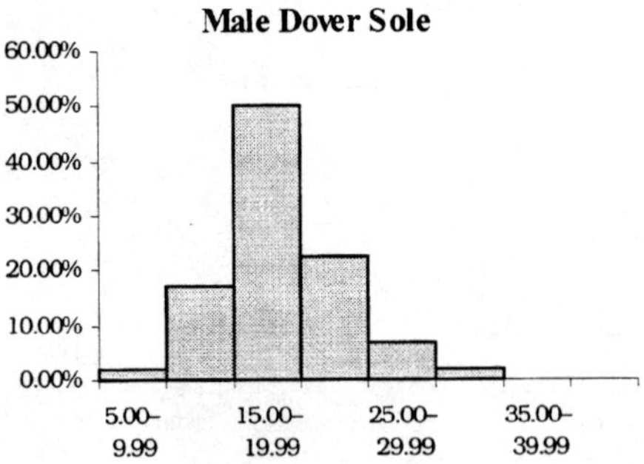

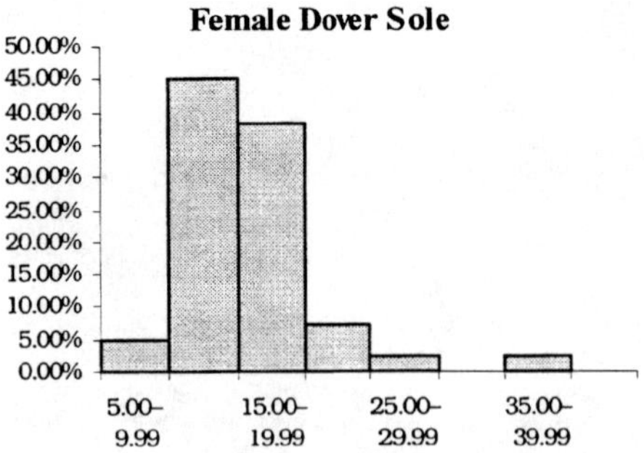

(d)

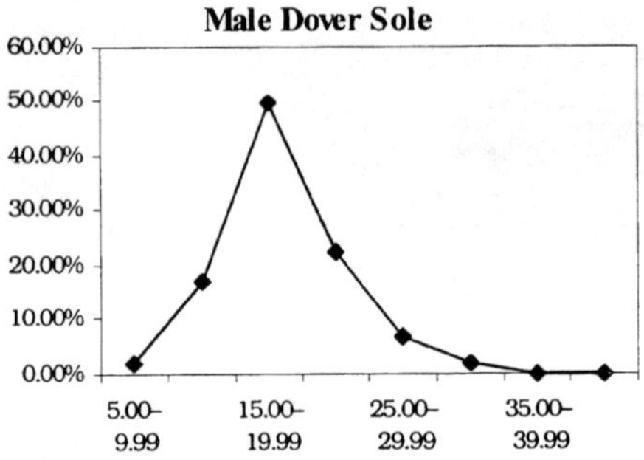

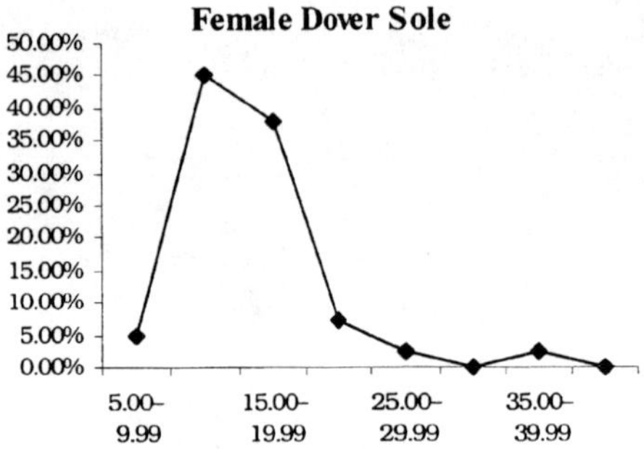

(e) Male Dover Sole

Bin	Cumulative %
5.00–9.99	1.72
10.00–14.99	18.97
15.00–19.99	68.97
20.00–24.99	91.38
25.00–29.99	98.28
30.00–34.99	100.00
35.00–39.99	100.00
More	100.00

Female Dover Sole

Bin	Cumulative %
5.00–9.99	4.76
10.00–14.99	50.00
15.00–19.99	88.10
20.00–24.99	95.24
25.00–29.99	97.62
30.00–34.99	97.62
35.00–39.99	100.00
More	100.00

(f)

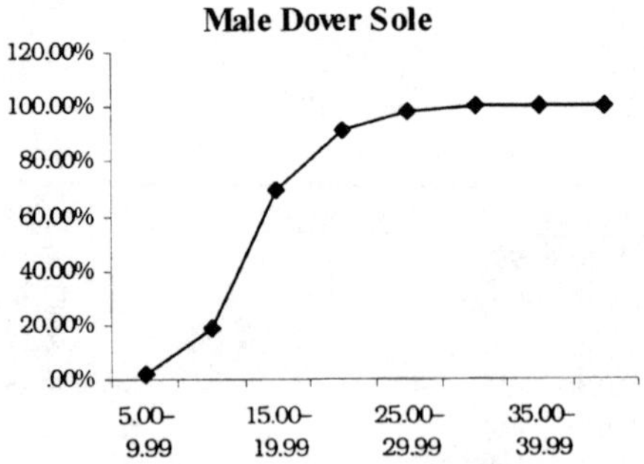

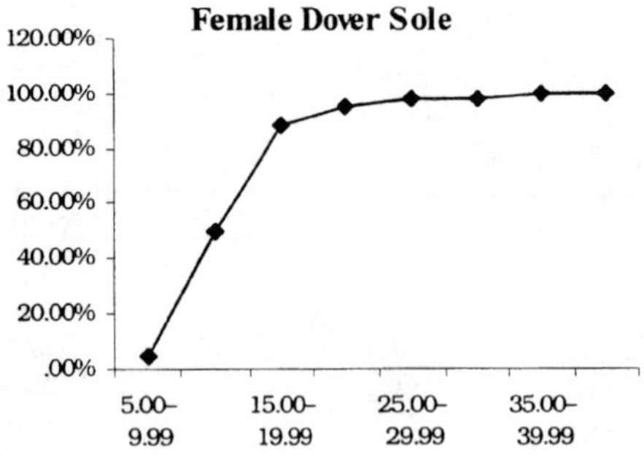

(g) Male Dover Sole have greater body depth, body width, and body weight than female Dover Sole.

(h) Body depth

Shallow water

Stem-and-Leaf Display for Depth

Stem unit: 10

```
 8 | 3 9
 9 | 1 2 4 7 7 8 10
10 | 3 3 3 3 4 4 6 7 7 9 9 9 10
11 | 0 0 1 1 2 2 2 2 3 3 3 4 4 4 5 7 9 9
12 | 0 1 1 3 4 5 6 6
13 | 1 6
```

Deep water

Stem-and-Leaf Display for Depth

Stem unit: 10

```
10 | 2 5
11 | 1 2 5 5 9
12 | 0 1 1 1 2 3 4 5 7 8
13 | 0 0 0 1 1 2 2 3 3 3 4 4 7 8 8 9 9 9 9 9
14 | 1 2 2 3 3 3 5 6 7 7
15 | 2 5
16 | 7
```

Shallow water

Bin	Frequency	Percentage
80.00–89.99	2	4.00
90.00–99.99	7	14.00
100.00–109.99	13	26.00
110.00–119.99	18	36.00
120.00–129.99	8	16.00
130.00–139.99	2	4.00
140.00–149.99	0	0.00
150.00–159.99	0	0.00
160.00–169.99	0	0.00
More	0	0.00

Deep water

Bin	Frequency	Percentage
80.00–89.99	0	0.00
90.00–99.99	0	0.00
100.00–109.99	2	4.00
110.00–119.99	5	10.00
120.00–129.99	10	20.00
130.00–139.99	20	40.00
140.00–149.99	10	20.00
150.00–159.99	2	4.00
160.00–169.99	1	2.00
More	0	0.00

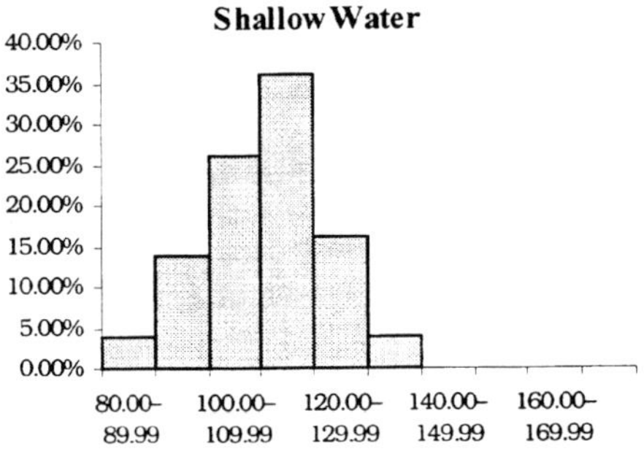

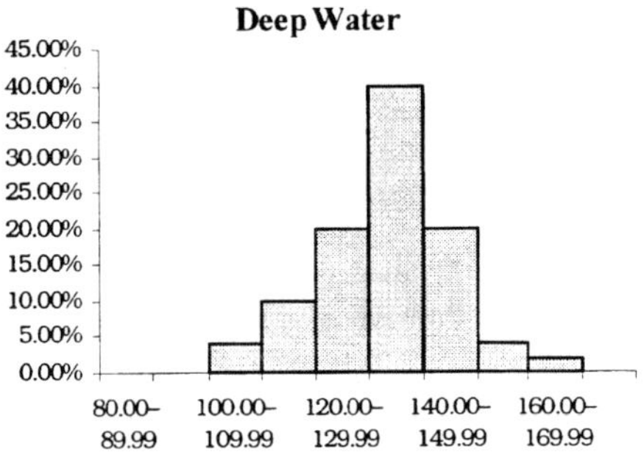

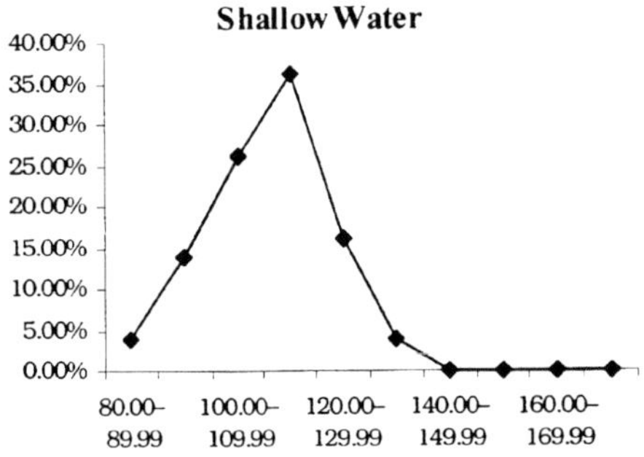

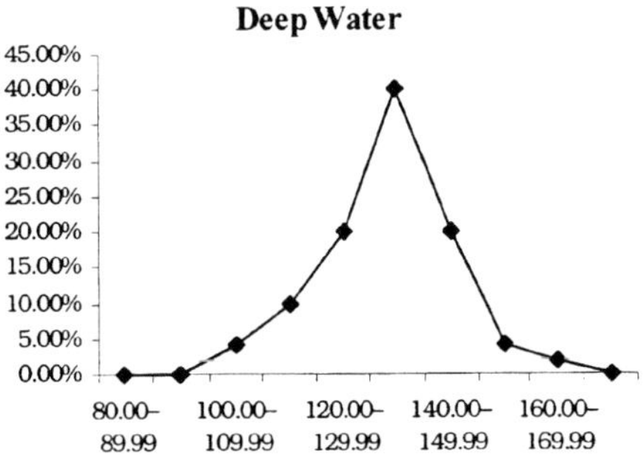

Shallow water

Bin	Cumulative %
80.00–89.99	4.00
90.00–99.99	18.00
100.00–109.99	44.00
110.00–119.99	80.00
120.00–129.99	96.00
130.00–139.99	100.00
140.00–149.99	100.00
150.00–159.99	100.00
160.00–169.99	100.00
More	100.00

Deep water

Bin	Cumulative %
80.00–89.99	.00
90.00–99.99	.00
100.00–109.99	4.00
110.00–119.99	14.00
120.00–129.99	34.00
130.00–139.99	74.00
140.00–149.99	94.00
150.00–159.99	98.00
160.00–169.99	100.00
More	100.00

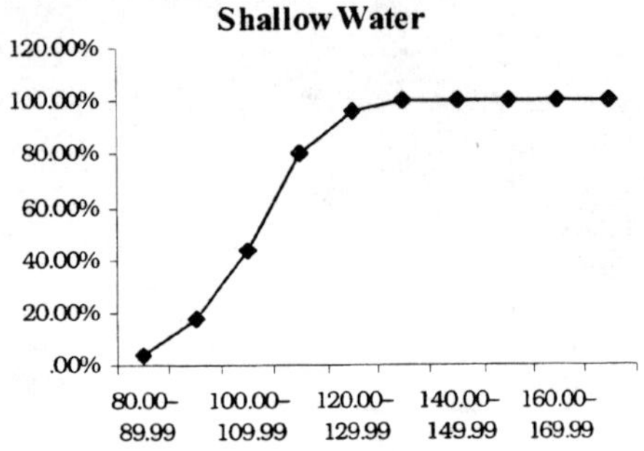

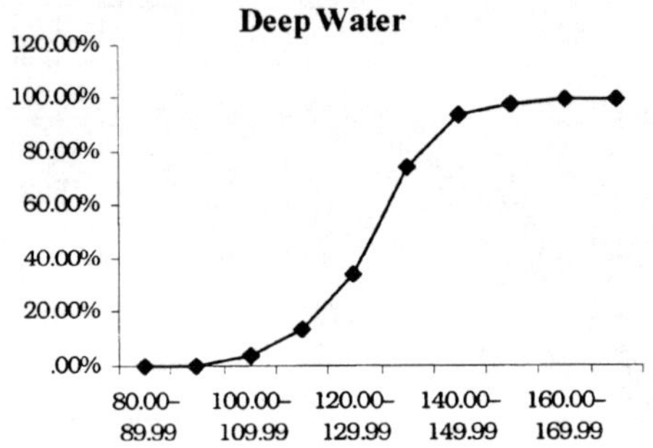

Body width.

Shallow water

Stem-and-Leaf Display for Width

Stem unit: 1

19	4
20	2
21	9
22	4
23	4 6 7 8
24	2 4 4 6 6 6 8 8 8
25	0 1 4 6 6 8 8 8 8
26	0 1 2 6 8
27	2 2 6 8
28	2 2 4 4 9
29	2 4 4 4 4 8
30	4 8
31	
32	
33	6
34	0

Deep water

Stem-and-Leaf Display for Width

Stem unit: 1

18	0 8
19	4 4 8
20	4
21	0 4 4 4 7
22	0 2 6 6 6 8
23	0 2 2 6 6 6 8 8
24	2 6 6 8 8
25	0 0 0 2 4 4 6 8
26	0 0 2 2 2 4 4 6 8
27	0 8
28	4

Shallow water

Bin	Frequency	Percentage
18.00–19.99	5	10.00
20.00–21.99	6	12.00
22.00–23.99	14	28.00
24.00–25.99	13	26.00
26.00–27.99	11	22.00
28.00–29.99	1	2.00
30.00–31.99	0	0.00
32.00–33.99	0	0.00
34.00–35.99	0	0.00
More	0	0.00

Deep water

Bin	Frequency	Percentage
18.00–19.99	1	2.00
20.00–21.99	2	4.00
22.00–23.99	5	10.00
24.00–25.99	18	36.00
26.00–27.99	9	18.00
28.00–29.99	11	22.00
30.00–31.99	2	4.00
32.00–33.99	1	2.00
34.00–35.99	1	2.00
More	0	0.00

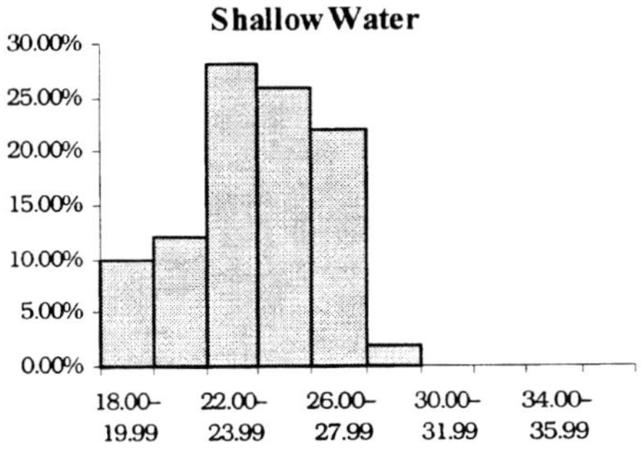

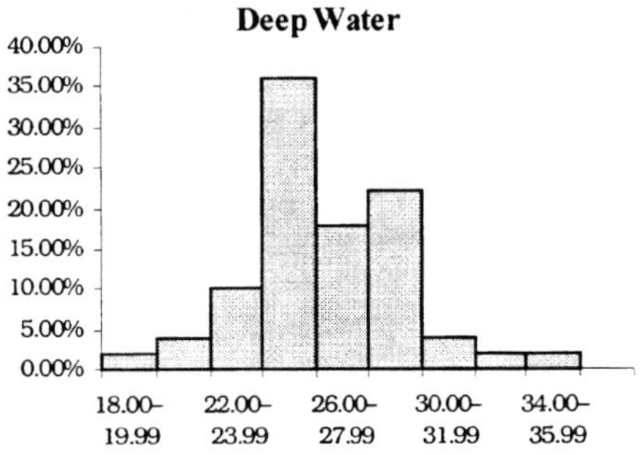

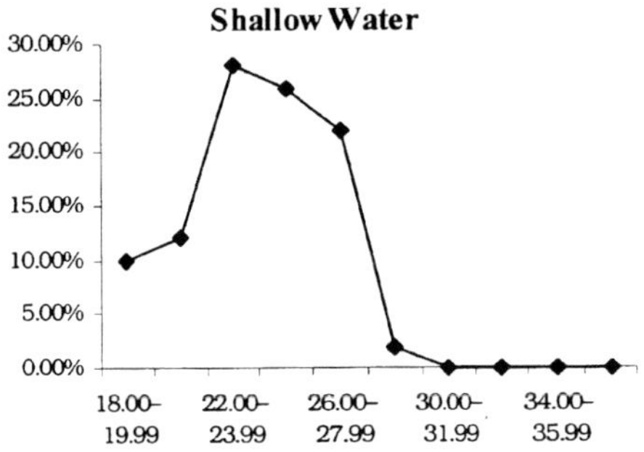

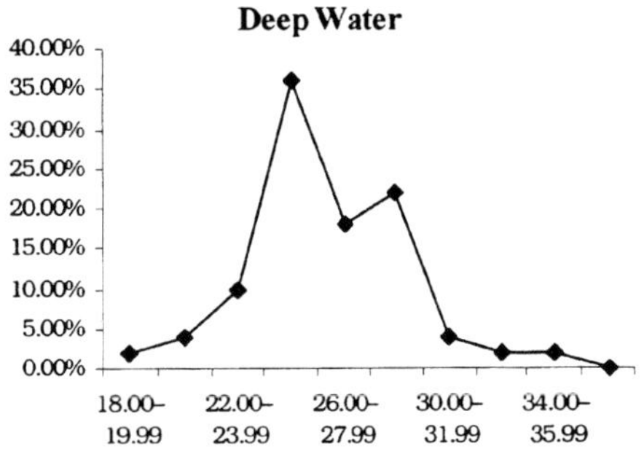

Shallow water

Bin	Cumulative %
18.00–19.99	10.00
20.00–21.99	22.00
22.00–23.99	50.00
24.00–25.99	76.00
26.00–27.99	98.00
28.00–29.99	100.00
30.00–31.99	100.00
32.00–33.99	100.00
34.00–35.99	100.00
More	100.00

Deep water

Bin	Cumulative %
18.00–19.99	2.00
20.00–21.99	6.00
22.00–23.99	16.00
24.00–25.99	52.00
26.00–27.99	70.00
28.00–29.99	92.00
30.00–31.99	96.00
32.00–33.99	98.00
34.00–35.99	100.00
More	100.00

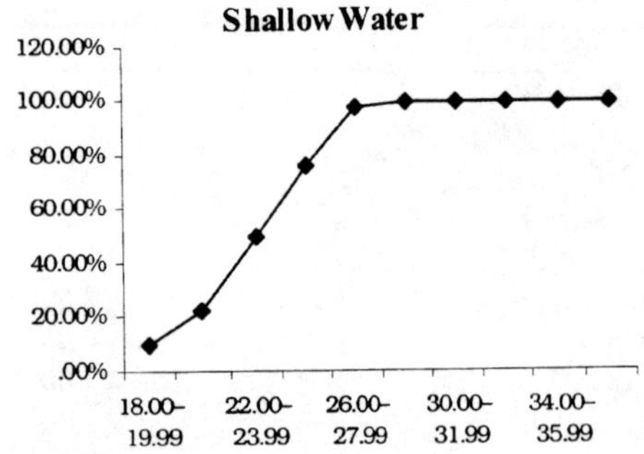

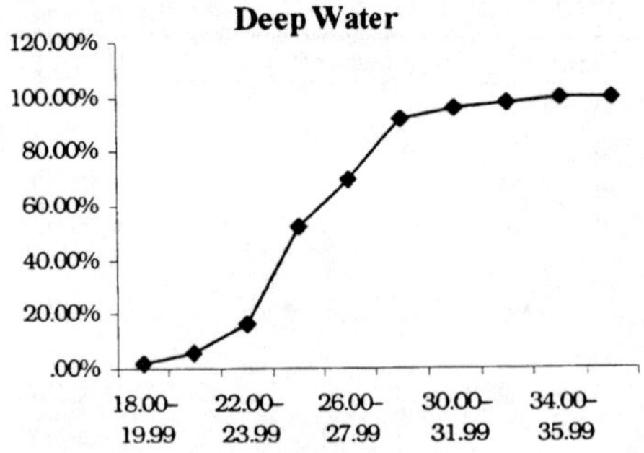

Body weight.

Shallow water

Stem-and-Leaf Display for Weight

Stem unit: 1

6	0
7	
8	0
9	
10	0 0 0 0 0 0
11	0 0 0 0
12	0 0 0 0 0 0 0
13	0 0 0 0
14	0 0
15	0 0 0 0 0
16	0 0 0 0 0 0 0 0 0 0 0
17	0
18	0
19	0 0
20	0 0
21	0
22	
23	0
24	
25	0

Deep water

Stem-and-Leaf Display for Weight

Stem unit: 10

0	9
1	0 1 3 3 3 4 5 5 5 6 6 6 6 7 7 7 7 7 7 8 8 8 8 8 9 9 9 9 9 9 9
2	1 1 1 1 1 2 2 3 3 3 3 4 5 7 8 9
3	2 5

Shallow water

Bin	Frequency	Percentage
5.00–9.99	2	4.00
10.00–14.99	23	46.00
15.00–19.99	20	40.00
20.00–24.99	4	8.00
25.00–29.99	1	2.00
30.00–34.99	0	0.00
35.00–39.99	0	0.00
More	0	0.00

Deep water

Bin	Frequency	Percentage
5.00–9.99	1	2.00
10.00–14.99	6	12.00
15.00–19.99	25	50.00
20.00–24.99	12	24.00
25.00–29.99	4	8.00
30.00–34.99	1	2.00
35.00–39.99	1	2.00
More	0	0.00

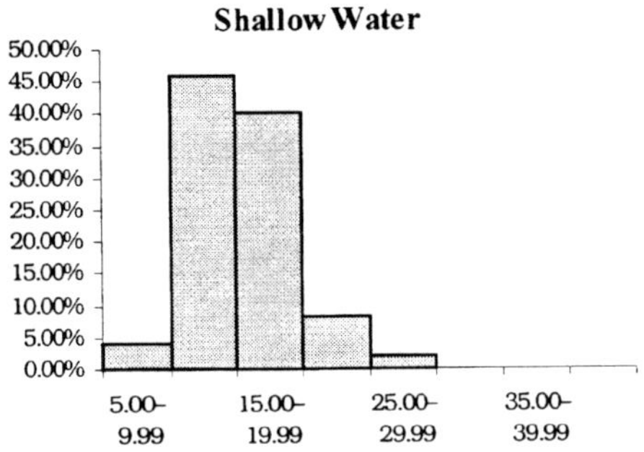

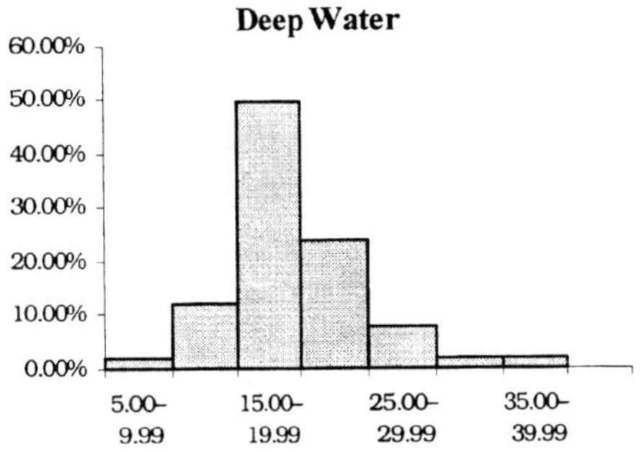

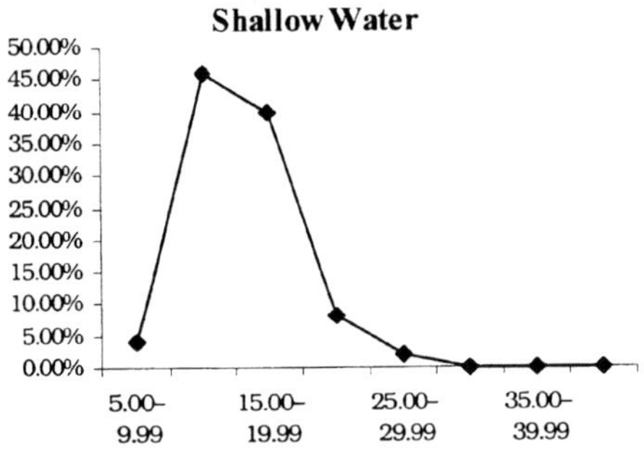

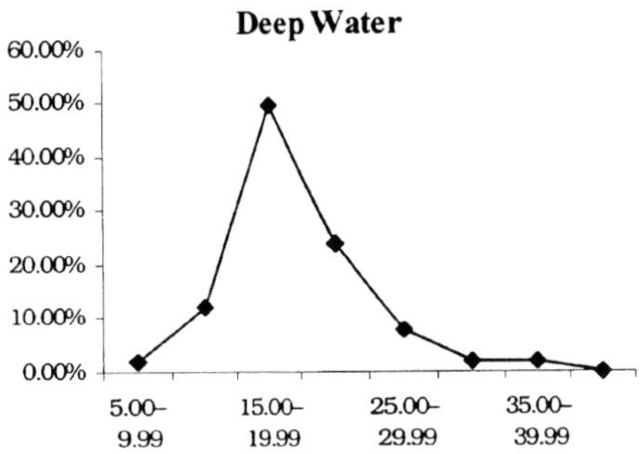

Shallow water

Bin	Cumulative %
5.00–9.99	4.00
10.00–14.99	50.00
15.00–19.99	90.00
20.00–24.99	98.00
25.00–29.99	100.00
30.00–34.99	100.00
35.00–39.99	100.00
More	100.00

Deep water

Bin	Cumulative %
5.00–9.99	2.00
10.00–14.99	14.00
15.00–19.99	64.00
20.00–24.99	88.00
25.00–29.99	96.00
30.00–34.99	98.00
35.00–39.99	100.00
More	100.00

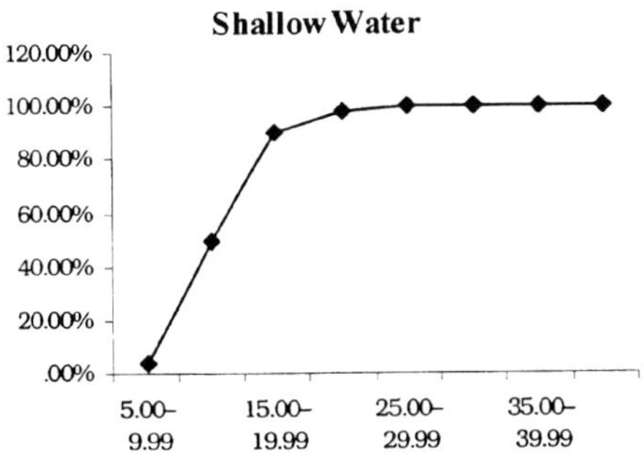

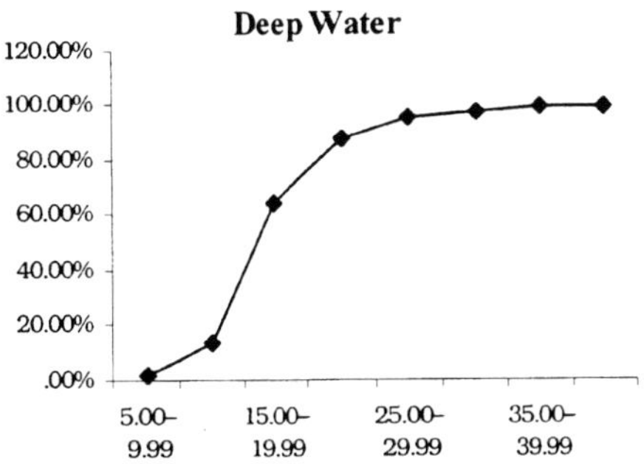

The Dover sole caught in deep water have greater body depth, width, and weight than the Dover sole caught in shallow water.

chapter 3

Describing and Summarizing Data

1. (a)

	Grade X	Grade Y
(1) Mean	575	575.4
(2) Median	575	575
(3) Standard Deviation	6.40	2.07

(b) If quality is measured by the average inner diameter, Grade X tires provide a better quality, because its mean and median are both equal to the expected value of 575 mm. If, however, quality is measured by consistency, Grade Y provides better quality, because its standard deviation is much smaller. The range in values for Grade Y is 5 mm compared to the range in values for Grade X, which is equal to 16 mm.

(c)

	Grade X	Grade Y
(1) Mean	575	577.4
(2) Median	575	575
(3) Standard Deviation	6.40	6.11

In the event that the fifth Y tire measures 588 mm rather than 578 mm, the Grade Y average inner diameter becomes 577.4 mm, which is much larger than Grade X average inner diameter. Also, the Grade Y standard deviation swells from 2.07 mm to 6.11 mm. Therefore, Grade X provides better quality in terms of the average inner diameter and has only slightly more variation than Grade Y. The range in values for Grade Y is now 15 mm, which is only slightly less than the range in values for Grade X.

2. (a)

(1) Arithmetic Mean	34.017
(2) Median	33.750
(3) Mode	No unique mode
(4) Midrange	$(37.23+29.63)/2 = 33.43$
(5) Quartiles	$Q_1 = 33.03$, $Q_3 = 36.14$
(6) Midhinge	$(33.03+36.14)/2 = 34.585$
(7) Range	$37.23-29.63 = 7.60$
(8) Interquartile Range	$36.14-33.03 = 3.11$
(9) Variance	4.914
(10) Standard Deviation	2.2168

(b) Mean $= 34.017 >$ median $= 33.750$. The distribution is positive or right-skewed, because the mean is pulled upward in the direction of positive values.

(c)

X_{smallest}	Q_1	Median	Q_3	X_{largest}
29.63	33.03	33.75	36.14	37.23

The distance from X_{smallest} to $Q_1 = 3.4$ exceeds the distance from Q_3 to $X_{\text{largest}} = 1.09$ and median $= 33.750 >$ midrange $= 33.43$. Therefore we may conclude that the distribution is left-skewed.

3. (a)

(1) Arithmetic Mean	25.677
(2) Median	25
(3) Mode	22

(4) Midrange $(40+17)/2 = 28.5$

(5) Quartiles $Q_1 = 21$, $Q_3 = 30$

(6) Midhinge $(30 + 21)/2 = 25.5$

(7) Range $40 - 17 = 23$

(8) Interquartile Range $30 - 21 = 9$

(9) Variance 37.959

(10) Standard Deviation 6.1611

(b) Mean $= 25.677 >$ median $= 25$. The distribution is positive or right-skewed, because the mean is pulled upward in the direction of positive values.

(c)

$X_{smallest}$	Q_1	Median	Q_3	$X_{largest}$
17	21	25	30	40

(1) The distance from $X_{smallest}$ to $Q_1 = 4$, the distance from Q_3 to $X_{largest} = 10$.

(2) Median $= 25 <$ midhinge $= 25.5 <$ midrange $= 28.5$, therefore we may conclude that the distribution is right-skewed.

4. (a) (1) Arithmetic Mean 1.5823

(2) Median 1.5825

(3) Mode 1.585

(4) Midrange $(1.570 + 1.593)/2 = 1.5815$

(5) Quartiles $Q_1 = 1.579$, $Q_3 = 1.586$

(6) Midhinge $(1.579 + 1.586)/2 = 1.5825$

(7) Range $1.593 - 1.570 = 0.023$

(8) Interquartile Range $1.586 - 1.579 = 0.007$

(9) Variance 0.000024

(10) Standard Deviation 0.0049

(b) Mean $= 1.5823 >$ median $= 1.5825$. The distribution may be slightly left-skewed, because the mean is slightly pulled in the direction of negative values.

(c)

$X_{smallest}$	Q_1	Median	Q_3	$X_{largest}$
1.570	1.579	1.5825	1.586	1.593

(1) The distance from $X_{smallest}$ to Q_1 is 0.009 and the distance from Q_3 to $X_{largest}$ is 0.007.

(2) The distance from Q_1 to the median is 0.0035 and the distance from the median to Q_3 is 0.0035.

(3) Median $= 1.5825 >$ midrange $= 1.5815 >$ midhinge $= 1.578$. The data is slightly left-skewed.

5. (a) (1) Arithmetic Mean 70.73

(2) Median 70

(3) Mode 70

(4) Midrange $(56 + 86)/2 = 71$

(5) Quartiles $Q_1 = 69.5$, $Q_3 = 72$

(6) Midhinge $(69.5 + 72)/2 = 70.75$

(7) Range $86 - 56 = 30$

(8) Interquartile Range $72 - 69.5 = 2.5$

(9) Variance 21.93

(10) Standard Deviation 4.6827

(b) Mean $= 70.73 >$ median $= 70$. The distribution is slightly right-skewed, because the mean is pulled upward in the direction of positive values.

(c)

$X_{smallest}$	Q_1	Median	Q_3	$X_{largest}$
56	69.5	70	72	86

(1) The distance from $X_{smallest}$ to Q_1 is 13.5 and the distance from Q_3 to $X_{largest}$ is 14.

(2) The distance from Q_1 to the median is 0.5 and the distance from the median to Q_3 is 2.

(3) Median $= 70 <$ midhinge $= 70.75 <$ midrange $= 71$.

Therefore we may conclude that the distribution is slightly right-skewed.

6. (a)

	General Office I	General Office II
(1) Arithmetic Mean	2.214	2.011
(2) Median	1.54	1.505
(3) Midrange	$(0.52+6.32)/2=3.42$	$(0.08+7.55)/2=3.815$
(4) First Quartile	0.93	0.6
(5) Third Quartile	3.93	3.75
(6) Midhinge	$(0.93+3.93)/2=2.43$	$(0.6+3.75)/2=2.175$
(7) Range	$6.32-0.52=5.8$	$7.55-0.08=7.47$
(8) Interquartile Range	$3.93-0.93=2.0$	$3.75-0.6=3.15$
(9) Variance	2.952	3.578
(10) Standard Deviation	1.718	1.891

(b)

	$X_{smallest}$	Q_1	Median	Q_3	$X_{largest}$
Central Office I	0.52	0.93	1.540	3.93	6.32
Central Office II	0.08	0.60	1.505	3.75	7.55

(c) For both distributions the distance from Q_3 to $X_{largest}$ greatly exceeds the distance from $X_{smallest}$ to Q_1 for midrange > midhinge >median, therefore the distributions are right-skewed.

(d) Both distributions have similar arithmetic means, medians and standard deviations, but their ranges are quite different. The data for the second central office are more evenly distributed.

(e)

	General Office II	General Office II (incorrect)
(1) Arithmetic Mean	2.011	3.011
(2) Median	1.505	1.505
(3) Midrange	3.815	$(27.55+0.08)/2=13.815$
(4) First Quartile	0.6	0.6
(5) Third Quartile	3.75	3.75
(6) Midhinge	2.175	2.175
(7) Range	7.47	$27.55-0.08=27.47$
(8) Interquartile Range	3.15	3.15
(9) Variance	3.579	35.238
(10) Standard Deviation	1.892	5.936

	$X_{smallest}$	Q_1	Median	Q_3	$X_{largest}$
Central Office II (incorrect)	0.08	0.6	1.505	3.75	27.55

The distance from Q_3 to $X_{largest}$ has increased, so this distribution is more right-skewed.

This incorrect value increased the variance and standard deviation, so the incorrect data are more evenly distributed.

7. (a)

	Plant A	Plant B
(1) Arithmetic Mean	9.382	11.354
(2) Median	8.515	11.96
(3) Midrange	$(4.42+21.62)/2=13.02$	$(2.33+25.75)/2=14.04$
(4) First Quartile	7.29	6.25
(5) Third Quartile	11.42	14.25
(6) Midhinge	$(11.42+7.29)/2=9.355$	$(6.25+14.25)/2=10.25$
(7) Range	$21.62-4.42=17.2$	$25.75-2.33=23.42$
(8) Interquartile Range	$11.42-7.29=4.13$	$14.25-6.25=8$
(9) Variance	15.981	26.277
(10) Standard Deviation	3.998	5.126
(11) Coefficient of Variation	42.61%	45.15%

(b)

	$X_{smallest}$	Q_1	Median	Q_3	$X_{largest}$
Plant A	4.42	7.29	8.515	11.42	21.62
Plant B	2.33	6.25	11.96	14.25	25.75

(c) (1) For both distributions the distance from Q_3 to $X_{largest}$ greatly exceeds the distance from $X_{smallest}$ to Q_1.

(2) Plant A: median = 8.515 < midhinge = 9.355 < midrange = 13.02
Plant B: midhinge = 10.25 < midrange = 14.04 > median = 11.96

Both the distributions are right-skewed. The data for Plant B requires a closer analysis because the mean of this data is less than the median, and the median is greater than the midhinge. This is typical of left skewed data. By constructing a chart similar to Figure 3.4 one can demonstrate more clearly that the data is slightly right skewed.

(d) Plant B has a greater range of processing times, much more dispersion among data values, a higher median, a higher value for the third quartile, and a greater extreme value than Plant A.

8. (a)

(1) Arithmetic Mean	37.44
(2) Median	33.9
(3) Midrange	$(22.3+74.1)/2=48.2$
(4) First Quartile	31.5
(5) Third Quartile	38.2
(6) Midhinge	$(31.5+38.2)/2=34.85$
(7) Range	$74.1-22.3=51.8$
(8) Interquartile Range	$38.2-31.5=6.7$
(9) Variance	145.2
(10) Standard Deviation	12.05

(b)

$X_{smallest}$	Q_1	Median	Q_3	$X_{largest}$
22.3	31.5	33.9	38.2	74.1

(c) (1) The distance from Q_3 to $X_{largest}=35.9$ greatly exceeds the distance from $X_{smallest}$ to $Q_1=9.2$.

(2) Median = 33.9 < midhinge = 34.85 < midrange = 48.2.
Therefore the development time distribution is right-skewed.

9. (a)

	Carnes 3-Way Diffusers	Krueger 4-Way Diffusers
(1) Arithmetic Mean	247.5	244.3
(2) Median	250	245
(3) Midrange	$(160+310)/2 = 235$	$(190+300)/2 = 245$
(4) First Quartile	215	225
(5) Third Quartile	285	265
(6) Midhinge	$(215+285)/2 = 250$	$(225+265)/2 = 245$
(7) Range	$310-160=150$	$300-190=110$
(8) Interquartile Range	$285-215=70$	$265-225=40$
(9) Variance	1557.407	732.677
(10) Standard Deviation	39.464	27.068

(b)

	$X_{smallest}$	Q_1	Median	Q_3	$X_{largest}$
Carnes 3-Way Diffusers	160	215	250	285	310
Krueger 4-Way Diffusers	190	225	245	265	300

(c) For Krueger 4-Way Diffusers

(1) The distance from $X_{smallest}$ to Q_1 is equal the distance from Q_3 to $X_{largest} = 35$.

(2) The distance from Q_1 to the median is equal the distance from the median to $Q_3 = 20$.

(3) Median = midrange = midhinge = 245 so the data are perfectly symmetrical.

For Carnes 3-Way Diffusers

(1) The distance from $X_{smallest}$ to $Q_1 = 55$ and the distance from Q_3 to $X_{largest} = 25$.

Midrange = 235 < midhinge = 250 so the distribution is left-skewed.

(d) The Carnes 3-Way Diffusers have a greater range, more dispersion among data values, a slightly higher mean and median, and a higher value for the third quartile than Krueger diffusers.

10. (a) Plot produced by PHstat agrees with the five-number summary of Problem 3.2 :

Box-and-Whisker Plot

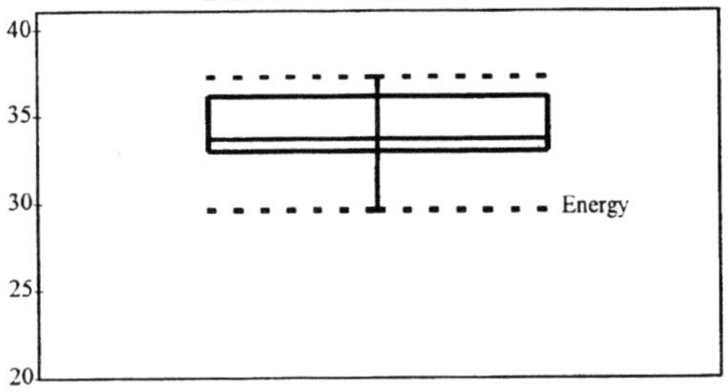

Note: Plot produced by MINITAB does **NOT** agree with the five-number summary (compare Q_1 for the two plots):

Boxplot of Energy

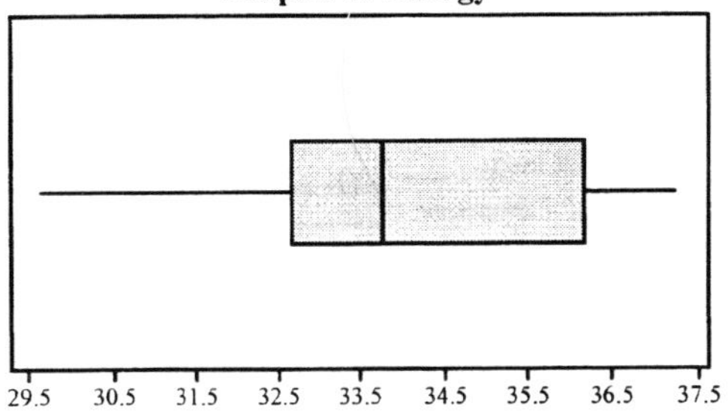

Note: This happens because MINITAB defines the values of Quartiles differently from the definition given in the textbook, page 111. See detailed explanation of the difference in Problem 3.26. In some situation it leads to different values of Quartiles (as in the present case); in some, to the same values of Quartiles. In this Chapter, when the differences can be easily noticed in the plots, we will present both MINITAB and PHStat plots.

(b) The center of the distribution is asymmetric, with the median located closer to Q_1 than to Q_3. On the other hand, the lower tail appears to be substantially longer than the upper tail. Therefore, the distribution is left-skewed.

11. (a)

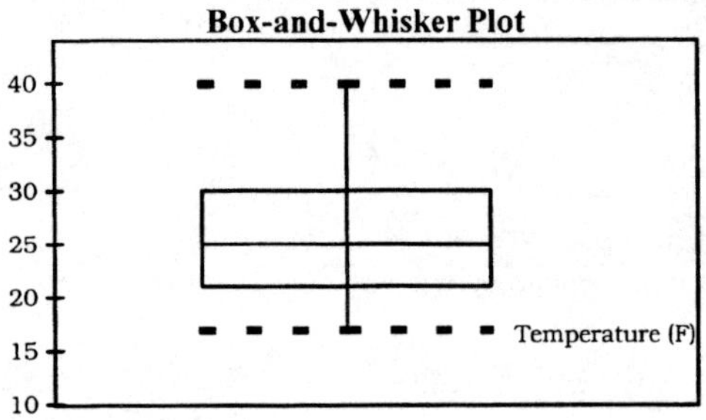

(b) The center of the distribution is asymmetric, with the median located a little closer to Q_1 than to Q_3. In addition, the upper tail appears to be substantially longer than the lower tail. Therefore, the distribution of temperature is right-skewed.

12. (a)

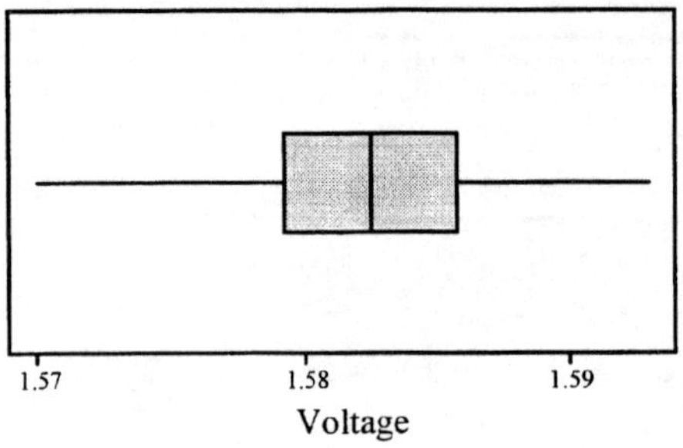

(b) The lower tail appears to be a little longer than the upper tail, showing that the distribution of voltage is slightly left-skewed.

13. (a)

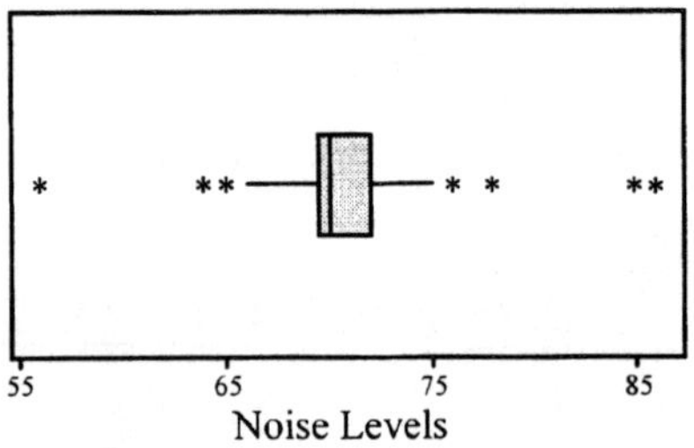

(b) The center of the distribution is asymmetric, with the median located much closer to Q_1 than to Q_3. Therefore, the distribution is slightly right-skewed.

14. (a)

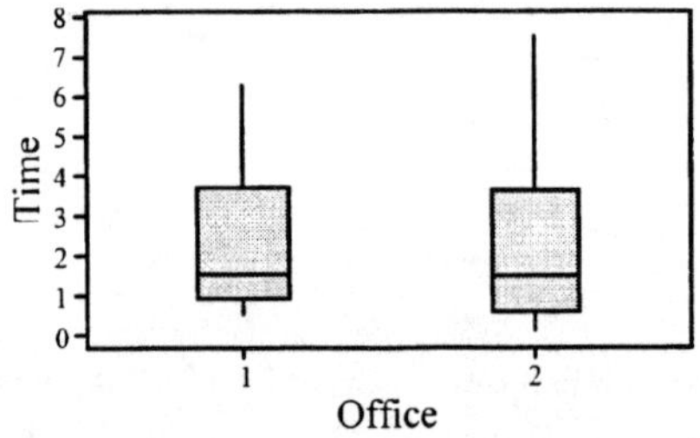

(b) Both distributions have asymmetric centers, with the median located much closer to Q_1 than to Q_3. In addition, the upper tails appear to be substantially longer than the lower tails. Therefore the distributions are right-skewed. The supervisors want to shift the distributions down around the means. They should focus their efforts on the types of problems that take the longest time to solve.

15. (a)

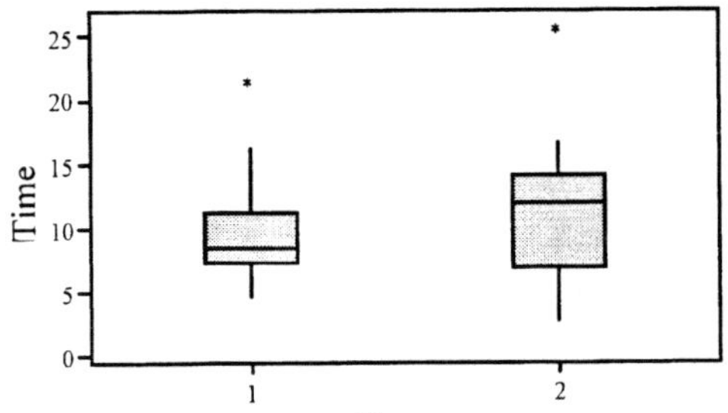

(b) The centers of the distributions are asymmetric. For plant A, the median is located much closer to Q_1 than to Q_3. For plant B, the median is located closer to Q_3 than to Q_1. In addition, the upper tails of distributions appear to be longer than the lower tails, so the distributions are right-skewed.
Note that estimating whether a distribution is right-or left-skewed is rather subjective (especially when graphical methods are employed). Thus, for verification Skewers provided by MINIT can be used for ambiguous cases (such as the Plant B case in the current problem).

16. (a)

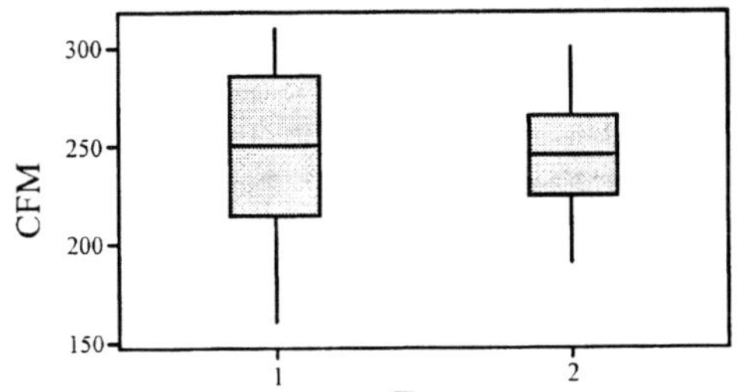

(b) The Krueger 4-Way distribution is symmetrical. The upper tail for the Carnes 3-Way distribution appears to be shorter than the lower tail, so this distribution is left-skewed.

(c) Although the median CFM of the two types of diffusers are similar, the first quartile and minimum values are greater, and the third quartile and the maximum values are less for the Krueger diffusers than for Carnes diffusers. In terms of dispersion, the range and interquartile range are less for the Krueger diffusers than for Carnes diffusers. In terms of symmetry, the Krueger diffuser's distribution appears to be symmetrical, whereas the distribution for the Carnes diffusers is left-skewed.

17. Central tendency, variability, skewness, and kurtosis are useful for describing a set of numerical data.

18. Measure of location is a typical value or average that represents or describes the entire set of data.

19. The **arithmetic mean** acts as a balancing point. It is the only measure of location based on all of the observations, and is greatly affected by extreme values.
The **median** is the middle value in an ordered sequence of data, dividing a distribution into two equal parts. Using the median may be more appropriate than the mean when extreme observations are present, because the median is not affected by a change in value of an observation if the order of the observations remain the same.
The **mode** is the most frequently occurring value in a data set. It is not useful if each value occurs only once or if there are several differing modes of different values.
Midrange shows the geometrical center of the data set. Because it involves only the smallest and largest observations in the data set, the midrange is greatly affected by an extreme value or values.
Midhinge represents the mean of the first and third quartiles and is not affected by extreme values in the data.

20. The measure of variation is the measure of the amount of dispersion or spread in the data.

21. The **range** measures the total spread in a set of data. It is an easily computed measure of variation, but takes into account only the largest and smallest values and fails to account for how the values are distributed between these two extremes. Unlike the range, **interquartile range** is not affected by extreme values and represents the range of the middle half of the data set. Unfortunately, like the range the interquartile range does not account for the distribution of the values in the set. **Variance** and **standard deviation** evaluate the spread or dispersion of data around the mean. The advantage of the standard deviation over the variance is that it has the same units as the original data.

22. The property of shape evaluates the manner in which the data are distributed around their mean.

23. Skewness represents the asymmetry of the distribution whereas kurtosis relates to the relative concentration of values in the center of the distribution as compared to the tails.

24. Variation shows spread or dispersion of the data around the mean. Kurtosis concerns the relative concentration of values in the center of the distribution as compared to the tails.

25. The box-and-whisker plot provides a graphical representation of the data through the five-number summary. This gives a more thorough understanding of the distribution of the data set than could be obtained from studying the mean, median, and standard deviation alone. The box-and-whisker plot is also a useful tool for comparing two or more groups graphically.

26.

	Ultra-Pure System		
	Conductivity	TAMP	TOC
(a) Mean	0.801	5.67	174.67
(b) Median	0.702	0.5	168.5
(c) Mode	No	0	No
(d) Midrange	$(0.517+1.365)/2=0.941$	$(0+44)/2=22$	$(340+19)/2=179.5$
(e) Quartiles	$Q_1=0.616$, $Q_3=0.958$	$Q_1=0$, $Q_3=6$	$Q_1=107$, $Q_3=240$
(f) Midhinge	$(0.616+0.958)/2=0.787$	$(0+6)/2=3$	$(107+240)/2=173.5$

	Deionizing System		
	Conductivity	TAMP	TOC
(a) Mean	0.59617	3.3333	173.5
(b) Median	0.556	0.5	180
(c) Mode	No	0	250
(d) Midrange	$(0.452+0.872)/2=0.662$	$(0+26)/2=13$	$(6+330)/2=168$
(e) Quartiles	$Q_1=0.476$, $Q_3=0.732$	$Q_1=0$, $Q_3=2$	$Q_1=45$, $Q_3=250$
(f) Midhinge	$(0.476+0.732)/2=0.604$	$(0+2)/2=1$	$(45+250)/2=147.5$

(g) The median and midhinge are the most useful for TAMP variables, because the others give distorted measures of central tendency due to the presence of outliers. The mean is the most useful for the conductivity and TOC variables, because it is based on all of the observations.

	Ultra-Pure System		
	Conductivity	TAMP	TOC
(h) Range	$1.365-0.517=0.848$	$44-0=44$	$340-19=321$
(i) Q_3-Q_1	$0.958-0.616=0.342$	$6-0=6$	$240-107=133$
(j) Variance	0.0781947	157.152	7752.97
Standard Deviation	0.279633	12.536	88.0509

	Deionizing System		
	Conductivity	TAMP	TOC
(h) Range	$0.872-0.452=0.42$	$26-0=26$	$330-6=324$
(i) Q_3-Q_1	$0.732-0.476=0.256$	$2-0=2$	$250-45=205$
(j) Variance	0.0178818	57.3333	10796.3
Standard Deviation	0.133723	7.57188	103.905

(k)

		$X_{smallest}$	Q_1	Median	Q_3	$X_{largest}$
	Conductivity	0.517	0.616	0.702	0.958	1.365
Ultra-Pure System	**TAMP**	0	0	0.5	6	44
	TOC	19	107	168.5	240	340
	Conductivity	0.452	0.476	0.556	0.732	0.872
Deionizing System	**TAMP**	0	0	0.5	2	26
	TOC	6	45	180	250	330

Ultra-Pure System
Conductivity
(1) The distance from $X_{smallest}$ to $Q_1 = 0.099$; the distance from Q_3 to $X_{largest} = 0.407$.
(2) Median = 0.702 < midhinge = 0.787 < midrange = 0.941, therefore we may conclude that the distribution is right-skewed.
TAMP
(1) The distance from $X_{smallest}$ to $Q_1 = 0$; the distance from Q_3 to $X_{largest} = 38$.
(2) Median = 0.5 < midhinge = 3 < midrange = 22, therefore we may conclude that the distribution is right-skewed.
TOC
(1) The distance from $X_{smallest}$ to $Q_1 = 88$; the distance from Q_3 to $X_{largest} = 100$.
(2) Median = 168.5 < midhinge = 173.5 < midrange = 179.5, therefore we may conclude that the distribution is right-skewed.
Deionizing System
Conductivity
(1) The distance from $X_{smallest}$ to $Q_1 = 0.024$; the distance from Q_3 to $X_{largest} = 0.142$.
(2) Median = 0.556 < midhinge = 0.604 < midrange = 0.662, therefore we may conclude that the distribution is right-skewed.
TAMP
(1) The distance from $X_{smallest}$ to $Q_1 = 0$; the distance from Q_3 to $X_{largest} = 24$.
(2) Median = 0.5 < midhinge = 1 < midrange = 13, therefore we may conclude that the distribution is right-skewed.
TOC
(1) The distance from $X_{smallest}$ to $Q_1 = 39$; the distance from Q_3 to $X_{largest} = 80$.
(2) Median = 180 > midhinge = 147.5 < midrange = 168, therefore we may conclude that the distribution is right-skewed.

(l)

Box-and-Whisker Plot of Conductivity

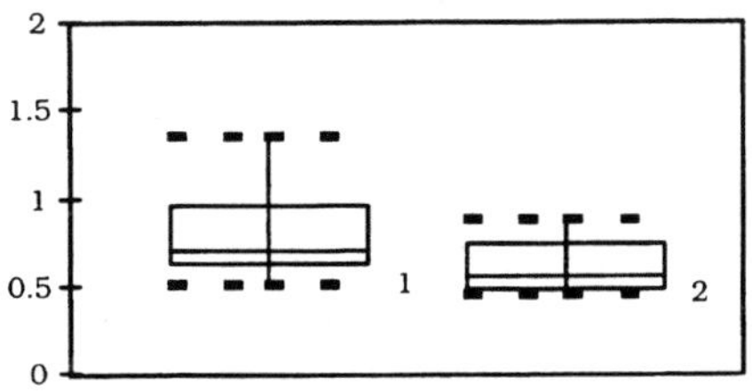

Box-and-Whisker Plot of TAMP

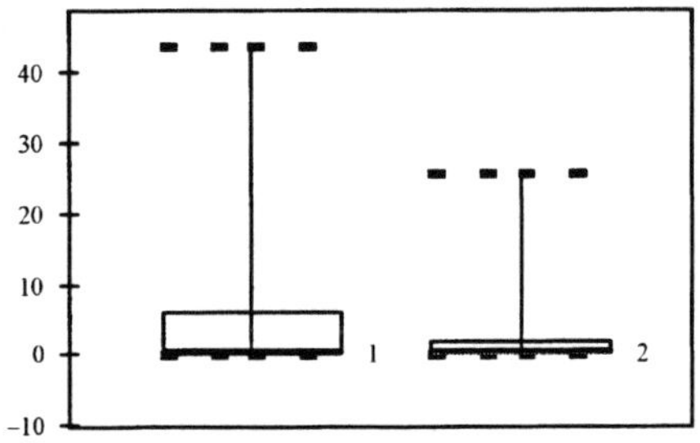

Box-and-whisker Plot of TOC

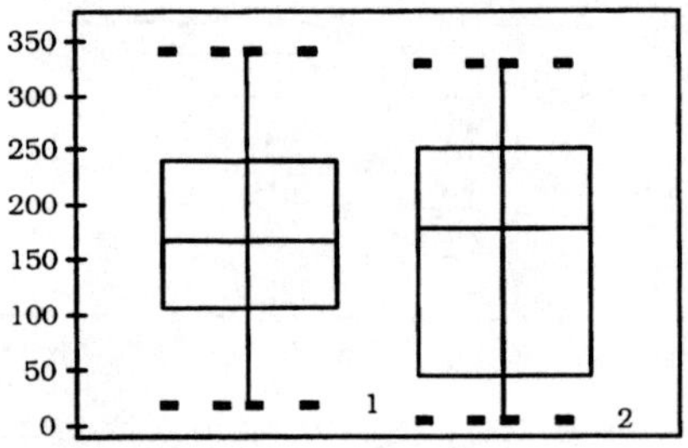

Note: The plot of TOC was produced by PHStat and agrees with the five-number summary. However, the plot produced by MINITAB does **<u>NOT</u>** agree with the five-number summary (compare Q_1 for the two plots and that of the five-number summary for deionizing system):

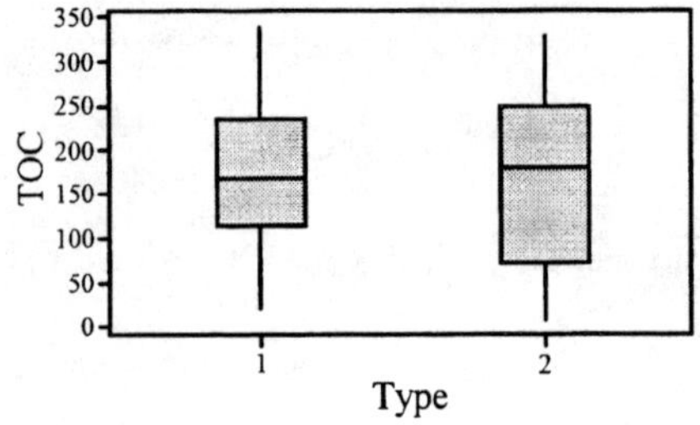

This occurs because MINITAB defines the values of Quartiles differently from the definition in the textbook, page 111. To see the difference, let us examine how the value of Q_1 for the deionizing system is computed.

Q_1 is defined as the value corresponding to the $(n+1)/4$ ordered observation. For this particular case $Q_1 = (12+1)/4 = 3.25$.

The textbook, (see page 111), demands that in this case the position point be rounded off to the nearest integer, 3, and the numerical value of the corresponding observation be selected, 45.

MINITAB, on the other hand, uses a more complicated procedure. It takes the 3rd and 4th ordered observations, finds their difference, calculates a quarter of this value, and adds the resulting value to the 3rd ordered observation. For the case under consideration, the 3rd and 4th ordered observations are 45 and 157, respectively, their difference is 112, its quarter is 112/4=28. The new value of Q_1 is 45+28=73.

Thus, the value of Q_1 computed by MINITAB is more than **<u>ONE AND A HALF</u>** times larger than the value of Q_1 calculated according to the textbook.

(m) **Conductivity.** In terms of location, the median, first and third quartiles, and the maximum and minimum values are larger for the Ultra-Pure System than for the Deionizing System. In terms of dispersion, the range and interquartile range are larger for the Ultra-Pure System than for the Deionizing System. Both distributions appear to be right-skewed.
TAMP. In terms of location, the median and first quartile are about the same, and the third quartile and maximum value are larger for the Ultra-Pure System than for the Deionizing System. In terms of dispersion, the interquartile range is smaller for the Ultra-Pure System than for the Deionizing System and the ranges are approximately the same. Both distributions appear to be slightly right-skewed.
TOC. In terms of location, the main characteristics are about the same, the first is larger for the Ultra-Pure System than for the Deionizing System. In terms of dispersion, the range and interquartile range are larger for the Ultra-Pure System than for the Deionizing System. Both distributions appear to be right-skewed.

27. (a)

	Rainfall Depth	**Runoff Depth**
(1) Arithmetic Mean	18.59	1.710
(2) Median	14.55	1.515
(3) Mode	No unique mode	No unique mode
(4) Midrange	$(7.2+41.2)/2=24.2$	$(4.05+0.07)/2=2.06$
(5) Quartiles	$Q_1=11.5$, $Q_3=27.3$	$Q_1=0.87$, $Q_3=2.49$

(6) Midhinge	$(11.5+27.3)/2 = 19.4$	$(0.87+2.49)/1.68$
(7) Range	$41.2-7.2 = 34$	$4.05-0.07 = 3.98$
(8) Interquartile Range	$27.3-11.5 = 15.8$	$2.49-0.87 = 1.62$
(9) Variance	109.782	1.22777
(10) Standard Deviation	10.4777	1.10805

(b) **Rainfall Depth:** Mean = 18.59 > median = 14.55. The distribution is positive or right-skewed, because the mean is pulled upward in the direction of positive values.
Runoff Depth: Mean = 1.71 > median = 1.515. The distribution is positive or right-skewed, because the mean is pulled upward in the direction of positive values.

(c)

	$X_{smallest}$	Q_1	Median	Q_3	$X_{largest}$
Rainfall Depth	7.2	11.5	14.55	27.3	41.2
Runoff Depth	0.07	0.87	1.515	2.49	4.05

Rainfall Depth

(1) The distance from $X_{smallest}$ to $Q_1 = 4.3$; the distance from Q_3 to $X_{largest} = 13.9$.

(2) Median = 14.55 < midhinge = 19.4 < midrange = 24.2, therefore we may conclude that the distribution is right-skewed.

Runoff Depth

(1) The distance from $X_{smallest}$ to $Q_1 = 0.8$; the distance from Q_3 to $X_{largest} = 1.56$.

(2) Median = 1.515 < midhinge = 1.68 < midrange = 2.06, therefore we may conclude that the distribution is right-skewed.

(d)

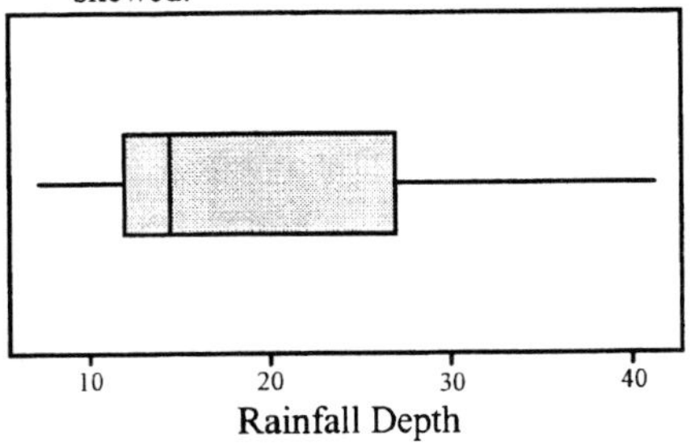

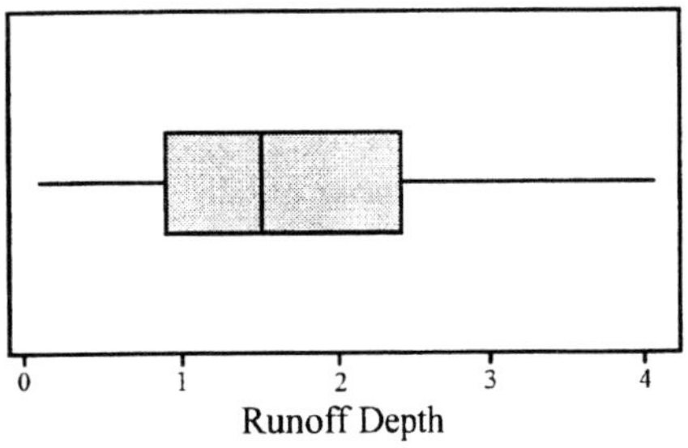

The center of the distribution is asymmetric, with the median located closer to Q_1 than to Q_3. In addition, the upper tail appears to be substantially longer than the lower tail, showing that the distribution is right-skewed.

The center of the distribution is asymmetric, with the median located a little closer to Q_1 than to Q_3. In addition, the upper tail appears to be longer than the lower tail, showing that the distribution is right-skewed.

(e) As the median of the Rainfall Depth distribution is located closer to Q_1 the distribution of Rainfall Depth is more right-skewed than in Runoff Depth.

28. (a)

	HC	CO	NO
(1) Arithmetic Mean	0.5517	7.968	1.3287
(2) Median	0.51	5.905	1.3100
(3) Mode	0.41	4.1, 6.02, 14.97	1.16, 1.31, 1.32, 1.47
(4) Midrange	$(0.34+1.1)/2 = 0.72$	$(1.85+23.53)/2 = 12.69$	$(0.49+2.94)/2 = 1.715$
(5) Quartiles	$Q_1 = 0.43$, $Q_3 = 0.61$	$Q_1 = 4.29$, $Q_3 = 11.2$	$Q_1 = 1.08$, $Q_3 = 1.49$
(6) Midhinge	$(0.43+0.61)/2 = 0.52$	$(4.29+11.2)/2 = 7.745$	$(1.08+1.49)/2 = 1.285$
(7) Range	$1.1-0.34 = 0.76$	$23.53-1.85 = 21.68$	$2.94-0.49 = 2.45$

(8) Interquartile Range	$0.61-0.43=0.18$	$11.2-4.29=6.91$	$1.49-1.08=0.41$
(9) Variance	0.0283	27.7891	0.235
(10) Standard Deviation	0.168	5.27154	0.484

(b) **HC** Mean = 0.5517 > median = 0.51 so the distribution is positive or right-skewed, because the mean is pulled upward in the direction of positive values.
CO Mean = 7.968 > median = 5.905 so the distribution is positive or right-skewed, because the mean is pulled upward in the direction of positive values.
NO Mean = 1.3287 > median = 1.31 so the distribution is positive or right-skewed, because the mean is pulled upward in the direction of positive values.

(c)

	$X_{smallest}$	Q_1	Median	Q_3	$X_{largest}$
HC	0.34	0.43	0.51	0.61	1.1
CO	1.85	4.29	5.905	11.2	23.53
NO	0.49	1.08	1.31	1.49	2.94

HC
(1) The distance from $X_{smallest}$ to $Q_1 = 0.09$ while the distance from Q_3 to $X_{largest} = 0.49$.
(2) Median = 0.51 < midhinge = 0.52 < midrange = 0.72, therefore we may conclude that the distribution is right-skewed.
CO
(1) The distance from $X_{smallest}$ to $Q_1 = 2.44$; the distance from Q_3 to $X_{largest} = 12.33$.
(2) Median = 5.905 < midhinge = 7.745 < midrange = 12.69, therefore we may conclude that the distribution is right-skewed.
NO
(1) The distance from $X_{smallest}$ to $Q_1 = 0.59$; the distance from Q_3 to $X_{largest} = 1.45$.
(2) Median = 1.31 > midhinge = 1.285 < midrange = 1.75 so the distribution may be right-skewed.
All three distributions are right-skewed, because the distance from Q_3 to $X_{largest}$ exceeds the distance from $X_{smallest}$ to Q_1.

(d)

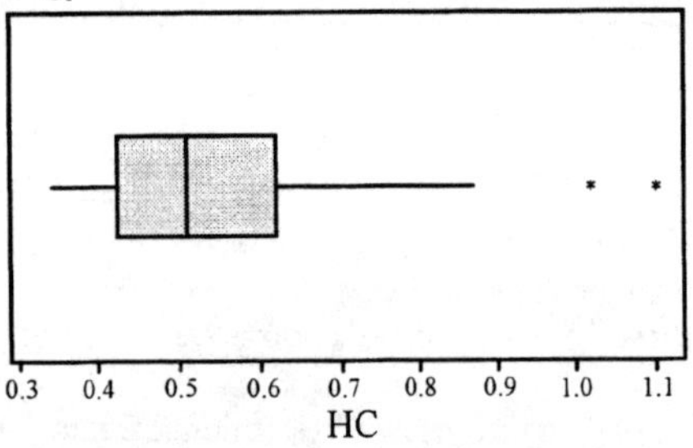

The center of the distribution is asymmetric, with the median located a little closer to Q_1 than to Q_3. In addition, the upper tail appears to be substantially longer than the lower tail, showing that the distribution is right-skewed.

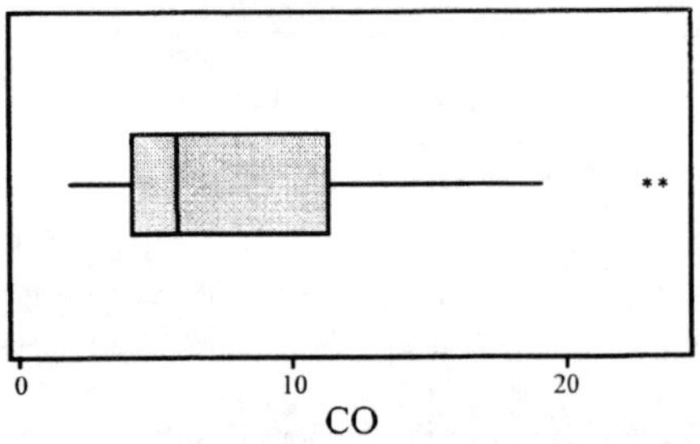

The center of the distribution is asymmetric, with the median located much closer to Q_1 than to Q_3. In addition, the upper tail appears to be substantially longer than the lower tail, showing that the distribution is right-skewed.

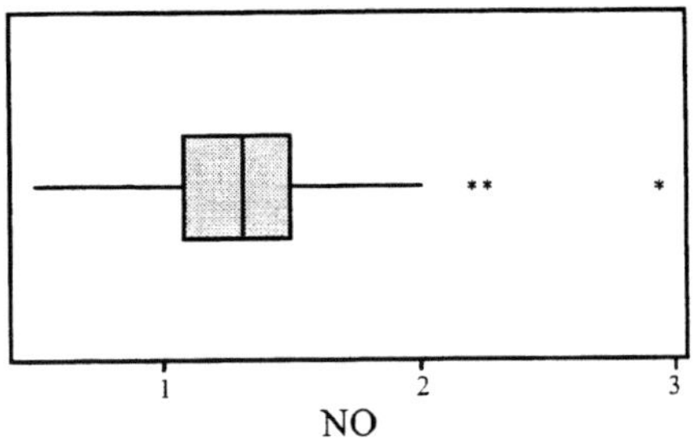

The center of the distribution is slightly asymmetric, with the median located a little closer to Q_3 than to Q_1. On the other hand, the upper tail appears to be substantially longer than the lower. Therefore we can conclude that the distribution is right-skewed.

(e) The central parts of these distributions are different. For example, the median of CO distribution is located much closer to Q_1 than in other distributions. In addition, the upper tails of the HC and CO distributions appear to be substantially longer than the lower tails, and for NO data they are comparable.

29. (a)

	DMY	NC
(1) Arithmetic Mean	16.713	13.643
(2) Median	17.1	13.4
(3) Mode	14.6, 20.7	12.7
(4) Midrange	$(11.6+22.2)/2 = 16.9$	$(11.8+16.0)/2 = 13.9$
(5) Quartiles	$Q_1 = 13.7$, $Q_3 = 19.5$	$Q_1 = 12.8$, $Q_3 = 14.7$
(6) Midhinge	$(13.7+19.5)/2 = 16.6$	$(12.8+14.7)/2 = 13.75$
(7) Range	$22.2-11.6 = 10.6$	$16.0-11.8 = 4.2$
(8) Interquartile Range	$19.5-13.7 = 5.8$	$14.7-12.8 = 1.9$
(9) Variance	10.4185	1.12711
(10) Standard Deviation	3.22776	1.06166

(b) **DMY** Mean = 16.713 < median = 17.1 so the distribution is left-skewed.
NC Mean = 13.643 < median = 13.4 so the distribution is left-skewed.

(c)

	X_{smallest}	Q_1	**Median**	Q_3	X_{largest}
DMY	11.6	13.7	17.1	19.5	22.2

(1) The distance from X_{smallest} to $Q_1 = 2.1$; the distance from Q_3 to $X_{\text{largest}} = 2.7$.

(2) Median = 17.1 < midhinge = 16.6 < midrange = 16.9, therefore we may conclude that the distribution is slightly right-skewed.

	X_{smallest}	Q_1	**Median**	Q_3	X_{largest}
NC	11.8	12.8	13.4	14.7	16.0

(1) The distance from X_{smallest} to $Q_1 = 1.0$; the distance from Q_3 to $X_{\text{largest}} = 1.3$.

(2) Median = 13.4 < midhinge = 13.75 < midrange = 13.9, therefore we may conclude that the distribution is slightly right-skewed.

(d) In terms of location, the median, the first and third quartiles, and the minimum values are larger for the DMY data than for the NC data. In terms of dispersion, the range and the interquartile range are larger for the DMY data than for the NC data. Both distributions appear to be slightly right-skewed.

(e)

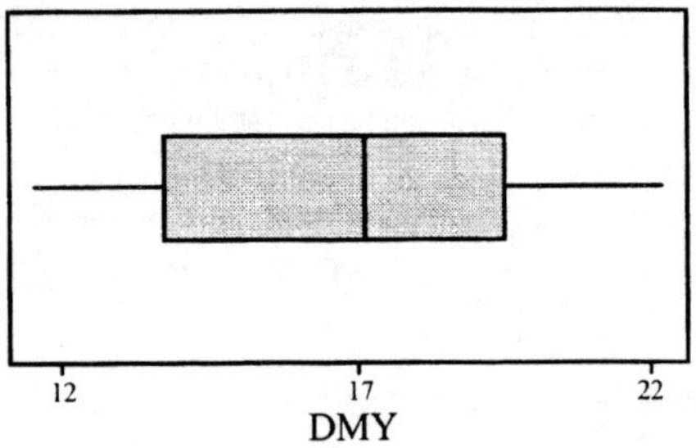

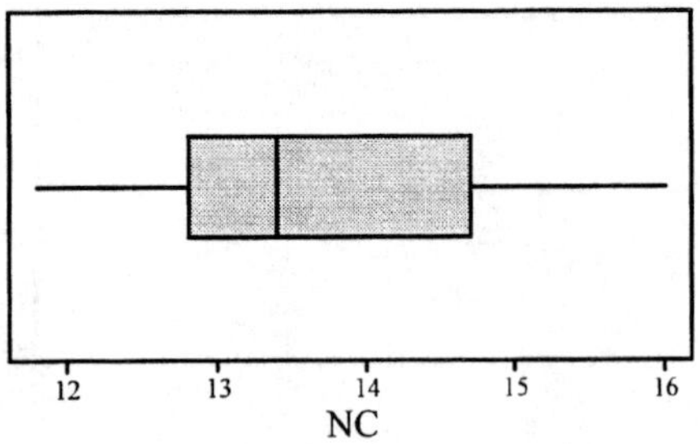

The center of the distribution is asymmetric, with the median located a little closer to Q_3 than to Q_1. But the upper tail appears to be a little longer than the lower tail. Therefore we can conclude that this distribution is approximately symmetrical.

The center of the distribution is asymmetric, with the median located closer to Q_1 than to Q_3. In addition, the upper tail appears to be a little longer than the lower tail. Therefore, the distribution is right-skewed.

(f) Both box-and-whisker plots have similar tails (the upper tail appears to be a little longer than the lower one), but the median for DMY distribution is shifted to the right and the median for DMY distribution is shifted to the left. In addition, the NC distribution is right-skewed, and the DMY distribution may be symmetrical.

30. Note: File RECLAIM is not found in the CD. Use the data in the textbook.

(a)

	1	2	3	4
(1) Arithmetic Mean	5.542	5.708	5.133	5.567
(2) Median	5.500	5.100	4.800	5.050
(3) Mode	4.4, 5.6, 6.0	5.1	4.7, 4.8, 5.8	5.0
(4) Midrange	$(4.4+7.7)/2=6.05$	$(4.4+10.7)/2=7.55$	$(4.2+7.8)/2=6.00$	$(3.6+8.6)/2=6.10$
(5) Quartiles	$Q_1=4.6$, $Q_3=6.0$	$Q_1=4.8$, $Q_3=5.5$	$Q_1=4.4$, $Q_3=5.8$	$Q_1=4.5$, $Q_3=6.7$
(6) Midhinge	$(4.6+6.0)/2=5.30$	$(4.8+5.5)/2=5.15$	$(4.4+5.8)/2=5.10$	$(4.5+6.7)/2=5.60$
(7) Range	$7.7-4.4=3.3$	$10.7-4.4=6.3$	$7.8-4.2=3.6$	$8.6-3.6=5.0$
(8) Interquartile Range	$6.0-4.6=1.4$	$5.5-4.8=0.7$	$5.8-4.4=1.4$	$6.7-4.5=2.2$
(9) Variance	0.986	2.948	0.973	2.246
(10) Standard Deviation	0.993	1.717	0.987	1.499

(b) **1st year**

Mean = 5.542 > median = 5.500 so the distribution may be right-skewed.

2nd year

Mean = 5.708 > median = 5.100 so the distribution may be right-skewed.

3rd year

Mean = 5.133 > median = 4.800 so the distribution may be right-skewed.

4th year

Mean = 5.567 > median = 5.050 so the distribution may be right-skewed.

(c)

	$X_{smallest}$	Q_1	**Median**	Q_3	$X_{largest}$
1st year	4.4	4.6	5.5	6.0	7.7
2nd year	4.4	4.8	5.1	5.5	10.7
3rd year	4.2	4.4	4.8	5.8	7.8
4th year	3.6	4.5	5.05	6.7	8.6

1st year

(1) The distance from X_{smallest} to $Q_1 = 0.2$; the distance from Q_3 to $X_{\text{largest}} = 1.7$.

(2) Median = 5.5 < midrange = 6.05, therefore we may conclude that the distribution is right-skewed.

2nd year

(1) The distance from X_{smallest} to $Q_1 = 0.4$; the distance from Q_3 to $X_{\text{largest}} = 5.2$.

(2) Median = 5.1 < midhinge = 5.15 < midrange = 7.55, therefore we may conclude that the distribution is right-skewed.

3rd year

(1) The distance from X_{smallest} to $Q_1 = 0.2$; the distance from Q_3 to $X_{\text{largest}} = 2.0$.

(2) Median = 4.8 < midhinge = 5.1 < midrange = 6.0, therefore we may conclude that the distribution is right-skewed.

4th year

(1) The distance from X_{smallest} to $Q_1 = 0.9$; the distance from Q_3 to $X_{\text{largest}} = 1.9$.

(2) Median = 5.05 < midhinge = 5.6 < midrange = 6.1, therefore we may conclude that the distribution is right-skewed.

(d) In terms of location, the median and Q_1 are about the same for all distributions. The fourth year distribution has the largest Q_3, the second year distribution has the largest maximum, and the fourth year distribution has the smallest minimum values. In terms of dispersion, the second year distribution has the largest range, but the smallest interquartile range, the fourth year distribution has the largest interquartile range. All distributions appear to be right-skewed.

(e)

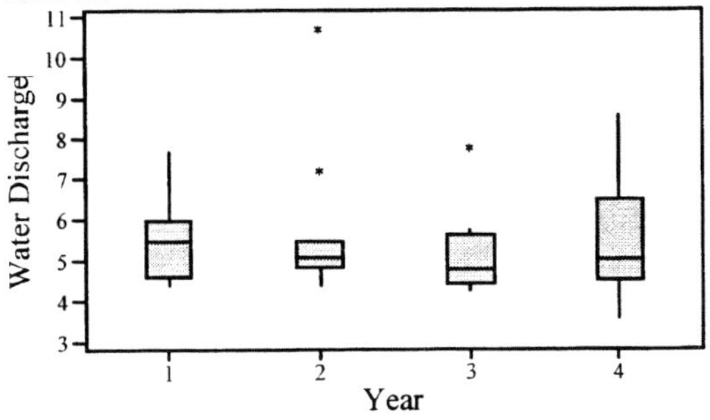

All distributions are right-skewed. The second year distribution has two outsiders, and the third year distribution has one outsider.

(f) The centers of the distributions are asymmetric. For the first year distribution the median is located closer to Q_3 than to Q_1 and for the others the median shifted to Q_1. For all distributions, the upper tail appears to be longer than the lower tail.

31. (a)

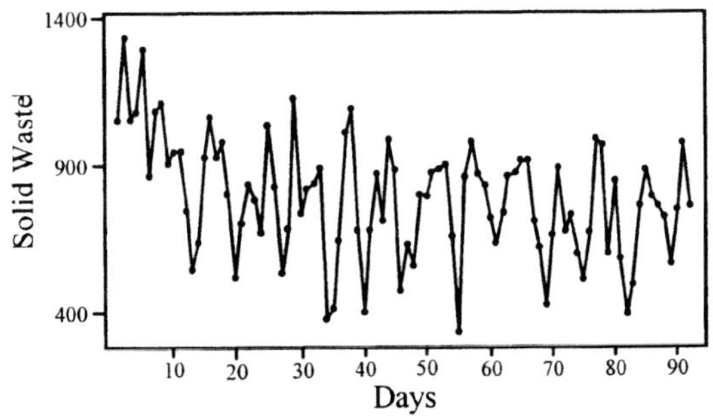

The data appear to be relatively stable with no evidence of a pattern over time.

(b) (1) Arithmetic Mean 787.9
(2) Median 796.5
(3) Mode 712, 859, 928
(4) Midrange $(333+1334)/2 = 833.5$
(5) Quartiles $Q_1 = 657$, $Q_3 = 913$
(6) Midhinge $(913+657)/2 = 785$
(7) Range $1334-333 = 1001$
(8) Interquartile Range $913-657 = 256$
(9) Variance 40861.4
(10) Standard Deviation 202.142

(c)

$X_{smallest}$	Q_1	Median	Q_3	$X_{largest}$
333.0	657.0	796.5	913.0	1334.0

(d)

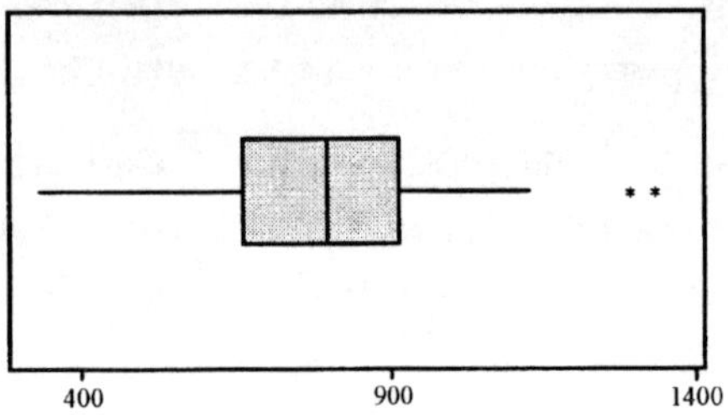

(e) (1) The distance from $X_{smallest}$ to $Q_1 = 324$; the distance from Q_3 to $X_{largest} = 421$.

(2) Median = 796.5 < midrange = 833.5, therefore we may conclude that the distribution is slightly right-skewed.

From the box-and-whisker plot we can see that the center of the distribution is slightly asymmetric, with the median located a little closer to Q_3 than to Q_1. On the other hand, the upper tail appears to be longer than the lower tail, therefore, the distribution may be slightly right-skewed.

(f)

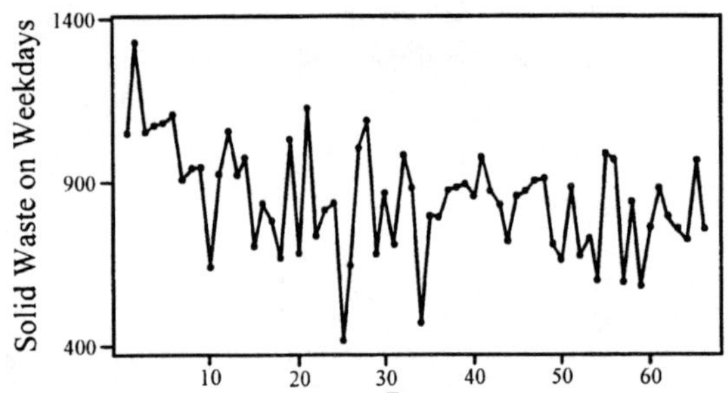

The data appear to be relatively stable with no evidence of a pattern over time.

(1) Arithmetic Mean 848.8
(2) Median 864.0
(3) Mode 712, 859, 928
(4) Midrange $(1334.0+414.0)/2 = 874$
(5) Quartiles $Q_1 = 726$, $Q_3 = 970$
(6) Midhinge $(970+726)/2 = 848$
(7) Range $1334.0-414.0 = 920$
(8) Interquartile Range $970-726 = 244$
(9) Variance 27817.6
(10) Standard Deviation 166.786

$X_{smallest}$	Q_1	Median	Q_3	$X_{largest}$
414.0	726	864.0	970	1334.0

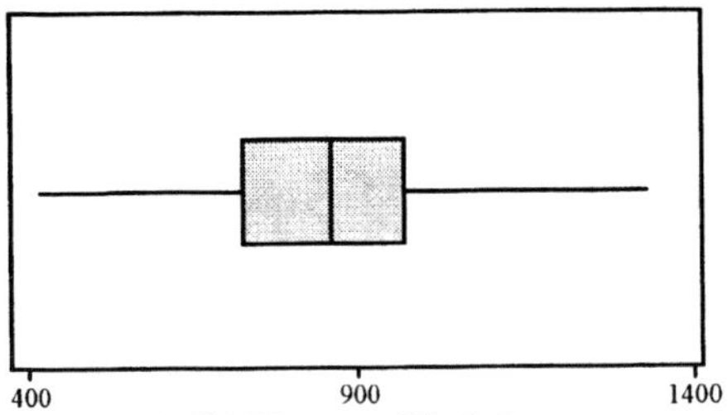

Solid Waste on Weekdays

(1) The distance from $X_{smallest}$ to $Q_1 = 312$; the distance from Q_3 to $X_{largest} = 364$.

(2) Median = 864 < midrange = 874, therefore we may conclude that the distribution is slightly right-skewed.
From the box-and-whisker plot we can see that the center of the distribution is slightly asymmetric, with the median located a little closer to Q_3 than to Q_1. On the other hand, the upper tail appears to be longer than the lower tail, therefore, the distribution may be slightly right-skewed.

(g)

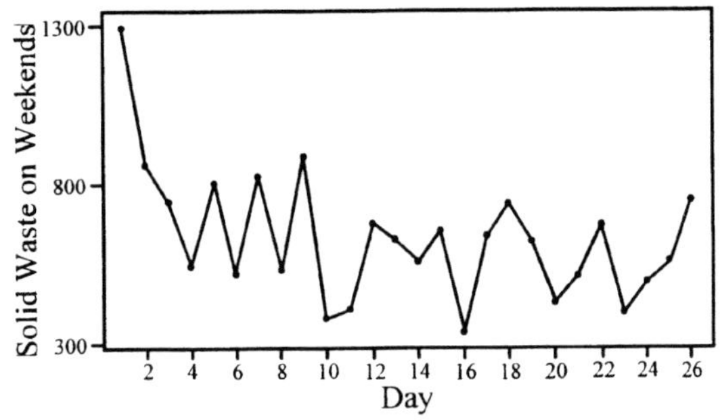

The data appear to be relatively stable with no evidence of a pattern over time.

(1)	Arithmetic Mean	633.3
(2)	Median	626.0
(3)	Mode	No unique mode
(4)	Midrange	$(333+1294)/2 = 813.5$
(5)	Quartiles	$Q_1 = 511$, $Q_3 = 747$
(6)	Midhinge	$(511+747)/2 = 629$
(7)	Range	$1294 - 333 = 961$
(8)	Interquartile Range	$747 - 511 = 236$
(9)	Variance	41748.1
(10)	Standard Deviation	204.324

$X_{smallest}$	Q_1	Median	Q_3	$X_{largest}$
333.0	511	626.0	747	1294.0

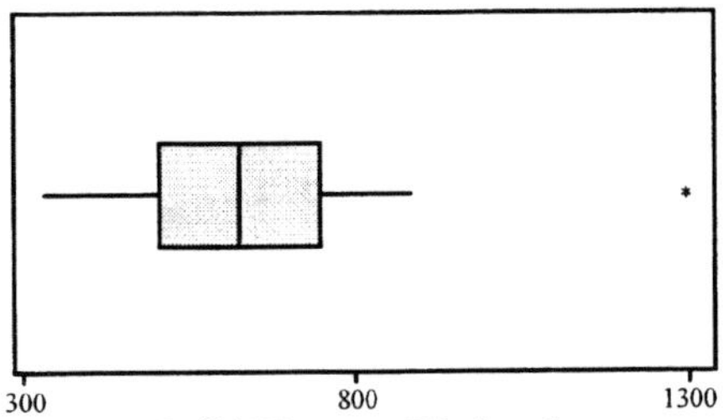

Solid Waste on Weekends

(1) The distance from $X_{smallest}$ to $Q_1 = 178$; the distance from Q_3 to $X_{largest} = 547$.

(2) Median = 626 < midhinge = 629 < midrange = 813.5, therefore we may conclude that the distribution is right-skewed.
From the box-and-whisker plot it can be seen that the center of the distribution is symmetric. On the other hand, the upper tail appears to be substantially longer than the lower tail, therefore, the distribution is right-skewed.

(h) All measures of location are larger for the weekday distribution than for the weekend distribution. Both distributions have approximately equal ranges and interquartile ranges. Both distributions are only slightly asymmetrical (The weekend distribution is more right-skewed due to an extreme value in the data set).

32. (a)

	Unweighted peak-to-peak	Weighted peak-to-peak	Rating
(1) Arithmetic Mean	76.72	21.61	4.891
(2) Median	68.94	19.93	5.000
(3) Mode	No unique mode	No unique mode	4.7
(4) Midrange	$(17.23+153.56)/2 = 85.395$	$(41.78+5.40)/2 = 23.59$	$(1.45+8.475)/2 = 4.9625$
(5) Quartiles	$Q_1 = 44.85$, $Q_3 = 97.65$	$Q_1 = 12.48$, $Q_3 = 29.78$	$Q_1 = 2.950$, $Q_3 = 6.075$
(6) Midhinge	$(44.85+97.65)/2 = 71.25$	$(29.78+12.48)/2 = 21.13$	$(2.95+6.075)/2 = 4.5125$
(7) Range	$153.56-17.23 = 136.33$	$41.78-5.40 = 36.38$	$8.475-1.45 = 7.025$
(8) Interquartile Range	$97.65-44.85 = 52.8$	$29.78-12.48 = 17.3$	$6.075-2.950 = 3.125$
(9) Variance	1570.37	111.971	4.03588
(10) Standard Deviation	39.6279	10.5816	2.00895

(b)

	$X_{smallest}$	Q_1	Median	Q_3	$X_{largest}$
Unweighted peak-to-peak	17.23	44.85	68.94	97.65	153.56
Weighted peak-to-peak	5.40	12.48	19.93	29.78	41.78
Rating	1.45	2.95	5.00	6.075	8.475

(c)

Box-and-Whisker Plot of Unweighted

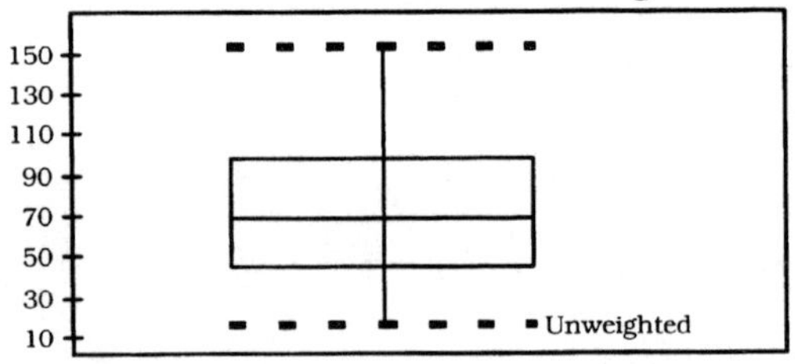

Note: This plot was produced by PHStat and agrees with the five-number summary. However, the plot produced by MINITAB does **NOT** agree with the five-number summary (compare Q_3 for two plots and that of the five-number summary):

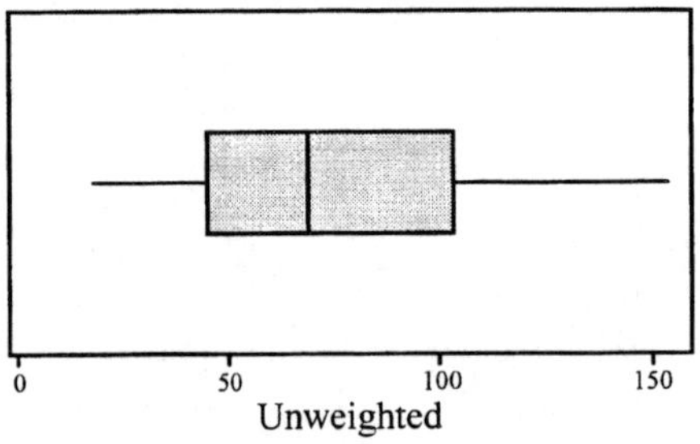

This occurs because MINITAB defines values of Quartiles differently from the definition in the textbook, (see page 111). See detailed explanation about this difference and the consequences in Problem 3.26.

Box-and-Whisker Plot of Weighted

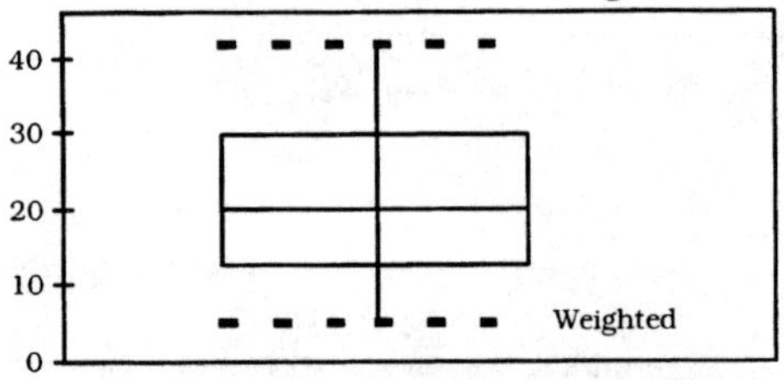

Note that this plot was produced by PHStat and agrees with the five-number summary. However, plot produced by MINITAB does **NOT** agree with the five-number summary (compare Q_3 for two plots and that of five-number summary):

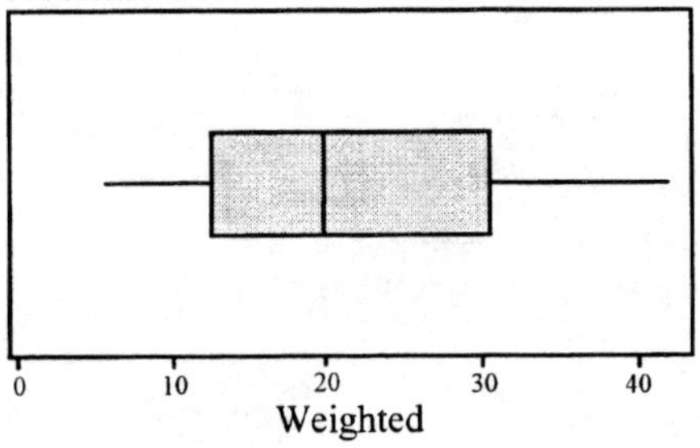

This occurs because MINITAB defines the values of Quartiles differently from the definition in the textbook, (see page 111). See detailed explanation about the difference and the consequences in Problem 3.26.

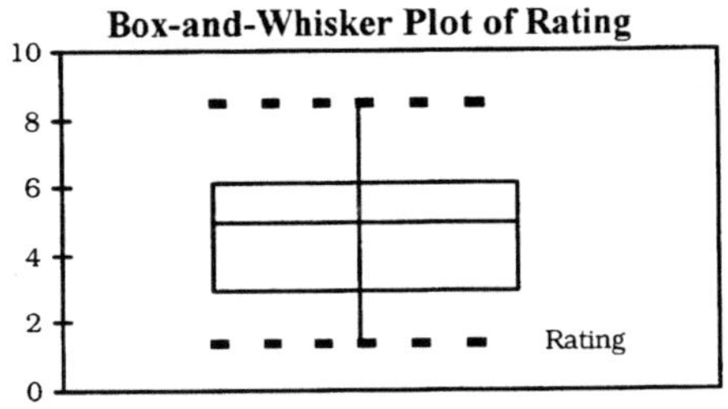

(d) **Unweighted peak-to-peak shock values**
The center of the distribution is asymmetric, with the median located a little closer to Q_1 than to Q_3. In addition, the upper tail appears to be longer than the lower tail, showing that the distribution is right-skewed.
Weighted peak-to-peak shock values
The center of the distribution is asymmetric, with the median located a little closer to Q_1 than to Q_3. In addition, the upper tail appears to be longer than the lower tail, showing that the distribution is right-skewed.
Rating of severity of shocks
The center of the distribution is asymmetric, with the median located closer to Q_3 than to Q_1, but the upper tail appears to be longer than the lower tail, therefore the distribution may be slightly right-skewed.

33. (a)

Jobs	Frequency	Percentage	Cumulative %
0–24	66	59.46%	59.46%
25–49	16	14.41%	73.87%
50–74	9	8.11%	81.98%
75–99	5	4.50%	86.48%
100–124	2	1.80%	88.28%
125–149	7	6.31%	94.59%
150–174	3	2.70%	97.29%
175–199	1	0.90%	98.19%
200–224	1	0.90%	99.09%
225–249	1	0.90%	99.99%

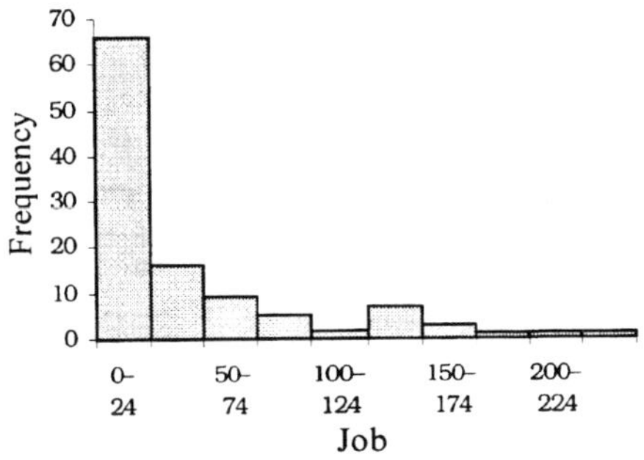

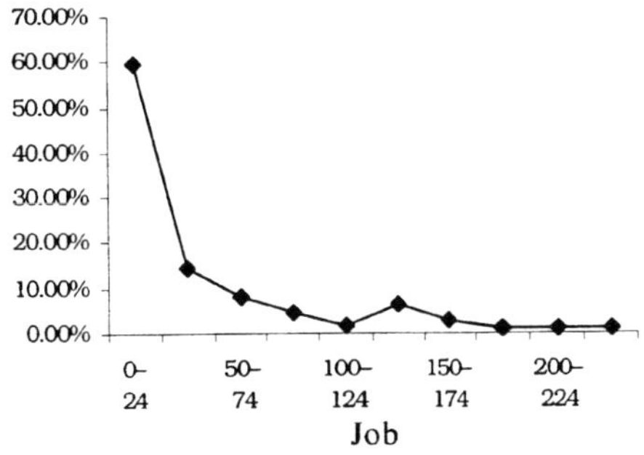

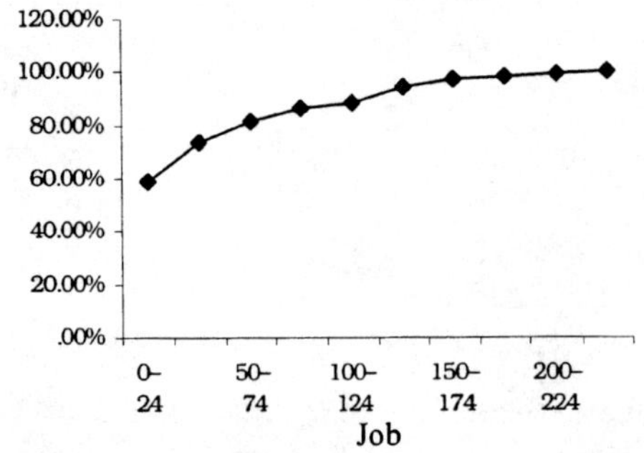

(b) Stem-and-Leaf Display for Data Cartridges

Stem unit: 10

0	1 1 1 1 1 1 2 2 2 2 2 3 3 3 3 4 4 4 4 4 4 5 5 5 5 5 5 6 6 6 7 7 7 7 8 8 8 8 9
1	0 0 0 0 0 1 2 2 3 4 4 5 7 8 8 8 8 9
2	0 0 0 0 1 2 3 4 8 8 9
3	0 0 0 0 1 2 3 5 7
4	0 0 2 3
5	0 2 5 6 9
6	0 0 7
7	4
8	0 6
9	1 4 6
10	0
11	1
12	6 7
13	1 7
14	0 4 7
15	
16	4 6
17	0
18	2
19	
20	
21	2
22	
23	7

(1) Arithmetic Mean 39.6847
(2) Median 18
(3) Mode 5
(4) Midrange $(1+237)/2 = 119$
(5) Quartiles $Q_1 = 5$, $Q_3 = 52$
(6) Midhinge $(5+52)/2 = 28.5$
(7) Range $237 - 1 = 236$
(8) Interquartile Range $52 - 5 = 47$
(9) Variance 2671.40
(10) Standard Deviation 51.6856

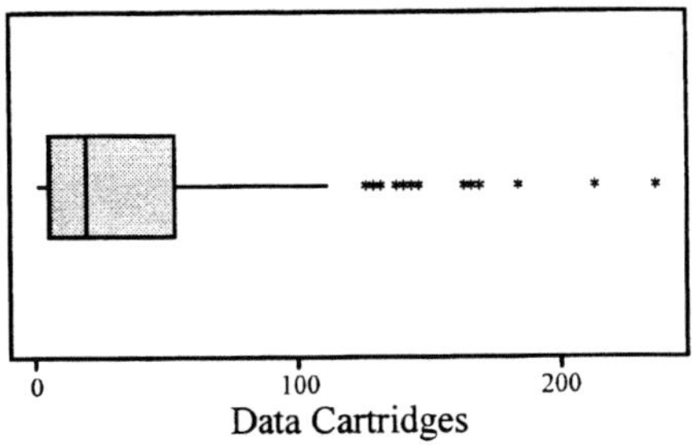

(c) The number of data cartridges required during a given day is distributed between 1 and 237. About 60% of all jobs are small and require only from 1 to 24 data cartridges. The most frequent requirement is 5 data cartridges. The "central half" of the data includes 5 to 52 data cartridges, with the median located much closer to the first quartile than to the third.

34. (a)

	With Magnets	Without Magnets
(1) Arithmetic Mean	19.723	20.402
(2) Median	19.950	20.4
(3) Mode	20.1, 20.4	20.2
(4) Midrange	$(13.5+20.8)/2=17.15$	$(19.5+21.4)/2=20.45$
(5) Quartiles	$Q_1=19.5$, $Q_3=20.4$	$Q_1=20.05$, $Q_3=20.65$
(6) Midhinge	$(19.5+20.4)/2=19.95$	$(20.05+20.65)/2=20.35$
(7) Range	$20.8-13.5=7.3$	$21.4-19.5=1.9$
(8) Interquartile Range	$20.4-19.5=0.9$	$20.65-20.05=0.6$
(9) Variance	1.60116	0.199768
(10) Standard Deviation	1.26537	0.446954

(b)

	$X_{smallest}$	Q_1	Median	Q_3	$X_{largest}$
With Magnets	13.5	19.5	19.95	20.4	20.8
Without Magnets	19.5	20.05	20.4	20.65	21.4

(c)

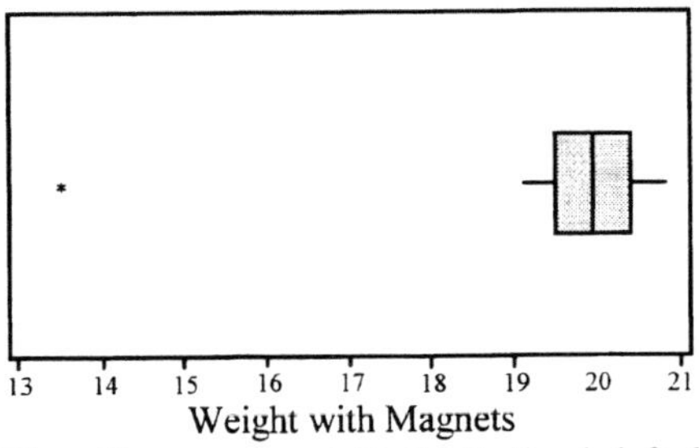

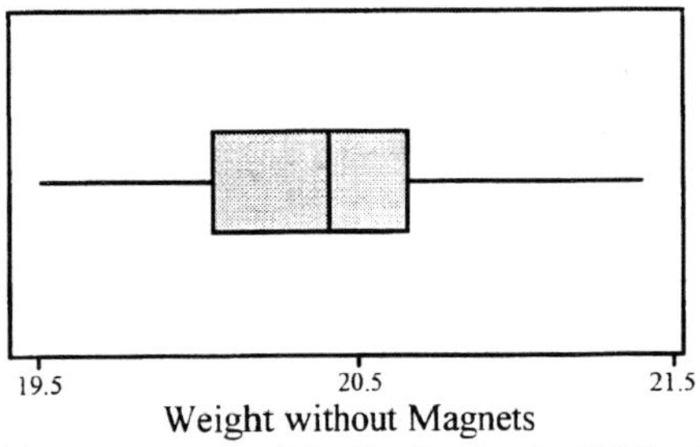

(d) The with magnets weight distribution is left-skewed, and the without magnets weight distribution is slightly right-skewed.

(e) In terms of location, all measures of location were smaller for the with magnets distribution.
In terms of dispersion, all measures of variation were larger for the with magnets distribution.
In terms of symmetry, the with magnets distribution is left-skewed, and the without magnets distribution is slightly right-skewed.

35. (a)

	Mpg	Fuel Capacity	Length	Width
(1) Arithmetic Mean	23.292	16.354	185.76	69.944
(2) Median	22	16.5	187	70
(3) Mode	20	18	175, 184, 188, 200	67
(4) Midrange	25.5	16.5	181.5	70.5
(5) Quartiles	$Q_1 = 20$, $Q_3 = 26$	$Q_1 = 14.5$, $Q_3 = 18.25$	$Q_1 = 175$, $Q_3 = 195$	$Q_1 = 67$, $Q_3 = 72.5$
(6) Midhinge	23	16.375	185	69.75
(7) Range	21	13	65	15
(8) Interquartile Range	6	3.75	20	5.5
(9) Variance	20.5728	7.65342	176.705	11.4400
(10) Standard Deviation	4.53572	2.76648	13.293	3.382

	Weight	Wheel base	Turning circle capacity
(1) Arithmetic Mean	3131.4	104.88	39.225
(2) Median	3175	105	39
(3) Mode	2865	103	39
(4) Midrange	3047.5	104.5	39.5
(5) Quartiles	$Q_1 = 2742.5$, $Q_3 = 3500.5$	$Q_1 = 101$, $Q_3 = 108$	$Q_1 = 38$, $Q_3 = 41$
(6) Midhinge	3121.5	104.5	39.75
(7) Range	2405	23	11
(8) Interquartile Range	758	7	3.5
(9) Variance	273498	30.1096	6.97165
(10) Standard Deviation	522.970	5.48722	2.64039

	Luggage capacity	Front leg room	Front head room
(1) Arithmetic Mean	14.247	41.871	3.635
(2) Median	14	42	3.5
(3) Mode	14	42	3
(4) Midrange	16	42.25	3.75
(5) Quartiles	$Q_1 = 12$, $Q_3 = 16$	$Q_1 = 41.25$, $Q_3 = 42.5$	$Q_1 = 3$, $Q_3 = 4$
(6) Midhinge	14	41.875	3.75
(7) Range	16	4.5	5.5
(8) Interquartile Range	4	1.25	1.5
(9) Variance	9.39275	0.781	1.226
(10) Standard Deviation	3.06476	0.884	1.107

(b)

	$X_{smallest}$	Q_1	Median	Q_3	$X_{largest}$
Mpg	15	20	22	26	36
Fuel Capacity	10	14.5	16.5	18.25	23
Length	149	175	187	195	214
Width	63	67	70	72.5	78
Weight	1845	2742.5	3175	3500.5	4250
Wheel base	93	101	105	108.	116
Turning Circle Capacity	34	38	39	41.5	45
Luggage Capacity	8	12	14	16	24
Front leg Room	40	41.25	42	42.5	44.5
Front head Room	1	3	3.5	4.5	6.5

(c)

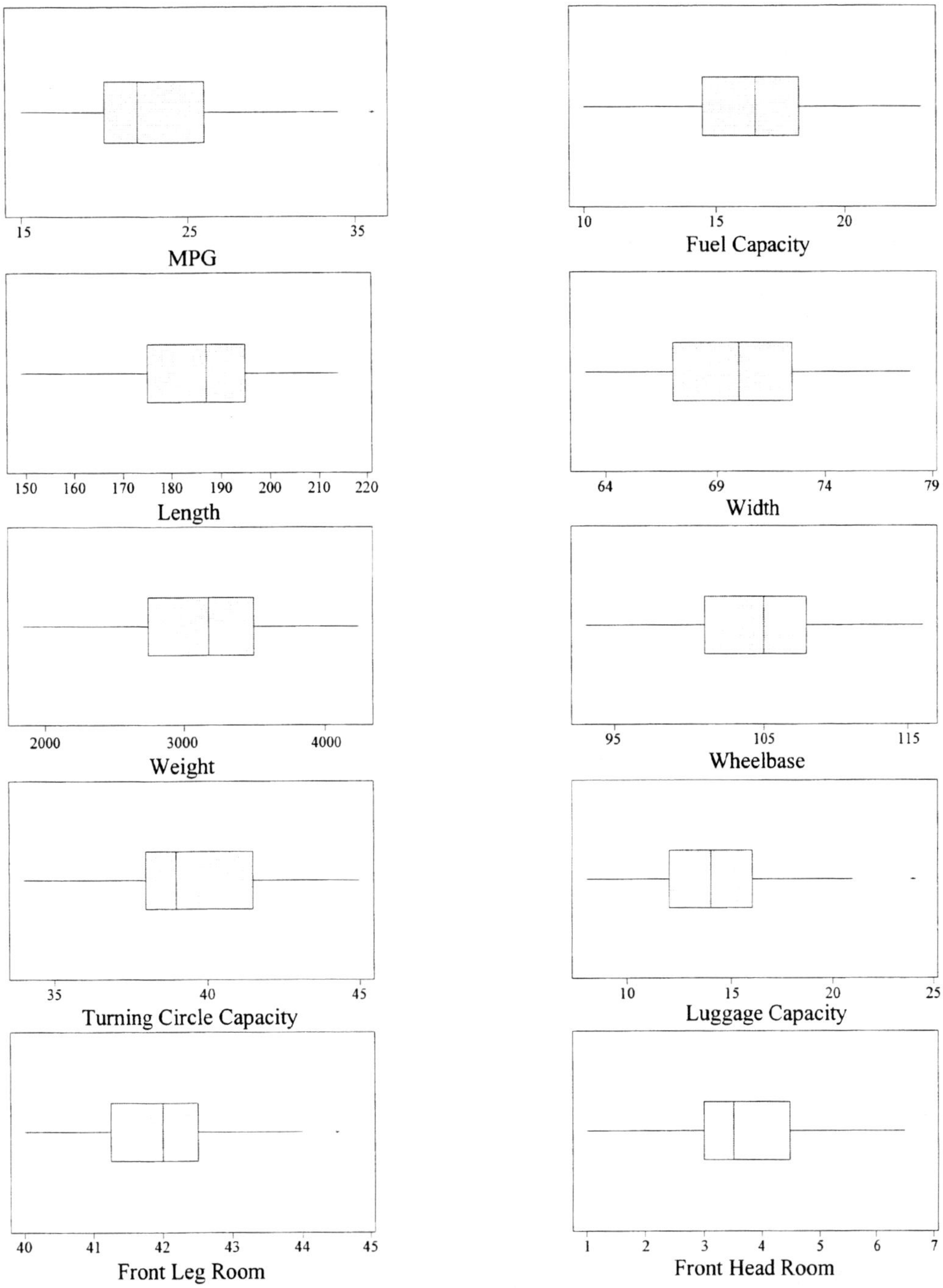
15 25 35
MPG
10 15 20
Fuel Capacity
150 160 170 180 190 200 210 220
Length
64 69 74 79
Width
2000 3000 4000
Weight
95 105 115
Wheelbase
35 40 45
Turning Circle Capacity
10 15 20 25
Luggage Capacity
40 41 42 43 44 45
Front Leg Room
1 2 3 4 5 6 7
Front Head Room

(d) The data for highway miles per gallon are right-skewed.
The data for fuel tank capacity are left-skewed.
The data for length are left-skewed.
The data for width are right-skewed.
The data for weight are left-skewed.
The data for wheel base are left skewed.
The data for turning circle capacity are right-skewed.
The data for luggage capacity are right-skewed.
The data for front leg room are right-skewed.
The data for front head room are right-skewed.

chapter 4

Probability and Discrete Probability Distributions

1. (a) Classical (b) Empirical, if the appropriate data are available; otherwise subjective
(c) Classical (d) Subjective

2. (a) A good wafer (b) A bad wafer with no particles (c) A bad wafer

(d) A good wafer with no particles is a joint event because it is defined by two characteristics; first the wafer is good and second, the wafer has no particles

(e) 1. $P(\text{the wafer is good}) = \dfrac{334}{450} = 0.742$ 2. $P(\text{the wafer has no particles}) = \dfrac{400}{450} = 0.889$

3. $P(\text{the wafer is good } or \text{ has no particles}) = P(\text{the wafer is good}) + P(\text{the wafer has no particles})$

$-P(\text{the wafer is good } and \text{ has no particles}) = \dfrac{334}{450} + \dfrac{400}{450} - \dfrac{320}{450} = \dfrac{414}{450} = 0.92$

4. $P(\text{the wafer is good } and \text{ has no particles}) = \dfrac{320}{450} = 0.711$

(f) $P(\text{the wafer is good}|\text{the wafer has no particles}) = \dfrac{P(\text{the wafer is good } and \text{ has no particles})}{P(\text{the wafer has no particles})} = \dfrac{320/450}{400/450} = \dfrac{320}{400} = 0.80$

(g) $P(\text{the wafer is good}|\text{the wafer has particles}) = \dfrac{P(\text{the wafer is good } and \text{ has particles})}{P(\text{the wafer has particles})} = \dfrac{14/450}{50/450} = \dfrac{14}{50} = 0.28$

(h) Most of the wafers that can be classified as "good" have no particles. Therefore, the probability that a wafer with no particles will be classified as "good" is relatively high, 0.80. On the other hand, the probability that a wafer *with* particles will be classified as "good" is much lower, 0.28.

(i) $P(\text{the wafer has no particles}|\text{the wafer is good}) = \dfrac{P(\text{the wafer is good } and \text{ has particles})}{P(\text{the wafer is good})} = \dfrac{320/450}{334/450} = \dfrac{320}{334} = 0.96$

(j) They are different because the probability that the wafer is good and the probability that it has no particles are not equal.

3. (a) The test diagnosis is positive.

(b) The test diagnosis is positive and the person has the disease.

(c) Three probabilities are given:

$P(\text{the test diagnosis is positive}) = 0.04$
$P(\text{the patient has the disease}|\text{the test diagnosis is positive}) = 0.95$
$P(\text{the patient does not have the disease}|\text{the test diagnosis is negative}) = 0.99$

(1) $P(\text{the test diagnosis is negative}) = 1 - P(\text{the test diagnosis is positive}) = 1 - 0.04 = 0.96$

(2) $P(\text{the test diagnosis is negative } and \text{ the patient does not have the disease})$
$= P(\text{the patient does not have the disease}|\text{the test diagnosis is negative}) \times P(\text{the test diagnosis is negative})$
$= 0.99 \times 0.96 = 0.9504$

(3) $P(\text{the test diagnosis is positive } and \text{ the patient has the disease})$
$= P(\text{the patient has the disease}|\text{the test diagnosis is positive}) \times P(\text{the test diagnosis is positive})$
$= 0.95 \times 0.04 = 0.0380$

(4) Step 1:
P(the test diagnosis is negative *and* the patient has the disease)
$= P$(the test diagnosis is negative) – P(the test diagnosis is negative *and* the patient does not have the disease)
$= 0.96 - 0.9504 = 0.0096$
Step 2:
P(the disease is present) = P(the test diagnosis is negative *and* the patient has the disease)
$+P$(the test diagnosis is positive *and* the patient has the disease) $= 0.0096 + 0.0380 = 0.0476$

(5) P(the test diagnosis is positive *or* the patient has the disease) = P(the test diagnosis is positive)
$+P$(the patient has the disease) – P(the test diagnosis is positive *and* the patient has the disease)
$= 0.04 + 0.0476 - 0.0380 = 0.0496$

(d) P(the test diagnosis is positive |the patient has the disease)

$$= \frac{P(\text{the test diagnosis is positive } \textit{and} \text{ the patient has the disease})}{P(\text{the patient has the disease})} = \frac{0.038}{0.0476} = 0.798$$

(e) P(the patient has the disease |the test diagnosis is positive) $= 0.95$. This probability is GIVEN.
Note that it could be computed using the following formula:
P(the patient has the disease |the test diagnosis is positive)

$$= \frac{P(\text{the test diagnosis is positive } \textit{and} \text{ the patient has the disease})}{P(\text{the test diagnosis is positive})} = \frac{0.038}{0.04} = 0.95$$

(f) These answers are different because the probability that "the test diagnosis is positive" and the probability that "the patient has the disease" are not equal.

A 2×2 cross-classification table for this problem takes the following form:

	Disease	No disease	Total
Positive	0.0380	0.0020	0.04
Negative	0.0096	0.9504	0.96
Total	0.0476	0.9524	1

4. (a) The bottle came from machine 2. (b) The bottle came from machine 1 and is nonconforming

(c) Four probabilities are given:
P(it is filled on machine 1 *and* is a nonconforming bottle) $= 0.01$
P(it is filled on machine 2 *and* is a nonconforming bottle) $= 0.025$
P(it is filled on machine 1) $= 0.5$
P(it is filled on machine 2) $= 0.5$

(1) P(it is a nonconforming bottle) = P(it is filled on machine 1 *and* is a nonconforming bottle)
$+P$(it is filled on machine 2 *and* is a nonconforming bottle) $= 0.01 + 0.025 = 0.035$

(2) P(it is filled on machine 2) $= 0.5$. This probability is given.

(3) P(it is filled on machine 1 *and* is a conforming bottle) = P(it is filled on machine 1)
$-P$(it is filled on machine 1 *and* is a nonconforming bottle) $= 0.5 - 0.01 = 0.49$

(4) P(it is filled on machine 2 *and* is a conforming bottle) = P(it is filled on machine 2)
$-P$(it is filled on machine 2 *and* is a nonconforming bottle) $= 0.5 - 0.025 = 0.475$

(5) Step 1:
P(it is a conforming bottle) = P(it is filled on machine 1 *and* is a conforming bottle)
$+P$(it is filled on machine 2 *and* is a conforming bottle) $= 0.49 + 0.475 = 0.965$
Step 2:
P(it is filled on machine 1 *or* is a conforming bottle) = P(it is filled on machine 1)
$+P$(it is a conforming bottle) – P(it is filled on machine 1 *and* is a conforming bottle)
$= 0.5 + 0.965 - 0.49 = 0.975$

(d) $P(\text{it is a conforming bottle}|\text{it is filled on machine 1}) = \dfrac{P(\text{it is filled on machine 1 } \textit{and} \text{ is a nonconforming bottle})}{P(\text{it is filled on machine 1})}$

$= \dfrac{0.01}{0.5} = 0.02$

(e) $P(\text{it is filled on machine 1}|\text{it is a nonconforming bottle}) = \dfrac{P(\text{it is filled on machine 1 } \textit{and} \text{ is a nonconforming bottle})}{P(\text{it is a nonconforming bottle})}$

$= \dfrac{0.01}{0.035} = 0.2857$

(f) These answers are different because the probability that "it is filled on machine 1" and the probability that "a bottle is a nonconforming bottle" are not equal.

A 2×2 cross-classification table for this problem takes the following form:

	Conforming	Nonconforming	Total
Machine 1	0.490	0.010	0.5
Machine 2	0.475	0.025	0.5
Total	0.965	0.035	1

5. (a) *P*(both cards are red) = *P*(the first card is red *and* the second card is red) = *P*(the 1st card is red) × *P*(the 2nd card is red), as the two events are independent. Further, *P*(the 1st card is red) $= 26/52$, because 26 of 52 cards are red. The event probabilities are multiplied because the cards are selected *without replacement*; the number of cards remaining after the first selection is 51, and the number of red cards is 25. Therefore, *P*(the second card is red) $= 25/51$ and *P*(both cards are red) $= 26/52 \times 25/51 = 0.2451$.

(b) *P*(the first card is an ace *and* the second card is ten *or* jack *or* queen *or* king) = *P*(the first card is an ace) × *P*(the second card is ten *or* jack *or* queen *or* king). The individual event probabilities are multiplied because the two events are independent. Further, *P*(the first card is an ace) $= 4/52$, because there are 4 aces in a standard deck of playing cards.

P(the second card is ten *or* jack *or* queen *or* king) = *P*(the second card is ten) + *P*(the second card is jack) + *P*(the second card is queen) + *P*(the second card is king). The individual event probabilities are added because these events are mutually exclusive . Because the cards are selected *without replacement*, the number of cards remaining after the first selection is 51, and the number of tens, jacks, queens or kings is 4. Therefore, *P*(the second card is ten *or* jack *or* queen *or* king) $= 4/51 + 4/51 + 4/51 + 4/51 = 16/51$ and *P*(the first card is an ace *and* the second card is ten *or* jack *or* queen *or* king) $= 4/52 \times 16/51 = 0.0241$.

(c) For Part (a): *P*(both cards are red) = *P*(the first card is red *and* the second card is red) = *P*(the first card is red) × *P*(the second card is red). The individual probabilities are multiplied because the two events are independent. Further, *P*(the first card is red) $= 26/52$, because 26 of 52 cards are red. The cards are selected *with replacement*, the second selection is the same as the first one. Therefore, *P*(the second card is red) $= 26/52$ and *P*(both cards are red) $= 26/52 \times 26/52 = 0.250$.

P(the first card is an ace *and* the second card is a ten *or* jack *or* queen *or* king) = *P*(the first card is an ace) × *P*(the second card is ten *or* jack *or* queen *or* king). The individual probabilities are multiplied because the two events are independent. Further *P*(the first card is an ace) $= 4/52$, because there are 4 aces in a standard deck of playing cards. In addition, *P*(the second card is ten *or* jack *or* queen *or* king) = *P*(the second card is ten) + *P*(the second card is jack) + *P*(the second card is queen) + *P*(the second card is king). The individual event probabilities are added because these events are mutually exclusive . The cards are selected *with replacement*, so the number of cards used in the second selection is 52, and the number of tens, jacks, queens or kings is 4. Therefore, *P*(the second card is ten *or* jack *or* queen *or* king) $= 4/52 + 4/52 + 4/52 + 4/52 = 16/52$ and *P*(the first card is an ace *and* the second card is ten *or* jack *or* queen *or* king) $= 4/52 \times 16/52 = 0.0237$.

6. *P*(you will get grades of B or above in both subjects) = *P*(you will get grades of B or above in statistics) × *P*(you will get grades of B or above in Calculus). The individual event probabilities are added because these events are independent. Given that *P*(you will get grades of B or above in statistics) = 0.6 and *P*(you will get grades of B or above in Calculus) = 0.5, *P*(you will get grades of B or above in both subjects) $= 0.6 \times 0.5 = 0.3$.
The answer to the question "why these two events might not be independent" will vary.

7. (a) *P*(both computers are intact) = *P*(the first computer is intact) × *P*(the second computer is intact). This is because these events are independent. Further, *P*(the first computer is intact) $= 40/50$, because 40 of 50 computers are intact. The computers are selected *without* replacement, so the number of computers remaining after the first selection is 49, and the number of intact computers is 39. Therefore, *P*(the second computer is intact) $= 39/49$ and *P*(both computers are intact) $= 40/50 \times 39/49 = 0.6367$.
   (b) *P*(both computers are damaged but operative) = *P*(the first computer is damaged but operative) × *P*(the second computer is damaged but operative). The individual events are multiplied because these events are independent. Further, *P*(the first computer is damaged but operative) $= 8/50$, because 8 of 50 computers are damaged, but operative. The computers are selected *without* replacement, so the number of computers remaining after the first selection is 49, and the number of damaged, but operative computers is 7. Therefore, *P*(the second computer is damaged, but operative) $= 7/49$ and *P*(both computers are damaged but operative) $= 8/50 \times 7/49 = 0.0229$.
   (c) For Part (a): *P*(both computers are intact) = *P*(the first computer is intact) × *P*(the second computer is intact). This is because these events are independent. Further, *P*(the first computer is intact) $= 40/50$, because 40 of 50 computers are intact. The computers are selected *with* replacement, so the number of computers in the second set remains 50, and the number of intact computers is 40. Therefore, *P*(the second computer is intact) $= 40/50$ and *P*(both computers are intact) $= 40/50 \times 40/50 = 0.640$.
   For Part (b): *P*(both computers are damaged but operative) = *P*(the first computer is damaged but operative) × *P*(the second computer is damaged but operative). The individual events are multiplied because these events are independent. Further, *P*(the first computer is damaged, but operative) $= 8/50$, because 8 of 50 computers are damaged, but operative. The computers are selected, *with* replacement, so the number of computers in the second set remains 50, and the number of damaged, but operative computers is 8. Therefore, *P*(the second computer is damaged but operative) $= 8/50$ and *P*(both computers are damaged but operative) $= 8/50 \times 8/50 = 0.0256$.
   (d) *P*(three computers are damaged but operative) = *P*(the first computer is damaged but operative) × *P*(the second computer is damaged but operative) × *P*(the 3rd computer is damaged but operative). The individual events are multiplied because these events are independent. Further, *P*(the first computer is damaged but operative) $= 8/50$, because 8 of 50 computers are damaged but operative. The computers are selected *without* replacement, the number of computers remaining after the first selection is 49, and the number of damaged but operative computers is 7. Therefore, *P*(the second computer is damaged but operative) $= 7/49$. The number of computers remaining after the second selection is 48, and the number of damaged but operative computers is 6. Therefore, *P*(the 3rd computer is damaged but operative) $= 6/48$, and *P*(all three computers are damaged but operative) $= 8/50 \times 7/49 \times 6/48 = 0.002857$.
   (e) *P*(three computers are damaged, but operative) = *P*(the first computer is damaged but operative) × *P*(the second computer is damaged, but operative) × *P*(the 3rd computer is damaged, but operative). The individual events are multiplied because these events are independent. Further, *P*(the first computer is damaged but operative) $= 8/50$, because 8 of 50 computers are damaged, but operative. The computers are selected *with* replacement, so the number of computers in the second and in the 3rd events remains 50, and the number of damaged but operative computers remains 8. Therefore, *P*(the second computer is damaged but operative) = *P*(the 3rd computer is damaged but operative) $= 8/50$, and P(all three computers are damaged but operative) $= 8/50 \times 8/50 \times 8/50 = 0.004096$.

8. (a) Distribution A:
   $\mu = 0(0.4) + 1(0.3) + 2(0.2) + 3(0.1) = 1$

   Distribution B:
   $\mu = 0(0.1) + 1(0.2) + 2(0.3) + 3(0.4) = 2$

(b) Distribution A:
$\sigma_x^2 = (0-1)^2(0.4)+(1-1)^2(0.3)+(2-1)^2(0.2)+(3-1)^2(0.1)=1$

$\sigma_x = \sqrt{\sigma_x^2} = 1$

Distribution B:
$\sigma_x^2 = (0-2)^2(0.1)+(1-2)^2(0.2)+(2-2)^2(0.3)+(3-2)^2(0.4)=1$

$\sigma_x = \sqrt{\sigma_x^2} = 1$

(c) The outcomes with larger values have larger probabilities for Distribution B than for Distribution A. As a result the expected value for Distribution B is greater than the expected value for Distribution A. Both distributions have the same standard deviation.

9. (a) Distribution A:
$\mu = 0(0.25)+1(0.25)+2(0.25)+3(0.25)=1.5$

Distribution B:
$\mu = 0(0.2)+1(0.4)+2(0.4)+3(0.2)=1.8$

(b) Distribution A:
$\sigma_x^2 = (0-1.5)^2(0.25)+(1-1.5)^2(0.25)+(2-1.5)^2(0.25)+(3-1.5)^2(0.25)=1.25$

$\sigma_x = \sqrt{\sigma_x^2} = \sqrt{1.25} = 1.118$

Distribution B:
$\sigma_x^2 = (0-1.8)^2(0.2)+(1-1.8)^2(0.4)+(2-1.8)^2(0.4)+(3-1.8)^2(0.2)=1.208$

$\sigma_x = \sqrt{\sigma_x^2} = \sqrt{1.208} = 1.099$

(c) The expected value for Distribution B is greater than the expected value for Distribution A. The standard deviation for Distribution A is larger than the standard deviation for Distribution B.

10. (a) $\mu = 0(0.35)+1(0.35)+2(0.25)+3(0.05)=1.0$

(b) $\sigma_x^2 = (0-1)^2(0.35)+(1-1)^2(0.35)+(2-1)^2(0.25)+(3-1)^2(0.05)=0.8$

$\sigma_x = \sqrt{\sigma_x^2} = \sqrt{0.8} = 0.894$

(c) The average value of the number of retransmissions is 1. The probability range is 1.0 ± 0.894.

11. (a) $\mu = 0(0.10)+1(0.20)+2(0.45)+3(0.15)+4(0.05)+5(0.05)=2.0$

(b) $\sigma_x^2 = (0-2)^2(0.1)+(1-2)^2(0.2)+(2-2)^2(0.45)+(3-2)^2(0.15)+(4-2)^2(0.05)+(5-2)^2(0.05)=1.4$

$\sigma_x = \sqrt{\sigma_x^2} = \sqrt{1.4} = 1.183$

(c) Average value of the traffic accidents is 2 per day. Probability range is 2.0 ± 1.183

12.

	Demand *(Thousands of pairs)*	**Sales, Small** *(Thousands of dollars)*	**Sales, Large** *(Thousands of dollars)*	**Profit, Small** *(Thousands of dollars)*	**Profit, Large** *(Thousands of dollars)*	***P***
E1	10	100	100	−100	−300	0.1
E2	20	200	200	0	−200	0.4
E3	50	500	500	300	100	0.2
E4	100	500	1000	300	600	0.3

(a) Small factory: $E(X) = -100(0.1)+0(0.4)+300(0.2)+300(0.3)=140$ (thousands of dollars)
Large factory: $E(X) = -300(0.1)+(-200)(0.4)+100(0.2)+600(0.3)=90$ (thousands of dollars)

(b) Small factory:
$\sigma_x^2 = (-100-140)^2(0.1)+(0-140)^2(0.4)+(300-140)^2(0.2)+(300-140)^2(0.3)=26{,}400$

$\sigma_x = 162.4808$ (thousands of dollars)

Large factory:

$\sigma_x^2 = (-300-90)^2(0.1)+(-200-90)^2(0.4)+(100-90)^2(0.2)+(600-90)^2(0.3) = 126{,}900$

$\sigma_x = 356.2303$ (thousands of dollars)

(c) The answers will vary, but building a small factory is the most logical as the expected value is higher and the standard deviation is lower.

13. (a) $P(X=1|n=4,\ p=0.20) = \frac{4!}{1!(4-1)!}0.2^1(1-0.2)^{4-1} = 0.4096$

(b) $P(X=3|n=4,\ p=0.80) = \frac{4!}{3!(4-3)!}0.8^3(1-0.8)^{4-3} = 0.4096$

(c) $P(X\le 1|n=5,\ p=0.30) = P(X=0|n=5,\ p=0.30)+P(X=1|n=5,\ p=0.30) = \frac{5!}{0!(5-0)!}0.3^0(1-0.3)^{5-0}$

$+\frac{5!}{1!(5-1)!}0.3^1(1-0.3)^{5-1} = 0.16807+0.36015 = 0.52822$

(d) $P(X>1|n=6,\ p=0.40) = 1-P(X\le 1|n=6,\ p=0.40) = 1-P(X=0|n=6,\ p=0.40)-P(X=1|n=6,\ p=0.40)$

$=1-\frac{6!}{0!(6-0)!}0.4^0(1-0.4)^{6-0}-\frac{6!}{1!(6-1)!}0.4^1(1-0.4)^{6-1} = 1-0.046656-0.186624 = 0.76672$

(e) $P(X<2|n=3,\ p=0.10) = P(X=0|n=3,\ p=0.10)+P(X=1|n=3,\ p=0.10)$

$=\frac{3!}{0!(3-0)!}0.1^0(1-0.1)^{3-0}+\frac{3!}{1!(3-1)!}0.1^1(1-0.1)^{3-1} = 0.729+0.243 = 0.972$

14. (a) $P(X=2|n=5,\ p=0.10) = \frac{5!}{2!(5-2)!}0.1^2(1-0.1)^{5-2} = 0.073$

(b) $P(X<3|n=5,\ p=0.10) = P(X=0|n=5,\ p=0.10)+P(X=1|n=5,\ p=0.10)+P(X=2|n=5,\ p=0.10)$

$=\frac{5!}{0!(5-0)!}0.1^0(1-0.1)^{5-0}+\frac{5!}{1!(5-1)!}0.1^1(1-0.1)^{5-1}+\frac{5!}{2!(5-2)!}0.1^2(1-0.1)^{5-2} = 0.59049+0.32805+0.0729$

$=0.99144$

(c) $P(X\le 1|n=6,\ p=0.30) = P(X=0|n=6,\ p=0.30)+P(X=1|n=6,\ p=0.30)$

$=\frac{6!}{0!(6-0)!}0.3^0(1-0.3)^{6-0}+\frac{6!}{1!(6-1)!}0.3^1(1-0.3)^{6-1} = 0.018+0.303 = 0.420$

(d) $P(X>1|n=6,\ p=0.30) = 1-P(X\le 1|n=6,\ p=0.30) = 1-0.420 = 0.580$; see (c).

(e) $P(X<3|n=3,\ p=0.15) = 1-P(X=3|n=3,\ p=0.15) = 1-\frac{3!}{3!(3-3)!}0.15^3(1-0.15)^{3-3} = 1-0.003375 = 0.997$

15. (a) $p=0.25,\ n=5$

1. $P(X=5|5,\ 0.25) = \frac{5!}{5!(5-5)!}0.25^5(1-0.25)^{5-5} = 0.001$

2. $P(X\ge 4|5,\ 0.25) = P(X=4|5,\ 0.25)+P(X=5|5,\ 0.25) = \frac{5!}{4!(5-4)!}0.25^4(1-0.25)^{5-4}$

$+\frac{5!}{5!(5-5)!}0.25^5(1-0.25)^{5-5} = 0.015+0.001 = 0.016$

3. $P(X=0|5,\ 0.25) = \frac{5!}{0!(5-0)!}0.25^0(1-0.25)^{5-0} = 0.237$

4. $P(X\le 2|5,\ 0.25) = P(X=0|5,\ 0.25)+P(X=2|5,\ 0.25) = \frac{5!}{0!(5-0)!}0.25^0(1-0.25)^{5-0}$

$+\frac{5!}{1!(5-1)!}0.25^2(1-0.25)^{5-1}+\frac{5!}{2!(5-2)!}0.25^2(1-0.25)^{5-2} = 0.896$

(b) Two assumptions are necessary: (1) The probabilities of selecting any given ball are all equal. (The probability of selecting a particular ball is 1/4 = 0.25.) (2) The outcome on a particular trial (a particular ball is selected) is independent of the outcome of any other trial (some other ball was selected).

(c) $\mu = np = 5 \times 0.25 = 1.25$, $\sigma = \sqrt{np(1-p)} = \sqrt{5 \times 0.25(1-0.25)} = 0.9682$

16. (a) 1. $P(X=5|5,\ 0.70) = \dfrac{5!}{5!(5-5)!}0.7^5(1-0.7)^{5-5} = 0.168$

2. $P(X \geq 3|5,\ 0.70) = P(X=5|5,\ 0.70) + P(X=4|5,\ 0.70) + P(X=3|5,\ 0.70) = \dfrac{5!}{5!(5-5)!}0.7^5(1-0.7)^{5-5}$

$+\dfrac{5!}{4!(5-4)!}0.7^4(1-0.7)^{5-4} + \dfrac{5!}{3!(5-3)!}0.7^3(1-0.7)^{5-3} = 0.168 + 0.360 + 0.309 = 0.837$

3. $P(X<2|5,\ 0.70) = P(X=0|5,\ 0.70) + P(X=1|5,\ 0.70) = \dfrac{5!}{0!(5-0)!}0.7^0(1-0.7)^{5-0}$

$+\dfrac{5!}{1!(5-1)!}0.7^1(1-0.7)^{5-1} = 0.002 + 0.028 = 0.030$

(b) Two assumptions are necessary: (1) All repairs are independent, and, (2) There are only two outcomes possible; troubles will either be repaired or not repaired.

(c) $\mu = np = 5 \times 0.70 = 3.5$, $\sigma = \sqrt{np(1-p)} = \sqrt{5 \times 0.7(1-0.7)} = 1.025$

(d) $n=5,\ p=0.80$

1. $P(X=5|5,\ 0.80) = \dfrac{5!}{5!(5-5)!}0.8^5(1-0.8)^{5-5} = 0.328$

2. $P(X \geq 3|5,\ 0.80) = P(X=5|5,\ 0.80) + P(X=4|5,\ 0.80) + P(X=3|5,\ 0.80) = \dfrac{5!}{5!(5-5)!}0.8^5(1-0.8)^{5-5}$

$+\dfrac{5!}{4!(5-4)!}0.8^4(1-0.8)^{5-4} + \dfrac{5!}{3!(5-3)!}0.8^3(1-0.8)^{5-3} = 0.32768 + 0.4096 + 0.2048 = 0.94208$

3. $P(X<2|5,\ 0.80) = P(X=0|5,\ 0.80) + P(X=1|5,\ 0.80) = \dfrac{5!}{0!(5-0)!}0.8^0(1-0.8)^{5-0}$

$+\dfrac{5!}{1!(5-1)!}0.8^1(1-0.8)^{5-1} = 0.00032 + 0.0064 = 0.00672$

(e) The probability that all five troubles will be repaired on the same day and the probability at least three will be repaired are increased, whereas the probability that fewer than two troubles will be repaired is decreased.

17. (a) $p = 0.05,\ n = 6$

1. $P(X=0|5,\ 0.05) = \dfrac{6!}{0!(6-0)!}0.05^0(1-0.05)^{6-0} = 0.735092$

2. $P(X<2|6,\ 0.05) = P(X=0|6,\ 0.05) + P(X=1|6,\ 0.05) = \dfrac{6!}{0!(6-0)!}0.05^0(1-0.05)^{6-0}$

$+\dfrac{6!}{1!(6-1)!}0.05^1(1-0.05)^{6-1} = 0.735092 + 0.232134 = 0.967226$

3. $P(X \geq 1|6,\ 0.05) = 1 - P(X=0|6,\ 0.05) = 1 - \dfrac{6!}{0!(6-0)!}0.05^0(1-0.05)^{6-0} = 1 - 0.735092 = 0.264908$

(b) Four assumptions are necessary. (1) All discharges are independent; and are possible (2) Only two outcomes are possible; an appliance is either discharging or it is not, (3) Discharge happens on a brief time interval, (4) The probability of an outcome p is the same for all the appliances and is constant from trial to trial.

(c) $\mu = np = 6 \times 0.05 = 0.3$, and $\sigma = \sqrt{np(1-p)} = \sqrt{6 \times 0.05(1-0.05)} = 0.534$

18. $n = 16,\ p = 0.15$

(a) $P(X = 2|16,\ 0.15) = \frac{16!}{2!(16-2)!}0.15^2(1-0.15)^{6-2} = 0.277$

(b) $P(X \geq 2|16,\ 0.15) = 1 - P(X = 0|16,\ 0.15) - P(X = 1|16,\ 0.15) = 1 - \frac{16!}{0!(16-0)!}0.15^0(1-0.15)^{16-0}$

$+\frac{16!}{1!(16-1)!}0.15^1(1-0.15)^{16-1} = 1 - 0.0742511 - 0.2096501 = 0.716099$

(c) $P(X \leq 1|16,\ 0.15) = P(X = 0|16,\ 0.15) + P(X = 1|16,\ 0.15) = \frac{16!}{0!(16-0)!}0.15^0(1-0.15)^{16-0}$

$+\frac{16!}{1!(16-1)!}0.15^1(1-0.15)^{16-1} = 0.0743 - 0.2010 = 0.284$

(d) $\mu = np = 16 \times 0.15 = 2.4$,

(e) $\sigma = \sqrt{np(1-p)} = \sqrt{16 \times 0.15(1-0.15)} = 1.43$

(f) $n = 16,\ p = 0.10$

$P(X = 2|16,\ 0.10) = \frac{16!}{2!(16-2)!}0.1^2(1-0.1)^{16-2} = 0.274522$

$P(X \geq 2|16,\ 0.10) = 1 - P(X = 0|16,\ 0.10) - P(X = 1|16,\ 0.10) = 1 - \frac{16!}{0!(16-0)!}0.1^0(1-0.1)^{16-0}$

$-\frac{16!}{1!(16-1)!}0.1^1(1-0.1)^{16-1} = 1 - 0.185 - 0.329 = 0.485$

$P(X \leq 1|16,\ 0.10) = P(X = 0|16,\ 0.10) + P(X = 1|16,\ 0.10) = \frac{16!}{0!(16-0)!}0.1^0(1-0.1)^{16-0}$

$+\frac{16!}{1!(16-1)!}0.1^1(1-0.1)^{16-1} = 0.185302 + 0.3294258 = 0.514728$

$\mu = np = 16 \times 0.10 = 1.6$, $\sigma = \sqrt{np(1-p)} = \sqrt{16 \times 0.1(1-0.1)} = 1.2$

19. (a) $n = 4,\ p = 0.9$

1. $P(X = 4|4,\ 0.9) = \frac{4!}{4!(4-4)!}0.9^4(1-0.9)^{4-4} = 0.6561$
2. $P(X = 0|4,\ 0.9) = \frac{4!}{0!(4-0)!}0.9^0(1-0.9)^{4-0} = 0.0001$
3. $P(X \geq 3|4,\ 0.9) = P(X = 3|4,\ 0.9) + P(X = 4|4,\ 0.9) = \frac{4!}{3!(4-3)!}0.9^3(1-0.15)^{4-3} + \frac{4!}{4!(4-4)!}0.9^4(1-0.15)^{4-4}$

   $= 0.2916 + 0.6561 = 0.9477$
4. $P(X < 2|4,\ 0.9) = P(X = 1|4,\ 0.9) + P(X = 0|4,\ 0.9) = \frac{4!}{1!(4-1)!}0.9^1(1-0.9)^{4-1} + \frac{4!}{0!(4-0)!}0.9^0(1-0.9)^{4-0}$

   $= 0.0036 + 0.0001 = 0.0037$

(b) Three assumptions are necessary: (1) All test results are independent, (2) Only two outcomes are possible; passing the first test or not, and (3) the probability of the passing the first test, p, is constant from trial to trial and is equal to the probability that a CD player passes the first test as evaluated from previous data. This probability, p, is 0.9.

(c) $\mu = np = 4 \times 0.9 = 3.6$, $\sigma = \sqrt{np(1-p)} = \sqrt{4 \times 0.9(1-0.9)} = 0.6$

(d) $n = 4,\ p = 0.99$

1. $P(X = 4|4,\ 0.99) = \frac{4!}{4!(4-4)!}0.99^4(1-0.99)^{4-4} = 0.9605$
2. $P(X = 4|4,\ 0.99) = \frac{4!}{0!(4-0)!}0.99^0(1-0.99)^{4-0} = 0.00000001$

3. $P(X \geq 3|4,\ 0.99) = P(X = 3|4,\ 0.99) + P(X = 4|4,\ 0.99) = \dfrac{4!}{3!(4-3)!}0.99^3(1-0.99)^{4-3}$

$+\dfrac{4!}{4!(4-4)!}0.99^4(1-0.99)^{4-4} = 0.0388 + 0.9601 = 0.999$

4. $P(X < 2|4,\ 0.99) = P(X = 1|4,\ 0.99) + P(X = 0|4,\ 0.99) = \dfrac{4!}{1!(4-1)!}0.99^1(1-0.99)^{4-1}$

$+\dfrac{4!}{0!(4-0)!}0.99^0(1-0.99)^{4-0} = 0.00000396 + 0.00000001 = 0.00000397$

20. (a) $p = 0.25,\ n = 4$

1. $P(X = 4|4,\ 0.25) = \dfrac{4!}{4!(4-4)!}0.25^4(1-0.25)^{4-4} = 0.00391$
2. $P(X = 0|4,\ 0.25) = \dfrac{4!}{0!(4-0)!}0.25^0(1-0.25)^{4-0} = 0.316406$
3. $P(X \geq 3|4,\ 0.25) = P(X = 3|4,\ 0.25) + P(X = 4|4,\ 0.25) = \dfrac{4!}{3!(4-3)!}0.25^3(1-0.25)^{4-3}$

$+\dfrac{4!}{4!(4-4)!}0.25^4(1-0.25)^{4-4} = 0.0469 + 0.00391 = 0.051$

4. $P(X < 2|4,\ 0.25) = P(X = 1|4,\ 0.25) + P(X = 0|4,\ 0.25) = \dfrac{4!}{1!(4-1)!}0.25^1(1-0.25)^{4-1}$

$+\dfrac{4!}{0!(4-0)!}0.25^0(1-0.25)^{4-0} = 0.422 + 0.316 = 0.738$

(b) Two assumptions are necessary: (1) All PCs are upgraded independently. (2) There are only two possible outcomes: the computer is upgraded or it is not.

(c) $\mu = np = 4 \times 0.25 = 1.0$, $\sigma = \sqrt{np(1-p)} = \sqrt{4 \times 0.25(1-0.25)} = 0.866$

(d) $p = 0.15,\ n = 4$

1. $P(X = 4|4,\ 0.15) = \dfrac{4!}{4!(4-4)!}0.15^4(1-0.15)^{4-4} = 0.000506$
2. $P(X = 0|4,\ 0.15) = \dfrac{4!}{0!(4-0)!}0.15^0(1-0.15)^{4-0} = 0.522$
3. $P(X \geq 3|4,\ 0.15) = P(X = 3|4,\ 0.15) + P(X = 4|4,\ 0.15) = \dfrac{4!}{3!(4-3)!}0.15^3(1-0.15)^{4-3}$

$+\dfrac{4!}{4!(4-4)!}0.15^4(1-0.15)^{4-4} = 0.0115 + 0.000506 = 0.0120$

4. $P(X < 2|4,\ 0.15) = P(X = 1|4,\ 0.15) + P(X = 0|4,\ 0.15) = \dfrac{4!}{1!(4-1)!}0.15^1(1-0.15)^{4-1}$

$+\dfrac{4!}{0!(4-0)!}0.15^0(1-0.15)^{4-0} = 0.368 + 0.522 = 0.890$

(e) The probabilities for (1) and (3) become smaller and the probabilities for (2) and (4) become larger as the probability that a computer is upgraded increases.

21. $n=10,\ p=0.10$

(a) $P(X>4|10,\ 0.10)=1-P(X=0|10,\ 0.10)-P(X=1|10,\ 0.10)-P(X=2|10,\ 0.10)-P(X=3|10,\ 0.10)$

$-P(X=4|10,\ 0.10)=1-\frac{10!}{0!(10-0)!}0.1^0(1-0.1)^{10-0}-\frac{10!}{1!(10-1)!}0.1^1(1-0.1)^{10-1}-\frac{10!}{2!(10-2)!}0.1^2(1-0.1)^{10-2}$

$-\frac{10!}{3!(10-3)!}0.1^3(1-0.1)^{10-3}-\frac{10!}{4!(10-4)!}0.1^4(1-0.1)^{10-4}=1-0.349-0.387-0.194-0.0574-0.0112$

$=0.00163$

(b) $P(2\le X\le 5|10,\ 0.10)=P(X=2|10,\ 0.10)+P(X=3|10,\ 0.10)+P(X=4|10,\ 0.10)+P(X=5|10,\ 0.10)$

$=\frac{10!}{2!(10-2)!}0.1^2(1-0.1)^{10-2}+\frac{10!}{3!(10-3)!}0.1^3(1-0.1)^{10-3}+\frac{10!}{4!(10-4)!}0.1^4(1-0.1)^{10-4}$

$+\frac{10!}{5!(10-5)!}0.1^5(1-0.1)^{10-5}=0.194+0.0574+0.0112+0.00149=0.264$

(c) $n=8,\ p=0.10$

$P(X>4|8,\ 0.10)=1-P(X=0|8,\ 0.10)-P(X=1|8,\ 0.10)-P(X=2|8,\ 0.10)-P(X=3|8,\ 0.10)$

$-P(X=4|8,\ 0.10)=1-\frac{8!}{0!(8-0)!}0.1^0(1-0.1)^{10-0}-\frac{8!}{1!(8-1)!}0.1^1(1-0.1)^{10-1}-\frac{8!}{2!(8-2)!}0.1^2(1-0.1)^{10-2}$

$-\frac{8!}{4!(8-4)!}0.1^4(1-0.1)^{10-4}=1-0.4305-0.383-0.149-0.0331-0.0045=0.000432$

$P(2\le X\le 5|8,\ 0.10)=P(X=2|8,\ 0.10)+P(X=3|8,\ 0.10)+P(X=4|8,\ 0.10)+P(X=5|8,\ 0.10)$

$=\frac{8!}{2!(8-2)!}0.1^2(1-0.1)^{10-2}+\frac{8!}{3!(8-3)!}0.1^3(1-0.1)^{10-3}+\frac{8!}{4!(8-4)!}0.1^4(1-0.1)^{10-4}$

$+\frac{8!}{5!(8-5)!}0.1^5(1-0.1)^{10-5}=0.1489+0.0331+0.00459+0.000408=0.187$

22. (a) $P(X=3|n=4,\ N=10,\ A=5)=\frac{\binom{5}{3}\binom{10-5}{4-3}}{\binom{10}{4}}=\frac{\frac{5!}{3!2!}\times\frac{5!}{1!4!}}{\frac{10!}{4!6!}}=0.238$

(b) $P(X<3|n=4,\ N=10,\ A=5)=P(X=0|n=4,\ N=10,\ A=5)+P(X=1|n=4,\ N=10,\ A=5)$

$+P(X=2|n=4,\ N=10,\ A=5)=\frac{\binom{5}{0}\binom{10-5}{4-0}}{\binom{10}{4}}+\frac{\binom{5}{1}\binom{10-5}{4-1}}{\binom{10}{4}}+\frac{\binom{5}{2}\binom{10-5}{4-2}}{\binom{10}{4}}=\frac{\frac{5!}{0!5!}\times\frac{5!}{4!1!}}{\frac{10!}{4!6!}}+\frac{\frac{5!}{1!4!}\times\frac{5!}{3!2!}}{\frac{10!}{4!6!}}$

$+\frac{\frac{5!}{2!3!}\times\frac{5!}{2!3!}}{\frac{10!}{4!6!}}=0.0238+0.2380+0.476=0.738$

(c) $P(X=1|n=3,\ N=20,\ A=2)=\frac{\binom{2}{1}\binom{20-2}{3-1}}{\binom{20}{3}}=\frac{\frac{2!}{1!1!}\times\frac{18!}{2!16!}}{\frac{20!}{3!7!}}=0.268$

(d) $P(X=3|n=5,\ N=15,\ A=5)=\frac{\binom{5}{3}\binom{15-5}{5-3}}{\binom{15}{5}}=\frac{\frac{5!}{3!2!}\times\frac{10!}{2!8!}}{\frac{15!}{5!10!}}=0.14985$

23. (a) $P(X=4|n=5,\ N=52,\ A=26)=\dfrac{\binom{26}{4}\binom{52-26}{5-4}}{\binom{52}{5}}=\dfrac{\dfrac{26!}{4!22!}\times\dfrac{26!}{1!25!}}{\dfrac{52!}{5!47!}}=0.150$

(b) $P(X=2|n=5,\ N=52,\ A=4)=\dfrac{\binom{4}{2}\binom{52-4}{5-2}}{\binom{52}{5}}=\dfrac{\dfrac{4!}{2!2!}\times\dfrac{48!}{3!45!}}{\dfrac{52!}{5!47!}}=0.0399298$

(c) $P(X=0|n=5,\ N=52,\ A=13)=\dfrac{\binom{13}{0}\binom{52-13}{5-0}}{\binom{52}{5}}=\dfrac{\dfrac{13!}{0!13!}\times\dfrac{39!}{5!34!}}{\dfrac{52!}{5!47!}}=0.2215336$

(d) There are only 4 aces in a standard deck of playing cards. $P(X=5|n=5,\ N=52,\ A=4)=0$

24. (a) $P(X=1|n=5,\ N=30,\ A=10)=\dfrac{\binom{10}{1}\binom{30-10}{5-1}}{\binom{30}{5}}=\dfrac{\dfrac{10!}{1!9!}\times\dfrac{20!}{4!16!}}{\dfrac{30!}{5!25!}}=0.340$

(b) $P(X\geq 1|n=5,\ N=30,\ A=10)=1-P(X=0|n=5,\ N=30,\ A=10)=\dfrac{\binom{10}{0}\binom{30-10}{5-0}}{\binom{30}{5}}=1-\dfrac{\dfrac{10!}{0!10!}\times\dfrac{20!}{5!15!}}{\dfrac{30!}{5!25!}}$

$=1-0.109=0.891$

(c) $P(X=3|n=5,\ N=30,\ A=10)=\dfrac{\binom{10}{3}\binom{30-10}{5-3}}{\binom{30}{5}}=\dfrac{\dfrac{10!}{3!7!}\times\dfrac{20!}{2!18!}}{\dfrac{30!}{5!25!}}=0.160$

(d) $P(X=5|n=5,\ N=30,\ A=10)=\dfrac{\binom{10}{5}\binom{30-10}{5-5}}{\binom{30}{5}}=\dfrac{\dfrac{10!}{5!5!}\times\dfrac{20!}{0!20!}}{\dfrac{30!}{5!25!}}=0.00177$

(e) Two assumptions are necessary.
 (1) The probability that a car will be purchased is the same for all 30 cars in the lot.
 In particular, the probability that "a purchased car is a compact car" is equal to the probability that "a purchased car is not a compact car". (This is only true when the demand for compact cars is equal to the demand for non-compact cars. For example, when gas prices are high, the demand for more economical compact cars is higher.)
 (2) The outcome of any particular trial does not depend on the outcomes of other trials.

25. (a) $P(X=1|n=4,\ N=15,\ A=5)=\dfrac{\binom{5}{1}\binom{15-5}{4-1}}{\binom{15}{4}}=\dfrac{\dfrac{5!}{1!4!}\times\dfrac{10!}{3!7!}}{\dfrac{15!}{4!11!}}=0.440$

(b) $P(X\geq 1|n=4,\ N=15,\ A=5)=1-P(X=0|n=4,\ N=15,\ A=5)=1-\dfrac{\binom{5}{0}\binom{15-5}{4-0}}{\binom{15}{4}}=1-\dfrac{\dfrac{5!}{0!5!}\times\dfrac{10!}{4!6!}}{\dfrac{15!}{4!11!}}$

$=1-0.154=0.846$

(c) $P(X \le 2|n=4,\ N=15,\ A=5) = P(X=0|n=4,\ N=15,\ A=5) + P(X=1|n=4,\ N=15,\ A=5)$

$$+P(X=2|n=4,\ N=15,\ A=5) = \frac{\binom{5}{0}\binom{15-5}{4-0}}{\binom{15}{4}} + \frac{\binom{5}{1}\binom{15-5}{4-1}}{\binom{15}{4}} + \frac{\binom{5}{2}\binom{15-5}{4-2}}{\binom{15}{4}} = \frac{\frac{5!}{0!5!}\times\frac{10!}{4!6!}}{\frac{15!}{4!11!}} + \frac{\frac{5!}{1!4!}\times\frac{10!}{3!7!}}{\frac{15!}{4!11!}}$$

$$+\frac{\frac{5!}{2!3!}\times\frac{10!}{2!8!}}{\frac{15!}{4!11!}} = 0.154 + 0.440 + 0.330 = 0.923$$

(d) $\mu = \frac{nA}{N} = \frac{4\times 5}{15} = 1.33$

26. (a) P(None of your messages was lost) = P(All your messages were received).

$$P(X=3|n=7,\ N=10,\ A=3) = \frac{\binom{3}{3}\binom{10-3}{7-3}}{\binom{10}{7}} = \frac{\frac{3!}{3!0!}\times\frac{7!}{4!3!}}{\frac{10!}{7!3!}} = 0.2916$$

(b) P(Exactly one of your messages was lost) = P(Two of your messages were received).

$$P(X=2|n=7,\ N=10,\ A=3) = \frac{\binom{3}{2}\binom{10-3}{7-2}}{\binom{10}{7}} = \frac{\frac{3!}{2!1!}\times\frac{7!}{5!2!}}{\frac{10!}{7!3!}} = 0.525$$

(c) P(All three of your messages were lost) = P(None of your messages was received).

$$P(X=0|n=7,\ N=10,\ A=3) = \frac{\binom{3}{0}\binom{10-3}{7-0}}{\binom{10}{7}} = \frac{\frac{3!}{3!0!}\times\frac{7!}{7!0!}}{\frac{10!}{7!3!}} = 0.00833$$

27. (a) $$P(X=6|n=6,\ N=54,\ A=6) = \frac{\binom{6}{6}\binom{54-6}{6-6}}{\binom{54}{6}} = \frac{\frac{6!}{6!0!}\times\frac{48!}{0!48!}}{\frac{54!}{6!48!}} = 3.87\times 10^{-8}$$

(b) $$P(X=5|n=6,\ N=54,\ A=6) = \frac{\binom{6}{5}\binom{54-6}{6-5}}{\binom{54}{6}} = \frac{\frac{6!}{5!1!}\times\frac{48!}{1!47!}}{\frac{54!}{6!48!}} = 1.12\times 10^{-5}$$

(c) $$P(X=4|n=6,\ N=54,\ A=6) = \frac{\binom{6}{4}\binom{54-6}{6-4}}{\binom{54}{6}} = \frac{\frac{6!}{4!2!}\times\frac{48!}{2!46!}}{\frac{54!}{6!48!}} = 0.000655$$

(d) $$P(X=0|n=6,\ N=54,\ A=6) = \frac{\binom{6}{0}\binom{54-6}{6-0}}{\binom{54}{6}} = \frac{\frac{6!}{0!6!}\times\frac{48!}{6!42!}}{\frac{54!}{6!48!}} = 0.475$$

(e) $\mu = \frac{nA}{N} = \frac{6\times 6}{54} = 0.667$

(f) $P(X=6|n=6,\ N=40,\ A=6)=\dfrac{\binom{6}{6}\binom{40-6}{6-6}}{\binom{40}{6}}=\dfrac{\dfrac{6!}{6!0!}\times\dfrac{34!}{0!34!}}{\dfrac{40!}{6!34!}}=2.61\times10^{-7}$

$P(X=5|n=6,\ N=40,\ A=6)=\dfrac{\binom{6}{5}\binom{40-6}{6-5}}{\binom{40}{6}}=\dfrac{\dfrac{6!}{5!1!}\times\dfrac{34!}{1!33!}}{\dfrac{40!}{6!34!}}=5.31\times10^{-5}$

$P(X=4|n=6,\ N=40,\ A=6)=\dfrac{\binom{6}{4}\binom{40-6}{6-4}}{\binom{40}{6}}=\dfrac{\dfrac{6!}{4!2!}\times\dfrac{34!}{2!32!}}{\dfrac{40!}{6!34!}}=0.00219$

$P(X=0|n=6,\ N=40,\ A=6)=\dfrac{\binom{6}{0}\binom{40-6}{6-0}}{\binom{40}{6}}=\dfrac{\dfrac{6!}{0!6!}\times\dfrac{34!}{6!28!}}{\dfrac{40!}{6!34!}}=0.350383$

$\mu=\dfrac{nA}{N}=\dfrac{6\times6}{40}=0.9$

28. (a) If $p=0.5$, and $X=2$, $P(n=5)=\binom{5-1}{2-1}0.5^2(1-0.5)^{5-2}=0.125$

(b) If $p=0.3$, and $X=2$, $P(n=5)=\binom{5-1}{2-1}0.3^2(1-0.3)^{5-2}=0.123$

(c) If $p=0.5$, and $X=4$, $P(n=10)=\binom{10-1}{4-1}0.5^4(1-0.5)^{10-4}=0.08203$

(d) If $p=0.2$, and $X=1$, $P(n=6)=\binom{6-1}{1-1}0.2^1(1-0.2)^{6-1}=0.0656$

(e) If $p=0.3$, and $X=1$, $P(n=6)=\binom{6-1}{1-1}0.3^1(1-0.3)^{6-1}=0.0504$

(f) If $p=0.3$, and $X=1$, $P(n=3)=\binom{3-1}{1-1}0.3^1(1-0.3)^{3-1}=0.147$

(g) (a) $\mu=2/0.5=4$, $\sigma=\sqrt{\dfrac{2(1-0.5)}{0.5^2}}=2$

(b) $\mu=2/0.3=6.667$, $\sigma=\sqrt{\dfrac{2(1-0.3)}{0.3^2}}=3.94$

(c) $\mu=4/0.5=8$, $\sigma=\sqrt{\dfrac{4(1-0.5)}{0.5^2}}=2.83$

(d) $\mu=1/0.2=5$, $\sigma=\sqrt{\dfrac{1(1-0.2)}{0.2^2}}=4.472$

(e) $\mu=1/0.3=3.33$, $\sigma=\sqrt{\dfrac{1(1-0.3)}{0.3^2}}=2.79$

(f) $\mu=1/0.3=3.33$, $\sigma=\sqrt{\dfrac{1(1-0.3)}{0.3^2}}=2.79$

29. (a) $p=0.35$, $X=2$

(1) $P(n=2)=\binom{2-1}{2-1}0.35^2(1-0.35)^{2-2}=0.123$

(2) $P(n=5)=\binom{5-1}{2-1}0.35^2(1-0.35)^{5-2}=0.135$

(3) $P(n=10)=\binom{10-1}{2-1}0.35^2(1-0.35)^{10-2}=0.0351$

(b) $\mu=2/0.35=5.714286$, $\sigma=\sqrt{\dfrac{2(1-0.35)}{0.35^2}}=3.258$

30. (a) $p = 0.10$, $X = 2$

(1) $P(n=3) = \binom{3-1}{2-1} 0.1^2(1-0.1)^{3-2} = 0.018$ (2) $P(n=5) = \binom{5-1}{2-1} 0.1^2(1-0.1)^{5-2} = 0.0292$

(3) $P(n=10) = \binom{10-1}{2-1} 0.1^2(1-0.1)^{10-2} = 0.0387$

(b) $\mu = 2/0.1 = 20$, $\sigma = \sqrt{\dfrac{2(1-0.1)}{0.1^2}} = 13.4$

(c) $p = 0.08$, $X = 2$

(1) $P(n=3) = \binom{3-1}{2-1} 0.08^2(1-0.08)^{3-2} = 0.0118$ (2) $P(n=5) = \binom{5-1}{2-1} 0.08^2(1-0.08)^{5-2} = 0.0200$

(3) $P(n=10) = \binom{10-1}{2-1} 0.08^2(1-0.08)^{10-2} = 0.0300$, $\mu = \dfrac{2}{0.08} = 25$, $\sigma = \sqrt{\dfrac{2(1-0.08)}{0.08^2}} = 16.95582$

31. (a) $p = 0.05$, $X = 1$

(1) $P(n=1) = \binom{1-1}{1-1} 0.05^1(1-0.05)^{1-1} = 0.05$ (2) $P(n=5) = \binom{5-1}{1-1} 0.05^1(1-0.05)^{1-1} = 0.040725$

(3) $P(n=10) = \binom{10-1}{1-1} 0.05^1(1-0.05)^{10-1} = 0.031512$

(b) $\mu = \dfrac{2}{0.05} = 40$, $\sigma = \sqrt{\dfrac{2(1-0.05)}{0.05^2}} = 27.5681$

(c) $p = 0.02$, $X = 1$

(1) $P(n=1) = \binom{1-1}{1-1} 0.02^1(1-0.02)^{1-1} = 0.2$ (2) $P(n=5) = \binom{5-1}{1-1} 0.02^1(1-0.02)^{5-1} = 0.0819$

(3) $P(n=10) = \binom{10-1}{1-1} 0.02^1(1-0.02)^{10-1} = 0.0268$, $\mu = \dfrac{2}{0.2} = 10$, $\sigma = \sqrt{\dfrac{2(1-0.2)}{0.2^2}} = 6.325$

32. (a) $p = 0.3$, $X = 1$

(1) $P(n=2) = \binom{2-1}{1-1} 0.03^1(1-0.03)^{2-1} = 0.21$ (2) $P(n=4) = \binom{4-1}{1-1} 0.03^1(1-0.03)^{4-1} = 0.103$

(3) $P(n=10) = \binom{10-1}{1-1} 0.03^1(1-0.03)^{10-1} = 0.0121$

(b) $p = 0.3$, $X = 2$

(1) $P(n=2) = \binom{2-1}{2-1} 0.03^2(1-0.03)^{2-2} = 0.09$ (2) $P(n=4) = \binom{4-1}{2-1} 0.03^2(1-0.03)^{4-2} = 0.1323$

(3) $P(n=10) = \binom{10-1}{2-1} 0.03^2(1-0.03)^{10-2} = 0.0467$

33. (a) $p = 0.6$, $X = 3$

(1) $P(n=3) = \binom{3-1}{3-1} 0.6^3(1-0.6)^{3-3} = 0.216$ (2) $P(n=5) = \binom{5-1}{3-1} 0.6^3(1-0.6)^{5-3} = 0.2073$

(3) $P(n=10) = \binom{10-1}{3-1} 0.6^3(1-0.6)^{10-3} = 0.0127$

(b) $\mu = \dfrac{3}{0.6} = 5$, $\sigma = \sqrt{\dfrac{3(1-0.6)}{0.6^2}} = 1.83$

(c) $p = 0.6,\ X = 1$

(1) $P(n=3) = \binom{3-1}{1-1} 0.6^1 (1-0.6)^{3-1} = 0.096$ (2) $P(n=5) = \binom{5-1}{1-1} 0.6^1 (1-0.6)^{5-1} = 0.0154$

(3) $P(n=10) = \binom{10-1}{1-1} 0.6^1 (1-0.6)^{10-1} = 0.000157$

(d) $\mu = \dfrac{1}{0.6} = 1.667,\ \sigma = \sqrt{\dfrac{1(1-0.6)}{0.6^2}} = 1.054$

34. (a) $p = 0.08,\ X = 1$

(1) $P(n=3) = \binom{3-1}{1-1} 0.08^1 (1-0.08)^{3-1} = 0.0677$ (2) $P(n=5) = \binom{5-1}{1-1} 0.08^1 (1-0.08)^{5-1} = 0.0573$

(3) $P(n=10) = \binom{10-1}{1-1} 0.08^1 (1-0.08)^{10-1} = 0.03778$

(b) $\mu = \dfrac{1}{0.08} = 12.5,\ \sigma = \sqrt{\dfrac{1(1-0.08)}{0.08^2}} = 11.98958$

(c) $p = 0.04,\ X = 1$

(1) $P(n=3) = \binom{3-1}{1-1} 0.04^1 (1-0.04)^{3-1} = 0.0369$ (2) $P(n=5) = \binom{5-1}{1-1} 0.04^1 (1-0.04)^{5-1} = 0.0340$

(3) $P(n=10) = \binom{10-1}{1-1} 0.04^1 (1-0.04)^{10-1} = 0.0277,\ \mu = \dfrac{1}{0.04} = 25,\ \sigma = \sqrt{\dfrac{1(1-0.04)}{0.04^2}} = 24.4949$

(d) $p = 0.08,\ X = 3$

(1) $P(n=3) = \binom{3-1}{3-1} 0.08^1 (1-0.08)^{3-3} = 0.000512$ (2) $P(n=5) = \binom{5-1}{3-1} 0.08^3 (1-0.08)^{5-3} = 0.00260$

(3) $P(n=10) = \binom{10-1}{3-1} 0.08^3 (1-0.08)^{10-3} = 0.0103,\ \mu = \dfrac{3}{0.08} = 37.5,\ \sigma = \sqrt{\dfrac{3(1-0.08)}{0.08^2}} = 20.76656$

35. (a) $P(X=0|\lambda=3.5) = \dfrac{e^{-3.5}3.5^0}{0!} = 0.0302$ (b) $P(X=3|\lambda=5.0) = \dfrac{e^{-5.0}5.0^0}{3!} = 0.1403$

(c) $P(X \geq 2|\lambda=0.5) = 1 - P(X=0|\lambda=0.5) - P(X=1|\lambda=0.5) = 1 - \dfrac{e^{-0.5}0.5^0}{0!} - \dfrac{e^{-0.5}0.5^1}{1!} = 1 - 0.607 - 0.303 = 0.0902$

(d) $P(X<0|\lambda=10) = 0.000000$

(e) $P(X=12\ or\ 13\ or\ 14) = P(X=12|\lambda=15) + P(X=13|\lambda=15) + P(X=14|\lambda=15)$

$P(X=12|\lambda=15) = \dfrac{e^{-15}15^{12}}{12!} = 0.0829$ $P(X=13|\lambda=15) = \dfrac{e^{-15}15^{13}}{13!} = 0.0956$

$P(X=14|\lambda=15) = \dfrac{e^{-15}15^{14}}{14!} = 0.1024$ $P(X=12\ or\ 13\ or\ 14) = 0.281$

36. (a) $P(X=2|\lambda=5.0) = \dfrac{e^{-5.0}5.0^2}{2!} = 0.0842$ (b) $P(X=0|\lambda=5.0) = \dfrac{e^{-5.0}5.0^0}{0!} = 0.00674$

(c) $P(X \leq 3|\lambda=5.0) = P(X=0|\lambda=5.0) + P(X=1|\lambda=5.0) + P(X=2|\lambda=5.0) + P(X=3|\lambda=5.0)$

$= \dfrac{e^{-5.0}5.0^0}{0!} + \dfrac{e^{-5.0}5.0^1}{1!} + \dfrac{e^{-5.0}5.0^2}{2!} + \dfrac{e^{-5.0}5.0^3}{3!} = 0.00674 + 0.03369 + 0.08422 + 0.14037 = 0.26503$

(d) $P(X<3|\lambda=5.0) = P(X=0|\lambda=5.0) + P(X=1|\lambda=5.0) = \dfrac{e^{-5.0}5.0^0}{0!} + \dfrac{e^{-5.0}5.0^1}{1!} = 0.00674 + 0.03369 = 0.040423$

37. (a) $P(X=0|\lambda=2.5) = \dfrac{e^{-2.5}2.5^2}{2!} = 0.0821$ (b) $P(X=2|\lambda=2.5) = \dfrac{e^{-2.5}2.5^2}{2!} = 0.257$

(c) $P(X \geq 1|\lambda = 2.5) = 1 - P(X = 0|\lambda = 2.5) = \dfrac{e^{-2.5}2.5^0}{0!} = 1 - 0.0821 = 0.918$

(d) $P(X \leq 1|\lambda = 2.5) = P(X = 0|\lambda = 2.5) + P(X = 0|\lambda = 2.5) = \dfrac{e^{-2.5}2.5^0}{0!} + \dfrac{e^{-2.5}2.5^1}{1!} = 0.082085 + 0.20521 = 0.287$

38. (a) $P(X = 0|\lambda = 6.0) = \dfrac{e^{-6.0}6.0^0}{0!} = 0.00248$ (b) $P(X = 5|\lambda = 6.0) = \dfrac{e^{-6.0}6.0^5}{5!} = 0.161$

(c) $P(X \geq 2|\lambda = 6.0) = 1 - P(X = 0|\lambda = 6.0) - P(X = 1|\lambda = 6.0) = 1 - \dfrac{e^{-6.0}6.0^0}{0!} - \dfrac{e^{-6.0}6.0^1}{1!} = 1 - 0.00248 - 0.0149 = 0.983$

(d) $P(X \leq 3|\lambda = 6.0) = P(X = 0|\lambda = 6.0) + P(X = 1|\lambda = 6.0) + P(X = 2|\lambda = 6.0) + P(X = 3|\lambda = 6.0) = \dfrac{e^{-6.0}6.0^0}{0!} + \dfrac{e^{-6.0}6.0^1}{1!}$

$+ \dfrac{e^{-6.0}6.0^2}{2!} + \dfrac{e^{-6.0}6.0^3}{3!} = 0.00248 + 0.0149 + 0.0892 = 0.151$

39. (a) $P(X = 8|\lambda = 10.0) = \dfrac{e^{10}10^8}{8!} = 0.113$

(b) $P(X = 8 \text{ or } X = 9|\lambda = 10.0) = P(X = 8|\lambda = 10.0) + P(X = 9|\lambda = 10.0) = \dfrac{e^{-10}10^8}{8!} + \dfrac{e^{-10}10^9}{9!} = 0.113 + 0.125110 = 0.238$

(c) $P(X = 0|\lambda = 10.0) = \dfrac{e^{10}10^0}{0!} = 0.0000450$

40. (a) (1) $P(X = 0|\lambda = 0.5) = \dfrac{e^{-0.5}0.5^0}{0!} = 0.607$

(2) $P(X \geq 1|\lambda = 0.5) = 1 - P(X = 0|\lambda = 0.5) = 1 - \dfrac{e^{-0.5}0.5^0}{0!} = 1 - 0.607 = 0.3934$

(3) $P(3 \leq X \leq 5|\lambda = 0.5) = P(X = 3|\lambda = 0.5) + P(X = 4|\lambda = 0.5) + P(X = 5|\lambda = 0.5) = \dfrac{e^{-0.5}0.5^3}{3!} + \dfrac{e^{-0.5}0.5^4}{4!}$

$+ \dfrac{e^{-0.5}0.5^5}{5!} = 0.012636 + 0.001580 + 0.000158 = 0.0144$

(b) $P(X = 3|\lambda = 5) + P(X = 4|\lambda = 5) + P(X = 5|\lambda = 5) = \dfrac{e^{-5}5^3}{3!} + \dfrac{e^{-5}5^4}{4!} + \dfrac{e^{-5}5^5}{5!}$

$= 0.140 + 0.175 + 0.1754 = 0.491$

(c) $\sigma = \sqrt{\lambda} = \sqrt{0.5} = 0.707$

41. (a) $P\left(X \geq 1\middle|\lambda = \dfrac{12}{5}\right) = 1 - P(X = 0|\lambda = 2.4) = 1 - \dfrac{e^{-2.4}2.4^0}{0!} = 1 - 0.090718 = 0.909282$

(b) $P(X = 5|\lambda = 10) + P(X = 6|\lambda = 10) + \ldots + P(X = 15|\lambda = 10) = \dfrac{e^{-10}10^5}{5!} + \ldots + \dfrac{e^{-10}10^8}{8!} + \dfrac{e^{-10}10^9}{9!} + \ldots + \dfrac{e^{-10}10^{15}}{15!}$

$= 0.0378 + 0.0631 + 0.0901 + 0.113 + 0.125 + 0.125 + 0.114 + 0.0948 + 0.0729 + 0.0521 + 0.0347 = 0.922$

42. Classical probability assumes that all elementary events are equally likely to occur. Empirical probability does not assume all elementary events are equally likely to occur. Subjective probabilities can be based on expert opinion or even gut feelings or hunches. Therefore, subjective probabilities depend on an individual opinion, whereas classical and empirical probabilities are objective.

43. A simple event is defined by one characteristic whereas a joint event is defined by two or more characteristics.

44. If two events, A and B, are mutually exclusive, then the probability of either event A or event B occurring is the sum of their separate probabilities.

45. Events are mutually exclusive if they cannot occur at the same time. Events are collectively exhaustive if one of them must occur.

46. Conditional probability is relevant if the probability that a given event will occur affects the probability that another event will occur. In other words, conditional probability is used if the events are not independent.

47. If two events are independent, then the probability of both events occurring is equal to the product of their respective probabilities. If two events are not independent, then the probability of both events occurring is the product of the probability of the first event and the conditional probability of the second event given that the first event has already occurred.

48. The expected value of a probability distribution is the average of a random variable.

49. (a) Each elementary event is classified into one of two mutually exclusive and collectively exhaustive categories.
(b) The probabilities of an outcome are constant from trial to trial.
(c) The outcome of a particular trial is independent of the outcome on any other trial.

50. (a) Each elementary event is classified into one of two mutually exclusive and collectively exhaustive categories.
(b) The data are selected *without replacement* from a finite (small) population.

51. The binomial distribution is used in situations in which the probability of success remains constant from trial to trial. This is true when the data are selected *with replacement* or when the data are selected from a very large population. The fact that an object was selected does not change the probabilities of other objects being selected. The hypergeometric distribution is used in situations in which the probability of success changes from trial to trial because the data are selected *without replacement* from a finite (small) population.

52. The binomial distribution is used to determine the probability of a certain number of successes in a certain number of trials. The negative binomial distribution determines the probability that x^{th} success occurs on the nth trial.

53. The negative binomial distribution is used to determine the probability that x^{th} success occurs on the nth trial whereas the geometric distribution is used to determine the probability that the first success occurs on the nth trial. Thus, the geometric distribution is a special case of the negative binomial distribution.

54. It is assumed that we can observe discrete events in an area of opportunity in such a manner that if we subdivide the area of opportunity into very small, equal-sized subareas of opportunity then the following is true:
(a) The probability of observing exactly one success in any subarea of opportunity is stable;
(b) the probability of observing two or more successes in any subarea of opportunity is zero;
(c) the occurrence of a success in any subarea of opportunity is statistically independent of that in any other subarea.

55. The binomial distribution analyzes the number of nonconforming items in a sample of n units; the Poisson distribution analyzes the number of nonconformities per sampled continuum (or per area opportunity).

56. (a) Consider a binomial distribution with $n = 3$, $p = 1/6$

$$P(\text{None of the three dice show the number selected}) = P(X = 0|n = 3,\ p = 0.167) = \frac{3!}{0!(3-0)!}0.167^{0}(1-0.167)^{3-0}$$

$= 0.579$

$P(\text{One of the three dice shows the number selected}) = P(X=1|n=3,\ p=0.167) = \frac{3!}{1!(3-1)!}0.167^1(1-0.167)^{3-1}$

$= 0.347$

$P(\text{Two of the three dice show the number selected}) = P(X=2|n=3,\ p=0.167) = \frac{3!}{2!(3-2)!}0.167^2(1-0.167)^{3-2}$

$= 0.0694$

$P(\text{All three dice show the number selected}) = P(X=3|n=3,\ p=0.167) = \frac{3!}{3!(3-3)!}0.167^3(1-0.167)^{3-3}$

$= 0.00463$

	Events	P	Profit
E1	None of the three dice show the number selected	0.579	−1
E2	One of the three dice shows the number selected	0.347	1
E3	Two of the three dice show the number selected	0.069	2
E4	All three dice show the number selected	0.00463	3

(b) $\mu = -1\times0.579+1\times0.0694+3\times0.00463 = -0.0787$. The average lost will be about \$0.08 for each bet.

(c) The answers will vary.

57. (a) Consider a binomial distribution, $n=5,\ p=0.6$

(1) $P(X=3|n=5,\ p=0.6) = \frac{5!}{3!(5-3)!}0.6^3(1-0.6)^{5-3} = 0.346$

(2) $P(X\ge3|n=5,\ p=0.6) = P(X=3|n=5,\ p=0.6)+P(X=4|n=5,\ p=0.6)+P(X=5|n=5,\ p=0.6)$

$= \frac{5!}{3!(5-3)!}0.6^3(1-0.6)^{5-3} + \frac{5!}{4!(5-4)!}0.6^4(1-0.6)^{5-4} + \frac{5!}{5!(5-5)!}0.6^5(1-0.6)^{5-5} = 0.346+0.259+0.078 = 0.683$

(3) $P(X=5|n=5,\ p=0.6) = \frac{5!}{5!(5-5)!}0.6^5(1-0.6)^{5-5} = 0.0778$

(4) $P(X=0|n=5,\ p=0.6) = \frac{5!}{0!(5-0)!}0.6^0(1-0.6)^{5-0} = 0.0102$

(b) $\mu = np = 5\times0.60 = 3,\ \sigma = \sqrt{np(1-p)} = \sqrt{5\times0.6(1-0.6)} = 1.0954$

(c) Consider a binomial distribution, $n=10,\ p=0.6$

(1) $P(X=3|n=10,\ p=0.6) = \frac{10!}{3!(10-3)!}0.6^3(1-0.6)^{10-3} = 0.0425$

(2) $P(X\ge3|n=10,\ p=0.6) = 1-P(X=0|n=10,\ p=0.6)-P(X=1|n=10,\ p=0.6)-P(X=2|n=10,\ p=0.6)$

$= 1-\frac{10!}{0!(10-0)!}0.6^0(1-0.6)^{10-0} - \frac{10!}{1!(10-1)!}0.6^1(1-0.6)^{10-1}\frac{10!}{2!(10-2)!}0.6^2(1-0.6)^{10-2}$

$= 1-0.00010-0.00157-0.01062 = 0.9878$

(3) $P(X=5|n=10,\ p=0.6) = \frac{10!}{5!(10-5)!}0.6^5(1-0.6)^{10-5} = 0.201$

(4) $P(X=0|n=10,\ p=0.6) = \frac{10!}{0!(10-0)!}0.6^0(1-0.6)^{10-0} = 0.000105,\ \mu = np = 10\times0.60 = 6$

$\sigma = \sqrt{np(1-p)} = \sqrt{10\times0.6(1-0.6)} = 1.55$

(d) Consider a binomial distribution, $n=5,\ p=0.7$

(1) $P(X=3|n=5,\ p=0.7) = \frac{5!}{3!(5-3)!}0.7^3(1-0.7)^{5-3} = 0.3087$

(2) $P(X\ge3|n=5,\ p=0.7) = P(X=3|n=5,\ p=0.7)+P(X=4|n=5,\ p=0.7)+P(X=5|n=5,\ p=0.7)$

$= \frac{5!}{3!(5-3)!}0.7^3(1-0.7)^{5-3} + \frac{5!}{4!(5-4)!}0.7^4(1-0.7)^{5-4} + \frac{5!}{5!(5-5)!}0.7^5(1-0.7)^{5-5}$

$= 0.30870+0.36015+0.16807 = 0.83692$

(3) $P(X=5|n=5,\ p=0.7)=\frac{5!}{5!(5-5)!}0.7^5(1-0.7)^{5-5}=0.168$

(4) $P(X=0|n=5,\ p=0.7)=\frac{5!}{0!(5-0)!}0.7^0(1-0.7)^{5-0}=0.00243$, $\mu=np=5\times 0.70=3.5$

$\sigma=\sqrt{np(1-p)}=\sqrt{5\times 0.7(1-0.7)}=1.024695$

58. (a) Hypergeometric distribution:

(1) $P(X=0|n=8,\ N=30,\ A=10)=\frac{\binom{10}{0}\binom{30-10}{8-0}}{\binom{30}{8}}=\frac{\frac{10!}{0!10!}\times\frac{20!}{8!2!}}{\frac{30!}{8!22!}}=0.0215$

(2) $P(X\geq 1|n=8,\ N=30,\ A=10)=1-P(X=0|n=8,\ N=30,\ A=10)=1-\frac{\binom{10}{0}\binom{30-10}{8-0}}{\binom{30}{8}}=1-\frac{\frac{10!}{0!10!}\times\frac{20!}{8!2!}}{\frac{30!}{8!22!}}$

$=1-0.0215=0.978$

(3) $P(X=8|n=8,\ N=30,\ A=10)=\frac{\binom{10}{8}\binom{30-10}{8-8}}{\binom{30}{8}}=\frac{\frac{10!}{8!2!}\times\frac{20!}{0!20!}}{\frac{30!}{8!22!}}=7.69\times 10^{-6}$

(b) $\mu=\frac{nA}{N}=\frac{8\times 10}{30}=2.67$

(c) The negative binomial distribution with $X=1$ (the geometric distribution):

$P(n=3|p=0.2,\ X=1)=\binom{3-1}{1-1}0.2^1(1-0.2)^{3-1}=0.128$

(d) The negative binomial distribution with $X=1$ (the geometric distribution):

$P(n=5|p=0.2,\ X=1)=\binom{5-1}{1-1}0.2^1(1-0.2)^{5-1}=0.0819$

(e) The negative binomial distribution: $P(n=8|p=0.2,\ X=3)=\binom{8-1}{3-1}0.2^3(1-0.2)^{3-1}=0.0551$

(f) The negative binomial distribution, $P(n=20|p=0.2,\ X=8)=\binom{20-1}{8-1}0.2^8(1-0.2)^{8-1}=0.008864$

(g) $\mu=\frac{8}{0.20}=40$

59. (a) Binomial distribution: $n=5$, $p=0.0002$

(1) $\mu=5\times 0.0002=0.001$

(2) $P(X\geq 1|n=5,\ p=0.0002)=1-P(X=0|n=5,\ p=0.0002)=1-\frac{5!}{0!(5-0)!}0.0002^0(1-0.0002)^{5-0}$

$=1-0.999=0.001$

(b) Binomial distribution: $n=10{,}000$, $p=0.0002$

(1) $P(X\geq 1|n=10{,}000,\ p=0.0002)=1-P(X=0|n=10{,}000,\ p=0.0002)$

$=1-\frac{10{,}000!}{0!(10{,}000-0)!}0.0002^0(1-0.0002)^{10{,}000-0}=1-0.135=0.865$

(2) $\mu=10{,}000\times 0.0002=2$

60. (a) Binomial distribution: $n = 4$, $p = 0.95$

(1) $P(X = 3|n = 4,\ p = 0.95) = \dfrac{4!}{3!(4-3)!}0.95^3(1-0.95)^{4-3} = 0.171$

(2) $P(X \geq 3|n = 4,\ p = 0.95) = P(X = 3|n = 4,\ p = 0.95) + P(X = 4|n = 4,\ p = 0.95) = \dfrac{4!}{3!(4-3)!}0.95^3(1-0.95)^{4-3}$

$+\dfrac{4!}{4!(4-4)!}0.95^4(1-0.95)^{4-4} = 0.171475 + 0.815 = 0.986$

(b) Binomial distribution: $n = 20$, $p = 0.95$

(1) $P(X = 18|n = 20,\ p = 0.95) = \dfrac{20!}{18!(20-18)!}0.95^{18}(1-0.95)^{20-18} = 0.189$

(2) $P(X \geq 18|n = 20,\ p = 0.95) = P(X = 18|n = 20,\ p = 0.95) + P(X = 19|n = 20,\ p = 0.95)$

$+P(X = 20|n = 20,\ p = 0.95) = \dfrac{20!}{18!(20-18)!}0.95^{18}(1-0.95)^{20-18} + \dfrac{20!}{19!(20-19)!}0.95^{19}(1-0.95)^{20-19}$

$+\dfrac{20!}{20!(20-20)!}0.95^{20}(1-0.95)^{20-20} = 0.1889 + 0.37735 + 0.35849 = 0.92452$

(3) $\mu = np = 20 \times 0.95 = 19$, $\sigma = \sqrt{np(1-p)} = \sqrt{20 \times 0.95(1-0.95)} = 0.975$

(c) The negative binomial distribution with $X = 1$ (the geometric distribution):

$P(n = 2|X = 1,\ p = 0.95) = \binom{2-1}{1-1}0.95^1(1-0.95)^{2-1} = 0.0475$

(d) The negative binomial distribution: $P(n = 5|X = 4,\ p = 0.95) = \binom{5-1}{4-1}0.95^4(1-0.95)^{5-4} = 0.163$

(e) The probability that a battery does not meet specifications is $p = 1 - 0.95 = 0.05$. If $X = 2$, then $\mu = \dfrac{2}{0.05} = 40$.

61. (a) The hypergeometrical distribution:

(1) $P(X = 0|N = 20,\ A = 8,\ n = 5) = \dfrac{\binom{8}{0}\binom{20-8}{5-0}}{\binom{20}{5}} = \dfrac{\dfrac{8!}{0!8!} \times \dfrac{12!}{5!7!}}{\dfrac{20!}{5!15!}} = 0.0511$

(2) $P(X \geq 1|N = 20,\ A = 8,\ n = 5) = 1 - P(X = 0|N = 20,\ A = 8,\ n = 5) = 1 - \dfrac{\binom{8}{0}\binom{20-8}{5-0}}{\binom{20}{5}} = 1 - \dfrac{\dfrac{8!}{0!8!} \times \dfrac{12!}{5!7!}}{\dfrac{20!}{5!15!}}$

$= 1 - 0.0511 = 0.949$

(3) $P(X = 5|N = 20,\ A = 8,\ n = 5) = \dfrac{\binom{8}{5}\binom{20-8}{5-5}}{\binom{20}{5}} = \dfrac{\dfrac{8!}{5!3!} \times \dfrac{12!}{0!12!}}{\dfrac{20!}{5!15!}} = 0.00361$

(b) $\mu = \dfrac{nA}{N} = \dfrac{5 \times 8}{20} = 2$, $\sigma_x = \sqrt{\dfrac{nA(N-A)}{N^2}}\sqrt{\dfrac{N-n}{N-1}} = \sqrt{\dfrac{5 * 8(20-8)}{20^2}}\sqrt{\dfrac{20-5}{20-1}} = 0.9733$

(c) The binomial distribution:

(1) $P(X = 0|p = 0.40,\ n = 5) = \dfrac{5!}{0!(5-0)!}0.4^0(1-0.4)^{5-0} = 0.0778$

(2) $P(X \geq 1|p = 0.40,\ n = 5) = 1 - P(X = 0|p = 0.40,\ n = 5) = 1 - \dfrac{5!}{0!(5-0)!}0.4^0(1-0.4)^{5-0} = 1 - 0.0778 = 0.922$

(3) $P(X = 5|p = 0.40,\ n = 5) = \dfrac{5!}{5!(5-5)!}0.4^5(1-0.4)^{5-5} = 0.0102$

(d) $\mu = np = 5 \times 0.40 = 2$, $\sigma = \sqrt{np(1-p)} = \sqrt{5 \times 0.4(1-0.4)} = 1.095445$

(e) The answers are close, but different due to the difference between the binomial and hypergeometrical distributions; see problem 4.51 above. Indeed, in the situation described in (a) and (b), the probability of success does not remain constant from trial to trial. Conversely, in part (c) we assume that the probability of success is the same for all trials, because the sample size is less than 5% of the population size (i.e., the population is large).

62. (a) The binomial distribution:

(1) $P(X = 3|p = 0.40,\ n = 8) = \dfrac{8!}{3!(8-3)!}0.4^3(1-0.4)^{8-3} = 0.279$

(2) $P(X \geq 3|p = 0.40,\ n = 8) = 1 - P(X = 0|p = 0.40,\ n = 8) - P(X = 1|p = 0.40,\ n = 8) - P(X = 2|p = 0.40,\ n = 8)$

$= 1 - \dfrac{8!}{0!(8-0)!}0.4^0(1-0.4)^{8-0} - \dfrac{8!}{1!(8-1)!}0.4^1(1-0.4)^{8-1} - \dfrac{8!}{2!(8-2)!}0.4^2(1-0.4)^{8-2}$

$= 1 - 0.01680 - 0.08958 - 0.20902 = 0.6846$

(b) The negative binomial distribution:

(1) $P(n = 8|p = 0.40,\ X = 3) = \binom{8-1}{3-1}0.4^3(1-0.4)^{8-3} = 0.105$

(2) $P(n = 10|p = 0.40,\ X = 3) = \binom{10-1}{3-1}0.4^3(1-0.4)^{10-3} = 0.0645$

63. (a) $P(X = 0|\lambda = 4) = \dfrac{e^{-4}4^0}{0!} = 0.018316$

(b) $P(X \geq 1|\lambda = 4) = 1 - P(X = 0|\lambda = 4) = 1 - \dfrac{e^{-4}4^0}{0!} = 1 - 0.0183 = 0.982$

(c) $P(X > 4|\lambda = 4) = 1 - P(X \leq 4|\lambda = 4) = 1 - P(X = 1|\lambda = 4) - P(X = 2|\lambda = 4) - P(X = 3|\lambda = 4) - P(X = 4|\lambda = 4)$

$= 1 - \dfrac{e^{-4}4^0}{0!} - \dfrac{e^{-4}4^1}{1!} - \dfrac{e^{-4}4^2}{2!} - \dfrac{e^{-4}4^3}{3!} - \dfrac{e^{-4}4^4}{4!} = 1 - 0.0183 - 0.0733 - 0.147 - 0.195 - 0.195 = 0.371$

64. (a) $P(X = 0|\lambda = 1) = \dfrac{e^{-1}1^0}{0!} = 0.368$ (b) $P(X = 2|\lambda = 1) = \dfrac{e^{-1}1^2}{2!} = 0.184$

(c) $P(X \geq 1|\lambda = 1) = 1 - P(X = 0|\lambda = 1) = 1 - \dfrac{e^{-1}1^0}{0!} = 1 - 0.367879 = 0.632121$

(d) $P(X \leq 1|\lambda = 1) = P(X = 0|\lambda = 1) + P(X = 1|\lambda = 1) = \dfrac{e^{-1}1^0}{0!} + \dfrac{e^{-1}1^1}{1!} = 0.368 + 0.368 = 0.736$

(e) (1) $P(X = 0|\lambda = 2) = \dfrac{e^{-2}2^0}{0!} = 0.135335$ (2) $P(X = 2|\lambda = 2) = \dfrac{e^{-2}2^2}{2!} = 0.271$

(3) $P(X \geq 1|\lambda = 2) = 1 - P(X = 0|\lambda = 2) = 1 - \dfrac{e^{-2}2^0}{0!} = 1 - 0.135335 = 0.865$

(4) $P(X \leq 1|\lambda = 2) = P(X = 0|\lambda = 2) + P(X = 1|\lambda = 2) = \dfrac{e^{-2}2^0}{0!} + \dfrac{e^{-2}2^1}{1!} = 0.135 + 0.271 = 0.406$

65. (a) $P(X = 1|\lambda = 1) = \dfrac{e^{-1}1^1}{1!} = 0.368$

(b) $P(X \geq 1|\lambda = 1) = 1 - P(X = 0|\lambda = 1) = 1 - \dfrac{e^{-1}1^0}{0!} = 1 - 0.368 = 0.632$

(c) $P(X = 5|\lambda = 5) = \dfrac{e^{-5}5^5}{5!} = 0.175$

(d) $P(X \geq 5|\lambda = 5) = 1 - P(X = 0|\lambda = 5) - P(X = 1|\lambda = 5) - P(X = 2|\lambda = 5) - P(X = 3|\lambda = 5) - P(X = 4|\lambda = 5)$

$$= 1 - \frac{e^{-5}5^0}{0!} - \frac{e^{-5}5^1}{1!} - \frac{e^{-5}5^2}{2!} - \frac{e^{-5}5^3}{3!} - \frac{e^{-5}5^4}{4!} = 1 - 0.00674 - 0.0337 - 0.084224 - 0.140374 - 0.175 = 0.560$$

(e) As the area of opportunity increases by a factor of 5, the average number of successes per area of opportunity increases 5 times as well (assuming that the average number of successes per unit area does not change). Note, however, that the increase in the number of all the combinations that lead to successes is *less* than the increase in the number of all of the combinations that do not result in successes.

chapter 5

Continuous Probability Distributions and Sampling Distributions

1. (a) $f(x)=\dfrac{1}{b-a}=\dfrac{1}{10-0}=0.1$

(1) $P(5<x<7)=0.1\times(7-5)=0.1\times 2=0.2$

(2) $P(2<x<3)=0.1\times(3-2)=0.1\times 1=0.1$

(b) $\mu=\dfrac{a+b}{2}=\dfrac{10+0}{2}=\dfrac{10}{2}=5.0$

(c) $\sigma^2=\dfrac{(b-a)^2}{12}=\dfrac{10^2}{12}=8.33$, $\sigma=\sqrt{8.33}=2.887$

2. (a) $f(x)=\dfrac{1}{b-a}=\dfrac{1}{2-0}=0.5$

(1) $P(x<0.6)=0.5\times(0.6-0)=0.3$

(2) $P(0.4<x<1.6)=0.5\times(1.6-0.4)=0.5\times 1.2=0.6$

(3) $P(x>1.8)=0.5\times(2.0-1.8)=0.5\times 0.2=0.1$

(4) $P(x>2)=0.5\times(2-2)=0$

(b) $\mu=\dfrac{a+b}{2}=\dfrac{2+0}{2}=1.0$

(c) $\sigma^2=\dfrac{(b-a)^2}{12}=\dfrac{2^2}{12}=0.33$, $\sigma=\sqrt{0.33}=0.577$

3. (a) $f(x)=\dfrac{1}{25-10}=\dfrac{1}{15}$

(1) $P(x<20)=\dfrac{1}{15}\times(20-10)=\dfrac{1}{15}\times 10=0.667$

(2) $P(20<x<22)=\dfrac{1}{15}\times(22-20)=\dfrac{1}{15}\times 2=0.133$

(b) $P(x>18)=\dfrac{1}{15}\times(25-18)=\dfrac{1}{15}\times 7=0.467$

(c) $\mu=\dfrac{a+b}{2}=\dfrac{25+10}{2}=\dfrac{35}{2}=17.5$

(d) $\sigma^2=\dfrac{(b-a)^2}{12}=\dfrac{15^2}{12}=18.75$, $\sigma=\sqrt{18.75}=4.33$

4. (a) $f(x)=\dfrac{1}{0.5-0}=2.0$

(1) $P(x<0.2)=0.2\times(0.2-0)=0.4$

(2) $P(0.1<x<0.3)=2.0\times(0.3-0.1)=2.0\times 0.2=0.4$

(3) $P(x>0.35)=2.0\times(0.5-0.35)=2.0\times 0.15=0.3$

(b) $\mu=\dfrac{a+b}{2}=\dfrac{0.5+0}{2}=0.25$

(c) $\sigma^2=\dfrac{(b-a)^2}{12}=\dfrac{0.5^2}{12}=0.021$, $\sigma=\sqrt{0.021}=0.144$

5. 24-hours $=24\times 60=1{,}440$ min, therefore $f(x)=\dfrac{1}{1440}=6.94\times 10^{-4}$

(a) 5:55 A.M. $=5\times 60+55=355$ min

7:38 P.M. $=19\times 60+38=1178$ min

$P(355<x<1{,}178)=\dfrac{1}{1{,}440}\times(1178-355)=\dfrac{1}{1{,}440}\times 823=0.5715$

(b) 10 P.M. $= 22\times 60 = 1{,}320$ min

5 A.M $= 5\times 60 = 300$ min

$P(10 \text{ P.M} < x < 5 \text{ A.M.}) = P(10 \text{ P.M.} < x < 12 \text{ P.M.}) + P(0 \text{ A.M.} < x < 5 \text{ A.M.}) = P(1{,}320 < x < 1440) + P(0 < x < 300)$

$= \frac{1}{1{,}440}\times 120 + \frac{1}{1{,}440}\times 300 = 0.0833 + 0.208 = 0.291$

(c) P (a failure will be detected within 10 minutes of its occurrence)

$= P(50 < x < 60) + P(110 < x < 120) + P(170 < x < 180) + \ldots + P(1{,}430 < x < 1{,}440)$

$= \frac{1}{1{,}440}\times 10 + \frac{1}{1{,}440}\times 10 + \frac{1}{1{,}440}\times 10 + \ldots + \frac{1}{1{,}440}\times 10$

$= 24\times\frac{1}{1{,}440}\times 10 = 0.167$

(d) P(it will take at least 40 minutes to detect that a failure has occurred)

$= P(0 < x < 20) + P(60 < x < 80) + P(120 < x < 140) + \ldots + P(1380 < x < 1400)$

$= \frac{1}{1{,}440}\times 20 + \frac{1}{1{,}440}\times 20 + \frac{1}{1{,}440}\times 20 + \ldots + \frac{1}{1{,}440}\times 20 = 24\times\frac{1}{1{,}440}\times 20 = 0.333$

6. (a) (1) $P(0 < Z < 1) = 0.3413 - 0 = 0.3413$

(2) $P(1.25 < Z < 1.75) = P(0 < Z < 1.75) - P(0 < Z < 1.25) = 0.4599 - 0.3944 = 0.0655$

(3) $P(-1.55 < Z < 1.55) = P(-1.55 < Z < 0) + P(0 < Z < 1.55) = 0.4394 + 0.4394 = 0.8788$

(4) $P(Z < -2.0) = P(Z > 2.0) = P(Z > 0) - P(0 < Z < 2) = 0.5 - 0.4772 = 0.0228$

(5) $P(Z > -1.0) = 0.5 + P(-1.0 < Z < 0) = 0.5 + 0.3413 = 0.8413$

(6) $P(Z < -2.0 \text{ or } Z > 1.0) = P(Z < -2.0) + P(Z > 1.0) = P(Z < 0) - P(0 < Z < -2.0) + P(Z > 0) - P(0 < Z < 1.0)$

$= 0.5 - 0.4772 + 0.5 - 0.3413 = 0.1815$

(b) 80% of the values exceed Z; 20% are less than Z, therefore Z is negative. If 20% of the values are below Z, then 30% of all the values must fall between Z and 0; subsequently the area between Z and 0 is 0.30, and $Z = -0.84$.

(c) Only 5% of the values exceed Z, therefore Z is positive. If 5% of the values are above Z then 45% of all the values must fall between Z and 0; subsequently the area between Z and 0 is 0.45, and $Z = 1.64$.

(d) The values of Z are symmetrically distributed around the mean, so 45% of all values fall between $-Z$ and 0 and 45% of all values fall between 0 and $+Z$. Therefore $Z^{\text{Lower}} = -1.65$, $Z^{\text{Upper}} = 1.65$.

7. (a) (1) $P(-2 < Z < 0) = P(0 < Z < 2) = 0.4772$

(2) $P(-1.25 < Z < 2.25) = P(-1.25 < Z < 0) + P(0 < Z < 2.25) = 0.3944 + 0.4878 = 0.8822$

(3) $P(-1.75 < Z < 1.75) = P(-1.75 < Z < 0) + P(0 < Z < 1.75) = 0.4599 + 0.4599 = 0.9198$

(4) $P(Z < -1.50) = P(Z < 0) - P(-1.50 < Z < 0) = 0.5 - 0.4332 = 0.0668$

(5) $P(Z > -1.50) = P(Z > 0) + P(-1.50 < Z < 0) = 0.5 + 0.4332 = 0.9332$

(6) $P(Z < -1.0 \text{ or } Z > 1.50) = P(Z < -1.0) + P(Z > 1.5) = P(Z < 0) - P(-1.0 < Z < 0) + P(Z > 0) - P(0 < Z < 1.5)$

$= 0.5 - 0.3413 + 0.5 - 0.4332 = 0.2255$

(7) $P(Z < -3.0 \text{ or } Z > 3.0) = P(Z < -3.0) + P(Z > 3.0) = P(Z < 0) - P(-3.0 < Z < 0) + P(Z > 0) - P(0 < Z < 3.0)$

$= 0.5 - 0.49865 + 0.5 - 0.49865 = 0.0027$

(b) 90% of the values exceed Z, 10% are less than Z; therefore Z is negative. If 10% of the values are below Z then 40% of all the values must fall between Z and 0; therefore the area between Z and 0 is 0.40, and $Z = -1.28$.

(c) Only 1% of the values exceed Z, therefore Z is positive. If 1% of the values are above Z then 49% of all the values must fall between Z and 0; subsequently the area between Z and 0 is 0.49, and $Z = 2.33$.

(d) The values of Z are symmetrically distributed around the mean, so 49.5% of all values fall between $-Z$ and 0 and 49.5% of all values fall between 0 and $+Z$. Therefore $Z^{\text{Lower}} = -2.58$, $Z^{\text{Upper}} = 2.58$.

8. (a) $P(-2 < Z < 0) + P(0 < Z < 2) = 0.4772 + 0.4772 = 0.9544$
(b) $P(-3 < Z < 0) + (0 < Z < 3) = 0.49865 + 0.49865 = 0.9973$

9. Mean 4.7 ounces
Standard Deviation 0.4 ounces

(a) (1) $Z = \frac{X - \mu_x}{\sigma_x} = \frac{5.00 - 4.70}{0.40} = 0.75$, $P(4.7 < X < 5) = 0.2734$

(2) $Z = \frac{X - \mu_x}{\sigma_x} = \frac{5.00 - 4.70}{0.40} = 0.75$, $P(X < 5) = P(X < 4.7) + P(4.7 < X < 5) = 0.5 + 0.2734 = 0.7734$,

$Z = \frac{X - \mu_x}{\sigma_x} = \frac{5.50 - 4.70}{0.40} = 2$, $P(X < 5.5) = P(X < 4.7) + P(4.7 < X < 5.5) = 0.5 + 0.4772 = 0.9772$,

$P(5 < X < 5.5) = P(X < 5.5) - P(X < 5) = 0.9772 - 0.7734 = 0.2038$

(3) $Z = \frac{X - \mu_x}{\sigma_x} = \frac{4.00 - 4.70}{0.40} = -1.75$, $P(X < 4) = P(X < 4.7) - P(4 < X < 4.7) = 0.5 - 0.4599 = 0.0401$,

$Z = \frac{X - \mu_x}{\sigma_x} = \frac{5.00 - 4.70}{0.40} = 0.75$, $P(X < 5) = P(X < 4.7) + P(4.7 < X < 5) = 0.5 + 0.2734 = 0.7734$,

$P(4 < X < 5) = P(X < 5) - P(X < 4) = 0.7734 - 0.0401 = 0.7333$

(4) $Z = \frac{X - \mu_x}{\sigma_x} = \frac{4.00 - 4.70}{0.40} = -1.75$, $P(X > 4) = P(4 < X < 4.7) + P(X > 4.7) = 0.4599 + 0.5 = 0.9599$

(5) $Z = \frac{X - \mu_x}{\sigma_x} = \frac{5.00 - 4.70}{0.40} = 0.75$, $P(X > 5) = P(X > 4.7) - P(4.7 < X < 5) = 0.5 - 0.2734 = 0.2266$

(b) 77% of all the values exceed *X*, therefore *X* is below the mean and *Z* is negative. If 23% of the values are below *X*, then 27% of all the values must fall between *X* and the mean; subsequently, the area between the mean and *X* is 0.27, and $Z = -0.74$. $X = \mu_x + z\sigma_x = 4.7 - 0.74 \times 0.40 = 4.404$

(c) The values of *X* are symmetrically distributed around the mean, so 45% of all values fall between X_L and the mean and 45% of all values fall between the mean and X_U. Therefore $Z_{\text{Lower}} = 1.65$, $Z_{\text{Upper}} = 1.65$.
$X_L = 4.70 - 1.65 \times 0.40 = 4.04$, $X_U = 4.70 + 1.65 \times 0.40 = 5.36$

10. Mean = 2 liters
Standard deviation = 0.05 liter

(a) (1) $Z = \frac{X - \mu_x}{\sigma_x} = \frac{1.9 - 2.0}{0.05} = -2.0$, $P(1.9 < X < 2) = 0.4772$

(2) $Z = \frac{X - \mu_x}{\sigma_x} = \frac{1.9 - 2.0}{0.05} = -2.0$, $P(X < 1.9) = P(X < 2.0) - P(1.9 < X < 2.0) = 0.5 - 0.4772 = 0.0228$,

$Z = \frac{X - \mu_x}{\sigma_x} = \frac{2.1 - 2.0}{0.05} = 2.0$, $P(X < 2.1) = P(X < 2.0) + P(2.0 < X < 2.1) = 0.5 + 0.4772 = 0.9772$,

$P(1.9 < X < 2.1) = P(X < 2.1) - P(X < 1.9) = 0.9772 - 0.0228 = 0.9544$

(3) $Z = \frac{X - \mu_x}{\sigma_x} = \frac{1.9 - 2.0}{0.05} = -2.0$, $P(X < 1.9) = P(X < 2.0) - P(1.9 < X < 2.0) = 0.5 - 0.4772 = 0.0228$

(4) $Z = \frac{X - \mu_x}{\sigma_x} = \frac{1.9 - 2.0}{0.05} = -2.0$, $P(X < 1.9) = P(X < 2.0) - P(1.9 < X < 2.0) = 0.5 - 0.4772 = 0.0228$,

$Z = \frac{X - \mu_x}{\sigma_x} = \frac{2.1 - 2.0}{0.05} = 2.0$, $P(X > 2.1) = P(X < 2.0) - P(2.0 < X < 2.1) = 0.5 - 0.4772 = 0.0228$,

$P(X \Leftarrow 1.9 \text{ or } X > 2.1) = P(X < 1.9) + P(X > 2.1) = 0.0228 + 0.0228 = 0.0456$

(5) $Z = \dfrac{X-\mu_x}{\sigma_x} = \dfrac{2.1-2.0}{0.05} = 2.0$, $P(X > 2.1) = P(X > 2.0) - P(2.0 < X < 2.1) = 0.5 - 0.4772 = 0.0228$

(6) $Z = \dfrac{X-\mu_x}{\sigma_x} = \dfrac{2.05-2.0}{0.05} = 1$, $P(X < 2.05) = P(X < 2.0) + P(2.0 < X < 2.05) = 0.5 + 0.3413 = 0.8413$,

$Z = \dfrac{X-\mu_x}{\sigma_x} = \dfrac{2.1-2.0}{0.05} = 2.0$, $P(X < 2.1) = P(X < 2.0) + P(2.0 < X < 2.1) = 0.5 + 0.4772 = 0.9772$,

$P(2.05 < X < 2.1) = P(X < 2.1) - P(X < 2.05) = 0.9772 - 0.8413 = 0.1359$

(b) 99% of all values exceed X, so only 1% of the values is less than X, therefore X is below the mean and Z is negative. The fact that 1% of values is below X tells us that 49% of all the values fall between X and the mean; thus the area between X and the mean is 0.49, therefore $Z = -2.33$, $X = \mu_x + Z\sigma_x = 2.0 - 2.33 \times 0.05 = 1.8835$

(c) The values of X are symmetrically distributed around the mean, so 49.5% of all values fall between X_L and the mean and 49.5% of all the values fall between the mean and X_U. Therefore $Z_{\text{Lower}} = -2.58$, $Z_{\text{Upper}} = 2.58$,

$X_L = 2.0 - 2.58 \times 0.05 = 1.871$, $X_U = 2.0 + 2.58 \times 0.05 = 2.129$

(d) The cumulative distribution function in part (b) calculated a value of X such that the area under the curve between it and the largest possible value of X equals 0.99. However in part (c) we are looking for the value of X such that the area under the curve between $-X$ and $+X$ is equal to 0.99.

(e) Mean 2.02
Standard Deviation 0.05

(a) (1) $Z = \dfrac{X-\mu_x}{\sigma_x} = \dfrac{1.90-2.02}{0.05} = -2.4$, $P(X < 1.9) = P(X < 2.02) - P(1.9 < X < 2.02) = 0.5 - 0.4918 = 0.0082$,

$Z = \dfrac{X-\mu_x}{\sigma_x} = \dfrac{2.0-2.02}{0.05} = -0.4$, $P(X < 2.0) = P(X < 2.02) - P(2.0 < X < 2.02) = 0.5 - 0.1554 = 0.3446$,

$P(1.9 < X < 2.0) = P(X < 2.0) - P(X < 1.9) = 0.3446 - 0.0082 = 0.3364$

(2) $Z = \dfrac{X-\mu_x}{\sigma_x} = \dfrac{1.90-2.02}{0.05} = -2.4$, $P(X < 1.9) = P(X < 2.02) - P(1.9 < X < 2.02) = 0.5 - 0.4918 = 0.0082$,

$Z = \dfrac{X-\mu_x}{\sigma_x} = \dfrac{2.1-2.02}{0.05} = 1.6$, $P(X < 2.1) = P(X < 2.02) + P(2.02 < X < 2.1) = 0.5 + 0.4452 = 0.9452$,

$P(1.9 < X < 2.1) = P(X < 2.1) - P(X < 1.9) = 0.9452 - 0.0082 = 0.937$

(3) $Z = \dfrac{X-\mu_x}{\sigma_x} = \dfrac{1.90-2.02}{0.05} = -2.4$, $P(X < 1.9) = P(X < 2.02) - P(1.9 < X < 2.02) = 0.5 - 0.4918 = 0.0082$

(4) $Z = \dfrac{X-\mu_x}{\sigma_x} = \dfrac{1.90-2.02}{0.05} = -2.4$, $P(X < 1.9) = P(X < 2.02) - P(1.9 < X < 2.02) = 0.5 - 0.4918 = 0.0082$,

$Z = \dfrac{X-\mu_x}{\sigma_x} = \dfrac{2.1-2.02}{0.05} = 1.6$, $P(X > 2.1) = P(X < 2.02) - P(2.02 < X < 2.1) = 0.5 - 0.4452 = 0.0548$,

$P(X \leq 1.9 \text{ or } X > 2.1) = P(X < 1.9) + P(X > 2.1) = 0.0082 + 0.0548 = 0.0630$

(5) $Z = \dfrac{X-\mu_x}{\sigma_x} = \dfrac{2.1-2.02}{0.05} = 1.6$, $P(X > 2.1) = P(X > 2.02) - P(2.02 < X < 2.1) = 0.5 - 0.4452 = 0.0548$

(6) $Z = \dfrac{X-\mu_x}{\sigma_x} = \dfrac{2.05-2.02}{0.05} = 0.6$, $P(X < 2.05) = P(X < 2.02) + P(2.02 < X < 2.05) = 0.5 + 0.2257 = 0.7257$,

$Z = \dfrac{X-\mu_x}{\sigma_x} = \dfrac{2.1-2.02}{0.05} = 1.6$, $P(X < 2.1) = P(X < 2.02) + P(2.0 < X < 2.1) = 0.5 + 0.4452 = 0.9452$,

$P(2.05 < X < 2.1) = 0.9452 - 0.7257 = 0.2195$

(b) 99% of all values exceed *X*, 1% of the values are less than *X*'s therefore *X* is below the mean and *Z* is negative. If 1% of the values is below *X* then 49% of all the values must fall between *X* and the mean; subsequently the area between *X* and the mean is 0.49, and $Z = -2.33$. $X = \mu_x + Z\sigma_x = 2.02 - 2.33 \times 0.05 = 1.9035$. The values of *X* are symmetrically distributed around the mean, so 49.5% of all values fall between X_L and the mean and 49.5% of all values fall between the mean and X_U. Therefore $Z_{\text{Lower}} = -2.58$ and $Z_{\text{Upper}} = 2.58$, $X_L = 2.02 - 2.58 \times 0.05 = 1.891$, $X_U = 2.02 + 2.58 \times 0.05 = 2.149$

11. (a) Mean 575 mm
Standard Deviation 5 mm

(1) $Z = \frac{X - \mu_x}{\sigma_x} = \frac{579 - 575}{5} = 0.8$, $P(575 < X < 579) = 0.2881$

(2) $Z = \frac{X - \mu_x}{\sigma_x} = \frac{572 - 575}{5} = -0.6$, $P(X < 572) = P(X < 575)\ P(572 < X < 575) = 0.5 - 0.2257 = 0.2743$,

$Z = \frac{X - \mu_x}{\sigma_x} = \frac{580 - 575}{5} = 1$, $P(X < 580) = P(X < 575) + P(575 < X < 580) = 0.5 + 0.3413 = 0.8413$,

$P(572 < X < 580) = P(X < 580) - P(X < 572) = 0.8413 - 0.2743 = 0.5670$

(3) $Z = \frac{X - \mu_x}{\sigma_x} = \frac{570 - 575}{5} = -1$, $P(X > 570) = P(570 < X < 575) + P(X > 575) = 0.3413 + 0.5 = 0.8413$

(4) $Z = \frac{X - \mu_x}{\sigma_x} = \frac{580 - 575}{5} = 1$, $P(X < 580) = P(X < 575) + P(575 < X < 580) = 0.5 + 0.3413 = 0.8413$

(b) 80% of all the values exceed *X*, therefore *X* is below the mean and *Z* is negative. If 20% of the values are below *X* then 30% of all the values must fall between the mean and *X*; subsequently the area between the mean and *X* is 0.30, and $Z = -0.84$. $X = \mu_x + Z\sigma_x = 575 - 0.84 \times 5 = 570.8$

(c) The values of *X* are symmetrically distributed around the mean, so 40% of all the values fall between X_L and mean and 40% of all values fall between the mean and X_U. Therefore $Z_{\text{Lower}} = -1.28$ and $Z_{\text{Upper}} = 1.28$.
$X_L = 575 - 1.28 \times 5 = 568.6$, $X_U = 575 + 1.28 \times 5 = 581.4$

(d) The cumulative distribution function in part (b) calculated a value of *X* such that the area under the curve between it and the largest possible value of *X* equals 0.8. However in part (c) we are looking for the value of *X* such that the area under the curve between –*X* and +*X* equals 0.8.

(e) Mean 575
Standard Deviation 0.04

(a) Using PHStat we obtain:

(1)	*Z* Value for 575	0
	Z Value for 579	100
	$P(X \le 575)$	0.5
	$P(X \le 579)$	1
	$P(575 \le X \le 579)$	0.5
(2)	*Z* Value for 572	–75
	Z Value for 580	125
	$P(X \le 572)$	0
	$P(X \le 580)$	1
	$P(572 \le X \le 580)$	1
(3)	*Z* Value	–125
	$P(X > 570)$	1
(4)	*Z* Value	125
	$P(X \le 580)$	1

(b) 80% of all the values exceed X, therefore X is below the mean and Z is negative. If 20% of the values are below X then 30% of all the values must fall between the mean and X; subsequently the area between the mean and X is 0.30, and $Z = -0.84$. $X = \mu_x + Z\sigma_x = 575 - 0.84 \times 0.04 = 574.9664$.

(c) The values of X are symmetrically distributed around the mean, so 40% of all the values fall between X_L and the mean and 40% of all values fall between the mean and X_U. Therefore $Z_{\text{Lower}} = -1.28$ and $Z_{\text{Upper}} = 1.28$. $X_L = 575 - 1.28 \times 0.04 = 574.9488$, $X_U = 575 + 1.28 \times 0.04 = 575.0512$. The cumulative distribution function in part (b) calculated a value of X such that the area under the curve between it and the largest possible value of X equals 0.8. However in part (c) we are looking for the value of X such that the area under the curve between $-X$ and $+X$ equals 0.8.

Mean	575
Standard Deviation	4
(1) Z Value for 575	0
Z Value for 579	1
$P(X \le 575)$	0.5
$P(X \le 579)$	0.841
$P(575 \le X \le 579)$	0.341
(2) Z Value for 572	–0.75
Z Value for 580	1.25
$P(X \le 572)$	0.2266
$P(X \le 580)$	0.8943
$P(572 \le X \le 580)$	0.6677
(3) Z Value	–1.25
$P(X > 570)$	0.8943
(4) Z Value	1.25
$P(X \le 580)$	0.8943

(d) 80% of all the values exceed X, therefore X is below the mean and Z is negative. If 20% of the values are below X then 30% of all the values must fall between the mean and X; subsequently the area between the mean and X is 0.30, and $Z = -0.84$. $X = \mu_x + Z\sigma_x = 575 - 0.84 \times 4 = 571.64$

(e) The values of X are symmetrically distributed around the mean, so 40% of all the values fall between X_L and mean and 40% of all the values fall between the mean and X_U. Therefore $Z_{\text{Lower}} = -1.28$ and $Z_{\text{Upper}} = 1.28$.
$X_L = 575 - 1.28 \times 4 = 569.88$, $X_U = 575 + 1.28 \times 4 = 580.12$

12. Mean 22.002
Standard Deviation 0.005

(a) $Z = \dfrac{X - \mu_x}{\sigma_x} = \dfrac{21.900 - 22.002}{0.005} = -20.4$, $P(X < 21.9) = 0$

$Z = \dfrac{X - \mu_x}{\sigma_x} = \dfrac{22.000 - 22.002}{0.005} = -0.4$

$P(X < 22.000) = P(X < 22.002) - P(22.000 < x < 22.002) = 0.5 - 0.1554 = 0.3446$

$P(21.9 < X < 22.0) = P(X < 22.0) - P(X < 21.9) = 0.3446$

Thus 34.46% of all shafts will have diameters between 21.90 and 22.00, while 65.54% of all shafts will have diameters less than 21.90 or more than 22.00.

(b) $Z = \frac{X-\mu_x}{\sigma_x} = \frac{21.900-22.002}{0.005} = -20.4$, $P(X < 21.9) = 0$

$Z = \frac{X-\mu_x}{\sigma_x} = \frac{22.010-22.002}{0.005} = 1.6$

$P(X < 22.01) = P(X < 22.002) + P(22.002 < X < 22.01) = 0.5 + 0.4452 = 0.9452$

$P(21.9 < X < 22.01) = P(X < 22.01) - P(X < 21.9) = 0.9452 - 0 = 0.9452$

(c) Only 2% of the values exceed X, therefore X is above the mean and Z is positive. If 2% of the values are above X then 48% of all the values must fall between X and the mean; subsequently the area between X and the mean is 0.48, and $Z = 2.05$.

$X = \mu_x + Z\sigma_x = 22.002 + 2.05 \times 0.005 = 22.01225$

(d) Using PHStat we obtain

Z Value for 21.9	–0.1016
Z Value for 22	–0.0020
$P(X \le 21.9)$	0.4595
$P(X \le 22)$	0.4992
$P(21.9 \le X \le 22)$	0.0397

Thus 3.97% of all shafts will have diameters between 21.90 and 22.00, while 96.03% of all shafts will have diameters less than 21.90 or more than 22.00.

Z Value for 21.9	–0.1016
Z Value for 22.01	0.0080
$P(X \le 21.9)$	0.4595
$P(X \le 22.01)$	0.5032
$P(21.9 \le X \le 22.01)$	0.0436

Z Value	2.0537
X Value	24.0640

13. Mean 80
Standard Deviation 20

(a) $Z = \frac{X-\mu_x}{\sigma_x} = \frac{77-80}{20} = -0.15$, $P(X < 77) = P(X < 80) - P(77 < X < 80) = 0.5 - 0.0596 = 0.4404$

(b) $Z = \frac{X-\mu_x}{\sigma_x} = \frac{74-80}{20} = -0.3$, $P(X < 74) = P(X < 80) = P(74 < X < 80) = 0.5 - 0.1179 = 0.3821$

$Z = \frac{X-\mu_x}{\sigma_x} = \frac{84-80}{20} = 0.2$

$P(X < 84) = P(X < 80) + P(80 < X < 84) = 0.5 + 0.0792 = 0.5793$

$P(74 < X < 84) = P(X < 84) - P(X < 74) = 0.5793 - 0.3821 = 0.1972$

(c) 25% of the values exceed X, therefore X is above the mean and Z is positive. If 25% of the values are above X then 25% of all the values must fall between X and the mean; subsequently the area between X and the mean is 0.25, and $Z = 0.67$.

$X = \mu_x + Z\sigma_x = 80 + 0.67 \times 20 = 93.4.$

14. Mean 6000 psi
Standard Deviation 240 psi

(a) $Z = \frac{X-\mu_x}{\sigma_x} = \frac{5500-6000}{240} = -2.08$, $P(X < 5500) = P(X < 6000) - P(5500 < X < 6000) = 0.5 - 0.4812 = 0.0188$

$Z = \frac{X-\mu_x}{\sigma_x} = \frac{6500-6000}{240} = 2.08$

$P(X<6500)=P(X<6000)+P(6000<X<6500)=0.5+0.4812=0.9812$

$P(5500<X<6500)=0.9812-0.0188=0.9624$

(b) $Z=\dfrac{X-\mu_x}{\sigma_x}=\dfrac{5000-6000}{240}=-4.17$, $P(X<5000)=P(X<6000)-P(5000<X<6000)=0$

$Z=\dfrac{X-\mu_x}{\sigma_x}=\dfrac{5900-6000}{240}=-0.42$

$P(X<5900)=P(X<6000)-P(5000<X<5900)=0.5-0.1628=0.3372$

$P(5000<X<5900)=P(X<5900)-P(X<5000)=0.3372-0=0.3372$

(c) $Z=\dfrac{X-\mu_x}{\sigma_x}=\dfrac{6750-6000}{240}=3.125$, $P(X<6750)=P(X<6000)+P(6000<X<6750)=0.5+0.49910=0.99910$

(d) $Z=\dfrac{X-\mu_x}{\sigma_x}=\dfrac{5800-6000}{240}=-0.83$, $P(X<5800)=P(X<6000)-P(5000<X<5800)=0.5-0.2963=0.2037$

(e) X exceeds 20% of all the values, therefore X is below the mean and Z is negative. If 20% of the values are below X then 30% of all the values must fall between X and the mean; subsequently the area between X and the mean is 0.30, therefore $Z=-0.84$.
$X=\mu_x+Z\sigma_x=6000-0.84\times 240=5798.4$

(f) 70% of all the values exceed X, therefore X is below the mean and Z is negative. If 30% of values are below X then 20% of all the values must fall between X and the mean; thus the area between X and the mean is 0.20, and $Z=0.52$.
$X=\mu_x+Z\sigma_x=6000-0.52\times 240=5875.2$

(g) Only 15% of all the values exceed X, therefore X is above the mean and Z is positive. If 15% of the values are below X then 35% of all the values must fall between X and the mean; subsequently the area between X and the mean is 0.35, therefore $Z=1.04$.
$X=\mu_x+Z\sigma_x=6000+1.04\times 240=6249.6$

15. $\mu_x=500\times 0.04=20$, $\sigma_x^2=np(1-p)=500\times 0.04(1-0.04)=19.2$

Because the variance is greater than 10, the normal distribution can be used to approximate the binomial distribution.

(a) $Z=\dfrac{X-np}{\sqrt{np(1-p)}}=\dfrac{10-500\times 0.04}{\sqrt{500\times 0.04(1-0.04)}}=-2.28$, $P(X<10)=P(X<20)-P(10<X<20)=0.5-0.4887=0.0113$

(b) $Z=\dfrac{X-np}{\sqrt{np(1-p)}}=\dfrac{15-500\cdot 0.04}{\sqrt{500\cdot 0.04(1-0.04)}}=-1.14$, $P(X<15)=P(X<20)-P(15<X<20)=0.5-0.3729=0.1271$

$Z=\dfrac{X-np}{\sqrt{np(1-p)}}=\dfrac{25-500\times 0.04}{\sqrt{500\times 0.04(1-0.04)}}=1.14$

$P(X<25)=P(X<20)+P(20<X<25)=0.5+0.3729=0.8729$

$P(15<X<25)=P(X<25)-P(X<15)=0.8729-0.1271=0.7458$

(c) $Z=\dfrac{X-np}{\sqrt{np(1-p)}}=\dfrac{15-500\cdot 0.04}{\sqrt{500\cdot 0.04(1-0.04)}}=-1.14$, $P(X>15)=P(15<X<20)+P(X<20)=0.3729+0.5=0.8729$

16. $p=\dfrac{1}{4}=0.25$, $\mu_x=100\times 0.25=25$, $\sigma_x^2=np(1-p)=100\times 0.25(1-0.25)=18.75$

Because the variance is greater than 10, the normal distribution can be used to approximate the binomial distribution.

(a) $Z=\dfrac{X-np}{\sqrt{np(1-p)}}=\dfrac{30-100\cdot 0.25}{\sqrt{100\cdot 0.25(1-0.25)}}=1.15$, $P(X>30)=P(X<25)-P(25<X<30)=0.5-0.3749=0.1251$

(b) $Z=\dfrac{X-np}{\sqrt{np(1-p)}}=\dfrac{20-100\cdot 0.25}{\sqrt{100\cdot 0.25(1-0.25)}}=-1.15$, $P(X<20)=P(X<25)-P(20<X<25)=0.5-0.3749=0.1251$

(c) $Z = \dfrac{X - np}{\sqrt{np(1-p)}} = \dfrac{15 - 100 \cdot 0.25}{\sqrt{100 \cdot 0.25(1-0.25)}} = -2.31$, $P(X < 15) = P(X < 25) - P(15 < X < 25) = 0.5 - 0.4896 = 0.0104$

$Z = \dfrac{X - np}{\sqrt{np(1-p)}} = \dfrac{35 - 100 \cdot 0.25}{\sqrt{100 \cdot 0.25(1-0.25)}} = 2.31$

$P(X < 35) = P(X < 25) + P(35 < X < 30) = 0.5 + 0.4896 = 0.9896$

$P(15 < X < 35) = P(X < 35) - P(X < 15) = 0.9896 - 0.0104 = 0.9792$

(d) $Z = \dfrac{X - np}{\sqrt{np(1-p)}} = \dfrac{60 - 100 \cdot 0.25}{\sqrt{100 \cdot 0.25(1-0.25)}} = 8.08$, $P(X > 60) = 0$

17. $\mu_x = 50 \times 0.7 = 35$, $\sigma_x^2 = np(1-p) = 50 \times 0.7(1 - 0.7) = 10.5$

Because the variance is greater than 10, the normal distribution can be used to approximate the binomial distribution.

(a) $Z = \dfrac{X - np}{\sqrt{np(1-p)}} = \dfrac{25 - 50 \cdot 0.70}{\sqrt{50 \cdot 0.70(1-0.70)}} = -3.08$, $P(X > 25) = P(25 < X < 35) + P(X > 35) = 0.49897 + 0.5 = 0.99897$

(b) $Z = \dfrac{X - np}{\sqrt{np(1-p)}} = \dfrac{40 - 50 \cdot 0.70}{\sqrt{50 \cdot 0.70(1-0.70)}} = 1.54$, $P(X > 40) = P(X > 35) - P(35 < X < 40) = 0.5 - 0.4382 = 0.0618$

(c) $Z = \dfrac{X - np}{\sqrt{np(1-p)}} = \dfrac{30 - 50 \cdot 0.70}{\sqrt{50 \cdot 0.70(1-0.70)}} = -1.54$, $P(X < 30) = P(X < 35) - P(30 < X < 35) = 0.5 - 0.4382 = 0.0618$

18. $\mu_x = 200 \times 0.9 = 180$, $\sigma_x^2 = np(1-p) = 200 \times 0.9(1 - 0.9) = 18.0$

Because the variance is greater than 10, the normal distribution can be used to approximate the binomial distribution.

(a) $Z = \dfrac{X - np}{\sqrt{np(1-p)}} = \dfrac{190 - 200 \cdot 0.90}{\sqrt{200 \cdot 0.90(1-0.90)}} = 2.36$, $P(X > 190) = P(X > 180) - P(180 < X < 190) = 0.5 - 0.4909 = 0.0091$

(b) $Z = \dfrac{X - np}{\sqrt{np(1-p)}} = \dfrac{175 - 200 \cdot 0.90}{\sqrt{200 \cdot 0.90(1-0.90)}} = -1.18$, $P(X < 175) = P(X < 180) - P(175 < X < 180) = 0.5 - 0.3810 = 0.119$

$Z = \dfrac{X - np}{\sqrt{np(1-p)}} = \dfrac{190 - 200 \cdot 0.90}{\sqrt{200 \cdot 0.90(1-0.90)}} = 2.36$

$P(X < 190) = 0.5 + P(180 < X < 190) = 0.5 + 0.4909 = 0.9909$

$P(175 < X < 190) = P(X < 190) - P(X < 175) = 0.9909 - 0.119 = 0.8719$

(c) $Z = \dfrac{X - np}{\sqrt{np(1-p)}} = \dfrac{185 - 200 \cdot 0.90}{\sqrt{200 \cdot 0.90(1-0.90)}} = 1.18$, $P(X < 185) = P(X < 180) + P(180 < X < 185) = 0.5 + 0.3810 = 0.8810$

19. $\mu_x = \lambda = 50$

Because λ is greater than 5, the normal distribution can be used to approximate the Poisson distribution.

(a) $Z = \dfrac{X - \lambda}{\sqrt{\lambda}} = \dfrac{35 - 50}{\sqrt{50}} = -2.12$, $P(X > 35) = P(35 < X < 50) + P(X > 50) = 0.4830 + 0.5 = 0.9830$

(b) $Z = \dfrac{X - \lambda}{\sqrt{\lambda}} = \dfrac{50 - 50}{\sqrt{50}} = 0$, $P(X > 50) = 0.5$

(c) $Z = \dfrac{X - \lambda}{\sqrt{\lambda}} = \dfrac{40 - 50}{\sqrt{50}} = -1.41$, $P(X < 40) = P(X < 50) - P(40 < X < 50) = 0.50 - 0.4207 = 0.0793$

$Z = \dfrac{X - \lambda}{\sqrt{\lambda}} = \dfrac{60 - 50}{\sqrt{50}} = 1.41$

$P(X < 60) = P(X < 50) + P(50 < X < 60) = 0.5 + 0.4207 = 0.9207$

$P(40 < X < 50) = P(X < 50) - P(X < 40) = 0.9207 - 0.0793 = 0.8414$

20. (a) $\mu_x = \lambda = 15$

Because λ is greater than 5, the normal distribution can be used to approximate the Poisson distribution.

(1) $Z = \frac{X-\lambda}{\sqrt{\lambda}} = \frac{5-15}{\sqrt{15}} = -2.58$, $P(X < 5) = P(X < 15) - P(5 < X < 15) = 0.5 - 0.4951 = 0.0049$

(2) $Z = \frac{X-\lambda}{\sqrt{\lambda}} = \frac{10-15}{\sqrt{15}} = -1.29$, $P(X > 10) = P(10 < X < 15) + P(X > 15) = 0.4015 + 0.5 = 0.9015$

(3) $Z = \frac{X-\lambda}{\sqrt{\lambda}} = \frac{10-15}{\sqrt{15}} = -1.29$, $P(X < 10) = P(X < 15) - P(10 < X < 15) = 0.5 - 0.4015 = 0.0985$

$Z = \frac{X-\lambda}{\sqrt{\lambda}} = \frac{20-15}{\sqrt{15}} = 1.29$

$P(X < 20) = P(X < 15) + P(15 < X < 20) = 0.5 + 0.4015 = 0.9015$

$P(10 < X < 20) = P(X < 20) - P(X < 10) = 0.9015 - 0.0985 = 0.803$

(b) $\sigma_x = \sqrt{\lambda} = \sqrt{15} = 3.873$

21. The length of paper is 50 feet; therefore $\lambda = 1 \times 10 = 10$. Because λ is greater than 5, the normal distribution can be used to approximate the Poisson distribution.

(a) $Z = \frac{X-\lambda}{\sqrt{\lambda}} = \frac{5-10}{\sqrt{10}} = -1.58$, $P(X > 5) = P(5 < X < 10) + P(X > 10) = 0.4429 + 0.5 = 0.9429$

(b) $Z = \frac{X-\lambda}{\sqrt{\lambda}} = \frac{5-10}{\sqrt{10}} = -1.58$, $P(X < 5) = P(X < 10) - P(5 < X < 10) = 0.5 - 0.4429 = 0.0571$

(c) $Z = \frac{X-\lambda}{\sqrt{\lambda}} = \frac{15-10}{\sqrt{10}} = 1.58$

$P(X < 15) = P(X < 10) + P(10 < X < 15) = 0.5 + 0.4429 = 0.9429$

$P(5 < X < 15) = P(X < 15) - P(X < 5) = 0.9429 - 0.0571 = 0.8858$

22. (a)

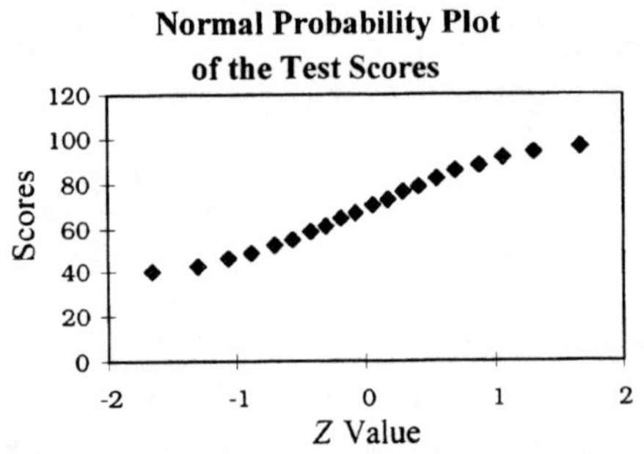

(b) Except for several points at the lower and upper ends of the scale, the plot seems to approximately follow a straight line. The test scores are approximately normally distributed.

23. (a)

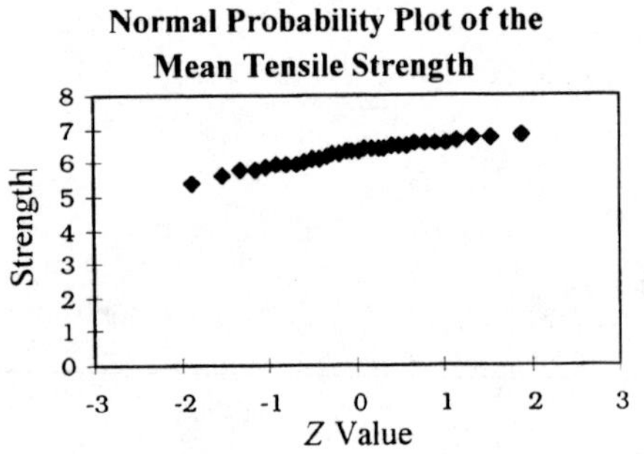

(b) The plot seems to approximately follow a straight line. The mean tensile strength appears to be normally distributed.

24. (a)

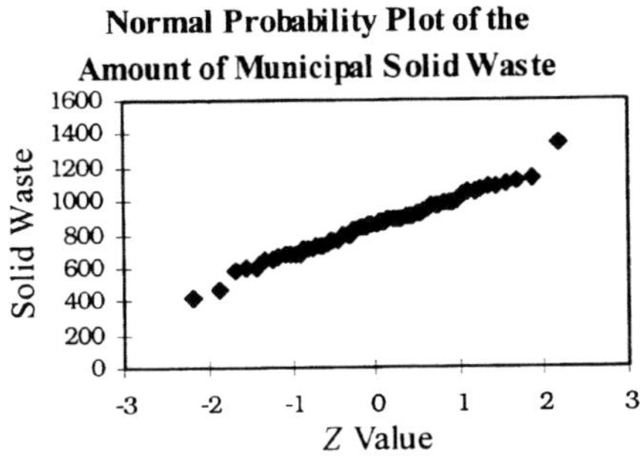

(b) Except for several points at the lower and upper ends of the scale, the plot seems to approximately follow a straight line. The amount of municipal solid waste appears to be approximately normally distributed.

25. (a)

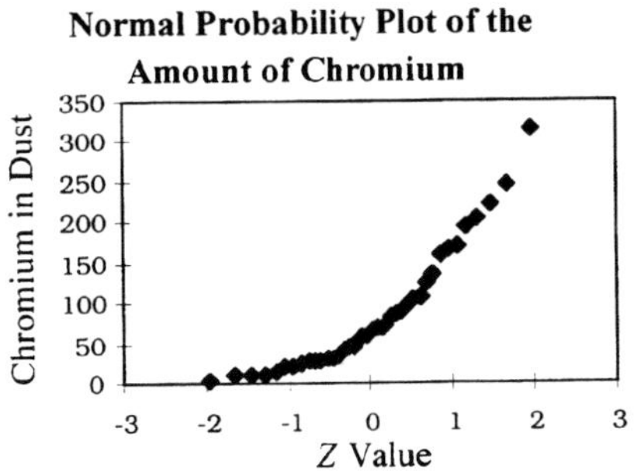

(b) This curve rises more slowly at first, and then the rate of increase grows rapidly. By examining the normal probability plot, it follows that the distribution of the amount of chromium is right-skewed.

26. (a)

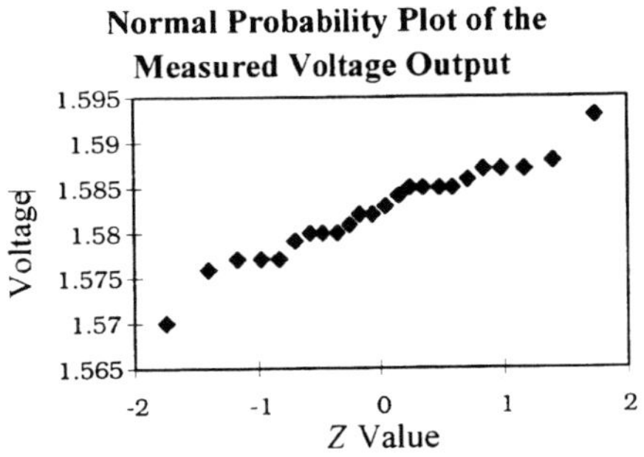

(b) This plot seems to approximately follow a straight line. The voltage output of the batteries appears to be approximately normally distributed.

27. (a)

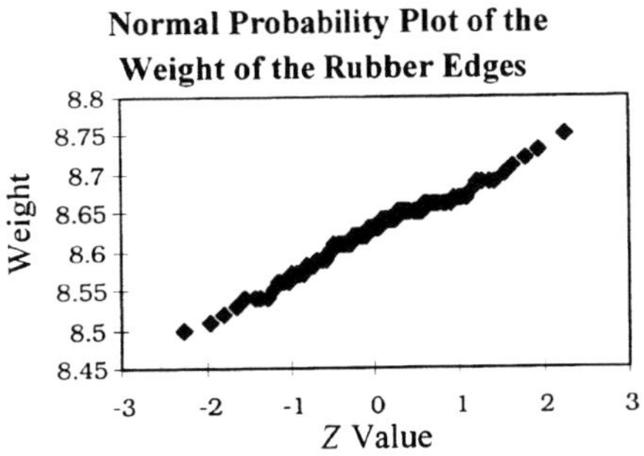

(b) The plot seems to approximately follow a straight line. The weights of the rubber edges appear to be approximately normally distributed.

28. (a) $\mu_x = e^{\mu_{\ln(x)} + \sigma^2_{\ln(x)}/2} = e^{5+4/2} = e^7 = 1096.633$

(b) $\sigma_x = \sqrt{e^{2(5)+4} \cdot (e^4 - 1)} = \sqrt{e^{14} \cdot (e^4 - 1)} = \sqrt{64457365} = 8028.534$

(c) (1) $Z = \frac{\ln(X) - \mu_{\ln(x)}}{\sigma_{\ln(x)}} = \frac{\ln(50) - 5}{2} = -0.54$, $P(X < 50) = 0.5 - 0.254 = 0.2946$

(2) $Z = \frac{\ln(X) - \mu_{\ln(x)}}{\sigma_{\ln(x)}} = \frac{\ln(30) - 5}{2} = -0.8$, $P(X > 30) = 0.5 + 0.2881 = 0.7281$

(3) $Z = \frac{\ln(X) - \mu_{\ln(x)}}{\sigma_{\ln(x)}} = \frac{\ln(30) - 5}{2} = -0.8$, $P(X < 30) = 0.5 - 0.2881 = 0.2119$

$Z = \frac{\ln(X) - \mu_{\ln(x)}}{\sigma_{\ln(x)}} = \frac{\ln(70) - 5}{2} = -0.38$

$P(X < 70) = 0.5 - 0.1480 = 0.3520$

$P(30 < X < 70) = P(X < 70) - P(X < 30) = 0.3520 - 0.2119 = 0.1401$

29. (a) $\mu_x = e^{\mu_{\ln(x)} + \sigma^2_{\ln(x)}/2} = e^{3.1+(1.2)^2/2} = e^{3.82} = 45.60421$

(b) $\sigma_x = \sqrt{e^{2(3.1)+(1.2)^2} \cdot \left(e^{(1.2)^2} - 1\right)} = \sqrt{e^{7.64} \cdot (e^{1.44} - 1)} = \sqrt{6698.222} = 81.84267$

(c) (1) $Z = \frac{\ln(X) - \mu_{\ln(x)}}{\sigma_{\ln(x)}} = \frac{\ln(5) - 3.1}{1.2} = -1.24$, $P(X < 5) = 0.5 - 0.3925 = 0.1075$

(2) $Z = \frac{\ln(X) - \mu_{\ln(x)}}{\sigma_{\ln(x)}} = \frac{\ln(10) - 3.1}{1.2} = -0.66$, $P(X > 10) = 0.5 + 0.2454 = 0.7454$

(3) $Z = \frac{\ln(X) - \mu_{\ln(x)}}{\sigma_{\ln(x)}} = \frac{\ln(5) - 3.1}{1.2} = -1.24$, $P(X < 5) = 0.5 - 0.3925 = 0.1075$

$Z = \frac{\ln(X) - \mu_{\ln(x)}}{\sigma_{\ln(x)}} = \frac{\ln(15) - 3.1}{1.2} = -0.33$

$P(X < 15) = 0.5 - 0.1293 = 0.3707$

$P(5 < X < 15) = P(X < 15) - P(X < 5) = 0.3707 - 0.1075 = 0.2632$

30. (a) $\mu_x = e^{\mu_{\ln(x)} + \sigma^2_{\ln(x)}/2} = e^{1.5+(0.1)^2/2} = e^{1.505} = 4.504154$

(b) $\sigma_x = \sqrt{e^{2(1.5)+(0.1)^2} \cdot \left(e^{(0.1)^2} - 1\right)} = \sqrt{e^{3.01} \cdot (e^{0.01} - 1)} = \sqrt{0.203892} = 0.451544$

(c) (1) $Z = \frac{\ln(X) - \mu_{\ln(x)}}{\sigma_{\ln(x)}} = \frac{\ln(1) - 1.5}{0.1} = -15$, $P(X < 1) = 0$

(2) $Z = \frac{\ln(X) - \mu_{\ln(x)}}{\sigma_{\ln(x)}} = \frac{\ln(2) - 1.5}{0.1} = -8.07$, $P(X > 2) = 1$

(3) $Z = \frac{\ln(X) - \mu_{\ln(x)}}{\sigma_{\ln(x)}} = \frac{\ln(1) - 1.5}{0.1} = -15$, $P(X < 1) = 0$

$Z = \frac{\ln(X) - \mu_{\ln(x)}}{\sigma_{\ln(x)}} = \frac{\ln(2) - 1.5}{0.1} = -8.07$

$P(X < 2) = 3.33067 \times 10^{-16}$

$P(1 < X < 2) = 3.33067 \times 10^{-16}$

31. (a) $\mu_x = e^{\mu_{\ln(x)} + \sigma^2_{\ln(x)}/2} = e^{2.5+(0.5)^2/2} = e^{2.625} = 13.80457$

(b) $\sigma_x = \sqrt{e^{2(2.5)+(0.5)^2} \cdot \left(e^{(0.5)^2} - 1\right)} = \sqrt{e^{5.25} \cdot (e^{0.25} - 1)} = \sqrt{54.12566} = 7.357015$

(c) (1) $Z = \dfrac{\ln(X) - \mu_{\ln(x)}}{\sigma_{\ln(x)}} = \dfrac{\ln(15) - 2.5}{0.5} = 0.42$, $P(X < 15) = 0.1628 + 0.5 = 0.6628$

$Z = \dfrac{\ln(X) - \mu_{\ln(x)}}{\sigma_{\ln(x)}} = \dfrac{\ln(20) - 2.5}{0.5} = 0.99$, $P(X > 20) = 0.5 - 0.3389 = 0.1611$

(3) $Z = \dfrac{\ln(X) - \mu_{\ln(x)}}{\sigma_{\ln(x)}} = \dfrac{\ln(15) - 2.5}{0.5} = 0.42$, $P(X < 15) = 0.1628 + 0.5 = 0.6628$

$Z = \dfrac{\ln(X) - \mu_{\ln(x)}}{\sigma_{\ln(x)}} = \dfrac{\ln(30) - 2.5}{0.5} = 1.8$

$P(X < 30) = 0.5 + 0.4641 = 0.9641$

$P(15 < X < 30) = P(X < 30) - P(X < 15) = 0.9641 - 0.6628 = 0.3013$

32. (a) $\mu = \dfrac{1}{\lambda} = \dfrac{1}{5} = 0.2$ (b) $\sigma = \dfrac{1}{\lambda} = \dfrac{1}{5} = 0.2$

(c) (1) $P(X < 1) = 1 - e^{-\lambda x} = 1 - e^{-5 \cdot 1} = 0.993262$ (2) $P(X > 3) = e^{-\lambda x} = e^{-15} = 1.52951 \cdot 10^{-6}$

(3) $P(3 < X < 5) = P(X < 5) - P(X < 3) = 1 - e^{-5(5)} - 1 + e^{-5(3)} = 3.05902 \cdot 10^{-7} - 1.38879 \cdot 10^{-11} = 3.05888 \cdot 10^{-7}$

33. $\lambda = 50$

(a) $P(\text{arrival time} < 0.05) = 1 - e^{-50(0.05)} = 0.917915$ (b) $P(\text{arrival time} < 0.0167) = 1 - e^{-50(0.0167)} = 0.566126$

(c) $\mu = \dfrac{1}{\lambda} = \dfrac{1}{50} = 0.02$ minute (d) $\sigma = \dfrac{1}{\lambda} = \dfrac{1}{50} = 0.02$ minute

(e) $\lambda = 60$

$P(\text{arrival time} < 0.05) = 1 - e^{-60(0.05)} = 0.950213$ $P(\text{arrival time} < 0.0167) = 1 - e^{-60(0.0167)} = 0.632856$

$\mu = \dfrac{1}{\lambda} = \dfrac{1}{60} = 0.0167$ minute = 1 second $\sigma = \dfrac{1}{\lambda} = \dfrac{1}{60} = 0.0167$ minute = 1 second

(f) $\lambda = 30$

$P(\text{arrival time} < 0.05) = 1 - e^{-30(0.05)} = 0.77687$ $P(\text{arrival time} < 0.0167) = 1 - e^{-30(0.0167)} = 0.394076$

$\mu = \dfrac{1}{\lambda} = \dfrac{1}{30} = 0.0333$ minute = 2 seconds $\sigma = \dfrac{1}{\lambda} = \dfrac{1}{30} = 0.0333$ minute = 2 seconds

34. $\lambda = 15$

(a) $P(\text{arrival time} < 0.05) = 1 - e^{-15(0.05)} = 0.527633$ (b) $P(\text{arrival time} < 0.25) = 1 - e^{-15(0.25)} = 0.976482$

(c) $\mu = \dfrac{1}{\lambda} = \dfrac{1}{15} = 0.0667$ hour = 4 minutes (d) $\sigma = \dfrac{1}{\lambda} = \dfrac{1}{15} = 0.0667$ hour = 4 minutes

35. $\lambda = 8$

(a) $P(\text{arrival time} < 0.25) = 1 - e^{-8(0.25)} = 0.864665$ (b) $P(\text{arrival time} < 0.05) = 1 - e^{-8(0.05)} = 0.32968$

(c) $\lambda = 15$

$P(\text{arrival time} < 0.25) = 1 - e^{-15(0.25)} = 0.976482$ $P(\text{arrival time} < 0.05) = 1 - e^{-15(0.25)} = 0.527633$

36. mean =10 days, therefore $\lambda = \dfrac{1}{10} = 0.1$

(a) $P(\text{time} < 5) = 1 - e^{-0.1(5)} = 0.393469$ (b) $P(\text{time} < 10) = 1 - e^{-0.1(10)} = 0.632121$

(c) $\mu = \dfrac{1}{\lambda} = \dfrac{1}{0.1} = 10$ days (d) $\sigma = \dfrac{1}{\lambda} = \dfrac{1}{0.1} = 10$ days

37. $\alpha = 2.5$, $\beta = 10$

(a) $P(X < 5) = 1 - e^{-(x/\beta)^{\alpha}} = 1 - e^{-(5/10)^{2.5}} = 1 - e^{-0.1767} = 0.162033$

(b) $P(X < 10) = 1 - e^{-(x/\beta)^{\alpha}} = 1 - e^{-(10/10)^{2.5}} = 0.632121$ (c) $P(X < 20) = 1 - e^{-(x/\beta)^{\alpha}} = 1 - e^{-(20/10)^{2.5}} = 0.996507$

38. $\alpha = 2,\ \beta = 6$

(a) $P(X<5) = 1-e^{-(x/\beta)^\alpha} = 1-e^{-(5/6)^2} = 0.500648$ (b) $P(X<10) = 1-e^{-(x/\beta)^\alpha} = 1-e^{-(10/6)^2} = 0.937823$

(c) $P(X<15) = 1-e^{-(x/\beta)^\alpha} = 1-e^{-(15/6)^2} = 0.99807$

39. $\alpha = 3,\ \beta = 10$

(a) $P(X<5) = 1-e^{-(x/\beta)^\alpha} = 1-e^{-(5/10)^3} = 0.117503$

(b) $P(X\geq 2) = 1-P(X<2) = 1-1+e^{-(x/\beta)^\alpha} = e^{-(2/10)^3} = 0.992031915$

(c) $P(X<6) = 1-e^{-(x/\beta)^\alpha} = 1-e^{-(6/10)^3} = 0.194265$

$P(X<15) = 1-e^{-(x/\beta)^\alpha} = 1-e^{-(15/10)^3} = 0.965782$

$P(6<X<15) = P(X<15)-P(X<6) = 0.965782-0.194265 = 0.771517$

(d) $\alpha = 5,\ \beta = 10$

$P(X<5) = 1-e^{-(x/\beta)^\alpha} = 1-e^{-(5/10)^5} = 0.030767$

$P(X\geq 2) = 1-P(X<2) = 1-1+e^{-(x/\beta)^\alpha} = e^{-(2/10)^5} = 0.999680051$

$P(X<6) = 1-e^{-(x/\beta)^\alpha} = 1-e^{-(6/10)^5} = 0.074814$

$P(X<15) = 1-e^{-(x/\beta)^\alpha} = 1-e^{-(15/10)^5} = 0.999496$

$P(6<X<15) = P(X<15)-P(X<6) = 0.999496-0.074814 = 0.924682$

40. $\alpha = 4,\ \beta = 40$

(a) $P(X<20) = 1-e^{-(x/\beta)^\alpha} = 1-e^{-(20/40)^4} = 0.060587$

(b) $P(X>50) = 1-P(X<50) = 1-1+e^{-(x/\beta)^\alpha} = e^{-(50/40)^4} = 0.087038368,\ \alpha = 4,\ \beta = 8$

(c) $P(X<5) = 1-e^{-(x/\beta)^\alpha} = 1-e^{-(5/8)^4} = 0.0141517$

$P(X<10) = 1-e^{-(x/\beta)^\alpha} = 1-e^{-(10/8)^4} = 0.912962$

$P(5<X<10) = P(X<10)-P(X<5) = 0.912962-0.141517 = 0.771445$

(d) $P(X>8) = 1-P(X<8) = 1-1+e^{-(x/\beta)^\alpha} = e^{-(8/8)^4} = 0.367879441$

(e) We can multiply the probabilities only if the wind velocity and wave height are independent. If these events are not independent (which seems reasonable), then the probability of both events occurring is the product of the probability that the wind velocity is more than 50 mph times the conditional probability that the wave height is greater than 8 feet, given that the wind velocity is more than 50 mph.

41. $\alpha = 1.5,\ \beta = 10$

(a) $P(X<10) = 1-e^{-(x/\beta)^\alpha} = 1-e^{-(10/10)^{1.5}} = 0.632121$

(b) $P(X\geq 5) = 1-P(X<5) = 1-1+e^{-(x/\beta)^\alpha} = e^{-(5/10)^{1.5}} = 0.702188501$

(c) $P(5<X<10) = P(X<10)-P(X<5) = 1-e^{-(10/10)^{1.5}}-1+e^{-(5/10)^{1.5}} = 0.33431$

(d) $\alpha = 1,\ \beta = 10$

$P(X<10) = 1-e^{-(x/\beta)^\alpha} = 1-e^{-(10/10)^1} = 0.632121$

$P(X\geq 5) = 1-P(X<5) = 1-1+e^{-(x/\beta)^\alpha} = e^{-(5/10)^1} = 0.60653066$

$P(X<5) = 1-e^{-(x/\beta)^\alpha} = 1-e^{-(5/10)^1} = 0.393469$

$P(5<X<10) = P(X<10)-P(X<5) = 0.632121-0.393469 = 0.238652$

42. (a) $Z = \dfrac{\overline{X}-\mu_{\overline{x}}}{\sigma_x/\sqrt{n}} = \dfrac{9.5-10}{2/\sqrt{16}} = -1,\ P(\overline{X}>9.5) = P(9.5<\overline{X}<10)+P(\overline{X}>10) = 0.3413+0.5 = 0.8413$

(b) $Z = \dfrac{\overline{X} - \mu_{\overline{x}}}{\sigma_{\overline{x}} / \sqrt{n}} = \dfrac{9-10}{2/\sqrt{16}} = -2$, $P(\overline{X} < 9) = P(\overline{X} < 10) - P(9 < \overline{X} < 10) = 0.5 - 0.4772 = 0.0228$

$Z = \dfrac{\overline{X} - \mu_{\overline{x}}}{\sigma_{\overline{x}} / \sqrt{n}} = \dfrac{10.5-10}{2/\sqrt{16}} = 1$

$P(\overline{X} < 10.5) = P(\overline{X} < 10) + P(10 < \overline{X} < 10.5) = 0.5 + 0.3413 = 0.8413$

$P(9 < \overline{X} < 10.5) = P(\overline{X} < 10.5) - P(\overline{X} < 9) = 0.8413 - 0.0228 = 0.8185$

(c) 20% of all the sample means should be below $\overline{X}$, therefore $\overline{X}$ is below the mean and Z is negative. If 20% of the values are below $\overline{X}$ then 30% of all the values must fall between $\overline{X}$ and the mean; subsequently the area between $\overline{X}$ and the mean is 0.30, and $Z = -0.84$.

$\overline{X} = \mu_x + Z\dfrac{\sigma_x}{\sqrt{n}} = 10 - 0.84\dfrac{2}{\sqrt{16}} = 9.58$

43. (a) $Z = \dfrac{\overline{X} - \mu_{\overline{x}}}{\sigma_x / \sqrt{n}} = \dfrac{14-14.1}{1.4/\sqrt{49}} = -0.5$, $P(\overline{X} > 14) = P(14 < \overline{X} < 14.1) + P(\overline{X} > 14.1) = 0.1915 + 0.5 = 0.6915$

(b) Only 1% of all the sample means should be below $\overline{X}$, therefore $\overline{X}$ is below the mean and Z is negative. If 1% of the values is below $\overline{X}$ then 49% of all the values must fall between $\overline{X}$ and the mean; subsequently the area between $\overline{X}$ and the mean is 0.49, and $Z = -2.33$.

$\overline{X} = \mu_x + Z\dfrac{\sigma_x}{\sqrt{n}} = 14.1 - 2.33\dfrac{1.4}{\sqrt{49}} = 13.634$

(c) The distribution of the sample mean must be normally distributed. This assumption is met because we are given a large enough sample.

(d) (a) $Z = \dfrac{\overline{X} - \mu_{\overline{x}}}{\sigma_x / \sqrt{n}} = \dfrac{14-14.1}{1.4/\sqrt{64}} = -0.57$, $P(\overline{X} > 14) = P(14 < \overline{X} < 14.1) + P(\overline{X} > 14.1) = 0.2157 + 0.5 = 0.7157$

(b) Only 1% of all the sample mean should be below $\overline{X}$, therefore $\overline{X}$ is below the mean and Z is negative. If 1% of the values are below $\overline{X}$ then 49% of all the values must fall between $\overline{X}$ and the mean; subsequently the area between $\overline{X}$ and the mean is 0.49, and $Z = -2.33$.

$\overline{X} = \mu_x + Z\dfrac{\sigma_x}{\sqrt{n}} = 14.1 - 2.33\dfrac{1.4}{\sqrt{64}} = 13.69225$

44. (a) $Z = \dfrac{\overline{X} - \mu_{\overline{x}}}{\sigma_x / \sqrt{n}} = \dfrac{38.5-40}{5/\sqrt{100}} = -3$, $P(\overline{X} > 38.5) = P(38.5 < \overline{X} < 40) + P(\overline{X} > 40) = 0.49865 + 0.5 = 0.99865$

(b) Only 5% of all the sample means should be below $\overline{X}$, therefore $\overline{X}$ is below the mean and Z is negative. If 5% of the values are below $\overline{X}$ then 45% of all the values must fall between $\overline{X}$ and the mean; subsequently the area between $\overline{X}$ and the mean is 0.45, and $Z = -1.64$.

$\overline{X} = \mu_x + Z\dfrac{\sigma_x}{\sqrt{n}} = 40 - 1.64\dfrac{5}{\sqrt{100}} = 39.18$

(c) The distribution of the sample mean must be normally distributed. This assumption is met because we are given a large enough sample.

(d) (a) $Z = \dfrac{\overline{X} - \mu_{\overline{x}}}{\sigma_x / \sqrt{n}} = \dfrac{38.5-40}{5/\sqrt{50}} = -2.12$, $P(\overline{X} > 38.5) = P(38.5 < \overline{X} < 40) + P(\overline{X} > 40) = 0.4830 + 0.5 = 0.9830$

(b) Only 5% of all the sample means should be below $\overline{X}$, therefore $\overline{X}$ is below the mean and Z is negative. If 5% of the values are below $\overline{X}$ then 45% of all the values must fall between $\overline{X}$ and the mean; subsequently the area between $\overline{X}$ and the mean is 0.45, and $Z = -1.64$.

$\overline{X} = \mu_x + Z\dfrac{\sigma_x}{\sqrt{n}} = 40 - 1.64\dfrac{5}{\sqrt{50}} = 38.84034$

45. (a) $Z = \dfrac{\overline{X} - \mu_{\overline{x}}}{\sigma_x / \sqrt{n}} = \dfrac{4.60 - 4.70}{0.40 / \sqrt{25}} = -1.25$, $P(\overline{X} > 4.6) = P(4.6 < \overline{X} < 4.7) + P(\overline{X} > 4.7) = 0.3944 + 0.5 = 0.8944$

(b) The areas between the lower X and the mean and the area between the mean and the upper X should be equal to 0.35. Thus the Z values are -1.04 and 1.04.

$$\overline{X}_L = \mu_x - Z\frac{\sigma_x}{\sqrt{n}} = 4.7 - 1.04\frac{0.4}{\sqrt{25}} = 4.6168$$

$$\overline{X}_U = \mu_x + Z\frac{\sigma_x}{\sqrt{n}} = 4.7 + 1.04\frac{0.4}{\sqrt{25}} = 4.7832$$

(c) 23% of all the sample means should be below $\overline{X}$, therefore $\overline{X}$ is below the mean and Z is negative. If 23% of the values are below $\overline{X}$ then 27% of all the values must fall between $\overline{X}$ and the mean; subsequently the area between $\overline{X}$ and the mean is 0.27, and $Z = -0.74$.

$$\overline{X} = \mu_x + Z\frac{\sigma_x}{\sqrt{n}} = 4.7 - 0.74\frac{0.4}{\sqrt{25}} = 4.6408$$

(d) In Problem 5.9(b), the X value = 4.404, whereas for this problem the X value = 4.6408. This is because the sampling distribution of the mean is less variable than the distribution of individual values.

46. (a) $Z = \dfrac{\overline{X} - \mu_{\overline{x}}}{\sigma_x / \sqrt{n}} = \dfrac{1.99 - 2.0}{0.05 / \sqrt{100}} = -2$, $P(\overline{X} > 1.99) = P(1.99 < \overline{X} < 2.0) + P(\overline{X} > 2.0) = 0.4772 + 0.5 = 0.9772$

(b) Only 1% of all the sample means should be below $\overline{X}$ therefore $\overline{X}$ is below the mean and Z is negative. If 1% of the values is below $\overline{X}$ then 49% of all the values must fall between $\overline{X}$ and the mean; subsequently the area between $\overline{X}$ and the mean is 0.49, therefore $Z = -2.33$.

$$\overline{X} = \mu_x + Z\frac{\sigma_x}{\sqrt{n}} = 2.0 - 2.33\frac{0.05}{\sqrt{100}} = 1.988$$

(c) In Problem 5.10(b), the X value = 1.8835, whereas for this problem X value = 1.98835. This is because the sampling distribution of the mean is more narrow than the distribution of individual values.

47. (a) $Z = \dfrac{p - \pi}{\sqrt{\dfrac{\pi(1-\pi)}{n}}} = \dfrac{0.25 - 0.20}{\sqrt{\dfrac{0.20(1-0.20)}{100}}} = 1.25$, $P(0.2 < p < 0.25) = 0.3944$

(b) $Z = \dfrac{p - \pi}{\sqrt{\dfrac{\pi(1-\pi)}{n}}} = \dfrac{0.25 - 0.20}{\sqrt{\dfrac{0.20(1-0.20)}{100}}} = 1.25$, $P(p < 0.25) = P(p < 0.2) + P(0.2 < p < 0.25) = 0.5 + 0.3944 = 0.8944$

$$Z = \frac{p - \pi}{\sqrt{\dfrac{\pi(1-\pi)}{n}}} = \frac{0.30 - 0.20}{\sqrt{\dfrac{0.20(1-0.20)}{100}}} = 2.5$$

$P(p < 0.30) = P(p < 0.2) + P(0.2 < p < 0.30) = 0.5 + 0.4938 = 0.9938$

$P(0.25 < p < 0.30) = P(p < 0.30) - P(p < 0.25) = 0.9938 - 0.8944 = 0.0994$

(c) $Z = \dfrac{p - \pi}{\sqrt{\dfrac{\pi(1-\pi)}{n}}} = \dfrac{0.25 - 0.20}{\sqrt{\dfrac{0.20(1-0.20)}{100}}} = 1.25$, $P(p < 0.25) = P(p < 0.2) + P(0.2 < p < 0.25) = 0.5 + 0.3944 = 0.8944$

(d) $\sigma_p = \sqrt{\dfrac{\pi(1-\pi)}{n}} = \sqrt{\dfrac{0.2(1-0.2)}{25}} = 0.08$

Using PHStat we obtain:

Z Value for 0.2	0	Z Value for 0.25	0.625
Z Value for 0.25	0.625	Z Value for 0.3	1.25
$P(p \le 0.2)$	0.5	$P(p \le 0.25)$	0.7340
$P(p \le 0.25)$	0.7340	$P(p \le 0.3)$	0.8944
$P(0.2 \le p \le 0.25)$	0.2340	$P(0.25 \le p \le 0.3)$	0.1603

Z Value	0.6250
$P(p \le 0.25)$	0.7340

48. (a) $Z = \dfrac{p-\pi}{\sqrt{\dfrac{\pi(1-\pi)}{n}}} = \dfrac{0.06-0.04}{\sqrt{\dfrac{0.04(1-0.04)}{400}}} = 2.04$, $P(0.04 < p < 0.06) = 0.4793$

(b) $Z = \dfrac{p-\pi}{\sqrt{\dfrac{\pi(1-\pi)}{n}}} = \dfrac{0.05-0.04}{\sqrt{\dfrac{0.04(1-0.04)}{400}}} = 1.02$, $P(p > 0.05) = P(p > 0.04) - P(0.04 < p < 0.05) = 0.5 - 0.3461 = 0.1539$

(c) $\sigma_p = \sqrt{\dfrac{\pi(1-\pi)}{n}} = \sqrt{\dfrac{0.04(1-0.04)}{300}} = 0.011$

Using PHStat we obtain

Z Value for 0.04	0
Z Value for 0.06	1.8182
$P(X \le 0.04)$	0.5
$P(X \le 0.06)$	0.9655
$P(0.04 \le X \le 0.06)$	0.4655

Z Value	0.9091
$P(X > 0.05)$	0.1817

49. (a) Mean 0.505

$Z = \dfrac{p-\pi}{\sqrt{\dfrac{\pi(1-\pi)}{n}}} = \dfrac{0.56-0.505}{\sqrt{\dfrac{0.505(1-0.505)}{100}}} = 1.10$

$P(p > 0.56) = P(p > 0.505) = P(0.505 < p < 0.56) = 0.5 - 0.3643 = 0.1357$

(b) Mean 0.6

$Z = \dfrac{p-\pi}{\sqrt{\dfrac{\pi(1-\pi)}{n}}} = \dfrac{0.56-0.6}{\sqrt{\dfrac{0.6(1-0.6)}{100}}} = -0.82$, $P(p > 0.56) = P(p < 0.60) + P(0.56 < p < 0.60) = 0.5 + 0.2939 = 0.7939$

(c) Mean 0.49

$Z = \dfrac{p-\pi}{\sqrt{\dfrac{\pi(1-\pi)}{n}}} = \dfrac{0.56-0.49}{\sqrt{\dfrac{0.49(1-0.49)}{100}}} = 1.4$, $P(p > 0.56) = P(p < 0.49) - P(0.49 < p < 0.56) = 0.5 - 0.4192 = 0.0808$

(d) (a) Mean 0.505

$Z = \dfrac{p-\pi}{\sqrt{\dfrac{\pi(1-\pi)}{n}}} = \dfrac{0.56-0.505}{\sqrt{\dfrac{0.505(1-0.505)}{400}}} = 2.20$

$P(p > 0.56) = P(p > 0.505) - P(0.505 < p < 0.56) = 0.5 - 0.4861 = 0.0139$

(b) Mean 0.6

$Z = \dfrac{p-\pi}{\sqrt{\dfrac{\pi(1-\pi)}{n}}} = \dfrac{0.56-0.6}{\sqrt{\dfrac{0.6(1-0.6)}{400}}} = -1.63$, $P(p > 0.56) = P(p < 0.60) + P(0.56 < p < 0.60) = 0.5 + 0.4484 = 0.9484$

(c) Mean 0.49

$Z = \dfrac{p-\pi}{\sqrt{\dfrac{\pi(1-\pi)}{n}}} = \dfrac{0.56-0.49}{\sqrt{\dfrac{0.49(1-0.49)}{400}}} = 2.80$,

$P(p > 0.56) = P(p > 0.49) - P(0.49 < p < 0.56) = 0.5 - 0.4974 = 0.0026$

50. (a) $Z = \dfrac{p-\pi}{\sqrt{\dfrac{\pi(1-\pi)}{n}}} = \dfrac{0.75-0.7}{\sqrt{\dfrac{0.7(1-0.7)}{100}}} = 1.09$, $P(0.7 < p < 0.75) = 0.3621$

(b) $Z = \dfrac{p-\pi}{\sqrt{\dfrac{\pi(1-\pi)}{n}}} = \dfrac{0.7-0.7}{\sqrt{\dfrac{0.7(1-0.7)}{100}}} = 0$, $P(p > 0.7) = 0.5$

(c) $Z = \dfrac{p-\pi}{\sqrt{\dfrac{\pi(1-\pi)}{n}}} = \dfrac{0.6-0.7}{\sqrt{\dfrac{0.7(1-0.7)}{100}}} = -2.17$, $P(p < 0.6) = P(p < 0.7) + P(0.6 < p < 0.7) = 0.5 - 0.4850 = 0.0150$

$Z = \dfrac{p-\pi}{\sqrt{\dfrac{\pi(1-\pi)}{n}}} = \dfrac{0.8-0.7}{\sqrt{\dfrac{0.7(1-0.7)}{100}}} = 2.17$

$P(p < 0.8) = P(p < 0.7) + P(0.7 < p < 0.8) = 0.5 + 0.4850 = 0.9850$

$P(0.6 < p < 0.8) = P(p < 0.8) - P(p < 0.6) = 0.9850 - 0.0150 = 0.9700$

(d) $\sigma_p = \sqrt{\dfrac{\pi(1-\pi)}{n}} = \sqrt{\dfrac{0.7(1-0.7)}{50}} = 0.065$

Using PHStat we obtain

Z Value for 0.7	0
Z Value for 0.75	0.7692
$P(p \le 0.7)$	0.5
$P(p \le 0.75)$	0.7791
$P(0.7 \le p \le 0.75)$	0.2791

Z Value	0
$P(p > 0.7)$	0.5

Z Value for 0.6	−1.5385
Z Value for 0.8	1.5385
$P(p \le 0.6)$	0.0620
$P(p \le 0.8)$	0.9380
$P(0.6 \le p \le 0.8)$	0.8761

51. (a) $Z = \dfrac{p-\pi}{\sqrt{\dfrac{\pi(1-\pi)}{n}}} = \dfrac{0.96-0.95}{\sqrt{\dfrac{0.95(1-0.95)}{1000}}} = 1.45$, $P(0.95 < p < 0.96) = 0.4265$

(b) $Z = \dfrac{p-\pi}{\sqrt{\dfrac{\pi(1-\pi)}{n}}} = \dfrac{0.94-0.95}{\sqrt{\dfrac{0.95(1-0.95)}{1000}}} = -1.45$, $P(p < 0.94) = P(p < 0.95) - P(0.94 < p < 0.95) = 0.5 - 0.4265 = 0.0735$

$Z = \dfrac{p-\pi}{\sqrt{\dfrac{\pi(1-\pi)}{n}}} = \dfrac{0.97-0.95}{\sqrt{\dfrac{0.95(1-0.95)}{1000}}} = 2.90$

$P(p < 0.97) = P(p < 0.95) + P(0.95 < p < 0.97) = 0.5 + 0.4981 = 0.9981$

$P(0.94 < p < 0.97) = P(p < 0.97) - P(p < 0.94) = 0.9981 - 0.0735 = 0.9246$

(c) $Z = \dfrac{p-\pi}{\sqrt{\dfrac{\pi(1-\pi)}{n}}} = \dfrac{0.93-0.95}{\sqrt{\dfrac{0.95(1-0.95)}{1000}}} = 2.90$, $P(p > 0.93) = P(0.93 < p < 0.95) + P(p > 0.95) = 0.4981 + 0.5 = 0.9981$

(d) $\sigma_p = \sqrt{\frac{\pi(1-\pi)}{n}} = \sqrt{\frac{0.95(1-0.95)}{1000}} = 0.01$

Using PHStat we obtain

Z Value for 0.95	0	Z Value for 0.94	−1
Z Value for 0.96	1	Z Value for 0.97	2
$P(X \leq 0.95)$	0.5	$P(X \leq 0.94)$	0.1587
$P(X \leq 0.96)$	0.8413	$P(X \leq 0.97)$	0.9772
$P(0.95 \leq X \leq 0.96)$	0.3413	$P(0.94 \leq X \leq 0.97)$	0.8186

Z Value	−2
$P(X > 0.93)$	0.9772

52. A rectangle.

53. Any normally distributed variable X can be converted to its standardized form by using the transformation formula for Z. We can then determine the desired probabilities from the table for the standard normal distribution (Table A.2).

54.
1. Determine the probability or area under the curve from the mean to the lower specification limit.
2. Determine the probability or area under the curve from the mean to the upper specification limit.
3. Subtract the smaller area from the larger area.

55.
1. Sketch the normal curve, and then place the values for the means on the X and Z axes, respectively.
2. Determine whether X is above or below the mean.
3. Split the appropriate half of the normal curve into two parts—the portion from the desired X to the mean, and the portion from the desired X to the tail.
4. Shade the area of interest.
5. By using Table A.2 for the standardized normal distribution, determine the appropriate Z value corresponding to the area under the normal curve from the desired X to the mean μ_x.
6. Solve the equation $X = \mu_x + Z\sigma_x$ for X.

56. The normal distribution can be used to approximate the binomial distribution when the variance, $np(1-p)$, is at least 10. The normal distribution can be used to approximate the Poisson distribution whenever the parameter λ is at least 5.

57. By standardizing the values, only one table for the probabilities of the standard normal distribution is needed.

58. The lognormal distribution is obtained when a right-skewed variable is transformed using natural logarithms and the transformed values are normally distributed. The lognormal distribution can be used only for a non-negative random variable X, whereas a normal distribution can be used for all X. In addition, the probability of obtaining a value below the mean is higher than 0.5. The latter occurs if the distribution were normally distributed instead of being lognormally distributed.

59. The average time between arrivals is inversely proportional to the average number of arrivals per unit time.

60. The α parameter indicates a shape factor and the β parameter is a scale factor that represents the size of the units in which X is measured.

61. The standard error of the mean decreases as the sample size increases, because the standard error of the mean is inversely proportional to the root of the sample size.

62. The sampling distribution of the mean follows a normal distribution for a large enough sample according to the central limit theorem.

63. (a) (1) $Z = \frac{X-\mu_x}{\sigma_x} = \frac{1.00-0.72}{0.10} = 2.8$, $P(X>1) = P(X>0.72) - P(0.72<X<1) = 0.5 - 0.4974 = 0.0026$

(2) $Z = \frac{X-\mu_x}{\sigma_x} = \frac{0.70-0.72}{0.10} = -0.2$, $P(X<0.7) = P(X<0.72) - P(0.7<X<0.72) = 0.5 - 0.0793 = 0.4207$

$Z = \frac{X-\mu_x}{\sigma_x} = \frac{0.80-0.72}{0.10} = 0.8$

$P(X<0.80) = P(X<0.72) + P(0.72<X<0.80) = 0.5 + 0.2881 = 0.7881$

$P(0.70<X<0.80) = P(X<0.80) - P(X<0.70) = 0.7881 - 0.4207 = 0.3674$

(b) 30% of all the values exceed X, therefore X is above the mean, and Z is positive. If 30% of the values are above X, then 20% of all the values must fall between X and the mean; subsequently the area between X and the mean is 0.20, and $Z = 0.52$.

$X = \mu_x + Z\sigma_x = 0.72 + 0.52 \times 0.10 = 0.772$

(c) 90% of all the values exceed X, therefore X is below the mean, and Z is negative. If 10% of the values are below X, then 40% of all the values fall between X and the mean; subsequently the area between X and the mean is 0.40, and $Z = -1.28$.

$X = \mu_x + Z\sigma_x = 0.72 - 1.28 \times 0.10 = 0.60$

(d) (1) $Z = \frac{\overline{X}-\mu_{\overline{x}}}{\sigma_x / \sqrt{n}} = \frac{0.7-0.72}{0.10/\sqrt{16}} = -0.8$, $P(\overline{X}>0.7) = P(0.7<\overline{X}<0.72) + P(\overline{X}>0.72) = 0.2881 + 0.5 = 0.7881$

(2) $Z = \frac{\overline{X}-\mu_{\overline{x}}}{\sigma_x / \sqrt{n}} = \frac{0.7-0.72}{0.10/\sqrt{16}} = -0.8$, $P(\overline{X}<0.7) = P(\overline{X}<0.72) - P(0.7<\overline{X}<0.72) = 0.5 - 0.2881 = 0.2119$

$Z = \frac{\overline{X}-\mu_{\overline{x}}}{\sigma_x / \sqrt{n}} = \frac{0.8-0.72}{0.10/\sqrt{16}} = 3.2$

$P(\overline{X}<0.8) = P(\overline{X}<0.72) + P(0.72<\overline{X}<0.8) = 0.5 + 0.49931 = 0.99931$

$P(0.7<\overline{X}<0.8) = P(\overline{X}<0.8) - P(\overline{X}<0.7) = 0.99931 - 0.2119 = 0.78741$

(e) The areas between the lower $\overline{X}$ and the mean, and the area between the mean and the upper $\overline{X}$ should be equal to 0.9/2 = 0.45. Thus the Z values are −1.65 and 1.65.

$\overline{X}_L = \mu_x - Z\frac{\sigma_x}{\sqrt{n}} = 0.72 - 1.65\frac{0.1}{\sqrt{16}} = 0.67875$

$\overline{X}_U = \mu_x + Z\frac{\sigma_x}{\sqrt{n}} = 0.72 + 1.65\frac{0.10}{\sqrt{16}} = 0.76125$

(f) This difference appears because the sampling distribution of the mean is less variable than the distribution of individual values.

64. (a) (1) $Z = \frac{X-\mu_x}{\sigma_x} = \frac{45-50}{10} = -0.5$, $P(X<45) = P(X<50) - P(45<X<50) = 0.5 - 0.1915 = 0.3085$

$Z = \frac{X-\mu_x}{\sigma_x} = \frac{55-50}{10} = 0.5$

$P(X<55) = P(X<50) + P(50<X<55) = 0.5 + 0.1915 = 0.6915$

$P(45<X<55) = P(X<55) - P(X<45) = 0.6915 - 0.3085 = 0.3830$

(2) $Z = \frac{X-\mu_x}{\sigma_x} = \frac{40-50}{10} = -1.0$, $P(X<40) = P(X<50) - P(40<X<50) = 0.5 - 0.3413 = 0.1587$

$Z = \frac{X-\mu_x}{\sigma_x} = \frac{60-50}{10} = 1.0$

$P(X<60) = P(X<50) + P(50<X<60) = 0.5 + 0.3413 = 0.8413$

$P(40<X<60) = P(X<60) - P(X<40) = 0.8413 - 0.1587 = 0.6826$

(3) $Z = \frac{X - \mu_x}{\sigma_x} = \frac{80 - 50}{10} = 3.0$, $P(X > 80) = P(X > 50) - P(50 < X < 80) = 0.5 - 0.49865 = 0.00135$

(b) X exceeds 20% of all the values, therefore X is below the mean, and Z is negative. If 20% of the values are below X then 30% of all the values must fall between X and the mean; subsequently the area between X and the mean is 0.30, and $Z = -0.84$.
$X = \mu_x + Z\sigma_x = 50 - 0.84 \times 10 = 41.6$

(c) 99% of all the values are below X, therefore X is above the mean, and Z is positive. If 1% of the values are above X, then 49% of all the values fall between X and the mean; subsequently the area between X and the mean is 0.49, and $Z = 2.33$.
$X = \mu_x + Z\sigma_x = 50 + 2.33 \times 10 = 73.3$

(d) (1) $n = 2 \times 8 = 16$

$$Z = \frac{\overline{X} - \mu_{\overline{x}}}{\sigma_{\overline{x}} / \sqrt{n}} = \frac{45 - 50}{10 / \sqrt{16}} = -2,\ P(\overline{X} < 45) = P(\overline{X} < 50) - P(45 < \overline{X} < 50) = 0.5 - 0.4772 = 0.0228$$

$$Z = \frac{\overline{X} - \mu_{\overline{x}}}{\sigma_{\overline{x}} / \sqrt{n}} = \frac{55 - 50}{10 / \sqrt{16}} = 2$$

$$P(\overline{X} < 55) = P(\overline{X} < 50) + P(50 < \overline{X} < 55) = 0.5 + 0.4772 = 0.9772$$

$$P(45 < \overline{X} < 55) = P(\overline{X} < 55) - P(\overline{X} < 45) = 0.9772 - 0.0228 = 0.9544$$

(2) $Z = \frac{\overline{X} - \mu_{\overline{x}}}{\sigma_{\overline{x}} / \sqrt{n}} = \frac{55 - 50}{10 / \sqrt{16}} = 2$, $P(\overline{X} > 55) = P(\overline{X} > 50) - P(50 < \overline{X} < 55) = 0.5 - 0.4772 = 0.0228$

(e) 98% of all the values are below X, therefore X is above the mean, and Z is positive. If 2% of the values are above X, then 48% of all the values must fall between X and the mean; subsequently the area between X and the mean is 0.48, and $Z = 2.05$.

$$\overline{X} = \mu_x + Z\frac{\sigma_x}{\sqrt{n}} = 50 + 2.05\frac{10}{\sqrt{16}} = 55.125$$

(f) This difference appears because the sampling distribution of the mean is less variable than the distribution of the individual values.

65. (a) (1) $Z = \frac{X - \mu_x}{\sigma_x} = \frac{60 - 70}{5} = -2.0$, $P(X < 60) = P(X < 70) - P(60 < X < 70) = 0.5 - 0.4772 = 0.0228$,

$$Z = \frac{X - \mu_x}{\sigma_x} = \frac{80 - 70}{5} = 2.0,\ P(X < 80) = P(X < 70) + P(70 < X < 80) = 0.5 + 0.4772 = 0.9772,$$

$$P(60 < X < 80) = P(X < 80) - P(X < 60) = 0.9772 - 0.0228 = 0.9544$$

(2) $Z = \frac{X - \mu_x}{\sigma_x} = \frac{85 - 70}{5} = 3.0$, $P(X > 85) = P(X > 70) - P(70 < X < 85) = 0.5 - 0.49865 = 0.00135$,

$$Z = \frac{X - \mu_x}{\sigma_x} = \frac{60 - 70}{5} = -2.0,\ P(X \geq 60) = P(60 < X < 70) + P(X > 70) = 0.4772 + 0.5 = 0.9772$$

(b) X exceeds 0.1% of the scuba divers, therefore X is below the mean and Z is negative. If 0.1% of the values is below X then 49.9% of all the values must fall between X and the mean; subsequently the area between X and the mean is 0.499, and $Z = -3.09$. $X = \mu_x + Z\sigma_x = 70 - 3.09 \times 5 = 54.55$

(c) 95% of all scuba divers exceed X, therefore X is below the mean and Z is negative. If 5% of the values are below X then 45% of all the values must fall between X and the mean; subsequently the area between X and the mean is 0.45, and $Z = -1.64$. $X = \mu_x + Z\sigma_x = 70 - 1.64 \times 5 = 61.8$

(d) (1) $Z = \frac{\overline{X} - \mu_{\overline{x}}}{\sigma_{\overline{x}} / \sqrt{n}} = \frac{65 - 70}{5 / \sqrt{4}} = -2$, $P(\overline{X} > 65) = P(65 < \overline{X} < 70) + P(\overline{X} > 70) = 0.4772 + 0.5 = 0.9772$

(2) $Z = \dfrac{\overline{X} - \mu_{\overline{x}}}{\sigma_{\overline{x}} / \sqrt{n}} = \dfrac{65-70}{5/\sqrt{4}} = -2$, $P(\overline{X} < 65) = P(\overline{X} < 70) - P(65 < \overline{X} < 70) = 0.5 - 0.4772 = 0.0228$,

$Z = \dfrac{\overline{X} - \mu_{\overline{x}}}{\sigma_{\overline{x}} / \sqrt{n}} = \dfrac{75-70}{5/\sqrt{4}} = 2$, $P(\overline{X} < 75) = P(\overline{X} < 70) + P(70 < \overline{X} < 75) = 0.50 + .4772 = 0.9772$,

$P(65 < \overline{X} < 75) = 0.9772 - 0.0228 = 0.9544$

(e) The areas between the lower $\overline{X}$ and the mean and the area between the mean and the upper $\overline{X}$ should be equal to $\dfrac{0.9}{2} = 0.45$. Thus the Z values are -1.65 and 1.65. $\overline{X}_L = \mu_x - Z\dfrac{\sigma_x}{\sqrt{n}} = 70 - 1.65\dfrac{5}{\sqrt{4}} = 65.875$,

$\overline{X}_U = \mu_x + Z\dfrac{\sigma_x}{\sqrt{n}} = 70 + 1.65\dfrac{5}{\sqrt{4}} = 74.125$

66. (a) $Z = \dfrac{X - \mu_x}{\sigma_x} = \dfrac{1.0 - 1.005}{0.10} = -0.05$, $P(X < 1.0) = P(X < 1.005) - P(1.0 < X < 1.005) = 0.5 - 0.0199 = 0.4801$

(b) $Z = \dfrac{X - \mu_x}{\sigma_x} = \dfrac{0.95 - 1.005}{0.10} = -0.55$, $P(X < 0.95) = P(X < 1.005) - P(0.95 < X < 1.005) = 0.5 - 0.2088 = 0.2912$,

$Z = \dfrac{X - \mu_x}{\sigma_x} = \dfrac{1.0 - 1.005}{0.10} = -0.05$, $P(X < 1.0) = P(X < 1.005) - P(1.0 < X < 1.005) = 0.5 - 0.0199 = 0.4801$,

$P(0.95 < Z < 1.0) = P(X < 1.0) - P(X < 0.95) = 0.4801 - 0.2912 = 0.1889$

(c) $Z = \dfrac{X - \mu_x}{\sigma_x} = \dfrac{1.0 - 1.005}{0.10} = -0.05$, $P(X < 1.0) = P(X < 1.005) - P(1.0 < X < 1.005) = 0.5 - 0.0199 = 0.4801$,

$Z = \dfrac{X - \mu_x}{\sigma_x} = \dfrac{1.05 - 1.005}{0.10} = 0.45$, $P(X < 1.05) = P(X < 1.005) + P(1.005 < X < 1.05) = 0.5 + 0.1736 = 0.6736$,

$P(1.0<X<1.05) = P(X<1.05) - P(X<1.0) = 0.6736 - 0.4801 = 0.1935$

(d) $P(X < 0.95 \text{ or } 1.05 < X) = P(X < 0.95) + P(X > 1.05)$, $Z = \dfrac{X - \mu_x}{\sigma_x} = \dfrac{0.95 - 1.005}{0.10} = -0.55$,

$P(X < 0.95) = P(X < 1.005) - P(0.95 < X < 1.005) = 0.5 - 0.2088 = 0.2912$, $Z = \dfrac{X - \mu_x}{\sigma_x} = \dfrac{1.05 - 1.005}{0.10} = 0.45$,

$P(X > 1.05) = P(X > 1.005) - P(1.005 < X < 1.05) = 0.5 - 0.1736 = 0.3264$,

$P(X < 0.95 \text{ or } 1.05 < X) = 0.2912 + 0.3264 = 0.6176$

(e) Mean 1

Standard Deviation 0.1

$Z = \dfrac{X - \mu_x}{\sigma_x} = \dfrac{0.95 - 1.0}{0.10} = -0.5$, $P(X < 0.95) = P(X < 1.0) - P(0.95 < X < 1.0) = 0.5 - 0.1915 = 0.3085$,

$Z = \dfrac{X - \mu_x}{\sigma_x} = \dfrac{1.05 - 1.0}{0.10} = 0.5$, $P(X > 1.05) = P(X > 1.0) - P(1.0 < X < 1.05) = 0.5 - 0.1915 = 0.3085$,

$P(X < 0.95 \text{ or } 1.05 < X) = 0.3085 + 0.3085 = 0.6170$

Mean 1.005

Standard Deviation 0.075

$Z = \dfrac{X - \mu_x}{\sigma_x} = \dfrac{0.95 - 1.005}{0.075} = -0.73$, $P(X < 0.95) = P(X < 1.005) - P(0.95 < X < 1.005) = 0.5 - 0.2673 = 0.2327$,

$Z = \dfrac{X - \mu_x}{\sigma_x} = \dfrac{1.05 - 1.005}{0.075} = 0.6$, $P(X > 1.05) = P(X > 1.005) - P(1.005 < X < 1.05) = 0.5 - 0.2257 = 0.2743$,

$P(X < 0.95 \text{ or } 1.05 < X) = 0.2327 + 0.2743 = 0.507$

Lowering the blackness to the target value of 1.0 gives us a probability of 0.6170 so the newspaper will be considered unacceptable. Reducing the standard deviation to 0.075 gives us a probability of 0.507 so the newspaper will be considered unacceptable. Therefore it would be more appropriate to focus on a process improvement that would reduce the standard deviation.

(f) $Z = \frac{\overline{X} - \mu_{\overline{x}}}{\sigma_{\overline{x}} / \sqrt{n}} = \frac{1.0 - 1.005}{0.10 / \sqrt{20}} = -0.23$, $P(\overline{X} < 1.0) = P(\overline{X} < 1.005) - P(1.0 < \overline{X} < 1.005) = 0.5 - 0.0910 = 0.4090$

(g) $Z = \frac{\overline{X} - \mu_{\overline{x}}}{\sigma_{\overline{x}} / \sqrt{n}} = \frac{0.95 - 1.005}{0.10 / \sqrt{20}} = -2.46$, $P(\overline{X} < 0.95) = P(\overline{X} < 1.005) - P(0.95 < \overline{X} < 1.005) = 0.5 - 0.4931 = 0.0069$,

$Z = \frac{\overline{X} - \mu_{\overline{x}}}{\sigma_{\overline{x}} / \sqrt{n}} = \frac{1.0 - 1.005}{0.10 / \sqrt{20}} = -0.23$, $P(\overline{X} < 1.0) = P(\overline{X} < 1.005) - P(1.0 < \overline{X} < 1.005) = 0.5 - 0.0910 = 0.4090$,

$P(0.95 < \overline{X} < 1.0) = P(\overline{X} < 1.0) - P(\overline{X} < 0.95) = 0.4090 - 0.0069 = 0.4021$

(h) $Z = \frac{\overline{X} - \mu_{\overline{x}}}{\sigma_{\overline{x}} / \sqrt{n}} = \frac{1.0 - 1.005}{0.10 / \sqrt{20}} = -0.23$, $P(\overline{X} < 1.0) = P(\overline{X} < 1.005) - P(1.0 < \overline{X} < 1.005) = 0.5 - 0.0910 = 0.4090$,

$Z = \frac{\overline{X} - \mu_{\overline{x}}}{\sigma_{\overline{x}} / \sqrt{n}} = \frac{1.05 - 1.005}{0.10 / \sqrt{20}} = 2.01$, $P(\overline{X} < 1.05) = P(\overline{X} < 1.005) + P(1.005 < \overline{X} < 1.05) = 0.5 + 0.4778 = 0.9778$,

$P(1.0 < \overline{X} < 1.05) = P(\overline{X} < 1.05) - P(\overline{X} < 1.0) = 0.9778 - 0.4090 = 0.5688$

(i) $P(\overline{X} < 0.95 \text{ or } 1.05 < \overline{X}) = P(\overline{X} < 0.95) + P(\overline{X} > 1.05)$, $Z = \frac{\overline{X} - \mu_{\overline{x}}}{\sigma_{\overline{x}} / \sqrt{n}} = \frac{0.95 - 1.005}{0.10 / \sqrt{20}} = -2.46$,

$P(\overline{X} < 0.95) = P(\overline{X} < 1.005) - P(0.95 < \overline{X} < 1.005) = 0.5 - 0.4931 = 0.0069$, $Z = \frac{\overline{X} - \mu_{\overline{x}}}{\sigma_{\overline{x}} / \sqrt{n}} = \frac{1.05 - 1.005}{0.10 / \sqrt{20}} = 2.01$,

$P(\overline{X} > 1.05) = P(\overline{X} > 1.005) - P(1.005 < \overline{X} < 1.05) = 0.5 - 0.4778 = 0.0222$,
$P(\overline{X} < 0.95 \text{ or } 1.05 < \overline{X}) = 0.0222 + 0.0069 = 0.0291$

67. (a) $\mu_x = e^{\mu_{\ln(x)} + \sigma^2_{\ln(x)}/2} = e^{4.5 + (1.3)^2/2} = e^{5.345} = 209.5579$

(b) $\sigma_x = \sqrt{e^{2(4.5)+(1.3)^2} \cdot \left(e^{(1.3)^2} - 1\right)} = \sqrt{e^{10.69} \cdot \left(e^{1.69} - 1\right)} = \sqrt{194079.316} = 440.544341$

(c) (1) $Z = \frac{\ln(X) - \mu_{\ln(x)}}{\sigma_{\ln(x)}} = \frac{\ln(100) - 4.5}{1.3} = 0.08$, $P(X < 100) = 0.5 + 0.0319 = 0.5319$

(2) $Z = \frac{\ln(X) - \mu_{\ln(x)}}{\sigma_{\ln(x)}} = \frac{\ln(200) - 4.5}{1.3} = 0.61$, $P(X < 200) = 0.5 + 0.2291 = 0.7291$

(3) $Z = \frac{\ln(X) - \mu_{\ln(x)}}{\sigma_{\ln(x)}} = \frac{\ln(100) - 4.5}{1.3} = 0.08$, $P(X < 100) = 0.5 + 0.0319 = 0.5319$,

$Z = \frac{\ln(X) - \mu_{\ln(x)}}{\sigma_{\ln(x)}} = \frac{\ln(200) - 4.5}{1.3} = 0.61$, $P(X < 200) = 0.5 + 0.2291 = 0.7291$,

$P(100 < X < 200) = P(X < 200) - P(X < 100) = 0.7291 - 05319 = 0.1972$

(d) $\mu_x = e^{\mu_{\ln(x)} + \sigma^2_{\ln(x)}/2} = e^{5 + (1.3)^2/2} = e^{5.845} = 345.5025$,

$\sigma_x = \sqrt{e^{2(5)+(1.3)^2} \cdot \left(e^{(1.3)^2} - 1\right)} = \sqrt{e^{11.69} \cdot \left(e^{1.69} - 1\right)} = \sqrt{527562.279} = 726.334826$

(1) $Z=\dfrac{\ln(X)-\mu_{\ln(x)}}{\sigma_{\ln(x)}}=\dfrac{\ln(100)-5}{1.3}=-0.3$, $P(X<100)=0.5-0.1179=0.3821$

(2) $Z=\dfrac{\ln(X)-\mu_{\ln(x)}}{\sigma_{\ln(x)}}=\dfrac{\ln(200)-5}{1.3}=0.23$, $P(X<200)=0.5+0.0910=0.5910$

(3) $Z=\dfrac{\ln(X)-\mu_{\ln(x)}}{\sigma_{\ln(x)}}=\dfrac{\ln(100)-5}{1.3}=-0.3$, $P(X<100)=0.5-0.1179=0.3821$,

$Z=\dfrac{\ln(X)-\mu_{\ln(x)}}{\sigma_{\ln(x)}}=\dfrac{\ln(200)-5}{1.3}=0.23$, $P(X<200)=0.5+0.0910=0.5910$,

$P(100<X<200)=P(X<200)-P(X<100)=0.5910-0.3821=0.2089$

(e) $\mu_x=e^{\mu_{\ln(x)}+\sigma^2_{\ln(x)}/2}=e^{4.5+(1.5)^2/2}=e^{5.625}=277.2723$,

$\sigma_x=\sqrt{e^{2(4.5)+(1.5)^2}\cdot\left(e^{(1.5)^2}-1\right)}=\sqrt{e^{11.25}\cdot\left(e^{2.25}-1\right)}=\sqrt{652536.45}=807.797283$

(1) $Z=\dfrac{\ln(X)-\mu_{\ln(x)}}{\sigma_{\ln(x)}}=\dfrac{\ln(100)-4.5}{1.5}=0.07$, $P(X<100)=0.5+0.0279=0.5279$

(2) $Z=\dfrac{\ln(X)-\mu_{\ln(x)}}{\sigma_{\ln(x)}}=\dfrac{\ln(200)-4.5}{1.5}=0.53$, $P(X<200)=0.5+0.2019=0.7019$

(3) $Z=\dfrac{\ln(X)-\mu_{\ln(x)}}{\sigma_{\ln(x)}}=\dfrac{\ln(100)-4.5}{1.5}=0.07$, $P(X<100)=0.5+0.0279=0.5279$,

$Z=\dfrac{\ln(X)-\mu_{\ln(x)}}{\sigma_{\ln(x)}}=\dfrac{\ln(200)-4.5}{1.5}=0.53$, $P(X<200)=0.5+0.2019=0.7019$,

$P(100<X<200)=P(X<200)-P(X<100)=0.7019-0.5279=0.174$

68. $\lambda=20$

(a) $P(\text{time}<14)=1-e^{-14/20}=1-e^{-0.7}=0.5034$

(b) $P(\text{time}>21)=e^{-21/20}=e^{-1.05}=0.3499$

(c) $P(\text{time}<7)=1-e^{-7/20}=1-e^{-0.35}=0.2953$

(d) $\alpha=1.5$, $\beta=20$

$P(\text{time}<14)=1-e^{-(x/\beta)^\alpha}=1-e^{-(14/20)^{1.5}}=0.4432$

$P(\text{time}>21)=1-1+e^{-(x/\beta)^\alpha}=e^{-(21/20)^{1.5}}=0.3409$

$P(\text{time}<7)=1-e^{-(x/\beta)^\alpha}=1-e^{-(7/20)^{1.5}}=0.1870$

The probabilities for the Weibull distribution are smaller than the corresponding probabilities for the exponential distribution.

69. (a)

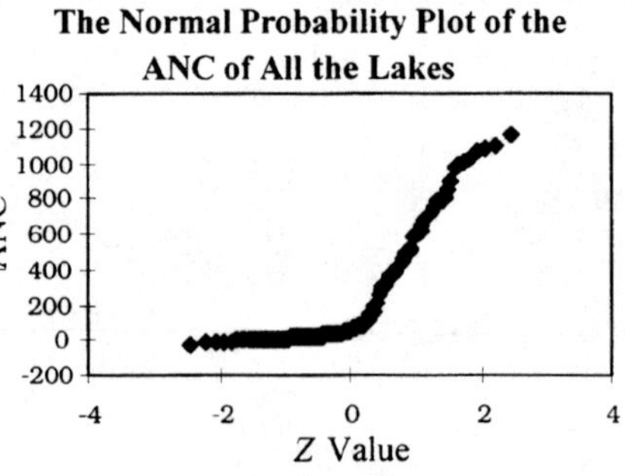

(b) The acid-neutralized capacities of all the lakes appear to be a right-skewed distribution, because the curve rises slowly at first, and then the rate of increase progresses rapidly.

(c)

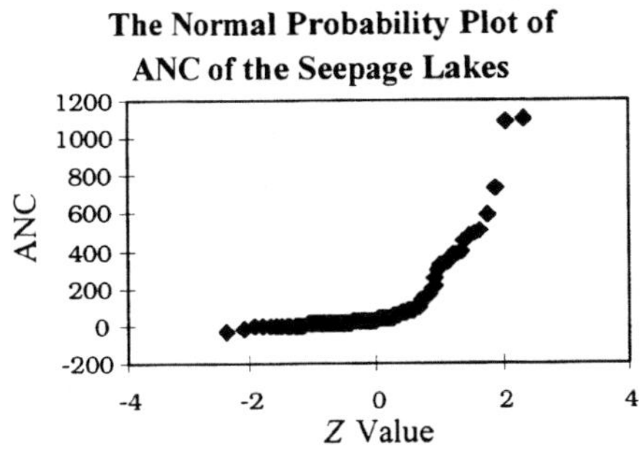

(d) The acid-neutralized capacities of the seepage lakes appear to belong to the right-skewed distribution, because the curve rises slowly at first, and then the rate of increase progresses rapidly.

(e)

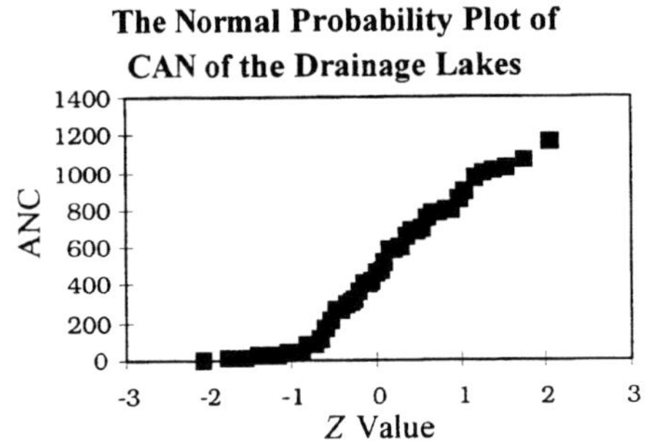

(f) The acid-neutralized capacities of the drainage lakes appear to belong to the right-skewed distribution, because the curve rises slowly at first, and then the rate of increase progresses rapidly.

(g)

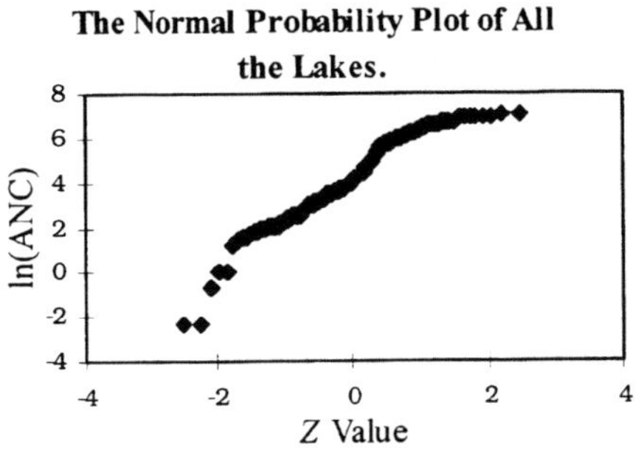

Except for several points at the lower and upper ends of the scale, the plot seems to approximately follow a straight line. Thus, it can be concluded that the data appears to be approximately normally distributed.

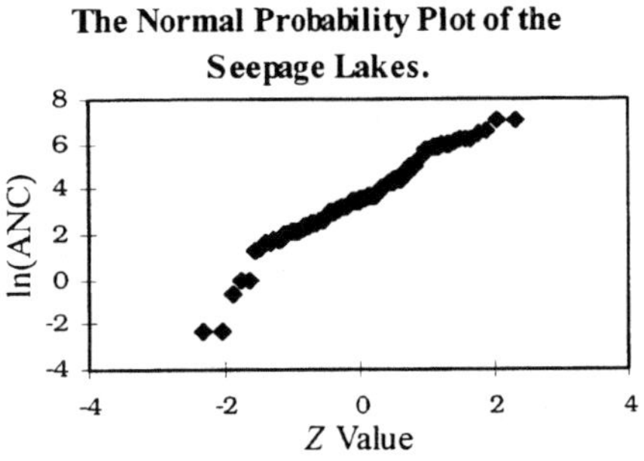

Except for several points at the lower and upper ends of the scale, the plot seems to approximately follow a straight line. Thus, it can be concluded that the data appears to be approximately normally distributed.

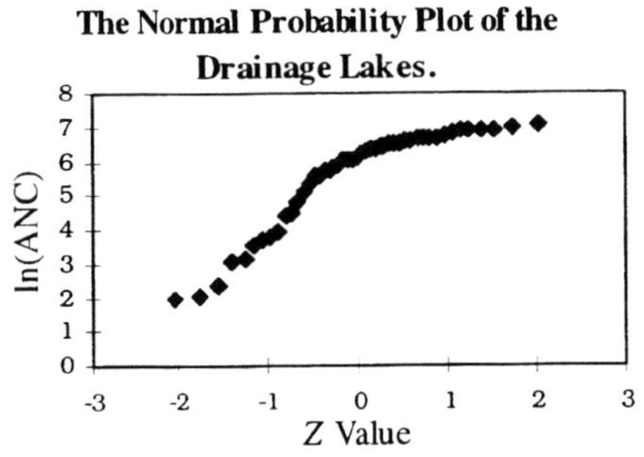

The acid-neutralized capacities of the drainage lakes appear to be left-skewed distribution, because the curve rises more rapidly at first, and then the rate of increase decreases.

(h) All distributions of (a)–(f) are right-skewed whereas the new variable consisting of the natural logarithm of the acid neutralizing capacity appears to be approximately normally distributed.

70. (a)

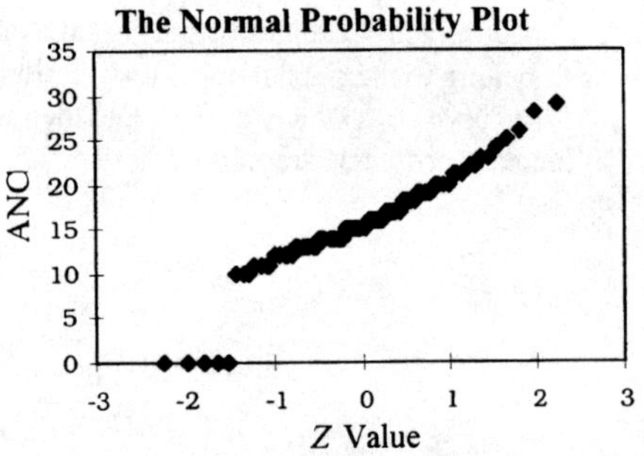

(b) Except for several points at the lower and upper ends of the scale, the plot approximately follows a straight line. The parts per million of impurities of a chemical appear to be approximately normally distributed.

chapter 6

Statistical Process Control Charts I: Basic Concepts and Attributes Charts

1. (a) ***NP* Chart for Abandoned Calls**

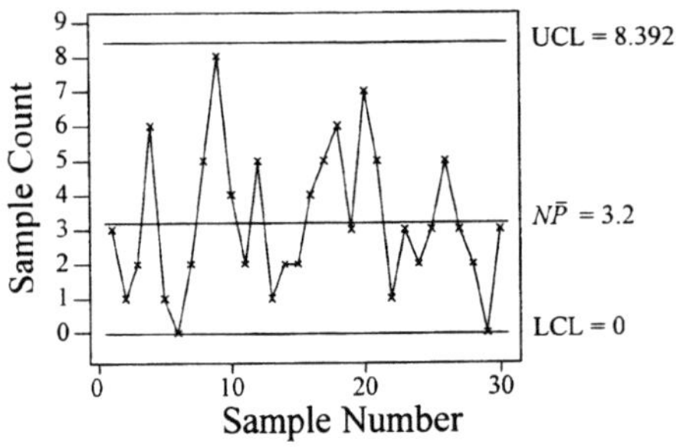

(b) Yes, rules 1–5 provide that this process is in a state of statistical control.

(c) Rules 1–5 provide that this process is in a state of statistical control.

(d) ***P* Chart for Abandoned Calls**

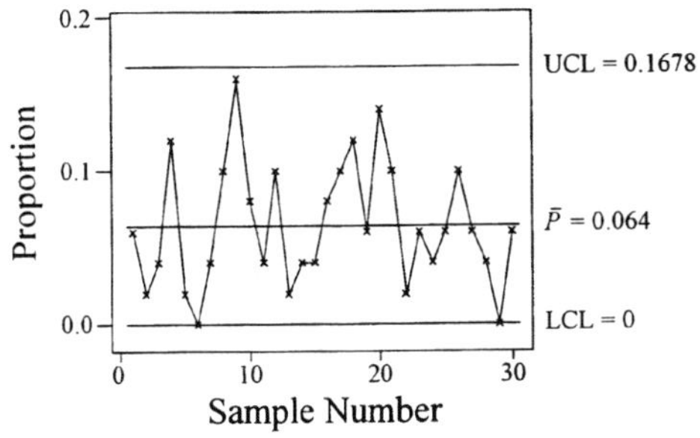

(e) Yes, rules 1–5 provide that this process is in a state of statistical control.

(f) Rules 1–5 provide that this process is in a state of statistical control.

(g) The results are the same.

2. (a) ***NP* Chart for Nonconforming Tools**

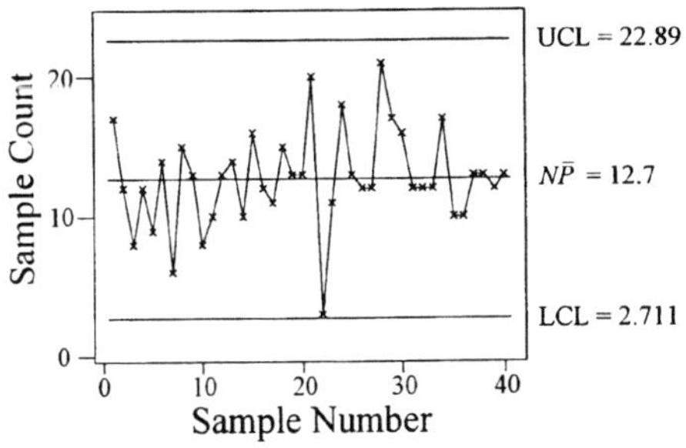

(b) Yes, rules 1–5 provide that this process is in a state of statistical control.

(c) Rules 1–5 provide that this process is in a state of statistical control.

(d) ***P* Chart for Nonconforming Tools**

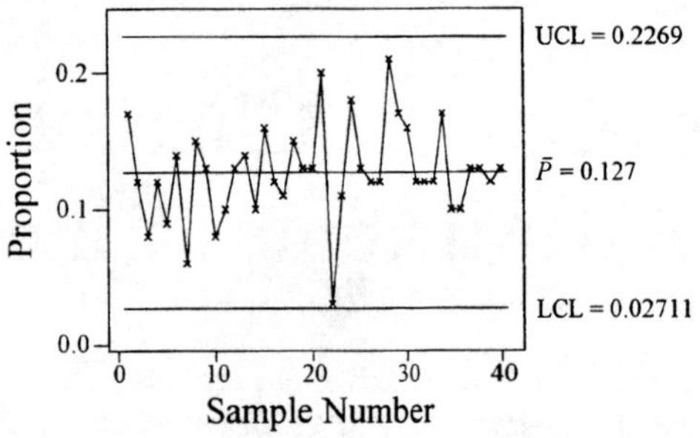

(e) Yes, rules 1–5 provide that this process is in a state of statistical control.
(f) Rules 1–5 provide that this process is in a state of statistical control.
(g) The results are the same.

3. (a) ***NP* Chart for Nonconforming Tiles**

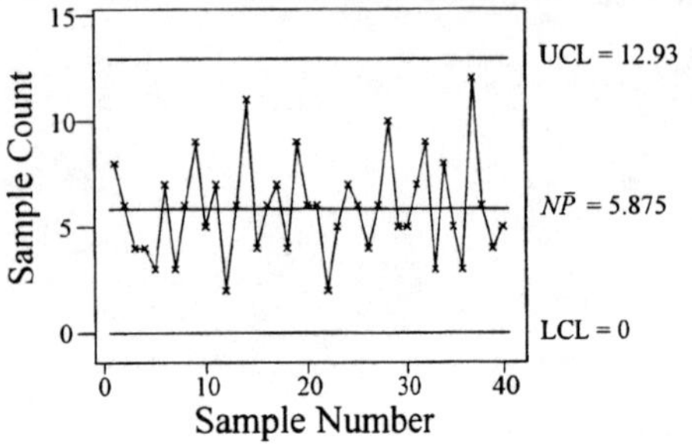

(b) Yes, rules 1–5 provide that this process is in a state of statistical control.
(c) Rules 1–5 provide that this process is in a state of statistical control.

(d) ***P* Chart for Nonconforming Tiles**

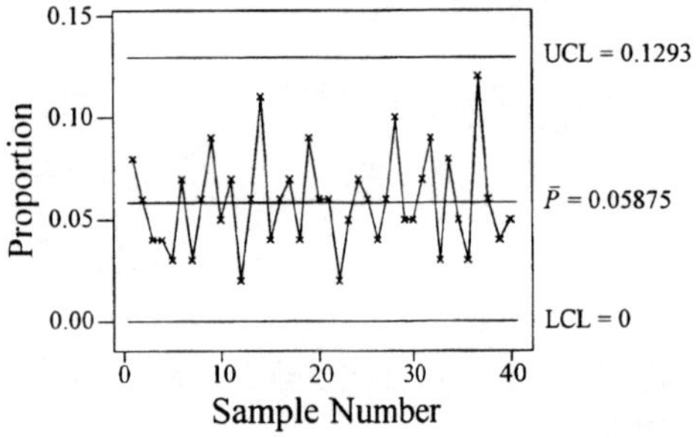

(e) Yes, rules 1–5 provide that this process is in a state of statistical control.
(f) Rules 1–5 provide that this process is in a state of statistical control.
(g) The results are the same.

4. (a) ***NP* Chart for Nonconforming Motor End Shields**

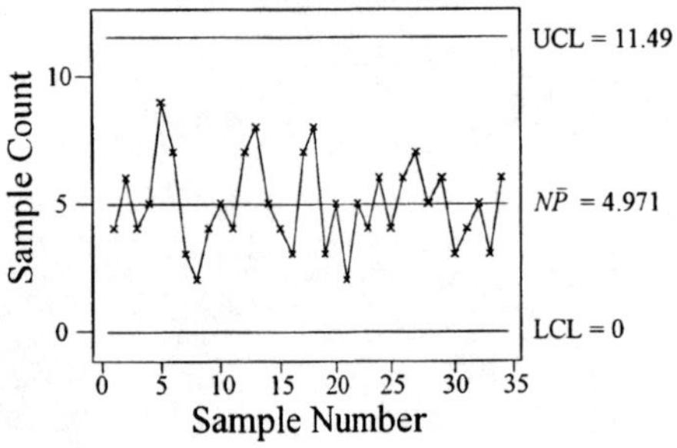

(b) Yes, rules 1–5 provide that this process is in a state of statistical control.
(c) Rules 1–5 provide that this process is in a state of statistical control.

(d) ***P* Chart for Nonconforming Motor End Shields**

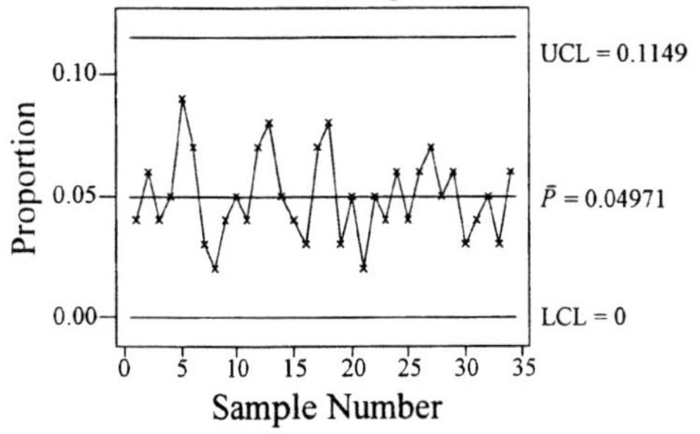

(e) Yes, rules 1–5 provide that this process is in a state of statistical control.
(f) Rules 1–5 provide that this process is in a state of statistical control.
(g) The results are the same.

5. (a) ***P* Chart for Nonconforming Components**

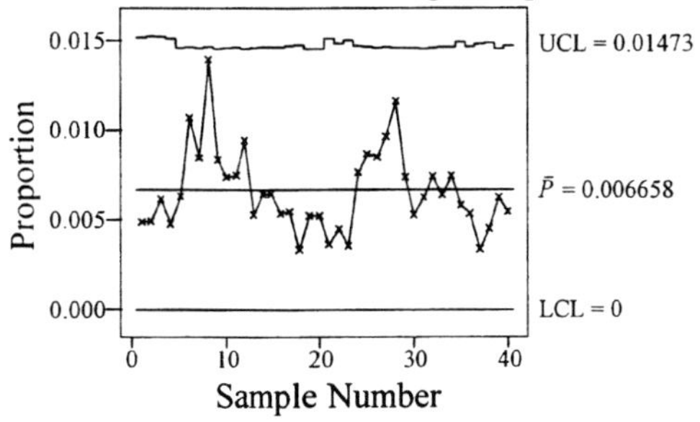

(b) Due to rule 4 (8 points below the centerline), the process is out of control.
(c) The process is out of control, but there are no exceptional points for removing.

6. (a) ***P* Chart for Scrap Reels**

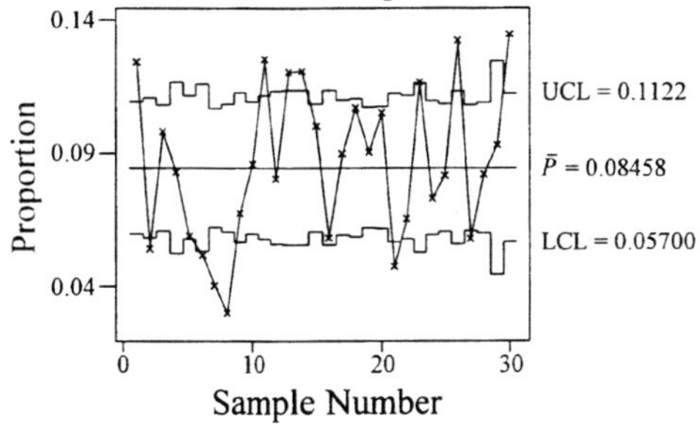

(b) There are points outside the control limits, so the process is out of control.
(c) There appears to be a mixture of patterns in these data, so it is necessary to determine the sources of this effect.

7. (a) ***P* Chart for Pending**

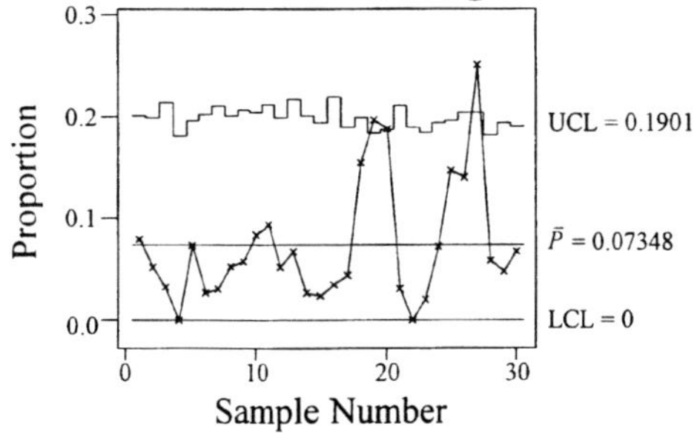

(b) There are points outside the control limits, so the process is out of control.
(c) It is necessary to determine the reason for the high proportions of unfocused, or pending samples on the 19th, 20th and 27th days.

8. (a) ***P* Chart for Nonconforming Subassemblies**

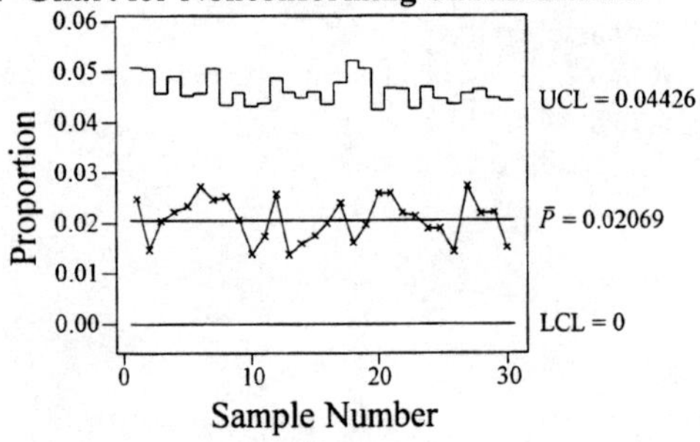

(b) Yes, rules 1–5 provide that this process is in a state of statistical control.

(c) Rules 1–5 provide that this process is in a state of statistical control.

9. (a) ***c* Chart for Imperfect Rolls**

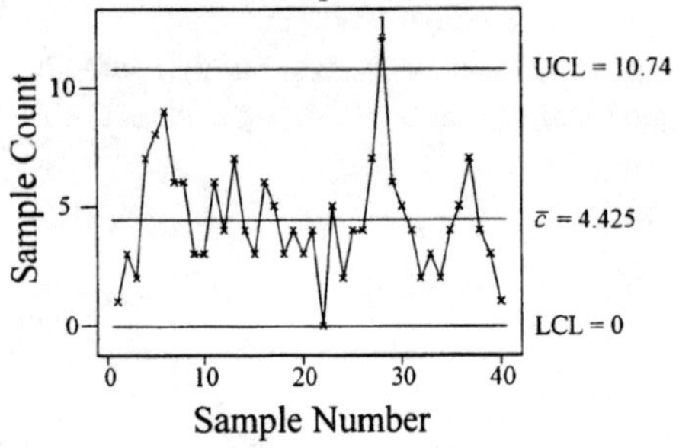

(b) There is a point above UCL, so this process is out of control.

(c) After removing the out-of-control point, (28), the process control chart appears as shown to the right. The revised process is in a better state of statistical control.

***c* Chart for Imperfect Rolls**

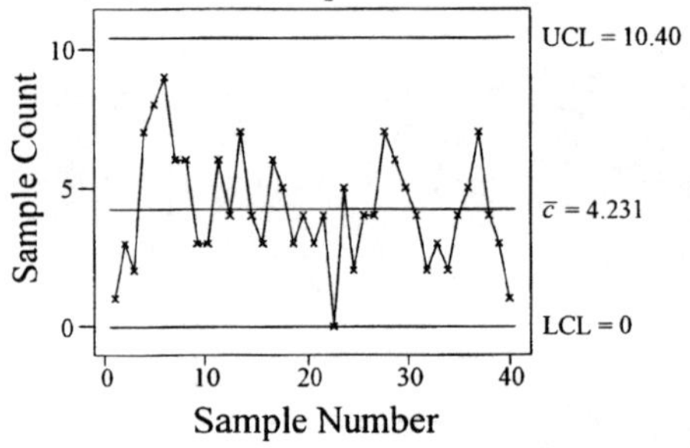

10. (a) ***c* Chart for Missing Rivets**

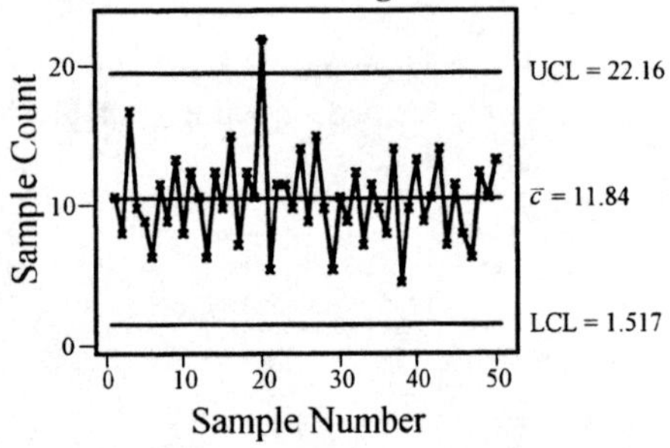

(b) There is one point above UCL, so this process is out of control.

(c) ***c* Chart for Missing Rivets**

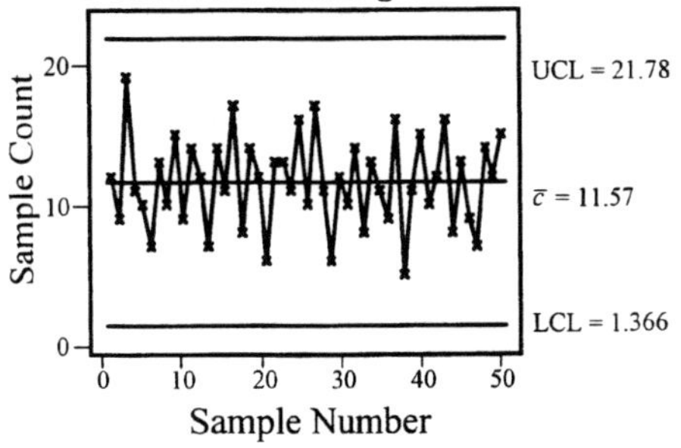

Now this process is in a state of statistical control.

11. (a) ***c* Chart for Vehicle Accident Data**

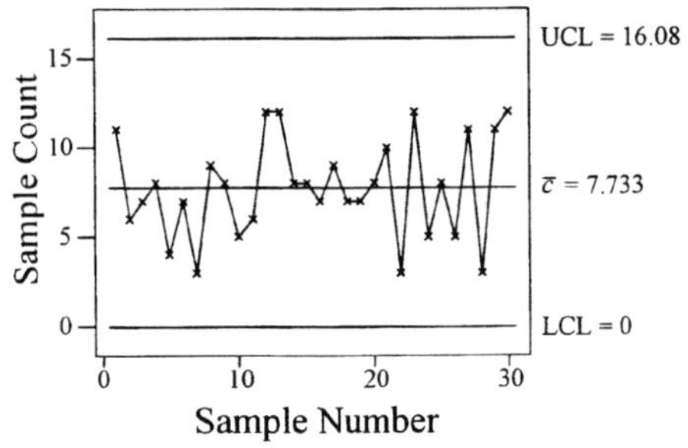

(b) Yes, rules 1–5 provide that this process is in a state of statistical control.

(c) Rules 1–5 provide that this process is in a state of statistical control.

(d) ***c* Chart for Vehicle Accident Data (With Expanded Control Limits)**

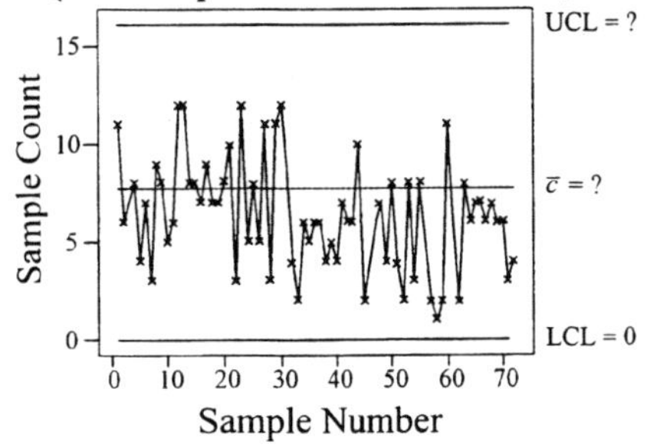

The process is out of statistical control (8 points below center line).

(e) This course leads to the decrease in the number of accidents, and shifts away from the mean.

(f) Calculate control limits for further monitoring using only data of 1993–1995 years.

(g) ***u* Chart for Vehicle Accident Data**

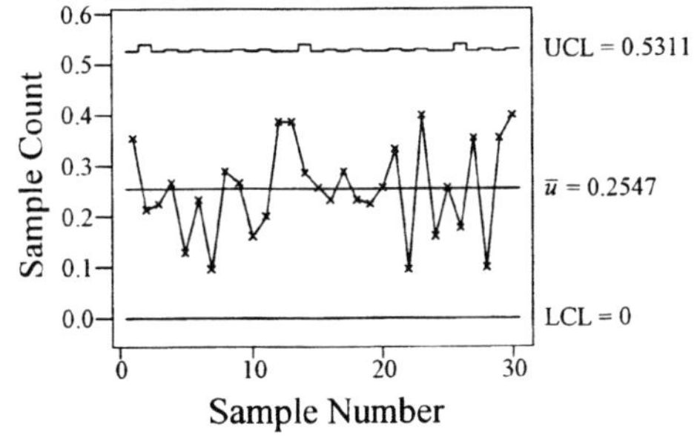

(h) There is a small variability in sample sizes, so *c* and *u* charts lead to the same result.

12. (a)

c Chart for Hits

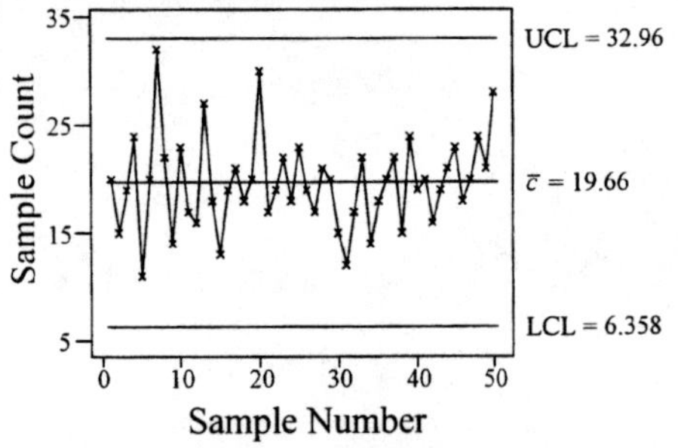

(b) Yes, rules 1–5 provide that this process is in a state of statistical control.

(c) Rules 1–5 provide that this process is in a state of statistical control.

13. (a)

***u* Chart for Code Errors**

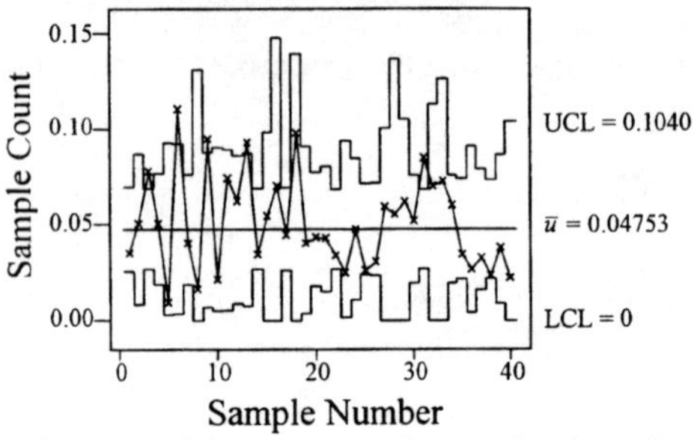

(b) There are points above UCL, so the process is out of control.

(c) After removing the 4 out-of-control points, the *u* chart appears as shown below.

***u* Chart for Code Errors**
(Recalculated Without Out-Of-Control Points)

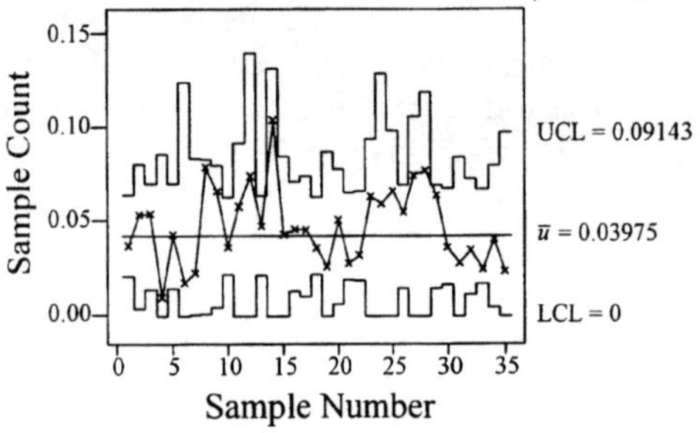

The revised process in in a state of statistical control.

14. (a)

***u* Chart for Flaws**

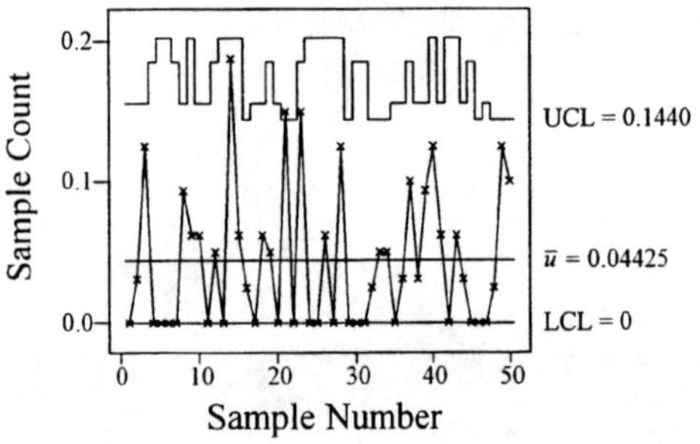

(b) There is one point above UCL, so this process is out of control.

(c) After removing the out-of-control control point, (21), the *u* chart appears as shown below.

u Chart for Flaws
(Recalculated Without Out-Of-Control Points)

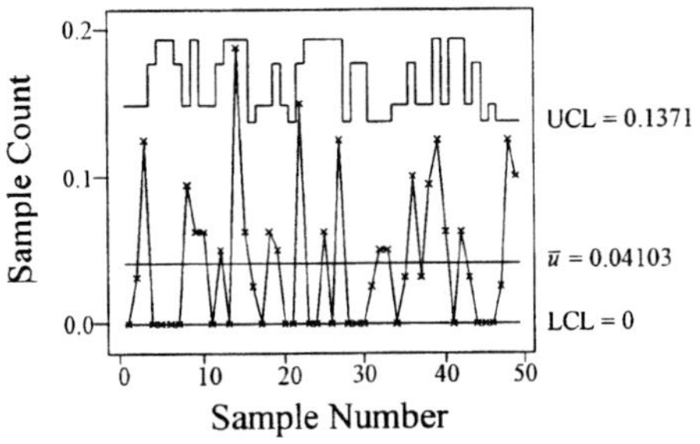

The revised process in in a state of statistical control.

15. (a) **c Chart for Cartridges Sent**

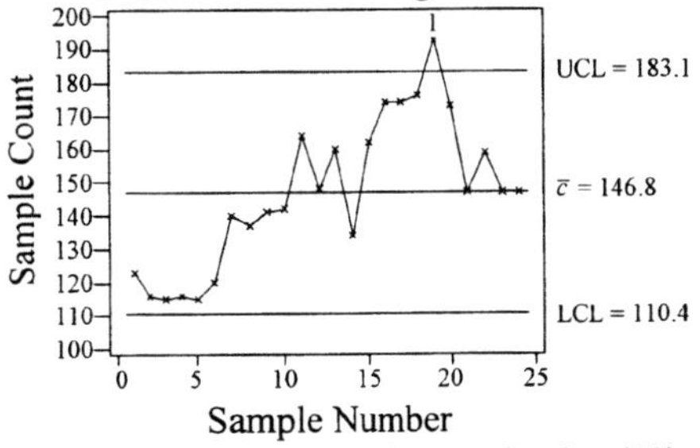

(b) Due to rules 1 and 4, the process is out if control.

(c) After removing the out-of-control point, (19), the control chart appears as shown below.

c Chart for Cartridges Sent
(Recalculated Without Out-Of-Control Points)

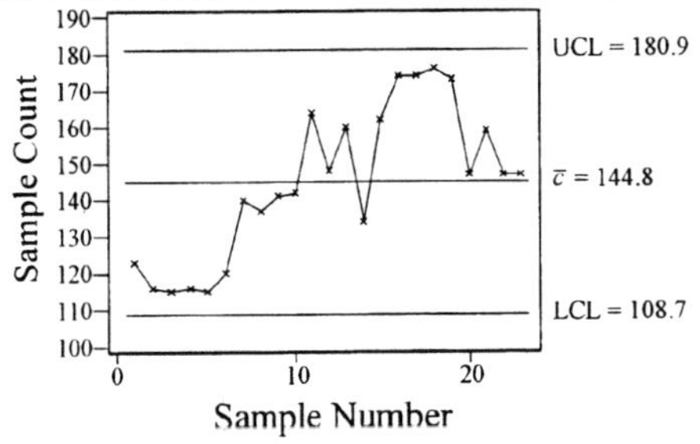

Due to rule 4, the process is still out of control.

16. Common causes are numerous small sources of variability that are inherent to a system or process and operate randomly (by chance). Special causes of variability usually have relatively large effects on the process and its output and occur sporadically.

17. When only chance or common cause affect the system, the process is said to be stable (that is, in a state of statistical control).

18. When only chance or common cause operate on the system, the process is said to be in a state of statistical control.

19. Control charts can detect special causes. Special causes are then eliminated to reduce the process variability. This results in improved product quality.

20. There are two types of errors. False alarms occur when the process is thought to be out of control when, in fact, it is not. Another type of error occurs whenever we fail to detect that a process is out of control.

21. One or more points plotted above the UCL or below the LCL indicate that the system is out of control. Should this occur, the process is interrupted and efforts are undertaken to identify the special cause that resulted in the signal.

22. Cyclic, mixture, and stratification patterns, as well as shifts in the process level indicate that the process is out of control.

23. Moment calculations in p and np charts are based on binomial distribution; the 3σ rule is derived from both the central limit theorem and from the normal distribution.

24. Moment calculations in c and u charts are based on the Poisson distribution; the 3σ rule is derived from both the central limit theorem and the normal distribution.

25. The assumptions are as follows:
(1) There are only two possible outcomes for an event. An item must be found to be either conforming or nonconforming. No intermediate values are possible.
(2) The probability of nonconforming items is constant.
(3) Successive items are independent.
(4) All samples contain the same number of items (p charts only).

26. If the number of conforming or acceptable items is counted instead of the number of nonconforming terms, then the chart is referred to as a yield chart.

27. In the United States, the upper control limit is usually placed three standard deviations above the mean, and the lower control limit is placed three standard deviations below the mean.

28. c charts and u charts are called area of opportunity charts. For c charts, areas of opportunity are of the same size, but for u charts, their sizes for the areas of opportunity may vary.

29. (a)

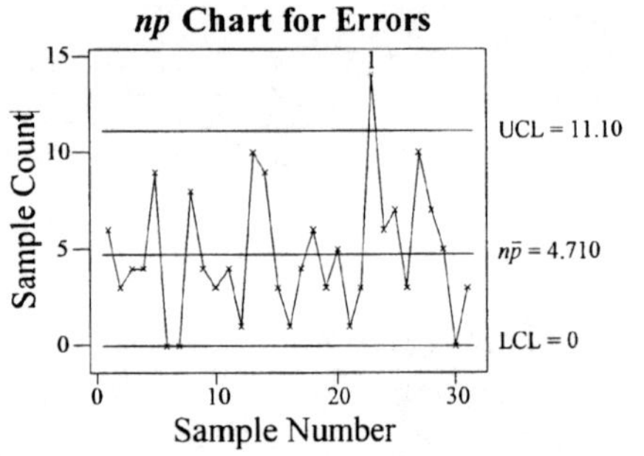

(b) There is one point above UCL, so this process is out of control. This day is probably the day after Labor Day (a holiday in the United States).

(c)

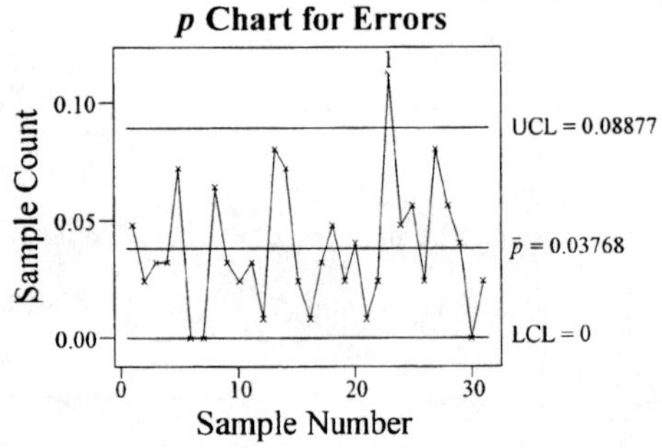

There is one point above UCL, so this process is out of control.

(d) The two charts differ only in their ordinates by the factor of 125. The shape of the plot and the relationship between the plotted values and the control limits are the same. Therefore, both charts convey the same information.

30. (a) ***np* Chart for Nonconforming Canisters**

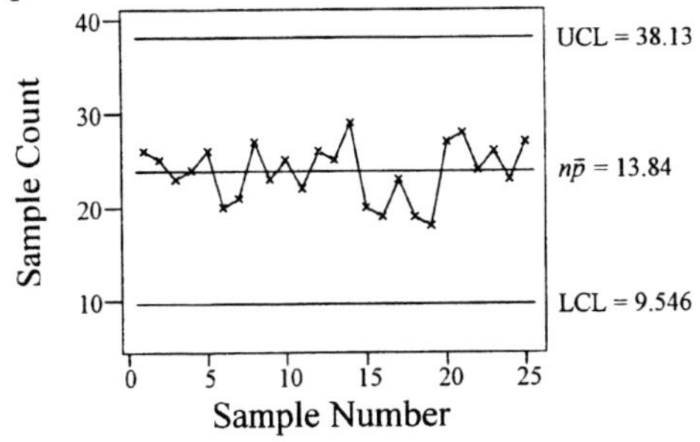

(b) Yes, rules 1–5 provide that this process is in a state of statistical control.

(c) ***p* Chart for Nonconforming Canisters**

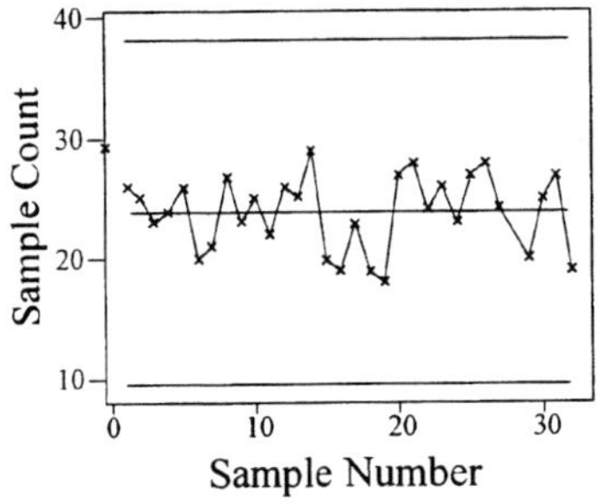

(d) ***p* Chart for Nonconforming Canisters**

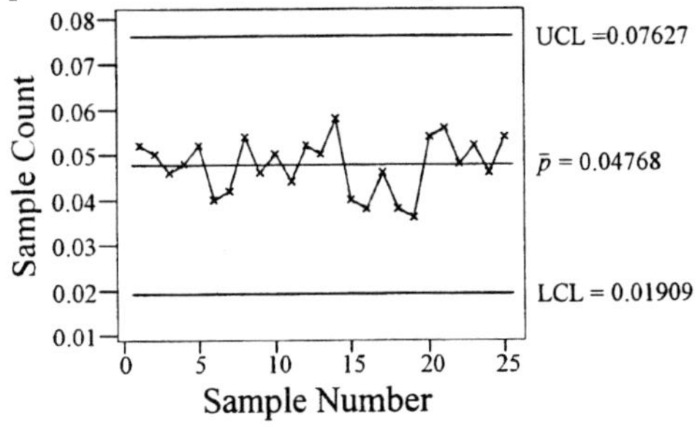

(e) The two charts differ only in their ordinates by the factor of 500, so the produced results must be the same.

31. (a) ***p* Chart for Records**

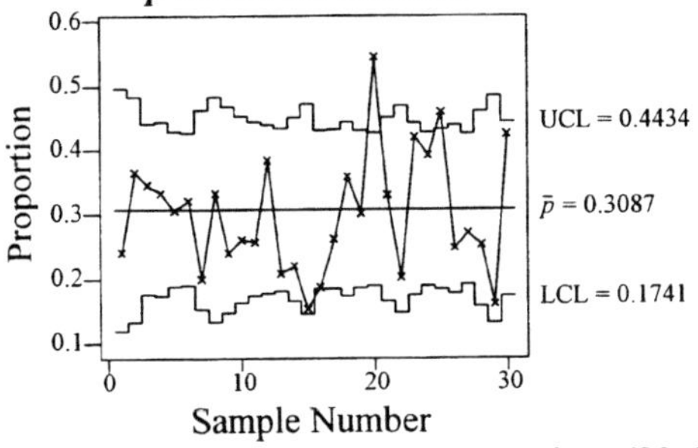

(b) There are two points above UCL, so this process is out of control.

(c) After removing the out-of-control points, (20, 25), the control chart appears as shown below.

***p* Chart for Records**

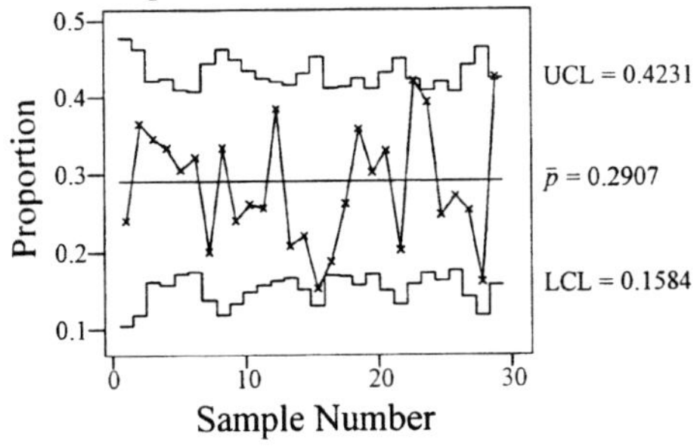

The revised process is in a state of statistical control.

32. (a) ***p* Chart for Passed**

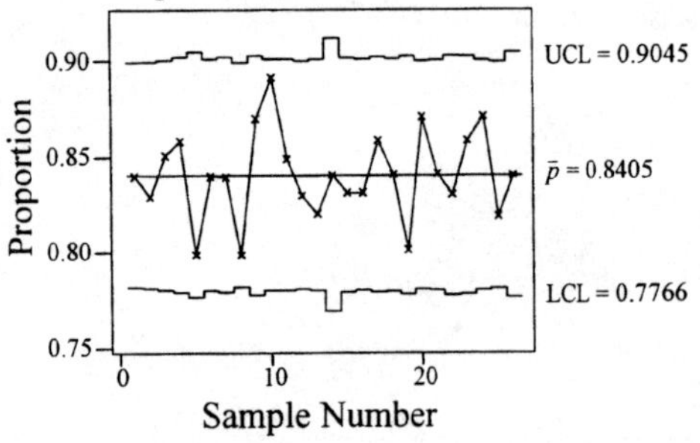

(b) Rules 1–5 provide that this process is in a state of statistical control.

33. (a) ***p* Chart for Returned Units**

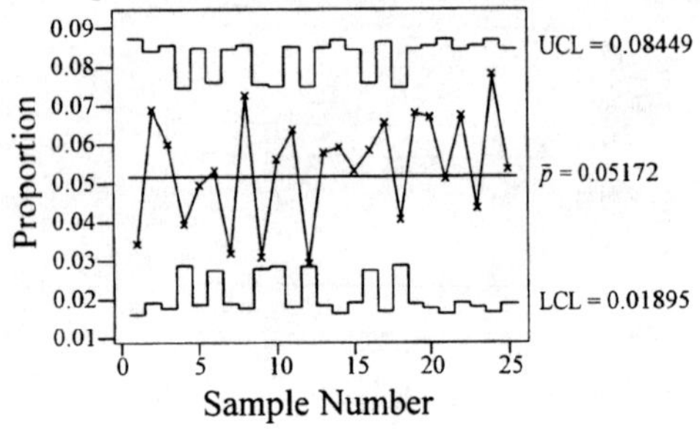

(b) Yes, rules 1–5 provide that this process is in a state of statistical control.

(c) Rules 1–5 provide that this process is in a state of statistical control.

34. (a) ***p* Chart for Incomplete Lab Slips**

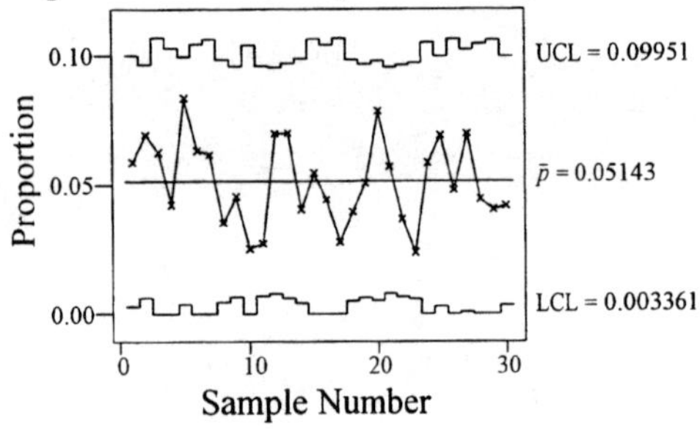

(b) Yes, rules 1–5 provide that this process is in a state of statistical control.

(c) Rules 1–5 provide that this process is in a state of statistical control.

35. (a) ***p* Chart for Problems**

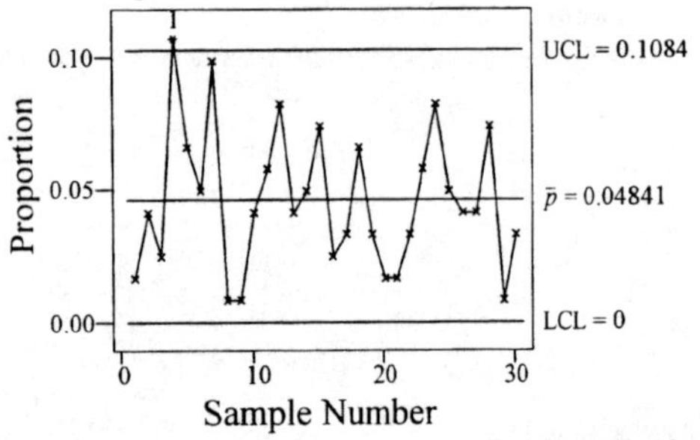

(b) Rules 1 and 2 provide that this process is out of control.

(c) After removing the out-of-control point, (4), the control chart appears as shown below.

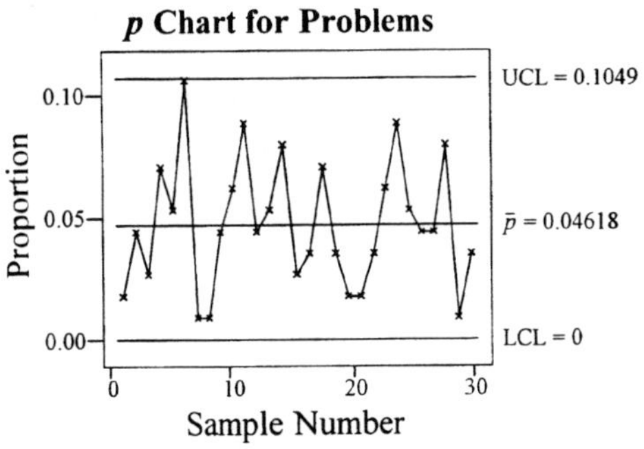

All points are inside the control limits, but due to rule 2 the process is out of control.

36. (a)

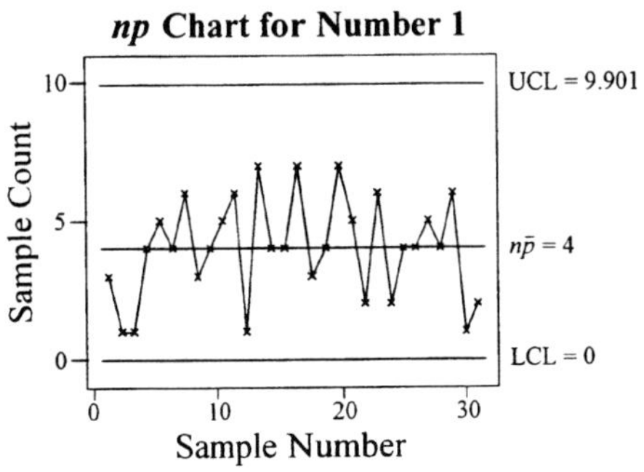

(b) Yes, rules 1–5 provide that this process is in a state of statistical control.

(c) Rules 1–5 provide that this process is in a state of statistical control.

(d)

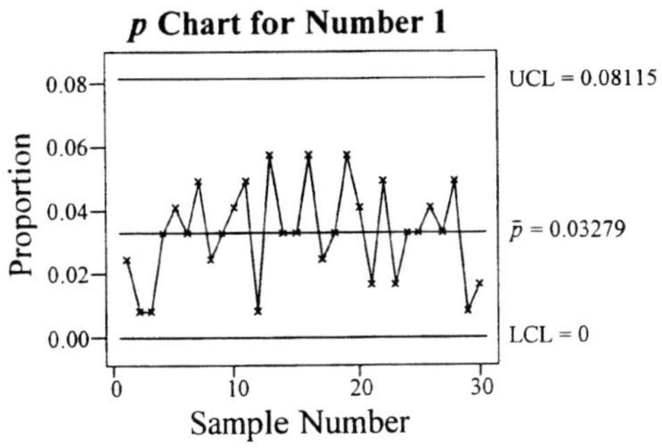

(e) Yes, rules 1–5 provide that this process is in a state of statistical control.

(f) Rules 1–5 provide that this process is in a state of statistical control.

(g) The two charts differ only in their ordinates by the factor of 122. The shape of the plot and the relationship between the plotted values and the control limits are the same. Therefore, both charts convey the same information.

37. (a)

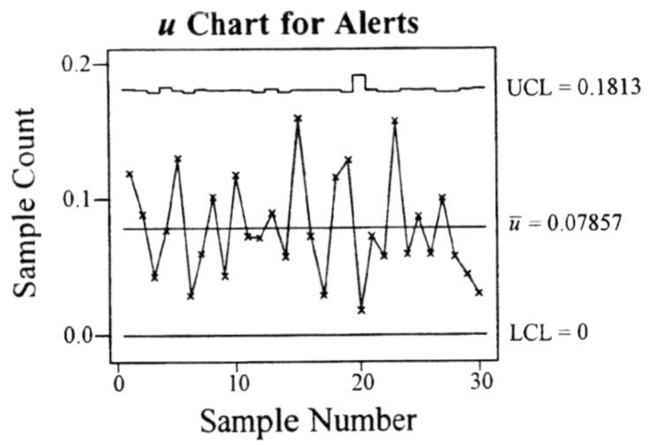

(b) Yes, rules 1–5 provide that this process is in a state of statistical control.

(c) Rules 1–5 provide that this process is in a state of statistical control.

38. (a) ***c* Chart for Accidents**

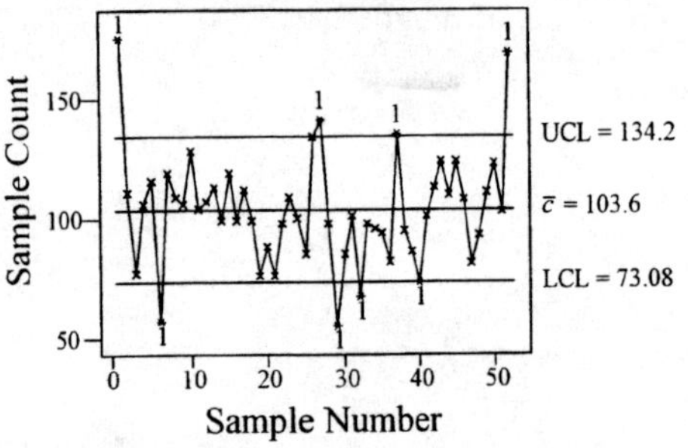

(b) There are many points outside the control limits, so this process is out of statistical control.

(c) A large number of accidents occur during the holidays and a smaller number occur during winter and summer vacations.

39. (a) ***c* Chart for Deliveries**

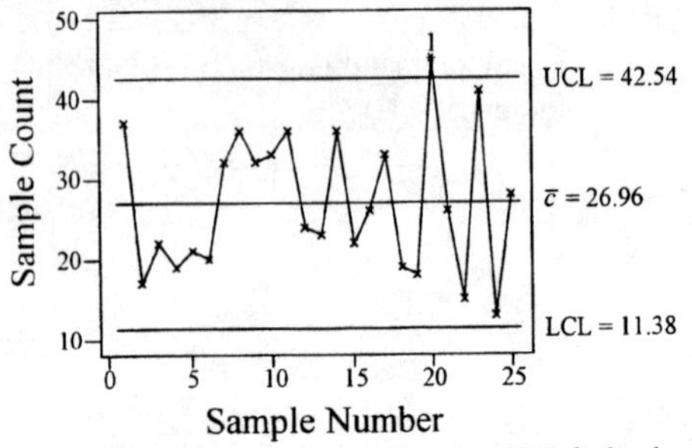

(b) There is one point above UCL, so this process is out of control.

(c) After removing the control point (20) is in the state of statistical control now.

***c* Chart for Deliveries**

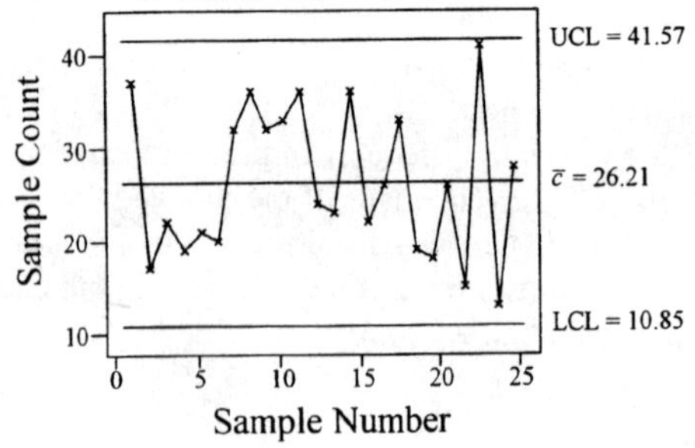

The revised process is in a state of statistical control.

(d) ***c* Chart for Deliveries**

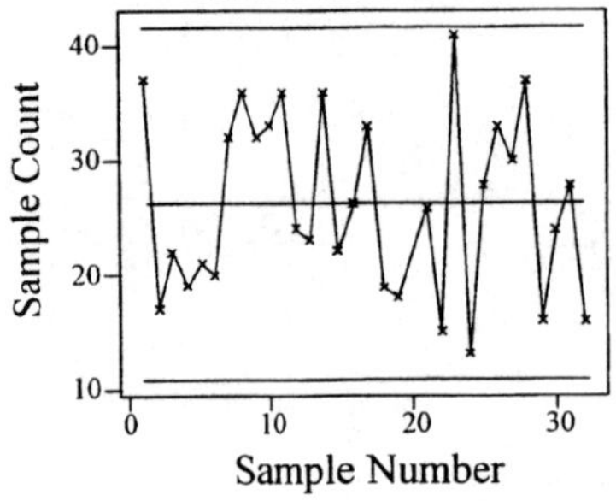

All points are within the revised control limits.

(e) Yes, because the revised process is stable.

40. (a) ***u* Chart for Incidents**

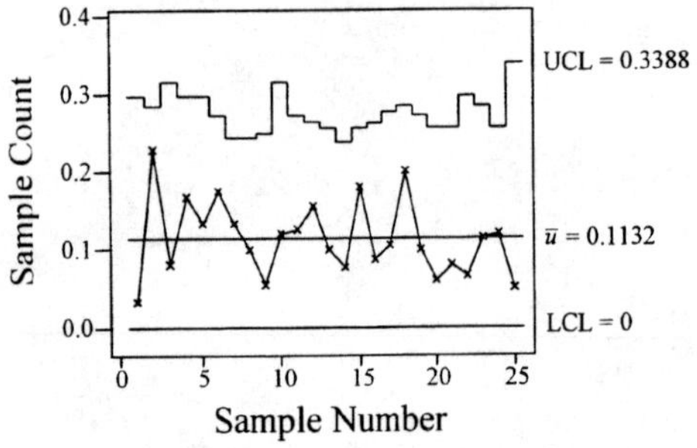

(b) Yes, rules 1–5 provide that inference is in the state of statistical control.

(c) Rules 1–5 provide that this process is in a state of statistical control.

41. (a) The LCL and UCL vary with sample size. When $n = 100$, the LCL $= 0.0119$ and the UCL $= 0.2133$. When $n = 112$, the LCL $= 0.0175$ and the UCL $= 0.2077$. When $n = 126$, the LCL $= 0.0229$ and the UCL $= 0.2022$.

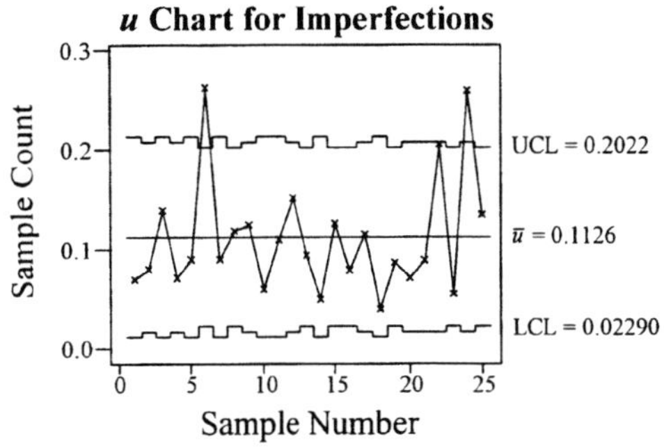

(b) There are two points representing roll 6 and roll 24 above the UCL, so the printing process is out of control.

(c) After the elimination of points 6 and 24, the control chart is shown below. The LCL and UCL vary with sample size. When $n = 500$, the LCL $= 0.0046$ and the UCL $= 0.1932$. When $n = 112$, the LCL $= 0.0098$ and the UCL $= 0.1880$. When $n = 126$, the LCL $= 0.0149$ and the UCL 0.1829.

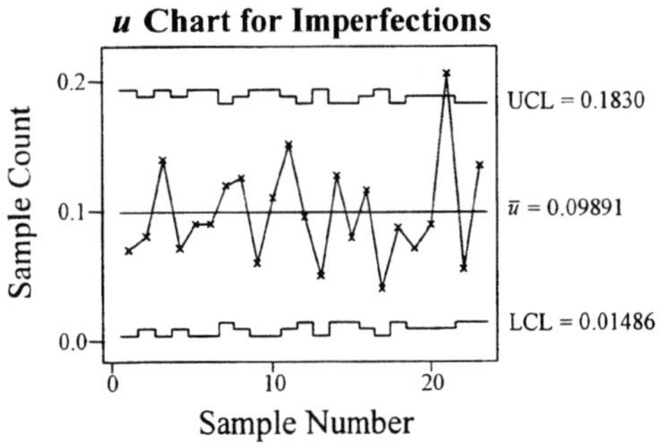

The process is still out of control.

42. (a)

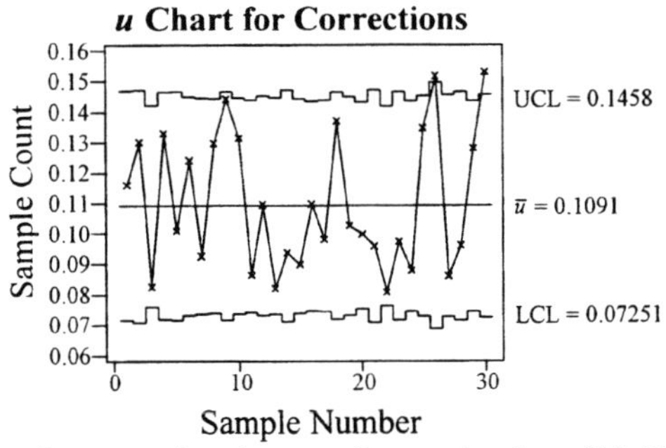

(b) There are two points above UCL, so this process is out of control.

(c) After removing the out-of-control points, (26, 30), the control chart appears as shown below. The revised process is still out of control.

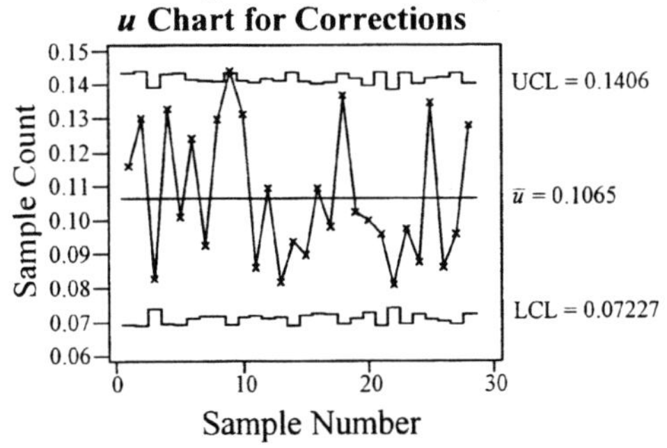

43. Answers will vary.

44. Answers will vary.

chapter 7

Statistical Process Control Charts II: Variable Control Charts

1. The data is in stacked format. Before using PHStat compute the mean and range for each group.

(a)

Control Chart	
Sample/Subgroup Size	5
$\bar{R}$	274.867
***R* Chart**	
D_3 Factor	0
D_4 Factor	2.114
Lower Control Limit	0
Center Line	274.867
Upper Control Limit	581.068

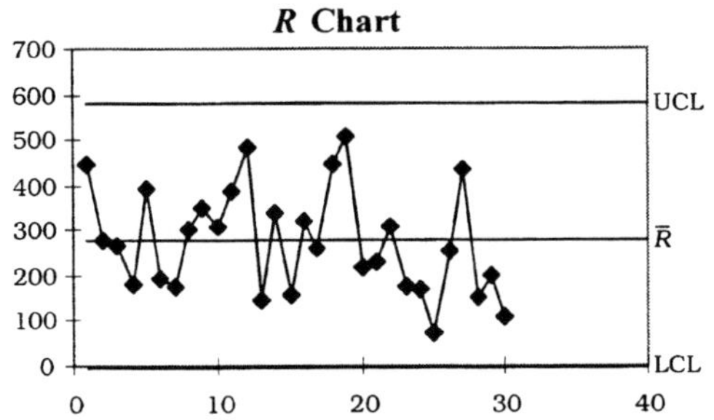

(b) There are no points outside of the control limits and there is no evidence of a pattern in the *R* chart. Therefore, we can conclude that the process is in a state of statistical control.

(c)

$\bar{X}$ Chart	
Average of Subgroup	197.887
A_2 Factor	0.577
Lower Control Limit	39.289
Center	197.887
Upper Control Limit	356.485

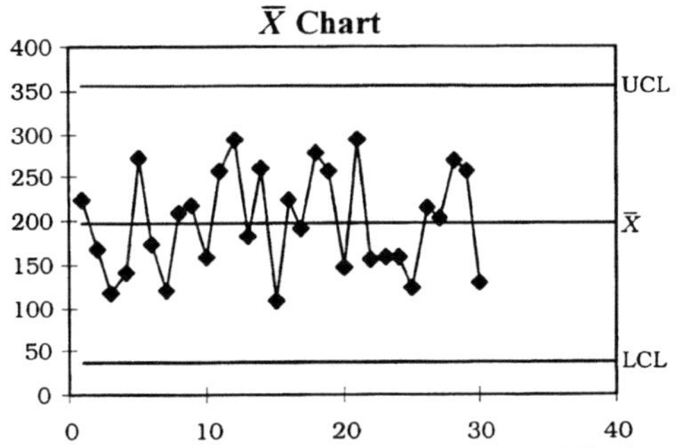

There are no points outside of the control limits, so the process is in a state of statistical control.

(d) There are no points outside of the control limits and there is no evidence of a pattern in the $\bar{X}$ chart. Therefore, we can conclude that the process is in a state of statistical control.

(e)

S Chart	
$\bar{S}$	108.771
B_3 factor	0
B_4 factor	2.089
Lower Control Limit	0
Center Line	108.771
Upper Control Limit	227.222

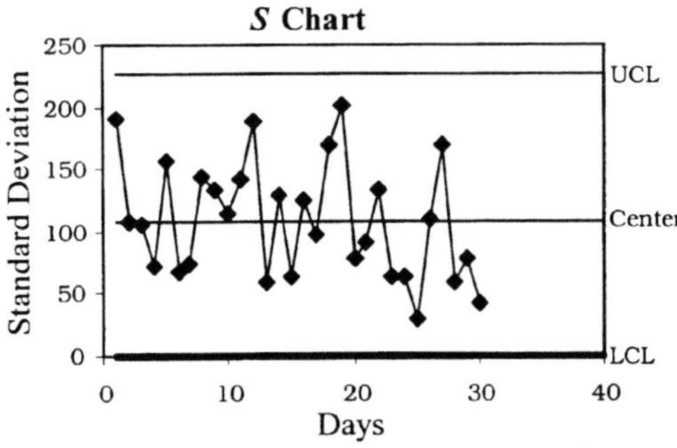

(f) There are no points outside of the control limits and there is no evidence of a pattern in the *S* chart. Therefore, we can conclude that the process is in a state of statistical control.

(g)

$\overline{X}$ Chart	
Average $\overline{X}$	197.887
A_3 factor	1.427
Lower Control Limit	42.671
Center Line	197.887
Upper Control Limit	353.103

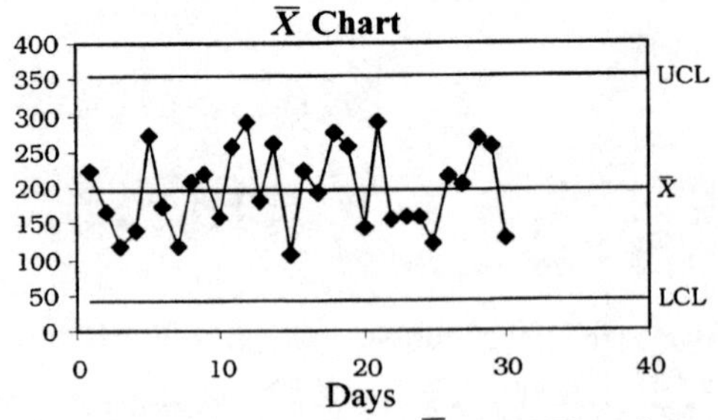

There are no points outside of the control limits and there is no evidence of a pattern in the $\overline{X}$ chart. Therefore, we can conclude that the process is in a state of statistical control.

(h) Results of (a) and (d) and (e–f) are the same. Process is stable and in a state of statistical control.

(i) Process is stable and is in a state of statistical control.

2. (a)

Control Chart	
Sample/Subgroup Size	4
$\overline{R}$	0.5911
***R* Chart**	
D_3 Factor	0
D_4 Factor	2.282
Lower Control Limit	0
Center	0.5911
Upper Control Limit	1.3490

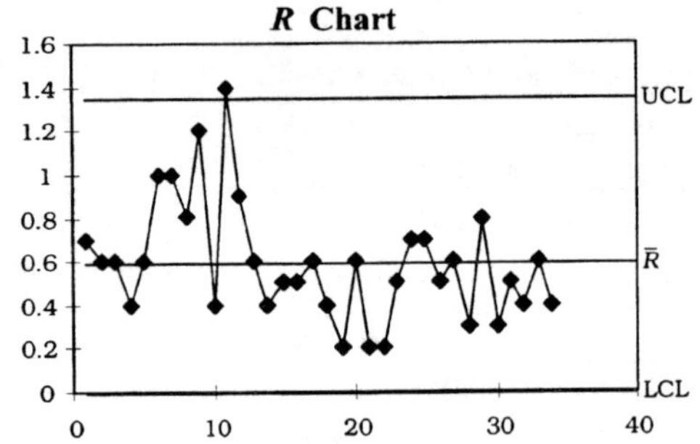

(b) Container 11 is above the upper control limit and should be removed.

Sample/Subgroup Size	4
$\overline{R}$	0.5667
***R* Chart**	
D_3 Factor	0
D_4 Factor	2.282
Lower Control Limit	0
Center	0.566667
Upper Control Limit	1.293133

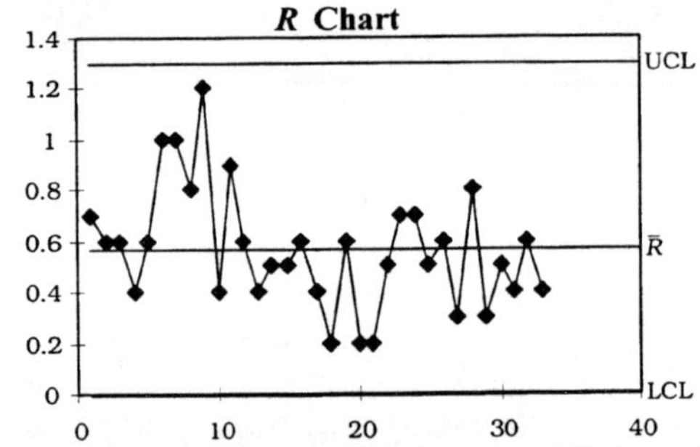

There are no points outside the control limits and no evidence of a pattern in the *R* chart.

(c)

$\bar{X}$ Chart	
Average of Subgroup	10.725
A_2 Factor	0.729
Lower Control Limit	10.311
Center	10.725
Upper Control Limit	11.138

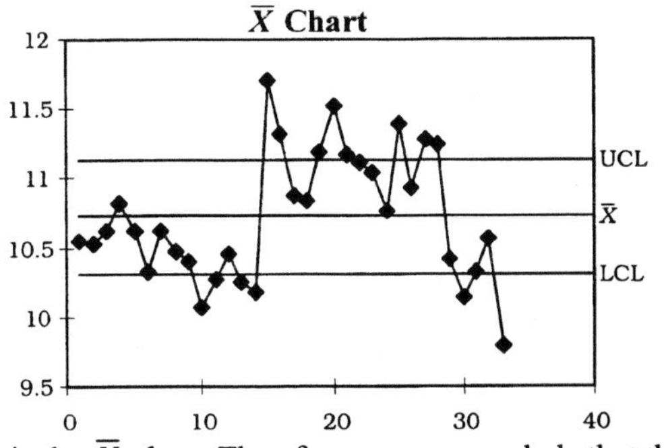

(d) The process is out of control. There is no evidence of a pattern in the $\bar{X}$ chart. Therefore, we can conclude that the process is in a state of statistical control.

(e)

S Chart	
$\bar{S}$	0.232398
B_3 factor	0
B_4 factor	2.266
Lower Control Limit	0
Center Line	0.232398
Upper Control Limit	0.526613

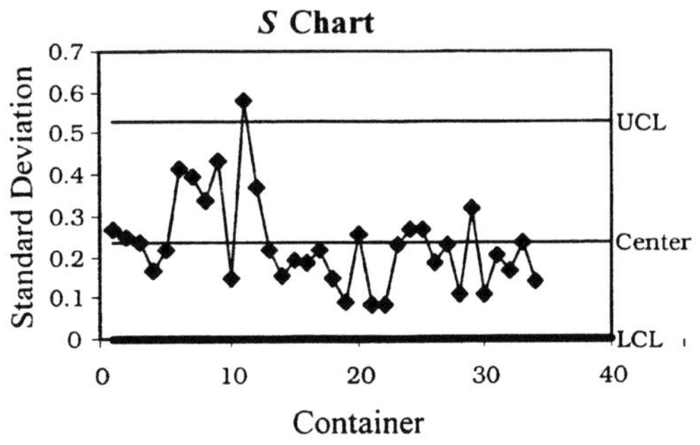

(f) After removing container 11

S Chart	
$\bar{S}$	0.2219
B_3 factor	0
B_4 factor	2.266
Lower Control Limit	0
Center Line	0.2219
Upper Control Limit	0.50283

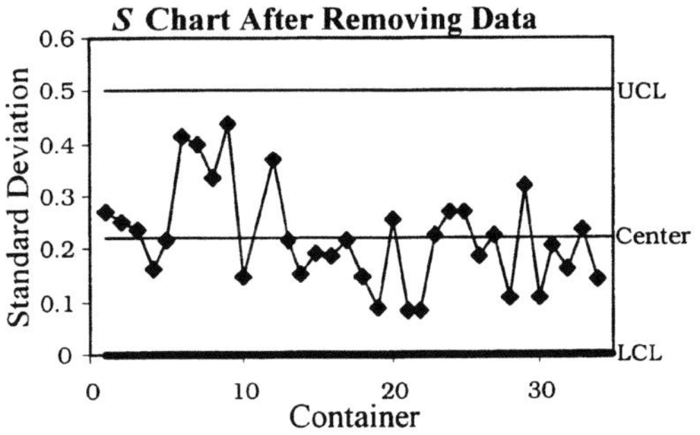

There are no points outside the control limits and there is no evidence of a pattern in the *S* chart.

(g)

$\bar{X}$ Chart	
Average $\bar{X}$	10.725
A_3 factor	1.628
Lower Control Limit	10.363
Center Line	10.725
Upper Control Limit	11.086

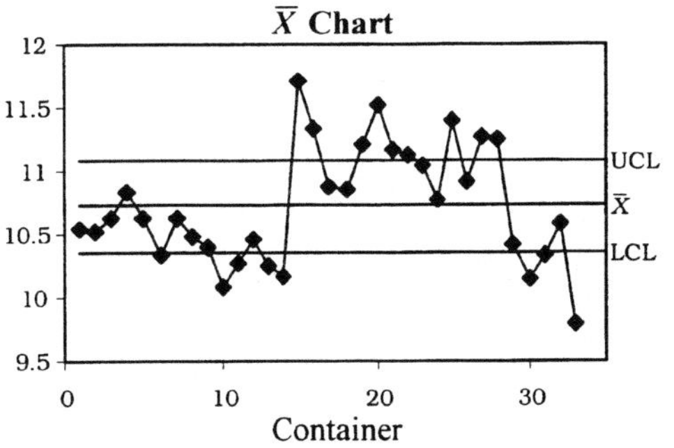

(h) The results of (a) and (d) and (e–f) are the same. Process is not stable and is out of statistical control.
(i) Process is not stable and is out of statistical control.

3. (a)

Control Chart	
Sample/Subgroup Size	6
$\overline{R}$	11.917
***R* Chart**	
D_3 Factor	0
D_4 Factor	2.004
Lower Control Limit	0
Center	11.9167
Upper Control Limit	23.881

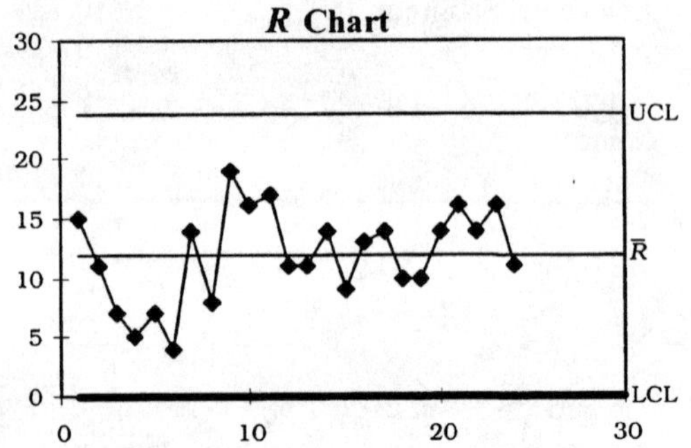

(b) There are no points outside of the control limits and there is no evidence of a pattern in the R chart.

(c)

$\overline{X}$ Chart	
Average of Subgroup	40.660
A_2 Factor	0.483
Lower Control Limit	34.90
Center	40.660
Upper Control Limit	46.415

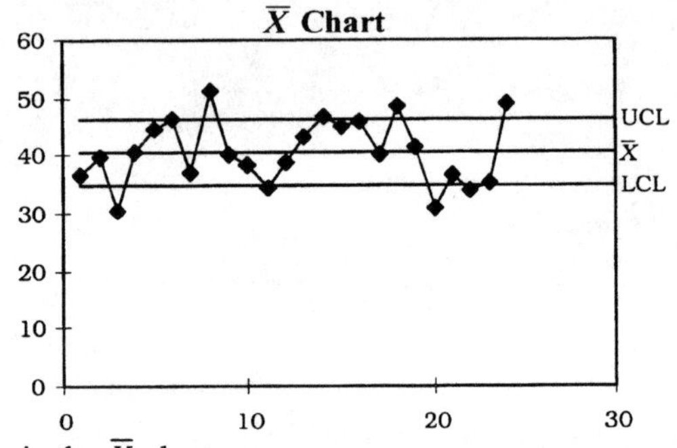

(d) The process is out of control. There is no evidence of a pattern in the $\overline{X}$ chart.

(e)

S Chart	
$\overline{S}$	4.625
B_3 factor	0.03
B_4 factor	1.97
Lower Control Limit	0.139
Center Line	4.625
Upper Control Limit	9.111

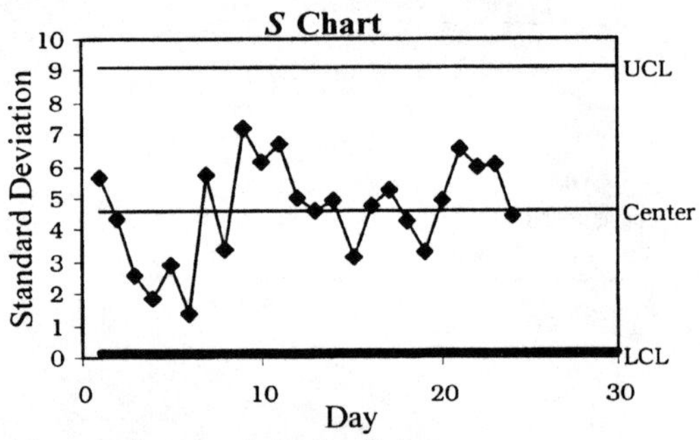

(f) There are no points outside the control limits and there is no evidence of a pattern in the S chart.

(g)

$\overline{X}$ Chart	
Average $\overline{X}$	40.656
A_3 factor	1.287
Lower Control Limit	34.708
Center Line	40.660
Upper Control Limit	46.612

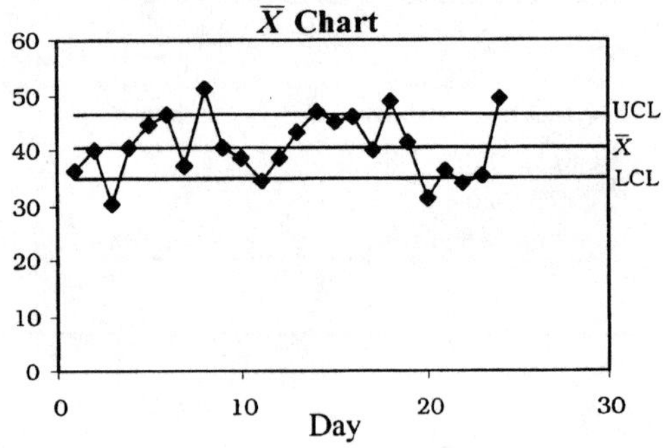

(h) The results of (a) and (d) and (e–f) are the same. Process is stable and out of statistical control.
(i) Process is stable and out of statistical control.

4. (a)

Control Chart	
Sample/Subgroup Size	24
$\overline{R}$	0.040
***R* Chart**	
D_3 Factor	0.452
D_4 Factor	1.548
Lower Control Limit	0.018
Center	0.040
Upper Control Limit	0.062

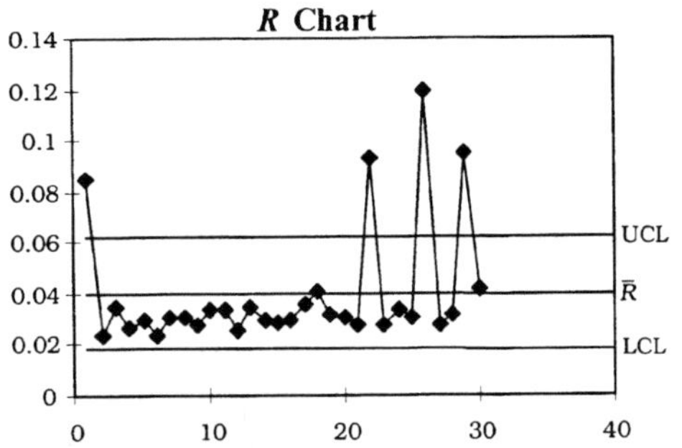

The process is out of control. Data from days 1, 22, 26 and 29 are outside of the upper control limits (without outliers) and should be removed from the data set.

(b)

Control Chart	
Sample/Subgroup Size	24
$\overline{R}$	0.031
***R* Chart**	
D_3 Factor	0.452
D_4 Factor	1.548
Lower Control Limit	0.014
Center	0.031
Upper Control Limit	0.048

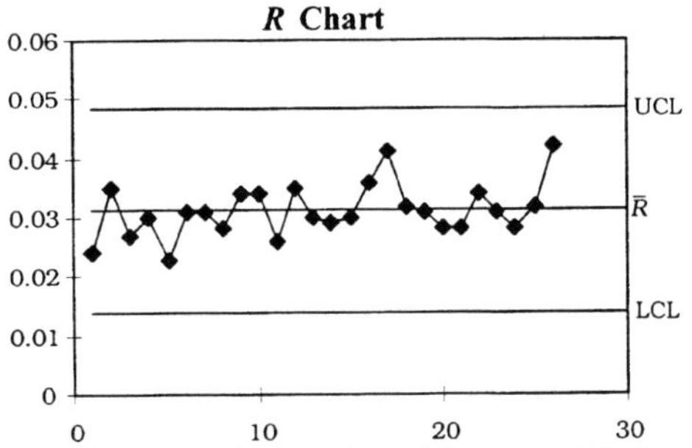

There are no points outside of the control limits and there is no evidence of a pattern in the *R* chart.

(c)

$\overline{X}$ Chart	
Average of Subgroup	0.045
A_2 Factor	0.157
Lower Control Limit	0.040
Center	0.045
Upper Control Limit	0.049

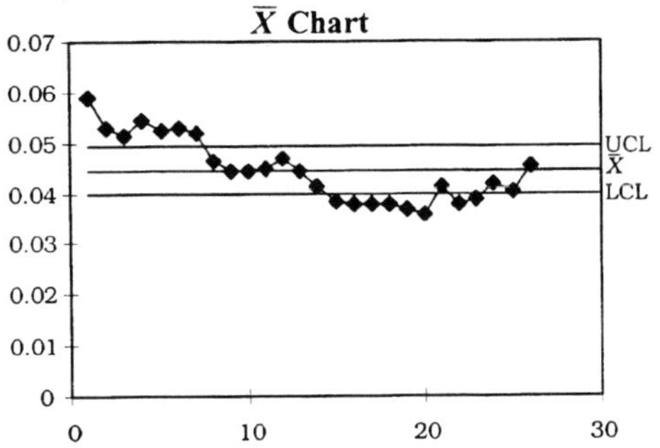

(d) The process is out of statistical control. There is a negative tendency in this data.

(e)

S Chart	
$\overline{S}$	0.010
B_3 factor	0.546
B_4 factor	1.454
Lower Control Limit	0.005
Center Line	0.005
Upper Control Limit	0.014

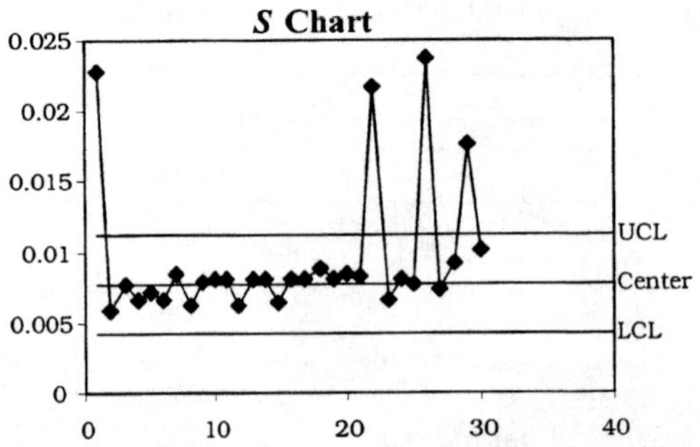

(f) The process is out of statistical control. Data points 1, 22, 26 and 29 are outside of the upper control limits (without outliers) and should be removed from the data set.

S Chart	
$\overline{S}$	0.008
B_3 factor	0.546
B_4 factor	1.454
Lower Control Limit	0.004
Center Line	0.008
Upper Control Limit	0.011

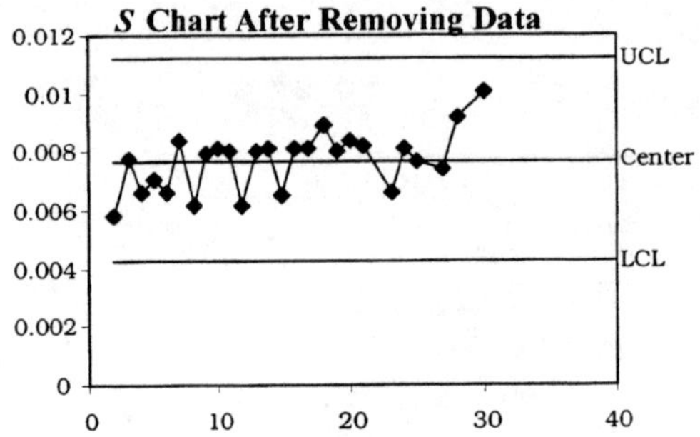

(g)

$\overline{X}$ Chart	
Average $\overline{X}$	0.045
A_3 factor	0.631
Lower Control Limit	0.040
Center Line	0.045
Upper Control Limit	0.049

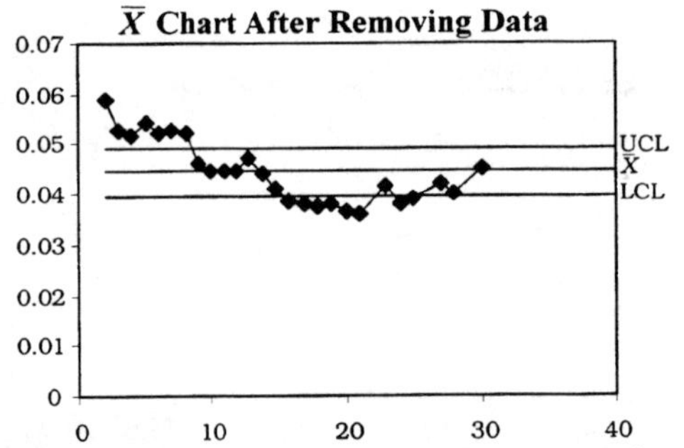

The process is out of control. There is a negative tendency in this data.

(h) The results of (a) and (d) and (e–f) are the same. The process is out of control. There is a negative tendency in this data.

(i) The process is out of control. There is a negative tendency in this data.

5. (a)

Control Chart	
Sample/Subgroup Size	4
$\overline{R}$	2.354
***R* Chart**	
D_3 Factor	0
D_4 Factor	2.282
Lower Control Limit	0
Center	2.354
Upper Control Limit	5.373

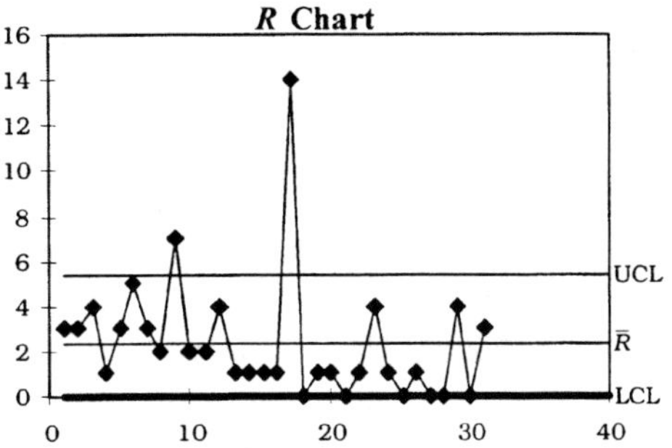

(b) The process is out of control. Data points 9 and 17 should be removed from the data set.

Control Chart	
Sample/Subgroup Size	4
$\overline{R}$	1.793
***R* Chart**	
D_3 Factor	0
D_4 Factor	2.282
Lower Control Limit	0
Center	1.793
Upper Control Limit	4.091

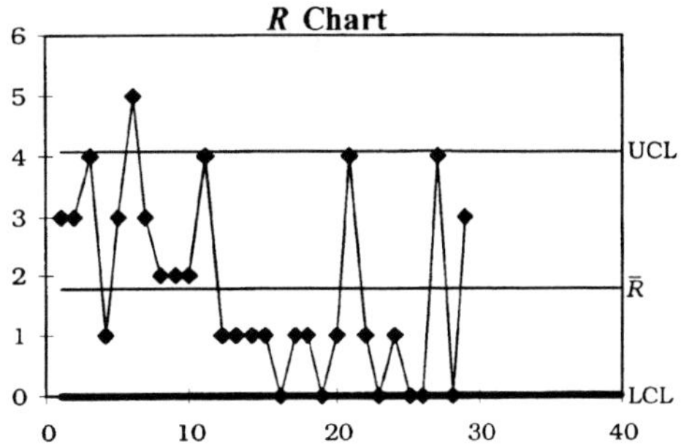

The process is out of control. Data point 6 should be removed from the data set because it is above the upper control limit.

Control Chart	
Sample/Subgroup Size	4
$\overline{R}$	1.678
***R* Chart**	
D_3 Factor	0
D_4 Factor	2.282
Lower Control Limit	0
Center	1.678
Upper Control Limit	3.830

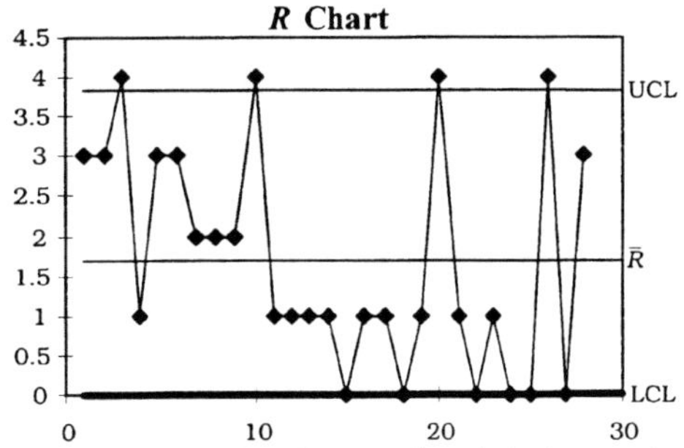

The process is globally out of statistical control.

(c)

$\overline{X}$ Chart	
Average $\overline{X}$	24.758
A_3 factor	0.729
Lower Control Limit	23.041
Center Line	24.758
Upper Control Limit	26.474

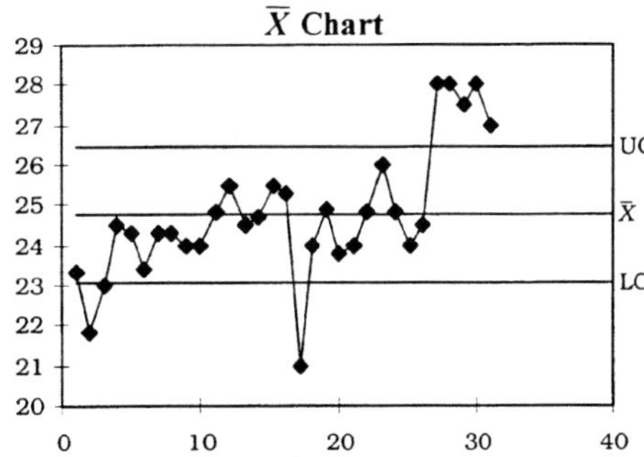

The process is out of statistical control.

(d) The process is globally out of statistical control.

(e)

S Chart	
$\overline{S}$	0.971
B_3 factor	0
B_4 factor	2.266
Lower Control Limit	0
Center Line	0.971
Upper Control Limit	2.201

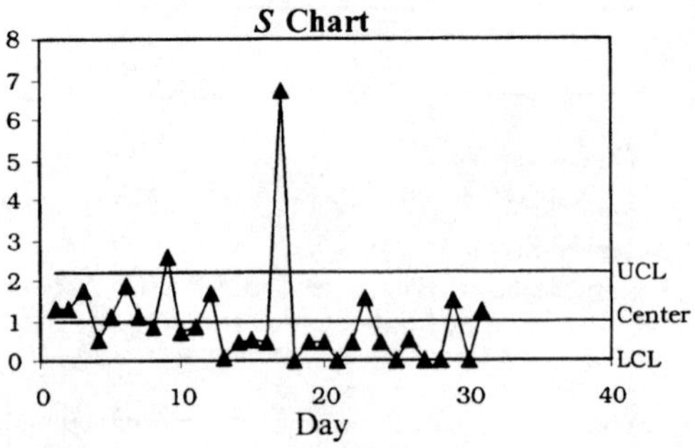

(f) The process is out of statistical control. Data points 9 and 17 should be removed fom the data set.

S Chart	
$\overline{S}$	0.720
B_3 factor	0
B_4 factor	2.266
Lower Control Limit	0
Center Line	0.720
Upper Control Limit	1.632

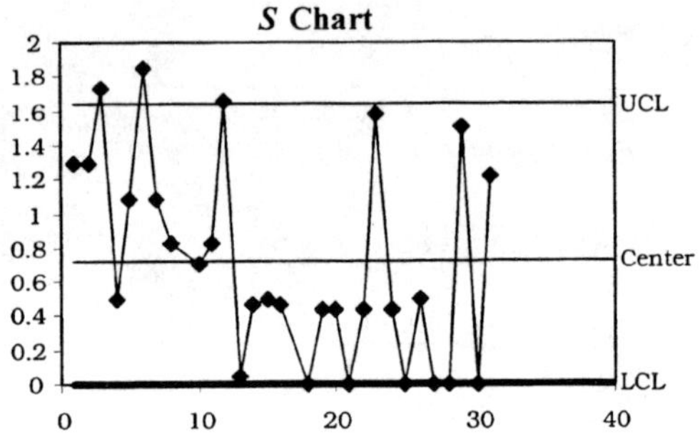

The process is out of statistical control.

(g)

$\overline{X}$ Chart	
Average $\overline{X}$	24.758
A_3 factor	1.628
Lower Control Limit	23.176
Center Line	24.758
Upper Control Limit	26.339

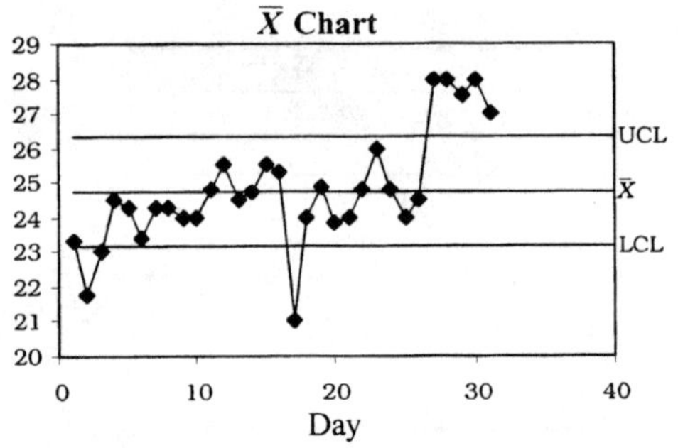

The process is out of statistical control.

(h) Results of (a) and (d) and (e–f) are the same. The process is out of statistical control.

(i) The process is out of statistical control.

6. (a)

Control Chart	
Sample/Subgroup Size	5
$\overline{R}$	0.864
***R* Chart**	
D_3 Factor	0
D_4 Factor	2.114
Lower Control Limit	0
Center	0.864
Upper Control Limit	1.826

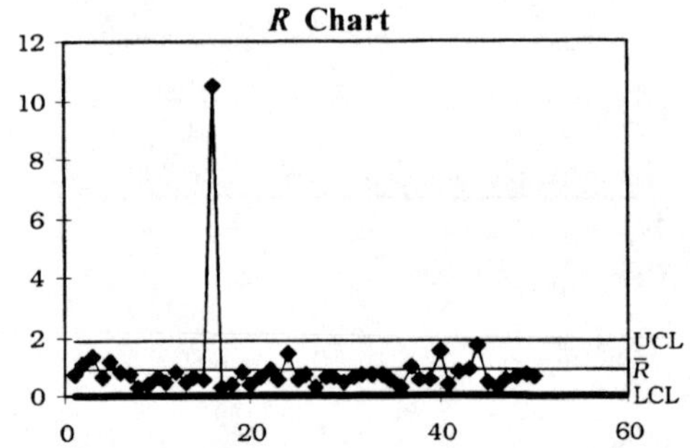

(b) The process is out of control. Data point 10 should be removed from the data set.

Control Chart	
Sample/Subgroup Size	5
$\overline{R}$	0.667
***R* Chart**	
D_3 Factor	0
D_4 Factor	2.114
Lower Control Limit	0
Center	0.667
Upper Control Limit	1.410

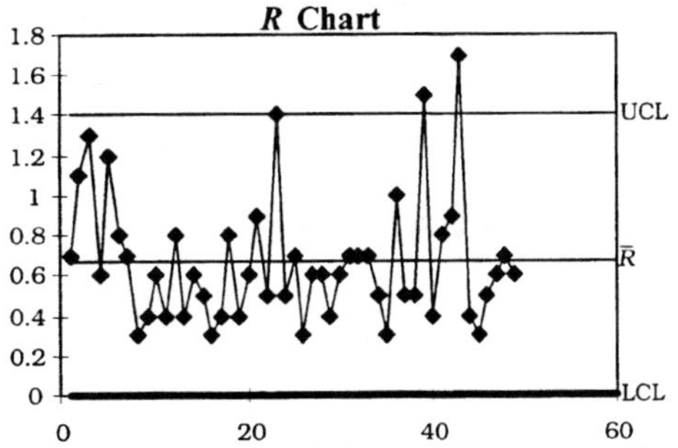

Data points 23, 39 and 43 should be removed from the data set because they are on or above the upper control limit.

Control Chart	
Sample/Subgroup Size	5
$\overline{R}$	0.610
***R* Chart**	
D_3 Factor	0
D_4 Factor	2.114
Lower Control Limit	0
Center	0.610
Upper Control Limit	1.291

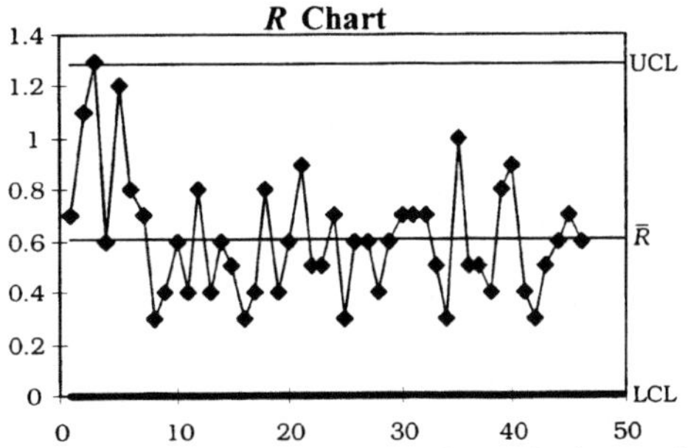

The process is now in a state of statistical control.

(c)

$\overline{X}$ Chart	
Average of Subgroup	20.274
A_2 factor	0.577
Lower Control Limit	19.775
Center	20.274
Upper Control Limit	20.772

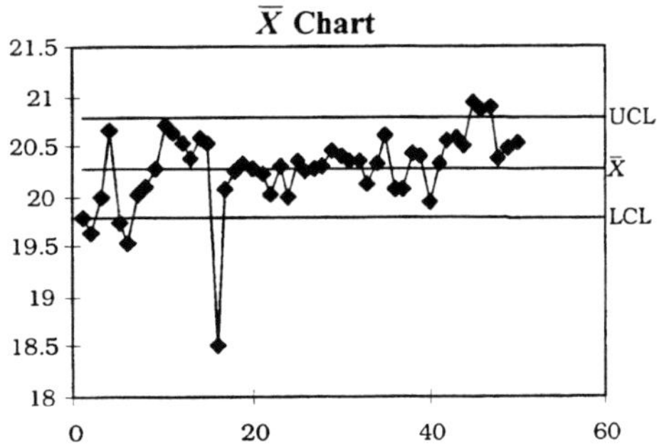

The process is out of statistical control. Data point 16 should be removed from the data set because it is below the lower control limit.

$\overline{X}$ Chart	
Average of Subgroup	20.310
A_2 factor	0.577
Lower Control Limit	19.925
Center	20.310
Upper Control Limit	20.695

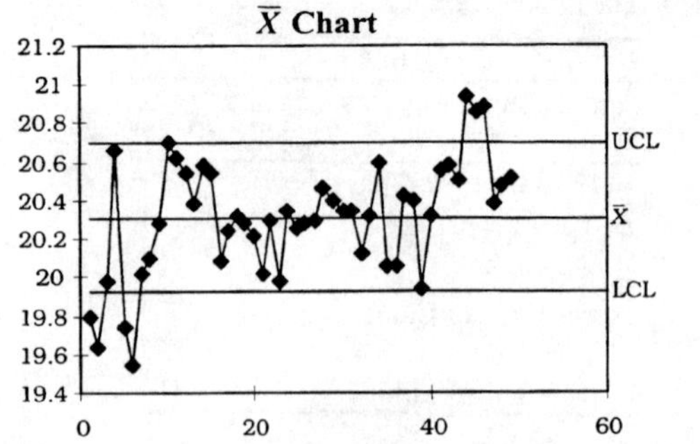

(d) The process is out of control. There is no pattern present in this data.

(e)

S Chart	
$\overline{S}$	0.351
B_3 factor	0
B_4 factor	2.089
Lower Control Limit	0
Center Line	0.351
Upper Control Limit	0.734

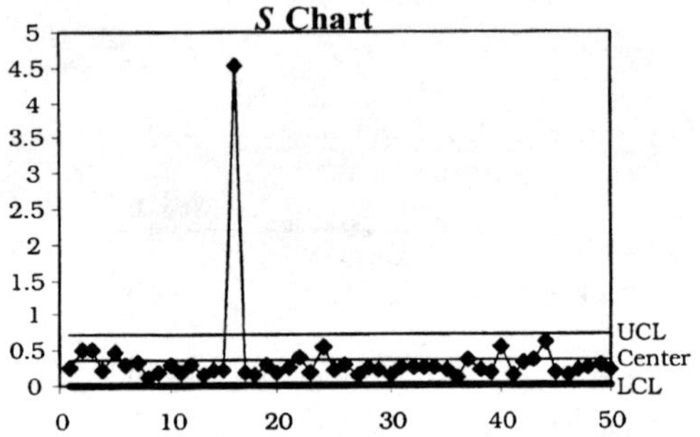

(f) The process is out of statistical control.

S Chart	
$\overline{S}$	0.266
B_3 factor	0
B_4 factor	2.089
Lower Control Limit	0
Center Line	0.266
Upper Control Limit	0.556

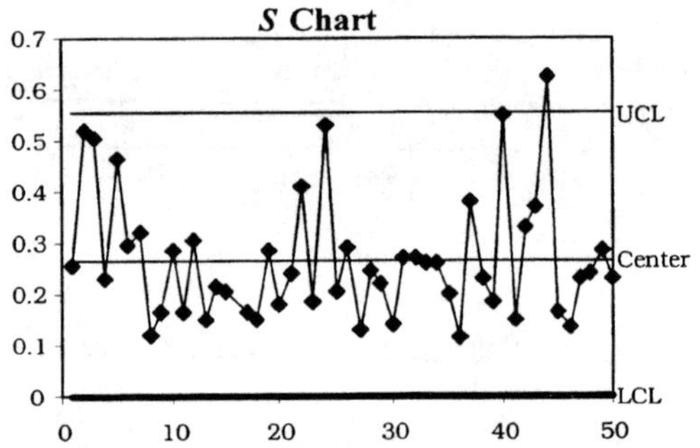

The process is out of statistical control. Data points 44 and 40 should be removed from the data set.

S Chart	
$\overline{S}$	0.252
B_3 factor	0
B_4 factor	2.089
Lower Control Limit	0
Center Line	0.252
Upper Control Limit	0.527

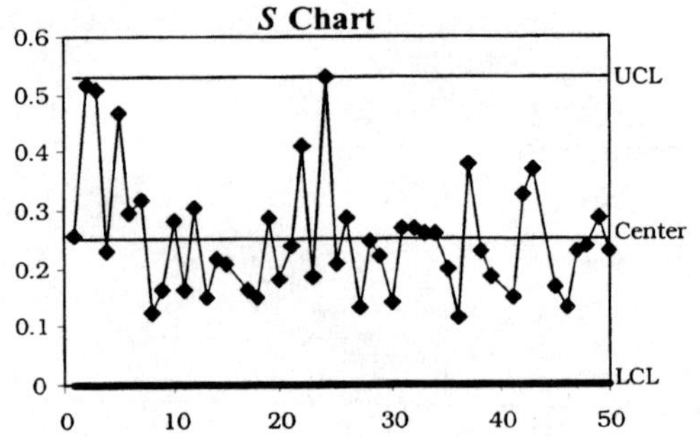

(g) The process should now be in a state of control.

$\overline{X}$ **Chart**	
Average of Subgroup	20.274
A_2 factor	0.577
Lower Control Limit	19.775
Center	20.274
Upper Control Limit	20.772

The process is out of statistical control.

(h) Results of (a) and (d) and (e–f) are the same. The process is out of statistical control.

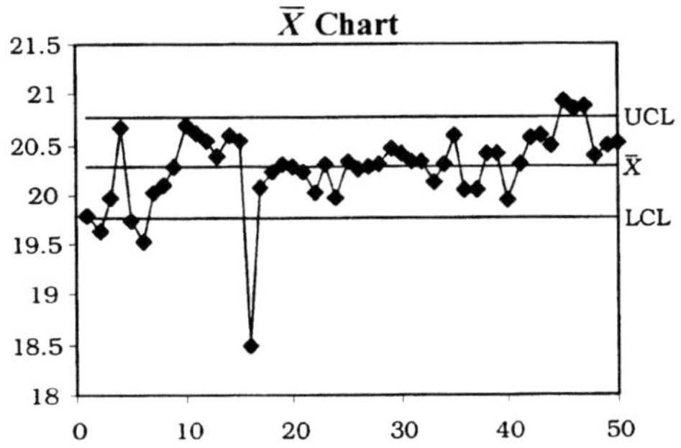

(i) The process is out of statistical control. There is no pattern in this data.

7. Before use PHStat compute the mean and range for each group.

(a)

Control Chart	
Sample/Subgroup Size	4
$\overline{R}$	0.042
***R* Chart**	
D_3 Factor	0
D_4 Factor	2.282
Lower Control Limit	0
Center	0.042
Upper Control Limit	0.096

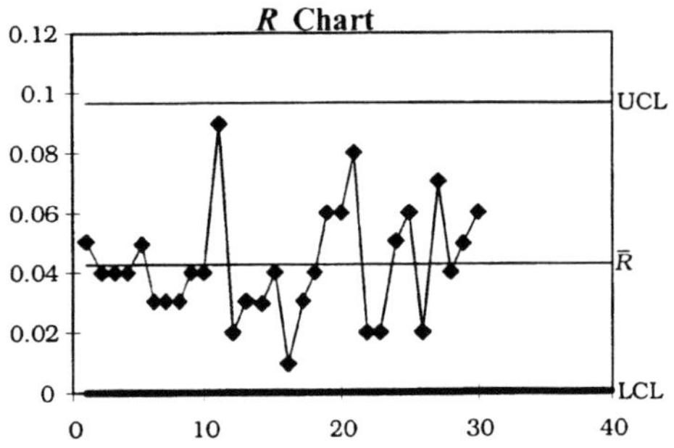

(b) The *R* chart does not indicate that the process is out of statistical control.

(c)

$\overline{X}$ **Chart**	
Average of Subgroup	4.128
A_2 factor	0.729
Lower Control Limit	4.097
Center	4.128
Upper Control Limit	4.158

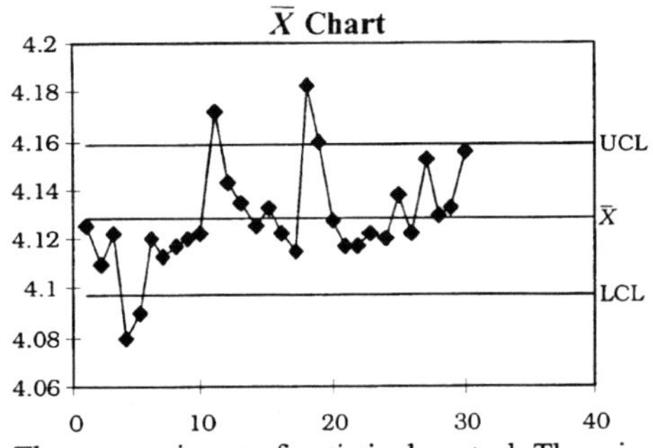

The process is out of statistical control. There is no evidence of a pattern in the $\overline{X}$-bar chart.

(d) The process is out of statistical control. There is no evidence of a pattern in the $\overline{X}$-bar chart.

(e)

S Chart	
$\overline{S}$	0.018
B_3 factor	0
B_4 factor	2.266
Lower Control Limit	0
Center Line	0.018
Upper Control Limit	0.042

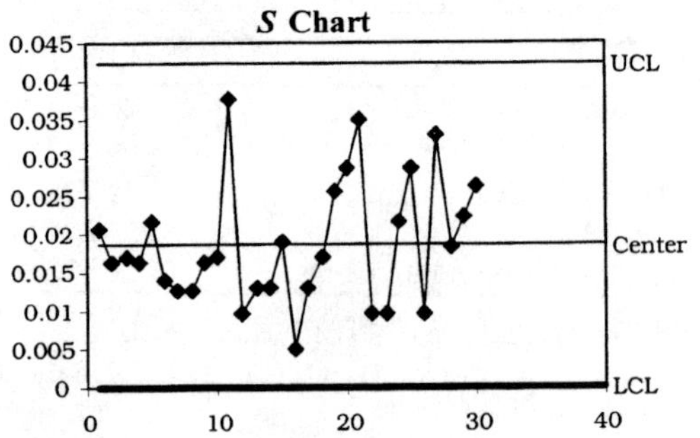

(f) The *S* chart does not indicate that the process is out of statistical control.

(g)

$\overline{X}$ Chart	
Average $\overline{X}$	4.128
A_3 factor	1.628
Lower Control Limit	4.097
Center Line	4.128
Upper Control Limit	4.158

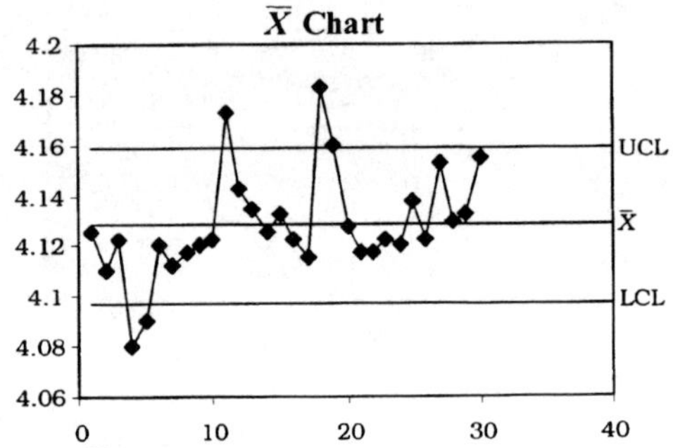

The $\overline{X}$ chart indicates that the process is out of statistical control.

(h) The results of B, $\overline{X}$ and $\overline{\overline{X}}$ charts are the same.

(i) The process is out of statistical control.

8. (a)

S Chart	
$\overline{S}$	28.213
B_3 factor	0.399
B_4 factor	1.600
Lower Control Limit	11.276
Center Line	28.213
Upper Control Limit	45.149

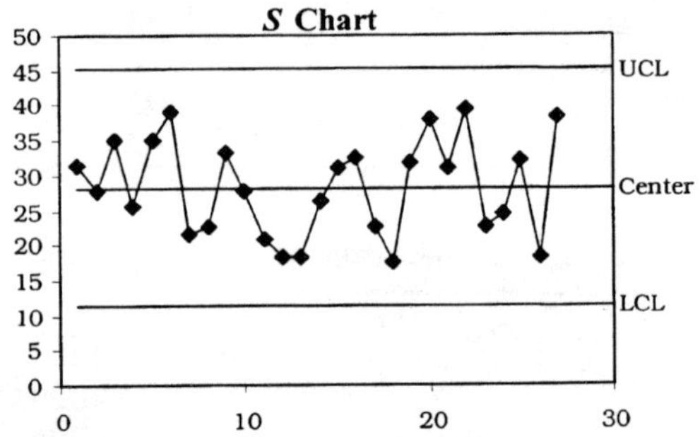

(b) The chart does not indicate that the process is out of statistical control.

(c)

$\overline{X}$ Chart	
Average $\overline{X}$	1907.368
A_3 factor	0.831
Lower Control Limit	1883.917
Center Line	1907.368
Upper Control Limit	1930.819

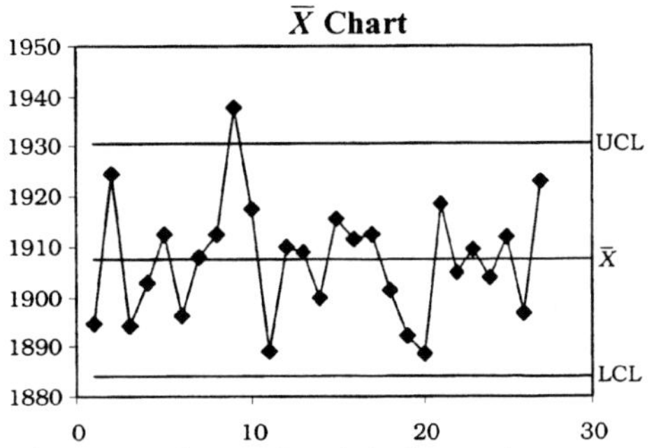

The process is out of statistical control.

(d) The only point outside the control limit corresponds to the end of the batch and must be taken into consideration.

9. (a)

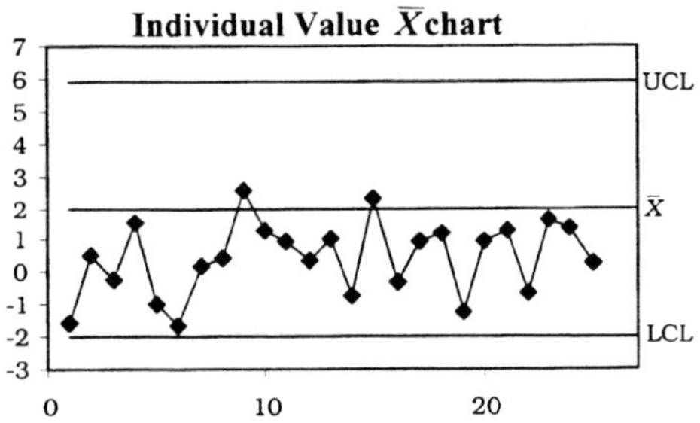

(b) There are no points outside of the control limits and no evidence of a pattern in the Individual Value chart.

(c)

Individual Value Chart	
$\overline{X}$	0.475
S	1.123
C_4 factor	0.990
Lower Control Limit	−2.929
Center Line	0.475
Upper Control Limit	3.880

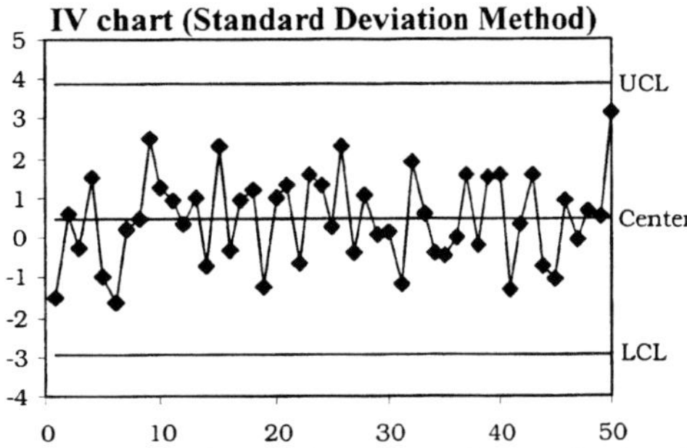

(d) The average flushness measurement has been reduced from 1.962 to 0.4752, the number of out-of-control points has been reduced from 32 to 12. Further work should provide an additional reduction of the average value and/or reduce the variability so that more points will be within the specification limits.

(e)

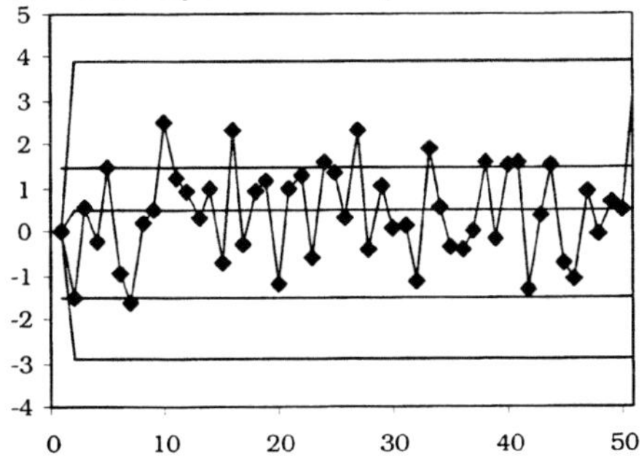

The average flushness measurement has been reduced from 1.962 to 0.4752. The number of control points has been reduced as well. Further work should provide additional reduction of these characteristics for a more stable process in which statistical control is more feasible.

10. (a)

Moving Range Chart	
$\overline{MR}$	0.521
D_3 factor	0.000
D_4 factor	3.267
Lower Control Limit	0.000
Center Line	0.521
Upper Control Limit	1.704

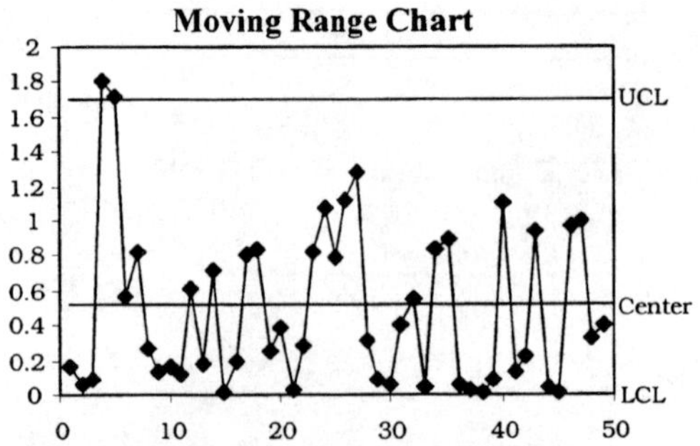

There are points outside of the control limits, so this process is out of statistical control.

(b) Data points 4 and 5 are above the upper control limit and should be removed from the data set.

Moving Range Chart	
$\overline{MR}$	0.468
D_3 factor	0.000
D_4 factor	3.267
Lower Control Limit	0.000
Center Line	0.468
Upper Control Limit	1.530

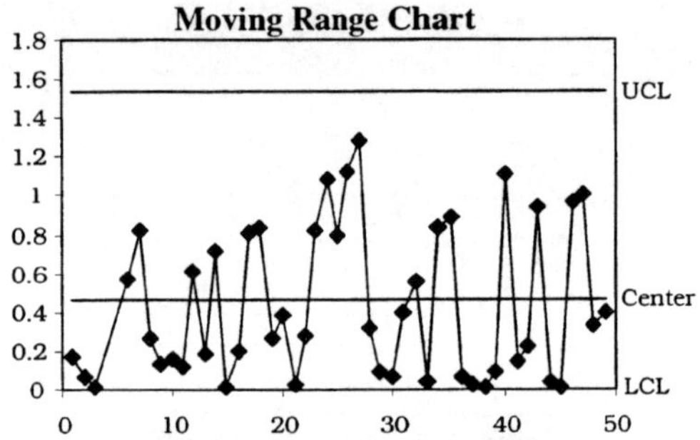

There are no points outside of the control limits, so this process is in a state of statistical control.

(c)

Individual Value Chart	
$\overline{X}$	2.690
E_2 factor	2.659
Lower Control Limit	1.303
Center Line	2.690
Upper Control Limit	4.077

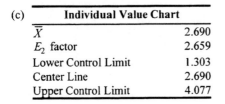

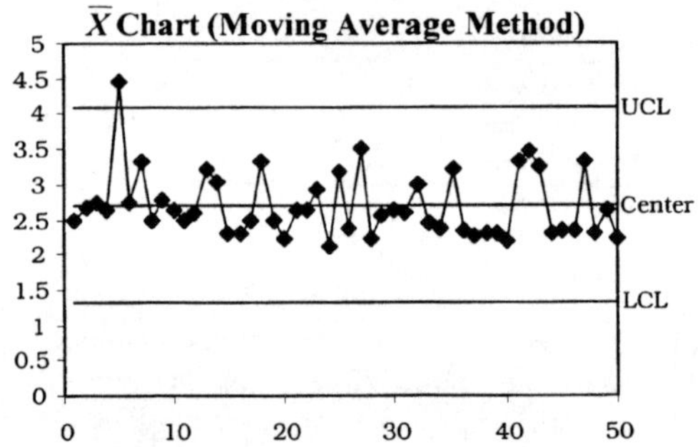

The process is out of statistical control.

(d)

Individual Value Chart	
$\overline{X}$	2.690
S	0.461
C_4 factor	0.990
Lower Control Limit	1.293
Center Line	2.690
Upper Control Limit	4.088

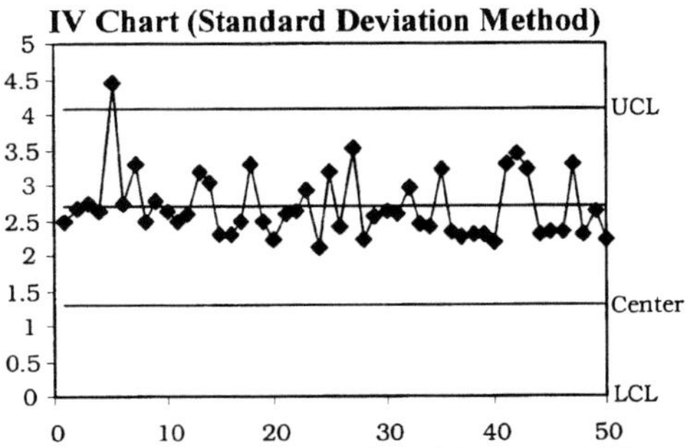

(e) The process is out of statistical control. Data point 5 is above the upper control limit and should be removed from that data set.

Individual Value Chart	
$\overline{X}$	2.654
S	0.388
C_4 factor	0.990
Lower Control Limit	1.475
Center Line	2.654
Upper Control Limit	3.833

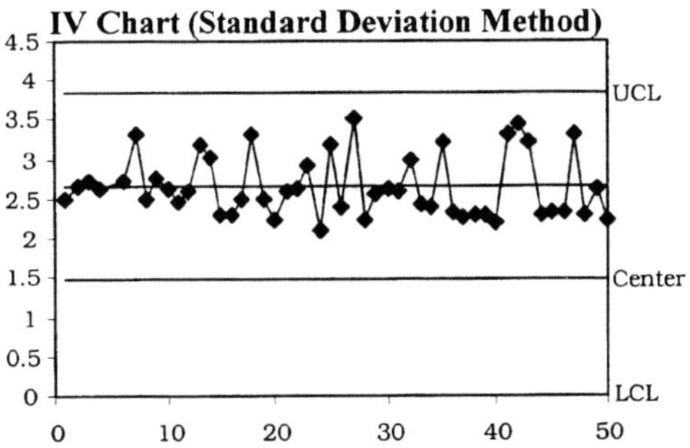

The process is in a state of the statistical control.

(f) Generally the process is out of statistical control ((a), (c), (d)). After removing point 5 from the data set, the process reaches a state of statistical control ((b), (e)).

11. (a)

Moving Range Chart	
$\overline{MR}$	2.081
D_3 factor	0.000
D_4 factor	3.267
Lower Control Limit	0.000
Center Line	2.081
Upper Control Limit	6.800

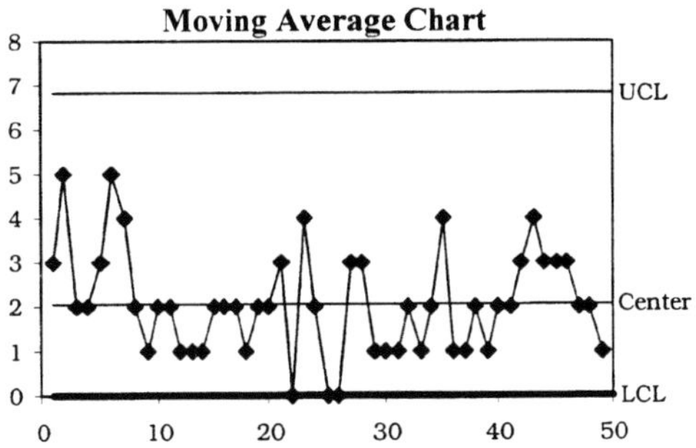

The process is in a state of statistical control.

(b) The process is in a state of statistical control.

(c)

Individual Value Chart	
$\overline{X}$	255.620
E_2 factor	2.659
Lower Control Limit	250.084
Center Line	255.620
Upper Control Limit	261.155

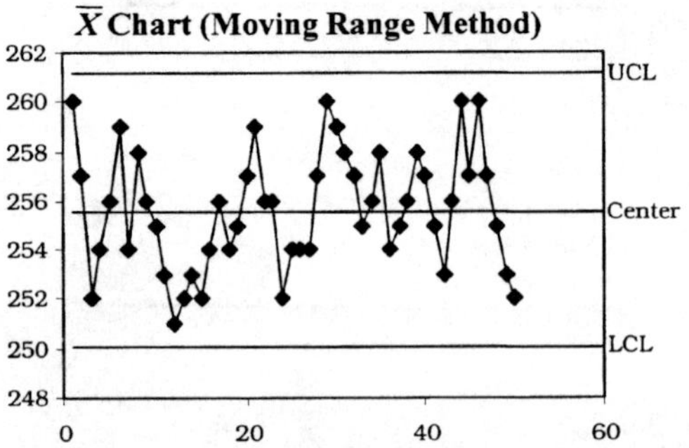

The process is in a state of statistical control.

(d)

Individual Value Chart	
$\overline{X}$	255.620
S	2.415
C_4 factor	0.990
Lower Control Limit	248.301
Center Line	255.620
Upper Control Limit	262.938

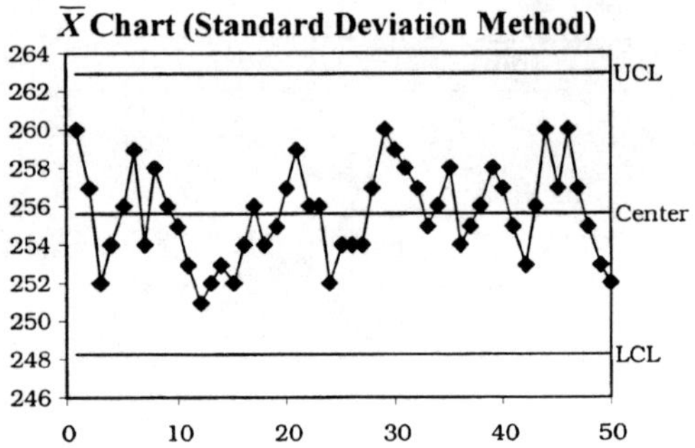

(e) The process is in a state of statistical control.

(f) All of the results are the same for parts (a) through (e)—the process is in a state of statistical control.

12. (a)

Moving Range Chart	
$\overline{MR}$	0.399
D_3 factor	0.000
D_4 factor	3.267
Lower Control Limit	0.000
Center Line	0.399
Upper Control Limit	1.305

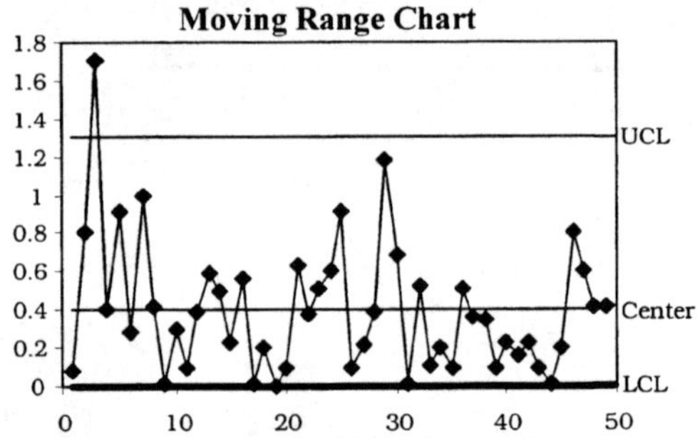

The process is out of statistical control.

(b) Data point 3 should be removed from the data set because it is above the upper control limit.

Moving Range Chart	
$\overline{MR}$	0.374
D_3 factor	0.000
D_4 factor	3.267
Lower Control Limit	0.000
Center Line	0.374
Upper Control Limit	1.223

Moving Range Chart

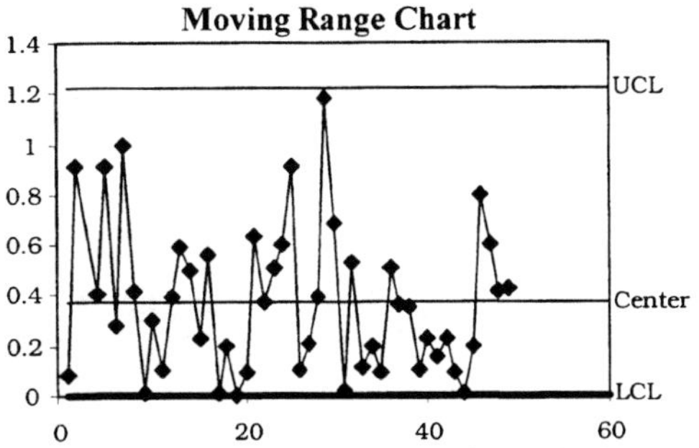

The revised process is in a state of statistical control.

(c)

Individual Value Chart	
$\overline{X}$	2.161
E_2 factor	2.659
Lower Control Limit	1.098
Center Line	2.161
Upper Control Limit	3.223

$\overline{X}$ Chart (Moving Range Method)

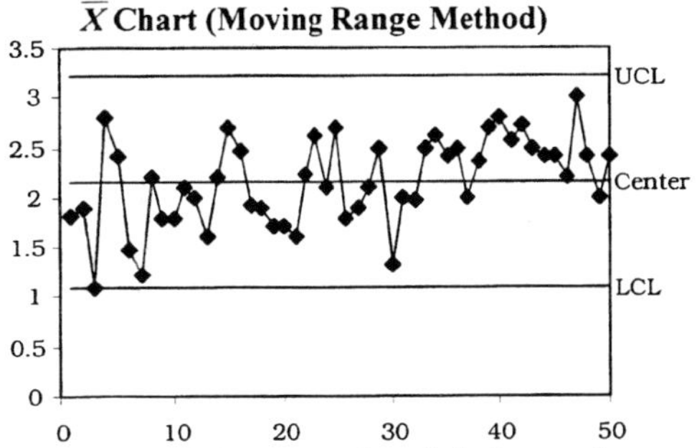

The process is in a state of statistical control.

(d)

Individual Value Chart	
$\overline{X}$	2.161
S	0.439
C_4 factor	0.990
Lower Control Limit	0.829
Center Line	2.161
Upper Control Limit	3.492

$\overline{X}$ Chart (Standard Deviation Method)

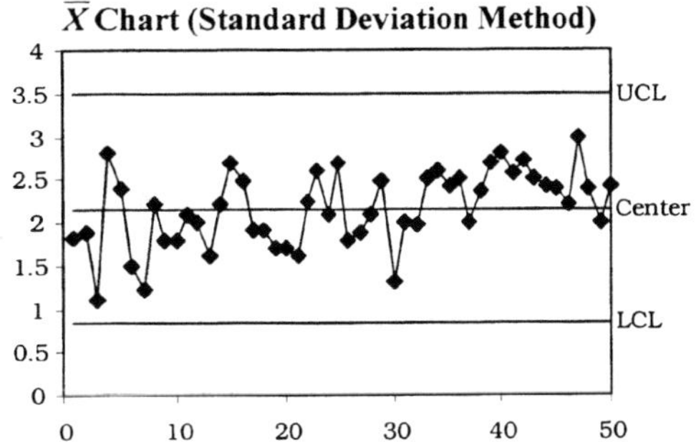

(e) The process is in a state of statistical control.

(f) The result of part (a) differs from all of the others ((b)–(e)), therefore, it is reasonable to conclude that the process is in a state of statistical control.

13. (a)

Moving Range Chart	
$\overline{MR}$	1.702
D_3 factor	0.000
D_4 factor	3.267
Lower Control Limit	0.000
Center Line	1.702
Upper Control Limit	5.561

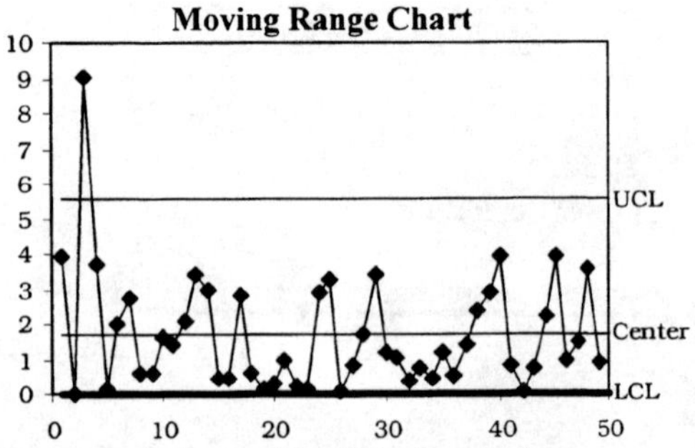

The process is out of statistical control.

(b) Data points 2 and 3 should be removed from the data set.

Moving Range Chart	
$\overline{MR}$	1.606
D_3 factor	0.000
D_4 factor	3.267
Lower Control Limit	0.000
Center Line	1.606
Upper Control Limit	5.248

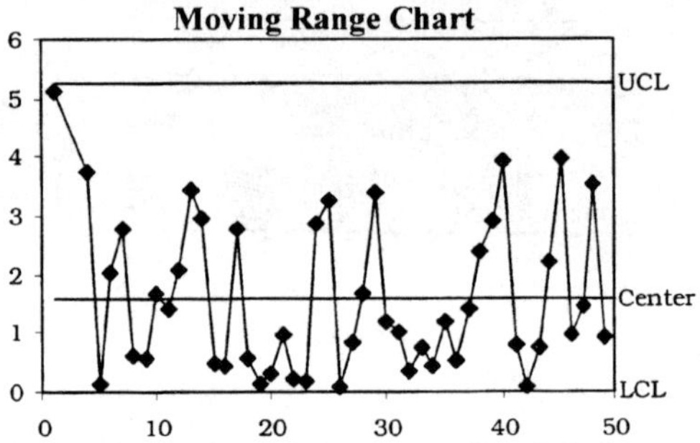

The revised process is in a state of statistical control.

(c)

Individual Value Chart	
$\overline{X}$	93.212
E_2 factor	2.659
Lower Control Limit	88.685
Center Line	93.212
Upper Control Limit	97.739

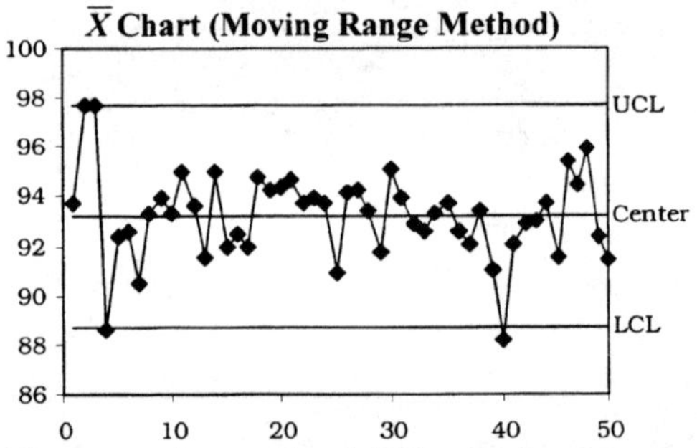

The process is out of statistical control.

(d)

Individual Value Chart	
$\overline{X}$	93.212
S	1.808
C_4 factor	0.990
Lower Control Limit	87.730
Center Line	93.212
Upper Control Limit	98.694

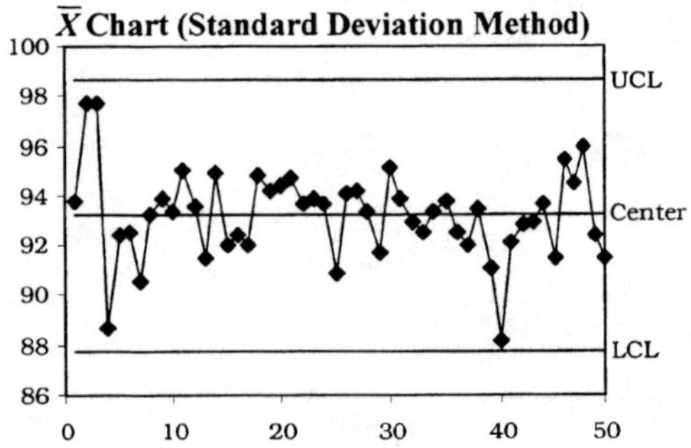

(e) The process is in a state of statistical control.

(f) The standard deviation method is the most efficient procedure and results in a controllable process; therefore, one should choose this method for the percent purity data.

14. (a)

Moving Range Chart	
$\overline{MR}$	3.633
D_3 factor	0.000
D_4 factor	3.267
Lower Control Limit	0.000
Center Line	3.633
Upper Control Limit	11.870

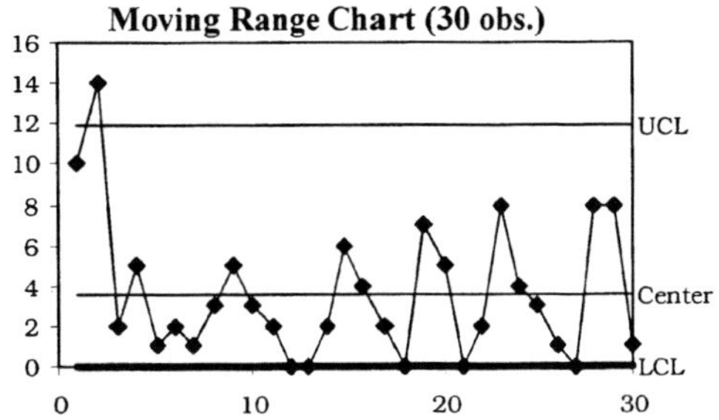

The process is out of statistical control.

(b) Data point 2 is above the upper control limt and should be removed from the data set.

Moving Range Chart	
$\overline{MR}$	3.068
D_3 factor	0.000
D_4 factor	3.267
Lower Control Limit	0.000
Center Line	3.068
Upper Control Limit	10.026

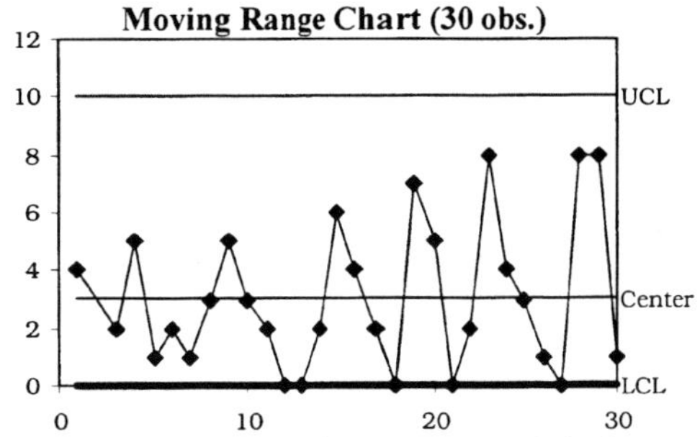

The revised process is in a state of statistical control.

(c)

Individual Value Chart	
$\overline{X}$	70.033
E_2 factor	2.659
Lower Control Limit	60.372
Center Line	70.033
Upper Control Limit	79.694

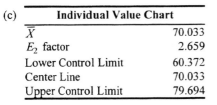

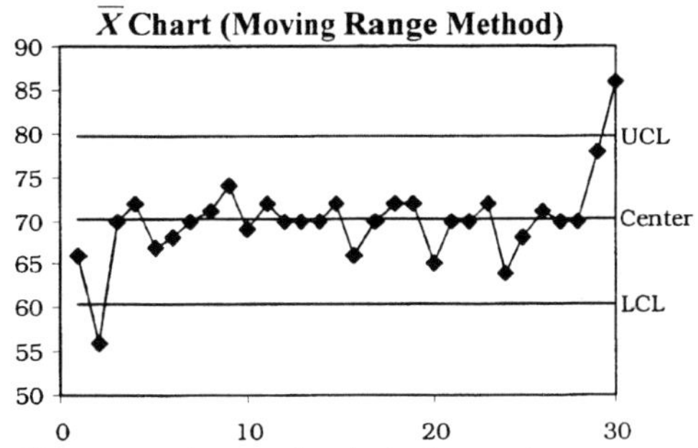

The process is out of statistical control.

(d)

Individual Value Chart	
$\overline{X}$	70.666
S	4.127
C_4 factor	0.990
Lower Control Limit	58.157
Center Line	70.666
Upper Control Limit	83.175

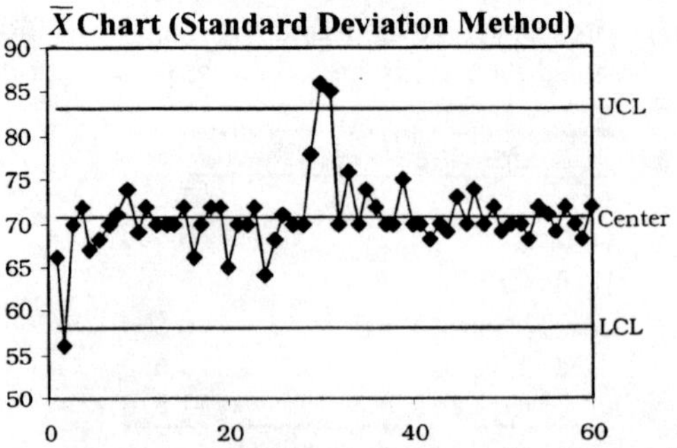

(e) The process is out of control. Data points 2, 30 and 31 should be removed form the data set because they fall outside the control limits.

Individual Value Chart	
$\overline{X}$	70.403
S	2.484
C_4 factor	0.990
Lower Control Limit	62.874
Center Line	70.403
Upper Control Limit	77.932

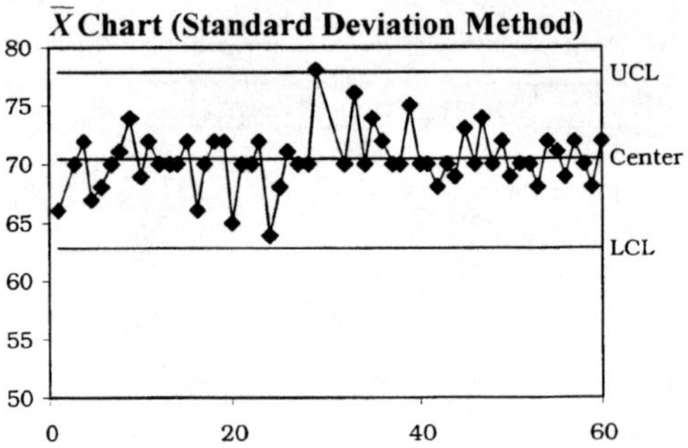

The revised process is in a state of statistical control.

(f) The results are the same for all of the parts.

15. (a)

Moving Range Chart	
$\overline{MR}$	578.566
D_3 factor	0.000
D_4 factor	3.267
Lower Control Limit	0.000
Center Line	578.566
Upper Control Limit	1890.177

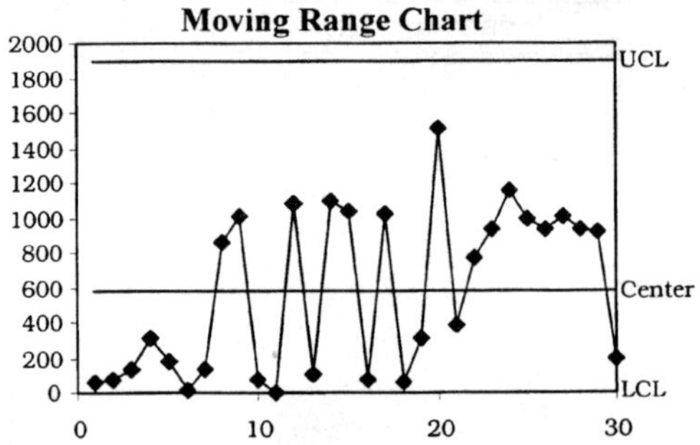

The process is in a state of statistical control.

(b) The process is in a state of statistical control.

(c)

Individual Value Chart	
$\overline{X}$	11756.23
E_2 factor	2.659
Lower Control Limit	10217.82
Center Line	11756.23
Upper Control Limit	13294.64

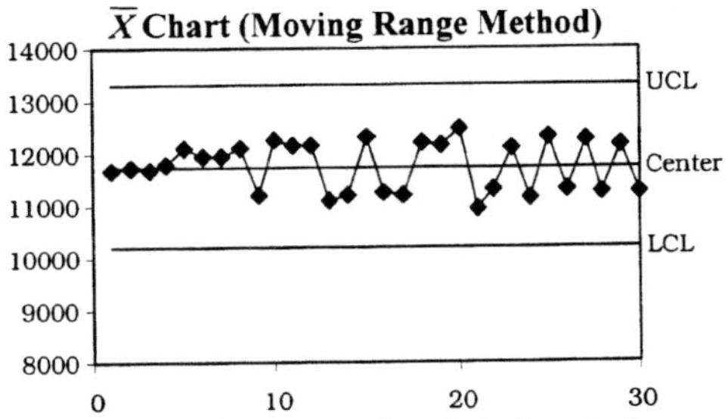

The process is in a state of statistical control.

(d)

Individual Value Chart	
$\overline{X}$	12038.880
S	494.047
C_4 factor	0.990
Lower Control Limit	10541.770
Center Line	12038.880
Upper Control Limit	13536.000

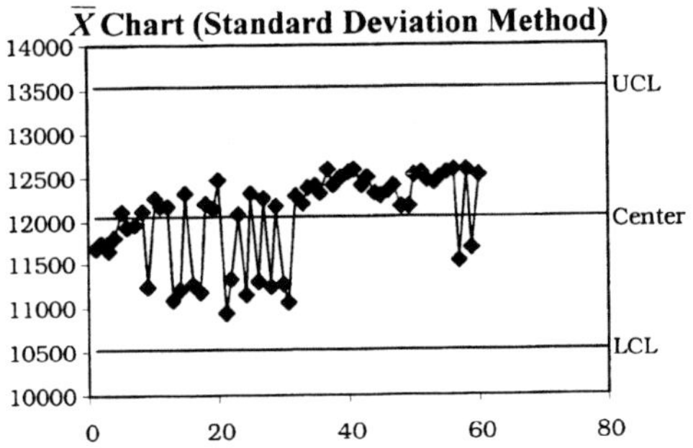

(e) The process is in a state of statistical control.

(f) The results are the same for all of the parts.

16. (a) CUSUM Chart

Day	Average	Standard Deviation	Z_i	S_{H_i}	S_{L_i}
1	223.200	189.820	0.489	0.000	0.000
2	166.200	108.810	−0.612	0.000	0.112
3	116.00	106.070	−1.582	0.000	1.195
4	139.600	71.811	−1.126	0.000	1.821
5	271.600	157.840	1.424	0.924	0.000
6	172.000	68.837	−0.500	0.000	0.000
7	118.800	73.619	−1.528	0.000	1.029
8	207.800	144.700	0.192	0.000	0.337
9	217.200	134.270	0.373	0.000	0.000
10	158.200	113.740	−0.767	0.000	0.267
11	256.600	141.010	1.135	0.635	0.000
12	291.600	187.550	1.811	1.946	0.000
13	181.800	58.290	−0.311	1.135	0.000
14	259.200	129.830	1.185	1.820	0.000
15	106.600	63.220	−1.764	0.000	1.264
16	224.400	125.600	0.512	0.012	0.252
17	190.600	96.984	−0.141	0.000	0.000
18	276.800	169.770	1.525	1.025	0.000
19	256.600	201.260	1.135	1.660	0.000
20	144.800	78.837	−1.026	0.134	0.526
21	291.200	91.448	1.803	1.437	0.000
22	155.400	134.350	−0.821	0.116	0.321
23	159.000	64.545	−0.751	0.000	0.573
24	159.400	63.885	−0.744	0.000	0.816
25	121.800	28.839	−1.470	0.000	1.787
26	213.600	109.220	0.304	0.000	0.983
27	202.000	169.450	0.080	0.000	0.403
28	269.800	60.288	1.390	0.890	0.000
29	257.400	77.893	1.150	1.540	0.000
30	127.400	41.332	−1.362	0.000	0.862
Overall mean	197.890				
$\overline{S}$	108.770				
C_4	0.940				
n	5.000				
k	0.500				

There are no S_{H_i} or S_{L_i} values greater than 4, hence there is no evidence that the process is out of statistical control.

(b) EWMA chart

Day	Average	Standard Deviation	W_i	LCL	UCL
1	223.200	189.823	204.215	159.075	236.698
2	166.200	108.810	194.711	149.372	246.401
3	116.000	106.068	175.033	144.687	251.087
4	139.600	71.810	166.175	142.224	253.550
5	271.600	157.836	192.531	139.209	256.564
6	172.000	68.837	187.399	139.209	256.564
7	118.800	73.619	170.249	139.209	256.564
8	207.800	144.695	179.637	139.209	256.564
9	217.200	134.265	189.028	139.209	256.564
10	158.200	113.744	181.321	139.209	256.564
11	256.600	141.008	200.141	139.209	256.564
12	291.600	187.552	223.005	139.209	256.564
13	181.800	58.290	212.704	139.209	256.564
14	259.200	129.833	224.328	139.209	256.564
15	106.600	63.220	194.896	139.209	256.564
16	224.400	125.600	202.272	139.209	256.564
17	190.600	96.983	199.354	139.209	256.564
18	276.800	169.770	218.716	139.209	256.564
19	256.600	201.264	228.187	139.209	256.564
20	144.800	78.837	207.340	139.209	256.564
21	291.200	91.448	228.305	139.209	256.564
22	155.400	134.351	210.079	139.209	256.564
23	159.000	64.545	197.309	139.209	256.564
24	159.400	63.885	187.832	139.209	256.564
25	121.800	28.839	171.324	139.209	256.564
26	213.600	109.223	181.893	139.209	256.564
27	202.000	169.451	186.920	139.209	256.564
28	269.800	60.288	207.640	139.209	256.564
29	257.400	77.893	220.080	139.209	256.564
30	127.400	41.332	196.910	139.209	256.564
Overall mean	197.887				
$\overline{S}$	108.770				
C_4	0.940				
n	5.000				
r	0.250				

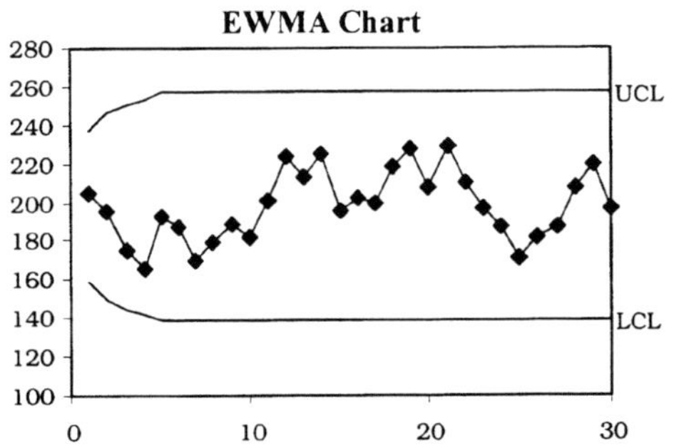

There are no W_i values outside of the LCL and UCL, hence there is no evidence that the process is out of control.

(c) The results are the same for all parts.

17. (a) CUSUM Chart

Container	Average	Standard Deviation	Z_i	S_{H_i}	S_{L_i}
1	10.550	0.311	−1.096	0.000	0.596
2	10.525	0.287	−1.267	0.000	1.363
3	10.625	0.275	−0.581	0.000	1.443
4	10.825	0.189	0.793	0.293	0.151
5	10.625	0.250	−0.581	0.000	0.231
6	10.325	0.479	−2.641	0.000	2.372
7	10.625	0.457	−0.581	0.000	2.453
8	10.475	0.386	−1.611	0.000	3.563
9	10.400	0.503	−2.126	0.000	5.189
10	10.075	0.171	−4.357	0.000	9.046
11	10.200	0.668	−3.499	0.000	12.045
12	10.275	0.427	−2.984	0.000	14.529
13	10.450	0.252	−1.782	0.000	15.811
14	10.250	0.173	−3.156	0.000	18.466
15	10.175	0.222	−3.671	0.000	21.637
16	11.700	0.216	6.801	6.301	14.336
17	11.325	0.250	4.226	10.027	9.610
18	10.875	0.171	1.136	10.663	7.974
19	10.850	0.100	0.964	11.127	6.510
20	11.200	0.294	3.368	13.995	2.642
21	11.525	0.096	5.599	19.094	0.000
22	11.175	0.096	3.196	21.790	0.000
23	11.125	0.263	2.853	24.142	0.000
24	11.050	0.311	2.338	25.980	0.000
25	10.775	0.310	0.449	25.929	0.000
26	11.400	0.216	4.741	30.170	0.000
27	10.925	0.263	1.479	31.149	0.000
28	11.275	0.126	3.883	34.532	0.000
29	11.250	0.370	3.711	37.743	0.000
30	10.425	0.126	−1.954	35.289	1.454
31	10.150	0.238	−3.842	30.947	4.796
32	10.325	0.189	−2.641	27.806	6.937
33	10.575	0.275	−0.924	26.382	7.361
34	9.800	0.163	−6.245	19.637	13.106
Overall mean	10.710				
$\overline{S}$	0.268				
C_4	0.921				
n	4.000				
k	0.500				

There are S_{H_i} and S_{L_i} values greater than 4, hence the process is out of control.

(b) EWMA chart

Container	Average	Standard Deviation	W_i	LCL	UCL
1	10.550	0.311	10.670	10.644	10.808
2	10.525	0.287	10.634	10.628	10.808
3	10.625	0.275	10.631	10.620	10.808
4	10.825	0.189	10.680	10.616	10.808
5	10.625	0.250	10.666	10.548	10.871
6	10.325	0.479	10.581	10.548	10.871
7	10.625	0.457	10.592	10.548	10.871
8	10.475	0.386	10.563	10.548	10.871
9	10.400	0.503	10.522	10.548	10.871
10	10.075	0.171	10.410	10.548	10.871
11	10.200	0.668	10.358	10.548	10.871
12	10.275	0.427	10.337	10.548	10.871
13	10.450	0.252	10.365	10.548	10.871
14	10.250	0.173	10.336	10.548	10.871
15	10.175	0.221	10.296	10.548	10.871
16	11.700	0.216	10.647	10.548	10.871
17	11.325	0.250	10.817	10.548	10.871
18	10.875	0.171	10.831	10.548	10.871
19	10.850	0.100	10.836	10.548	10.871
20	11.200	0.294	10.927	10.548	10.871
21	11.525	0.096	11.076	10.548	10.871
22	11.175	0.096	11.101	10.548	10.871
23	11.125	0.263	11.107	10.548	10.871
24	11.050	0.311	11.093	10.548	10.871
25	10.775	0.310	11.013	10.548	10.871
26	11.400	0.216	11.110	10.548	10.871
27	10.925	0.263	11.064	10.548	10.871
28	11.275	0.126	11.117	10.548	10.871
29	11.250	0.370	11.150	10.548	10.871
30	10.425	0.126	10.969	10.548	10.871
31	10.150	0.238	10.764	10.548	10.871
32	10.325	0.189	10.654	10.548	10.871
33	10.575	0.275	10.634	10.548	10.871
34	9.800	0.163	10.426	10.548	10.871
Overall mean	10.710				
$\overline{S}$	0.268				
C_4	0.940				
n	4.000				
r	0.250				

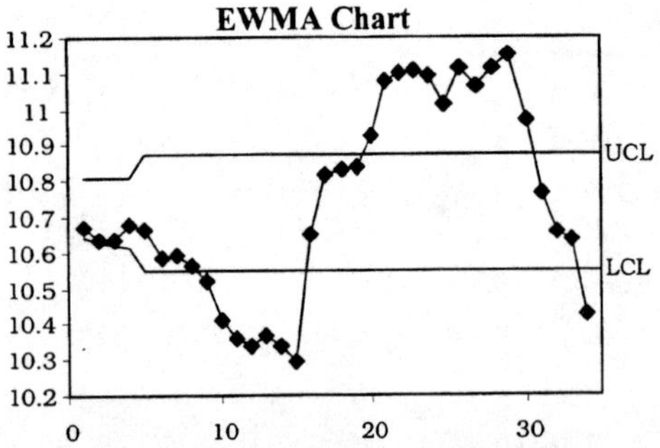

There are W_i values below the LCL and above the UCL, hence the process is out of statistical control.

(c) The results are the same for all of the parts. The process is out of statistical control.

18. (a)

Month	Average	Standard Deviation	Z_i	S_{H_i}	S_{L_i}
1	36.500	5.612	−2.096	0.000	1.596
2	39.833	4.355	−0.416	0.000	1.513
3	30.333	2.582	−5.204	0.000	6.217
4	40.500	1.871	−0.080	0.000	5.797
5	44.667	2.875	2.019	1.519	3.278
6	46.333	1.366	2.859	3.879	0.00
7	37.167	5.742	−1.760	1.618	1.260
8	51.000	3.406	5.211	6.329	0.000
9	40.333	7.174	−0.164	5.665	0.000
10	38.500	6.156	−1.088	4.076	0.588
11	34.500	6.656	−3.104	0.472	3.193
12	38.833	5.037	−0.920	0.000	3.613
13	43.167	4.622	1.263	0.763	1.850
14	46.833	4.956	3.111	3.375	0.000
15	45.167	3.125	2.271	5.146	0.000
16	45.833	4.792	2.607	7.253	0.000
17	40.167	5.231	−0.248	6.505	0.000
18	48.667	4.274	4.035	10.040	0.000
19	41.500	3.332	0.423	9.963	0.000
20	31.000	4.899	−4.868	4.595	4.368
21	36.500	6.534	−2.096	1.999	5.964
22	34.167	5.947	−3.272	0.000	8.737
23	35.167	6.047	−2.768	0.000	11.005
24	49.167	4.401	4.287	3.787	6.218
Overall mean	40.660				
$\overline{S}$	4.625				
C_4	0.952				
n	6.000				
k	0.500				

There are S_{H_i} and S_{L_i} values greater than 4, hence the process is out of statistical control.

(b) EWMA Chart

Month	Average	Standard Deviation	W_i	LCL	UCL
1	36.500	5.612	39.620	39.172	42.148
2	39.833	4.355	40.453	38.799	42.520
3	30.333	2.582	38.078	38.620	42.700
4	40.500	1.871	40.620	38.525	42.794
5	44.667	2.875	41.661	38.410	42.910
6	46.333	1.366	42.078	38.410	42.910
7	37.167	5.742	39.786	38.410	42.910
8	51.000	3.406	43.245	38.410	42.910
9	40.333	7.174	40.578	38.410	42.910
10	38.500	6.156	40.120	38.410	42.910
11	34.500	6.656	39.120	38.410	42.910
12	38.833	5.037	40.203	38.410	42.910
13	43.167	4.622	41.286	38.410	42.910
14	46.833	4.956	42.203	38.410	42.910
15	45.167	3.125	41.786	38.410	42.910
16	45.833	4.792	41.953	38.410	42.910
17	40.167	5.231	40.536	38.410	42.910
18	48.667	4.274	42.661	38.410	42.910
19	41.500	3.332	40.870	38.410	42.910
20	31.000	4.899	38.245	38.410	42.910
21	36.500	6.535	39.620	38.410	42.910
22	34.167	5.947	39.036	38.410	42.910
23	35.167	6.047	39.286	38.410	42.910
24	49.167	4.401	42.786	38.410	42.910
Overall mean	40.660				
$\overline{S}$	4.625				
C_4	0.952				
n	6.000				
r	0.250				

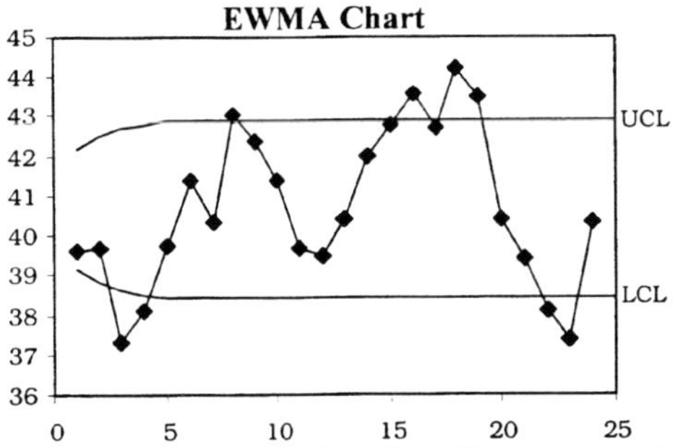

There are W_i values below the LCL and above the UCL, hence the process is out statistical of control.

(c) The results are the same for all of the parts. The process is out of statistical control.

19. (a) CUSUM Chart

Day	Mean Flow	Flow Standard Deviation	Z_i	S_{H_i}	S_{L_i}
1	0.065	0.023	10.050	9.550	0.000
2	0.059	0.006	7.050	16.100	0.000
3	0.053	0.008	4.001	19.601	0.000
4	0.052	0.007	3.340	22.440	0.000
5	0.054	0.007	4.763	26.703	0.000
6	0.053	0.007	3.848	30.051	0.000
7	0.053	0.008	4.001	33.552	0.000
8	0.052	0.006	3.645	36.696	0.000
9	0.046	0.008	0.747	36.944	0.000
10	0.045	0.008	−0.219	36.225	0.000
11	0.044	0.008	−0.269	35.456	0.000
12	0.045	0.006	−0.066	34.890	0.000
13	0.047	0.008	1.052	35.442	0.000
14	0.044	0.008	−0.422	34.520	0.000
15	0.041	0.007	−1.845	32.175	1.345
16	0.038	0.008	−3.370	28.305	4.215
17	0.038	0.008	−3.574	24.231	7.289
18	0.038	0.009	−3.675	20.056	10.464
19	0.038	0.008	−3.624	15.931	13.588
20	0.037	0.008	−4.234	11.197	17.323
21	0.036	0.008	−4.539	6.158	21.362
22	0.041	0.022	−2.150	3.508	23.012
23	0.042	0.007	−1.744	1.264	24.256
24	0.038	0.008	−3.624	0.000	27.380
25	0.039	0.008	−3.065	0.000	29.945
26	0.044	0.024	−0.320	0.000	29.766
27	0.042	0.007	−1.489	0.000	30.755
28	0.040	0.009	−2.404	0.000	32.660
29	0.041	0.018	−1.947	0.000	34.106
30	0.045	0.010	0.086	0.000	33.520
Overall mean	0.045				
$\overline{S}$	0.010				
C_4	0.989				
n	24.000				
k	0.500				

There are S_{H_i} and S_{L_i} values greater than 4, hence the process is out of statistical control.

(b) EWMA Chart

Day	Mean Flow	Flow Standard Deviation	W_i	LCL	UCL
1	0.065	0.023	0.050	0.042	0.048
2	0.059	0.006	0.052	0.041	0.049
3	0.053	0.008	0.052	0.040	0.050
4	0.052	0.007	0.052	0.040	0.050
5	0.054	0.007	0.053	0.040	0.050
6	0.053	0.007	0.053	0.034	0.050
7	0.053	0.008	0.053	0.040	0.050
8	0.052	0.006	0.053	0.040	0.050
9	0.046	0.008	0.052	0.040	0.050
10	0.045	0.008	0.049	0.040	0.050
11	0.044	0.008	0.048	0.040	0.050
12	0.045	0.006	0.047	0.040	0.050
13	0.047	0.008	0.047	0.040	0.050
14	0.044	0.008	0.046	0.040	0.050
15	0.041	0.007	0.045	0.040	0.050
16	0.038	0.008	0.043	0.040	0.050
17	0.038	0.008	0.042	0.040	0.050
18	0.038	0.009	0.041	0.040	0.050
19	0.038	0.008	0.040	0.040	0.050
20	0.037	0.008	0.039	0.040	0.050
21	0.036	0.008	0.038	0.040	0.050
22	0.041	0.022	0.039	0.040	0.050
23	0.042	0.007	0.040	0.040	0.050
24	0.038	0.008	0.039	0.040	0.050
25	0.039	0.008	0.039	0.040	0.050
26	0.044	0.024	0.040	0.040	0.050
27	0.042	0.007	0.041	0.040	0.050
28	0.040	0.009	0.041	0.040	0.050
29	0.041	0.018	0.041	0.040	0.050
30	0.045	0.010	0.042	0.040	0.050
Overall mean	0.045				
$\overline{S}$	0.010				
C_4	0.940				
n	5.000				
r	0.250				

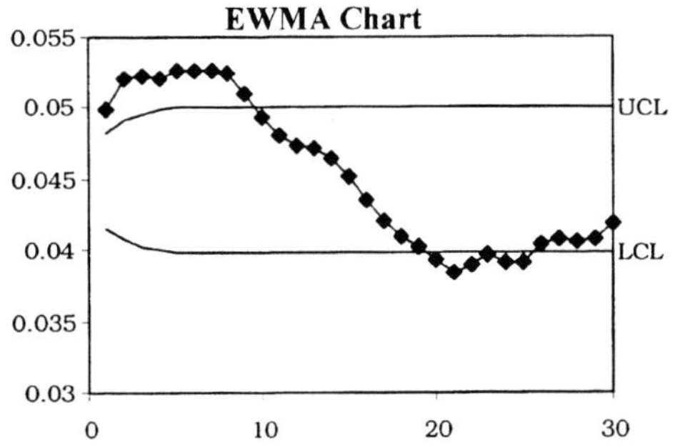

There are W_i values below the LCL and above the UCL, hence the process is out of statistical control.

(c) The results are the same for all of the parts. The process is out of statistical control.

20. (a) CUSUM Chart

Day	Mean Time	Standard Deviation (Time)	Z_i	S_{H_i}	S_{L_i}
1	23.300	1.300	–2.890	0.000	2.390
2	21.800	1.300	–5.767	0.000	7.657
3	23.000	1.730	–3.465	0.000	10.622
4	24.500	0.500	–0.588	0.000	10.710
5	24.300	1.090	–0.972	0.000	11.182
6	23.400	1.850	–2.698	0.000	13.380
7	24.300	1.090	–0.972	0.000	13.852
8	24.300	0.830	–0.972	0.000	14.324
9	24.000	2.550	–1.547	0.000	15.371
10	24.000	0.700	–1.547	0.000	16.418
11	24.800	0.830	–0.013	0.000	15.931
12	25.500	1.660	1.330	0.830	14.101
13	24.500	0.050	–0.588	0.000	14.189
14	24.700	0.470	–0.205	0.000	13.894
15	25.500	0.500	1.330	0.830	12.064
16	25.300	0.470	0.946	1.276	10.618
17	21.000	6.680	–7.301	0.000	17.419
18	24.000	0.000	–1.547	0.000	18.466
19	24.900	0.430	0.179	0.000	17.787
20	23.800	0.430	–1.931	0.000	19.218
21	24.000	0.000	–1.547	0.000	20.265
22	24.800	0.430	–0.013	0.000	19.778
23	26.000	1.580	2.289	1.789	16.989
24	24.800	0.430	–0.013	1.276	16.502
25	24.000	0.000	–1.547	0.000	17.549
26	24.500	0.500	–0.588	0.000	17.638
27	28.000	0.000	6.125	5.625	11.013
28	28.000	0.000	6.125	11.250	4.388
29	27.500	1.500	5.166	15.916	0
30	28.000	0.000	6.125	21.541	0
31	27.000	1.220	4.207	25.248	0
Overall mean	24.807				
$\overline{S}$	0.961				
C_4	0.921				
n	4.000				
k	0.500				

There are S_{H_i} and S_{L_i} values greater than 4, hence the process is out of control.

(b) EWMA Chart

Day	Mean Time	Standard Deviation (Time)	W_i	LCL	UCL
1	23.300	1.300	24.430	24.464	25.149
2	21.800	1.300	23.773	24.378	25.235
3	23.000	1.730	23.580	24.337	25.277
4	24.500	0.500	23.810	24.315	25.298
5	24.300	1.090	23.932	24.288	25.325
6	23.400	1.850	23.799	24.288	25.325
7	24.300	1.090	23.924	24.288	25.325
8	24.300	0.830	24.018	24.288	25.325
9	24.000	2.550	24.014	24.288	25.325
10	24.000	0.700	24.010	24.288	25.325
11	24.800	0.830	24.208	24.288	25.325
12	25.500	1.660	24.531	24.288	25.325
13	24.500	0.050	24.523	24.288	25.325
14	24.700	0.470	24.567	24.288	25.325
15	25.500	0.500	24.800	24.288	25.325
16	25.300	0.470	24.925	24.288	25.325
17	21.000	6.680	23.944	24.288	25.325
18	24.000	0.000	23.958	24.288	25.325
19	24.900	0.430	24.194	24.288	25.325
20	23.800	0.430	24.095	24.288	25.325
21	24.000	0.000	24.071	24.288	25.325
22	24.800	0.430	24.254	24.288	25.325
23	26.000	1.580	24.690	24.288	25.325
24	24.800	0.430	24.718	24.288	25.325
25	24.000	0.000	24.538	24.288	25.325
26	24.500	0.500	24.529	24.288	25.325
27	28.000	0.000	25.396	24.288	25.325
28	28.000	0.000	26.047	24.288	25.325
29	27.500	1.500	26.411	24.288	25.325
30	28.000	0.000	26.808	24.288	25.325
31	27.000	1.220	26.856	24.288	25.325
Overall mean	24.807				
$\overline{S}$	0.961				
C_4	0.940				
n	5.000				
r	0.250				

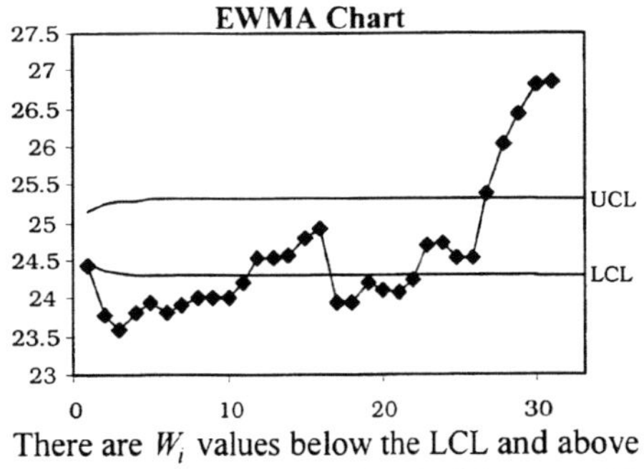

There are W_i values below the LCL and above the UCL, hence the process is out of statistical control.

(c) The results are the same for all of the parts. The process is out of statistical control.

21. (a) CUSUM Chart

Sample	Average	Standard Deviation	Z_i	S_{H_i}	S_{L_i}
1	19.800	0.255	−2.986	0.000	2.486
2	19.640	0.518	−3.993	0.000	5.978
3	19.980	0.507	−1.853	0.000	7.331
4	20.660	0.230	2.427	1.927	4.404
5	19.740	0.467	−3.363	0.000	7.267
6	19.540	0.297	−4.622	0.000	11.389
7	20.020	0.319	−1.601	0.000	12.490
8	20.100	0.122	−1.098	0.000	13.088
9	20.280	0.164	0.035	0.000	12.552
10	20.700	0.283	2.678	2.178	9.374
11	20.620	0.164	2.175	3.853	6.699
12	20.540	0.305	1.672	5.025	4.528
13	20.380	0.148	0.665	5.190	3.363
14	20.580	0.217	1.923	6.613	0.940
15	20.540	0.207	1.672	7.784	0.000
16	18.500	4.535	−11.167	0.000	10.667
17	20.080	0.164	−1.223	0.000	11.390
18	20.240	0.152	−0.216	0.000	11.107
19	20.320	0.286	0.287	0.000	10.320
20	20.280	0.179	0.035	0.000	9.785
21	20.220	0.239	−0.342	0.000	9.627
22	20.020	0.408	−1.601	0.000	10.728
23	20.300	0.187	0.161	0.000	10.067
24	19.980	0.531	−1.853	0.000	11.420
25	20.340	0.207	0.413	0.000	10.507
26	20.260	0.288	−0.091	0.000	10.097
27	20.280	0.130	0.035	0.000	9.562
28	20.300	0.245	0.161	0.000	8.901
29	20.460	0.219	1.168	0.668	7.233
30	20.400	0.141	0.790	0.958	5.943
31	20.340	0.270	0.413	0.871	5.030
32	20.340	0.270	0.413	0.784	4.117
33	20.120	0.259	−0.972	0.000	4.589
34	20.320	0.259	0.287	0.000	3.802
35	20.600	0.200	2.049	1.549	1.253
36	20.060	0.114	−1.349	0.000	2.102
37	20.060	0.378	−1.349	0.000	2.951
38	20.420	0.228	0.916	0.416	1.535
39	20.400	0.187	0.790	0.707	0.244
40	19.940	0.550	−2.104	0.000	1.849
41	20.320	0.148	0.287	0.000	1.062
42	20.560	0.329	1.797	1.297	0.000
43	20.580	0.370	1.923	2.721	0.000
44	20.500	0.625	1.420	3.640	0.000
45	20.940	0.167	4.189	7.329	0.000
46	20.860	0.134	3.685	10.515	0.000
47	20.880	0.228	3.811	13.826	0.000
48	20.380	0.239	0.665	13.991	0.000
49	20.480	0.286	1.294	14.784	0.000
50	20.520	0.228	1.546	15.830	0.000
Overall mean	20.274				
$\overline{S}$	0.352				
C_4	0.990				
n	5.000				
k	0.500				

There are S_{H_i} and S_{L_i} values greater than 4, hence the process is out of statistical control.

(b) EWMA chart

Sample	Average	Standard Deviation	W_i	Lower Control Limit	Upper Control Limit
1	19.800	0.255	20.156	20.155	20.394
2	19.640	0.518	20.027	20.125	20.423
3	19.980	0.507	20.015	20.111	20.438
4	20.660	0.230	20.176	20.103	20.445
5	19.740	0.467	20.067	20.094	20.455
6	19.540	0.297	19.935	20.094	20.455
7	20.020	0.319	19.957	20.094	20.455
8	20.100	0.122	19.992	20.094	20.455
9	20.280	0.164	20.064	20.094	20.455
10	20.700	0.283	20.223	20.094	20.455
11	20.620	0.164	20.322	20.094	20.455
12	20.540	0.305	20.377	20.094	20.455
13	20.380	0.148	20.378	20.094	20.455
14	20.580	0.217	20.428	20.094	20.455
15	20.540	0.207	20.456	20.094	20.455
16	18.500	4.535	19.967	20.094	20.455
17	20.080	0.164	19.995	20.094	20.455
18	20.240	0.152	20.057	20.094	20.455
19	20.320	0.286	20.122	20.094	20.455
20	20.280	0.179	20.162	20.094	20.455
21	20.220	0.239	20.176	20.094	20.455
22	20.020	0.409	20.137	20.094	20.455
23	20.300	0.187	20.178	20.094	20.455
24	19.980	0.531	20.128	20.094	20.455
25	20.340	0.207	20.181	20.094	20.455
26	20.260	0.288	20.201	20.094	20.455
27	20.280	0.130	20.221	20.094	20.455
28	20.300	0.245	20.241	20.094	20.455
29	20.460	0.219	20.295	20.094	20.455
30	20.400	0.141	20.322	20.094	20.455
31	20.340	0.270	20.326	20.094	20.455
32	20.340	0.270	20.330	20.094	20.455
33	20.120	0.259	20.277	20.094	20.455
34	20.320	0.259	20.288	20.094	20.455
35	20.600	0.200	20.366	20.094	20.455
36	20.060	0.114	20.289	20.094	20.455
37	20.060	0.378	20.232	20.094	20.455
38	20.420	0.228	20.279	20.094	20.455
39	20.400	0.187	20.309	20.094	20.455
40	19.940	0.550	20.217	20.094	20.455
41	20.320	0.148	20.243	20.094	20.455
42	20.560	0.329	20.322	20.094	20.455
43	20.580	0.370	20.387	20.094	20.455
44	20.500	0.625	20.415	20.094	20.455
45	20.940	0.167	20.546	20.094	20.455
46	20.860	0.134	20.625	20.094	20.455
47	20.880	0.228	20.688	20.094	20.455
48	20.380	0.239	20.611	20.094	20.455
49	20.480	0.286	20.579	20.094	20.455
50	20.520	0.228	20.564	20.094	20.455
Overall mean	20.274				
$\overline{S}$	0.352				
C_4	0.990				
n	5.000				
r	0.250				

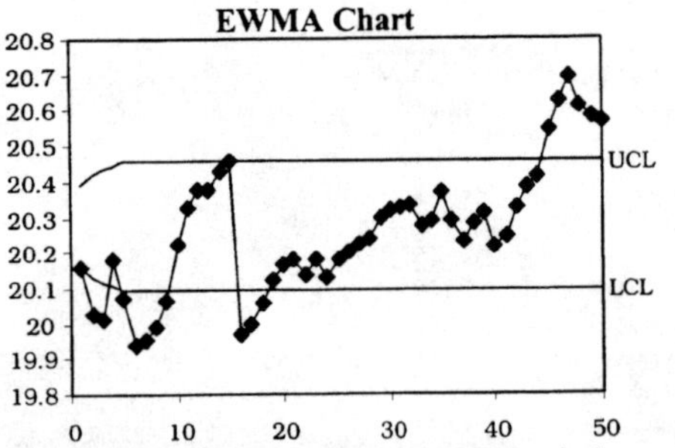

There are W_i values below the LCL and above the UCL, hence the process is out of statistical control.

(c) The results are the same for all of the parts. The process is out of statistical control.

22. (a) CUSUM Chart

Day	Average	Standard Deviation	Z_i	S_{H_i}	S_{L_i}
1	4.125	0.021	−0.304	0.000	0.000
2	4.110	0.016	−1.784	0.000	1.284
3	4.123	0.017	−0.551	0.000	1.334
4	4.080	0.016	−4.742	0.000	5.577
5	4.090	0.022	−3.756	0.000	8.833
6	4.120	0.014	−0.797	0.000	9.130
7	4.113	0.013	−1.537	0.000	10.167
8	4.118	0.013	−1.044	0.000	10.711
9	4.120	0.016	−0.797	0.000	11.008
10	4.123	0.017	−0.551	0.000	11.059
11	4.173	0.038	4.381	3.881	6.178
12	4.143	0.010	1.422	4.803	4.256
13	4.135	0.013	0.682	4.985	3.074
14	4.125	0.013	−0.304	4.181	2.878
15	4.133	0.019	0.436	4.116	1.943
16	4.123	0.005	−0.551	3.066	1.993
17	4.115	0.013	−1.290	1.275	2.784
18	4.183	0.017	5.367	6.143	0.000
19	4.160	0.026	3.148	8.790	0.000
20	4.128	0.0288	−0.058	8.233	0.000
21	4.118	0.035	−1.044	6.689	0.544
22	4.118	0.010	−1.044	5.145	1.088
23	4.123	0.010	−0.551	4.095	1.138
24	4.120	0.022	−0.797	2.797	1.436
25	4.138	0.029	0.929	3.226	0.007
26	4.123	0.010	−0.551	2.175	0.058
27	4.153	0.033	2.408	4.084	0.000
28	4.130	0.018	0.189	3.773	0.000
29	4.133	0.022	0.436	3.708	0.000
30	4.155	0.026	2.655	5.863	0.000
Overall mean	4.128				
$\overline{S}$	0.019				
C_4	0.921				
n	4.000				
k	0.500				

There are S_{H_i} and S_{L_i} values greater than 4, hence the process is out of statistical control.

(b) EWMA Chart

Day	Average	Standard Deviation	W_i	LCL	UCL
1	4.125	0.021	4.127	4.120	4.136
2	4.110	0.016	4.123	4.119	4.138
3	4.123	0.017	4.123	4.118	4.139
4	4.080	0.016	4.112	4.117	4.139
5	4.090	0.022	4.107	4.117	4.140
6	4.120	0.014	4.110	4.117	4.140
7	4.113	0.013	4.111	4.117	4.140
8	4.118	0.013	4.112	4.117	4.140
9	4.120	0.016	4.114	4.117	4.140
10	4.123	0.017	4.116	4.117	4.140
11	4.173	0.038	4.130	4.117	4.140
12	4.143	0.010	4.133	4.117	4.140
13	4.135	0.013	4.134	4.117	4.140
14	4.125	0.013	4.132	4.117	4.140
15	4.133	0.019	4.132	4.117	4.140
16	4.123	0.005	4.129	4.117	4.140
17	4.115	0.013	4.126	4.117	4.140
18	4.183	0.017	4.140	4.117	4.140
19	4.160	0.026	4.145	4.117	4.140
20	4.128	0.029	4.141	4.117	4.140
21	4.118	0.035	4.135	4.117	4.140
22	4.118	0.010	4.131	4.117	4.140
23	4.123	0.010	4.129	4.117	4.140
24	4.120	0.022	4.126	4.117	4.140
25	4.138	0.029	4.129	4.117	4.140
26	4.123	0.010	4.127	4.117	4.140
27	4.153	0.033	4.134	4.117	4.140
28	4.130	0.018	4.133	4.117	4.140
29	4.133	0.022	4.133	4.117	4.140
30	4.155	0.026	4.138	4.117	4.140
Overall mean	4.128				
$\overline{S}$	0.019				
C_4	0.921				
n	4.000				
r	0.250				

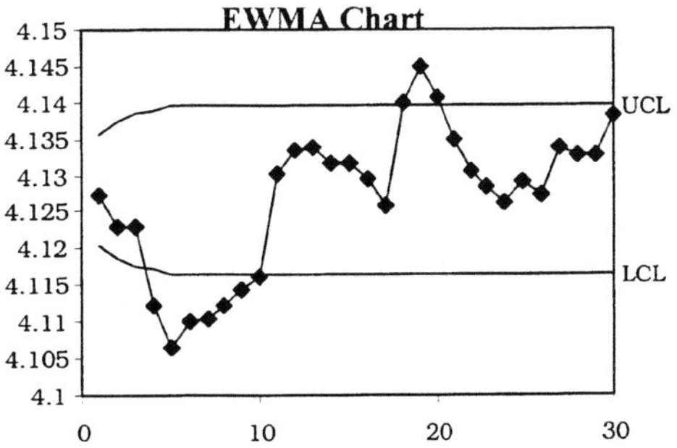

There are W_i values below the LCL and above the UCL, hence the process is out of statistical control.

(c) The results are the same for all of the parts. The process is out of statistical control.

23. (a) CUSUM Chart

Day	Mean Weight	Standard Deviation Weight	Z_i	S_{H_i}	S_{L_i}
1	1894.670	31.330	−1.520	0.000	1.020
2	1924.670	27.600	2.071	1.571	0.000
3	1894.000	34.980	−1.600	0.000	1.100
4	1902.670	25.380	−0.562	0.000	1.163
5	1912.670	34.860	0.635	0.135	0.028
6	1896.000	39.120	−1.361	0.000	0.889
7	1908.000	21.570	0.076	0.000	0.313
8	1912.670	22.490	0.635	0.135	0.000
9	1937.920	33.090	3.657	3.292	0.000
10	1917.330	27.890	1.193	3.985	0.000
11	1889.330	20.840	−2.159	1.325	1.659
12	1910.000	18.090	0.315	1.140	0.844
13	1909.000	18.090	0.195	0.836	0.149
14	1900.000	26.200	−0.882	0.000	0.531
15	1915.330	31.160	0.953	0.453	0.000
16	1911.330	32.620	0.474	0.427	0.000
17	1912.680	22.750	0.636	0.563	0.000
18	1901.330	17.670	−0.723	0.000	0.223
19	1892.000	31.820	−1.840	0.000	1.563
20	1888.670	38.060	−2.238	0.000	3.301
21	1918.670	31.140	1.353	0.853	1.448
22	1904.670	39.260	−0.323	0.030	1.271
23	1909.330	22.590	0.235	0.000	0.536
24	1904.000	24.480	−0.403	0.000	0.439
25	1912.000	32.270	0.554	0.054	0.000
26	1896.670	18.200	−1.281	0.000	0.781
27	1923.330	38.210	1.911	1.411	0.000
Overall mean	1907.368				
$\bar{S}$	28.213				
C_4	0.975				
n	12.000				
k	0.500				

There are no S_{H_i} or S_{L_i} values greater than 4, hence there is no evidence that the process is out of statistical control.

(b) EWMA chart

Day	Mean Weight	Standard Deviation Weight	W_i	LCL	UCL
1	1894.670	31.330	1904.194	1901.103	1913.633
2	1924.670	27.600	1909.313	1899.537	1915.199
3	1894.000	34.980	1905.485	1898.781	1915.956
4	1902.670	25.380	1904.781	1898.383	1916.353
5	1912.670	34.860	1906.753	1897.896	1916.840
6	1896.000	39.120	1904.065	1897.896	1916.840
7	1908.000	21.570	1905.049	1897.896	1916.840
8	1912.670	22.490	1906.954	1897.896	1916.840
9	1937.920	33.090	1914.695	1897.896	1916.840
10	1917.330	27.890	1915.354	1897.896	1916.840
11	1889.330	20.840	1908.848	1897.896	1916.840
12	1910.000	18.090	1909.136	1897.896	1916.840
13	1909.000	18.090	1909.102	1897.896	1916.840
14	1900.000	26.200	1906.827	1897.896	1916.840
15	1915.330	31.160	1908.952	1897.896	1916.840
16	1911.330	32.620	1909.547	1897.896	1916.840
17	1912.680	22.750	1910.330	1897.896	1916.840
18	1901.330	17.670	1908.080	1897.896	1916.840
19	1892.000	31.820	1904.060	1897.896	1916.840
20	1888.670	38.060	1900.213	1897.896	1916.840
21	1918.670	31.140	1904.827	1897.896	1916.840
22	1904.670	39.260	1904.788	1897.896	1916.840
23	1909.330	22.590	1905.923	1897.896	1916.840
24	1904.000	24.480	1905.442	1897.896	1916.840
25	1912.000	32.270	1907.082	1897.896	1916.840
26	1896.670	18.200	1904.479	1897.896	1916.840
27	1923.330	38.210	1909.192	1897.896	1916.840
Overall mean	1907.368				
$\overline{S}$	28.213				
C_4	0.975				
n	12.000				
r	0.250				

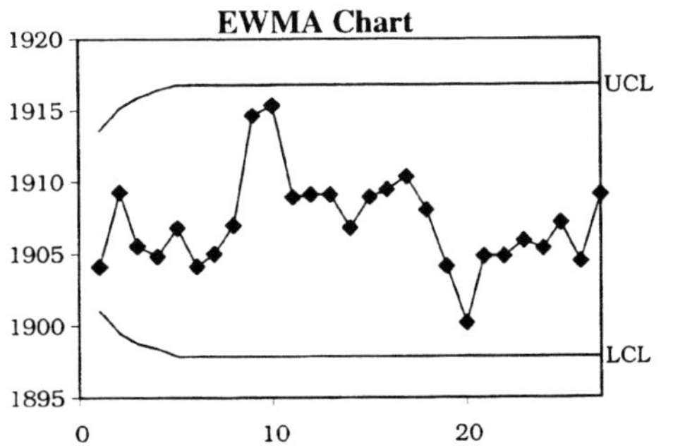

There are no W_i values out of LCL and UCL, hence there is no evidence that the process is out of statistical control.

(c) The results in general are the same for all of the parts.

24. $USL = 103$, $LSL = 97$, $USL - LSL = 6$, $6\sigma = UCL - LCL = 102.553 - 97.453 = 5.1$, $\sigma = 0.85$

(a) $C_p = \dfrac{USL - LSL}{6\sigma} = \dfrac{6}{5.1} = 1.176$. $C_p > 1$, so the process is unlikely to produce nonconforming units.

$Z_{LSL} = \dfrac{LSL - \overline{X}}{\sigma} = \dfrac{-3}{0.85} = -3.529$, $Z_{USL} = \dfrac{USL - \overline{X}}{\sigma} = \dfrac{3}{0.85} = 3.529$, $|Z_{\min}| = |Z_{LSL}| = |Z_{USL}| = 3.529$,

$C_{pk} = \left|\dfrac{Z_{\min}}{3}\right| = \dfrac{3.529}{3} = 1.176$. The specification limits are equidistant from the mean, so $C_p = C_{pk}$.

(b) proportion too small $= 0.5 - 0.49979 = 0.00021$.
proportion too large $= 0.5 - 0.49979 = 0.00021$.
proportion too small + proportion too large $= 0.00042$.

(c) $Z_{LSL} = \dfrac{LSL - \overline{X}}{\sigma} = \dfrac{97 - 101}{0.85} = \dfrac{-4}{0.85} = 4.706$, $Z_{USL} = \dfrac{USL - \overline{X}}{\sigma} = \dfrac{103 - 101}{0.85} = \dfrac{2}{0.85} = 2.353$,
proportion too small $= 0.5 - 0.49999876 = 0.00000124$
proportion too large $= 0.5 - 0.4906 = 0.0094$
proportion too small + proportion too large $= 0.00940124$

25. $USL = 210$, $LSL = 190$, $USL - LSL = 20$, $6\sigma = UCL - LCL = 220 - 180 = 40$, $\sigma = 6.667$

(a) $C_p = \dfrac{USL - LSL}{6\sigma} = \dfrac{20}{40} = 0.5$, $C_p < 1$, so the process can be expected to produce many nonconforming units.

$Z_{LSL} = \dfrac{LSL - \overline{X}}{\sigma} = \dfrac{190 - 200}{6.667} = -\dfrac{10}{6.667} = -1.5$, $Z_{USL} = \dfrac{USL - \overline{X}}{\sigma} = \dfrac{210 - 200}{6.667} = \dfrac{10}{6.667} = 1.5$,

$|Z_{\min}| = |Z_{LSL}| = |Z_{USL}| = 1.5$, $C_{pk} = \left|\dfrac{Z_{\min}}{3}\right| = \dfrac{1.5}{3} = 0.5$. The specification limits are equidistant from the mean, so

$C_p = C_{pk}$.

(b) proportion too small $= 0.5 - 0.4332 = 0.0668$
proportion too large $= 0.5 - 0.4332 = 0.0668$
proportion too small + proportion too large $= 0.1336$

(c) $Z_{LSL} = \dfrac{LSL - \overline{X}}{\sigma} = \dfrac{190 - 200}{3} = -\dfrac{10}{3} = -3.33$, $Z_{USL} = \dfrac{USL - \overline{X}}{\sigma} = \dfrac{210 - 200}{3} = \dfrac{10}{3} = 3.33$
proportion too small $= 0.5 - 0.49957 = 0.00043$
proportion too large $= 0.5 - 0.49957 = 0.00043$
proportion too small + proportion too large $= 0.00086$

(d) $|Z_{\min}| = 3 * C_{pk} = 3 * 1.33 = 3.99$. For the same specification limits and the same sample mean we have $\sigma = \dfrac{10}{|Z_{\min}|} = \dfrac{10}{3.99} = 2.5$ and $UCL - LCL = 6\sigma = 15$, hence $LCL = 200 - 7.5 = 192.5$, $UCL = 200 + 7.5 = 207.5$. For the same standard deviation and the same sample mean we have $LSL = \overline{X} - \sigma \times Z_{\min} = 200 - 3 \times 3.99 = 188$, $USL = \overline{X} + \sigma \times Z_{\min} = 200 + 3 \times 3.99 = 212$

26. $LSL = 64.25$, $USL = 66.75$, $USL - LSL = 2.5$, $6\sigma = UCL - LCL = 66.86 - 64.34 = 2.52$, $\sigma = 0.42$

(a) $C_p = \dfrac{USL - LSL}{6\sigma} = \dfrac{2.5}{2.52} = 0.992$, $C_p < 1$, so the process can be expected to produce many nonconforming units.

$Z_{LSL} = \dfrac{LSL - \overline{X}}{\sigma} = \dfrac{64.25 - 65.6}{0.42} = -\dfrac{1.35}{0.42} = -3.214$, $Z_{USL} = \dfrac{USL - \overline{X}}{\sigma} = \dfrac{66.75 - 65.6}{0.42} = \dfrac{1.15}{0.42} = 2.738$, $|Z_{\min}| = 2.738$,

$C_{pk} = \left|\dfrac{Z_{\min}}{3}\right| = \dfrac{2.738}{3} = 0.913$

(b) proportion too small $= 0.5 - 0.49934 = 0.00066$
proportion too large $= 0.5 - 0.4969 = 0.0031$
proportion too small + proportion too large $= 0.00376$

(c) $LSL = 64.19$, $USL = 66.81$, $USL - LSL = 2.62$, $6\sigma = UCL - LCL = 66.81 - 64.19 = 2.62$, $\sigma = 0.437$,
$C_p = \frac{USL - LSL}{6\sigma} = \frac{2.62}{2.62} = 1$. The process can be expected to produce 0.0027 units beyond the specification limits.
$Z_{LSL} = \frac{LSL - \overline{X}}{\sigma} = \frac{64.19 - 65.5}{0.437} = -\frac{1.31}{0.437} = -3$, $Z_{USL} = \frac{USL - \overline{X}}{\sigma} = \frac{66.81 - 65.5}{0.437} = \frac{1.31}{0.437} = 3$, $|Z_{min}| = 3$, $C_{pk} = 1$.
The specification limits are equidistant from the mean, hence $C_p = C_{pk}$.

(d) The process can be expected to produce 0.0027 units beyond the specification limits.

(e) $|Z_{min}| = 3 \times C_{pk} = 3 \times 1.33 = 3.99$. For the same specification limits and the same sample mean, the following holds
$\sigma = \frac{1.31}{|Z_{min}|} = \frac{1.31}{3.99} = 0.328$ and $UCL - LCL = 6\sigma = 1.97$, so $LCL = 65.5 - 0.985 = 64.515$,
$UCL = 65.5 + 0.985 = 66.485$. For the same standard deviation and the same sample mean we have
$LSL = \overline{X} - \sigma \times Z_{min} = 65.5 - 0.437 \times 3.99 = 63.756$, $USL = \overline{X} + \sigma \times Z_{min} = 65.5 + 0.437 \times 3.99 = 67.244$

27. $LSL = 0.4$, $USL = 0.55$, $USL - LSL = 0.15$

(a) $C_p = \frac{USL - LSL}{6\sigma} = \frac{0.15}{6 \times 0.05} = \frac{0.15}{0.3} = 0.5$; $C_p < 1$, so the process can be expected to produce many nonconforming units. $Z_{LSL} = \frac{LSL - \overline{X}}{\sigma} = \frac{0.4 - 0.5}{0.05} = -2$, $Z_{USL} = \frac{USL - \overline{X}}{\sigma} = \frac{0.55 - 0.5}{0.05} = 1$, $|Z_{min}| = 1$, $C_{pk} = \left|\frac{Z_{min}}{3}\right| = \frac{1}{3}$

(b) proportion too small $= 0.5 - 0.4772 = 0.0228$
proportion too large $= 0.5 - 0.3413 = 0.1587$
proportion too small + proportion too large $= 0.1815$

(c) $|Z_{min}| = 3 \times C_{pk} = 3 \times 1.33 = 3.99$. For the same specification limits and the same sample mean the following should hold $\sigma = \frac{0.05}{|Z_{min}|} = \frac{0.05}{3.99} = 0.0125$ and $UCL - LCL = 6\sigma = 0.075$, so $LCL = 0.5 - 0.0375 = 0.4625$,
$UCL = 0.5 + 0.0375 = 0.5375$

28. $LSL = 4.5$, $USL = \infty$, $C_p = \infty$

(a) $Z_{LSL} = \frac{LSL - \overline{X}}{\sigma} = \frac{4.5 - 5.3}{0.12} = -6.67$, $|Z_{min}| = 6.67$, $C_{pk} = \left|\frac{Z_{min}}{3}\right| = 2.22$

(b) proportion too small ≈ 0
proportion too large $= 0$
proportion too small + proportion too large ≈ 0

(c) $|Z_{min}| = 3 \times C_{pk} = 3 \times 1.33 = 3.99$, $\sigma = \frac{0.8}{|Z_{min}|} = \frac{0.8}{3.99} = 0.2$ or $LSL = \overline{X} - \sigma \times Z_{min} = 5.3 - 0.12 \times 3.99 = 4.82$

29. The R chart evaluates the process stability and tests the out-of-control points. The $\overline{X}$ chart shows the existence of the central tendency. For correct process monitoring, both characteristics should be studied. Only when the control chart, which measures the variability within a group (R or s chart) indicates that inherent process variability is stable, is it possible to study the central tendency ($\overline{X}$ or $\overline{\overline{X}}$ chart).

30. For sample size of 10 or more it is more appropriate to use s and $\overline{\overline{X}}$ charts than R and $\overline{X}$ charts.

31. The $\overline{X}$ chart indicates the shifts between the group averages, the CUSUM and EWMA charts indicate small shifts within the group averages.

32. This sampling method is appropriate for detecting process shifts if one wants to minimize the variation within a subgroup and increase the chances of detecting the variability among different groups.

33. This method is appropriate whenever sample data is used to make a decision about the acceptability of all units of production within an interval. Unfortunately, this method maximizes variations within a sample and is ineffective in detecting the shifts in process average.

34. For an unknown process monitoring, it is important to monitor near the beginning of the process to detect the presence of a shift as soon as possible.

35. If the cause of the out-of-control points has been found and eliminated, it is possible to remove the out-of-control points from the control limits calculations.

36. Calculations of control limits are based on normal assumptions. If these assumptions are not valid, it is still possible for the process to be stable and to produce a large number of units outside of the control limits.

37. Calculation of the $\overline{\overline{X}}$ includes more items than one of the $\overline{X}$. Due to the central limit theorem, $\overline{\overline{X}}$ has a probability distribution closer to the normal distribution.

38. Process capability is the ability of a process to produce output that meets or exceeds the requirements set in the design specification.

39. Specified tolerance limits are the boundaries beyond which the process should not function or perform main operations. These are the limits of process existence. Natural tolerance limits show the boundaries of the most typical process values.

40. (a)

Control Chart	
Sample/Subgroup Size	4.000
$\overline{R}$	8.516
***R* Chart**	
D_3 Factor	0.000
D_4 Factor	2.282
Lower Control Limit	0.000
Center	8.516
Upper Control Limit	19.435

$\overline{X}$ Chart	
Average of Subgroup Averages	18.555
A_2 Factor	0.729
Lower Control Limit	12.346
Center	18.555
Upper Control Limit	24.763

(b)

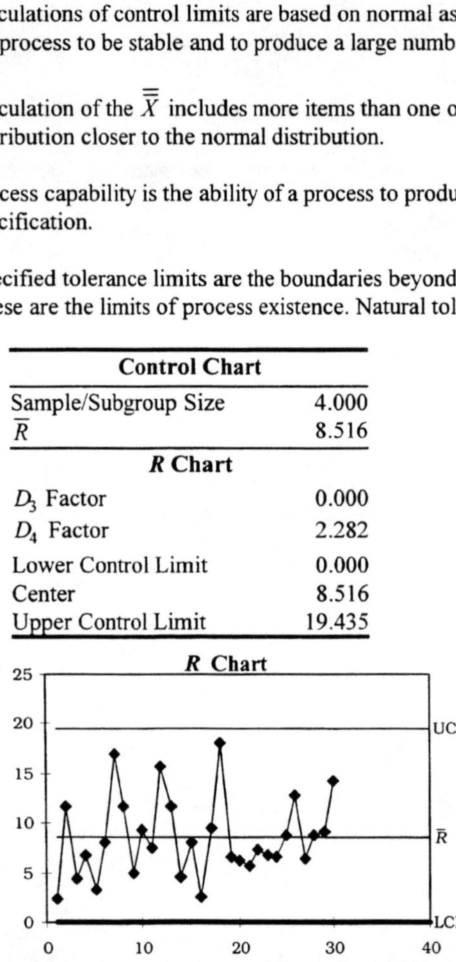

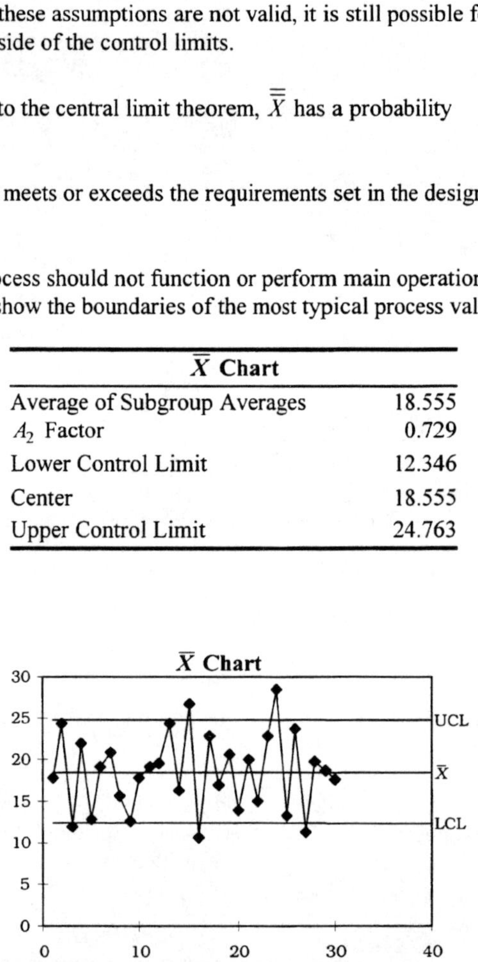

(c) There are no points outside of the control limits and no evidence of a pattern in the *R* chart. The process is stable.
(d) There are points outside of the control limits on the $\overline{X}$ chart, hence the process is out of statistical control.
(e) It is not possible to construct the CUSUM chart because the standard deviations are not known.
(f) It is not possible to construct the EWMA chart because the standard deviations are not known.
(g) There are no results to compare.
(h) For example, it is possible to control the number of waiting patients and delay time per patient.

41. (a)

Control Chart	
Sample/Subgroup Size	4.000
$\overline{R}$	3.314
***R* Chart**	
D_3 Factor	0.000
D_4 Factor	2.282
Lower Control Limit	0.000
Center	3.314
Upper Control Limit	7.563

$\overline{X}$ Chart	
Average of Subgroup Averages	56.235
A_2 Factor	0.729
Lower Control Limit	53.819
Center	56.235
Upper Control Limit	58.651

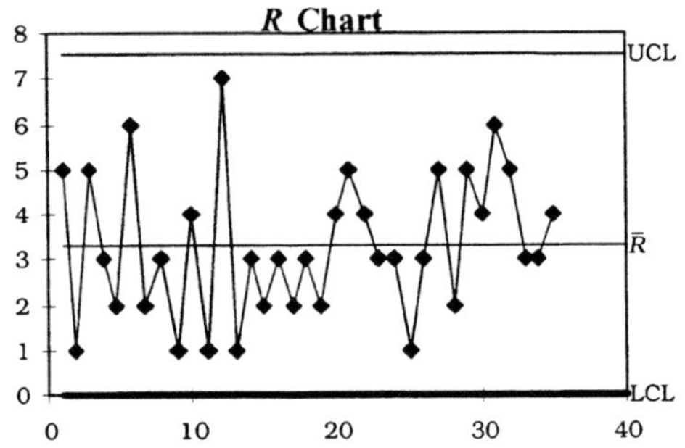

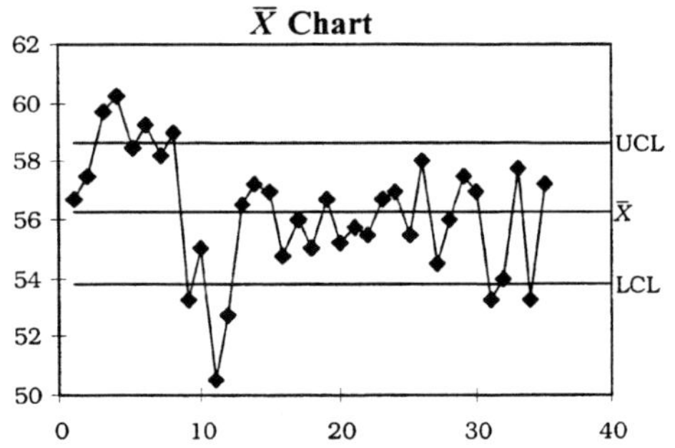

(b) There are no points outside of the control limits and there is no evidence of a pattern in the *R* chart. The process is stable.

(c) There are points outside of the control limits on the $\overline{X}$ chart, hence the process is out of statistical control.

(d)

S Chart	
$\overline{S}$	1.471
B_3 factor	0.000
B_4 factor	2.266
Lower Control Limit	0.000
Center Line	1.471
Upper Control Limit	3.335

$\overline{X}$ Chart	
Average $\overline{X}$	56.235
A_3 factor	1.628
Lower Control Limit	53.839
Center Line	56.235
Upper Control Limit	58.632

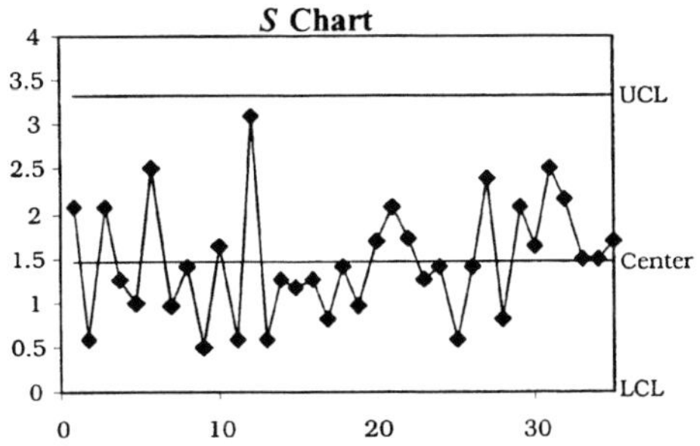

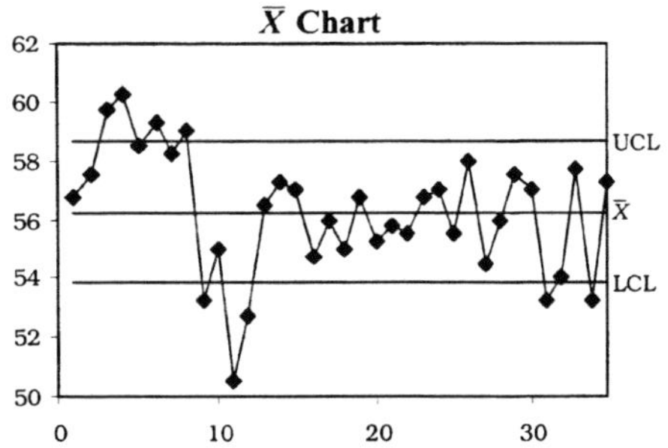

(e) There are no points outside of the control limits on the *s* chart, hence the process is in a state of statistical control.

(f) There are points outside of the control limits on the $\overline{\overline{X}}$ chart, hence the process is out of statistical control.

(g) The results are the same for all of the parts.

(h) CUSUM chart

Sample	Average	Standard Deviation	Z_i	S_{H_i}	S_{L_i}
1	56.750	2.062	0.644	0.144	0.000
2	57.500	0.577	1.583	1.226	0.000
3	59.750	2.062	4.399	5.126	0.000
4	60.250	1.258	5.025	9.651	0.000
5	58.500	1.000	2.834	11.985	0.000
6	59.250	2.500	3.773	15.258	0.000
7	58.250	0.957	2.521	17.280	0.000
8	59.000	1.414	3.460	20.240	0.000
9	53.250	0.500	−3.738	16.003	3.238
10	55.000	1.633	−1.547	13.956	4.284
11	50.500	0.577	−7.180	6.276	10.964
12	52.750	3.096	−4.363	1.412	14.828
13	56.500	0.577	0.331	1.243	13.997
14	57.250	1.258	1.270	2.013	12.227
15	57.000	1.155	0.957	2.470	10.771
16	54.750	1.258	−1.860	0.110	12.130
17	56.000	0.816	−0.295	0.000	11.925
18	55.000	1.414	−1.547	0.000	12.972
19	56.750	0.957	0.644	0.144	11.829
20	55.250	1.708	−1.234	0.000	12.562
21	55.750	2.062	−0.608	0.000	12.670
22	55.500	1.732	−0.921	0.000	13.091
23	56.750	1.258	0.644	0.144	11.948
24	57.000	1.414	0.957	0.601	10.491
25	55.500	0.577	−0.921	0.000	10.912
26	58.000	1.414	2.209	1.709	8.203
27	54.500	2.380	−2.173	0.000	9.876
28	56.000	0.816	−0.295	0.000	9.671
29	57.500	2.082	1.583	1.083	7.589
30	57.000	1.633	0.957	1.539	6.132
31	53.250	2.500	−3.738	0.000	9.369
32	54.000	2.160	−2.799	0.000	11.668
33	57.750	1.500	1.896	1.396	9.272
34	53.250	1.500	−3.738	0.000	12.510
35	57.250	1.708	1.270	0.770	10.740
Overall mean	56.236				
$\overline{S}$	1.472				
C_4	0.921				
n	4.000				
k	0.500				

(i) EWMA chart

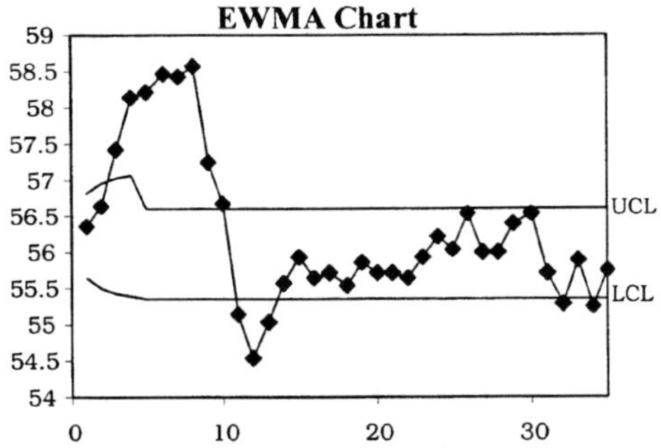

There is a shift in the process mean.

(j) The results are the same for all of the parts. The process is stable and out of statistical control. The EWMA chart indicates a shift in the process mean with the magnitude of one standard deviation.

(k) $LSL = 53$, $USL = 57$, $USL - LCL = 4$,
$C_p = \dfrac{USL - LSL}{6\sigma} = \dfrac{4}{6 \times 1.47} = 0.45$, $C_p < 1$, so the process can be expected to produce many nonconforming units.

$$Z_{LSL} = \frac{LSL - \overline{X}}{\sigma} = \frac{53 - 56.236}{1.47} = -2.2,$$

$$Z_{USL} = \frac{USL - \overline{X}}{\sigma} = \frac{57 - 56.236}{1.47} = 0.52, \ |Z_{\min}| = 0.52,$$

$$C_{pk} = \left|\frac{Z_{\min}}{3}\right| = \frac{0.52}{3} = 0.173$$

42. (a)

Control Chart	
Sample/Subgroup Size	6.000
$\overline{R}$	0.002
***R* Chart**	
D_3 Factor	0.000
D_4 Factor	2.004
Lower Control Limit	0.000
Center	0.002
Upper Control Limit	0.004

$\overline{X}$ Chart	
Average of Subgroup Averages	0.055
A_2 Factor	0.483
Lower Control Limit	0.055
Center	0.056
Upper Control Limit	0.057

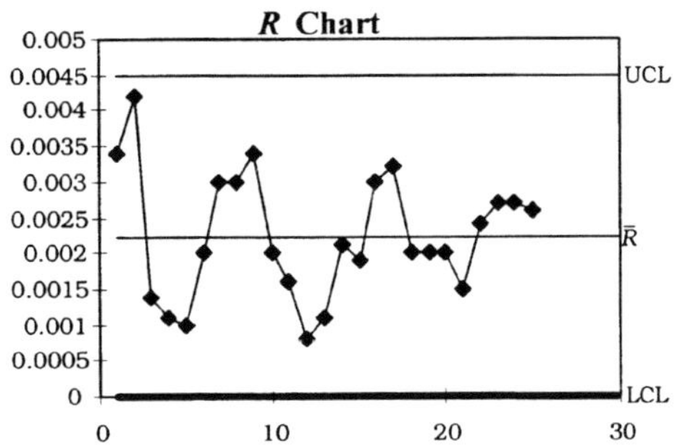

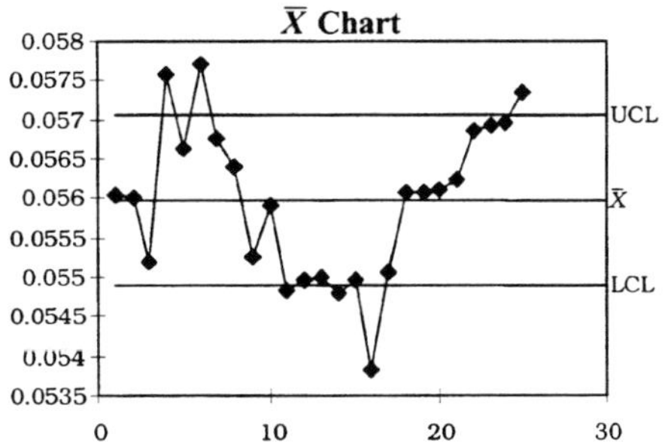

(b) There are no points outside of the control limits and there is no evidence of a pattern in the R chart. The process is stable.

(c) There are points outside of the control limits on the $\overline{X}$ chart, hence the process is out of statistical control.

(d)

S Chart	
$\overline{S}$	0.000
B_3 factor	0.565
B_4 factor	1.435
Lower Control Limit	0.000
Center Line	0.000
Upper Control Limit	0.001

$\overline{X}$ Chart	
Average $\overline{X}$	0.055
A_3 factor	0.606
Lower Control Limit	0.055
Center Line	0.055
Upper Control Limit	0.056

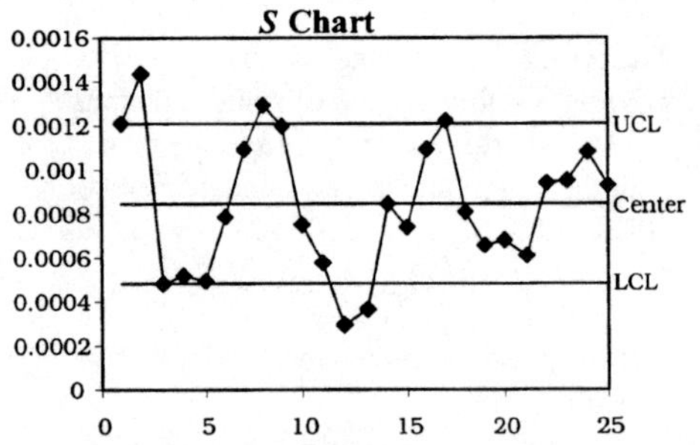

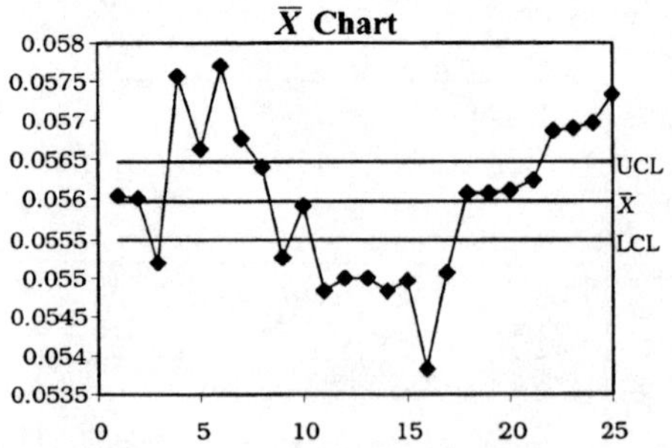

(e) There are points outside of the control limits on the s chart, hence the process is out of statistical control.

(f) There are points outside of the control limits on the $\overline{X}$ chart, hence the process is out of statistical control.

(g) The results for the $\overline{X}$ charts are the same. The R chart does not indicate that the process is out of control. A more sensitive s chart should demonstrate this effect.

(h) CUSUM chart

Sample	Average	Standard Deviation	Z_i	S_{H_i}	S_{L_i}
1	0.056	0.001	0.347	0.000	0.000
2	0.056	0.001	0.208	0.000	0.000
3	0.055	0.000	−2.010	0.000	1.510
4	0.058	0.001	4.597	4.097	0.000
5	0.057	0.000	1.964	5.561	0.000
6	0.058	0.001	4.920	9.981	0.000
7	0.057	0.001	2.333	11.814	0.000
8	0.056	0.001	1.317	12.631	0.000
9	0.055	0.001	−1.871	10.260	1.371
10	0.056	0.001	−0.069	9.691	0.940
11	0.055	0.001	−3.026	6.164	3.467
12	0.055	0.000	−2.610	3.054	5.577
13	0.055	0.000	−2.564	0.000	7.641
14	0.055	0.001	−3.072	0.000	10.214
15	0.055	0.001	−2.657	0.000	12.370
16	0.054	0.001	−5.845	0.000	17.715
17	0.055	0.001	−2.426	0.000	19.640
18	0.056	0.001	0.393	0.000	18.748
19	0.056	0.001	0.439	0.000	17.809
20	0.056	0.001	0.485	0.000	16.824
21	0.056	0.001	0.901	0.401	15.423
22	0.057	0.001	2.610	2.511	12.312
23	0.057	0.001	2.749	4.760	9.063
24	0.057	0.001	2.888	7.148	5.676
25	0.057	0.001	3.904	10.552	1.272
Overall mean	0.056				
$\overline{S}$	0.001				
C_4	0.952				
n	6.000				
k	0.500				

(i) EWMA chart

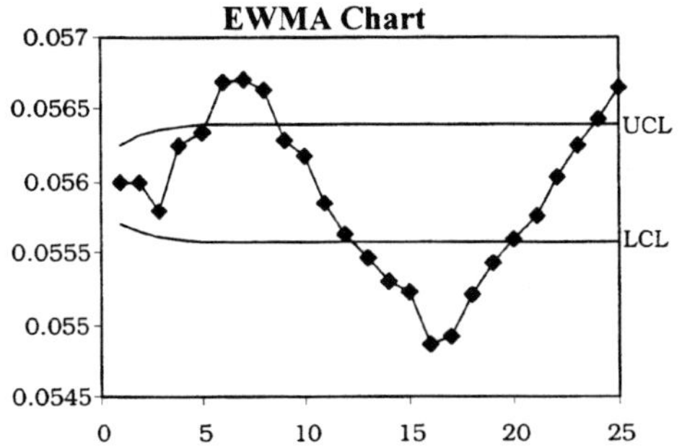

There is a shift in the process mean.

(j) The process is not stable, and out of control. The EWMA chart indicates a shift in the process mean with a magnitude of one standard deviation.

(k) The process is not stable, hence the calculation of the capability index is not correct.

(l) The process is not stable, hence the calculation of the nonconforming item proportions is not correct.

(m) There is a large variance in the sample standard deviations. This violates the homogeneous sampling assumption.

43. (a)

Control Chart	
Sample/Subgroup Size	3.000
$\overline{R}$	9.960
***R* Chart**	
D_3 Factor	0.000
D_4 Factor	2.575
Lower Control Limit	0.000
Center	9.960
Upper Control Limit	25.647

$\overline{X}$ Chart	
Average of Subgroup Averages	35.680
A_2 Factor	1.0230
Lower Control Limit	25.491
Center	35.680
Upper Control Limit	45.869

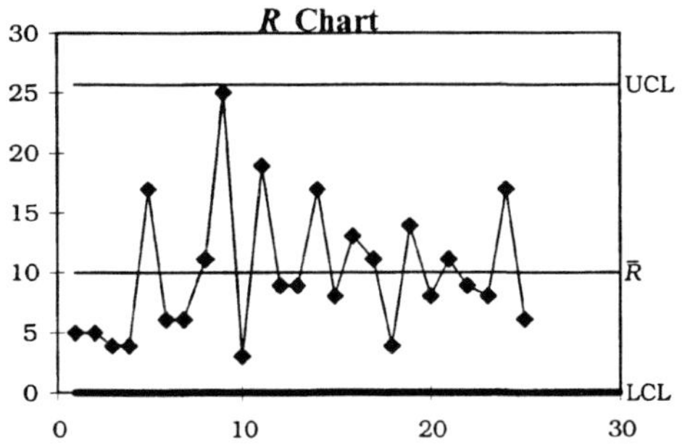

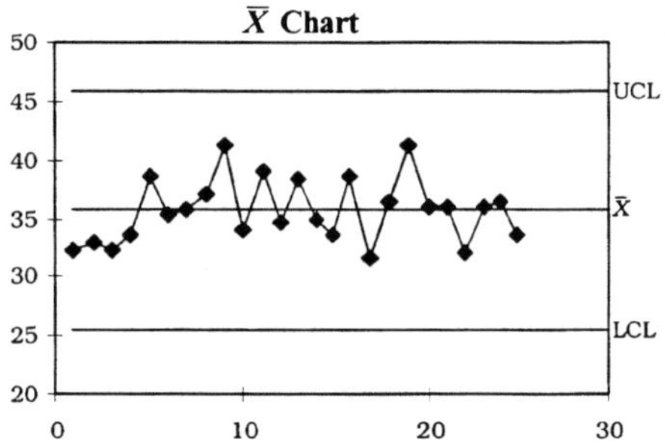

(b) There are no points outside of the control limits and there is no evidence of a pattern in the *R* chart. The process is stable.

(c) There are no points outside of the control limits on the $\overline{X}$ chart, hence the process is in a state of statistical control.

(d)

***S* Chart**	
$\overline{S}$	5.223
B_3 factor	0.000
B_4 factor	2.568
Lower Control Limit	0.000
Center Line	5.223
Upper Control Limit	13.413

$\overline{X}$ Chart	
Average $\overline{X}$	35.680
A_3 factor	1.953
Lower Control Limit	25.479
Center Line	35.680
Upper Control Limit	45.881

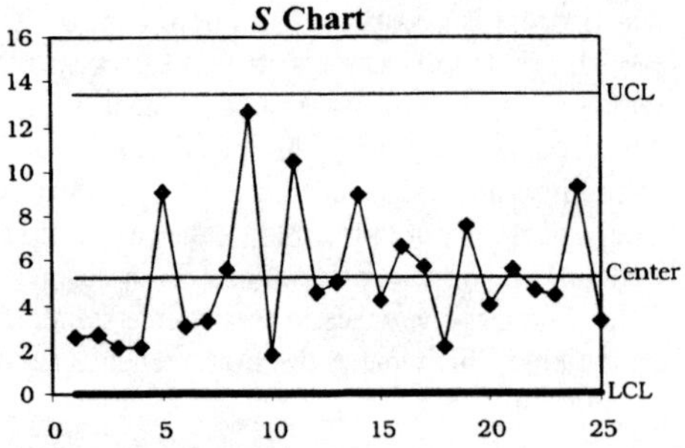

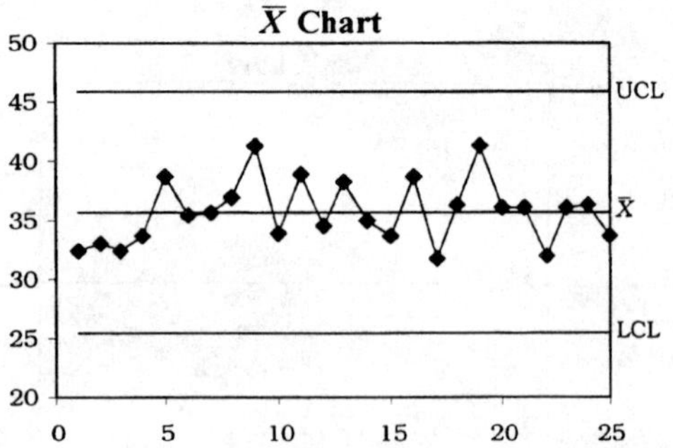

(e) There are no points outside of the control limits and there is no evidence of a pattern in the s chart. The process is stable.

(f) There are no points outside of the control limits on the $\overline{X}$ chart, hence the process is in a state of statistical control.

(g) The results are the same for all of the parts.

(h) CUSUM chart

Sample	Average	Standard Deviation	Z_i	S_{H_i}	S_{L_i}
1	32.333	2.517	−1.065	0.000	0.565
2	33.000	2.646	−0.858	0.000	0.358
3	32.333	2.082	−1.065	0.000	0.565
4	33.667	2.082	−0.651	0.000	0.151
5	38.667	9.074	0.901	0.401	0.000
6	35.333	3.055	−0.134	0.000	0.000
7	35.667	3.215	−0.030	0.000	0.000
8	37.000	5.568	0.384	0.000	0.000
9	41.333	12.662	1.730	1.230	0.000
10	34.000	1.732	−0.548	0.000	0.048
11	39.000	10.440	1.005	0.505	0.000
12	34.667	4.509	−0.341	0.000	0.000
13	38.333	4.933	0.798	0.298	0.000
14	35.000	8.888	−0.237	0.000	0.000
15	33.667	4.163	−0.651	0.000	0.151
16	38.667	6.658	0.901	0.401	0.000
17	31.667	5.686	−1.272	0.000	0.772
18	36.333	2.082	0.177	0.000	0.000
19	41.333	7.572	1.730	1.230	0.000
20	36.000	4.000	0.073	0.000	0.000
21	36.000	5.568	0.073	0.000	0.000
22	32.000	4.583	−1.169	0.000	0.669
23	36.000	4.359	0.073	0.000	0.000
24	36.333	9.292	0.177	0.000	0.000
25	33.667	3.215	−0.651	0.000	0.151
Overall mean	35.764				
$\overline{S}$	5.307				
C_4	0.952				
n	3.000				
k	0.500				

(i) EWMA chart

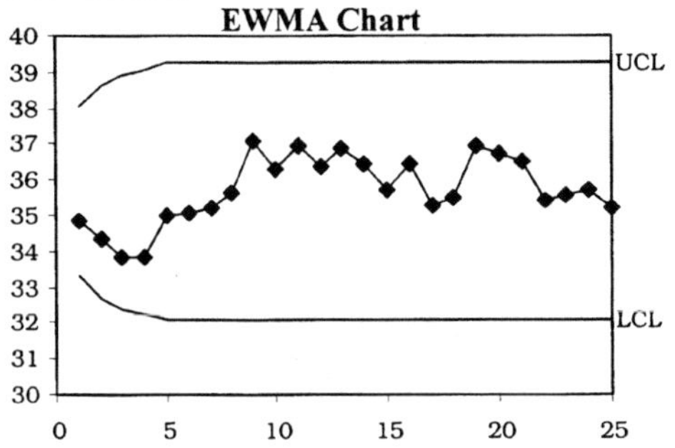

(j) The process is stable and in a state of statistical control. The EWMA chart does not indicate a shift in the process mean with the magnitude of one standard deviation.

44. (a)

Moving Range Chart	
$\overline{MR}$	15.327
D_3 factor	0.000
D_4 factor	3.267
Lower Control Limit	0.000
Center Line	15.327
Upper Control Limit	50.072

Individual Value Chart	
$\overline{X}$	292.740
E_2 factor	2.659
Lower Control Limit	251.987
Center Line	292.740
Upper Control Limit	333.493

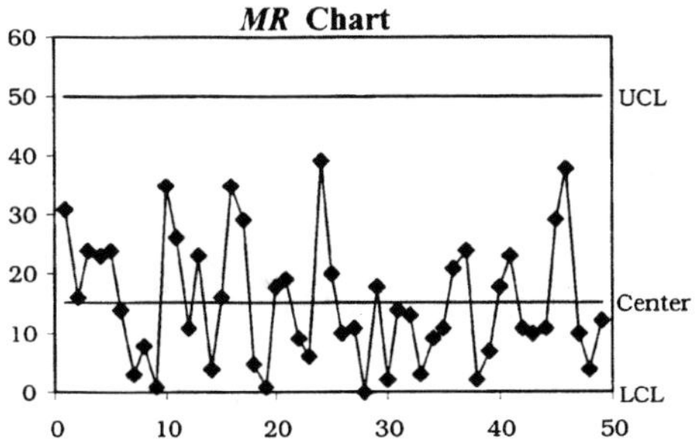

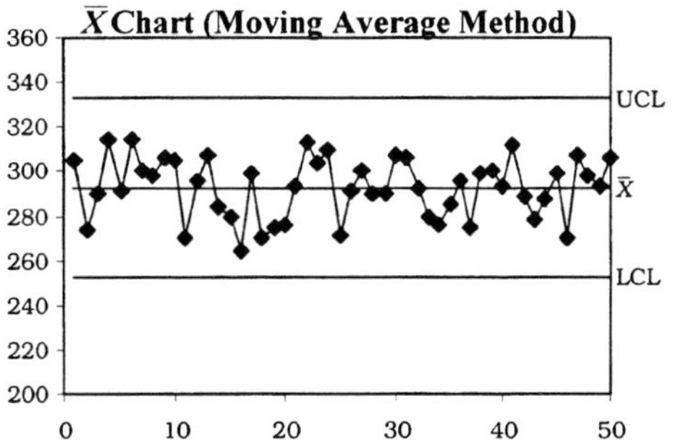

(b) There are no points outside of the control limits on the MR chart, hence the process is in a state of statistical control.

(c) There are no points outside of the control limits on the X chart, hence the process is in a state of statistical control.

(d)

Individual Value Chart	
$\overline{X}$	292.740
S	10.439
C_4 factor	0.990
Lower Control Limit	261.106
Center Line	292.740
Upper Control Limit	324.374

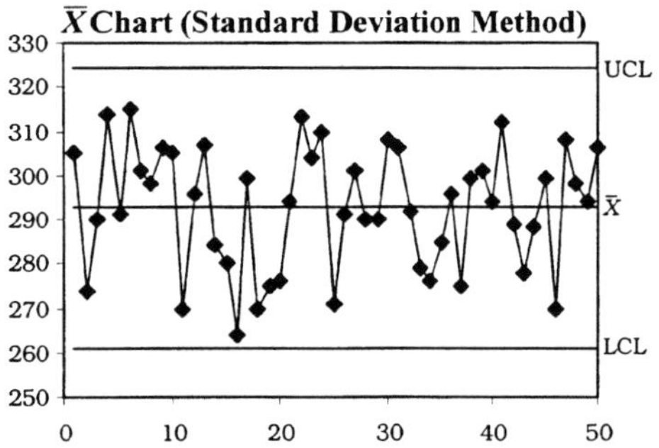

(e) There are no points outside of the control limits on the X chart, hence the process is in a state of statistical control.

(f) The results are the same for all of the parts.

45. (a)

Moving Range Chart	
$\overline{MR}$	1.018
D_3 factor	0.000
D_4 factor	3.267
Lower Control Limit	0.000
Center Line	1.018
Upper Control Limit	3.325

Individual Value Chart	
$\overline{X}$	1.496
E_2 factor	2.659
Lower Control Limit	−1.210
Center Line	1.496
Upper Control Limit	4.202

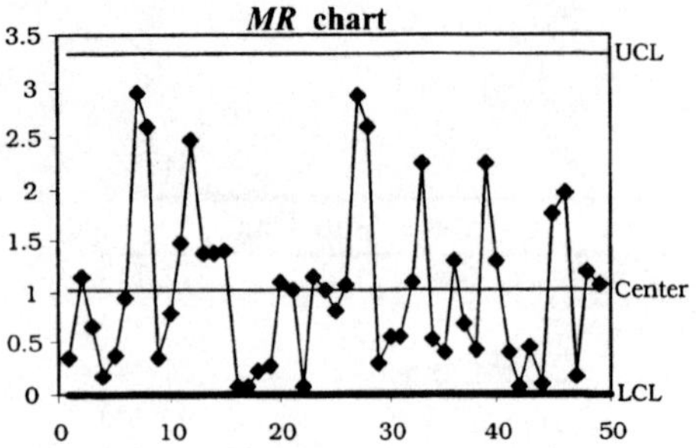

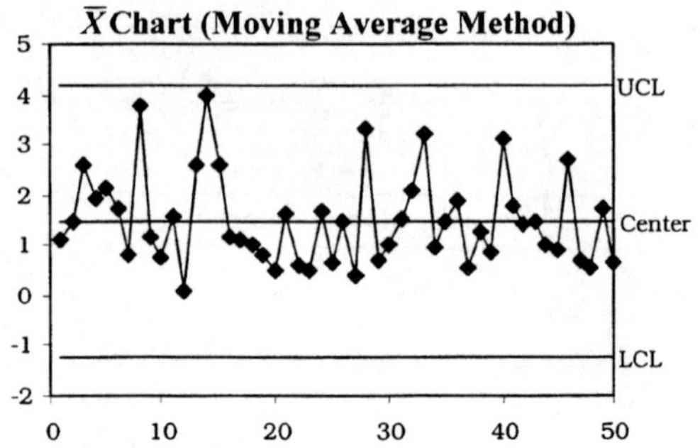

(b) There are no points outside of the control limits on the *MR* chart, hence the process is in a state of statistical control.
(c) There are no points outside of the control limits on the *X* chart, hence the process is in a state of statistical control.

(d)

Individual Value Chart	
$\overline{X}$	1.496
S	0.908
C_4 factor	0.990
Lower Control Limit	−1.257
Center Line	1.496
Upper Control Limit	4.249

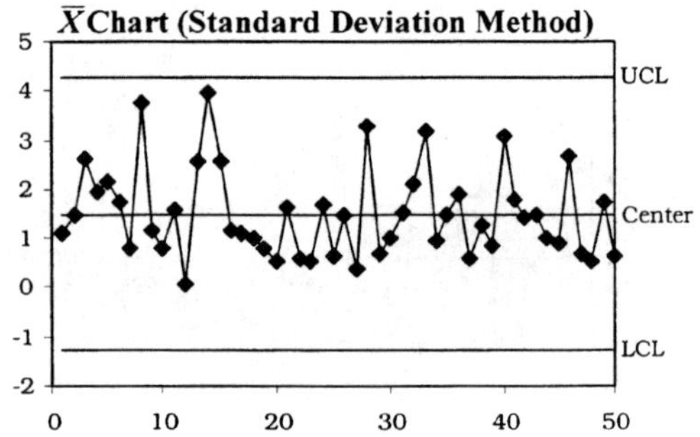

(e) There are no points outside of the control limits on the *X* chart, hence the process is in a state of statistical control.
(f) The results are the same for all of the parts.

46. (a)

Control Chart	
Sample/Subgroup Size	5.000
$\overline{R}$	0.242
***R* Chart**	
D_3 Factor	0.000
D_4 Factor	2.114
Lower Control Limit	0.000
Center	0.242
Upper Control Limit	0.512

$\overline{X}$ Chart	
Average of Subgroup	1.000
A_2 Factor	0.577
Lower Control Limit	0.860
Center	1.000
Upper Control Limit	1.140

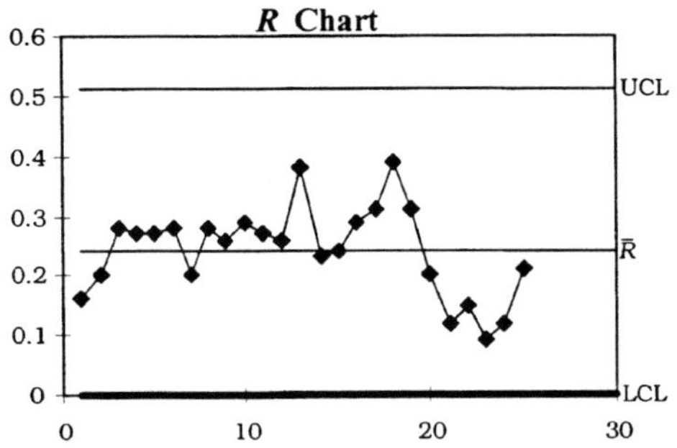

The process is stable.

***S* Chart**	
$\bar{S}$	0.092
B_3 factor	0.000
B_4 factor	2.089
Lower Control Limit	0.000
Center Line	0.092
Upper Control Limit	0.191

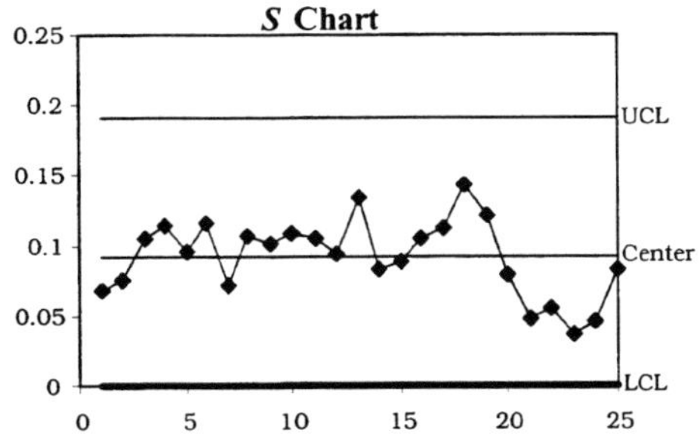

The process is stable.

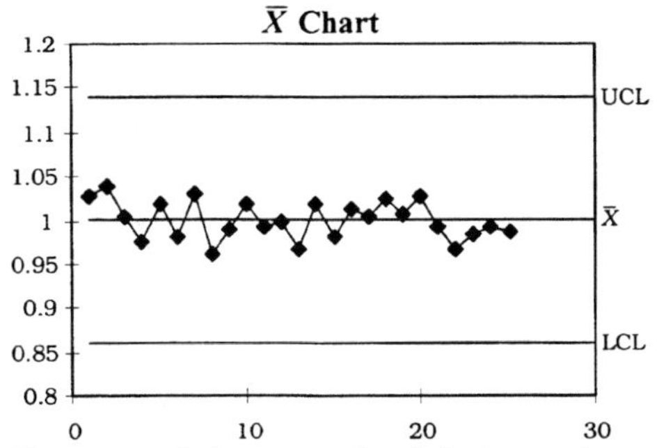

The process is in a state of statistical control.

$\bar{X}$ Chart	
Average $\bar{X}$	1.000
A_3 factor	1.427
Lower Control Limit	0.870
Center Line	1.000
Upper Control Limit	1.131

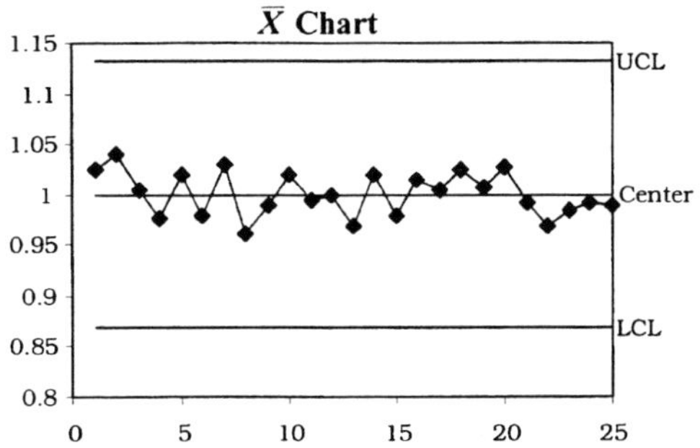

The process is in a state of statistical control.

CUSUM chart

Day	Average	Standard Deviation	Z_i	S_{H_i}	S_{L_i}
1	1.026	0.068	0.589	0.089	0.000
2	1.040	0.076	0.910	0.500	0.000
3	1.004	0.105	0.084	0.084	0.000
4	0.976	0.113	−0.558	0.000	0.058
5	1.020	0.096	0.452	0.000	0.000
6	0.980	0.116	−0.466	0.000	0.000
7	1.030	0.072	0.681	0.181	0.000
8	0.960	0.107	−0.925	0.000	0.425
9	0.990	0.101	−0.237	0.000	0.162
10	1.020	0.108	0.452	0.000	0.000
11	0.994	0.104	−0.145	0.000	0.000
12	1.000	0.093	−0.007	0.000	0.000
13	0.968	0.135	−0.742	0.000	0.242
14	1.020	0.082	0.452	0.000	0.000
15	0.980	0.088	−0.466	0.000	0.000
16	1.014	0.104	0.314	0.000	0.000
17	1.004	0.112	0.084	0.000	0.000
18	1.024	0.143	0.543	0.043	0.000
19	1.006	0.121	0.130	0.000	0.000
20	1.028	0.078	0.635	0.135	0.000
21	0.992	0.047	−0.191	0.000	0.000
22	0.968	0.055	−0.741	0.000	0.242
23	0.984	0.036	−0.374	0.000	0.116
24	0.992	0.045	−0.191	0.000	0.000
25	0.988	0.083	−0.283	0.000	0.000
Overall mean	1.000				
$\overline{S}$	0.092				
C_4	0.940				
n	5.000				
k	0.500				

There are no shifts in the process mean with the magnitude of one standard deviation.

EWMA chart

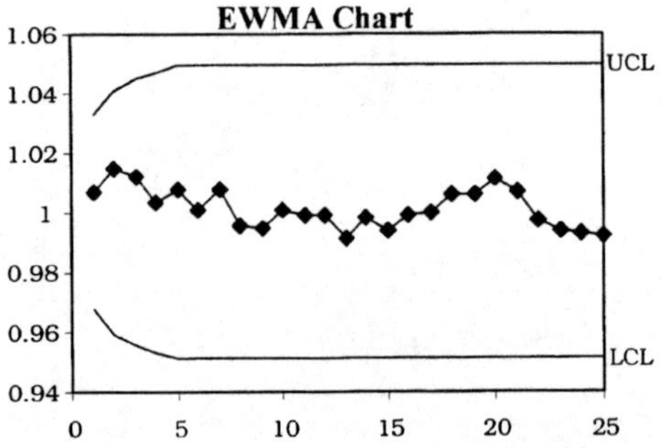

There are no shifts in the process mean with a magnitude of one standard deviation.

(b) There are no points outside of the control limits, so this process is in a state of statistical control.

47. (a)

Moving Range Chart	
$\overline{MR}$	0.005
D_3 factor	0.000
D_4 factor	3.267
Lower Control Limit	0.000
Center Line	0.005
Upper Control Limit	0.017

Individual Value Chart	
$\overline{X}$	2.000
E_2 factor	2.659
Lower Control Limit	1.987
Center Line	2.000
Upper Control Limit	2.015

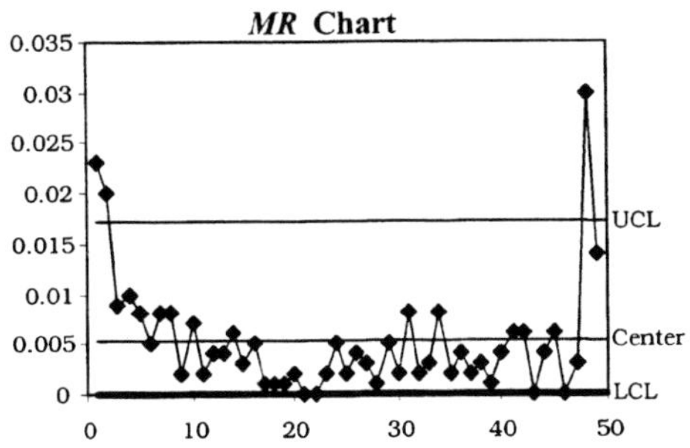

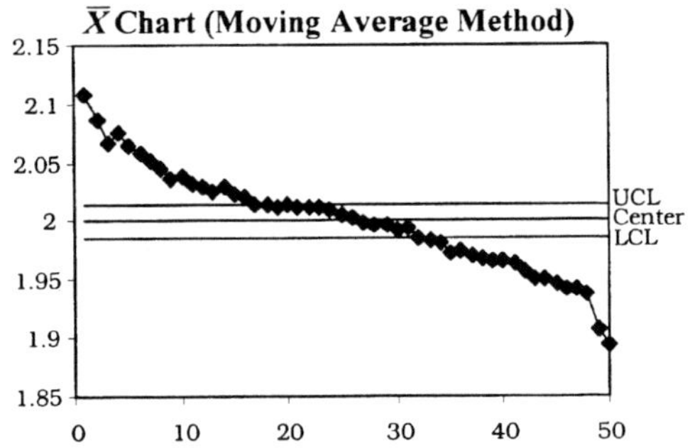

(b) There are points outside of the control limits on the *MR* chart, hence the process is out of statistical control.

(c) There are points outside of the control limits on the X chart, hence the process is out of statistical control. There is a negative trend in this process.

(d)

Individual Value Chart	
$\overline{X}$	2.000
S	0.045
C_4 factor	0.990
Lower Control Limit	1.866
Center Line	2.001
Upper Control Limit	2.136

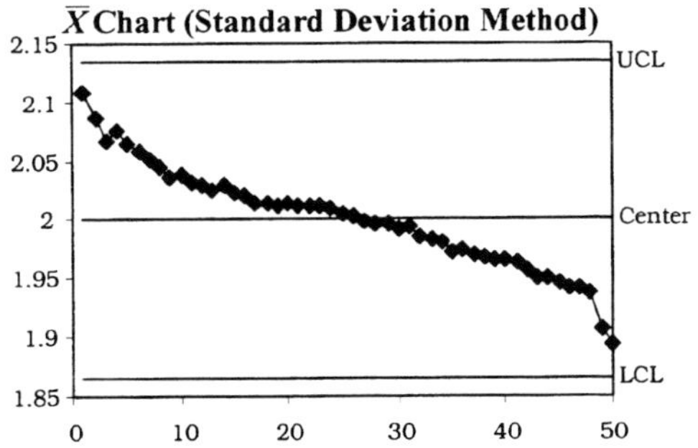

(e) There are no points outside of the control limits. The process is in a state of statistical control.

(f) The *MR* method controls the neighbor points variability and can be small or large for the trend processes. The SD method controls common variability, and its results are more accurate.

(g) There is a trend in this data that may indicate problems with either the data production or measurement.

(h) Based on the *MR* chart, we conclude that the process is not stable, and therefore, the calculation of the capability index is not correct.

(i) The process is not stable, therefore, the calculation of the proportions of the nonconforming items is not correct.

48. (a)

Control Chart	
Sample/Subgroup Size	5.000
$\overline{R}$	0.600
***R* Chart**	
D_3 Factor	0.000
D_4 Factor	2.114
Lower Control Limit	0.000
Center	0.600
Upper Control Limit	1.268

$\overline{X}$ Chart	
Average of Subgroup	62.586
A_2 Factor	0.577
Lower Control Limit	62.239
Center	62.586
Upper Control Limit	62.932

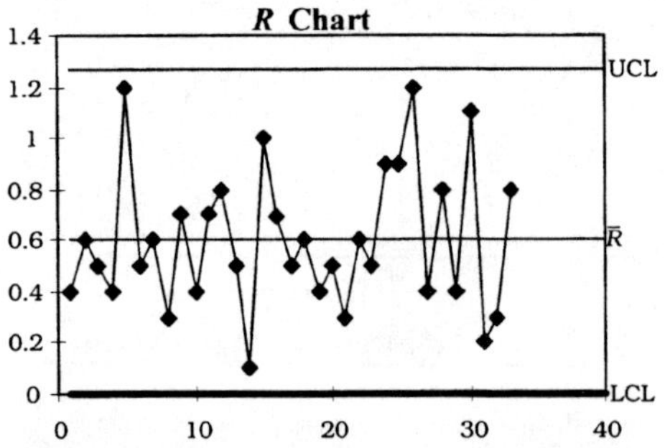

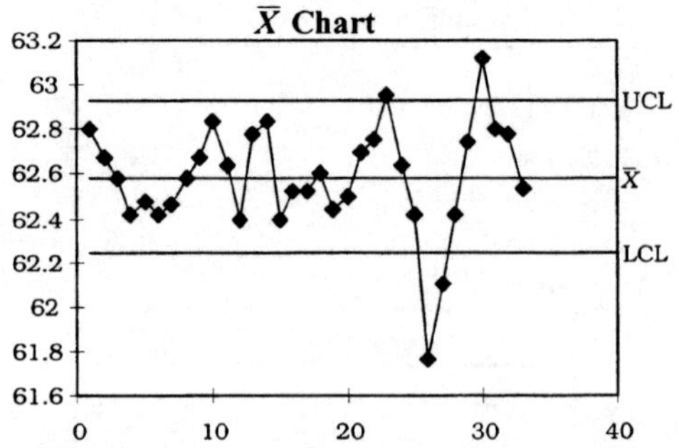

(b) There are no points outside of the control limits on the R chart, hence the process is stable.

(c) There are points outside of the control limits in the $\overline{X}$ chart, hence the process is out of statistical control.

(d)

S Chart	
$\overline{S}$	0.242
B_3 factor	0.000
B_4 factor	2.089
Lower Control Limit	0.000
Center Line	0.242
Upper Control Limit	0.506

$\overline{X}$ Chart	
Average $\overline{X}$	62.585
A_3 factor	1.427
Lower Control Limit	62.240
Center Line	62.585
Upper Control Limit	62.931

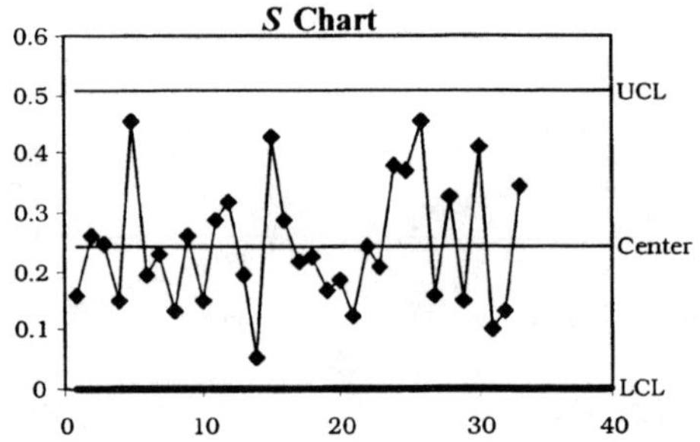

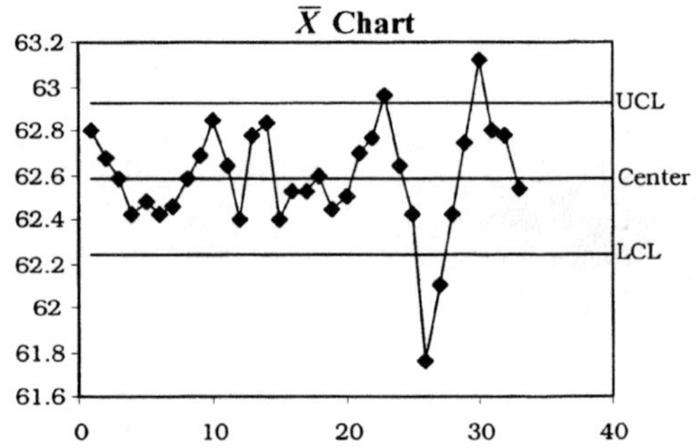

(e) There are no points outside of the control limits on the s chart, hence the process is stable.

(f) There are points outside of the control limits on the $\overline{\overline{X}}$ chart, hence the process is out of statistical control.

(g) The results are the same for all of the parts.

(h) CUSUM chart

Sample	Average	Standard Deviation	Z_i	S_{H_i}	S_{L_i}
1	62.800	0.158	1.863	1.363	0.000
2	62.680	0.259	0.821	1.683	0.000
3	62.580	0.249	−0.047	1.683	0.000
4	62.420	0.148	−1.436	1.683	0.936
5	62.480	0.455	−0.915	1.683	1.352
6	62.420	0.192	−1.436	1.683	2.288
7	62.460	0.230	−1.089	1.683	2.877
8	62.580	0.130	−0.047	1.683	2.877
9	62.680	0.259	0.821	2.004	2.877
10	62.840	0.152	2.210	3.714	2.877
11	62.640	0.288	0.474	3.714	2.877
12	62.400	0.316	−1.610	3.714	3.987
13	62.780	0.192	1.689	4.903	3.987
14	62.840	0.055	2.210	6.613	3.987
15	62.400	0.430	−1.610	6.613	5.097
16	62.520	0.286	−0.568	6.613	5.166
17	62.520	0.217	−0.568	6.613	5.234
18	62.600	0.224	0.126	6.613	5.234
19	62.440	0.167	−1.263	6.613	5.996
20	62.500	0.187	−0.742	6.613	6.238
21	62.700	0.122	0.994	7.107	6.238
22	62.760	0.241	1.515	8.122	6.238
23	62.960	0.207	3.252	10.874	6.238
24	62.640	0.378	0.474	10.874	6.238
25	62.420	0.370	−1.436	10.874	7.175
26	61.760	0.456	−7.166	10.874	13.841
27	62.100	0.158	−4.214	10.874	17.555
28	62.420	0.327	−1.436	10.874	18.491
29	62.740	0.152	1.342	11.715	18.491
30	63.120	0.409	4.641	15.856	18.491
31	62.800	0.100	1.863	17.219	18.491
32	62.780	0.130	1.689	18.407	18.491
33	62.540	0.344	−0.395	18.407	18.491
Overall mean	62.585				
$\bar{S}$	0.242				
C_4	0.940				
n	5.000				
k	0.500				

There is a shift in the process mean with the magnitude of one standard deviation.

(i) EWMA chart

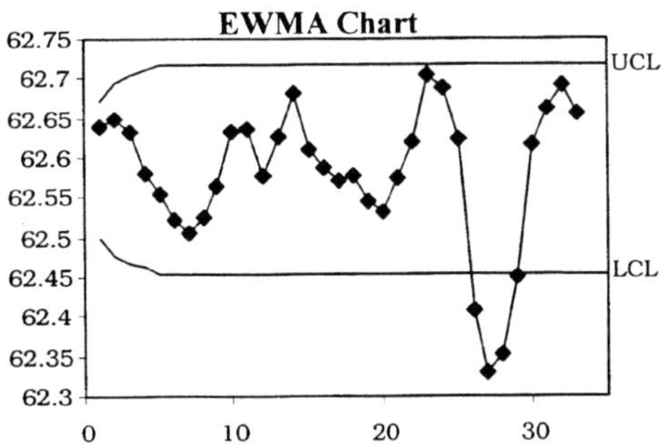

There is a shift in the process mean with the magnitude of one standard deviation.

(j) The results are the same for all of the parts. The process is stable, out of control, and there is a shift in the process mean with the magnitude of one standard deviation.

(k) $LSL = 61.25$, $USL = 63.75$, $USL - LSL = 2.5$, $\overline{X} = 62.585$, $\sigma \approx 0.242$, $C_p = \dfrac{USL - LSL}{6\sigma} = \dfrac{2.5}{6 \times 0.242} = 1.72$, $C_p > 1$,

so the process is unlikely to produce nonconforming units. $Z_{LSL} = \dfrac{LSL - \overline{X}}{\sigma} = \dfrac{61.25 - 62.585}{0.242} = -5.5$,

$Z_{USL} = \dfrac{USL - \overline{X}}{\sigma} = \dfrac{63.75 - 62.585}{0.242} = 4.8$, $|Z_{\min}| = 4.8$, $C_{pk} = \left|\dfrac{Z_{\min}}{3}\right| = \dfrac{4.8}{3} = 1.6$

(l) proportion too small $= 0.5 - 0.49999978 = 0.00000022$.
proportion too large $= 0.5 - 0.4999992 = 0.0000008$.
proportion too small + proportion too large $= 0.00000102$.

49. Thickness for Tablet 54 is 0.115.

(a) Hardness

Moving Range Chart	
$\overline{MR}$	0.319
D_3 factor	0.000
D_4 factor	3.267
Lower Control Limit	0.000
Center Line	0.319
Upper Control Limit	1.041

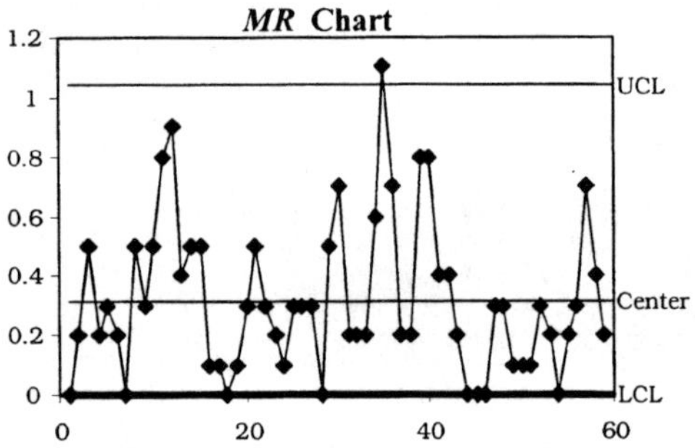

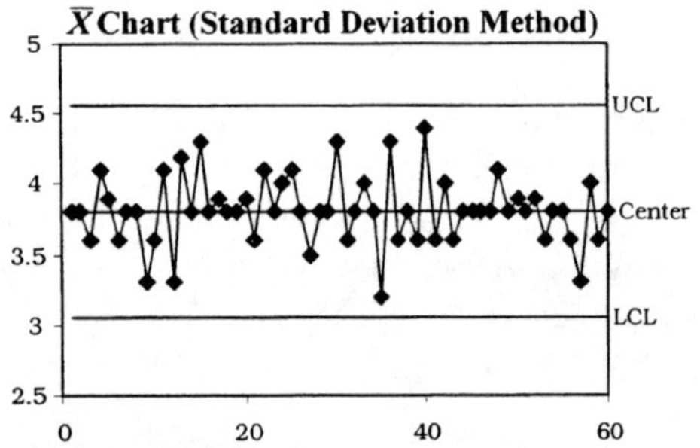

There are points outside of control limits, hence the process is not stable. The process is in a state of statistical control.

Individual Value Chart	
$\overline{X}$	3.808
E_2 factor	2.659
Lower Control Limit	2.961
Center Line	3.808
Upper Control Limit	4.656

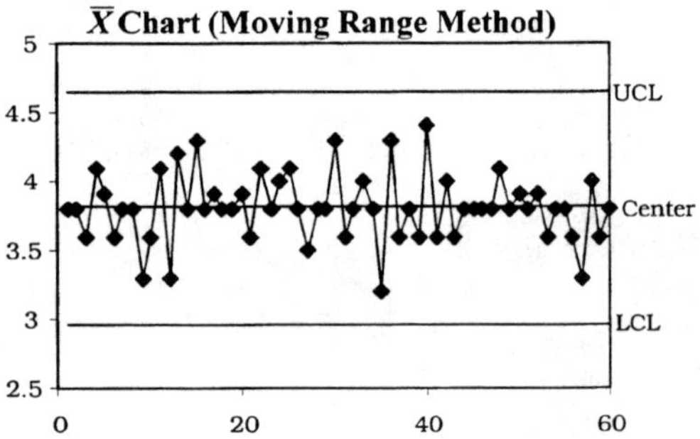

(b) There are points outside of the control limits on the *MR* chart, hence the process is not stable.

(c) Based on the *MR* chart, the process is not stable, hence the calculation of the capability index is not correct.

(d) Thickness

Moving Range Chart	
$\overline{MR}$	0.001
D_3 factor	0.000
D_4 factor	3.267
Lower Control Limit	0.000
Center Line	0.001
Upper Control Limit	0.004

Individual Value Chart	
$\overline{X}$	0.112
E_2 factor	2.659
Lower Control Limit	0.109
Center Line	0.112
Upper Control Limit	0.115

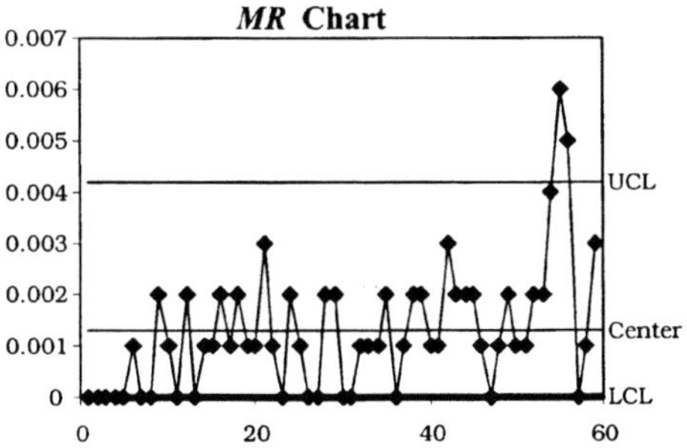

There are points outside of the control limits, hence the process is not stable.

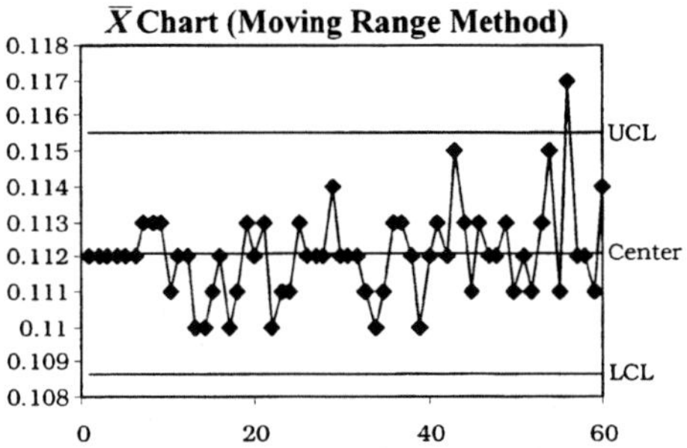

There are points outside of the control limits, hence this process is out of statistical control.

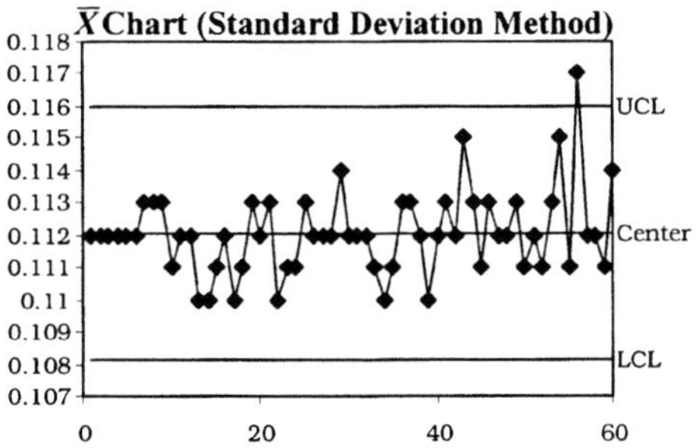

There are points outside of the control limits, hence this process is out of statistical control.

(e) There are points outside of the control limits on the *MR* chart, hence the process is not stable.

(f) Based on the *MR* chart, the process is not stable, hence the calculation of the capability index is not correct.

50. (a)

S Chart	
$\overline{S}$	0.101
B_3 factor	0.284
B_4 factor	1.716
Lower Control Limit	0.029
Center Line	0.101
Upper Control Limit	0.174

$\overline{X}$ Chart	
Average $\overline{X}$	7.198
A_3 factor	0.975
Lower Control Limit	7.099
Center Line	7.198
Upper Control Limit	7.297

S Chart

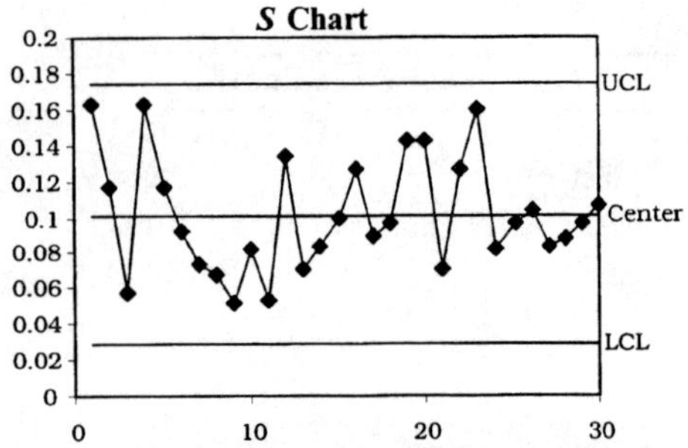

$\overline{X}$ Chart

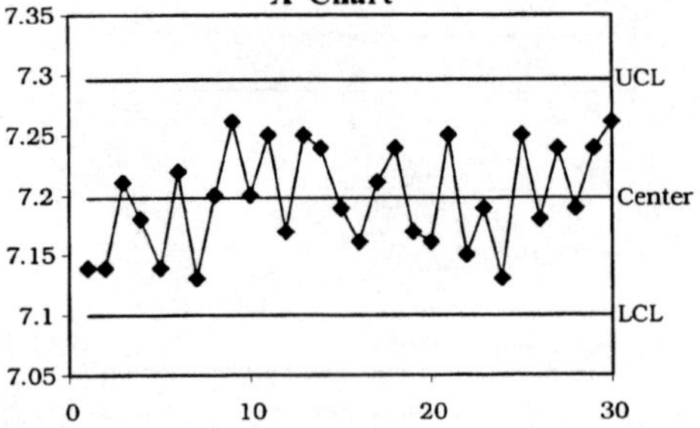

(c) There are no points outside of the control limits on the S chart, hence the process is stable.

(d) There are no points outside of the control limits on the $\overline{\overline{X}}$ chart, hence the process is in a state of statistical control.

(e) CUSUM chart

Day	Mean	Standard Deviation	Z_i	S_{H_i}	S_{L_i}
1	7.140	0.163	−1.763	0.000	1.263
2	7.140	0.117	−1.763	0.000	2.526
3	7.210	0.057	0.365	0.000	2.526
4	7.180	0.162	−0.547	0.000	2.573
5	7.140	0.117	−1.763	0.000	3.836
6	7.220	0.092	0.669	0.169	3.836
7	7.130	0.074	−2.067	0.169	5.403
8	7.200	0.067	0.061	0.169	5.403
9	7.260	0.052	1.884	1.553	5.403
10	7.200	0.082	0.061	1.553	5.403
11	7.250	0.053	1.581	2.634	5.403
12	7.170	0.134	−0.851	2.634	5.754
13	7.250	0.071	1.581	3.714	5.754
14	7.240	0.084	1.277	4.491	5.754
15	7.190	0.099	−0.243	4.491	5.754
16	7.160	0.126	−1.155	4.491	6.409
17	7.210	0.089	0.365	4.491	6.409
18	7.240	0.097	1.277	5.267	6.409
19	7.170	0.142	−0.851	5.267	6.760
20	7.160	0.143	−1.155	5.267	7.415
21	7.250	0.071	1.581	6.348	7.415
22	7.150	0.127	−1.459	6.348	8.374
23	7.190	0.159	−0.243	6.348	8.374
24	7.130	0.082	−2.067	6.348	9.941
25	7.250	0.097	1.581	7.428	9.941
26	7.180	0.103	−0.547	7.428	9.988
27	7.240	0.084	1.277	8.205	9.988
28	7.190	0.088	−0.243	8.205	9.988
29	7.240	0.097	1.277	8.982	9.988
30	7.260	0.107	1.884	10.366	9.988
Overall mean	7.198				
$\overline{S}$	0.101				
C_4	0.973				
n	10.000				
k	0.500				

There is a shift in the mean of the process with a magnitude of one standard deviation.

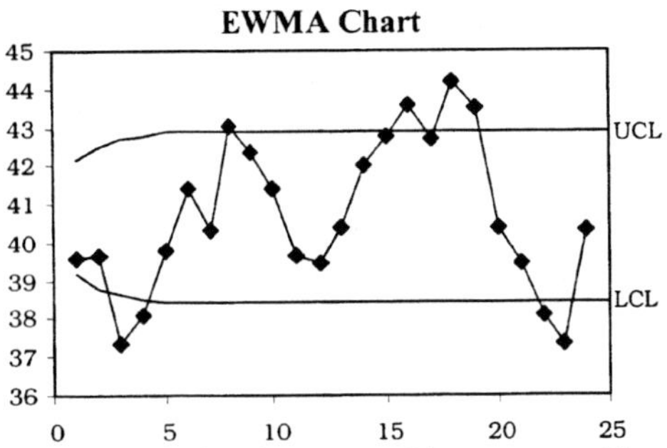

There is a shift in the mean of the process with a magnitude of one standard deviation.

(f) The process is stable and in a state of statistical control. There is a shift in the mean of the process with a magnitude of one standard deviation.

(g) $LSL = 7.12$, $USL = 7.28$, $USL - LSL = 0.16$, $\overline{X} = 7.198$, $\sigma \approx 0.1012$, $C_p = \dfrac{USL - LSL}{6\sigma} = \dfrac{0.16}{6 \times 0.1012} = 0.264$, $C_p < 1$, so the process can be expected to produce many nonconforming units. $Z_{LSL} = \dfrac{LSL - \overline{X}}{\sigma} = \dfrac{7.12 - 7.198}{0.1012} = -0.77$, $Z_{USL} = \dfrac{USL - \overline{X}}{\sigma} = \dfrac{7.28 - 7.198}{0.1012} = 0.81$, $|Z_{\min}| = 0.77$, $C_{pk} = \left|\dfrac{Z_{\min}}{3}\right| = \dfrac{0.77}{3} = 0.257$

51. Answers will vary. **52.** Answers will vary. **53.** Answers will vary.

chapter 8

Estimation Procedures

1. $\overline{X} \pm Z\frac{\sigma}{\sqrt{n}} = 85 \pm 1.96\frac{8}{\sqrt{64}} = 85 \pm 1.96$; $83.04 < \mu < 86.96$

2. (a) $t = 2.228$ (b) $t = 3.169$ (c) $t = 2.037$ (d) $t = 1.997$ (e) $t = 1.746$

3. $\overline{X} \pm t_{n-1}\frac{S}{\sqrt{n}} = 75 \pm 2.03\frac{24}{\sqrt{36}} = 75 \pm 8.12$; $66.88 < \mu < 83.12$

4. (a) $\overline{X} \pm Z\frac{\sigma}{\sqrt{n}} = 350 \pm 1.96\frac{100}{\sqrt{64}} = 350 \pm 24.5$; $325.5 < \mu < 374.5$
   (b) No, the probability that the light bulb's life has an average of more than 374.5 hrs is ~ 0.025.
   (c) No, but for $n = 64$ due to the central limit theorem it is approximately normally distributed.
   (d) Any individual value in the interval $\mu \pm 3\sigma$ is typical.
   (e) $\overline{X} \pm Z\frac{\sigma}{\sqrt{n}} = 350 \pm 1.96\frac{80}{\sqrt{64}} = 350 \pm 19.6$; $330.4 < \mu < 369.4$
   The probability that the light bulbs' life has an average of more than 369.4 is $\sim$ 0.025, so the average of 400 hours is unusual.

5. (a) $\overline{X} \pm Z\frac{\sigma}{\sqrt{n}} = 1.99 \pm 1.96\frac{0.05}{\sqrt{100}} = 1.99 \pm 0.0098$; $1.9802 < \mu < 1.9998$
   (b) No. As σ is known and $n = 100$, based on the central limit theorem, we may assume that the sampling distribution of $\overline{X}$ is approximately normal.
   (c) An individual value of 2.02 is 0.60 of the standard deviation above the sample mean of 1.99. The confidence interval represents bounds on the estimate of a sample of 100, not an individual value.
   (d) $\overline{X} \pm Z\frac{\sigma}{\sqrt{n}} = 1.97 \pm 1.96\frac{0.05}{\sqrt{100}} = 1.97 \pm 0.0098$; $1.9602 < \mu < 1.9798$
   A shift of 0.02 units in the sample average shifts the confidence interval by the same distance without affecting the width of the resulting interval.

6. (a) $\overline{X} \pm t_{n-1}\frac{S}{\sqrt{n}} = 195.3 \pm 2.11\frac{21.4}{\sqrt{18}} = 195.3 \pm 10.64$; $184.66 < \mu < 205.94$
   (b) No. An average value 200 is valid.
   (c) Any individual value in the interval $\mu \pm 3\sigma$ is typical.

7. $\overline{X} = 1069.563$; $S = 227.4276$; $n = 35$
   (a) $\overline{X} \pm t_{n-1}\frac{S}{\sqrt{n}} = 1069.563 \pm 2.03\frac{227.4276}{\sqrt{35}} = 1069.563 \pm 78.124$; $991.439 < \mu < 1147.687$
   (b) All individual observations must be represented by independent, identically distributed normal random values, i.e., they must be a random Gaussian sample. The assumption is probably correct, because the sample kurtosis and sample skewness are equal to 0.72283 and 0.29377, respectively, for sample size of 35. The same conclusion may be derived from a normal probability plot.

8. $\overline{X} = 6.7328$; $S = 0.0658$; $n = 25$

(a) $\overline{X} \pm t_{n-1}\frac{S}{\sqrt{n}} = 6.7328 \pm 2.06\frac{0.0658}{\sqrt{25}} = 6.7328 \pm 0.02716$; $6.71 < \mu < 6.76$

(b) All individual observations must be represented by independent, identically distributed normal random values, i.e., they must be a random Gaussian sample. The assumption is probably correct, because the sample kurtosis and sample skewness are equal to –0.15123 and –0.43823, respectively, for a sample size of 25. The same conclusion may be derived from a normal probability plot.

9. $\overline{X} = 64.484$; $S = 2.41106$; $n = 50$

(a) $\overline{X} \pm t_{n-1}\frac{S}{\sqrt{n}} = 64.484 \pm 2.0096\frac{2.41106}{\sqrt{50}} = 64.484 \pm 0.685$; $63.80 < \mu < 65.17$

(b) All individual observations must be represented by independent, identically distributed normal random values, i.e., they must be a random Gaussian sample. The assumption is probably correct, because the sample kurtosis and sample skewness are equal to –0.8846 and 0.180138, respectively, for a sample size of 50. The same conclusion may be derived from a normal probability plot.

10. $\overline{X} = 273.085$; $S = 25.21135$; $n = 40$

(a) $\overline{X} \pm t_{n-1}\frac{S}{\sqrt{n}} = 273.085 \pm 2.023\frac{25.21135}{\sqrt{40}} = 273.085 \pm 8.063$; $265.02 < \mu < 281.15$

(b) All individual observations must be represented by independent, identically distributed normal random values, i.e., they must be a random Gaussian sample. The assumption is probably correct, because the sample kurtosis and sample skewness are equal to –0.04289 and –0.12563, respectively, for a sample size of 40. The same conclusion may be derived from a normal probability plot.

11. $\overline{X} = 9.08$; $S = 0.81584$; $n = 36$

(a) $\overline{X} \pm t_{n-1}\frac{S}{\sqrt{n}} = 9.08 \pm 2.03\frac{0.81584}{\sqrt{36}} = 9.08 \pm 0.276$; $8.80 < \mu < 9.36$

(b) All individual observations must be represented by independent, identically distributed random values, i.e., they must be a random Gaussian sample. A closer approximation would be obtained if this were a sample from a normal distribution. The assumption is probably correct, because the sample kurtosis and sample skewness are equal to 0.571098 and –0.57151, respectively, for a sample size of 36. The same conclusion may be derived from a normal probability plot.

12. (a) $\chi^2_U = 26.296$, $\chi^2_L = 7.962$ (b) $\chi^2_U = 21.920$, $\chi^2_L = 3.816$ (c) $\chi^2_U = 21.955$, $\chi^2_L = 1.344$

13. (a)

Confidence Interval for Variance	
Sample Standard Deviation	2.1
Sample Size	30
Confidence Level	95%
df	29
Sum of Squares	127.89
Lower Chi-Square Value	16.04705
Upper Chi-Square Value	45.72228
Interval Lower Limit for Variance	2.797105
Interval Upper Limit for Variance	7.969689
Interval Lower Limit for Standard Deviation	1.672455
Interval Upper Limit for Standard Deviation	2.823064

$2.797 < \sigma^2 < 7.97$; $1.672 < \sigma < 2.823$

(b) All individual observations must be independent, identically distributed random values, i.e., they must be a random Gaussian sample.

14. (a)

Confidence Interval for Variance	
Sample Standard Deviation	0.025
Sample Size	25
Confidence Level	99%
df	24
Sum of Squares	0.015
Lower Chi-Square Value	9.886199
Upper Chi-Square Value	45.55836
Interval Lower Limit for Variance	0.000329
Interval Upper Limit for Variance	0.001517
Interval Lower Limit for Standard Deviation	0.018145
Interval Upper Limit for Standard Deviation	0.038952

$0.000329 < \sigma^2 < 0.001517$; $0.018 < \sigma < 0.039$

(b) All individual observations must be independent, identically distributed random values, i.e., they must be a random Gaussian sample.

(c) The redesigned process does not significantly reduce the standard deviation because 0.035 is within the confidence interval for σ.

15.

Confidence Interval for Variance	
Sample Standard Deviation	21.4
Sample Size	18
Confidence Level	95%
df	17
Sum of Squares	7785.32
Lower Chi-Square Value	7.564179
Upper Chi-Square Value	30.19098
Interval Lower Limit for Variance	257.8691
Interval Upper Limit for Variance	1029.235
Interval Lower Limit for Standard Deviation	16.0583
Interval Upper Limit for Standard Deviation	32.0817

$257.879 < \sigma^2 < 1029.235$; $16.058 < \sigma < 32.082$

16. (a)

Confidence Interval for Variance	
Sample Standard Deviation	0.065798
Sample Size	25
Confidence Level	95%
df	24
Sum of Squares	0.103905
Lower Chi-Square Value	12.40115
Upper Chi-Square Value	39.36406
Interval Lower Limit for Variance	0.00264
Interval Upper Limit for Variance	0.008379
Interval Lower Limit for Standard Deviation	0.051377
Interval Upper Limit for Standard Deviation	0.091535

$0.00264 < \sigma^2 < 0.00838$; $0.051 < \sigma < 0.092$

(b) All individual observations must be represented by independent, identically distributed normal random values, i.e., they must be a random Gaussian sample. The assumption is probably correct, because the sample kurtosis and sample skewness are equal to –0.15123 and –0.43823, respectively, for a sample size of 25. The same conclusion may be derived from a normal probability plot.

17. (a)

Confidence Interval for Variance	
Sample Standard Deviation	0.405763
Sample Size	30
Confidence Level	95%
df	29
Sum of Squares	4.774667
Lower Chi-Square Value	16.04705
Upper Chi-Square Value	45.72228
Interval Lower Limit for Variance	0.104428
Interval Upper Limit for Variance	0.297542
Interval Lower Limit for Standard Deviation	0.323153
Interval Upper Limit for Standard Deviation	0.545474

$0.1044 < \sigma^2 < 0.2975$; $0.323 < \sigma < 0.545$

(b) All individual observations must be represented by independent identically distributed normal random values, i.e., they must be a random Gaussian sample. There are some doubts about the validity of this assumption because both sample kurtosis and sample skewness are not close to zero (they are equal to –0.44915 and –0.62772, respectively, for a sample size of 30). From the normal probability plot, we conclude that the initial sample can be normal as well. A more precise answer to this question can be provided by testing the corresponding hypothesis (see chapter 9).

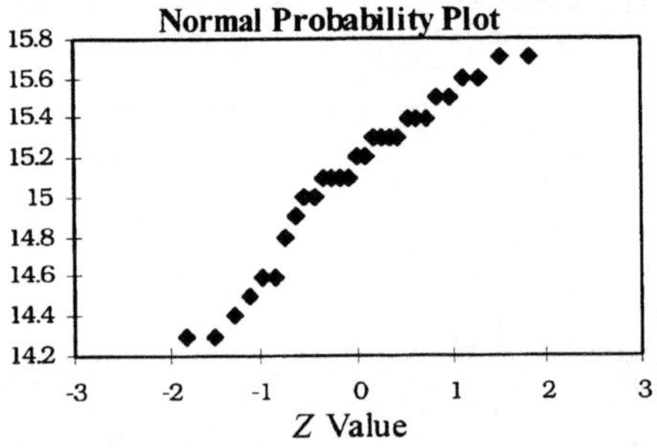

(c) No. The standard deviation is greater than 0.323 with a probability greater than 0.95.

18. (a)

Confidence Interval for Variance	
Sample Standard Deviation	2.658868
Sample Size	20
Confidence Level	95%
df	19
Sum of Squares	134.322
Lower Chi-Square Value	8.906514
Upper Chi-Square Value	32.85234
Interval Lower Limit for Variance	4.088659
Interval Upper Limit for Variance	15.08132
Interval Lower Limit for Standard Deviation	2.022043
Interval Upper Limit for Standard Deviation	3.883468

$4.089 < \sigma^2 < 15.081$; $2.022 < \sigma < 3.883$

(b) All individual observations must be represented by independent, identically distributed normal random values, i.e., they must be a random Gaussian sample. The assumption is probably correct because the sample kurtosis and sample skewness are equal to 0.159217 and 0.123385, respectively, for a sample size of 20. The same conclusion may be derived from a normal probability plot.

(c) No, because $2.5 < S$, $P(\sigma \le 2.5) < 0.5$.

19. (a) $\bar{X} \pm t_{n-1}S\sqrt{1+\frac{1}{n}} = 195.3 \pm 2.11 \cdot 21.4\sqrt{1+\frac{1}{18}} = 195.3 \pm 46.39$; $148.81 < X_f < 241.69$

(b) Part (a) is an interval estimation for an individual value rather than for a mean, therefore, it is wider than the confidential interval in 8.6 (a). Both of the intervals are centered at 195.3.

20. (a) $\bar{X} \pm t_{n-1}S\sqrt{1+\frac{1}{n}} = 1069.563 \pm 2.03 \cdot 227.43\sqrt{1+\frac{1}{35}} = 1069.563 \pm 468.232$; $601.331 < X_f < 1537.795$

(b) This is an interval estimation for an individual value rather than for a mean, therefore, it is wider than the confidential interval in 8.7 (a). Both of the intervals are centered at 1069.563.

21. (a) $\bar{X} \pm t_{n-1}S\sqrt{1+\frac{1}{n}} = 6.7328 \pm 2.06 \cdot 0.0658\sqrt{1+\frac{1}{25}} = 6.7328 \pm 0.4518$; $6.281 < X_f < 7.185$

(b) This is an interval estimation for an individual value rather than for a mean, therefore, it is wider than the confidential interval in 8.8 (a). Both of the intervals are centered at 6.7328.

22. (a) $\bar{X} \pm t_{n-1}S\sqrt{1+\frac{1}{n}} = 64.484 \pm 2.0096 \cdot 2.411\sqrt{1+\frac{1}{50}} = 64.484 \pm 4.893$; $59.591 < X_f < 69.377$

(b) This is an interval estimation for an individual value, not for a mean, therefore, it is wider than the confidential interval in 8.8 (a). Both of the intervals are centered at 64.484.

23. (a) $\bar{X} \pm t_{n-1}S\sqrt{1+\frac{1}{n}} = 273.085 \pm 2.023 \cdot 25.21135\sqrt{1+\frac{1}{40}} = 273.085 \pm 51.636$; $221.449 < X_f < 324.721$

(b) This is an interval estimation for an individual value, not for a mean, therefore, it is wider than the confidential interval in 8.8 (a). Both of the intervals are centered at 273.085.

24. (a) $\bar{X} \pm t_{n-1}S\sqrt{1+\frac{1}{n}} = 9.08 \pm 2.03 \cdot 0.81584\sqrt{1+\frac{1}{36}} = 9.08 \pm 1.679$; $7.401 < X_f < 10.759$

(b) This is an interval estimation for an individual value, not for a mean, therefore, it is wider than the confidential interval in 8.8 (a). Both of the intervals are centered at 9.08.

25. $\bar{X} = 195.3$; $S = 21.4$; $n = 18$

(a) $p = 0.90$, $n = 18$, $K_2 = 2.376$

$\bar{X} \pm K_2 = 195.3 \pm 2.376 \times 21.4 = 195.3 \pm 50.846$

Tolerance estimate is (144.454; 246.146).

(b) $p = 0.1$, $n = 18$, $K_1 = 1.974$

$\bar{X} - K_1S = 195.3 - 1.974 \times 21.4 = 195.3 - 42.24$

$= 153.06$

(c) The result of 8.6 (a) provides an interval estimate for a mean, the result of 8.19 (a) gives the prediction interval for the single future observation (it is, therefore, wider than the former), whereas this result gives an interval estimate for a given portion (90%) of the observations; therefore, it is the largest.

26. $\bar{X} = 1069.563$; $S = 227.4276$; $n = 35$

(a) $p = 0.9$, $K_2 = 2.094$

$\bar{X} \pm K_2S = 1069.563 \pm 2.094 \times 227.4276$

$= 1069 \pm 476.233$

Tolerance estimate is (593.33; 1545.796)

(b) $p = 0.1$, $K_1 = 1.732$

$\bar{X} + K_1S = 1069.563 + 1.732 \cdot 227.4276$

$= 1069.563 + 393.9 = 1433.463$

(c) The result of 8.7 (a) provides an interval estimate for a mean, the result of 8.20 (a) shows the prediction interval for the single future observation (it is, therefore, wider then the former), whereas this result gives an interval estimate for a certain portion (90%) of the observations. For this reason it is the largest.

27. $\overline{X} = 6.7328$; $S = 0.0658$; $n = 25$

(a) $p = 0.95$, $K_2 = 2.984$

$\overline{X} \pm K_2 S = 6.7328 \pm 2.984 \times 0.0658 = 6.7328 \pm 0.1963$

Tolerance estimate is (6.5365; 6.9291)

(b) It is not correct to compare this tolerance interval with the previous two because they have different confidence levels.

28. $\overline{X} = 64.484$; $S = 2.41106$; $n = 50$

(a) $p = 0.95$, $K_2 = 2.382$

$\overline{X} \pm K_2 S = 64.484 \pm 2.382 \times 2.411 = 64.484 \pm 5.743$

Tolerance estimate is (58.741; 70.227).

(b) $p = 0.99$, $K_1 = 2.862$

$\overline{X} + K_1 S = 64.484 + 2.862 \times 2.411 = 64.484 + 6.900 = 71.384$

(c) The result of 8.9 (a) provides an interval estimate for a mean, the result of 8.22 (a) shows the prediction interval for the single future observation (it is, therefore, wider than the former) whereas this result gives an interval estimate for a certain portion (95%) of the observations. It is, therefore, the largest.

29. $\overline{X} = 273.085$; $S = 25.21135$; $n = 40$

(a) $p = 0.9$, $K_2 = 2.253$

$\overline{X} \pm K_2 S = 273.085 \pm 2.253 \times 25.21 = 273.085 \pm 56.344$

Tolerance estimate is (216.741; 329.429).

(b) $p = 0.05$, $K_1 = 2.125$

$\overline{X} + K_1 S = 273.085 + 2.125 \times 25.21 = 273.085 + 53.571 = 326.656$

(c) It is not correct to compare this tolerance interval with the previous two because they have different confidence levels.

30. $\overline{X} = 9.08$; $S = 0.81584$; $n = 36$

(a) $p = 0.99$, $K_2 = 3.276$

$\overline{X} \pm K_2 S = 9.08 \pm 3.276 \cdot 0.816 = 9.08 \pm 2.673$

Tolerance estimate is (6.407; 11.753).

(b) $p = 0.99$, $K_1 = 3.334$

$\overline{X} + K_1 S = 9.08 + 3.334 \times 0.816 = 9.08 + 2.72 = 11.8$

(c) The result of 8.11 (a) provides an interval estimate for a mean, the result of 8.24 (a) shows the prediction interval for the single future observation (it is, therefore, wider than the former), whereas this result gives an interval estimate for a certain portion (99%) of the observations. It is, therefore, the largest.

31.

Confidence Interval Estimate for the Mean	
Sample Size	63
Number of Successes	40
Confidence Level	95%
Sample Proportion	0.634920635
Z Value	−1.95996108
Standard Error of the Proportion	0.060657302
Interval Half Width	0.118885951
Interval Lower Limit	0.516034684
Interval Upper Limit	0.753806586

$0.516 < \pi < 0.754$

32. (a)

Confidence Interval Estimate for the Mean	
Sample Size	450
Number of Successes	116
Confidence Level	95%
Sample Proportion	0.257777778
Z Value	−1.95996108
Standard Error of the Proportion	0.020619753
Interval Half Width	0.040413913
Interval Lower Limit	0.217363864
Interval Upper Limit	0.298191691

(b)

Confidence Interval Estimate for the Mean	
Sample Size	116
Number of Successes	36
Confidence Level	95%
Sample Proportion	0.310344828
Z Value	−1.95996108
Standard Error of the Proportion	0.042954559
Interval Half Width	0.084189263
Interval Lower Limit	0.226155565
Interval Upper Limit	0.394534091

33.

Confidence Interval Estimate for the Mean	
Sample Size	1126
Number of Successes	114
Confidence Level	99%
Sample Proportion	0.101243339
Z Value	−2.57583451
Standard Error of the Proportion	0.008989491
Interval Half Width	0.023155441
Interval Lower Limit	0.078087898
Interval Upper Limit	0.12439878

$0.078 < \pi < 0.124$

34. (a)

Confidence Interval Estimate for the Mean	
Sample Size	276
Number of Successes	86
Confidence Level	95%
Sample Proportion	0.311594203
Z Value	−1.95996108
Standard Error of the Proportion	0.027878051
Interval Half Width	0.054639894
Interval Lower Limit	0.256954309
Interval Upper Limit	0.366234097

(b)

Confidence Interval Estimate for the Mean	
Sample Size	111
Number of Successes	72
Confidence Level	95%
Sample Proportion	0.648648649
Z Value	−1.95996108
Standard Error of the Proportion	0.045312089
Interval Half Width	0.088809931
Interval Lower Limit	0.559838718
Interval Upper Limit	0.737458579

35. (a)

Confidence Interval Estimate for the Mean	
Sample Size	1425
Number of Successes	722
Confidence Level	95%
Sample Proportion	0.506666667
Z Value	−1.95996108
Standard Error of the Proportion	0.013244146
Interval Half Width	0.025958011
Interval Lower Limit	0.480708656
Interval Upper Limit	0.532624678

(b)

Confidence Interval Estimate for the Mean	
Sample Size	1425
Number of Successes	115
Confidence Level	90%
Sample Proportion	0.080701754
Z Value	−1.644853
Standard Error of the Proportion	0.007215431
Interval Half Width	0.011868323
Interval Lower Limit	0.068833431
Interval Upper Limit	0.092570078

(c)

Confidence Interval Estimate for the Mean	
Sample Size	1425
Number of Successes	588
Confidence Level	99%
Sample Proportion	0.412631579
Z Value	–2.57583451
Standard Error of the Proportion	0.013041547
Interval Half Width	0.033592866
Interval Lower Limit	0.379038713
Interval Upper Limit	0.446224445

36. For a confidence level of 100%, the entire domain for the parameters of interest would be used as a confidence estimate. This results in less precise and less useful estimates.

37. The *t* distribution is used in the interval estimate procedure when information about the variance is not available.

38. An increase in the confidence level means an increase in the probability of finding the characteristic of interest in some intervals. An increase in the probability leads to a wider interval estimate.

39. The estimated objects are different, so the estimators are different as well. Both of the point estimates are the same (sample average), but the interval for the mean estimate is narrower.

40. The estimated objects are different, so the estimators are different as well. The first provides an estimate for the first moment of the random variable, and the second gives an estimate for a fixed portion of observation.

41. It depends on the problem context and the type pf results derived. If we are interested in lower or upper values, we need to construct one-sided tolerance and confidence intervals. For a model without any preference for the positive or negative differences of the observed values and their mean, it is appropriate to construct two-sided confidence and tolerance intervals.

42.

Mean	199.452
Standard Deviation	5.967769
Sample Variance	35.61427
Kurtosis	–0.84602
Skewness	–0.07292
Count	25
Confidence Level (95.0%)	2.463373

(a)

Confidence Interval Estimate for the Mean	
Sample Standard Deviation	5.967769
Sample Mean	199.452
Sample Size	25
Confidence Level	95%
Standard Error of the Mean	1.1935538
Degrees of Freedom	24
t Value	2.063898137
Interval Half Width	2.463373464
Interval Lower Limit	196.99
Interval Upper Limit	201.92

(b)

Confidence Interval For Variance	
Sample Standard Deviation	5.967769
Sample Size	25
Confidence Level	95%
df	24
Sum of Squares	854.7424
Lower Chi-Square Value	12.40115
Upper Chi-Square Value	39.36406
Interval Lower Limit for Variance	21.71378
Interval Upper Limit for Variance	68.92447
Interval Lower Limit for Standard Deviation	4.659804
Interval Upper Limit for Standard Deviation	8.302076

(c) All individual observations must be represented by independent, identically distributed normal random values, i.e., they must represent a random Gaussian sample. The assumption is probably correct, because the sample kurtosis and sample skewness are equal to −0.84602 and −0.07292, respectively, for the sample size of 25. The same conclusion may be derived from a normal probability plot.

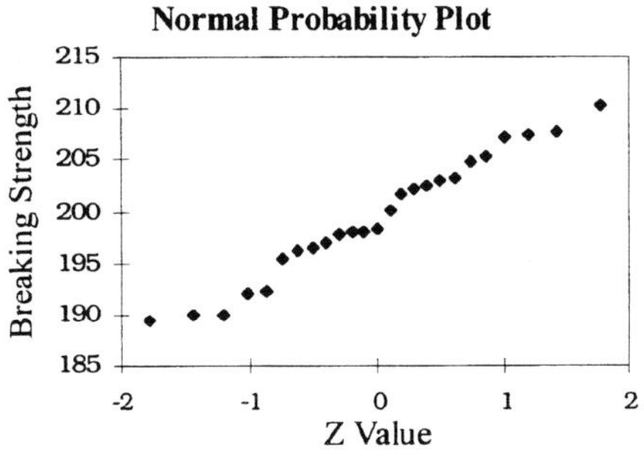

(d) $\bar{X} \pm t_{n-1} S\sqrt{1+\frac{1}{n}} = 199.452 \pm 2.064 \times 5.968\sqrt{1+\frac{1}{25}} = 199.452 \pm 12.562$, $186.89 < X_f < 212.014$

(e) $\bar{X} \pm K_2 S = 199.452 \pm 3.462 \times 5.968 = 199.452 \pm 20.661$, $K_2 = 3.462$, (178.791; 220.113)

(f) $\bar{X} - K_1 S = 199.452 - 3.158 \times 5.968 = 199.452 - 18.847 = 180.605$, $K_1 = 3.158$

(g) The result of part (a) provides an interval estimate for a mean, the result of part (d) gives the prediction interval for the single future observation (so it is wider than the previous one) and the result of part (e) gives an interval estimate for a certain portion (99%) of the observations. It is, therefore, the largest.

43.

Mean	438.3333
Standard Deviation	261.5013
Sample Variance	68382.91
Kurtosis	5.753448
Skewness	2.060448
Count	36
Confidence Level(95.0%)	88.47941

(a)

Confidence Interval Estimate for the Mean	
Sample Standard Deviation	261.5013
Sample Mean	438.3333
Sample Size	36
Confidence Level	95%
Standard Error of the Mean	43.58355
Degrees of Freedom	35
t Value	2.030110409
Interval Half Width	88.4794185
Interval Lower Limit	349.85
Interval Upper Limit	526.81

(b)

Confidence Interval For Variance	
Sample Standard Deviation	261.5013
Sample Size	36
Confidence Level	95%
df	35
Sum of Squares	2393403
Lower Chi-Square Value	20.56938
Upper Chi-Square Value	53.20331
Interval Lower Limit for Variance	44985.97
Interval Upper Limit for Variance	116357.5
Interval Lower Limit for Standard Deviation	212.099
Interval Upper Limit for Standard Deviation	341.1122

(c) All individual observations must be represented by independent, identically distributed normal random values, i.e., they must be a random Gaussian sample. The assumption is probably correct, because the sample kurtosis is equal to 5.753448 for a sample size of 36. The same conclusion may be derived from a normal probability plot.

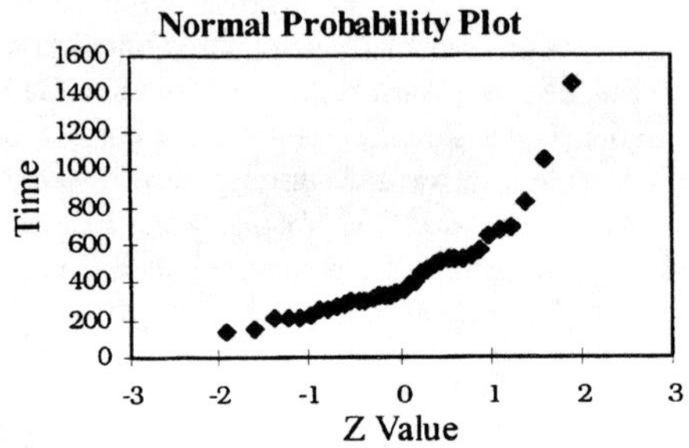

(d) $\overline{X} \pm t_{n-1} S \sqrt{1+\frac{1}{n}} = 438.333 \pm 2.03 \times 261.5\sqrt{1+\frac{1}{36}} = 438.333 \pm 538.17$, (0; 976.5)

(e) $\overline{X} \pm K_2 S = 438.333 \pm 3.276 \times 261.5 = 438.333 \pm 856.674$, $K_2 = 3.276$, (0; 1295.007)

(f) The result of part (a) provides an interval estimate for a mean, the result of part (d) gives the prediction interval for the single future observation whereas the result of part (e) gives an interval estimate for a certain portion (99%) of the observations.

44.

Mean	273.2308
Standard Deviation	9.763107
Sample Variance	95.31825
Kurtosis	–0.75629
Skewness	0.136865
Count	52
Confidence Level(95.0%)	2.718064

(a)

Confidence Interval Estimate for the Mean	
Sample Standard Deviation	9.763107
Sample Mean	273.2308
Sample Size	52
Confidence Level	95%
Standard Error of the Mean	1.353899342
Degrees of Freedom	51
t Value	2.007582225
Interval Half Width	2.718064254
Interval Lower Limit	270.51
Interval Upper Limit	275.95

(b)

Confidence Interval For Variance	
Sample Standard Deviation	9.763107
Sample Size	52
Confidence Level	95%
df	51
Sum of Squares	4861.231
Lower Chi-Square Value	33.1618
Upper Chi-Square Value	72.61603
Interval Lower Limit for Variance	66.94432
Interval Upper Limit for Variance	146.5913
Interval Lower Limit for Standard Deviation	8.181951
Interval Upper Limit for Standard Deviation	12.10749

(c) All individual observations must be represented by independent, identically distributed normal random values, i.e., they must represent random Gaussian sample. The assumption is probably correct because the sample kurtosis and sample skewness are equal to –0.75629 and 0.136865, respectively, for a sample size of 52. The same conclusion may be derived from a normal probability plot.

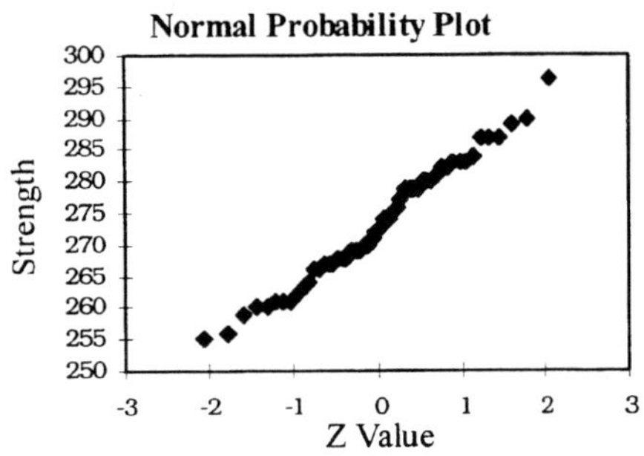

(d) $\overline{X} \pm t_{n-1}S\sqrt{1+\frac{1}{n}} = 273.231 \pm 2.008 \times 9.763\sqrt{1+\frac{1}{52}} = 273.231 \pm 19.792$, (253.439; 293.023)

(e) $\overline{X} \pm K_2 S = 273.231 \pm 1.999 \times 9.763 = 273.231 \pm 19.516$, $K_2 = 1.999$, (253.715; 292.747)

(f) $X - K_1 S = 273.231 - 2.862 \times 9.763 = 245.289$

(g) The result of part (a) provides an interval estimate for a mean, the result of part (d) gives the prediction interval for the single future observation, whereas the result of part (e) gives an interval estimate for a certain portion (99%) of the observations.

45. Height

Mean	157.0833
Standard Deviation	46.3199
Sample Variance	2145.533
Kurtosis	–0.91332
Skewness	–0.27951
Count	21
Confidence Level (95.0%)	21.08456

(a)

Confidence Interval Estimate for the Mean	
Sample Standard Deviation	46.3199
Sample Mean	157.0833
Sample Size	21
Confidence Level	95%
Standard Error of the Mean	10.10783085
Degrees of Freedom	20
t Value	2.085962478
Interval Half Width	21.0845559
Interval Lower Limit	136.00
Interval Upper Limit	178.17

(b)

Confidence Interval For Variance	
Sample Standard Deviation	46.3199
Sample Size	21
Confidence Level	95%
df	20
Sum of Squares	42910.66
Lower Chi-Square Value	9.590772
Upper Chi-Square Value	34.16958
Interval Lower Limit for Variance	1255.815
Interval Upper Limit for Variance	4474.161
Interval Lower Limit for Standard Deviation	35.43748
Interval Upper Limit for Standard Deviation	66.88917

(c) All individual observations must be independent, identically distributed normal random values, i.e., they must represent a random Gaussian sample. The same conclusion may be derived from a normal probability plot.

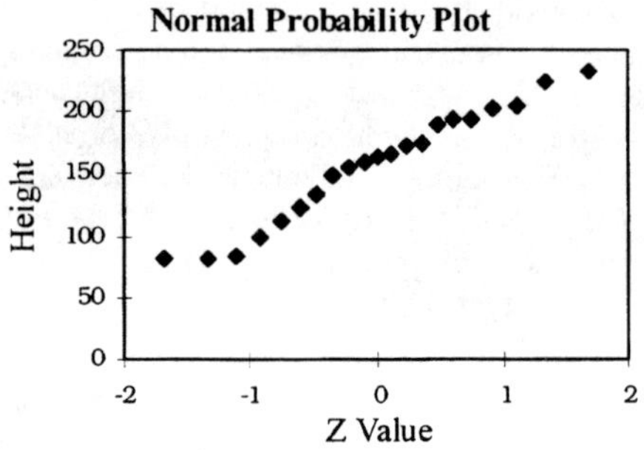

(d) $\overline{X} \pm t_{n-1} S \sqrt{1+\frac{1}{n}} = 157.08 \pm 2.086 \times 46.32 \sqrt{1+\frac{1}{21}} = 157.08 \pm 98.898$, (58.182; 255.978)

(e) $\overline{X} \pm K_2 S = 157.08 \pm 3.621 \times 46.32 = 157.08 \pm 167.72$, (0; 324.8)

(f) The result of part (a) provides an interval estimate for a mean, the result of part (d) gives the prediction interval for the single future observation, whereas the result of part (e) gives an interval estimate for a certain portion (99%) of the observations.

dbh

Mean	29.28571
Standard Deviation	14.79237
Sample Variance	218.8143
Kurtosis	−1.22175
Skewness	0.172381
Count	21
Confidence Level (95.0%)	6.733404

(a)

Confidence Interval Estimate for the Mean	
Sample Standard Deviation	14.79237
Sample Mean	29.28577
Sample Size	21
Confidence Level	95%
Standard Error of the Mean	3.227959773
Degrees of Freedom	20
t Value	2.085962478
Interval Half Width	6.733402968
Interval Lower Limit	22.55
Interval Upper Limit	36.02

(b)

Confidence Interval For Variance	
Sample Standard Deviation	14.79273
Sample Size	21
Confidence Level	95%
df	20
Sum of Squares	4376.497
Lower Chi-Square Value	9.590772
Upper Chi-Square Value	34.16958
Interval Lower Limit for Variance	128.0817
Interval Upper Limit for Variance	456.3237
Interval Lower Limit for Standard Deviation	11.31732
Interval Upper Limit for Standard Deviation	21.36174

(c) All individual observations must be independent, identically distributed normal random values, i.e., they must represent a random Gaussian sample. The same conclusion may be derived from a normal probability plot.

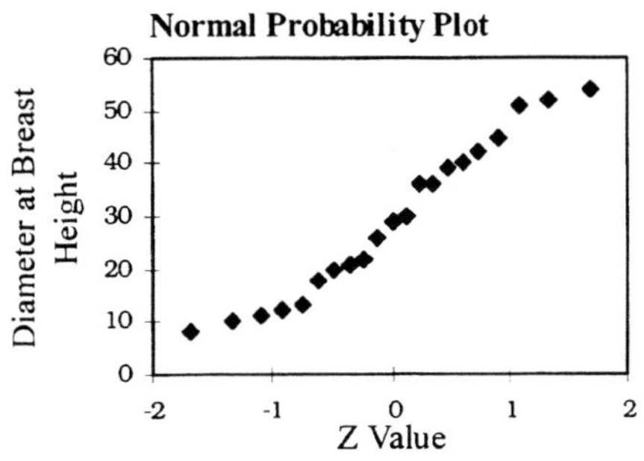

(d) $\overline{X} \pm t_{n-1} S\sqrt{1+\frac{1}{n}} = 29.286 \pm 2.086 \times 14.79\sqrt{1+\frac{1}{21}} = 29.286 \pm 31.578$, (0; 60.864)

(e) $\overline{X} \pm K_2 S = 29.286 \pm 3.621 \times 14.79 = 29.286 \pm 53.554$, (0; 82.84)

(f) The result of part (a) provides an interval estimate for a mean, the result of part (d) gives the prediction interval for the single future observation, whereas the result of part (e) gives an interval estimate for a certain portion (99%) of the observations.

Bark

Mean	2.219048
Standard Deviation	0.916307
Sample Variance	0.839619
Kurtosis	0.121937
Skewness	0.829526
Count	21
Confidence Level (95.0%)	0.417098

(a)

Confidence Interval Estimate for the Mean	
Sample Standard Deviation	0.916307
Sample Mean	2.219048
Sample Size	21
Confidence Level	95%
Standard Error of the Mean	0.19995458
Degrees of Freedom	20
t Value	2.085962478
Interval Half Width	0.417097752
Interval Lower Limit	1.80
Interval Upper Limit	2.64

(b)

Confidence Interval For Variance	
Sample Standard Deviation	0.9163
Sample Size	21
Confidence Level	95%
df	20
Sum of Squares	16.79211
Lower Chi-Square Value	9.590772
Upper Chi-Square Value	34.16958
Interval Lower Limit for Variance	0.491435
Interval Upper Limit for Variance	1.750861
Interval Lower Limit for Standard Deviation	0.701024
Interval Upper Limit for Standard Deviation	1.323201

(c) All individual observations must be independent, identically distributed normal random values, i.e., they must represent a random Gaussian sample. The same conclusion may be derived from a normal probability plot.

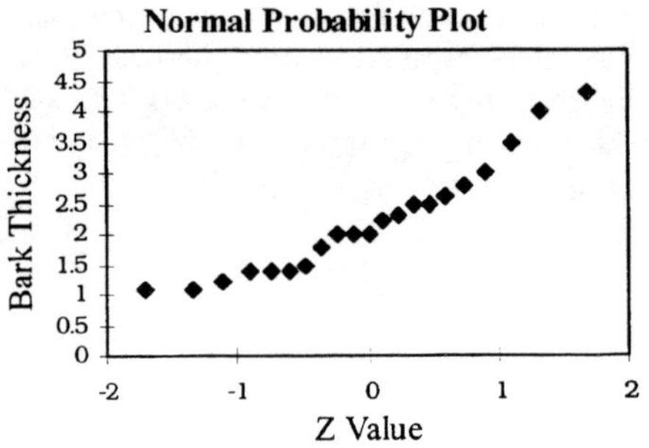

(d) $\bar{X} \pm t_{n-1} S \sqrt{1+\frac{1}{n}} = 2.22 \pm 2.086 \times 0.92 \sqrt{1+\frac{1}{21}} = 2.22 \pm 1.96$, (0.26; 4.18)

(e) $\bar{X} \pm K_2 S = 2.22 \pm 3.621 \times 0.92 = 2.22 \pm 3.33$, (0; 5.55)

(f) The result of part (a) provides an interval estimate for a mean, the result of part (d) gives the prediction interval for the single future observation, whereas the result of part (e) gives an interval estimate for a certain portion (99%) of the observations.

chapter 9

Introduction to Hypothesis Testing

1. (a) $H_0: \mu = 70$ pounds; the cloth has an average breaking strength of 70 pounds.
$H_1: \mu \neq 70$ pounds; the cloth has an average breaking strength that differs from 70 pounds.

(b)

Z Test of Hypothesis for the Mean	
Null Hypothesis	$\mu = 70$
Level of Significance	0.05
Population Standard Deviation	3.5
Sample Size	49
Sample Mean	69.1
Standard Error of the Mean	0.5
Z Test Statistic	−1.8

Two-Tail Test	
Lower Critical Value	−1.95996108
Upper Critical Value	1.959961082
p-value	0.071860531
Do not reject the null hypothesis	

Decision rule: Reject H_0 if $Z < -1.96$ or $Z > 1.96$. Test statistic: $Z = \frac{\overline{X} - \mu}{\sigma/\sqrt{n}} = \frac{69.1 - 70}{3.5/\sqrt{49}} = -1.8$. Decision: Because $-1.96 < Z < 1.96$, do not reject H_0. There is insufficient evidence to conclude that the cloth has an average breaking strength that differs from 70 pounds for the 0.05 significance level.

(c) p-value $= 0.072$. This is the probability of obtaining a test statistic $|Z|$ equal to or greater than the result obtained from the sample data given that the null hypothesis is true.

(d)

Z Test of Hypothesis for the Mean	
Null Hypothesis	$\mu = 70$
Level of Significance	0.05
Population Standard Deviation	1.75
Sample Size	49
Sample Mean	69.1
Standard Error of the Mean	0.25
Z Test Statistic	−3.6

Two-Tail Test	
Lower Critical Value	−1.95996108
Upper Critical Value	1.959961082
p-value	0.000318291
Reject the null hypothesis	

Decision rule: Reject H_0 if $Z < -1.96$ or $Z > 1.96$. Test statistic: $Z = \frac{\overline{X} - \mu}{\sigma/\sqrt{n}} = \frac{69.1 - 70}{1.75/\sqrt{49}} = -3.6$. Decision: Because $Z < -1.96$, reject H_0. There is sufficient evidence to conclude that the cloth has an average breaking strength that differs from 70 pounds for the 0.05 significance level.

(e)

Z Test of Hypothesis for the Mean	
Null Hypothesis	$\mu = 70$
Level of Significance	0.05
Population Standard Deviation	3.5
Sample Size	49
Sample Mean	69
Standard Error of the Mean	0.5
Z Test Statistic	−2

Two-Tail Test	
Lower Critical Value	−1.95996108
Upper Critical Value	1.959961082
p-value	0.045500124
Reject the null hypothesis	

Decision rule: Reject H_0 if $Z < -1.96$ or $Z > 1.96$. Test statistic: $Z = \frac{\bar{X} - \mu}{\sigma/\sqrt{n}} = \frac{69 - 70}{3.5/\sqrt{49}} = -2$. Decision: Because $Z < -1.96$, reject H_0. There is sufficient evidence to conclude that the cloth has an average breaking strength that is different from the 70 pound breaking strength.

2. (a) $H_0: \mu = 8$ ounces; the population average amount of salad dressing dispensed into the bottles is 8 ounces.
$H_1: \mu \neq 8$ ounces; the population average amount of salad dressing dispensed into the bottles differs from 8 ounces.

(b)

Z Test of Hypothesis for the Mean	
Null Hypothesis	$\mu = 8$
Level of Significance	0.05
Population Standard Deviation	0.15
Sample Size	50
Sample Mean	7.983
Standard Error of the Mean	0.021213203
Z Test Statistic	–0.80138769

Two-Tail Test	
Lower Critical Value	–1.95996108
Upper Critical Value	1.959961082
p-value	0.422907113
Do not reject the null hypothesis	

Decision rule: Reject H_0 if $Z < -1.96$ or $Z > 1.96$. Test statistic: $Z = \frac{\bar{X} - \mu}{\sigma/\sqrt{n}} = \frac{7.983 - 8}{0.15/\sqrt{50}} = -0.8$. Decision: Because $-1.96 < Z < 1.96$, do not reject H_0. There is insufficient evidence to conclude that the population average amount of salad dressing dispensed is different from 8 ounces for the 0.05 significance level.

(c) p-value $= 0.423$. This is the probability of obtaining a test statistic $|Z|$ equal to or greater than the result obtained from the sample data given that the null hypothesis is true.

(d)

Z Test of Hypothesis for the Mean	
Null Hypothesis	$\mu = 8$
Level of Significance	0.05
Population Standard Deviation	0.05
Sample Size	50
Sample Mean	7.983
Standard Error of the Mean	0.007071068
Z Test Statistic	–2.40416306

Two-Tail Test	
Lower Critical Value	–1.95996108
Upper Critical Value	1.959961082
p-value	0.016209529
Reject the null hypothesis	

Decision rule: Reject H_0 if $Z < -1.96$ or $Z > 1.96$. Test statistic: $Z = \frac{\bar{X} - \mu}{\sigma/\sqrt{n}} = \frac{7.983 - 8}{0.05/\sqrt{50}} = -2.4$. Decision: Because $Z < -1.96$, reject H_0. There is sufficient evidence to conclude that the population average amount of salad dressing dispensed is different from 8 ounces for the 0.05 significance level.

(e)

Z Test of Hypothesis for the Mean	
Null Hypothesis	$\mu = 8$
Level of Significance	0.05
Population Standard Deviation	0.15
Sample Size	50
Sample Mean	7.952
Standard Error of the Mean	0.021213203
Z Test Statistic	–2.2627417

Two-Tail Test	
Lower Critical Value	–1.95996108
Upper Critical Value	1.959961082
p-value	0.023651543
Reject the null hypothesis	

Decision rule: Reject H_0 if $Z < -1.96$ or $Z > 1.96$. Test statistic: $Z = \frac{\bar{X} - \mu}{\sigma/\sqrt{n}} = \frac{7.952 - 8}{0.15/\sqrt{50}} = -2.26$. Decision: Because $Z < -1.96$, reject H_0. There is sufficient evidence to conclude that the population average amount of salad dressing dispensed is different from 8 ounces for the 0.05 significance level.

3. (a) $H_0: \mu = 375$ hours; the light bulbs in a large shipment have an average life of 375 hours.
$H_1: \mu \neq 375$ hours; the light bulbs in a large shipment have an average life that differs from 375 hours.

(b)

Z Test of Hypothesis for the Mean	
Null Hypothesis	$\mu = 375$
Level of Significance	0.05
Population Standard Deviation	100
Sample Size	50
Sample Mean	350
Standard Error of the Mean	14.14213562
Z Test Statistic	−1.76776695

Two-Tail Test	
Lower Critical Value	−1.95996108
Upper Critical Value	1.959961082
p-value	0.077099777
Do not reject the null hypothesis	

Decision rule: Reject H_0 if $Z < -1.96$ or $Z > 1.96$. Test statistic: $Z = \frac{\overline{X} - \mu}{\sigma/\sqrt{n}} = \frac{350 - 375}{100/\sqrt{50}} = -1.77$. Decision: Because $-1.96 < Z < 1.96$, do not reject H_0. There is insufficient evidence that the average light bulb life is different from 375 hours for the 0.05 significance level.

(c) Based on the result of Chapter 8, problem 4, the null hypothesis is rejected, because 375 hours does not belong to the central confidence interval. The conclusions for each problem will be different due to the different sample sizes.

4. (a) $H_0: \mu = 2$ liters; the average amount of soft drink placed in the bottles is 2 liters.
$H_1: \mu \neq 2$ liters; the average amount of soft drink placed in the bottles differs from 2 liters.

(b)

Z Test of Hypothesis for the Mean	
Null Hypothesis	$\mu = 2$
Level of Significance	0.05
Population Standard Deviation	0.05
Sample Size	100
Sample Mean	1.99
Standard Error of the Mean	0.005
Z Test Statistic	−2

Two-Tail Test	
Lower Critical Value	−1.95996108
Upper Critical Value	1.959961082
p-value	0.045500124
Reject the null hypothesis	

Decision rule: Reject H_0 if $Z < -1.96$ or $Z > 1.96$. Test statistic: $Z = \frac{\overline{X} - \mu}{\sigma/\sqrt{n}} = \frac{1.99 - 2}{0.05/\sqrt{50}} = -2$. Decision: Because $Z < -1.96$, reject H_0. There is sufficient evidence to conclude that the population average amount of soft drink placed in bottles is different from 2.0 liters for the 0.05 significance level.

(c) Based on the confidence interval constructed in Chapter 8, problem 5, we must reject the null hypothesis because 2.0 liters does not belong to this confidence interval. These two procedures lead to the construction of *the same* confidence interval, and therefore lead to *the same* conclusion.

5. (a) $H_0: \mu = 9.0$; the average energy efficiency rating of window-mounted large-capacity air-conditioning units is 9.0.
$H_1: \mu \neq 9.0$; the average energy efficiency rating of window-mounted large-capacity air-conditioning units differs from 9.0.
Decision rule: Reject H_0 if $|t| > 2.03$.
Test statistic: $t = \frac{\overline{X} - \mu}{S/\sqrt{n}} = \frac{9.211 - 9}{0.3838/\sqrt{36}} = 3.30$
Decision: Because $|t| > 2.03$, reject H_0.
There is sufficient evidence to conclude that the average energy rating of window-mounted large-capacity air-conditioning units is not equal to 9.0 for the 0.05 significance level.

(b) The following assumptions are made: (1) The computed numerical data are independently drawn and represent a random sample from a population that is normally distributed. (2) The sample population is not very small or very skewed. Note that the t test is robust, so if the sample size is large and the central limit theorem applies, the t test does not loose much power even if the distribution departs from normal.

(c) p-value = 0.002. This is the probability of obtaining a test statistic $|t|$ equal to or greater than the result obtained from the sample data given that the null hypothesis is true.

(d)

t Test of Hypothesis for the Mean	
Null Hypothesis	$\mu = 9$
Level of Significance	0.05
Sample Size	36
Sample Mean	9.155555556
Sample Standard Deviation	0.410187723
Standard Error of the Mean	0.068364621
Degrees of Freedom	35
t Test Statistic	2.275380955

Two-Tail Test	
Lower Critical Value	−2.03011041
Upper Critical Value	2.030110409
p-value	0.029115712
Reject the null hypothesis	

Decision rule: Reject H_0 if $|t| > 2.03$. Test statistic: $t = \dfrac{\overline{X}-\mu}{S/\sqrt{n}} = \dfrac{9.155-9}{0.41/\sqrt{36}} = 2.275$. Decision: Because $|t| > 2.03$, reject H_0. There is sufficient evidence to conclude that the average energy rating of window-mounted large-capacity air-conditioning units is not equal to 9.0 and EER for the 0.05 significance level.

6. (a) $H_0: \mu = 260$ Brinell units; the average hardness of the plastic blocks is 260 (in Brinell units).
$H_1: \mu > 260$ Brinell units; the average hardness of the plastic blocks is greater than 260 (in Brinell units).

t Test of Hypothesis for the Mean	
Null Hypothesis	$\mu = 260$
Level of Significance	0.05
Sample Size	50
Sample Mean	267.64
Sample Standard Deviation	24.44193452
Standard Error of the Mean	3.456611529
Degrees of Freedom	49
t Test Statistic	2.210257049

Upper Tail Test	
Upper Critical Value	1.676551165
p-value	0.015894144
Reject the null hypothesis	

Decision rule: Reject H_0 if $|t| > 1.677$.

Test statistic: $t = \dfrac{\overline{X}-\mu}{S/\sqrt{n}} = \dfrac{267.64-260}{24.44/\sqrt{50}} = 2.21$.

Decision: Because $|t| > 1.677$, reject H_0.

The average hardness of the plastic block exceeds 260 (in Brinell units) for the 0.05 significance level.

(b) The following assumptions are made: (1) The computed numerical data are drawn independently and represent a random sample from the population that is normally distributed. (2) The sample population is not very small or very skewed. Note that the t test is robust, so if the sample size is large and the central limit theorem applies, the t test does not loose much power even if the distribution departs from normal.

(c) p-value = 0.016. This is the probability of obtaining the test statistic $|t|$ equal to or greater than the result obtained from the sample data given that the null hypothesis is true.

(d)

t Test of Hypothesis for the Mean	
Null Hypothesis	$\mu = 260$
Level of Significance	0.05
Sample Size	50
Sample Mean	266.64
Sample Standard Deviation	24.79590157
Standard Error of the Mean	3.506670029
Degrees of Freedom	49
t Test Statistic	1.893534306

Upper Tail Test	
Upper Critical Value	1.676551165
p-value	0.03209957
Reject the null hypothesis	

Decision rule: Reject H_0 if $t > 1.677$. Test statistic: $t = \frac{\bar{X} - \mu}{S/\sqrt{n}} = \frac{266.64 - 260}{24.8/\sqrt{50}} = 1.89$. Decision: Because $t > 1.677$, reject H_0. The average hardness of the plastic block exceeds 260 (in Brinell units) for the 0.05 significance level.

7. (a) $H_0: \mu = 15$ ounces; the average weight of the raisin boxes is 15 ounces.
$H_1: \mu \neq 15$ ounces; the average weight of the raisin boxes differs from 15 ounces.

t Test of Hypothesis for the Mean	
Null Hypothesis	$\mu = 15$
Level of Significance	0.05
Sample Size	30
Sample Mean	15.11333333
Sample Standard Deviation	0.405763081
Standard Error of the Mean	0.074081864
Degrees of Freedom	29
t Test Statistic	1.529839112

Two-Tail Test	
Lower Critical Value	–2.04523076
Upper Critical Value	2.045230758
p-value	0.136892688
Do not reject the null hypothesis	

Decision rule: Reject H_0 if $|t| > 2.05$.

Test statistic: $t = \frac{\bar{X} - \mu}{S/\sqrt{n}} = \frac{15.1133 - 15}{0.4058/\sqrt{30}} = 1.53$.

Decision: Because $|t| < 2.05$, do not reject H_0.

There is insufficient evidence to conclude that the average weight of the raisin boxes is different from 15 ounces for the 0.05 significance level.

(b) The following assumptions are made: (1) The computed numerical data must be independently drawn and represent a random sample from a population that is normally distributed. (2) The sample population is not very small or very skewed. Note that the *t* test is robust, so if the sample size is large and the central limit theorem applies, the *t* test does not loose much power even if the distribution departs from normal.

(c)

t Test of Hypothesis for the Mean	
Null Hypothesis	$\mu = 15$
Level of Significance	0.05
Sample Size	30
Sample Mean	15.18
Sample Standard Deviation	0.490882386
Standard Error of the Mean	0.089622452
Degrees of Freedom	29
t Test Statistic	2.008425299

Two-Tail Test	
Lower Critical Value	–2.04523076
Upper Critical Value	2.045230758
p-value	0.05399146
Do not reject the null hypothesis	

Decision rule: Reject H_0 if $|t| > 2.045$. Test statistic: $t = \dfrac{\overline{X}-\mu}{S/\sqrt{n}} = \dfrac{15.18-15}{0.4909/\sqrt{30}} = 2.008$. Decision: Because $|t| < 2.045$, do not reject H_0. There is insufficient evidence to conclude that the mean weight per box is different from 15 ounces for the 0.05 significance level.

8. (a) $H_0: \mu = 140$ ampere-hours; the average battery capacity is 140 ampere hours.
$H_1: \mu \neq 140$ ampere-hours; the average battery capacity differs from 140 ampere hours.

t Test of Hypothesis for the Mean	
Null Hypothesis	$\mu = 140$
Level of Significance	0.05
Sample Size	20
Sample Mean	138.47
Sample Standard Deviation	2.658867982
Standard Error of the Mean	0.594540955
Degrees of Freedom	19
t Test Statistic	–2.57341397

Lower-Tail Test	
Lower Critical Value	–1.72913133
p-value	0.00930502
Reject the null hypothesis	

Decision rule: Reject H_0 if $t < -1.73$.

Test statistic: $t = \dfrac{\overline{X}-\mu}{S/\sqrt{n}} = \dfrac{138.47-140}{2.659/\sqrt{20}} = -2.57$.

Decision: Because $t < -1.73$, reject H_0.

The average number of ampere-hours is less than 140 for the 0.05 significance level.

(b) The following assumptions are made: (1) The computed numerical data must be independently drawn and represent a random sample from a population that is normally distributed. (2) The sample population is not very small or very skewed. Note that the *t* test is robust, so if the sample size is large and the central limit theorem applies, the *t* test does not loose much power even if the distribution departs from normal.

(c)

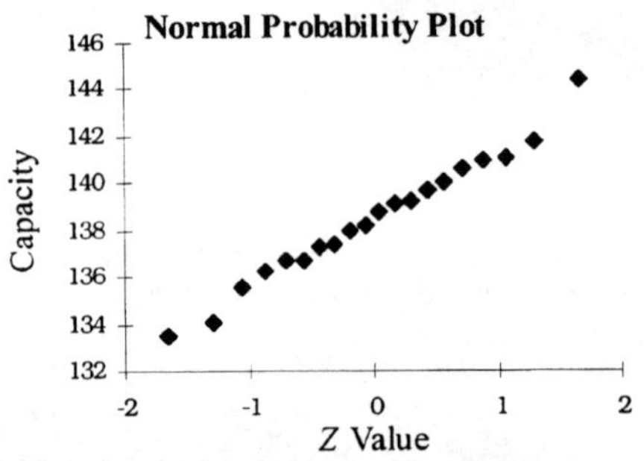

The normal probability plot shows an approximately linear increase in capacity with increasing z values. This suggests that the assumptions made are not violated and that the results of the *t* test are valid.

(d)

t Test of Hypothesis for the Mean	
Null Hypothesis	$\mu = 140$
Level of Significance	0.05
Sample Size	20
Sample Mean	139.1
Sample Standard Deviation	3.03505831
Standard Error of the Mean	0.67865967
Degrees of Freedom	19
t Test Statistic	–1.32614334

Lower-Tail Test	
Lower Critical Value	–1.72913133
p-value	0.100257215
Do not reject the null hypothesis	

Decision rule: Reject H_0 if $t < -1.729$. Test statistic: $t = \dfrac{\overline{X} - \mu}{S/\sqrt{n}} = \dfrac{138.47 - 140}{2.659/\sqrt{20}} = -2.573$. Decision: Because $t > -1.729$, do not reject H_0. There is sufficient evidence to conclude that the average number of ampere-hours is less than 140 for the 0.05 significance level.

9. (a) $H_0: \mu = 350$ psi; the mean bursting pressure of the PVC irrigation pipe is 350 psi.
$H_1: \mu < 350$ psi; the mean bursting pressure of the PVC irrigation pipe is less than 350 psi.

t Test of Hypothesis for the Mean	
Null Hypothesis	$\mu = 350$
Level of Significance	0.05
Sample Size	10
Sample Mean	407.3
Sample Standard Deviation	28.86385668
Standard Error of the Mean	9.127552915
Degrees of Freedom	9
t Test Statistic	6.277695734

Lower-Tail Test	
Lower Critical Value	−1.83311386
p-value	0.999927613
Do not reject the null hypothesis	

Decision rule: Reject H_0 if $t < -1.83$.

Test statistic: $t = \dfrac{\overline{X} - \mu}{S/\sqrt{n}} = \dfrac{407.3 - 350}{28.864/\sqrt{10}} = 6.28$.

Decision: Because $t > -1.83$, do not reject H_0.

There is insufficient evidence to conclude that the average bursting pressure is less than 350 psi for the 0.05 significance level.

(b) The following assumptions are made: (1) The numerical data must be independently drawn and represent a random sample from a population that is normally distributed. (2) The sample population is not very small or very skewed. Note that the *t* test is robust, so if the sample size is large and the central limit theorem applies, the *t* test does not loose much power even if the distribution departs from normal.

10. $H_0: \mu_1 = \mu_2$; the mean surface hardness of the polished plates is the same as the mean surface hardness of the untreated plates.
$H_1: \mu_1 \neq \mu_2$; the mean surface hardness of the polished plates is different from the mean surface hardness of the untreated plates.

t Test for Differences in Two Means	
Hypothesized Difference	0
Level of Significance	0.05

Population 1 Sample	
Sample Mean	163.4
Sample Size	20
Sample Standard Deviation	10.2

Population 2 Sample	
Sample Mean	156.9
Sample Size	20
Sample Standard Deviation	6.4
Population 1 Sample Degrees of Freedom	19
Population 2 Sample Degrees of Freedom	19
Total Degrees of Freedom	38
Pooled Variance	72.5
Difference in Sample Means	6.5
t-Test Statistic	2.414039

Two-Tail Test	
Lower Critical Value	−2.02439
Upper Critical Value	2.024394
p-value	0.020702
Reject the null hypothesis	

Decision rule: Reject H_0 if $|t| > 2.02439$.

Test statistic: $t = \dfrac{(\bar{X}_1 - \bar{X}_2) - (\mu_1 - \mu_2)}{\sqrt{S_p^2(1/n_1 + 1/n_2)}} = \dfrac{163.4 - 156.9}{\sqrt{72.5(1/20 + 1/20)}} = 2.41$.

Decision: Because $|t| > 2.02$, reject H_0.

There is a significant difference in the average surface hardness between the untreated and the polished steel plates for the 0.05 significance level.

11. (a) $H_0: \mu_1 = \mu_2$; the mean talking time of the nickel-cadmium batteries is the same as the mean talking time of the nickel-metal hydride batteries.

$H_1: \mu_1 \neq \mu_2$; the mean talking time of the nickel-cadmium batteries is different than the mean talking time of the nickel-metal hydride batteries.

t-Test: Two-Sample Assuming Equal Variances

	Cadmium	Metal Hydride
Mean	70.748	79.728
Variance	195.7884	226.0296
Observations	25	25
Pooled Variance	210.909	
Hypothesized Mean Difference	0	
df	48	
t Stat	–2.18617	
$p(T \leq t)$ one-tail	0.016856	
t Critical one-tail	1.677224	
$p(T \leq t)$ two-tail	0.033712	
t Critical two-tail	2.010634	

Decision rule: Reject H_0 if $|t| > 2.01$.

Test statistic: $t = \dfrac{(\bar{X}_1 - \bar{X}_2) - (\mu_1 - \mu_2)}{\sqrt{S_p^2(1/n_1 + 1/n_2)}} = \dfrac{70.748 - 79.728}{\sqrt{210.909(1/25 + 1/25)}} = -2.18$.

Decision: Because $t < -2.01$, reject H_0.

There is a significant difference between the two means because the two-tail p-value is less than 0.05.

(b) In part (a) it is assumed that numerical data are sampled from normally distributed populations having equal variances. The pooled t test is not sensitive to moderate departures from normality if the sample size is large.

(c) $p(T \leq t) = 0.034$. This is the probability of obtaining a test statistic $|t|$ equal to or greater than the result obtained from the sample data given that the null hypothesis is true.

(d) $H_0: \mu_1 = \mu_2$, $H_1: \mu_1 \neq \mu_2$

t-Test: Two-Sample Assuming Unequal Variances

	Cadmium	Metal Hydride
Mean	70.748	79.728
Variance	195.7884	226.0296
Observations	25	25
Hypothesized Mean Difference	0	
df	48	
t Stat	–2.18617	
$p(T \leq t)$ one-tail	0.016856	
t Critical one-tail	1.677224	
$p(T \leq t)$ two-tail	0.033712	
t Critical two-tail	2.010634	

Decision rule: Reject H_0 if $|t| > 2.010634$. Test statistic: $t = \frac{(\bar{X}_1 - \bar{X}_2) - (\mu_1 - \mu_2)}{\sqrt{S_p^2(1/n_1 + 1/n_2)}} = -2.18617$. Decision: Because $|t| < -2.010634$, reject H_0. There is a significant difference between the two means because the two-tail p-value is less than 0.05.

(e) In the separate variance t test, it is assumed that the data are sampled from two normally distributed populations.

(f) $p(T \le t)$ two-tail = 0.034. This is the probability of obtaining a test statistic $|t|$ equal to or greater than the result obtained from the sample data, given that the null hypothesis is true.

(g) We must reject the null hypothesis and conclude that the population means are unequal. This is true whether we assume that the populations have equal variances.

12. (a) $H_0: \mu_1 = \mu_2$; the average weight of coffee filter packs filled without magnets is the same as the weight of packs filled with magnets.
$H_1: \mu_1 \ne \mu_2$; the average weight of coffee filter packs filled without magnets is the same as the weight of packs filled with magnets.

t-Test: Two-Sample Assuming Equal Variances

	With Magnets	Without Magnets
Mean	19.72333	20.40222
Variance	1.601161	0.199768
Observations	30	45
Pooled Variance	0.756486	
Hypothesized Mean Difference	0	
df	73	
t Stat	−3.31158	
$p(T \le t)$ one-tail	0.000722	
t Critical one-tail	1.665996	
$p(T \le t)$ two-tail	0.001445	
t Critical two-tail	1.992998	

Decision rule: Reject H_0 if $|t| > 1.99$.

Test statistic: $t = \frac{(\bar{X}_1 - \bar{X}_2) - (\mu_1 - \mu_2)}{\sqrt{S_p^2(1/n_1 + 1/n_2)}} = \frac{19.7233 - 20.4022}{\sqrt{0.7564(1/30 + 1/45)}} = -3.31$.

Decision: Because $t < -1.99$, reject H_0.

There is a significant difference between the two means because the two-tail p-value is less than 0.05.

(b) It is assumed that the data are sampled from normally distributed populations having equal variances.

(c) $p(T \le t)$ two-tail = 0.001. This is the probability of obtaining a test statistic $|t|$ equal to or greater than the result obtained from the sample data given that the null hypothesis is true.

13. (a) $H_0: \mu_1 = \mu_2$; the mean airflow value observed for Carnes 3-Way diffusers is the same as the mean airflow value observed for Krueger 4-Way diffusers.
$H_1: \mu_1 \ne \mu_2$; the mean airflow value observed for Carnes 3-Way diffusers is different than the mean airflow value observed for Krueger 4-Way diffusers.

t-Test: Two-Sample Assuming Equal Variances	Carnes	Kruger
Mean	247.5	244.3
Variance	1557.398	732.6633
Observations	50	50
Pooled Variance	1145.031	
Hypothesized Mean Difference	0	
df	98	
t Stat	0.472837	
$p(T \le t)$ one-tail	0.31869	
t Critical one-tail	1.660551	
$p(T \le t)$ two-tail	0.637381	
t Critical two-tail	1.984467	

Decision rule: Reject H_0 if $|t| > 1.98$.

Test statistic: $t = \dfrac{(\bar{X}_1 - \bar{X}_2) - (\mu_1 - \mu_2)}{\sqrt{S_p^2(1/n_1 + 1/n_2)}} = \dfrac{247.5 - 244.3}{\sqrt{1145.031(1/50 + 1/50)}} = 0.473$.

Decision: Because $|t| < 1.98$, do not reject H_0.

There is no significant difference between the two means because the two-tail p-value is greater than 0.05.

(b) It is assumed that the data are sampled from normally distributed populations having equal variances.

(c) $p(T \le t)$ two-tail $= 0.637$. This is the probability of obtaining a test statistic $|t|$ equal to or greater than the result obtained from the sample data given that the null hypothesis is true.

14. (a) $H_0: \mu_1 = \mu_2$; the mean time to clear problems for Central Office 1 is the same as the mean time for Central Office 2.
$H_1: \mu_1 \ne \mu_2$; the mean time to clear problems for Central Office 1 is different than the mean time for Central Office 2.

t-Test: Two-Sample Assuming Equal Variances	Office 1	Office 2
Mean	2.214	2.0115
Variance	2.951657	3.57855
Observations	20	20
Pooled Variance	3.265104	
Hypothesized Mean Difference	0	
df	38	
t Stat	0.354386	
$p(T \le t)$ one-tail	0.362504	
t Critical one-tail	1.685953	
$p(T \le t)$ two-tail	0.725009	
t Critical two-tail	2.024394	

Decision rule: Reject H_0 if $|t| > 2.02$.

Test statistic: $t = \dfrac{(\bar{X}_1 - \bar{X}_2) - (\mu_1 - \mu_2)}{\sqrt{S_p^2(1/n_1 + 1/n_2)}} = \dfrac{2.214 - 2.0115}{\sqrt{3.265(1/20 + 1/20)}} = 0.354$.

Decision: Since $|t| < 2.02$, do not reject H_0.

There is no significant difference between the two means because the two-tail p-value is greater than 0.05.

(b) It is assumed that the pressing time in each office is normally distributed and that the variances in the two offices are equal.

(c) There are some doubts about the validity of the assumptions made in part (b) because the box-and-whisker plots both have long tails.

(c)

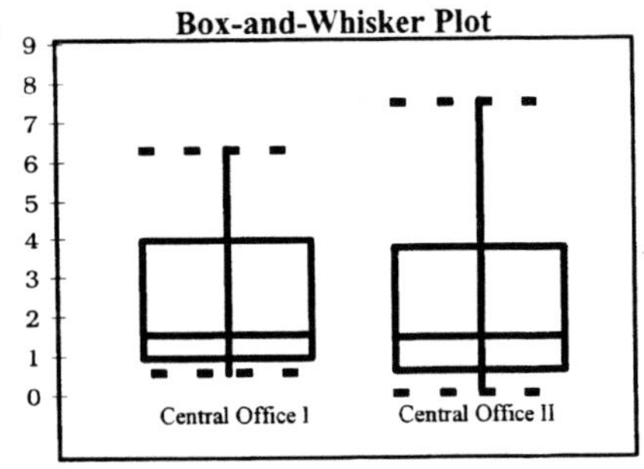

(d) $p(T \leq t)$ two-tail = 0.725. This is the probability of obtaining a test statistic $|t|$ equal to or greater than the result obtained from the sample data, given that the null hypothesis is true.

15. (a) $H_0: \mu_1 = \mu_2$; the average processing time in Plant A is the same as the average processing time in Plant B.
$H_1: \mu_1 \neq \mu_2$; the average processing time in Plant A is different than the average processing time in Plant B.

***t*-Test: Two-Sample Assuming Equal Variances**

	Plant A	Plant B
Mean	9.382	11.3535
Variance	15.98123	26.27748
Observations	20	20
Pooled Variance	21.12935	
Hypothesized Mean Difference	0	
df	38	
t Stat	−1.35629	
$p(T \leq t)$ one-tail	0.091505	
t Critical one-tail	1.685953	
$p(T \leq t)$ two-tail	0.18301	
t Critical two-tail	2.024394	

Decision rule: Reject H_0 if $|t| > 2.02$.

Test statistic: $t = \dfrac{(\bar{X}_1 - \bar{X}_2) - (\mu_1 - \mu_2)}{\sqrt{S_p^2(1/n_1 + 1/n_2)}} = \dfrac{9.382 - 11.3535}{\sqrt{21.2935(1/20 + 1/20)}} = -1.36$.

Decision: Since $|t| < 2.02$, do not reject H_0.

There is no significant difference between the two means because the two-tail *p*-value is greater than 0.05.

(b) It is assumed that the processing time in each plant is normally distributed and that the variances in the two plants are equal.

(c) There are some doubts about the validity of the assumptions made in part (b) because the data from both plants are slightly skewed. This is shown below in the box-and-whisker plot. The skewness is probably not enough to seriously affect the results..

(c)

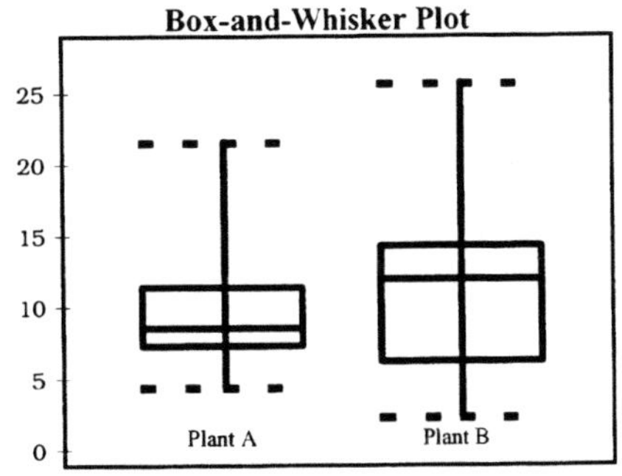

(d) $p(T \leq t)$ two-tail = 0.183. This is the probability of obtaining a test statistic $|t|$ equal to or greater than the result obtained from the sample data, given that the null hypothesis is true.

16. $H_0: \mu_1 = \mu_2$; the average weight of cans filled on line A is the same as the average weight of cans filled on line B.
$H_1: \mu_1 \neq \mu_2$; the average weight of cans filled on line A is different than the average weight of cans filled on line B.

t Test for Differences in Two Means	
Hypothesized Difference	0
Level of Significance	0.05

Population 1 Sample	
Sample Mean	8.005
Sample Size	11
Sample Standard Deviation	0.012

Population 2 Sample	
Sample Mean	7.997
Sample Size	16
Sample Standard Deviation	0.005
Population 1 Sample Degrees of Freedom	10
Population 2 Sample Degrees of Freedom	15
Total Degrees of Freedom	25
Pooled Variance	8.45×10^{-5}
Difference in Sample Means	0.008
t-Test Statistic	2.22196

Two-Tail Test	
Lower Critical Value	–2.05954
Upper Critical Value	2.059537
p-value	0.024318
Reject the null hypothesis	

Decision rule: Reject H_0 if $|t| > 2.06$.

Test statistic: $t = \dfrac{(\bar{X}_1 - \bar{X}_2) - (\mu_1 - \mu_2)}{\sqrt{S_p^2(1/n_1 + 1/n_2)}} = \dfrac{8.005 - 7.997}{\sqrt{8.45\times10^{-5}(1/11 + 1/16)}} = 2.22$.

Decision: Since $|t| > 2.06$, reject H_0.
There is a significant difference between the mean weights of cans filled on different lines because the two-tail *p*-value is less than 0.05.

17. (a) $f_l = 0.429$; $f_u = 2.20$. (b) $f_l = 0.362$; $f_u = 2.57$. (c) $f_l = 0.297$; $f_u = 3.09$.
(d) $f_l = 0.258$; $f_u = 3.50$.

18. $H_0: \sigma_1^2 = \sigma_2^2$; the two computer models have the same population variance.
$H_1: \sigma_1^2 \neq \sigma_2^2$; the two computer models have different population variances.

F-Test Two-Sample for Variances	Model 1	Model 2
Mean	–1.07833	–2.18083
Variance	1.036706	5.350717
Observations	12	12
df	11	11
F	0.193751	
$P(F \leq f)$ one-tail	0.005649	
F Lower Critical one-tail	0.35487	

Decision rule: Reject H_0 if $F < 0.355$.

Test statistic: $F = \dfrac{s_1^2}{s_2^2} = \dfrac{1.036706}{5.350717} = 0.194$.

Decision: Since $F < 0.355$, reject H_0.
There is a significant difference between the two variances because the *p*-value is less than 0.05.

19. $H_0: \sigma_1^2 = \sigma_2^2$; the two pumping plants have the same population variance.
$H_1: \sigma_1^2 \neq \sigma_2^2$; the two pumping plants have different population variances.

F-Test Two-Sample for Variances	Polonio Pass	Devil's Den
Mean	4076.5	4275.25
Variance	277676.6	334540.7
Observations	20	20
df	19	19
F	0.830023	
$P(F \le f)$ one-tail	0.344415	
F Lower Critical one-tail	0.461201	

Decision rule: Reject H_0 if $F < 0.461$.

Test statistic: $F = \frac{s_1^2}{s_2^2} = \frac{277676.6}{334540.7} = 0.830$.

Decision: Since $F > 0.830$, reject H_0.

There is no significant difference between the two variances because the p-value is greater than 0.05.

20. (a) $H_0: \sigma_1^2 = \sigma_2^2$; the two cleaning methods have the same population variance.
$H_1: \sigma_1^2 \neq \sigma_2^2$; the two cleaning methods have different population variances.

F Test for Differences in Two Means	
Level of Significance	0.05

Population 1 Sample	
Sample Size	10
Sample Standard Deviation	80452.4

Population 2 Sample	
Sample Size	5
Sample Standard Deviation	44328.8
F-Test Statistic	3.293867
Population 1 Sample Degrees of Freedom	9
Population 2 Sample Degrees of Freedom	4

Two-Tail Test	
Lower Critical Value	0.211951
Upper Critical Value	8.904635
p-value	0.263094
Do not reject the null hypothesis	

Decision rule: Reject H_0 if $F < 0.212$ or if $F > 8.90$.

Test statistic: $F = \frac{s_1^2}{s_2^2} = \frac{80452.4^2}{44328.8^2} = 3.29$.

Decision: Since $0.212 < F < 8.90$, do not reject H_0.

There is no significant difference between the two variances because the p-value is greater than 0.05.

(b) It is assumed that the observed numerical data are independently sampled from the normally distributed populations.

21. (a) $H_0: \sigma_1^2 = \sigma_2^2$; the two battery types have the same population variance in talking time.
$H_1: \sigma_1^2 \neq \sigma_2^2$; the two battery types have different population variances in talking time.

F-Test Two-Sample for Variances	Cadmium	Metal Hydride
Mean	70.748	79.728
Variance	195.7884	226.0296
Observations	25	25
df	24	24
F	0.866207	
$P(F \le f)$ one-tail	0.363909	
F Lower Critical one-tail	0.504093	

Decision rule: Reject H_0 if $F < 0.504$.

Test statistic: $F = \frac{s_1^2}{s_2^2} = \frac{195.7884}{226.0296} = 0.866$.

Decision: Since $F > 0.504$, do not reject H_0.

There is no significant difference between the two variances because the p-value is greater than 0.05.

(b) Do not reject the null hypothesis, $\sigma_1^2 = \sigma_2^2$; it is, therefore, necessary to use a pooled-variance t test to calculate the difference in the two means.

22. (a) $H_0: \sigma_1^2 = \sigma_2^2$; the two diffuser types have the same population variance in airflow measurements.
$H_1: \sigma_1^2 \neq \sigma_2^2$; the two diffuser types have different population variances in airflow measurements.

F-Test Two-Sample for Variances

	Carnes	Krueger
Mean	247.5	244.3
Variance	1557.398	732.6633
Observations	50	50
df	49	49
F	2.125667	
$P(F \geq f)$ one-tail	0.004718	
F Upper Critical one-tail	1.60729	

Decision rule: Reject H_0 if $F > 1.61$.

Test statistic: $F = \frac{s_1^2}{s_2^2} = \frac{1557.398}{732.6633} = 2.13$.

Decision: Since $F > 1.61$, reject H_0.

There is a significant difference between the two variances in air flow measurements because the p-value is less than 0.05.

(b) Reject the null hypothesis, $\sigma_1^2 = \sigma_2^2$; it is therefore necessary to use a separate-variance t test to calculate the difference in the two means.

23. (a) $H_0: \sigma_1^2 = \sigma_2^2$; the two lines have the same population variance.
$H_1: \sigma_1^2 > \sigma_2^2$; the variance in line A is greater than the variance in line B.

F Test for Differences in Two Means	
Level of Significance	0.05

Population 1 Sample	
Sample Size	11
Sample Standard Deviation	0.012

Population 2 Sample	
Sample Size	16
Sample Standard Deviation	0.005
F-Test Statistic	5.76
Population 1 Sample Degrees of Freedom	10
Population 2 Sample Degrees of Freedom	15

Upper-Tail Test	
Upper Critical Value	2.543715
p-value	0.001333
Reject the null hypothesis	

Decision rule: Reject H_0 if $F > 2.54$.

Test statistic: $F = \frac{s_1^2}{s_2^2} = \frac{0.012^2}{0.005^2} = 5.76$.

Decision: Since $F > 2.54$, reject H_0.

The variance in Line A is greater than the variance in Line B because the p-value for the upper-tail test is less than 0.05.

24. (a) $H_0: \mu_1 = \mu_2$; the average flow rate measurements taken by the rotameter and the weigh tank are the same
$H_1: \mu_1 \neq \mu_2$; the average flow rate measurements taken by the rotameter and the weigh tank are different.

t-Test: Paired Two Sample for Means	Rotameter	Weight Tank
Mean	0.19597	0.19581
Variance	0.004448	0.004671
Observations	10	10
Pearson Correlation	0.988132	
Hypothesized Mean Difference	0	
df	9	
t Stat	0.048041	
$p(T \le t)$ one-tail	0.481366	
t Critical one-tail	1.833114	
$p(T \le t)$ two-tail	0.962733	
t Critical two-tail	2.262159	

Decision rule: Reject H_0 if $|t| > 2.26$.

Test statistic: $t = \dfrac{\overline{D} - \mu_{\overline{D}}}{S_{\overline{D}}/\sqrt{n}} = \dfrac{1.6 \times 10^{-4} - 0}{0.010532/\sqrt{10}} = 0.0480$.

Decision: Because $|t| < 2.26$, do not reject H_0.

There is no significant difference between the two means because the p-value is greater than 0.05.

(b) Two series of observations are obtained from the same set of items or individuals. The sample of the pair wise differences between two observations drawn for the same items must be a set of independent, identically normally distributed values.

(c) $p(T \le t)$ two-tail $= 0.963$. This is the probability of obtaining a test statistic $|t|$ equal to or greater than the result obtained from the sample data given that the null hypothesis is true.

25. (a) $H_0: \mu_1 = \mu_2$; the average thickness measurements obtained by the nondestructive and the destructive method are the same.
$H_1: \mu_1 \neq \mu_2$; the average thickness measurements obtained by the nondestructive and the destructive method are different.

t-Test: Paired Two Sample for Means	Nondestructive Method	Destructive Method
Mean	229.1818	249.3636
Variance	29277.16	38313.85
Observations	11	11
Pearson Correlation	0.991909	
Hypothesized Mean Difference	0	
df	10	
t Stat	−1.97488	
$p(T \le t)$ one-tail	0.03826	
t Critical one-tail	1.812462	
$p(T \le t)$ two-tail	0.076521	
t Critical two-tail	2.228139	

Decision rule: Reject H_0 if $|t| > 2.23$.

Test statistic: $t = \dfrac{\overline{D} - \mu_{\overline{D}}}{S_{\overline{D}}/\sqrt{n}} = \dfrac{-20.1818 - 0}{33.89242/\sqrt{11}} = -1.97$.

Decision: Because $|t| < 2.23$, do not reject H_0.

There is no significant difference in the average measurement of thickness between the two methods because the p-value is greater than 0.05.

(b) It is assumed that the thickness in each method is normally distributed and that the variances in the two methods are equal.

(c) $p(T \le t)$ two-tail = 0.077. This is the probability of obtaining a test statistic $|t|$ equal to or greater than the result obtained from the sample data given that the null hypothesis is true.

(d) $H_0: \mu_1 = \mu_2$, $H_1: \mu_1 \ne \mu_2$

t-Test: Two-Sample Assuming Unequal Variances

	Nondestructive Method	**Destructive Method**
Mean	229.1818	249.3636
Variance	29277.16	38313.85
Observations	11	11
Hypothesized Mean Difference	0	
df	20	
t Stat	–0.25746	
$p(T \le t)$ one-tail	0.399727	
t Critical one-tail	1.724718	
$p(T \le t)$ two-tail	0.799453	
t Critical two-tail	2.085962	

There is no significant difference in the average thickness between the two methods because the p-value is greater than 0.05.

(e) For the significance level 0.05 (a) and (d) provides the same results.

(f) It is most appropriate to use the paired test because the data is obtained from repeated measurements of the same sample.

26. (a) $H_0: \mu_1 = \mu_2$; the average compressive strength of 40 samples of concrete at 2 days is the same as at 7 days.
$H_1: \mu_1 < \mu_2$; the average compressive strength of 40 samples of concrete at 2 days is less than at 7 days.

t-Test: Paired Two Sample for Means

	Two days	**Seven days**
Mean	2.991	3.544125
Variance	0.246102	0.25359
Observations	40	40
Pearson Correlation	0.721256	
Hypothesized Mean Difference	0	
df	39	
t Stat	–9.37209	
$p(T \le t)$ one-tail	7.77×10^{-12}	
t Critical one-tail	1.684875	
$p(T \le t)$ two-tail	1.55×10^{-11}	
t Critical two-tail	2.022689	

Decision rule: Reject H_0 if $|t| > 2.02$.

Test statistic: $t = \dfrac{\overline{D} - \mu_{\overline{D}}}{S_{\overline{D}}/\sqrt{n}} = \dfrac{-0.55279 - 0}{0.373329/\sqrt{40}} = -9.37$.

Decision: Because $|t| > 2.02$, reject H_0.

There is sufficient evidence to conclude that the average strength is less at 2 days than at seven days because of the very small one-tail p-value.

(b) Two series of observations are obtained from the same set of items or individuals. The sample of the pair wise difference between two observations drawn for the same set of items must be a set of independent identically normally distributed random values.

(c) $p(T \le t)$ one-tail $= 7.77 \times 10^{-12}$. This is the probability of obtaining a test statistic t less than the result obtained from the sample data given that the null hypothesis is true.

27. (a) $H_0: \mu_1 = \mu_2$; the average time for the two sorting methods is the same.
$H_1: \mu_1 \ne \mu_2$; the average time for the two sorting methods is different.

***t*-Test: Paired Two Sample for Means**

	Insert Sort	**Selection Sort**
Mean	5.05525	8.89175
Variance	0.031359	0.068681
Observations	40	40
Pearson Correlation	0.243727	
Hypothesized Mean Difference	0	
df	39	
t Stat	−87.2055	
$p(T \le t)$ one-tail	1.27×10^{-46}	
t Critical one-tail	1.684875	
$p(T \le t)$ two-tail	2.55×10^{-46}	
t Critical two-tail	2.022689	

Decision rule: Reject H_0 if $|t| > 2.02$.

Test statistic: $t = \dfrac{\overline{D} - \mu_{\overline{D}}}{S_{\overline{D}}/\sqrt{n}} = \dfrac{-3.8365 - 0}{0.27824/\sqrt{40}} = -87.2055$.

Decision: Because $|t| > 2.02$, reject H_0.

There is significant difference between the 2 average times because of the very small p-value.

(b) Two series of observations are obtained from the same set of items or individuals. The sample of the pair wise differences between two observations drawn for the same items must be a set of independent, identically normal distributed random values.

(c) $p(T \le t)$ two-tail $= 2.55 \times 10^{-46}$. This is the probability of obtaining a test statistic $|t|$ equal to or greater than the result obtained from the sample data given that the null hypothesis is true.

28. (a) $H_0: \mu_1 = \mu_2$; the average wear for the new material is the same as for the old material.
$H_1: \mu_1 < \mu_2$; the average wear for the new material is less than the wear for the old material.

t-Test: Paired Two Sample for Means

	New	Old
Mean	6.2	5.9
Variance	4.622222	4.1
Observations	10	10
Pearson Correlation	0.643192	
Hypothesized Mean Difference	0	
df	9	
t Stat	0.536895	
$p(T \le t)$ one-tail	0.302178	
t Critical one-tail	1.833114	
$p(T \le t)$ two-tail	0.604357	
t Critical two-tail	2.262159	

Decision rule: Reject H_0 if $|t| > 2.26$.

Test statistic: $t = \dfrac{\overline{D} - \mu_{\overline{D}}}{S_{\overline{D}}/\sqrt{n}} = \dfrac{0.3 - 0}{1.766981/\sqrt{10}} = 0.537$.

Decision: Because $|t| < 2.26$, do not reject H_0.

There is no significant difference between the two average wears, because the p-value is greater than 0.05.

(b) Two series of observations are obtained from the same set of items or individuals. The sample of pair wise differences between two observations drawn for the same items must be a set of independent, identically normal distributed random values.

(c) $p(T \le t)$ two-tail = 0.604. This is the probability of obtaining a test statistic $|t|$ equal to or greater than the result obtained from the sample data given that the null hypothesis is true.

29. (a) $H_0: \mu_1 = \mu_2$; the average gasoline mileage is the same for regular and high-octane gas.
$H_1: \mu_1 \ne \mu_2$; the average gasoline mileage is different for regular and high-octane gas.

t-Test: Paired Two Sample for Means

	Regular	High-octane
Mean	27	27.5
Variance	66.66667	82.05556
Observations	10	10
Pearson Correlation	0.925401	
Hypothesized Mean Difference	0	
df	9	
t Stat	–0.45964	
$p(T \le t)$ one-tail	0.328338	
t Critical one-tail	1.833114	
$p(T \le t)$ two-tail	0.656677	
t Critical two-tail	2.262159	

Decision rule: Reject H_0 if $|t| > 2.26$.

Test statistic: $t = \dfrac{\overline{D} - \mu_{\overline{D}}}{S_{\overline{D}}/\sqrt{n}} = \dfrac{0.5 - 0}{3.44/\sqrt{10}} = -0.460$.

Decision: Because $|t| < 2.26$, do not reject H_0.

There is not significant difference between two average gasoline mileage values because the p-value is greater than 0.05.

(b) It is assumed that the distribution of the difference in the average gas mileage between regular and high-octane gas is approximately normal.

(c) $p(T \leq t)$ two-tail = 0.657. This is the probability of obtaining a test statistic $|t|$ equal to or greater than the result obtained from the sample data given that the null hypothesis is true.

30. (a)

Two-Way Table

Count of Gender		**Major**		
Gender	**C**	**E**	**O**	**Grand Total**
Female	6	6	3	15
Male	9	14	2	25
Grand Total	15	20	5	40

(b) $H_0: \pi_C = \pi_E = \pi_O$; the proportions of students of each gender that major in computer science, electrical engineering, and other engineering majors are equal.
H_1: At least one proportion differs.

Observed Frequencies:

Count of Gender		**Major**		
Gender	**C**	**E**	**O**	**Grand Total**
Female	6	6	3	15
Male	9	14	2	25
Grand Total	15	20	5	40

Expected Frequencies:

Count of Gender		**Major**		
Gender	**C**	**E**	**O**	**Grand Total**
Female	5.625	7.5	1.875	15
Male	9.375	12.5	3.125	25
Grand Total	15	20	5	40

Level of Significance	**0.05**
Number of Rows	2
Number of Columns	3
Degrees of Freedom	2
Critical Value	5.99148
Chi-Square Test Statistic	1.6
p-value	0.44933
Do not reject the null hypothesis	

Decision rule: Reject H_0 if $\chi^2 > 5.99$.
Test statistic: $\chi^2 = 1.6$.
Decision: Because $\chi^2 < 5.99$, do not reject H_0.
There is no relationship between gender and major for the 0.05 significance level.

(c) *p*-value = 0.449. This is the probability of obtaining a test statistic chi-square equal to or greater than the result obtained from the sample data given that the null hypothesis is true.

31. (a) $H_0: \pi_1 = \pi_2$; the proportions of smokers that develop osteoporosis and non-smokers that develop osteoporosis are equal.
$H_1: \pi_1 \neq \pi_2$; the proportions of smokers that develop osteoporosis and non-smokers that develop osteoporosis differ.

Observed Frequencies: Smoking			
Osteoporosis	**Yes**	**No**	**Total**
Yes	22	16	38
No	10	28	38
Total	32	44	76

Expected Frequencies:Smoking			
Osteoporosis	**Yes**	**No**	**Total**
Yes	16	22	38
No	16	22	38
Total	32	44	76

Level of Significance	**0.05**
Number of Rows	2
Number of Columns	2
Degrees of Freedom	1
Critical Value	3.84146
Chi-Square Test Statistic	7.7728
p-value	0.0053
Reject the null hypothesis	

Decision rule: Reject H_0 if $\chi^2 > 3.841$. Test statistic: $\chi^2 = 7.773$. Decision: Because $\chi^2 < 3.841$, reject H_0. There is a significant relationship between lifestyle and osteoporosis for the 0.05 significance level.

(b) *p*-value = 0.005. This is the probability of obtaining a test statistic chi-square equal to or greater than the result obtained from the sample data given that the null hypothesis is true.

32. (a) $H_0 : \pi_1 = \pi_2$; the proportion of good wafers produced from dies in good condition is the same as the proportion of good wafers produced from dies in poor condition.
$H_1 : \pi_1 \neq \pi_2$; the proportion of good wafers produced from dies in good condition is different than the proportion of good wafers produced from dies in poor condition.

Observed Frequencies: Condition of Die			
Quality of Wafer	**No Particles**	**Particles**	**Total**
Good	320	14	334
Bad	80	36	116
Total	400	50	450

Expected Frequencies:Condition of Die			
Quality of Wafer	**No Particles**	**Particles**	**Total**
Good	296.8888889	37.1111111	334
Bad	103.1111111	12.8888889	116
Total	400	50	450

Level of Significance	**0.05**
Number of Rows	2
Number of Columns	2
Degrees of Freedom	1
Critical Value	3.841455
Chi-Square Test Statistic	#NUM!
p-value	2.27×10^{-15}
Reject the null hypothesis	

There is evidence of a significant relationship between the condition of the die and the quality of the wafer.

(b) p-value $= 2.27 \times 10^{-15}$. This is the probability of obtaining a test statistic chi-square equal to or greater than the result obtained from the sample data given that the null hypothesis is true.

(c) There is evidence of a relationship between the condition of the die and the quality of the wafer.

33. (a) $H_0: \pi_1 = \pi_2 = \pi_3$; the proportions of each type of reference found are equal in both types of program.
H_1: At least one proportion differs.

	Observed Frequencies: References			
Optimization	**Register**	**Immediate**	**Indirect**	**Total**
Yes	88	29	47	164
No	186	45	88	319
Total	274	74	135	483

	Expected Frequencies: References			
Optimization	**Register**	**Immediate**	**Indirect**	**Total**
Yes	93.0352	25.12629	45.83851	164
No	180.9648	48.87371	89.16149	319
Total	274	74	135	483

Level of Significance	**0.05**
Number of Rows	2
Number of Columns	3
Degrees of Freedom	2
Critical Value	5.991476
Chi-Square Test Statistic	1.361408
p-value	0.50626
Do not reject the null hypothesis	

Decision rule: Reject H_0 if $\chi^2 > 5.991$. Test statistic: $\chi^2 = 1.361$. Decision: Because $\chi^2 < 5.991$, do not reject H_0. There is no relationship between the type of the program and the type of references for the 0.05 significance level.

(b) p-value $= 0.506$. This is the probability of obtaining a test statistic chi-square equal to or greater than the result obtained from the sample data given that the null hypothesis is true.

34. (a) $H_0: \pi_1 = \pi_2$; the proportions of nonconforming lab tests performed between the two shifts are equal.
$H_1: \pi_1 \neq \pi_2$; the proportions of nonconforming lab tests performed between the two shifts are different.

	Observed Frequencies: Shift		
Lab Test Performed	**Day**	**Evening**	**Total**
Nonconforming	16	24	40
Conforming	654	306	960
Total	670	330	1000

	Expected Frequencies: Shift		
Lab Test Performed	**Day**	**Evening**	**Total**
Nonconforming	26.8	13.2	40
Conforming	643.2	316.8	960
Total	670	330	1000

Level of Significance	0.05
Number of Rows	2
Number of Columns	2
Degrees of Freedom	1
Critical Value	3.841455
Chi-Square Test Statistic	13.73943
p-value	0.00021
Reject the null hypothesis	

Decision rule: Reject H_0 if $\chi^2 > 3.841$. Test statistic: $\chi^2 = 13.739$. Decision: Because $\chi^2 > 3.841$, reject H_0. There is a significant difference in the proportion of nonconforming lab tests performed between two shifts for the significance level of 0.05.

(b) p-value = 0.00021. This is the probability of obtaining a test statistic chi-square equal to or greater than the result obtained from the sample data given that the null hypothesis is true.

35. (a) $H_0: \pi_A = \pi_B = \pi_C = \pi_D$; the proportions of patients on each of the four drug regimens suffering severe adverse effects are all equal.
H_1: At least one proportion is different.

		Observed Frequencies: Drug Regimen			
Result	**A**	**B**	**C**	**D**	**Total**
Severe	714	785	754	820	3073
Not Severe	9630	9543	9042	9557	37772
Total	10344	10328	9796	10377	40845

		Expected Frequencies: Drug Regimen			
Result	**A**	**B**	**C**	**D**	**Total**
Severe	778.2375	777.0338	737.0084	780.7203	3073
Not Severe	9565.762	9550.966	9058.992	9596.28	37772
Total	10344	10328	9796	10377	40845

Level of Significance	0.05
Number of Rows	2
Number of Columns	4
Degrees of Freedom	3
Critical Value	7.814725
Chi-Square Test Statistic	8.382645
p-value	0.038731
Reject the null hypothesis	

Decision rule: Reject H_0 if $\chi^2 > 7.815$. Test statistic: $\chi^2 = 8.383$. Decision: Because $\chi^2 > 7.815$, reject H_0. There is a significant difference among the 4 drug regimens with respect to the proportion of patients suffering severe adverse effects for the 0.05 significance level.

(b) There are 64.2 fewer severe reactions observed than expected with drug regimen A. Other regimens were less effective at reducing observed severe reactions compared to expected values. From the p-values shown in the above table for $\alpha = 0.05$ it can be concluded that the A and B drug regimens are not statsitically different. However, because regimen B is more expensive, regimen A is preferred.

36. (a) $H_0: \pi_1 = \pi_2 = \pi_3 = \pi_4 = \pi_5$; the proportions of defective parts produced on the various days of the week are all equal.
H_1: At least one proportion is different.

Result	Observed Frequencies: Day Mon.	Tues.	Wed.	Thurs.	Fri.	Total
Number of defective parts	12	7	7	10	14	50
Number of acceptable parts	88	93	93	90	86	450
Total	100	100	100	100	100	500

Result	Expected Frequencies: Day Mon.	Tues.	Wed.	Thurs.	Fri.	Total
Number of defective parts	10	10	10	10	10	50
Number of acceptable parts	90	90	90	90	90	450
Total	100	100	100	100	100	500

Level of Significance	0.05
Number of Rows	2
Number of Columns	5
Degrees of Freedom	4
Critical Value	9.487728
Chi-Square Test Statistic	4.222222
p-value	0.376766
Do not reject the null hypothesis	

Decision rule: Reject H_0 if $\chi^2 > 9.487$. Test statistic: $\chi^2 = 4.222$. Decision: Because $\chi^2 < 9.487$, do not reject H_0. There is no difference in the proportion of defective parts produced on the various days of the week for the 0.05 significance level.

(b) $H_0: \pi_1 = \pi_2 = \pi_3 = \pi_4 = \pi_5$; the proportions of defective parts produced on the various days of the week are all equal.
H_1: At least one proportion is different.

Result	Observed Frequencies: Day Mon.	Tues.	Wed.	Thurs.	Fri.	Total
Number of defective parts	12	7	7	10	24	60
Number of acceptable parts	88	93	93	90	76	440
Total	100	100	100	100	100	500

Result	Expected Frequencies: Day Mon.	Tues.	Wed.	Thurs.	Fri.	Total
Number of defective parts	12	12	12	12	12	60
Number of acceptable parts	88	88	88	88	88	440
Total	100	100	100	100	100	500

Level of Significance	0.05
Number of Rows	2
Number of Columns	5
Degrees of Freedom	4
Critical Value	9.487728
Chi-Square Test Statistic	18.75013
p-value	0.00088
Reject the null hypothesis	

Decision rule: Reject H_0 if $\chi^2 > 9.488$. Test statistic: $\chi^2 = 18.750$. Decision: Because $\chi^2 > 9.488$, reject H_0. There is a difference in the proportion of defective parts produced on various days of the week for the 0.05 significance level.

37. (a) $\chi_L^2 = 10.520$, $\chi_U^2 = 46.928$ (b) $\chi_L^2 = 6.908$, $\chi_U^2 = 28.845$ (c) $\chi_L^2 = 5.892$, $\chi_U^2 = 22.362$

38. (a) $H_0: \sigma = 1.20$ F; The standard deviation is equal to 1.2° F.
$H_1: \sigma > 1.20$ F; The standard deviation is greater than 1.2° F.

Chi-Square Test of Hypothesis for the Variance	
Null Hypothesis	$\sigma^2 = 1.44$
Level of Significance	0.05
Sample Size	30
Sample Standard Deviation	2.1
df	29
Chi-Square Test Statistic	88.8125

Upper-Tail Test	
Upper Critical Value	42.55695
p-value	5.54×10^{-8}
Reject the null hypothesis	

Decision rule: Reject H_0 if $\chi^2 > 42.56$. Test statistic: $\chi^2 = 88.81$. Decision: Because $\chi^2 > 42.56$, reject H_0. The standard deviation of the population is greater than 1.2° F for the 0.05 significance level.

(b) It is assumed that the observed numerical data are sampled from a normally distributed population.

(c) *p*-value = 5.54×10^{-8}. This is the probability of obtaining a test statistic of magnitude greater than the result obtained from the sample data, given that the null hypothesis is true.

39. (a) $H_0: \sigma = 0.035$ inches; the standard deviation is equal to 0.035 inches.
$H_0: \sigma < 0.035$ inches; the standard deviation is less than 0.035 inches.

Chi-Square Test of Hypothesis for the Variance	
Null Hypothesis	$\sigma^2 = 0.001225$
Level of Significance	0.05
Sample Size	25
Sample Standard Deviation	0.025
df	24
Chi-Square Test Statistic	12.2449

Upper-Tail Test	
Lower Critical Value	13.84842
p-value	0.022994
Reject the null hypothesis	

Decision rule: Reject H_0 if $\chi^2 < 13.848$. Test statistic: $\chi^2 = 12.245$. Decision: Because $\chi^2 < 13.848$, reject H_0. The standard deviation of the population is less than 0.035 inch for the 0.05 significant level.

(b) It is assumed that the observed numerical data are sampled from a normally distributed population.

(c) *p*-value = 0.022994.
This is the probability of obtaining a test statistic of magnitude lower than the result obtained from the sample data given that the null hypothesis is true.

40. $H_0: \sigma = 875$ psi; the standard deviation is equal to 875 psi.
$H_1: \sigma > 875$ psi; the standard deviation is greater than 875 psi.

Chi-Square Test of Hypothesis for the Variance	
Null Hypothesis	$\sigma^2 = 765625$
Level of Significance	0.05
Sample Size	6
Sample Standard Deviation	323.9097
df	5
Chi-Square Test Statistic	0.685175

Upper-Tail Test	
Upper Critical Value	11.07048
p-value	0.983772
Do not reject the null hypothesis	

Decision rule: Reject H_0 if $\chi^2 > 11.070$. Test statistic: $\chi^2 = 0.685$. Decision: Because $\chi^2 < 11.070$, do not reject H_0. The sample standard deviation is not greater than 875 psi for 0.05 significance level.

41. $H_0{:}\sigma = 0.100$; the standard deviation is equal to 0.100.
$H_1{:}\sigma > 0.100$; the standard deviation is greater than 0.100.

Chi-Square Test of Hypothesis for the Variance	
Null Hypothesis	$\sigma^2 = 0.01$
Level of Significance	0.05
Sample Size	31
Sample Standard Deviation	0.068303
df	30
Chi-Square Test Statistic	13.99603

Upper-Tail Test	
Upper Critical Value	43.77295
p-value	0.994297
Do not reject the null hypothesis	

Decision rule: Reject H_0 if $\chi^2 > 43.773$. Test statistic: $\chi^2 = 13.996$. Decision: Because $\chi^2 < 43.773$, do not reject H_0. The sample standard deviation is not greater than 0.100 percent For 0.05 significance level.

42. $H_0{:}\sigma = 1.00$ K; the standard deviation is equal to 1.00 K.
$H_1{:}\sigma > 1.00$ K; the standard deviation is greater than 1.00 K.

Chi-Square Test of Hypothesis for the Variance	
Null Hypothesis	$\sigma^2 = 1$
Level of Significance	0.05
Sample Size	12
Sample Standard Deviation	1.752274
df	11
Chi-Square Test Statistic	33.77509

Upper-Tail Test	
Upper Critical Value	19.67515
p-value	0.000394
Reject the null hypothesis	

Decision rule: Reject H_0 if $\chi^2 > 19.675$. Test statistic: $\chi^2 = 33.775$. Decision: Because $\chi^2 > 19.675$, reject H_0. The sample standard deviation is greater than 1.00 K for 0.05 significance level.

43. $H_0{:}\sigma = 100$; the standard deviation is equal to 100.
$H_1{:}\sigma \neq 100$; the standard deviation is not equal to 100.

Chi-Square Test of Hypothesis for the Variance	
Null Hypothesis	$\sigma^2 = 10000$
Level of Significance	0.05
Sample Size	12
Sample Standard Deviation	235.8256
df	11
Chi-Square Test Statistic	61.17507

Two-Tail Test	
Lower Critical Value	3.815742
Upper Critical Value	21.92002
p-value	1
Do not reject the null hypothesis	

Decision rule: Reject H_0 if $\chi^2 < 3.816$ or $\chi^2 > 21.920$. Test statistic: $\chi^2 = 61.175$. Decision: Because $\chi^2 > 21.920$, reject H_0. Standard deviation is significantly different from 100 for the 0.05 significance level.

44. (a) $H_0{:}M_1 = M_2$; the population medians are equal.
$H_1{:}M_1 \neq M_2$; the population medians are different.

Wilcoxon Rank Sum Test	
Level of Significance	0.05

Population 1 Sample	
Sample Size	10
Sample Standard Deviation	91

Population 2 Sample	
Sample Size	5
Sum of Ranks	29
Warning: Large-scale approximation formula not designed for small sample sizes.	
Total Sample Size n	15
T_1 Test Statistic	29
T_1 Mean	40
Standard Error of T_1	8.164966
Z Test Statistic	–1.34722

Two-Tail Test	
Lower Critical Value	–1.95996
Upper Critical Value	1.959961
p-value	0.17791
Do not reject the null hypothesis	

Decision rule: Reject H_0 if $|Z| > 1.96$. Test statistic: $Z = -1.347$. Decision: Because $|Z| < 1.96$, do not reject H_0. These two methods have the same population median for 0.05 significance level.

(b) It is assumed that the two observed series are independent and sampled from the continuously distributed random variables.

45. $H_0: M_1 = M_2$; the population medians are equal.
$H_1: M_1 \neq M_2$; the population medians are different.
Ballast Efficiency Factor

Wilcoxon Rank Sum Test	
Level of Significance	0.05

Population 1 Sample	
Sample Size	4
Sum of Ranks	10

Population 2 Sample	
Sample Size	6
Sum of Ranks	45
Warning: Large-scale approximation formula not designed for small sample sizes.	
Total Sample Size n	10
T_1 Test Statistic	10
T_1 Mean	22
Standard Error of T_1	4.690416
Z Test Statistic	–2.55841

Two-Tail Test	
Lower Critical Value	–1.95996
p-value	1.959961
Upper Critical Value	0.010515
Reject the null hypothesis	

Decision rule: Reject H_0 if $|Z| > 1.96$. Test statistic: $Z = -2.558$. Decision: Because $|Z| > 1.96$, reject H_0. These two methods have different population medians for 0.05 significance level.

Light Output

Wilcoxon Rank Sum Test	
Level of Significance	0.05

Population 1 Sample	
Sample Size	4
Sum of Ranks	34

Population 2 Sample	
Sample Size	6
Sum of Ranks	21
Warning: Large-scale approximation formula not designed for small sample sizes.	
Total Sample Size n	10
T_1 Test Statistic	34
T_1 Mean	22
Standard Error of T_1	4.690416
Z Test Statistic	2.558409

Two-Tail Test	
Lower Critical Value	−1.95996
Upper Critical Value	1.959961
p-value	0.010515
Reject the null hypothesis	

Decision rule: Reject H_0 if $|Z| > 1.96$. Test statistic: $Z = 2.558409$. Decision: Because $|Z| > 1.96$, reject H_0. These two methods have different population medians for 0.05 significance level.

Total Harmonic Distortion

Wilcoxon Rank Sum Test	
Level of Significance	0.05

Population 1 Sample	
Sample Size	4
Sum of Ranks	17

Population 2 Sample	
Sample Size	6
Sum of Ranks	38
Warning: Large-scale approximation formula not designed for small sample sizes.	
Total Sample Size n	10
T_1 Test Statistic	17
T_1 Mean	22
Standard Error of T_1	4.690416
Z Test Statistic	−1.066

Two-Tail Test	
Lower Critical Value	−1.95996
Upper Critical Value	1.959961
p-value	0.286422
Do not reject the null hypothesis	

Decision rule: Reject H_0 if $|Z| > 1.96$. Test statistic: $Z = -1.066$. Decision: Because $|Z| < 1.96$, do not reject H_0. These two methods have the same population median for the 0.05 significance level.

Power Factor

Wilcoxon Rank Sum Test	
Level of Significance	0.05

Population 1 Sample	
Sample Size	4
Sum of Ranks	31.5

Population 2 Sample	
Sample Size	6
Sum of Ranks	23.5
Warning: Large-scale approximation formula not designed for small sample sizes.	
Total Sample Size n	10
T_1 Test Statistic	31.5
T_1 Mean	22
Standard Error of T_1	4.690416
Z Test Statistic	2.025407

Two-Tail Test	
Lower Critical Value	−1.95996
Upper Critical Value	1.959961
p-value	0.042825
Reject the null hypothesis	

Decision rule: Reject H_0 if $|Z| > 1.96$. Test statistic: Z=2.025407. Decision: Because $|Z| > 1.96$, reject H_0. These two methods have different population medians for 0.05 significance level.

Lamp Temperature

Wilcoxon Rank Sum Test	
Level of Significance	0.05

Population 1 Sample	
Sample Size	4
Sum of Ranks	32

Population 2 Sample	
Sample Size	6
Sum of Ranks	23
Total Sample Size n	10
T_1 Test Statistic	32
T_1 Mean	22
Standard Error of T_1	4.690416
Z Test Statistic	2.132007

Two-Tail Test	
Lower Critical Value	−1.95996
Upper Critical Value	1.959961
p-value	0.033006
Reject the null hypothesis	

Decision rule: Reject H_0 if $|Z| > 1.96$. Test statistic: Z=2.132007. Decision: Because $|Z| > 1.96$, reject H_0. These two methods have different population medians for 0.05 significance level.

Ballast Temperature

Wilcoxon Rank Sum Test	
Level of Significance	0.05

Population 1 Sample	
Sample Size	4
Sum of Ranks	34

Population 2 Sample	
Sample Size	6
Sum of Ranks	21
Warning: Large-scale approximation formula not designed for small sample sizes.	
Total Sample Size n	10
T_1 Test Statistic	34
T_1 Mean	22
Standard Error of T_1	4.690416
Z Test Statistic	2.558409

Two-Tail Test	
Lower Critical Value	−1.95996
Upper Critical Value	1.959961
p-value	0.010515
Reject the null hypothesis	

Decision rule: Reject H_0 if $|Z| > 1.96$. Test statistic: $Z = 2.558409$. Decision: Because $|Z| > 1.96$, reject H_0. These two methods have different population medians for the 0.05 significance level.

46. (a) $H_0: M_1 = M_2$; the population medians are equal.
$H_1: M_1 \neq M_2$; the population medians are different.

Wilcoxon Rank Sum Test	
Level of Significance	0.05

Population 1 Sample	
Sample Size	25
Sum of Ranks	502.5

Population 2 Sample	
Sample Size	25
Sum of Ranks	772.5
Warning: Large-scale approximation formula not designed for small sample sizes.	
Total Sample Size n	50
T_1 Test Statistic	502.5
T_1 Mean	637.5
Standard Error of T_1	51.53882
Z Test Statistic	−2.61938

Two-Tail Test	
Lower Critical Value	−1.95996
Upper Critical Value	1.959961
p-value	0.008809
Reject the null hypothesis	

Decision rule: Reject H_0 if $|Z| > 1.96$. Test statistic: $Z = -2.619$. Decision: Because $|Z| > 1.96$, reject H_0. These two batteries have different population medians for the 0.05 significance level.

(b) p-value = 0.009. This is the probability of obtaining a test statistic of magnitude equal to or greater than the result obtained from the sample data given that the null hypothesis is true.
(c) These two batteries have both different means and different medians for the 0.05 significance level.

47. (a) $H_0: M_1 = M_2$; the population medians are equal.
$H_1: M_1 \neq M_2$; the population medians are different.

Wilcoxon Rank Sum Test	
Level of Significance	0.05

Population 1 Sample	
Sample Size	30
Sum of Ranks	790

Population 2 Sample	
Sample Size	45
Sum of Ranks	2060
Total Sample Size n	75
T_1 Test Statistic	790
T_1 Mean	1140
Standard Error of T_1	92.46621
Z Test Statistic	–3.78517

Two-Tail Test	
Lower Critical Value	–1.95996
Upper Critical Value	1.959961
p-value	0.000154
Reject the null hypothesis	

Decision rule: Reject H_0 if $|Z| > 1.96$. Test statistic: $Z = -3.785$. Decision: Because $|Z| > 1.96$, reject H_0. These two variables have different population medians for the 0.05 significance level.
(b) p-value = 0.0002. This is the probability of obtaining a test statistic of magnitude equal to or greater than the result obtained from the sample data given that the null hypothesis is true.
(c) These two batteries have both different means and different medians for 0.05 significance level.

48. (a) $H_0: M_1 = M_2$; the population medians are equal.
$H_1: M_1 \neq M_2$; the population medians are different.

Wilcoxon Rank Sum Test	
Level of Significance	0.05

Population 1 Sample	
Sample Size	20
Sum of Ranks	434.5

Population 2 Sample	
Sample Size	20
Sum of Ranks	385.5
Total Sample Size n	40
T_1 Test Statistic	434.5
T_1 Mean	410
Standard Error of T_1	36.96846
Z Test Statistic	0.662727

Two-Tail Test	
Lower Critical Value	−1.95996
Upper Critical Value	1.959961
p-value	0.507505
Do not reject the null hypothesis	

Decision rule: Reject H_0 if $|Z| > 1.96$. Test statistic: $Z = 0.662727$. Decision: Because $|Z| < 1.96$, do not reject H_0. These two variables have the same population medians for the 0.05 significance level.

(b) p-value = 0.508. This is the probability of obtaining a test statistic of magnitude equal to or greater than the result obtained from the sample data given that the hypothesis H_0 is true.

(c) These two variables have both equal means and equal medians for the 0.05 significance level.

49. (a) $H_0: M_1 = M_2$; the population medians are equal.
$H_1: M_1 \neq M_2$; the population medians are different.

Wilcoxon Rank Sum Test	
Level of Significance	0.05

Population 1 Sample	
Sample Size	20
Sum of Ranks	345.5

Population 2 Sample	
Sample Size	20
Sum of Ranks	474.5
Total Sample Size n	40
T_1 Test Statistic	345.5
T_1 Mean	410
Standard Error of T_1	36.96846
Z Test Statistic	−1.74473

Two-Tail Test	
Lower Critical Value	−1.95996
Upper Critical Value	1.959961
p-value	0.081032
Do not reject the null hypothesis	

Decision rule: Reject H_0 if $|Z| > 1.96$. Test statistic: $Z = -1.745$. Decision: Because $|Z| < 1.96$, do not reject H_0. These two variables have the same population medians for 0.05 significance level.

(b) p-value = 0.081. This is the probability of obtaining a test statistic of magnitude equal to or greater than the result obtained from the sample data given that the null hypothesis is true.

(c) These two variables have both equal means and equal medians for 0.05 significance level.

50. The null hypothesis is the hypothesis that is always tested. The alternative hypothesis is the hypothesis that is supported if the null hypothesis is rejected.

51. A Type I error occurs when the null hypothesis is rejected when in fact it is true and should not be rejected. The probability of occurrence of Type I error is the level of significance. A Type II error occurs when the null hypothesis is not rejected when in fact it is false and should be rejected.

52. The power of a statistical test is the conditional probability of rejecting the null hypothesis when it is false and should therefore be rejected.

53. For the one-side alternatives it is necessary to use a one-tailed test procedure. For the $H_1: \theta \neq \theta_0$ alternatives one should perform a two-tailed test.

54. The p-value is the probability of obtaining a test statistic of magnitude equal to or greater than the result obtained from the same data given that the null hypothesis is true.

55. If the $(1-\alpha)\%$ confidence interval does not contain the parameter value tested in the null hypothesis, this null hypothesis should be rejected for the confidence level α. For a one-tailed test it is necessary to construct a one-tailed confidence intervals.

56. The following criteria are used to select a hypothesis testing procedure:
(a) Nature of the problem (one-, two-, or c-sample).
(b) Nature of the population (i.e., normally distributed random varabiles).
(c) Nature of the data—dependent or independent.
(d) Assumptions about the mean(s) or variance(s).
(e) Scale of the data (nominal, ordinal or quantitative).

57. The pooled-variance t test is selected when two samples are randomly and independently drawn from populations such that the populations are normally distributed and have equal variances.

58. The separate-variance t test is selected when two samples are randomly and independently drawn from populations that are normally distributed without any additional assumptions about the population variances.

59. The Wilcoxon rank sum test can be used with ordinal data when sample sizes are small and it cannot be assumed that the data in each group are taken from normally distributed populations.

60. The F test is used when observed numerical data are independently sampled from normally distributed populations.

61. For related populations the results obtained from one group are not independent of those obtained from all other groups.

62. Repeated measurements are measurements that are taken more than once from the same set of items or individuals. Paired or matched items are items that share similar characteristics and are linked to control the effect of that characteristic on the study.

63. The paired t test is used when two sets of data are selected for the same set of items or individuals and when the sample of difference scores is randomly and independently drawn from a population that is normally distributed.

64. The chi-square test when dealing with $2\times c$ contingency tables should be used when all of the expected frequencies are large or at least 1.

65. By performing a chi-square test for various sample pairs of contingency tables and by taking into account their p-values, one can select groups with significantly different proportions of success.

66. (a) $H_0: \mu = 10$ minutes; the population average time is 10 minutes.
$H_1: \mu > 10$ minutes; the population average time is greater than 10 minutes.

***t* Test of Hypothesis for the Mean**	
Null Hypothesis	$\mu = 10$
Level of Significance	0.05
Sample Size	9
Sample Mean	12
Sample Standard Deviation	1.802775638
Standard Error of the Mean	0.600925213
Degrees of Freedom	8
t Test Statistic	3.328201177

Upper-Tail Test	
Upper Critical Value	1.85954832
p-value	0.005206113
Reject the null hypothesis	

Decision rule: Reject H_0 if $t > 1.860$. Test statistic: $t = 3.328$. Decision: Because $t > 1.860$, reject H_0. The population average is greater than 10 minutes for the 0.05 significance level.

(b) $H_0: \mu = 10$ minutes; the population average time is 10 minutes.

$H_1: \mu > 10$ minutes; the population average time is greater than 10 minutes.

t Test of Hypothesis for the Mean	
Null Hypothesis	$\mu = 10$
Level of Significance	0.05
Sample Size	9
Sample Mean	16
Sample Standard Deviation	13.20037878
Standard Error of the Mean	4.400126261
Degrees of Freedom	8
t Test Statistic	1.363597234

Upper-Tail Test	
Upper Critical Value	1.85954832
p-value	0.104912851
Do not reject the null hypothesis	

Decision rule: Reject H_0 if $t > 1.860$. Test statistic: $t = 1.364$. Decision: Because $t < 1.860$, do not reject H_0. The population average is not greater than 10 minutes for the 0.05 significance level.

(c) The large value of 51 used in part (b) leads to a significant increase in the sample standard deviation and to a significant decrease in the *t* test statictic. *p* values are small for the initial sample and large for the revised data; therefore, the answer for part (b) is different from the answer for part (a).

(d) $H_0: \mu_1 = \mu_2$; the average time taken for computer majors to write a program is the same as other majors.

$H_1: \mu_1 > \mu_2$; the average time taken for other majors to write a program is greater for computer majors.

t Test for Differences in Two Means	
Hypothesized Difference	0
Level of Significance	0.05

Population 1 Sample	
Sample Mean	12
Sample Size	9
Sample Standard Deviation	1.8

Population 2 Sample	
Sample Mean	8.5
Sample Size	11
Sample Standard Deviation	2
Population 1 Sample Degrees of Freedom	8
Population 2 Sample Degrees of Freedom	10
Total Degrees of Freedom	18
Pooled Variance	3.662222
Difference in Sample Means	3.5
t-Test Statistic	4.069099

Upper-Tail Test	
Upper Critical Value	1.734063
p-value	0.00036
Reject the null hypothesis	

Decision rule: Reject H_0 if $t > 1.734$. Test statistic: $t = 4.069$. Decision: Because $t > 1.734$, reject H_0. On average, the computer majors can write a Visual Basic program in a shorter time than the introductory students can.

(e) $H_0: \sigma_1 = \sigma_2$; the variances are equal.

$H_0: \sigma_1 \neq \sigma_2$; the variances are not equal.

F Test for Differences in Two Variances	
Level of Significance	0.05

Population 2 Sample	
Sample Size	11
Sample Standard Deviation	2
F-Test Statistic	0.81
Population 1 Sample Degrees of Freedom	8
Population 2 Sample Degrees of Freedom	10

Population 1 Sample	
Sample Size	9
Sample Standard Deviation	1.8

Two-Tail Test	
Lower Critical Value	0.232822
Upper Critical Value	3.854893
p-value	0.780357
Reject the null hypothesis	

Decision rule: Reject H_0 if $F < 0.233$ or $F > 3.855$. Test statistic: $F = 0.81$. Decision: Because $0.233 < F < 3.855$, do not reject H_0.

There is no significant difference between the two variances. The p-value of this decision is 0.780. This is a probability of obtaining a test statistic F less than the lower critical value of 0.233 or greater than the upper critical value of 3.85 when the null hypothesis is true (variances are equal). The p value in part (a) is very small (0.0052). This means there is a small probability of obtaining a test statistic t greater than the upper critical value of 1.86 when the null hypothesis is true ($\mu = 10$ minutes).

67. $H_0: \sigma_1 = \sigma_2$; the variances are equal.
$H_1: \sigma_1 \neq \sigma_2$; the variances are not equal.

F-Test Two-Sample for Variances	Variable 1	Variable 2
Mean	909.65	1018.35
Variance	8893.464	9389.874
Observations	40	40
df	39	39
F	0.947133	
$P(F \leq f)$ one-tail	0.433093	
F Critical one-tail	0.586694	

There is no significant difference between the two variances.

$H_0: \mu_1 = \mu_2$; the two means are equal.
$H_1: \mu_1 \neq \mu_2$; the two means are not equal.

t-Test: Two-Sample Assuming Equal Variances	Variable 1	Variable 2
Mean	909.65	1018.35
Variance	8893.464	9389.874
Observations	40	40
Pooled Variance	9141.669	
Hypothesized Mean Difference	0	
df	78	
t Stat	−5.08431	
$p(T \leq t)$ one-tail	1.24×10^{-6}	
t Critical one-tail	1.664625	
$p(T \leq t)$ two-tail	2.47×10^{-6}	
t Critical two-tail	1.990848	

There is a significant difference between the two means.

68. $H_0: \sigma_1 = \sigma_2$; the variances are equal.

$H_1: \sigma_1 \neq \sigma_2$; the variances are not equal.

F-Test Two-Sample for Variances		
	Variable 1	**Variable 2**
Mean	51.625	61.3
Variance	353.0493	264.0367
Observations	12	7
df	11	6
F	1.337122	
$P(F \le f)$one-tail	0.376318	
F Critical one-tail	4.027441	

There is no significant difference between the two variances.

$H_0: \mu_1 = \mu_2$; the two means are equal.

$H_1: \mu_1 \neq \mu_2$; the two means are not equal.

t-Test: Two-Sample Assuming Equal Variances		
	Variable 1	**Variable 2**
Mean	51.625	61.3
Variance	353.0493	264.0367
Observations	12	7
Pooled Variance	321.6331	
Hypothesized Mean Difference	0	
df	17	
t Stat	−1.13431	
$p(T \le t)$ one-tail	0.136202	
t Critical one-tail	1.739606	
$p(T \le t)$ two-tail	0.272405	
t Critical two-tail	2.109819	

There is no significant difference between the two means.

69. ***pH***

$H_0: \sigma_1 = \sigma_2$; the variances are equal.

$H_1: \sigma_1 \neq \sigma_2$; the variances are not equal.

F-Test Two-Sample for Variances		
	Variable 1	**Variable 2**
Mean	5.203333	5.3
Variance	0.096479	0.100291
Observations	12	12
df	11	11
F	0.961989	
$P(F \le f)$one-tail	0.474955	
F Critical one-tail	0.35487	

There is no significant difference between the two variances.

$H_0: \mu_1 = \mu_2$; the two means are equal.

$H_1: \mu_1 \neq \mu_2$; the two means are not equal.

t-Test: Two-Sample Assuming Equal Variances

	Variable 1	Variable 2
Mean	5.203333	5.3
Variance	0.096479	0.100291
Observations	12	12
Pooled Variance	0.098385	
Hypothesized Mean Difference	0	
df	22	
t Stat	–0.7549	
$p(T \le t)$ one-tail	0.229158	
t Critical one-tail	1.717144	
$p(T \le t)$ two-tail	0.458316	
t Critical two-tail	2.073875	

There is no significant difference between the two means.

Conductivity

$H_0: \sigma_1 = \sigma_2$; the variances are equal.

$H_1: \sigma_1 \ne \sigma_2$; the variances are not equal.

F-Test Two-Sample for Variances

	Variable 1	Variable 2
Mean	0.80125	0.596167
Variance	0.078195	0.017882
Observations	12	12
df	11	11
F	4.372871	
$P(F \le f)$one-tail	0.010805	
F Critical one-tail	2.817927	

There is a significant difference between the two variances.

$H_0: \mu_1 = \mu_2$; the two means are equal.

$H_1: \mu_1 \ne \mu_2$; the two means are not equal.

t-Test: Two-Sample Assuming Unequal Variances

	Variable 1	Variable 2
Mean	0.80125	0.596167
Variance	0.078195	0.017882
Observations	12	12
Pooled Volume	0	
Hypothesized Mean Difference	16	
t Stat	2.291988	
t stat	0.017902	
$p(T \le t)$ one-tail	1.745884	
t Critical one-tail	0.035805	
$p(T \le t)$ two-tail	2.119905	

There is a significant difference between the two means.

Total Aerobic Microbial Population

$H_0: \sigma_1 = \sigma_2$; the variances are equal.

$H_1: \sigma_1 \neq \sigma_2$; the variances are not equal.

F-Test Two-Sample for Variances	Variable 1	Variable 2
Mean	5.666667	3.333333
Variance	157.1515	57.33333
Observations	12	12
df	11	11
F	2.741015	
$P(F \leq f)$one-tail	0.054512	
F Critical one-tail	2.817927	

There are some doubts about the significance of the difference between the two variances, because the *p*-value is approximately 0.05. Therefore, consider both procedures for testing the hypothesis about the mean equality.

$H_0: \mu_1 = \mu_2$; the two means are equal.

$H_1: \mu_1 \neq \mu_2$; the two means are not equal.

t-Test: Two-Sample Assuming Equal Variances	Variable 1	Variable 2
Mean	5.666667	3.333333
Variance	157.1515	57.33333
Observations	12	12
Pooled Variance	107.2424	
Hypothesized Mean Difference	0	
df	22	
t Stat	0.551911	
$p(T \leq t)$ one-tail	0.293286	
t Critical one-tail	1.717144	
$p(T \leq t)$ two-tail	0.586573	
t Critical two-tail	2.073875	

t-Test: Two-Sample Assuming Unequal Variances	Variable 1	Variable 2
Mean	5.666667	3.333333
Variance	157.1515	57.33333
Observations	12	12
Hypothesized Mean Difference	0	
df	18	
t Stat	0.551911	
$p(T \leq t)$ one-tail	0.293898	
t Critical one-tail	1.734063	
$p(T \leq t)$ two-tail	0.587797	
t Critical two-tail	2.100924	

The result is the same for both assumptions; there is no significant difference between the two means.

Total Organic Carbon (TOC)

$H_0: \sigma_1 = \sigma_2$; the variances are equal.

$H_1: \sigma_1 \neq \sigma_2$; the variances are not equal.

F-Test Two-Sample for Variances

	Variable 1	Variable 2
Mean	174.6667	173.5
Variance	7752.97	10796.27
Observations	12	12
df	11	11
F	0.718115	
$P(F \leq f)$one-tail	0.296119	
F Critical one-tail	0.35487	

There is no significant difference between the two variances.

$H_0: \mu_1 = \mu_2$; the two means are equal.

$H_1: \mu_1 \neq \mu_2$; the two means are not equal.

t-Test: Two-Sample Assuming Equal Variances

	Variable 1	Variable 2
Mean	174.6667	173.5
Variance	7752.97	10796.27
Observations	12	12
Pooled Variance	9274.621	
Hypothesized Mean Difference	0	
df	22	
t Stat	0.029674	
$p(T \leq t)$ one-tail	0.488297	
t Critical one-tail	1.717144	
$p(T \leq t)$ two-tail	0.976595	
t Critical two-tail	2.073875	

There is no significant difference between the two means.

70. (a) $H_0: \mu = 50$ hours per year; the mean is equal to 50 hours per year.

$H_1: \mu > 50$ hours per year; the mean is not equal to 50 hour per year.

t Test of Hypothesis for the Mean

Null Hypothesis	$\mu = 50$
Level of Significance	0.05
Sample Size	43
Sample Mean	54.14395349
Sample Standard Deviation	38.92837477
Standard Error of the Mean	5.936521498
Degrees of Freedom	42
T Test Statistic	0.698044046

Upper-Tail Test

Upper Critical Value	1.681951289
p-value	0.244498268
Do not reject the null hypothesis	

The population mean does not differ from 50 hours per year for the 0.05 significance level

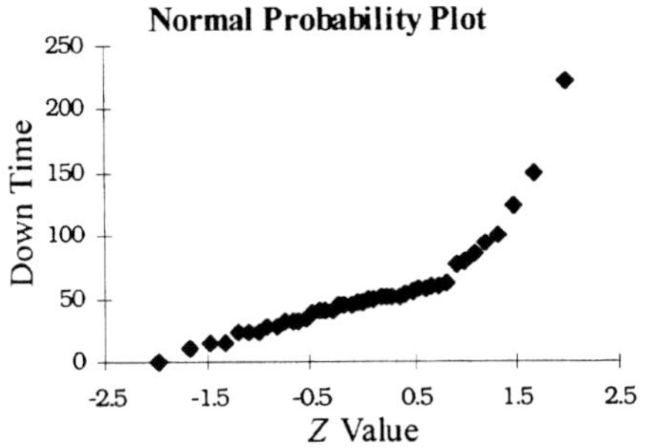

(b) $H_0: \sigma = 25$ hours per year; the variance is equal to 25 hours per year.
$H_1: \sigma \neq 25$ hours per year; the variance is not equal to 25 hour per year.

Chi-Square Test of Hypothesis for the Variance	
Null Hypothesis	$\sigma^2 = 625$
Level of Significance	0.1
Sample Size	43
Sample Standard Deviation	38.928
df	42
Chi-Square Test Statistic	101.8342

Two-Tail Test	
Lower Critical Value	28.14405
Upper Critical Value	58.12403
p-value	0.999999
Do not reject the null hypothesis	

The standard deviation of the population does not differ from 25 hours per year for the 0.10 significance level.

(c) In parts (a) and (b) it is assumed that the observed numerical data are drawn from the normally distributed population.

(d) Assumptions about the data being normally distributed are false, so the analysis in parts (a) and (b) is not correct.

71. (a) $H_0: \pi_1 = \pi_2$; the two proportions are equal.
$H_1: \pi_1 \neq \pi_2$; the two proportions are not equal.

Observed Frequencies: Hearing Loss Caused by Hib

Country	Yes	No	Total
Canada	57	44	101
US	83	60	143
Total	140	104	244

Expected Frequencies: Hearing Loss Caused by Hib

Country	Yes	No	Total
Canada	57.95081967	43.0491803	101
US	82.04918033	60.9508197	143
Total	140	104	244

Level of Significance	0.05
Number of Rows	2
Number of Columns	2
Degrees of Freedom	1
Critical Value	3.841455
Chi-Square Test Statistic	0.062452
p-value	0.802661
Do not reject the null hypothesis	

There is no significant difference between the two population proportions.

(b)

Observed Frequencies: Treated with Dexamethasone			
Result	**Yes**	**No**	**Total**
Severe	8	27	35
Not severe	252	206	458
Total	260	233	493

Expected Frequencies: Treated with Dexamethasone			
Result	**Yes**	**No**	**Total**
Severe	18.45841785	16.5415822	35
Not severe	241.5415822	216.458418	458
Total	260	233	493

Level of Significance	**0.01**
Number of Rows	2
Number of Columns	2
Degrees of Freedom	1
Critical Value	6.634891
Chi-Square Test Statistic	13.49803
p-value	0.000239
Reject the null hypothesis	

There is a significant difference between the two population proportions.

(c)

Observed Frequencies: Treated with Dexametazone			
Problem	**Yes**	**No**	**Total**
Neurological deficit	25	38	63
Hearing loss	365	329	694
Total	390	367	757

Expected Frequencies: Treated with Dexametazone			
Problem	**Yes**	**No**	**Total**
Neurological deficit	32.45706737	30.5429326	63
Hearing loss	357.5429326	336.457067	694
Total	390	367	757

Level of Significance	**0.01**
Number of Rows	2
Number of Columns	2
Degrees of Freedom	1
Critical Value	6.634891
Chi-Square Test Statistic	3.854724
p-value	0.049606
Do not reject the null hypothesis	

There is no significant difference between the two population proportions.

72. *Mercury*

$H_0: \sigma_1 = \sigma_2$; the variances are equal.

$H_1: \sigma_1 \neq \sigma_2$; the variances are not equal.

F-Test Two-Sample for Variances		
	Variable 1	Variable 2
Mean	0.728571	0.714286
Variance	0.002381	0.021429
Observations	7	7
df	6	6
F	0.111111	
$P(F \le f)$one-tail	0.00856	
F Critical one-tail	0.233435	

There is a significant difference between the two variances.

$H_0: \mu_1 = \mu_2$; the two means are equal.

$H_1: \mu_1 \ne \mu_2$; the two means are not equal.

t-Test: Two-Sample Assuming Unequal Variances		
	Variable 1	Variable 2
Mean	0.728571	0.714286
Variance	0.002381	0.021429
Observations	7	7
Hypothesized Mean Difference	0	
df	7	
t Stat	0.244949	
$p(T \le t)$ one-tail	0.406761	
t Critical one-tail	1.894578	
$p(T \le t)$ two-tail	0.813522	
t Critical two-tail	2.364623	

There is no significant difference between the two means.

Silver

$H_0: \sigma_1 = \sigma_2$; the variances are equal.

$H_1: \sigma_1 \ne \sigma_2$; the variances are not equal.

F-Test Two-Sample for Variances		
	Variable 1	Variable 2
Mean	0.6	0.585714
Variance	0.003333	0.038095
Observations	7	7
df	6	6
F	0.0875	
$P(F \le f)$one-tail	0.0046	
F Critical one-tail	0.233435	

There is a significant difference between the two variances.

$H_0: \mu_1 = \mu_2$; the two means are equal.

$H_1: \mu_1 \ne \mu_2$; the two means are not equal.

t-Test: Two-Sample Assuming Unequal Variances		
	Variable 1	**Variable 2**
Mean	0.6	0.585714
Variance	0.003333	0.038095
Observations	7	7
Hypothesized Mean Difference	0	
df	7	
t Stat	0.185695	
$p(T \le t)$ one-tail	0.428975	
t Critical one-tail	1.894578	
$p(T \le t)$ two-tail	0.85795	
t Critical two-tail	2.364623	

There is no significant difference between the two means.

Cadmium

$H_0: \sigma_1 = \sigma_2$; the variances are equal.

$H_1: \sigma_1 \ne \sigma_2$; the variances are not equal.

F-Test Two-Sample for Variances		
	Variable 1	**Variable 2**
Mean	0.728571	0.757143
Variance	0.012381	0.002857
Observations	7	7
df	6	6
F	4.333333	
$P(F \le f)$one-tail	0.048769	
F Critical one-tail	4.283862	

There is a significant difference between the two variances for the 0.05 significance level.

$H_0: \mu_1 = \mu_2$; the two means are equal.

$H_1: \mu_1 \ne \mu_2$; the two means are not equal.

t-Test: Two-Sample Assuming Unequal Variances		
	Variable 1	**Variable 2**
Mean	0.728571	0.757143
Variance	0.012381	0.002857
Observations	7	7
Hypothesized Mean Difference	0	
df	9	
t Stat	–0.61237	
$p(T \le t)$ one-tail	0.277723	
t Critical one-tail	1.833114	
$p(T \le t)$ two-tail	0.555445	
t Critical two-tail	2.262159	

There is no significant difference between the two means for the 0.05 significance level.

Lead

$H_0: \sigma_1 = \sigma_2$; the variances are equal.

$H_1: \sigma_1 \neq \sigma_2$; the variances are not equal.

F-Test Two-Sample for Variances	Variable 1	Variable 2
Mean	7.142857	3.814286
Variance	2.809524	0.094762
Observations	7	7
df	6	6
F	29.64824	
$P(F \leq f)$one-tail	0.000331	
F Critical one-tail	4.283862	

There is a significant difference between the two variances for the 0.05 significance level.

$H_0: \mu_1 = \mu_2$; the two means are equal.

$H_1: \mu_1 \neq \mu_2$; the two means are not equal.

t-Test: Two-Sample Assuming Unequal Variances	Variable 1	Variable 2
Mean	7.142857	3.814286
Variance	2.809524	0.094762
Observations	7	7
Hypothesized Mean Difference	0	
df	6	
t Stat	5.16758	
$p(T \leq t)$ one-tail	0.00104	
t Critical one-tail	1.943181	
$p(T \leq t)$ two-tail	0.002079	
t Critical two-tail	2.446914	

There is a significant difference between the two means for the 0.05 significance level.

Copper

$H_0: \sigma_1 = \sigma_2$; the variances are equal.

$H_1: \sigma_1 \neq \sigma_2$; the variances are not equal.

F-Test Two-Sample for Variances	Variable 1	Variable 2
Mean	7	15.42857
Variance	3.666667	28.28571
Observations	7	7
df	6	6
F	0.12963	
$P(F \leq f)$one-tail	0.01263	
F Critical one-tail	0.233435	

There is a significant difference between the two variances for the 0.05 significance level.

$H_0: \mu_1 = \mu_2$; the two means are equal.

$H_1: \mu_1 \neq \mu_2$; the two means are not equal.

t-Test: Two-Sample Assuming Unequal Variances		
	Variable 1	**Variable 2**
Mean	7	15.42857
Variance	3.666667	28.28571
Observations	7	7
Hypothesized Mean Difference	0	
df	8	
t Stat	–3.94504	
$p(T \le t)$ one-tail	0.002133	
t Critical one-tail	1.859548	
$p(T \le t)$ two-tail	0.004266	
t Critical two-tail	2.306006	

There is significant difference between the two means for the 0.05 significance level.

73. To check the assumptions let us construct the multiple Box-and-Whisker plot. The normal distribution assumption appears valid based on the plot.

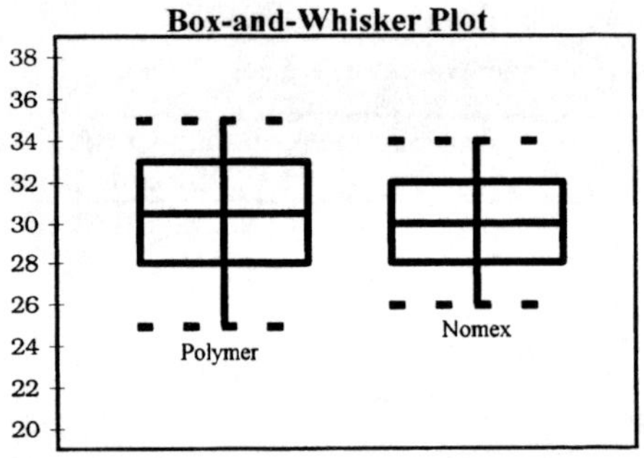

$H_0: \sigma_1 = \sigma_2$; the variances are equal.

$H_1: \sigma_1 \ne \sigma_2$; the variances are not equal.

F-Test Two-Sample for Variances		
	Variable 1	**Variable 2**
Mean	30.44828	29.89655
Variance	7.327586	5.238916
Observations	29	29
df	28	28
F	1.398684	
$P(F \le f)$one-tail	0.190023	
F Critical one-tail	1.882078	

There is no significant difference between the two variances for the 0.05 significance level.

$H_0: \mu_1 = \mu_2$; the two means are equal.

$H_1: \mu_1 \ne \mu_2$; the two means are not equal.

t-Test: Two-Sample Assuming Equal Variances

	Variable 1	Variable 2
Mean	30.44828	29.89655
Variance	7.327586	5.238916
Observations	29	29
Pooled Variance	6.283251	
Hypothesized Mean Difference	0	
df	56	
t Stat	0.838135	
$p(T \le t)$ one-tail	0.202759	
t Critical one-tail	1.672522	
$p(T \le t)$ two-tail	0.405518	
t Critical two-tail	2.003239	

There is no significant difference between the two means for the 0.05 significance level.

74. ***Systolic Blood Pressure (SBP)***

$H_0: \mu_1 = \mu_2$; the two means are equal.

$H_1: \mu_1 \neq \mu_2$; the two means are not equal.

t-Test: Paired Two Sample for Means

	Variable 1	Variable 2
Mean	154.8333	130.1667
Variance	393.7879	420.697
Observations	12	12
Pearson Correlation	0.096116	
Hypothesized Mean Difference	0	
df	11	
t Stat	3.149131	
$p(T \le t)$ one-tail	0.004628	
t Critical one-tail	1.795884	
$p(T \le t)$ two-tail	0.009257	
t Critical two-tail	2.200986	

There is no significant difference between the two means for the 0.05 significance level.

Diastolic Blood Pressure (DBP)

$H_0: \mu_1 = \mu_2$; the two means are equal.

$H_1: \mu_1 \neq \mu_2$; the two means are not equal.

t-Test: Paired Two Sample for Means

	Variable 1	Variable 2
Mean	90.5	86.58333
Variance	115.7273	357.5379
Observations	12	12
Pearson Correlation	–0.02212	
Hypothesized Mean Difference	0	
df	11	
t Stat	0.617823	
$p(T \le t)$ one-tail	0.274634	
t Critical one-tail	1.795884	
$p(T \le t)$ two-tail	0.549269	
t Critical two-tail	2.200986	

There is a significant difference between the two means for the 0.05 significance level.

Serum Sodium Concentration (SNa)

$H_0: \mu_1 = \mu_2$; the two means are equal.

$H_1: \mu_1 \neq \mu_2$; the two means are not equal.

t-Test: Paired Two Sample for Means

	Variable 1	Variable 2
Mean	144.3333	141.9167
Variance	5.333333	3.719697
Observations	12	12
Pearson Correlation	0.63953	
Hypothesized Mean Difference	0	
df	11	
t Stat	4.56975	
$p(T \le t)$ one-tail	0.000402	
t Critical one-tail	1.795884	
$p(T \le t)$ two-tail	0.000804	
t Critical two-tail	2.200986	

There is no significant difference between the two means for the 0.05 significance level.

Serum Potassium Concentration (SK)

$H_0: \mu_1 = \mu_2$; the two means are equal.

$H_1: \mu_1 \neq \mu_2$; the two means are not equal.

t-Test: Paired Two Sample for Means	Variable 1	Variable 2
Mean	3.383333	4.525
Variance	0.457879	0.418409
Observations	12	12
Pearson Correlation	0.289738	
Hypothesized Mean Difference	0	
df	11	
t Stat	−5.01196	
$p(T \leq t)$ one-tail	0.000198	
t Critical one-tail	1.795884	
$p(T \leq t)$ two-tail	0.000395	
t Critical two-tail	2.200986	

There is no significant difference between the two means for the 0.05 significance level.

Plasma aldosterone concentration (PAC)

$H_0: \mu_1 = \mu_2$; the two means are equal.

$H_1: \mu_1 \neq \mu_2$; the two means are not equal.

t-Test: Paired Two Sample for Means	Variable 1	Variable 2
Mean	1194.167	159.1667
Variance	1198972	35444.7
Observations	12	12
Pearson Correlation	0.864973	
Hypothesized Mean Difference	0	
df	11	
t Stat	3.826797	
$p(T \leq t)$ one-tail	0.001405	
t Critical one-tail	1.795884	
$p(T \leq t)$ two-tail	0.00281	
t Critical two-tail	2.200986	

There is no significant difference between the two means for the 0.05 significance level.

chapter 10

The Design of Experiments: One Factor and Randomized Block Experiments

1. (a) $H_0: \mu_1 = \mu_2 = \mu_3$, H_1: Not all of the means are equal

Anova: Single Factor

Summary				
Groups	**Count**	**Sum**	**Average**	**Variance**
Vegetable	5.000	2199.000	439.800	4435.200
Canola	5.000	2834.000	566.800	2443.700
Safflower	5.000	2139.000	427.800	2149.200

ANOVA						
Source of Variation	**SS**	**df**	**MS**	***F***	***p*-value**	F_{crit}
Between Groups	59323.330	2.000	29661.670	9.856	0.030	3.885
Within Groups	36112.400	12.000	3009.367			
Total	95435.730	14.000				

Decision rule: Reject H_0 if $F > 3.885$. Test statistic: $F = 9.856$. Decision: Because $F > 3.885$, reject H_0. There is a significant difference between the average number of popped kernels for these three oils.

(b)

Tukey Kramer Multiple Comparisons	
Group 1	
Sample Mean	439.800
Sample Size	5.000
Group 2	
Sample Mean	566.800
Sample Size	5.000
Group 3	
Sample Mean	427.800
Sample Size	5.000
MSW	3009.367
Q Statistic	3.060

Group 1 to Group 2 Comparison	
Absolute Difference	127.000
Standard Error of Difference	24.533
Critical Range	75.071
Means are different	

Group 1 to Group 3 Comparison	
Absolute Difference	12.000
Standard Error of Difference	24.533
Critical Range	75.071
Means are not different	

Group 2 to Group 3 Comparison	
Absolute Difference	139.000
Standard Error of Difference	24.533
Critical Range	75.071
Means are different	

Groups	**Group-to-group Means Comparison**		
	1–2	1–3	2–3
Means	different	not different	different

There is a significant difference between the means μ_1 and μ_2, and the means μ_2 and μ_3. Due to the absence of a significant difference between μ_1 and μ_3, one can conclude that μ_2 is significantly different from all others.

(c) Canola oil should be used to maximize the number of popped kernels. The average number of popped kernels is the greatest for Canola oil. Canola oil significantly differs from the average number of popped kernels from the other oils. (Canola oil is the best for the popcorn making if we do not take into account other parameters of these oils.)

2. (a) $H_0: \mu_1 = \mu_2 = \mu_3 = \mu_4$, H_1: Not all of the means are equal

Anova: Single Factor

Summary

Groups	Count	Sum	Average	Variance
Column 1	10.000	2066.140	206.614	5.246
Column 2	10.000	2185.160	218.516	30.667
Column 3	10.000	2265.880	226.588	23.182
Column 4	10.000	2286.220	228.622	16.107

ANOVA

Source of Variation	SS	df	MS	F	p-value	F_{crit}
Between Groups	2990.990	3.000	996.997	53.030	2.73×10^{-13}	2.866
Within Groups	676.824	36.000	18.801			
Total	3667.814	39.000				

Decision rule: Reject H_0 if $F > 2.866$. Test statistic: $F = 53.030$. Decision: Because $F > 2.866$, reject H_0. There is evidence of a difference between the average distances traveled by the golf balls produced by different design models.

(b)

Tukey Kramer Multiple Comparisons	
Group 1	
Sample Mean	206.614
Sample Size	10.000
Group 2	
Sample Mean	218.516
Sample Size	10.000
Group 3	
Sample Mean	226.588
Sample Size	10.000
Group 4	
Sample Mean	228.622
Sample Size	10.000
MSW	18.801
Q Statistic	3.810

Group 1 to Group 2 Comparison	
Absolute Difference	11.902
Standard Error of Difference	1.371
Critical Range	5.224
Means are different	

Group 1 to Group 3 Comparison	
Absolute Difference	19.974
Standard Error of Difference	1.371
Critical Range	5.224
Means are different	

Group 1 to Group 4 Comparison	
Absolute Difference	22.008
Standard Error of Difference	1.371
Critical Range	5.224
Means are different	

Group 2 to Group 3 Comparison	
Absolute Difference	8.072
Standard Error of Difference	1.371
Critical Range	5.224
Means are different	

Group 2 to Group 4 Comparison	
Absolute Difference	10.106
Standard Error of Difference	1.371
Critical Range	5.224
Means are different	

Group 3 to Group 4 Comparison	
Absolute Difference	2.034
Standard Error of Difference	1.371
Critical Range	5.224
Means are not different	

Group-to-group Means Comparison						
Groups	1–2	1–3	1–4	2–3	2–4	3–4
Means	Different	Different	Different	Different	Different	Not Different

There is no significant difference between μ_3 and μ_4 for the 0.05 significance level.

(c) (1) The assumptions of randomness and independence appear to be valid. These assumptions are necessary for the sampling procedure.
(2) The assumption of normality of errors appears to be valid.
(3) The assumption of homogeneity of variance appears to be valid for the second, third, and fourth samples. The first sample may not hold to the assumption. Bartlet's test may be used to test this hypothesis.

Box-and-Whisker Plot

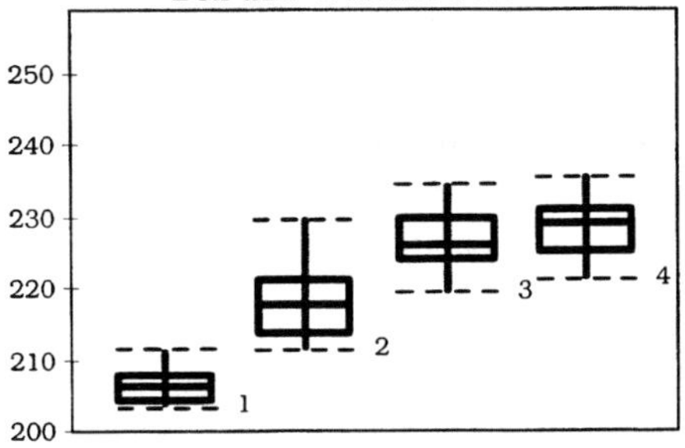

(d) The manufacturing manager must compare the third and fourth designs using all of the other parameters. Based on the average traveling distance, they are the best; however, there is no significant difference between μ_3 and μ_4.

3. (a) $H_0: \mu_1 = \mu_2 = \mu_3$, H_1: Not all of the means are equal.

Anova: Single Factor

Summary				
Groups	**Count**	**Sum**	**Average**	**Variance**
Run 1	10.000	6.620	0.662	0.024
Run 2	10.000	7.520	0.752	0.045
Run 3	10.000	6.860	0.686	0.028

ANOVA						
Source of Variation	**SS**	**df**	**MS**	***F***	***p*-value**	F_{crit}
Between Groups	0.043	2.000	0.022	0.674	0.518	3.354
Within Groups	0.870	27.000	0.032			
Total	0.914	29.000				

Decision rule: Reject H_0 if $F > 3.354$. Test statistic: $F = 0.674$. Decision: Because $F < 3.354$, do not reject H_0. There is no significant difference between the average amounts of sulfides for the three runs for the 0.05 level.

(b) Although no significant difference between the averages were found, a Tukey Kramer Multiple Comparisons should still be completed.

Tukey Kramer Multiple Comparisons	
Group 1	
Sample Mean	0.662
Sample Size	10.000
Group 2	
Sample Mean	0.752
Sample Size	10.000
Group 3	
Sample Mean	0.686
Sample Size	10.000
MSW	0.0322
Q Statistic	2.900

Group 1 to Group 2 Comparison	
Absolute Difference	0.090
Standard Error of Difference	0.057
Critical Range	0.165
Means are different	

Group 1 to Group 3 Comparison	
Absolute Difference	0.024
Standard Error of Difference	0.057
Critical Range	0.165
Means are not different	

Group 1 to Group 4 Comparison	
Absolute Difference	22.008
Standard Error of Difference	1.371
Critical Range	5.224
Means are not different	

Group 2 to Group 3 Comparison	
Absolute Difference	0.066
Standard Error of Difference	0.057
Critical Range	0.165
Means are not different	

Group-to-Group Means Comparison			
Groups	1–2	1–3	2–3
Means	Not different	Not different	Not different

There are no significant differences between any of the pairs of means.

(c) (1) The assumptions of randomness and independence appear to be valid. These assumptions are necessary for the sampling procedure.

(2) The assumption of normality of errors appears to be valid.

(3) The assumption of homogeneity of variance appears to be valid for the first and second samples. The third sample does not appear to hold to the assumption. Bartlet's test may be used to test this hypothesis.

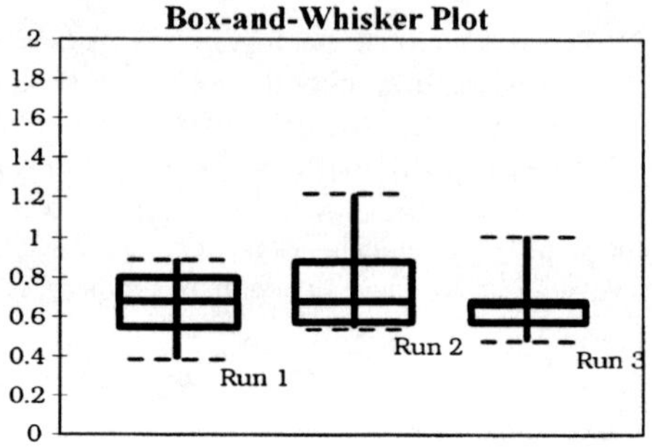

4. (a) $H_0: \mu_1 = \mu_2 = \mu_3 = \mu_4 = \mu_5$, H_1: Not all of the means are equal

Anova: Single Factor

Summary				
Groups	**Count**	**Sum**	**Average**	**Variance**
Normal	3.000	131.500	43.833	0.583
25% Dirty	3.000	100.800	33.600	5.070
35% Dirty	3.000	92.000	30.667	0.203
25% Clean	3.000	130.800	43.600	3.370
35% Clean	3.000	130.200	43.400	1.120

ANOVA						
Source of Variation	**SS**	**df**	**MS**	***F***	***p*-value**	F_{crit}
Between Groups	487.451	4.000	121.863	58.890	6.49×10^{-7}	3.478
Within Groups	20.693	10.000	2.069			
Total	508.144	14.000				

Decision rule: Reject H_0 if $F > 3.478$. Test statistic: $F = 58.890$. Decision: Because $F > 3.478$, reject H_0. There is evidence of a difference between the average compressive strengths for the different mixes.

(b) critical range $= 4.65\sqrt{\frac{2.069333}{2}\left(\frac{1}{3}+\frac{1}{3}\right)} = 3.861$. Let us denote $d_{ij} = |\bar{X}_i - \bar{X}_j|$

	i–j									
Groups	1–2	1–3	1–4	1–5	2–3	2–4	2–5	3–4	3–5	4–5
d_{ij}	10.230	13.170	0.233	0.433	2.933	10.000	9.800	12.930	12.730	0.200
Decision	Different	Different	Not different	Not different	Not different	Different	Different	Different	Different	Not different

(c) The first, fourth, and fifth mixes have the largest average compressive strengths and do not differ significantly. Therefore, one of these three mixes must be recommended. The best one out of these three should be chosen after other relevant parameters are compared. For example, the fourth and fifth mixes are more expensive than the first one; in this case it would be reasonable to recommend the first (normal) mix.

5. (a) $H_0: \mu_A = \mu_B = \mu_C$, H_1: Not all of the means are equal.

Anova: Single Factor

		Summary		
Groups	**Count**	**Sum**	**Average**	**Variance**
A	5.000	450.100	90.020	0.877
B	5.000	455.300	91.060	1.093
C	5.000	467.500	93.500	2.325

			ANOVA			
Source of Variation	**SS**	**df**	**MS**	***F***	***p*-value**	F_{crit}
Between Groups	31.909	2.000	15.955	11.144	0.002	3.885
Within Groups	17.180	12.000	1.432			
Total	49.089	14.000				

Decision rule: Reject H_0 if $F > 3.885$. Test statistic: $F = 11.144$. Decision: Because $F > 3.885$, reject H_0. There is significant difference between the average reflectance for the different machines for the 0.05 level.

(b)

Tukey Kramer Multiple Comparisons	
Group 1	
Sample Mean	90.020
Sample Size	5.000
Group 2	
Sample Mean	91.060
Sample Size	5.000
Group 3	
Sample Mean	93.500
Sample Size	5.000
MSW	1.432
Q Statistic	3.770

Group 1 to Group 2 Comparison	
Absolute Difference	1.040
Standard Error of Difference	0.535
Critical Range	2.017
Means are not different	

Group 1 to Group 3 Comparison	
Absolute Difference	3.480
Standard Error of Difference	0.535
Critical Range	2.017
Means are different	

Group 2 to Group 3 Comparison	
Absolute Difference	2.440
Standard Error of Difference	0.535
Critical Range	2.017
Means are different	

Groups	**Group-to-group Means Comparison**		
	1–2	1–3	2–3
Means	Not different	Different	Different

There is a significant difference between the third mean and all others.

(c) Machine C should be recommended because its average reflectance is significantly greater than the averages of the other two.

6. (a) $H_0: \mu_1 = \mu_2 = \mu_3 = \mu_4 = \mu_5 = \mu_6$, H_1: Not all of the means are equal.

Anova: Single Factor

Summary

Groups	Count	Sum	Average	Variance
0	3.000	13835.000	4611.667	52684.330
20	3.000	15305.000	5101.667	12444.330
30	3.000	16413.000	5471.000	98863.000
40	3.000	17520.000	5840.000	36109.000
50	3.000	17247.000	5749.000	999.000
60	3.000	14573.000	4857.667	37526.330

ANOVA

Source of Variation	SS	df	MS	*F*	*p*-value	F_{crit}
Between Groups	3679438.000	5.000	735887.700	18.503	2.88×10^{-5}	3.106
Within Groups	477252.000	12.000	39771.000			
Total	4156691.000	17.000				

Decision rule: Reject H_0 if $F > 3.106$. Test statistic: $F = 18.503$. Decision: Because $F > 3.106$, reject H_0. There is evidence of a difference between the average compressive strengths.

(b) critical range $= 4.75\sqrt{\dfrac{39771}{2}\left(\dfrac{1}{8}+\dfrac{1}{8}\right)} = 334.91$. Let us denote $d_{ij} = |\bar{X}_{.i} - \bar{X}_{.j}|$

Groups	1–2	1–3	1–4	1–5	1–6
d_{ij}	1470.000	2578.000	3685.000	3485.000	738.000
Decision	Different	Different	Different	Different	Different

Groups	2–3	2–4	2–5	2–6	3–4
d_{ij}	1108.000	2215.000	1942.000	732.000	1107.000
Decision	Different	Different	Different	Different	Different

Groups	3–5	3–6	4–5	4–6	5–6
d_{ij}	834.000	1840.000	273.000	2947.000	2674.000
Decision	Different	Different	Not different	Different	Different

(c) It will be reasonable to recommend either 40% or 50% because these percentages correspond to the greatest average compressive strengths. These average strengths do not differ significantly between themselves. In order to choose the best one of the two, further comparisons using another characteristic would be necessary.

7. (a) $H_0: \mu_1 = \mu_2 = \mu_3 = \mu_4 = \mu_5 = \mu_6$, H_1: Not all of the means are equal.

Anova: Single Factor

Summary

Groups	Count	Sum	Average	Variance
Column 1	8.000	4117.000	514.625	17228.840
Column 2	8.000	3893.000	486.625	20580.840
Column 3	8.000	3923.000	490.375	3708.554
Column 4	8.000	4058.000	507.250	11095.070
Column 5	8.000	3676.000	459.500	15778.000
Column 6	8.000	3596.000	449.500	18549.710

ANOVA

Source of Variation	SS	df	MS	*F*	*p*-value	F_{crit}
Between Groups	26511.850	5.000	5302.371	0.366	0.869	2.438
Within Groups	608587.100	42.000	14490.170			
Total	635099.000	47.000				

Decision rule: Reject H_0 if $F > 2.438$. Test statistic: $F = 0.366$. Decision: Because $F < 2.438$, do not reject H_0. There is no significant difference between the average tensile strengths for the different time period.

(b) Although no significant difference between the averages was found, a Tukey Kramer Multiple Comparisons should be done to complete the analysis.

Critical range $= 4.23\sqrt{\frac{14490.17}{2}\left(\frac{1}{8}+\frac{1}{8}\right)} = 180$.

Let us denote $d_{ij} = \left|\overline{X}_{.i} - \overline{X}_{.j}\right|$

	i–j				
Groups	1–2	1–3	1–4	1–5	1–6
d_{ij}	224.000	194.000	59.000	441.000	521.000
Decision	Different	Different	Not different	Different	Different

	i–j				
Groups	2–3	2–4	2–5	2–6	3–4
d_{ij}	30.000	165.000	217.000	297.000	135.000
Decision	Not different	Not different	Different	Different	Not different

	i–j				
Groups	3–5	3–6	4–5	4–6	5–6
d_{ij}	247.000	337.000	382.000	462.000	80.000
Decision	Different	Different	Different	Different	Not different

(c)

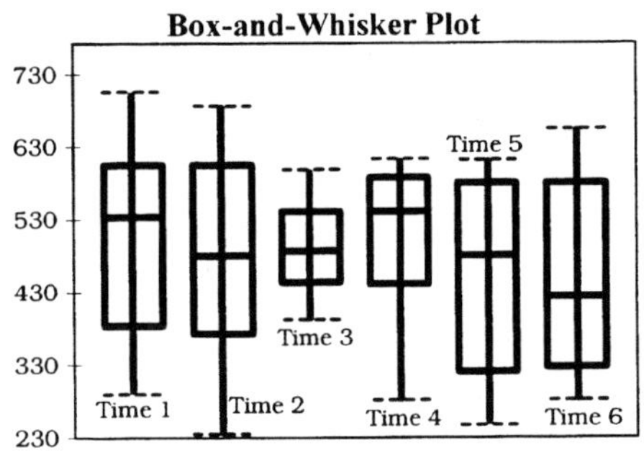

(d) There are no clear patterns in this data. From the box-and-whisker plot it can be concluded that the average stresses measured over time periods 5 and 6 are significantly lower than those measured over time periods 1, 2, 3 and 4. However, because there are no significant differences between the average stresses measured over time periods 5 and 6, we cannot determine which of these two average stresses is the lowest. Further, the average stress measured over time period 1 is significantly higher than those measured over time periods 2, 3, 5, and 6. Although the average stress measured over time period 1 is also higher than that measured over time period 4, this result is not significant.

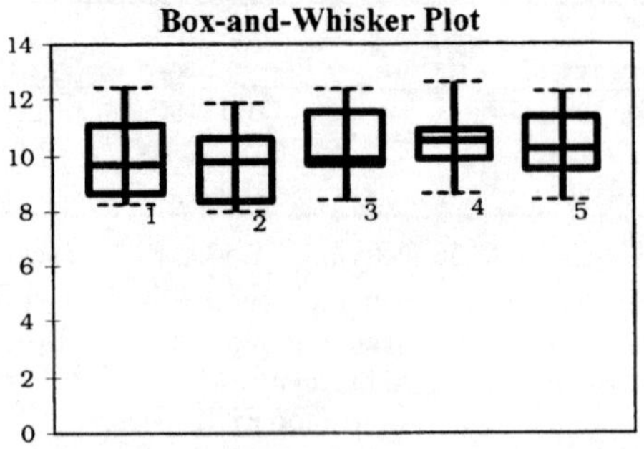

8. (a) $H_0: \mu_1 = \mu_2 = \mu_3 = \mu_4 = \mu_5$, H_1: At least one of the means differs. The answer to the question "describe any trends or relationships that might be apparent among the treatment groups and among the blocks" will vary.

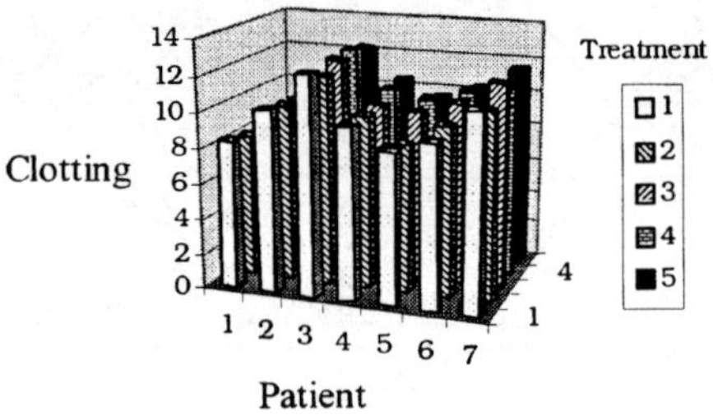

(b) ***Anova: Two-Factor Without Replication***

Summary	Count	Sum	Average	Variance
Patient 1	5.000	42.100	8.420	0.037
Patient 2	5.000	51.000	10.200	0.075
Patient 3	5.000	61.200	12.240	0.073
Patient 4	5.000	50.200	10.040	0.113
Patient 5	5.000	46.100	9.220	0.457
Patient 6	5.000	49.900	9.980	0.257
Patient 7	5.000	55.600	11.120	0.157
TS 1	7.000	69.800	9.971	2.026
TS 2	7.000	68.300	9.757	1.593
TS 3	7.000	72.200	10.314	1.601
TS 4	7.000	73.400	10.486	1.358
TS 5	7.000	72.400	10.343	1.453

ANOVA

Source of Variation	SS	df	MS	F	p-value	F_{crit}
Rows	46.031	6.000	7.672	85.446	5.35×10^{-15}	2.508
Columns	2.521	4.000	0.630	7.020	0.001	2.776
Error	2.155	24.000	0.090			
Total	50.707	34.000				

Decision rule: Reject H_0 if $F > 2.776$. Test statistic: $F = 7.020$. Decision: Because $F > 2.776$, reject H_0. There is evidence of a difference among the average plasma clotting times for the five treatment substances.

(c) critical range $= 4.54\sqrt{\dfrac{0.089786}{5}} = 0.60838$. Let us denote $d_{ij} = \left|\overline{X}_{.i} - \overline{X}_{.j}\right|$

	i–j									
Groups	1–2	1–3	1–4	1–5	2–3	2–4	2–5	3–4	3–5	4–5
d_{ij}	1.500	2.400	3.600	2.600	3.900	5.100	4.100	1.200	0.200	1.000
Decision	Different	Different	Different	Different	Different	Different	Different	Different	Not different	Different

(d) There is evidence of a difference among the average plasma clotting times for the five treatment substances, but not all pair comparisons show significant differences.

(e) Estimated relative efficiency: $RE = \dfrac{(r-1)MSBL + r(c-1)MSE}{(rc-1)MSE} = \dfrac{(7-1)7.67181 + 7(5-1)0.089786}{(35-1)0.089786} = 17.964$

(f) The result of part (e) shows that 17.964 times as many observations in each treatment group of a one-way ANOVA design would be needed to obtain the same precision for the comparison of treatment group means as for the randomized block design.

9. (a) $H_0: \mu_1 = \mu_2 = \mu_3$, H_1: At least one of the means is different.

Anova: Two-Factor Without Replication

Summary	Count	Sum	Average	Variance
Two days	40.000	119.640	2.991	0.246
Seven days	40.000	141.765	3.544	0.254
28 days	40.000	182.380	4.560	0.232

ANOVA

Source of Variation	SS	df	MS	F	p-value	F_{crit}
Rows	21.170	39.000	0.543	5.752	2.92×10^{-11}	1.553
Columns	50.628	2.000	25.314	268.256	1.09×10^{-35}	3.114
Error	7.361	78.000	0.094			
Total	79.159	119.000				

Decision rule: Reject H_0 if $F > 3.114$. Test statistic: $F = 268.256$. Decision: Because $F > 3.114$, reject H_0. There is evidence of a difference among the average compressive strengths after 2, 7 and 28 days.

(b) critical range $= 3.38\sqrt{\dfrac{0.094366}{40}} = 0.16417$. Let us denote $d_{ij} = |\bar{X}_{.i} - \bar{X}_{.j}|$

	i–j		
Groups	1–2	1–3	2–3
d_{ij}	0.553	1.569	1.015
Decision	Different	Different	Different

There are significant differences for all pairs of means for the 0.05 level.

(c) Estimated relative efficiency: $RE = \dfrac{(r-1)MSBL + r(c-1)MSE}{(rc-1)MSE} = \dfrac{39\cdot 0.54822 + 40\cdot 2\cdot 0.094366}{119\cdot 0.094366} = 2.576$

(d) **Box-and-Whisker Plot**

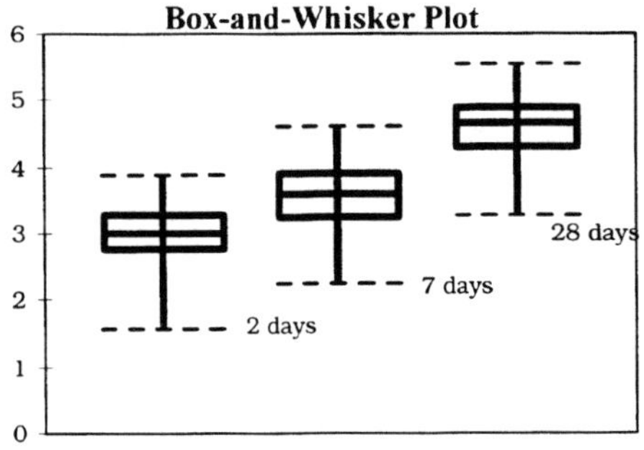

(e) Compressive strength increases as the number of days after pouring increases, within a range of 2 to 28 days.

10. (a)

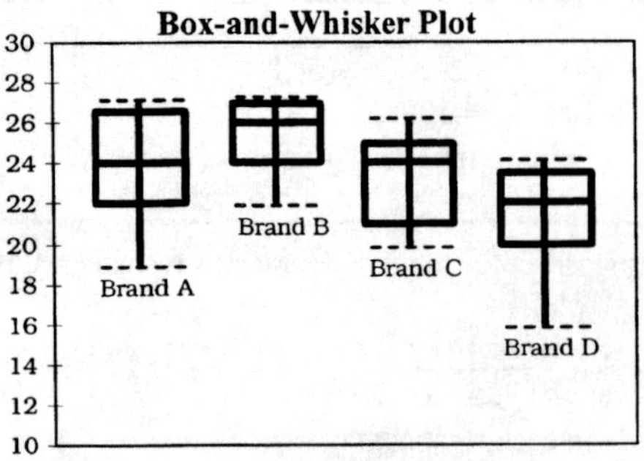

The answer to the question "describe any differences that might be apparent among the treatment groups and among the blocks" will vary.

(b) $H_0: \mu_A = \mu_B = \mu_C = \mu_D$, H_1: At least one of the means is different.

Anova: Two-Factor Without Replication

Summary	Count	Sum	Average	Variance
C.C.	4.000	97.000	24.250	2.917
S.E.	4.000	104.000	26.000	2.000
E.G.	4.000	77.000	19.250	6.250
B.L.	4.000	99.000	24.750	2.917
C.M.	4.000	90.000	22.500	3.000
C.N.	4.000	101.000	25.250	2.250
G.N.	4.000	98.000	24.500	5.667
R.M.	4.000	97.000	24.250	6.250
P.V.	4.000	84.000	21.000	3.333
Brand A	9.000	216.000	24.000	7.000
Brand B	9.000	230.000	25.556	3.528
Brand C	9.000	208.000	23.111	4.861
Brand D	9.000	193.000	21.444	6.778

ANOVA

Source of Variation	SS	df	MS	F	p-value	F_{crit}
Rows	153.222	8.000	19.153	19.065	1.21×10^{-8}	3.363
Columns	79.639	3.000	26.546	26.424	8.86×10^{-8}	4.718
Error	24.111	24.000	1.005			
Total	256.972	35.000				

Decision rule: Reject H_0 if $F > 4.718$. Test statistic: $F = 26.424$. Decision: Because $F > 4.718$, reject H_0. There is evidence of a difference among the average ratings of the four brands of Colombian coffee.

critical range $= 4.91\sqrt{\dfrac{1.00463}{9}} = 1.64$. Let us denote $d_{ij} = |\bar{X}_{.i} - \bar{X}_{.j}|$

	i–j					
Groups	1–2	1–3	1–4	2–3	2–4	3–4
d_{ij}	1.556	0.889	2.556	2.44	4.111	1.667
Means	Not different	Not different	Different	Different	Different	Different

There are no significant differences between μ_1 and μ_2 and between μ_1 and μ_3 for the 0.01 level. Brand B appears to be the best. Brand B is significantly better than Brands C and D. Although this difference is insignificant, the average score of Brand B is greater than that of Brand A.

11. (a) $H_0: \mu_1 = \mu_2 = \mu_3 = \mu_4$, H_1: At least one of the means is different.

Anova: Two-Factor Without Replication

Summary	Count	Sum	Average	Variance
1	4.000	90.900	22.725	0.069
2	4.000	217.600	54.400	4.620
3	4.000	39.300	9.825	1.249
4	4.000	85.900	21.475	2.729
5	4.000	52.700	13.175	0.769
6	4.000	177.900	44.475	64.369
7	4.000	63.100	15.775	12.429
8	4.000	75.000	18.750	15.843
Fear	8.000	222.600	27.825	328.656
Happiness	8.000	203.300	25.413	258.313
Depression	8.000	191.000	23.875	224.196
Calmness	8.000	185.500	23.188	221.216

ANOVA

Source of Variation	SS	df	MS	F	p-value	F_{crit}
Rows	7021.865	7.000	1003.124	102.858	8.3×10^{-15}	2.488
Columns	101.433	3.000	33.811	3.467	0.034	3.072
Error	204.803	21.000	9.753			
Total	7328.100	31.000				

Decision rule: Reject H_0 if $F > 3.072$. Test statistic: $F = 3.467$. Decision: Because $F > 3.072$, reject H_0. There is a significant difference among the average measured skin potentials for the emotions for the 0.05 level.

(b) critical range $= 3.95\sqrt{\frac{9.7525}{8}} = 4.361$. Let us denote $d_{ij} = |\bar{X}_{.i} - \bar{X}_{.j}|$

	i–j					
Groups	1–2	1–3	1–4	2–3	2–4	3–4
d_{ij}	2.413	3.950	4.638	1.538	2.225	0.688
Decision	Not different	Not different	Different	Not different	Not different	Not different

There is a significant difference between μ_1 and μ_4 for the 0.05 level.

(c) Estimated relative efficiency: $RE = \frac{(r-1)MSBL + r(c-1)MSE}{(rc-1)MSE} = \frac{7\cdot 1003.121 + 8\cdot 3\cdot 9.7525}{31\cdot 9.7525} = 24$

(d) There is a significant difference among the average measured skin potentials for the emotions for the 0.05 level. Paired comparisons show that this effect exists for the fear and the calmness groups at a significant level.

12. (a) $H_0: \mu_1 = \mu_2 = \mu_3$, H_1: At least one of the means is different.

Anova: Two-Factor Without Replication

Summary	Count	Sum	Average	Variance
1	3.000	16.650	5.550	0.018
2	3.000	17.450	5.817	0.011
3	3.000	15.400	5.133	0.016
4	3.000	17.350	5.783	0.006
5	3.000	16.450	5.483	0.013
6	3.000	16.450	5.483	0.006
Round out	6.000	33.600	5.600	0.064
Narrow angle	6.000	33.450	5.575	0.063
Wide angle	6.000	32.700	5.450	0.070

ANOVA						
Source of Variation	**SS**	**df**	**MS**	***F***	***p*-value**	F_{crit}
Rows	0.923	5.000	0.185	30.342	9.8×10^{-6}	3.326
Columns	0.078	2.000	0.039	6.370	0.0164	4.103
Error	0.061	10.000	0.006			
Total	1.061	17.000				

Decision rule: Reject H_0 if $F > 3.072$. Test statistic: $F = 6.370$. Decision: Because $F > 3.072$, reject H_0. There is a significant difference among the times to run to the second base for the three methods for the 0.05 level.

(b) critical range $= 3.88\sqrt{\dfrac{0.006083}{6}} = 0.1309$. Let us denote $d_{ij} = |\bar{X}_{.i} - \bar{X}_{.j}|$

	i–j		
Groups	1–2	1–3	2–3
d_{ij}	0.025	0.150	0.125
Decision	Not different	Different	Not different

There is a significant difference between μ_1 and μ_3 for the 0.05 level.

(c) Estimated relative efficiency: $RE = \dfrac{(r-1)\text{MSBL} + r(c-1)\text{MSE}}{(rc-1)\text{MSE}} = \dfrac{5\cdot 0.184583 + 6\cdot 2\cdot 0.006083}{17\cdot 0.006083} = 9.631$

(d) There is a significant difference among the times to run to second base for the three methods for the 0.05 level. The wide angle method provides a significantly lower mean time value than the round out method. The wide angle method also provides a lower mean time than the narrow angle method, although the difference is insignificant. It appears that the player should use the wide angle method for better results.

(e) The purpose of blocking is to remove as much variability as possible. Then the focus of the test is on the differences among the treatment conditions.

13. (a) $H_0: M_1 = M_2 = M_3$, H_1: At least one of the medians is different.

Kruskal Wallis Rank Test	
Level of Significance	0.050
Group 1	
Sum of Ranks	119.000
Sample Size	8.000
Group 2	
Sum of Ranks	112.000
Sample Size	8.000
Group 3	
Sum of Ranks	69.000
Sample Size	8.000
Sum of Squared Ranks/Sample Size	3933.250
Sum of Sample Sizes	24.000
Number of groups	3.000
H Test Statistic	3.665
Critical Value	5.991
p-Value	0.160
Do not reject the null hypothesis	

Decision rule: reject H_0 if $H > 5.991$. Test statistic: $H = 3.665$. Decision: Because $H < 5.991$, do not reject H_0. There is no significant temperature effect on the median life of the three types of electronic components.

(b) Temperature does not have a significant effect on the failure time because of the large *p*-value of 0.16.

14. (a) $H_0: M_1 = M_2 = M_3$, H_1: At least one of the medians is different.

Kruskal Wallis Rank Test	
Level of Significance	0.050
Group 1	
Sum of Ranks	100.500
Sample Size	8.000
Group 2	
Sum of Ranks	80.000
Sample Size	8.000
Group 3	
Sum of Ranks	119.500
Sample Size	8.000
Sum of Squared Ranks/Sample Size	3847.563
Sum of Sample Sizes	24.000
Number of groups	3.000
H Test Statistic	1.951
Critical Value	5.991
p-Value	0.377
Do not reject the null hypothesis	

Decision rule: reject H_0 if $H > 5.991$. Test statistic: $H = 1.951$. Decision: Because $H < 5.991$, do not reject H_0. There is no significant difference in the median lead concentration for the three types of water.

(b) **Box-and-Whisker Plot**

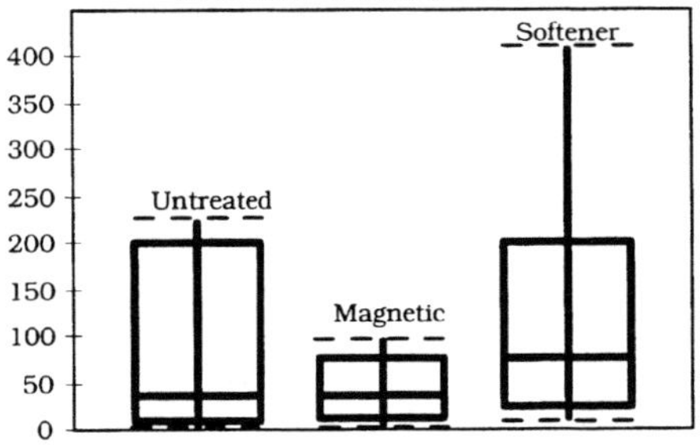

There is a significant difference in the variances, so it is not appropriate to use the ANOVA procedure. For the same reason, there are some doubts concerning the appropriateness of the Kruskel-Wallis test, but the sampling median is more robust than the sampling average. With respect to the ANOVA, the initial data do not have zero skewness, therefore the normal assumption is not satisfied.

15. (a) $H_0: M_1 = M_2 = M_3 = M_4$, H_1: At least one of the medians is different

Kruskal Wallis Rank Test	
Level of Significance	0.050
Group 1	
Sum of Ranks	55.000
Sample Size	10.000
Group 2	
Sum of Ranks	174.000
Sample Size	10.000
Group 3	
Sum of Ranks	277.000
Sample Size	10.000
Group 4	
Sum of Ranks	314.000
Sample Size	10.000
Sum of Squared Ranks/Sample Size	20862.600
Sum of Sample Sizes	40.000
Number of groups	4.000
H Test Statistic	29.653
Critical Value	7.815
p-Value	1.63×10^{-6}
Reject the null hypothesis	

Decision rule: reject H_0 if $H > 7.815$. Test statistic: $H = 29.653$. Decision: Because $H > 7.815$, reject H_0. There is evidence of a difference in the median distance traveled by the golf balls of different design.

(b) There are no differences in the results of 10.2 and 10.15 because the initial assumptions of the ANOVA appear to be valid (see the Box-and-Whisker Plot). There is no significant difference between the means and the medians.

Box-and-Whisker Plot

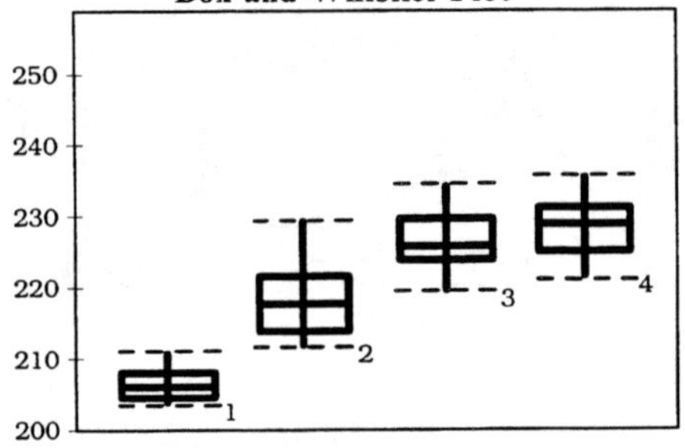

16. (a) $H_0: M_1 = M_2 = M_3$, H_1: At least one of the medians is different.

Kruskal Wallis Rank Test	
Level of Significance	0.050
Group 1	
Sum of Ranks	144.000
Sample Size	10.000
Group 2	
Sum of Ranks	172.500
Sample Size	10.000
Group 3	
Sum of Ranks	148.500
Sample Size	10.000
Sum of Squared Ranks/Sample Size	7254.450
Sum of Sample Sizes	30.000
Number of groups	3.000
H Test Statistic	0.606
Critical Value	5.991
p-Value	0.739
Do not reject the null hypothesis	

Decision rule: Reject H_0 if $H > 5.991$. Test statistic: $H = 0.606$. Decision: Because $H < 5.991$, do not reject H_0. There is no significant difference in the median amount of sulfides for the three different runs.

(b) There are no differences between the results of 10.3 and 10.16 because the initial assumptions of the ANOVA appear to be valid (see the Box-and-Whisker Plot. There is no significant difference between the means and the medians.

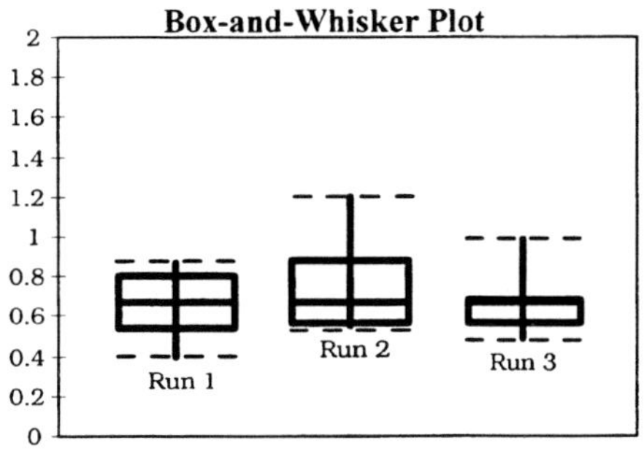

17. (a) $H_0: M_1 = M_2 = M_3 = M_4 = M_5 = M_6$, H_1: At least one of the medians is different.

j	1	2	3	4	5	6
T_j	224.000	199.500	189.000	221.500	179.500	162.500
n_j	8.000	8.000	8.000	8.000	8.000	8.000

$$H = \left[\frac{12}{n(n+1)}\sum_{j=1}^{6}\frac{T_j^2}{n_j}\right] - 3(n+1) = \left[\frac{12}{48\cdot 49}\cdot\frac{1}{8}(224^2 + 199.5^2 + 189^2 + 221.5^2 + 179.5^2 + 162.5^2)\right] - 3\cdot 49 = 1.8431.$$

Decision rule: Reject H_0 if $H > 11.071$. Decision: Because $H < 11.071$, do not reject H_0. There is no significant difference in the median tensile strengths for the six time periods.

(b) There are no differences in the results of 10.7 and 10.17 because the initial assumptions of the ANOVA appear to be valid. There is no significant difference between the means and the medians.

18. The among-group variation is measured by the sum of the squared differences between the sample mean of each group and the overall mean. The within-group variation measures the difference between each individual observation and the mean of its own group and sums the square of these differences over all of the groups.

19. Only two assumptions can be tested graphically—the normality and homogeneity of variance. It is possible to see skewness, kurtosis, mean squared displacement using the multiple Box-and-Whisker Plot.

20. In the completely randomized design models, n homogeneous items or individuals are randomly assigned to c levels of the study factor (one-way ANOVA test). In the randomized block design models there are repeated measurements or matched samples (blocks) for various levels of the study factor (treatments).

21. The main assumptions of the ANOVA are:
(a) Randomness and Independence.
(b) Normality.
(c) Homogeneity of variance.

22. The hypothesis about equal means with common alternative can be tested using the ANOVA assumptions. Thus, the one-way ANOVA F test has more stringent assumptions than the Kruskal-Wallis test. As a result, for situations involving completely randomized designs, the more stringent assumptions of the F test hold. The F test is preferred over the Kruskal-Wallis test because it is slightly more powerful in its ability to detect significant treatment effects.

23. The Kruskal-Wallis should be selected when the measurements are ordinal over all of the sample groups, and the common population distributions are continuous. Under these assumptions, the hypothesis about equal medians with common alternative can be tested. Thus, the Kruskal-Wallis procedure makes less stringent assumptions than the F test. As a result, for completely randomized designs, the Kruskal-Wallis test is more powerful than the F test, when the more stringent assumptions of the F test cannot be met.

24. Once it has been determined that a difference exists among the group means, it is important to determine which particular groups are different. The multiple-comparison procedures for evaluating pairwise combinations of the group means should be used for this determination. In particular, the Tukey-type procedure provides comparisons among all of the pairs of groups simultaneously. With this procedure, the pairs of significantly different groups are identified.

25. In the randomized block design models, there are repeated measurements or matched samples (blocks) for the various levels of the study factor (treatments). The purpose of blocking is to remove as much block or subject variability as possible, so that the focus is on differences among the c treatment conditions. Thus, the reason for selecting a randomized block F test (instead of a completely randomized test) is to provide a more efficient analysis by reducing the experimental error and thereby obtaining more precise results. Obviously, a randomized block F test makes more stringent assumptions than does a completely randomized test: in addition to the assumptions of the one-way analysis of variance listed in Problem 21, it should also be assumed that there is no interacting effects between the treatments and the blocks.

26. (a) $H_0: \mu_A = \mu_B = \mu_C = \mu_D$, H_1: At least one of the means is different.

Summary

Groups	Count	Sum	Average	Variance
A	6.000	572.000	95.333	23.067
B	6.000	509.000	84.833	16.567
C	6.000	452.000	75.333	17.467
D	6.000	491.000	81.833	14.567

ANOVA

Source of Variation	SS	df	MS	F	p-value	F_{crit}
Between Groups	1251.000	3.000	417.000	23.274	9.9×10^{-7}	3.098
Within Groups	358.333	20.000	17.917			
Total	1609.333	23.000				

Decision rule: Reject H_0 if $F > 3.010$. Test statistic: $F = 23.274$. Decision: Because $F > 3.010$, reject H_0. There is evidence of a difference in the shelf life between the formulations.

(b)

Tukey Kramer Multiple Comparisons	
Group 1	
Sample Mean	95.333
Sample Size	6.000
Group 2	
Sample Mean	84.833
Sample Size	6.000
Group 3	
Sample Mean	75.333
Sample Size	6.000
Group 4	
Sample Mean	81.833
Sample Size	6.000
MSW	17.917
Q Statistic	3.960

Group 1 to Group 2 Comparison	
Absolute Difference	10.500
Standard Error of Difference	1.728
Critical Range	6.843
Means are different	

Group 1 to Group 3 Comparison	
Absolute Difference	20.000
Standard Error of Difference	1.728
Critical Range	6.843
Means are not different	

Group 1 to Group 4 Comparison	
Absolute Difference	13.500
Standard Error of Difference	1.728
Critical Range	6.843
Means are different	

Group 2 to Group 3 Comparison	
Absolute Difference	9.500
Standard Error of Difference	1.728
Critical Range	6.843
Means are different	

Group 2 to Group 4 Comparison	
Absolute Difference	3.000
Standard Error of Difference	1.728
Critical Range	6.843
Means are not different	

Group 3 to Group 4 Comparison	
Absolute Difference	6.500
Standard Error of Difference	1.728
Critical Range	6.843
Means are not different	

critical range = 6.843026. Let us denote $d_{ij} = |\bar{X}_{.i} - \bar{X}_{.j}|$.

				i–j		
Groups	1–2	1–3	1–4	2–3	2–4	3–4
d_{ij}	10.500	20.000	13.500	9.500	3.000	6.500
Decision	Different	Different	Different	Different	Not different	Not different

There is no significant difference between the means μ_2 and μ_4, and the means μ_3 and μ_4 for 0.05 level.

(c) There is a significant difference among the four methods. The maximum shelf life is provided by method A and it is significantly different from all others.

27. (a) $H_0: \mu_1 = \mu_2 = \mu_3 = \mu_4$, H_1: At least one of the means is different.

Anova: Single Factor

Summary				
Groups	**Count**	**Sum**	**Average**	**Variance**
0.0 cc	10.000	6519.000	651.900	3390.989
0.5 cc	10.000	5897.000	589.700	4256.678
1.0 cc	10.000	5629.000	562.900	3727.878
2.0 cc	10.000	5705.000	570.500	2490.722

ANOVA						
Source of Variation	**SS**	**df**	**MS**	***F***	***p*-value**	F_{crit}
Between Groups	48901.100	3.000	16300.370	4.702	0.007	2.866
Within Groups	124796.400	36.000	3466.567			
Total	173697.500	39.000				

Decision rule: Reject H_0 if $F > 2.866$. Test statistic: $F = 4.702$. Decision: Because $F > 2.866$, reject H_0 for the 0.05 level.

(b)

Tukey Kramer Multiple Comparisons	
Group 1	
Sample Mean	651.900
Sample Size	10.000
Group 2	
Sample Mean	589.700
Sample Size	10.000
Group 3	
Sample Mean	562.900
Sample Size	10.000
Group 4	
Sample Mean	570.500
Sample Size	10.000
MSW	3466.567
Q Statistic	3.810

Group 1 to Group 2 Comparison	
Absolute Difference	62.200
Standard Error of Difference	18.619
Critical Range	70.937
Means are not different	

Group 1 to Group 3 Comparison	
Absolute Difference	89.000
Standard Error of Difference	18.619
Critical Range	70.937
Means are different	

Group 1 to Group 4 Comparison	
Absolute Difference	81.400
Standard Error of Difference	18.619
Critical Range	70.937
Means are different	

Group 2 to Group 3 Comparison	
Absolute Difference	26.800
Standard Error of Difference	18.619
Critical Range	70.937
Means are not different	

Group 2 to Group 4 Comparison	
Absolute Difference	19.200
Standard Error of Difference	18.619
Critical Range	70.937
Means are not different	

Group 3 to Group 4 Comparison	
Absolute Difference	7.600
Standard Error of Difference	18.619
Critical Range	70.937
Means are not different	

critical range = 70.93732. Let us denote $d_{ij} = |\bar{X}_{.i} - \bar{X}_{.j}|$

	i–j					
Groups	1–2	1–3	1–4	2–3	2–4	3–4
d_{ij}	62.200	89.000	81.400	26.800	19.200	7.600
Decision	Not different	Different	Different	Not different	Not different	Not different

There is a significant difference between the means μ_1 and μ_3, and the means μ_1 and μ_4 for the 0.05 level.

(c) **Box-and-Whisker Plot**

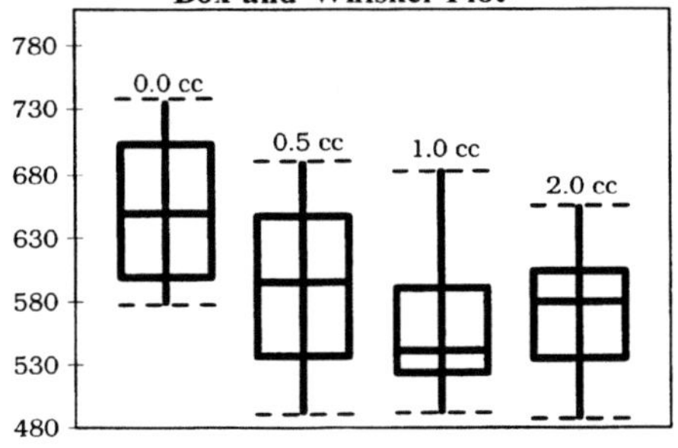

(d) The drug reading for the 0.0 cc formulation is significantly larger than those for the 1.0 cc and the 2.0 cc formulations. The drug reading for the 0.0 cc formulation is also larger than that for the 0.5 cc formulation; this result, however, is not significant.

28. (a) $H_0: \mu_1 = \mu_2 = \mu_3$, H_1: At least one of the means is different.

Anova: Single Factor

Summary

Groups	Count	Sum	Average	Variance
30	6.000	149.000	24.833	0.799
40	6.000	141.200	23.533	1.399
50	6.000	139.900	23.317	0.766

ANOVA

Source of Variation	SS	df	MS	*F*	*p*-value	F_{crit}
Between Groups	8.074	2.000	4.037	4.088	0.038	3.682
Within Groups	14.815	15.000	0.988			
Total	22.889	17.000				

Decision rule: Reject H_0 if $F > 3.682$. Test statistic: $F = 4.088$. Decision: Because $F > 3.682$, reject H_0. There is a significant difference in the mean breaking strengths for the three air-jet pressures for the 0.05 level.

(b)

Tukey Kramer Multiple Comparisons		
	Group 1	
Sample Mean		24.833
Sample Size		6.000
	Group 2	
Sample Mean		23.533
Sample Size		6.000
	Group 3	
Sample Mean		23.317
Sample Size		6.000
MSW		0.988
Q Statistic		3.670

Group 1 to Group 2 Comparison	
Absolute Difference	1.300
Standard Error of Difference	0.406
Critical Range	1.489
Means are not different	

Group 1 to Group 3 Comparison	
Absolute Difference	1.517
Standard Error of Difference	0.406
Critical Range	1.489
Means are different	

Group 2 to Group 3 Comparison	
Absolute Difference	0.217
Standard Error of Difference	0.406
Critical Range	1.489
Means are not different	

critical range = 1.489003. Let us denote $d_{ij} = |\overline{X}_{.i} - \overline{X}_{.j}|$

		i–j	
Groups	1–2	1–3	2–3
d_{ij}	1.300	1.517	0.217
Decision	Not different	Different	Not different

There is a significant difference between μ_1 and μ_3 for the 0.05 level.

(c) $H_0: M_1 = M_2 = M_3$, H_1: At least one of the medians is different.

Kruskal Wallis Rank Test	
Level of Significance	0.050
Group 1	
Sum of Ranks	82.000
Sample Size	6.000
Group 2	
Sum of Ranks	50.000
Sample Size	6.000
Group 3	
Sum of Ranks	39.000
Sample Size	6.000
Sum of Squared Ranks/Sample Size	1790.833
Sum of Sample Sizes	18.000
Number of groups	3.000
H Test Statistic	5.836
Critical Value	5.991
p-Value	0.054
Do not reject the null hypothesis	

There is no significant difference among the medians for the 0.05 level.

(d) Increase in the air-jet pressure from 30 psi to 50 psi leads to significant decrease in breaking strength.

(e) $H_0: \mu_1 = \mu_2 = \mu_3$, H_1: At least one of the means is different.

Anova: Two-Factor Without Replication

Summary	Count	Sum	Average	Variance
1	3.000	73.500	24.500	1.390
2	3.000	72.300	24.100	0.480
3	3.000	73.200	24.400	2.890
4	3.000	70.900	23.633	1.103
5	3.000	70.300	23.433	0.503
6	3.000	69.900	23.300	3.130
30 psi	6.000	149.000	24.833	0.799
40 psi	6.000	141.200	23.533	1.399
50 psi	6.000	139.900	23.317	0.766

ANOVA

Source of Variation	SS	df	MS	*F*	*p*-value	F_{crit}
Rows	3.896	5.000	0.779	0.714	0.627	3.326
Columns	8.074	2.000	4.037	3.697	0.063	4.103
Error	10.919	10.000	1.092			
Total	22.889	17.000				

Decision rule: Reject H_0 if $F > 4.103$. Test statistic: $F = 3.697$. Decision: Because $F < 4.103$, do not reject H_0. There is no significant difference in the mean breaking strengths for the 0.05 level.

(f) There is no significant difference in the mean breaking strengths. Nonetheless, for the sake of completeness, the Tukey procedure should be applied. critical range $= 3.88\sqrt{\dfrac{1.091889}{6}} = 1.655$. Let us denote $d_{ij} = |\overline{X}_i - \overline{X}_j|$

	i–j		
Groups	1–2	1–3	2–3
d_{ij}	1.300	1.517	0.217
Decision	Not different	Not different	Not different

There are no significant differences in the pairs of means.

(g) $H_0: \mu_1' = \mu_2' = \mu_3' = \mu_4' = \mu_5' = \mu_6'$, H_1: At least one of the means is different. Decision rule: Reject H_0 if $F > 3.326$. Test statistic: $F = 0.714$. Decision: Because $F < 3.326$, do not reject H_0. There is no blocking effect.

(h) Estimated relative efficiency: $RE = \dfrac{(r-1)\text{MSBL} + r(c-1)\text{MSE}}{(rc-1)\text{MSE}} = \dfrac{5 \cdot 0.779222 + 6 \cdot 2 \cdot 1.091889}{17 \cdot 1.091889} = 0.9158$

(i) There is no significant difference between the mean breaking strengths part (e) for the 0.05 level. The difference between the observed and critical statistics are not large (0.405) and the *p*-value (0.063) is close to the 0.05. Pairwise comparisons part (b) show a significant difference between μ_1 and μ_3. At the same time, the difference between the observed and critical statistics is small (0.028). This is the critical case for the decision rule and it does not provide globally different results. There is no blocking effect in part (g) and the relative efficiency is about $0.92 < 1$ part (h), so the one-way ANOVA is the appropriate method. Eliminating the blocking effects causes the absence of the significant differences for all pairwise means comparisons.

29. ***Conductivity***

(a) $H_0: \mu_1 = \mu_2 = \mu_3 = \mu_4 = \mu_5$, H_1: At least one of the means is different.
Anova: Single Factor

Summary				
Groups	**Count**	**Sum**	**Average**	**Variance**
6	9.000	13237.000	1470.778	103990.400
7	9.000	15392.000	1710.222	11880.440
8	9.000	11902.000	1322.444	6697.528
9	9.000	16100.000	1788.889	28479.860
10	9.000	9551.000	1061.222	15093.440
11	9.000	11410.000	1267.778	4619.444

ANOVA						
Source of Variation	**SS**	**df**	**MS**	***F***	***p*-value**	F_{crit}
Between Groups	3443266.000	5.000	688653.200	24.197	4.51×10^{-12}	2.409
Within Groups	1366089.000	48.000	28460.190			
Total	4809355.000	53.000				

Decision rule: Reject H_0 if $F > 2.409$. Test statistic: $F = 24.197$. Decision: Because $F > 2.409$, reject H_0.

(b) There is evidence of a difference in the conductivity of the wells.

Hardness

(a) $H_0: \mu_1 = \mu_2 = \mu_3 = \mu_4 = \mu_5$, H_1: At least one of the means is different.
Anova: Single Factor

Summary				
Groups	**Count**	**Sum**	**Average**	**Variance**
7	9.000	8553.000	950.333	10698.250
8	9.000	6742.000	749.111	1224.361
9	9.000	9785.000	1087.222	21044.440
10	9.000	2289.000	254.333	94.000
11	9.000	2730.000	303.333	471.750

ANOVA						
Source of Variation	**SS**	**df**	**MS**	***F***	***p*-value**	F_{crit}
Within Groups	5095229.000	4.000	1273807.000	189.935	1.92×10^{-25}	2.606
Within Groups	268262.400	40.000	6706.561			
Total	5363491.000	44.000				

Decision rule: Reject H_0 if $F > 2.606$. Test statistic: $F = 189.935$. Decision: Because $F > 2.606$, reject H_0.

(b) There is evidence of a difference in the hardness of the wells.

Chloride

(a) $H_0: \mu_1 = \mu_2 = \mu_3 = \mu_4 = \mu_5$, H_1: At least one of the means is different.
Anova: Single Factor

Summary				
Groups	**Count**	**Sum**	**Average**	**Variance**
6	9.000	3160.000	351.111	2221.611
7	9.000	1459.000	162.111	646.611
8	9.000	896.000	99.556	13.278
9	9.000	1448.000	160.889	1018.361
10	9.000	1989.000	221.000	207.500
11	9.000	1209.000	134.333	196.250

ANOVA

Source of Variation	SS	df	MS	F	p-value	F_{crit}
Within Groups	358216.600	5.000	71643.320	99.883	3.57×10^{-24}	2.409
Within Groups	34428.890	48.000	717.269			
Total	392645.500	53.000				

Decision rule: Reject H_0 if $F > 2.409$. Test statistic: $F = 99.883$. Decision: Because $F > 2.409$, reject H_0.

(b) There is evidence of a difference in the level of chloride of the wells.

30. (a) $H_0: \mu_1 = \mu_2 = \mu_3 = \mu_4 = \mu_5 = \mu_6 = \mu_7 = \mu_8$, H_1: At least one of the means is different.

Anova: Two-Factor Without Replication

Summary	Count	Sum	Average	Variance
A	8.000	93.000	11.625	14.268
B	8.000	79.000	9.875	25.268
C	8.000	86.000	10.750	24.786
D	8.000	94.000	11.750	7.643
E	8.000	92.000	11.500	13.429
F	8.000	46.000	5.750	21.357
G	8.000	70.000	8.750	9.643
H	8.000	82.000	10.250	7.357
I	8.000	104.000	13.000	10.286
J	8.000	106.000	13.250	9.643
K	8.000	113.000	14.125	4.125
L	8.000	115.000	14.375	5.125
1	12.000	125.000	10.417	9.356
2	12.000	176.000	14.667	8.970
3	12.000	134.000	11.167	9.242
4	12.000	112.000	9.333	7.697
5	12.000	173.000	14.417	17.720
6	12.000	101.000	8.417	20.265
7	12.000	142.000	11.833	19.970
8	12.000	117.000	9.750	11.477

ANOVA

Source of Variation	SS	df	MS	F	p-value	F_{crit}
Rows	521.500	11.000	47.409	5.793	9.57×10^{-7}	2.487
Columns	440.333	7.000	62.905	7.686	5.07×10^{-7}	2.881
Error	630.167	77.000	8.184			
Total	1592.000	95.000				

Decision rule: Reject H_0 if $F > 2.881$. Test statistic: $F = 7.686$. Decision: Because $F > 2.881$, reject H_0. There is evidence of a difference among the wines.

(b) There are repeated measurements or matched samples (blocks) for the various levels of the study factor (treatments) in the randomized block design models. A randomized block design model is selected rather than the completely randomized design model to provide a more efficient analysis by reducing the experimental error and thereby obtain more precise results. For this problem the respondents are the blocks (matched variables) and wines are the treatments (the study factors). A respondent's individual taste influences her rating decisions.

(c) There is evidence of a difference in the average rating scores between wines 2 and 5 and all of the others. Testing of this hypothesis gives the following results:

Anova: Two-Factor Without Replication

Summary	Count	Sum	Average	Variance
A	6.000	64.000	10.667	13.067
B	6.000	49.000	8.167	20.967
C	6.000	50.000	8.333	6.667
D	6.000	66.000	11.000	4.400
E	6.000	58.000	9.667	2.267
F	6.000	26.000	4.333	5.867
G	6.000	49.000	8.167	10.967
H	6.000	55.000	9.167	3.767
I	6.000	70.000	11.667	5.467
J	6.000	79.000	13.167	5.367
K	6.000	82.000	13.667	4.667
L	6.000	83.000	13.833	5.367
1	12.000	125.000	10.417	9.356
3	12.000	134.000	11.167	9.242
4	12.000	112.000	9.333	7.697
6	12.000	101.000	8.417	20.265
7	12.000	142.000	11.833	19.970
8	12.000	117.000	9.750	11.477

ANOVA

Source of Variation	SS	df	MS	*F*	*p*-value	F_{crit}
Rows	507.153	11.000	46.105	7.226	1.93×10^{-7}	2.589
Columns	93.236	5.000	18.647	2.923	0.021	3.370
Error	350.931	55.000	6.381			
Total	951.319	71.000				

Decision rule: Reject H_0 if $F > 3.370$. Test statistic: $F = 2.923$. Decision: Because $F < 3.370$, do not reject H_0. There is no significant difference among the average rating scores of wines 1, 3, 4, 6, 7 and 8 for the 0.01 level. Now let as compare the means μ_2 and μ_5 with all of the others. critical range $= 5.21\sqrt{\frac{8.183983}{12}} = 4.30$. Let us denote $d_{ij} = |\overline{X}_{.i} - \overline{X}_{.j}|$

				i–j			
Groups	1–2	2–3	2–4	2–5	2–6	2–7	2–8
d_{ij}	4.250	3.500	5.330	0.250	6.250	2.830	4.920
Decision	Not different	Not different	Different	Not different	Different	Not different	Different

			i–j			
Groups	1–5	3–5	4–5	5–6	5–7	5–8
d_{ij}	4.000	3.250	5.080	6.000	2.580	4.670
Decision	Not different	Not different	Different	Different	Not different	Different

(d) (1) The country does not have an effect on this rating.
(2) The type of the wine does not affect the rating
(3) The wine price does affect the rating. A significant difference in price leads to a significant difference in the rating.

(e) Estimated relative efficiency: $RE = \frac{(r-1)\text{MSBL} + r(c-1)\text{MSE}}{(rc-1)\text{MSE}} = \frac{11\cdot 47.40909 + 12\cdot 7\cdot 8.183983}{95\cdot 8.183983} = 1.555$

(f) $H_0: \mu_1 = \mu_2 = \mu_3 = \mu_4 = \mu_5 = \mu_6 = \mu_7 = \mu_8$, H_1: At least one of the means is different.
Anova: Single Factor

Summary	Count	Sum	Average	Variance
1	12.000	125.000	10.417	9.356
2	12.000	176.000	14.667	8.970
3	12.000	134.000	11.167	9.242
4	12.000	112.000	9.333	7.697
5	12.000	173.000	14.417	17.720
6	12.000	101.000	8.417	20.265
7	12.000	142.000	11.833	19.970
8	12.000	117.000	9.750	11.477

ANOVA

Source of Variation	SS	df	MS	F	p-value	F_{crit}
Between Groups	440.333	7.000	62.905	4.807	0.000	2.115
Within Groups	1151.667	88.000	13.087			
Total	1592.000	95.000				

Decision rule: Reject H_0 if $F > 2.115$. Test statistic: $F = 4.807$. Decision: Because $F > 2.115$, reject H_0. There is evidence of a difference in the average rating scores among the wines.

(g) $SSBL = 521.5$, $SSE = 630.1667$, $SSW = 1151.667$, $SSBL + SSE = SSW$. The within-group variation is decomposed based on among-block and error variation. This effect is due to the "thin" procedure.

(h) In the best case (when all tendencies are evident) all methods will yield the same results. In general, the results of the calculations will not have any correct interpretation. For example, the ANOVA and RBD procedures are not correct for ordinal-scaled data, such as ratings. Therefore, their results do not have a reasonable interpretation. For these special cases, it is appropriate to use nonparametric procedures, like the Kruskal-Wallis or Friedman test.

chapter 11

The Design of Experiments: Factorial Designs

1.

Two-way ANOVA: Breaking Strength versus Operator; Machine

Analysis of Variance for Breaking Strength

Source	DF	SS	MS	F	P
Operator	3	301.11	100.37	26.57	0.000
Machine	2	329.39	164.69	43.60	0.000
Interaction	6	86.39	14.40	3.81	0.008
Error	24	90.67	3.78		
Total	35	807.56			

(a) $H_0: \mu_A = \mu_B = \mu_C = \mu_D$, H_1: At least one of the means is different.
Decision rule: Reject H_0 if $F > 3.01$. Test statistic: $F = 26.57$. Decision: Because $F > 3.01$, reject H_0. There is evidence of a difference in the breaking strengths of wool serge material due to the operator.

(b) $H_0: \mu_I = \mu_{II} = \mu_{III}$, H_1: At least one of the means is different.
Decision rule: Reject H_0 if $F > 3.40$. Test statistic: $F = 43.60$. Decision: Because $F > 3.40$, reject H_0. There is evidence of a difference in the breaking strengths of wool serge material due to the machine.

(c) H_0: There is no interaction between the operator and the machine.
H_1: There is interaction between the operator and the machine.
Decision rule: Reject H_0 if $F > 2.51$. Test statistic: $F = 3.81$. Decision: Because $F > 2.51$, reject H_0. There is a significant interaction between operator and machine for the 0.05 level.

(d) (1)

```
                          Individual 95% CI
Operator        Mean      ---------+---------+---------+---------+--
A             112.00                                   (----*----)
B             110.56                              (----*-----)
C             104.33       (----*-----)
D             109.56                          (----*-----)
                          ---------+---------+---------+---------+--
                              105.00    107.50    110.00    112.50
```

(2)

```
                          Individual 95% CI
Machine         Mean      --+---------+---------+---------+---------
I             113.08                                  (---*----)
II            105.75      (----*----)
III           108.50                (----*----)
                          --+---------+---------+---------+---------
                         105.00    107.50    110.00    112.50
```

(e) (1) critical range $= Q_U\sqrt{\frac{MSE}{rn'}} = 3.90\sqrt{\frac{3.78}{4\cdot 3}} = 2.189$. Let us denote $d_{ij} = |\overline{X}_{i.} - \overline{X}_{j.}|$

Group-to-Group Means Comparison

Groups	A–B	A–C	A–D	B–C	B–D	C–D
d_{ij}	1.44	7.67	2.44	5.67	1	5.23
Means	Not different	Different	Different	Different	Not different	Different

There are significant differences between average breaking strengths produced by operator C and average breaking strengths produced by each of the others for the 0.05 level. The average breaking strengths produced by Operations A and D are also different at this significance level.

(2) critical range $= Q_U\sqrt{\frac{MSE}{rn'}} = 3.53\sqrt{\frac{3.78}{4\cdot 3}} = 1.98$. Let us denote $\Delta_{ij} = |\overline{X}_{.i} - \overline{X}_{.j}|$

Group-to-Group Means Comparison

Groups	I—II	I—III	II—III
Δ_{ij}	7.33	4.58	5.75
Means	Different	Different	Different

There are significant differences in average breaking strengths for all pairs of machines for the 0.05 significance level.

(f) Operators create fabric of varying strengths depending on which machines individuals use. One suggestion is to use the 12 operator-machine combinations as the levels of a single factor and completely analyze the data by performing a one-way ANOVA.

(g) For the random effect model one can provide test statistic $F = \frac{MSFA}{MSAB} = \frac{100.37}{14.40} = 6.97$. Decision rule: reject H_0 if $F > 4.76$. Decision: Because $F = 6.97 > 4.76$, reject H_0. There is a significant difference in the breaking strengths of wool serge material due to the operator for both fixed-effects and random-effects models for the 0.05 significance level.

2. **Two-way ANOVA: Output versus Receiver; Amplifier**

```
Analysis of Variance for Output
Source          DF        SS        MS        F        P
Receiver         1     112.7     112.7    10.48    0.005
Amplifier        3     103.0      34.3     3.19    0.052
Interaction      3       6.3       2.1     0.20    0.897
Error           16     172.0      10.8
Total           23     394.0
```

(a) $H_0: \mu_{R1} = \mu_{R2}$, $H_1: \mu_{R1} \neq \mu_{R2}$
Decision rule: reject H_0 if $F > 8.35$. Test statistic: $F = 10.48$. Decision: Because $F > 8.35$, reject H_0. There is a significant difference in the amplification of the stereo recording due to the receiver for the 0.01 significance level.

(b) $H_0: \mu_A = \mu_B = \mu_C = \mu_D$, H_1: At least one of the means is different.
Decision rule: reject H_0 if $F > 5.29$. Test statistic: $F = 3.19$. Decision: Because $F < 5.29$, do not reject H_0. There is no significant difference in the amplification of the stereo recording due to the amplifier for the 0.01 significance level.

(c) H_0: There is no interaction between the receiver and the amplifier.
H_1: There is interaction between the receiver and the amplifier.
Decision rule: reject H_0 if $F > 5.29$. Test statistic: $F = 0.20$. Decision: Because $F < 5.29$, do not reject H_0. There is no significant interaction between the receiver and the amplifier.

(d) (1)

```
                                Individual 95% CI
Receiver          Mean    ------+---------+---------+---------+-----
R1                9.17                               (---------*---------)
R2                4.83     (---------*---------)
                          ------+---------+---------+---------+-----
                              4.00      6.00      8.00     10.00
```

(2)

```
                                Individual 95% CI
Amplifier         Mean    -------+---------+---------+---------+----
A                 6.2                (---------*--------)
B                 9.2                          (---------*--------)
C                 4.0      (--------*---------)
D                 8.7                        (---------*--------)
                          -------+---------+---------+---------+----
                                3.0       6.0       9.0      12.0
```

(e) There is no significant difference in the amplification of the stereo recording due to the amplifier; however, for the sake of completeness, the Tukey procedure should be applied. critical range = $Q_U\sqrt{\frac{MSE}{rn'}} = 4.05\sqrt{\frac{10.8}{2\cdot 4}} = 4.706$. Let us denote $\Delta_{ij} = \left|\bar{X}_{.i} - \bar{X}_{.j}\right|$

Group-to-Group Means Comparison

Groups	A–B	A–C	A–D	B–C	B–D	C–D
Δ_{ij}	3	2.2	2.5	5.2	0.5	4.7
Means	Not different	Not different	Not different	Different	Not different	Not different

There is a significant difference between amplifiers B and C for the 0.01 significance level.

(f) A significantly higher decibel output is achieved when receiver R_1 is used. Among the amplifiers, B gives the best results.

3. **Two-way ANOVA: Fabric Removed versus Fabric; Treatment**

```
Analysis of Variance for Fabric r
Source          DF        SS        MS        F        P
Fabric           1      49.0      49.0     4.88    0.047
Treatment        1     756.3     756.3    75.31    0.000
Interaction      1      42.3      42.3     4.21    0.063
Error           12     120.5      10.0
Total           15     968.0
```

(a) $H_0: \mu_C = \mu_P,\ H_1: \mu_C = \mu_P$
Decision rule: Reject H_0 if $F > 4.75$. Test statistic: $F = 4.88$. Decision: Because $F > 4.75$, reject H_0. There is a significant difference in the average number of inches of a fabric burned after a flame test due to the type of fabric for the 0.05 significance level.

(b) $H_0: \mu_X = \mu_Y,\ H_1: \mu_X \neq \mu_Y$
Decision rule: Reject H_0 if $F > 4.75$. Test statistic: $F = 75.31$. Decision: Because $F > 75.31$, reject H_0. There is evidence of a difference in the average number of inches of a fabric burned after a flame test due to the treatment applied.

(c) H_0: There is no interaction between the fabric and the treatment.
H_1: There is interaction between the fabric and the treatment.
Decision rule: Reject H_0 if $F > 4.75$. Test statistic: $F = 4.21$. Decision: Because $F < 4.75$, do not reject H_0. There is no significant interaction between the fabric and the treatment for the 0.05 significance level.

(d) (1)

```
                                  Individual 95% CI
Fabric              Mean     ------+---------+---------+---------+-----
C                   35.3     (-----------*-----------)
P                   38.8                  (-----------*-----------)
                             ------+---------+---------+---------+-----
                                 34.0      36.0      38.0      40.0
```

(2)

```
                                  Individual 95% CI
Treatment           Mean     -----+---------+---------+---------+------
X                   43.9                                (----*----)
Y                   30.1     (----*----)
                             -----+---------+---------+---------+------
                                30.0      35.0      40.0      45.0
```

(e) There is a significant difference in the average number of inches of fabric burned after a flame test, due to both the type of fabric and the treatment applied, but there is no significant interaction between the fabric and the treatment effects for the 0.05 significance level.

4. **Two-way ANOVA: Density versus Strength; Time**

Analysis of Variance for Density

Source	DF	SS	MS	F	P
Strength	1	52.56	52.56	23.58	0.000
Time	1	1.56	1.56	0.70	0.419
Interaction	1	3.06	3.06	1.37	0.264
Error	12	26.75	2.23		
Total	15	83.94			

(a) $H_0: \mu_1 = \mu_2$, $H_1: \mu_1 \neq \mu_2$
Decision rule: Reject H_0 if $F > 4.75$. Test statistic: $F = 23.58$. Decision: Because $F > 4.75$, reject H_0. There is evidence of a difference in the average density of photographic plate film due to strength.

(b) $H_0: \mu_{10} = \mu_{14}$, $H_1: \mu_{10} \neq \mu_{14}$
Decision rule: Reject H_0 if $F > 4.75$. Test statistic: $F = 0.70$. Decision: Because $F < 4.75$, do not reject H_0. There is no difference in the average density of photographic plate film due to development time.

(c) H_0: There is no interaction between strength and development time.
H_1: There is interaction between strength and development time.
Decision rule: Reject H_0 if $F > 4.75$. Test statistic: $F = 1.37$. Decision: Because $F < 4.75$, do not reject H_0. There is no significant interaction between strength and development time.

(d) (1)

```
                                  Individual 95% CI
Strength            Mean     -+---------+---------+---------+---------+
1                   2.63       (-------*------)
2                   6.25                             (-------*------)
                             -+---------+---------+---------+---------+
                            1.50      3.00      4.50      6.00      7.50
```

(2)

```
                                  Individual 95% CI
Time                Mean     --------+---------+---------+---------+---
10                  4.13     (----------------*----------------)
14                  4.75              (----------------*----------------)
                             --------+---------+---------+---------+---
                                   3.50      4.20      4.90      5.60
```

(e) There is evidence of a difference in the average density of photographic plate film due to strength, but there is no difference in the average density of photographic plate film due to development time. There is also no significant interaction between strength and development time.

5.

Two-way ANOVA: Particle Size versus Operator; Resin Railcar

```
Analysis of Variance for Particle
Source          DF        SS        MS        F        P
Operator         2     20.90     10.45     7.18    0.004
Resin railcar    7    283.87     40.55    27.85    0.000
Interaction     14     14.14      1.01     0.69    0.759
Error           24     34.94      1.46
Total           47    353.86
```

(a) $H_0: \mu_1 = \mu_2 = \mu_3$, H_1: At least one of the means is different.

Decision rule: Reject H_0 if $F > 3.74$. Test statistic: $F = \frac{MSFA}{MSAB} = \frac{10.5}{1.01} = 10.4$. Decision: Because $F > 3.74$, reject H_0. There is evidence of a difference in the average particle size of the resin due to the operator.

(b) $H_0: \mu_1 = \mu_2 = ... = \mu_8$, H_1: At least one of the means is different.

Decision rule: Reject H_0 if $F > 2.76$. Test statistic: $F = \frac{MSFB}{MSAB} = \frac{40.6}{1.01} = 40.2$. Decision: Because $F > 2.76$, reject H_0. There is evidence of a difference in the average particle size of the resin due to the resin railcar.

(c) H_0: There is no interaction between the operator and the resin railcar.

H_1: There is interaction between the operator and the resin railcar.

Decision rule: Reject H_0 if $F > 2.13$. Test statistic: $F = 0.69$. Decision: Because $F < 2.13$, do not reject H_0. There is no significant interaction between the operator and the resin railcar.

(d) (1)

```
                               Individual 95% CI
Operator          Mean    ----------+---------+---------+---------+-
1                32.94                          (---------*---------)
2                32.68                    (---------*---------)
3                31.43    (---------*---------)
                          ----------+---------+---------+---------+-
                                31.50     32.20     32.90     33.60
```

(2)

```
                               Individual 95% CI
Resin railcar     Mean    --------+---------+---------+---------+---
1                35.65                                    (----*----)
2                34.62                              (----*----)
3                29.85       (----*----)
4                29.47    (----*----)
5                30.85            (----*----)
6                30.20        (----*----)
7                32.72                       (-----*----)
8                35.47                                   (----*----)
                          --------+---------+---------+---------+---
                              30.00     32.00     34.00     36.00
```

(e) There is evidence of a difference in the average particle size of the resin both due to the operator and due to the resin railcar. However, there is no significant interaction between the operator and resin railcar.

(f) (1) $H_0: \mu_1 = \mu_2 = \mu_3$, H_1: At least one of the means is different

Decision rule: Reject H_0 if $F > 3.40$. Test statistic: $F = 7.18$. Decision: Because $F > 3.40$, reject H_0. There is a significant difference in the average particle size of the resin due to the operator for the 0.05 significance level.

(2) $H_0: \mu_1 = \mu_2 = ... = \mu_8$, H_1: At least one of the means is different
Decision rule: Reject H_0 if $F > 2.42$. Test statistic: $F = 27.85$. Decision: Because $F > 2.42$, reject H_0. There is evidence of a difference in the average particle size of the resin due to the resin railcar.

(3) H_0: There is no interaction between the operator and the resin railcar.
H_1: There is interaction between the operator and the resin railcar.
Decision rule: Reject H_0 if $F > 2.13$. Test statistic: $F = 0.69$. Decision: Because $F < 2.13$, do not reject H_0. There is no significant interaction between the operator and resin railcar.

CONCLUSION: Results of (a)–(c) and (f) are the same. *There is no difference in testing H_0 for random and fixed effects.*

6. **ANOVA: Deviation from Target versus % Carbonation; Operating Pressure and Line Speed**

Factor	Type	Levels	Values	
% Carbonation	fixed	2	10	12
Operating pr	fixed	2	25	30
Line speed	fixed	2	200	300

Analysis of Variance for Deviation from Target

Source	DF	SS	MS	F	P
% Carbonation	1	180.625	180.625	93.47	0.000
Operating pr	1	50.625	50.625	26.20	0.000
Line speed	1	57.600	57.600	29.81	0.000
%carbona*Operating pr	1	0.100	0.100	0.05	0.821
%carbona*Line speed	1	0.025	0.025	0.01	0.910
Operating pr*Line speed	1	0.625	0.625	0.32	0.574
%carbona*Operating pr*Line speed	1	2.500	2.500	1.29	0.264
Error	32	61.840	1.932		
Total	39	353.940			

(a) $H_0: \mu_{10} = \mu_{12}$, $H_1: \mu_{10} \neq \mu_{12}$
Decision rule: Reject H_0 if $F > 4.15$. Test statistic: $F = 93.47$. Decision: Because $F > 4.15$, reject H_0. There is evidence of an effect on the deviation from the target due to percent of carbonation.

(b) $H_0: \mu_{25} = \mu_{30}$, $H_1: \mu_{25} \neq \mu_{30}$
Decision rule: Reject H_0 if $F > 4.15$. Test statistic: $F = 26.20$. Decision: Because $F > 4.15$, reject H_0. There is evidence of an effect on the deviation from the target due to operating pressure.

(c) $H_0: \mu_{200} = \mu_{300}$, $H_1: \mu_{200} \neq \mu_{300}$
Decision rule: Reject H_0 if $F > 4.15$. Test statistic: $F = 29.81$. Decision: Because $F > 4.15$, reject H_0. There is evidence of an effect on the deviation from the target due to line speed.

(d) Based on large p-values, there are no significant interactions of the factors.

(e) **Main Effects Plot—Data Means for Deviation from Target**

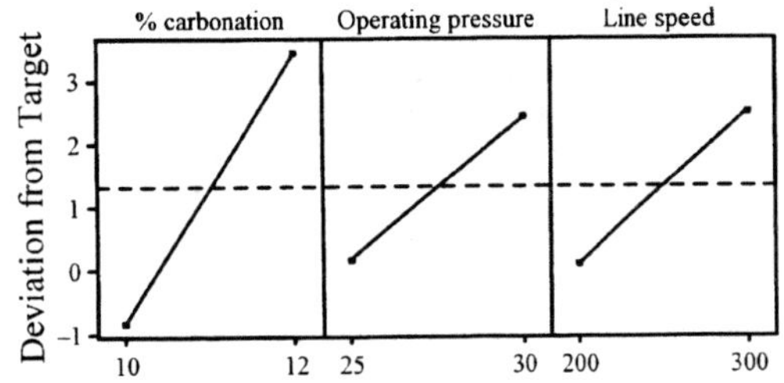

(f) **Interaction Plot—Data Means for Deviation from Target**

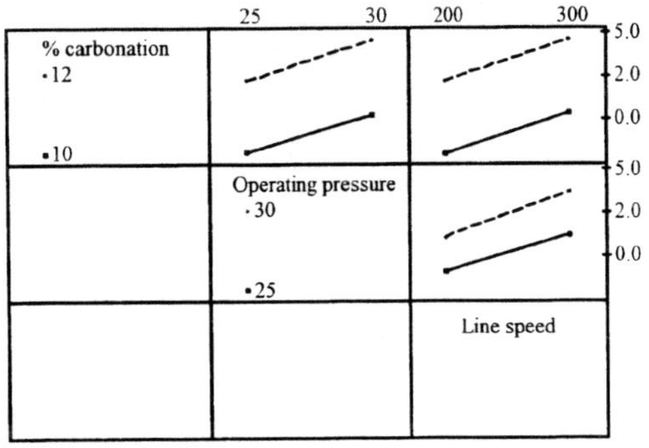

(g)

Treatment Combinations	Notation	Average Response
Carb.10, op.*p*.25, l.s.200	*abc*	−3.22
Carb.10, op.*p*.25, l.s.300	*abC*	−0.60
Carb.10, op.*p*.30, l.s.200	*aBc*	−0.80
Carb.10, op.*p*.30, l.s.300	*aBC*	1.30
Carb.12, op.*p*.25, l.s.200	*Abc*	1.40
Carb.12, op.*p*.25, l.s.300	*AbC*	3.10
Carb.12, op.*p*.30, l.s.200	*ABc*	3.00
Carb.12, op.*p*.30, l.s.300	*ABC*	6.20

$$A = \frac{1}{4n'}[Abc + AbC + ABc + ABC - abc - abC - aBc - aBC] = 0.851$$

$$B = \frac{1}{4n'}[aBc + aBC + ABc + ABC - abc - abC - Abc - AbC] = 0.451$$

$$C = \frac{1}{4n'}[abC + aBC + AbC + ABC - abc - aBc - Abc - ABc] = 0.481$$

$$AB = \frac{1}{4n'}[abc + abC + ABc + ABC - Abc - aBc - AbC - aBC] = 0.019$$

$$AC = \frac{1}{4n'}[abc + aBc + AbC + ABC - abC - aBC - Abc - ABc] = 0.009$$

$$BC = \frac{1}{4n'}[abc + Abc + aBC + ABC - abC - aBc - ABc - AbC] = 0.049$$

$$ABC = \frac{1}{4n'}[abC + aBc + Abc + ABC - ABc - AbC - aBC - abc] = 0.101$$

Main effects are *A*, *B* and *C*.

(h)

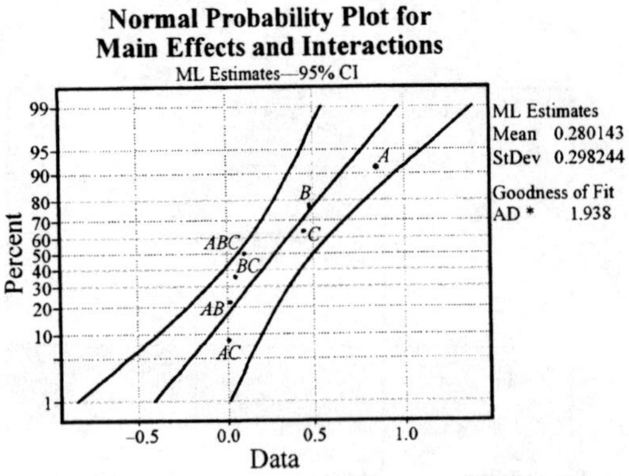

(i) There is no significant dependence on AB, AC, and ABC factor combinations. A, B, and C factors are significant.

(j) In parts (a)–(d) the actual effects of significant factors A, B, and C were obscured by the use of insignificant factor combination terms in the ANOVA model.

(k) Based on part (g), 10% carbonation, 25 psi operating pressure and 300 bottles per minute line speed levels should be used to reduce the deviation from the target.

7. **ANOVA: Distance versus Design; Weight and Size**

Factor	Type	Levels	Values	
Design	fixed	2	C	S
Weight	fixed	2	H	L
Size	fixed	2	L	S

Analysis of Variance for Distance

Source	DF	SS	MS	F	P
Design	1	7906.5	7906.5	11.45	0.002
Weight	1	116.3	116.3	0.17	0.685
Size	1	14663.3	14663.3	21.24	0.000
Design*Weight	1	657.0	657.0	0.95	0.339
Design*Size	1	24255.0	24255.0	35.14	0.000
Weight*Size	1	4027.5	4027.5	5.83	0.024
Design*Weight*Size	1	318.8	318.8	0.46	0.503
Error	24	16566.3	690.3		
Total	31	68510.7			

(a) $H_0: \mu_S = \mu_C$, $H_1: \mu_S \neq \mu_C$
Decision rule: Reject H_0 if $F > 4.26$. Test statistic: $F = 11.45$. Decision: Because $F > 4.26$, reject H_0. There is a significant effect on the distance due to design for the 0.05 significance level.

(b) $H_0: \mu_L = \mu_H$, $H_1: \mu_L \neq \mu_H$
Decision rule: Reject H_0 if $F > 4.26$. Test statistic: $F = 0.17$. Decision: Because $F < 4.26$, do not reject H_0. There is no significant effect on the distance due to weight.

(c) $H_0: \mu_s = \mu_l$, $H_1: \mu_s \neq \mu_l$
Decision rule: Reject H_0 if $F > 4.42$. Test statistic: $F = 21.24$. Decision: Because $F > 4.26$, reject H_0. There is evidence of an effect on the distance due to size.

(d) Based on small p-values, there are significant interactions between the design and the size and between the weight and the size.

(e) **Main Effects Plot—Data Means Distance**

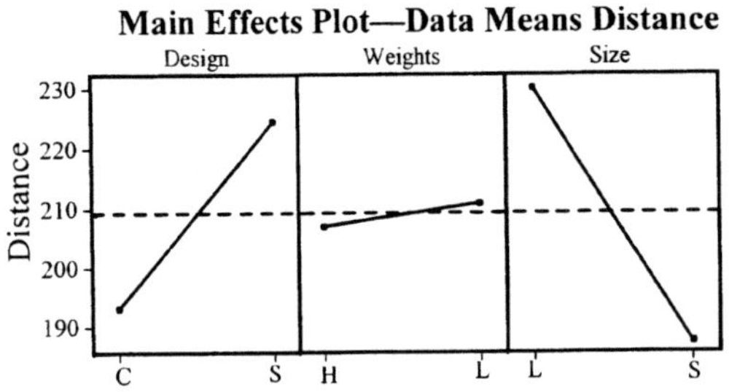

(f) **Interaction Plot—Data Means for Distance**

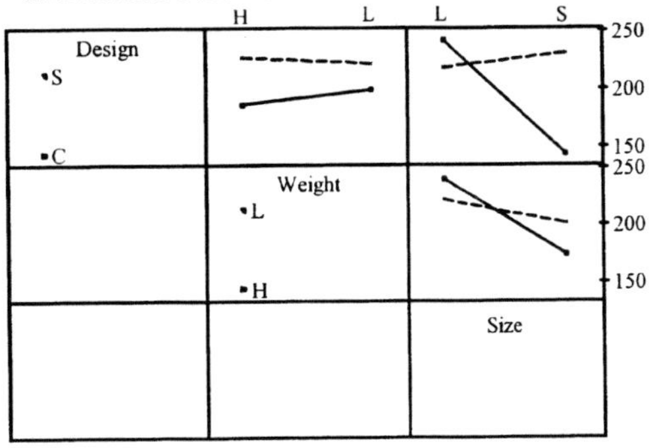

(g)

Treatment Combinations	Notation	Average Response
Simple, light, small	*abc*	242.5
Simple, light, large	*abC*	158.8
Simple, heavy, small	*aBc*	219.0
Simple, heavy, large	*aBC*	201.5
Complex, light, small	*Abc*	129.8
Complex, light, large	*AbC*	240.5
Complex, heavy, small	*ABc*	235.5
Complex, heavy, large	*ABC*	243.8

$$A = \frac{1}{4n'}[Abc + AbC + ABc + ABC - abc - abC - aBc - aBC] = 1.73$$

$$B = \frac{1}{4n'}[aBc + aBC + ABc + ABC - abc - abC - Abc - AbC] = 8.02$$

$$C = \frac{1}{4n'}[abC + aBC + AbC + ABC - abc - aBc - Abc - ABc] = 1.11$$

$$AB = \frac{1}{4n'}[abc + abC + ABc + ABC - Abc - aBc - AbC - aBC] = 5.61$$

$$AC = \frac{1}{4n'}[abc + aBc + AbC + ABC - abC - aBC - Abc - ABc] = 13.77$$

$$BC = \frac{1}{4n'}[abc + Abc + aBC + ABC - abC - aBc - ABc - AbC] = -2.27$$

$$ABC - \frac{1}{4n'}[abC + aBc + Abc + ABC - ABc - AbC - aBC - abc] = -10.55$$

(h) **Normal Probability Plot for Main Effects and Interactions**

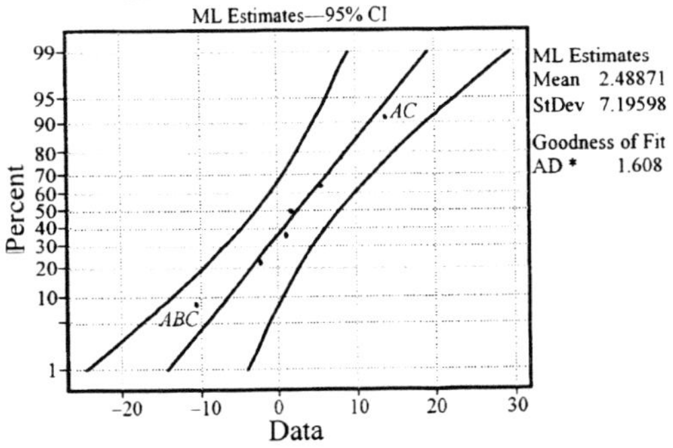

(i) Effects ABC and AC are farthest from the line $x = 0$. These factor combinations must be included in the ANOVA model.

(j) In parts (a)–(d) the actual effects of significant factors were obscured by the use of insignificant factor combination terms in the ANOVA model.

(k) Based on average distances in part (g), complex design, heavy weight and large size (average distance is 243.8 inch) or simple design, light weight and small size (average distance is 242.5 inch) should be used.

8. (a)

Battery Type	Connector Design	Temperature	Notation	Time
L	S	A	*abc*	93
H	S	A	*Abc*	489
L	G	A	*abc*	94
H	G	A	*ABC*	493
L	S	C	*abc*	72
H	S	C	*Abc*	612
L	G	C	*abc*	75
H	G	C	*Abc*	490

$$A = \frac{1}{4n'}[Abc + AbC + ABc + ABC - abc - abC - aBc - aBC] = 438$$

$$B = \frac{1}{4n'}[aBc + aBC + ABc + ABC - abc - abC - Abc - AbC] = -29$$

$$C = \frac{1}{4n'}[abC + aBC + AbC + ABC - abc - aBc - Abc - ABc] = -20$$

$$AB = \frac{1}{4n'}[abc + abC + ABc + ABC - Abc - aBc - AbC - aBC] = -31$$

$$AC = \frac{1}{4n'}[abc + aBc + AbC + ABC - abC - aBC - Abc - ABc] = -40$$

$$BC = \frac{1}{4n'}[abc + Abc + aBC + ABC - abC - aBc - ABc - AbC] = 31$$

$$ABC = \frac{1}{4n'}[abC + aBc + Abc + ABC - ABc - AbC - aBC - abc] = 32$$

(b) **Main Effects Plot—Data Means for Time**

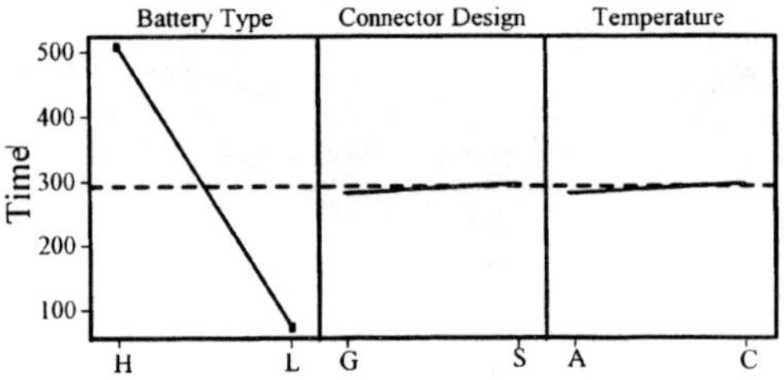

(c) **Interaction Plot—Data Means for Time**

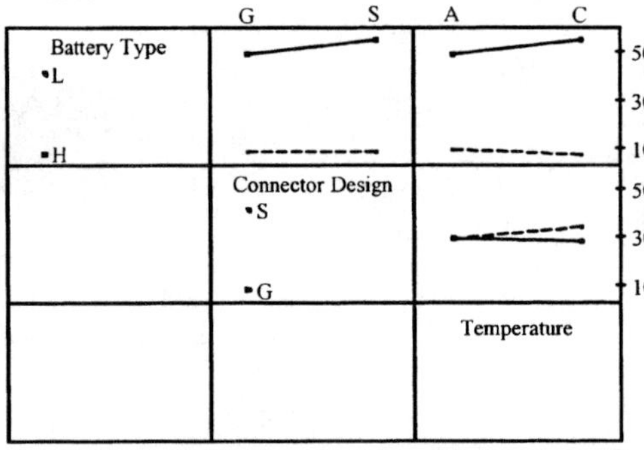

(d) **Normal Probability Plot for Main Effects and Interactions**

ML Estimates—95% CI

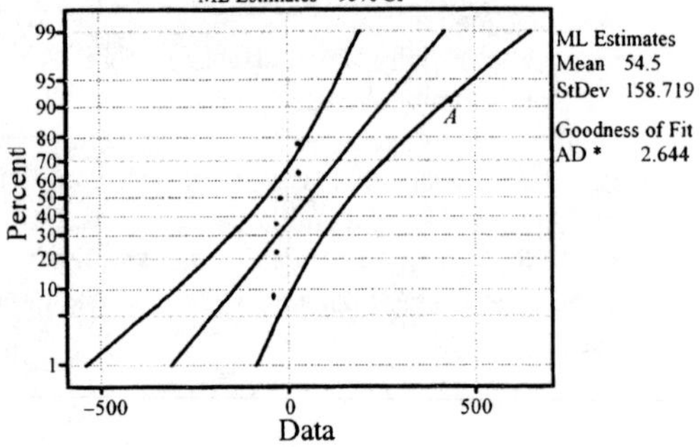

(e) The battery quality factor, A, has the most significant effect on battery lifetime.

(f) **Analysis of Variance for Time**

Source	DF	SS	MS	F	P
Type	1	382813	382813	169.56	0.000
Design	1	1625	1625	0.72	0.444
Temperature	1	800	800	0.35	0.584
Error	4	9031	2258		
Total	7	394268			

Only the battery quality factor is significant.

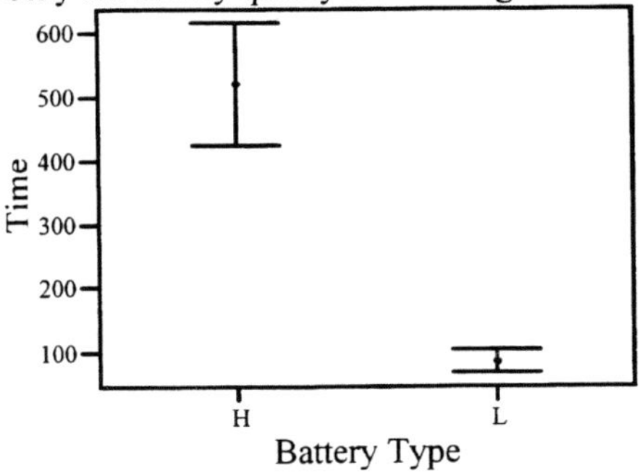

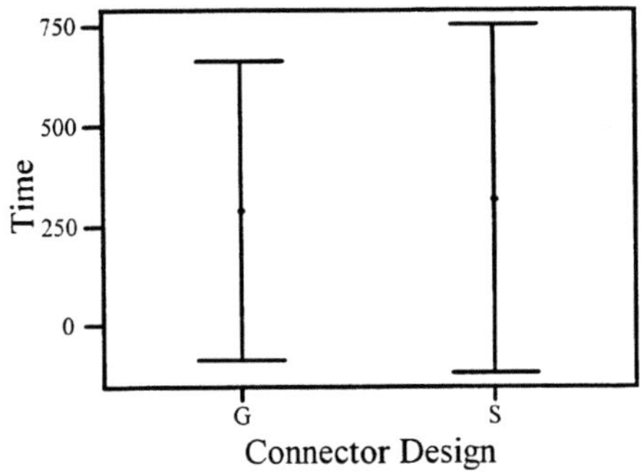

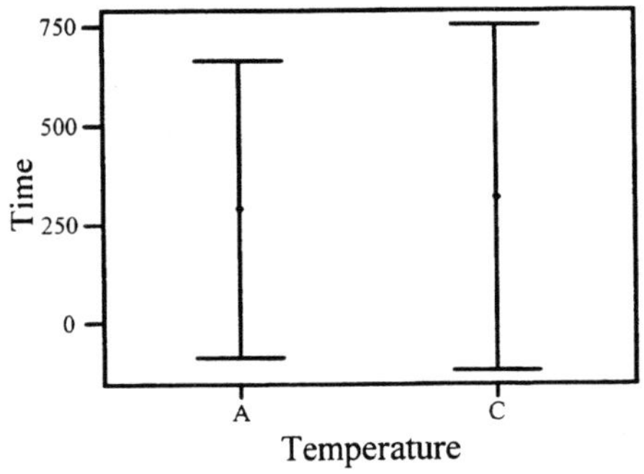

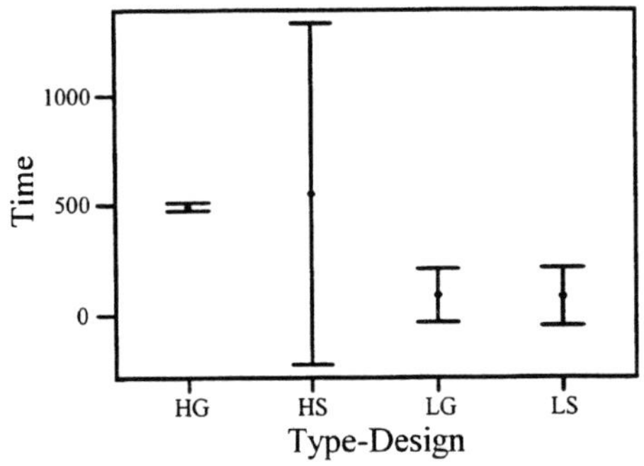

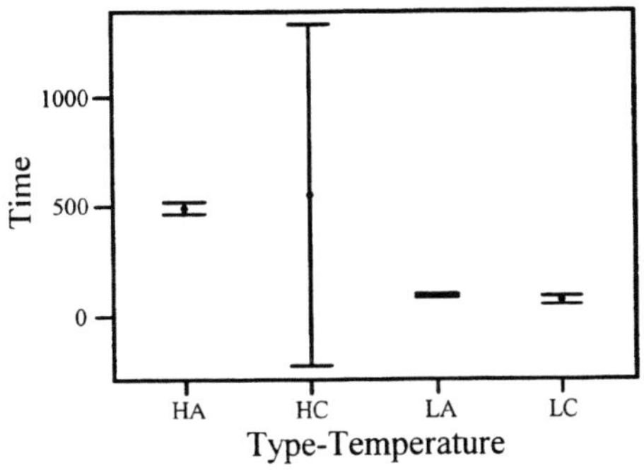

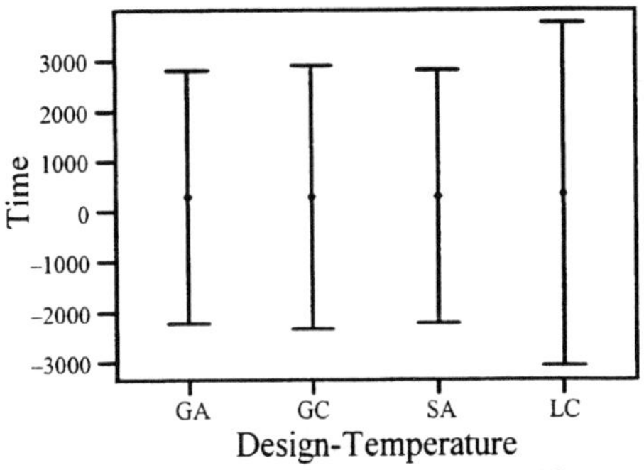

A (battery quality), *AB* (battery type—connector design) and *AC* (battery type—temperature) are significant.

(g) The most significant effect is provided by factor *A* (battery quality).

9. (a)

Ring Osculation	Cage Design	Heat Treatment	Relative Life	Notation
L	L	L	17	*abc*
H	L	L	25	*Abc*
L	H	L	19	*aBc*
L	L	H	26	*abC*
H	H	L	21	*ABc*
H	L	H	85	*AbC*
L	H	H	16	*aBC*
H	H	H	128	*ABC*

$$A=\frac{1}{4n'}[Abc+AbC+ABc+ABC-abc-abC-aBc-aBC]=45$$

$$B=\frac{1}{4n'}[aBc+aBC+ABc+ABC-abc-abC-Abc-AbC]=8$$

$$C=\frac{1}{4n'}[abC+aBC+AbC+ABC-abc-aBc-Abc-ABc]=43$$

$$AB=\frac{1}{4n'}[abc+abC+ABc+ABC-Abc-aBc-AbC-aBC]=12$$

$$AC=\frac{1}{4n'}[abc+aBc+AbC+ABC-abC-aBC-Abc-ABc]=40$$

$$BC=\frac{1}{4n'}[abc+Abc+aBC+ABC-abC-aBc-ABc-AbC]=9$$

$$ABC=\frac{1}{4n'}[abC+aBc+Abc+ABC-ABc-AbC-aBC-abc]=15$$

(b) **Main Effects Plot—Data Means for Relative Life**

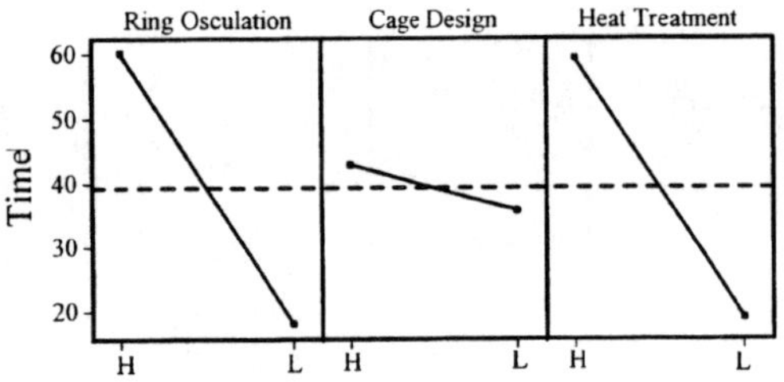

(c) **Interaction Plot—Data Means for Relative Life**

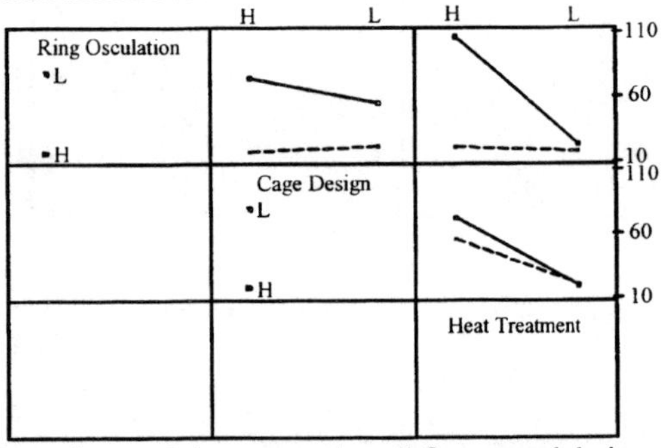

(d) **Normal Probability Plot for Main Effects and Interactions**

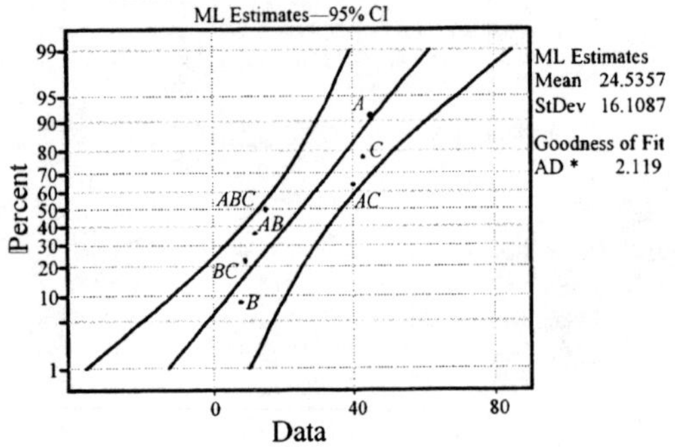

(e) From the graph it appears that all factors and their combinations have significant effects on the relative life of the bearings.

(f)

Analysis of Variance for Relative

Source	DF	SS	MS	F	P
Ring osc	1	4095	4095	3.99	0.116
Cage des	1	120	120	0.12	0.749
Heat tre	1	3741	3741	3.65	0.129
Error	4	4105	1026		
Total	7	12061			

There are no significant factors.

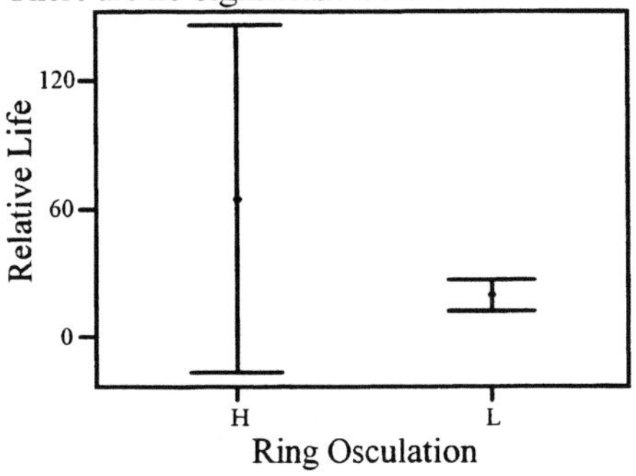

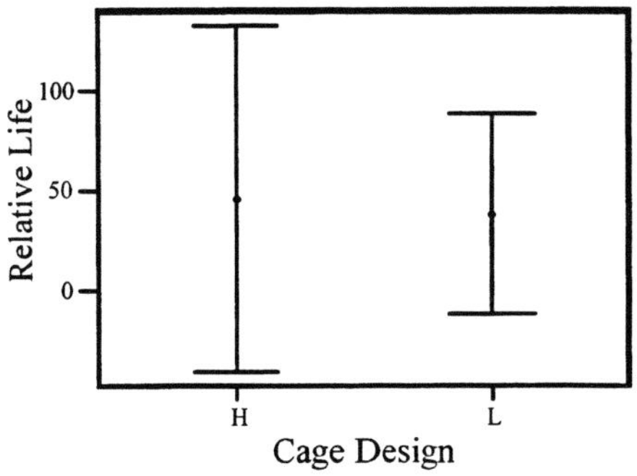

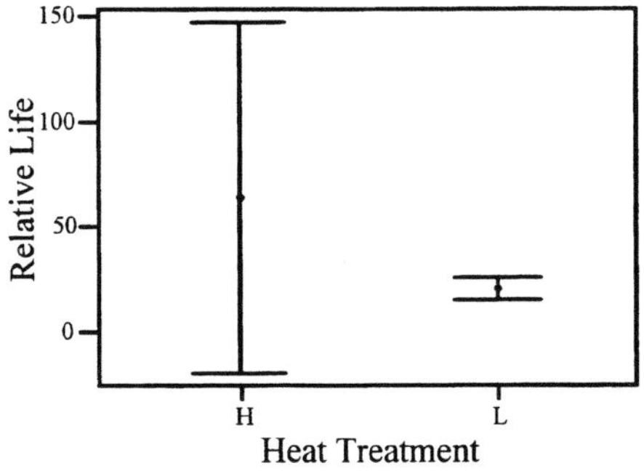

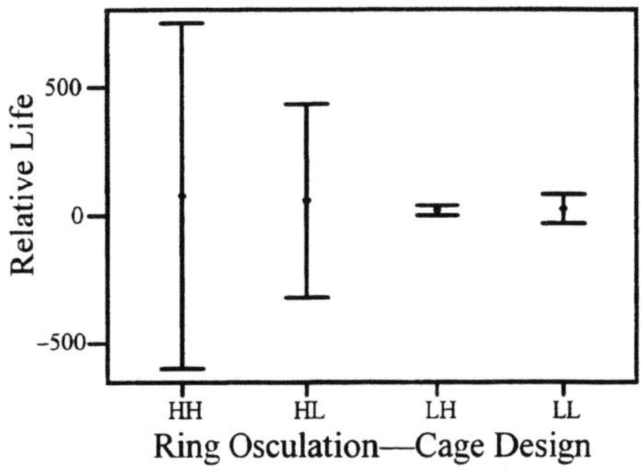

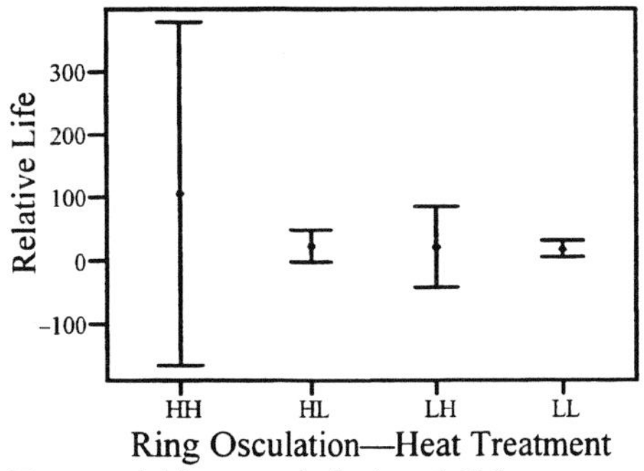

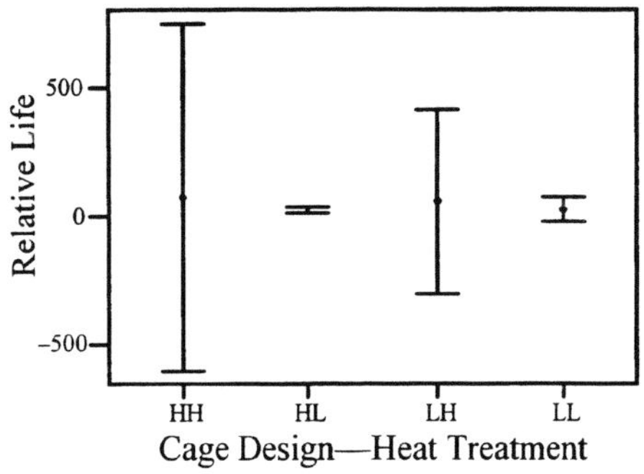

(g) Factors *A* (ring osculation) and *C* (heat treatment) are significant.

10. (a)

Temperature	Pressure	Catalyst	Tensile Strength	Notation
300	40	20	30	*abc*
400	40	20	20	*Abc*
300	70	20	20	*aBc*
300	40	30	10	*abC*
400	70	20	30	*ABc*
400	40	30	60	*AbC*
300	70	30	10	*aBC*
400	70	30	10	*ABC*

$$A = \frac{1}{4n'}[Abc + AbC + ABc + ABC - abc - abC - aBc - aBC] = 12.5$$

$$B = \frac{1}{4n'}[aBc + aBC + ABc + ABC - abc - abC - Abc - AbC] = -12.5$$

$$C = \frac{1}{4n'}[abC + aBC + AbC + ABC - abc - aBc - Abc - ABc] = -2.5$$

$$AB = \frac{1}{4n'}[abc + abC + ABc + ABC - Abc - aBc - AbC - aBC] = -7.5$$

$$AC = \frac{1}{4n'}[abc + aBc + AbC + ABC - abC - aBC - Abc - ABc] = 12.5$$

$$BC = \frac{1}{4n'}[abc + Abc + aBC + ABC - abC - aBc - ABc - AbC] = -12.5$$

$$ABC = \frac{1}{4n'}[abC + aBc + Abc + ABC - ABc - AbC - aBC - abc] = -17.5$$

(b) **Main Effects Plot—Data Means for Tensile Strength**

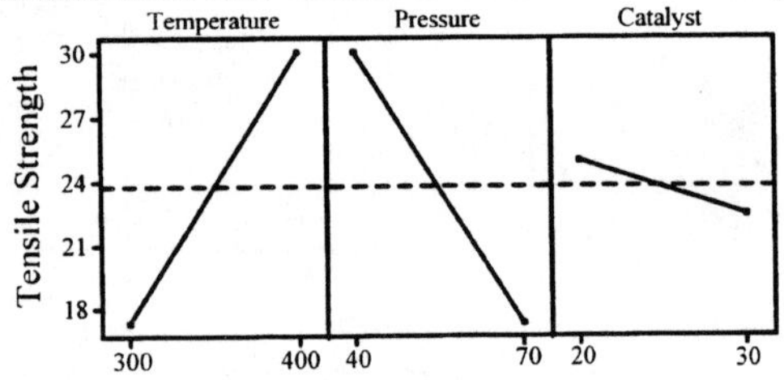

(c) **Interaction Plot—Data Means for Tensile Strength**

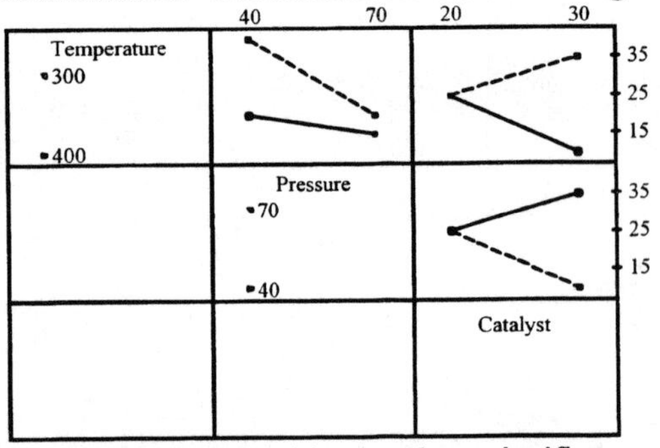

(d) **Normal Probability Plot for Main Effects and Interactions**

ML Estimates—95% CI

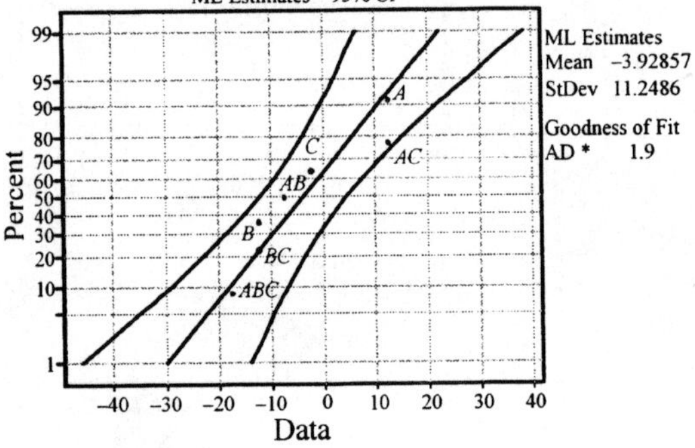

(e) All factors and their combinations have significant effects on the tensile strength.

(f) **Analysis of Variance for Tensile**

Source	DF	SS	MS	F	P
Temperat	1	312.5	312.5	0.93	0.390
Pressure	1	312.5	312.5	0.93	0.390
Catalyst	1	12.5	12.5	0.04	0.857
Error	4	1350.0	337.5		
Total	7	1987.5			

There are no significant factors.

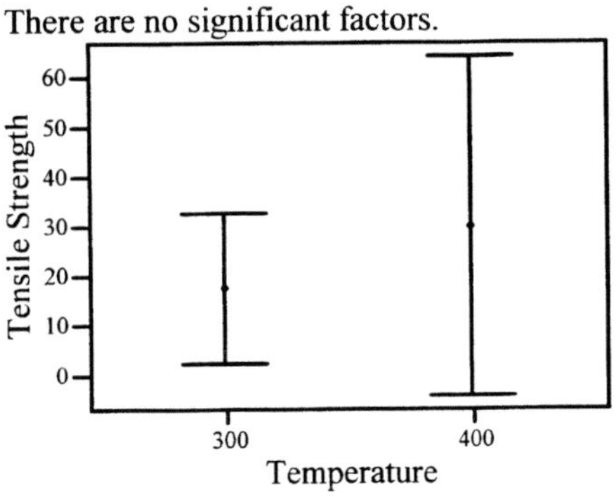

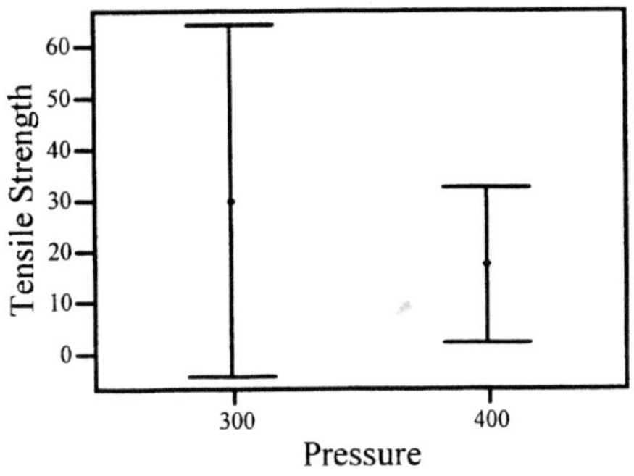

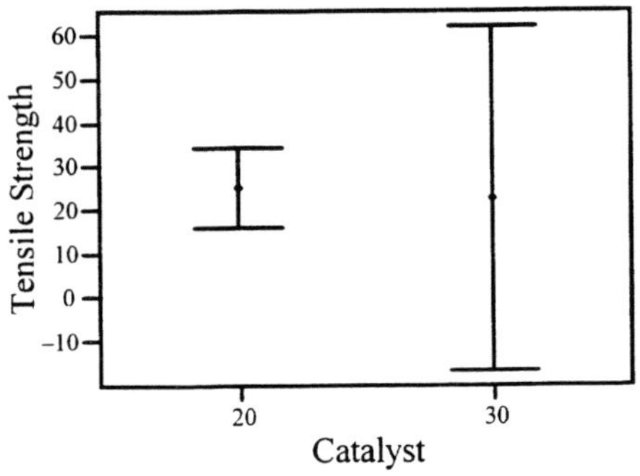

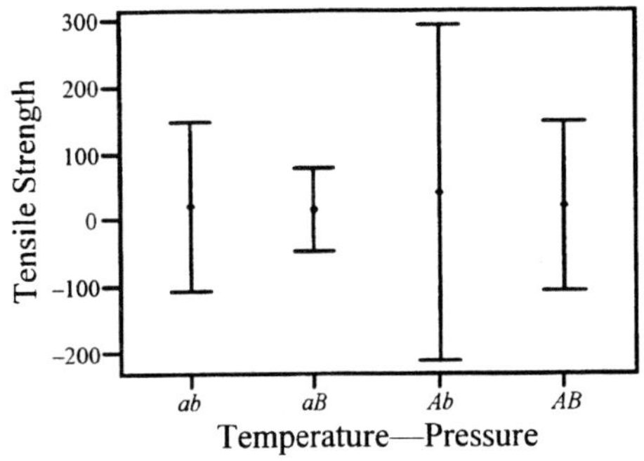

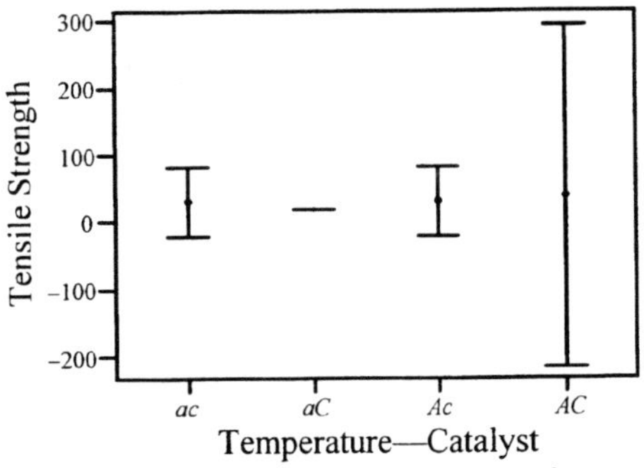

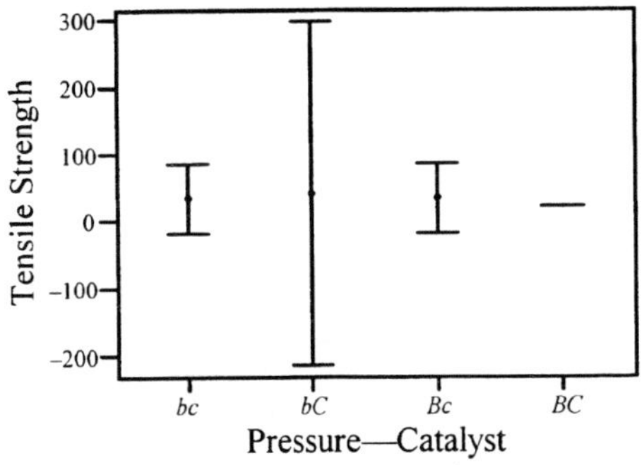

(g) There are significant effects of the single temperature and pressure factors on the tensile strength.

11. (a)

Relative Volatility	Bottom Composition	Top Composition	Feed Composition	Measured Efficiency	Notation
1.1	0.005	0.70	0.3	88	*abcd*
2.0	0.005	0.70	0.3	11	*Abcd*
1.1	0.200	0.70	0.3	31	*aCcd*
1.1	0.005	0.99	0.3	138	*abCd*
1.1	0.005	0.70	0.6	84	*abcD*
2.0	0.200	0.70	0.3	4	*ABcd*
2.0	0.005	0.99	0.3	18	*AbCd*
2.0	0.005	0.70	0.6	12	*AbcD*
1.1	0.200	0.99	0.3	80	*aBCd*
1.1	0.200	0.70	0.6	31	*aBcD*
1.1	0.005	0.99	0.6	138	*abCD*
2.0	0.200	0.99	0.3	11	*ABCd*
2.0	0.200	0.70	0.6	4	*ABcD*
2.0	0.005	0.99	0.6	19	*AbCD*
1.1	0.200	0.99	0.6	85	*aBCD*
2.0	0.200	0.99	0.6	11	*ABCD*

Factors	Main Effect
A	73.125
B	31.375
C	29.375
D	0.387
AB	23.875
AC	22.375
AD	0.158
BC	0.158
BD	0.880
CD	1.129
ABC	0.158
ABD	1.378
ACD	1.129
BCD	0.158
ABCD	0.158

(b)

Main Effects Plot—Data Means for Measured Efficiency

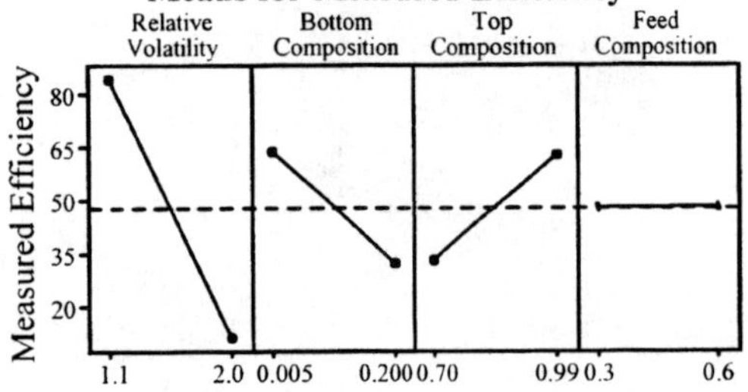

(c)

Interaction Plot—Data Means for Measured Efficiency

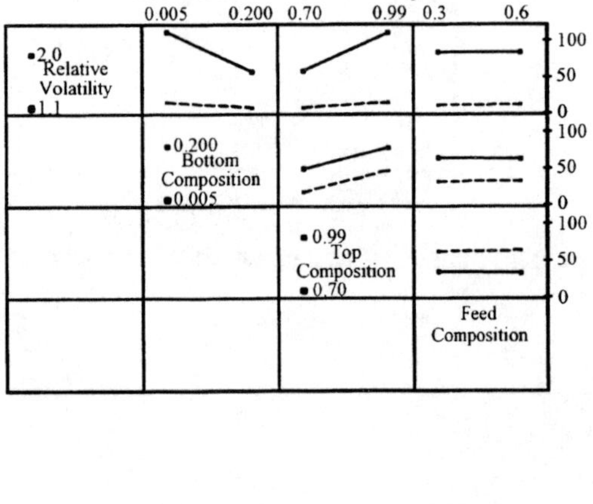

(d)

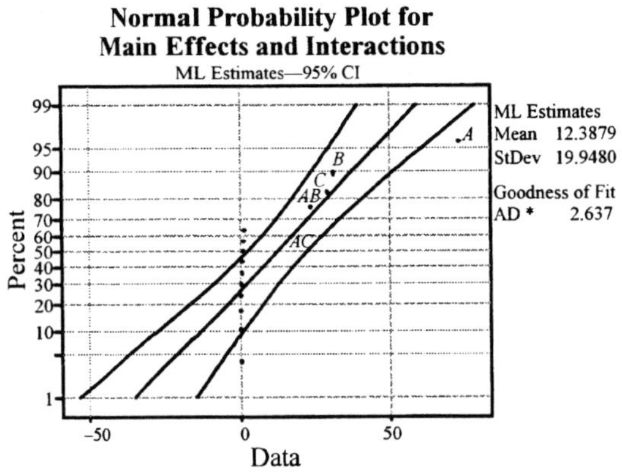

(e) There are significant effects of *A*, *B*, *C*, *AB* and *AC*.

(f)

Analysis of Variance for Measured

Source	DF	SS	MS	F	P
Relative	1	21389.1	21389.1	54.67	0.000
Bottom c	1	3937.6	3937.6	10.06	0.009
Top comp	1	3451.6	3451.6	8.82	0.013
Feed com	1	0.6	0.6	0.00	0.970
Error	11	4303.7	391.2		
Total	15	33082.4			

The single factors *A*, *B*, and *C* have significant effects for the 0.05 significance level. Factor *D* is not significant at this level.

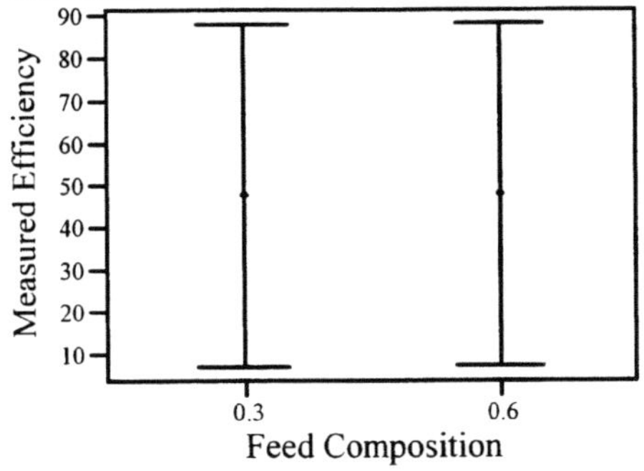

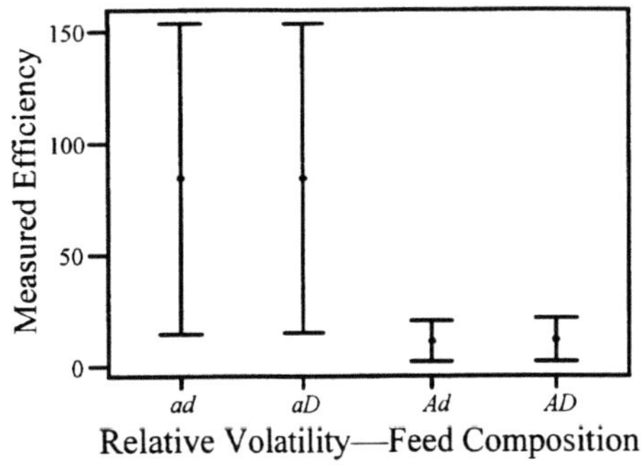

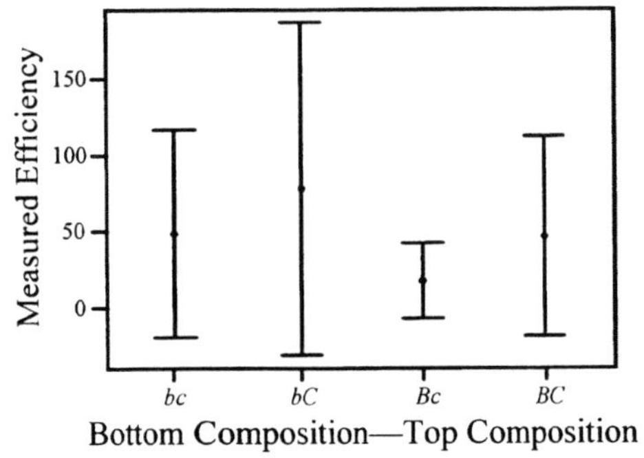

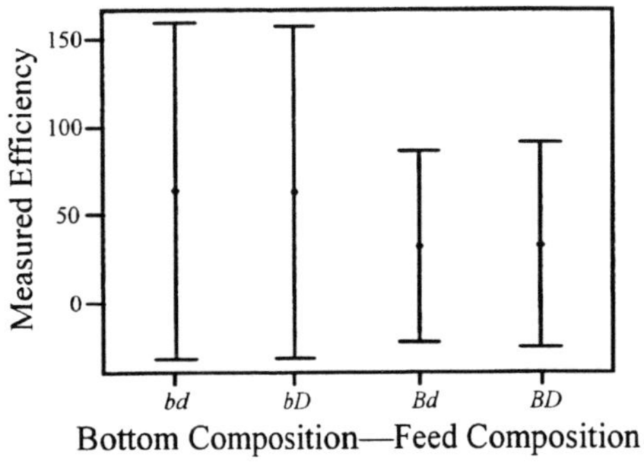

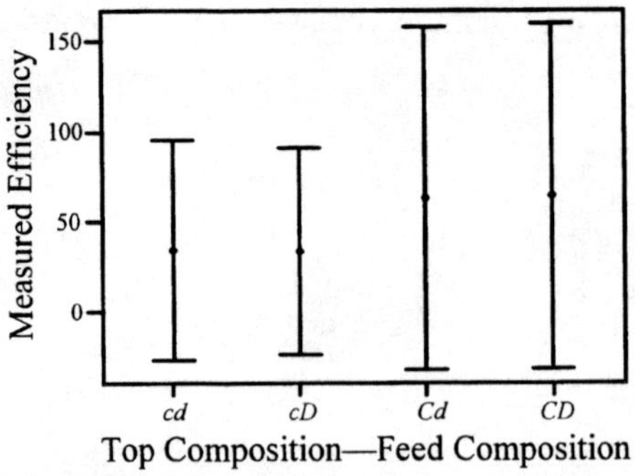

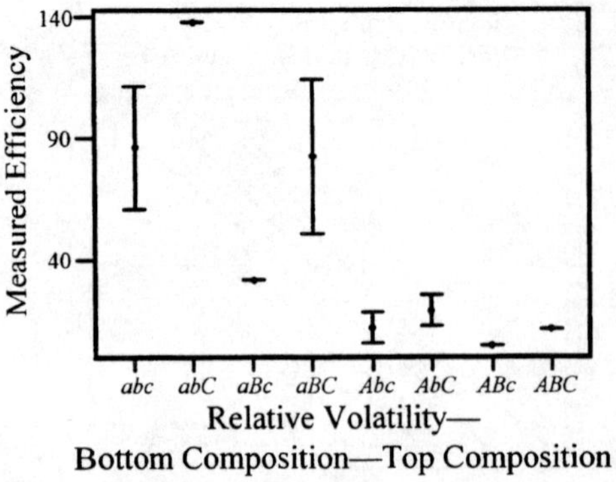

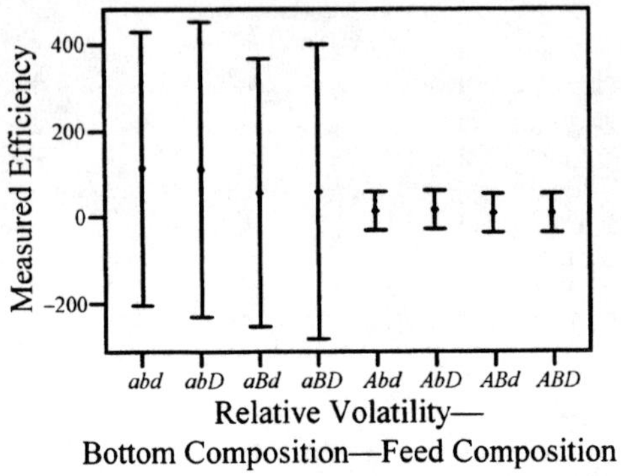

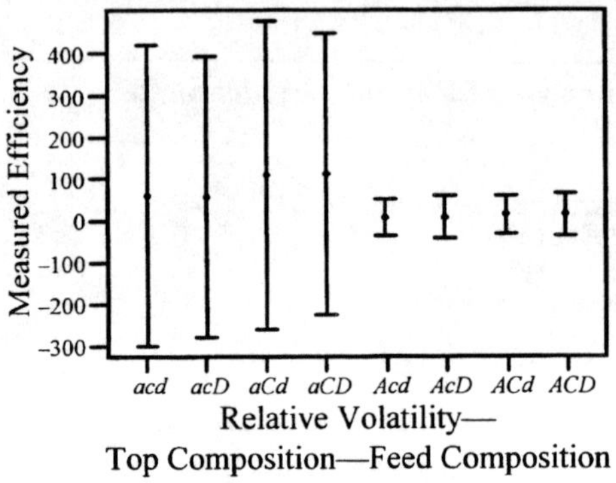

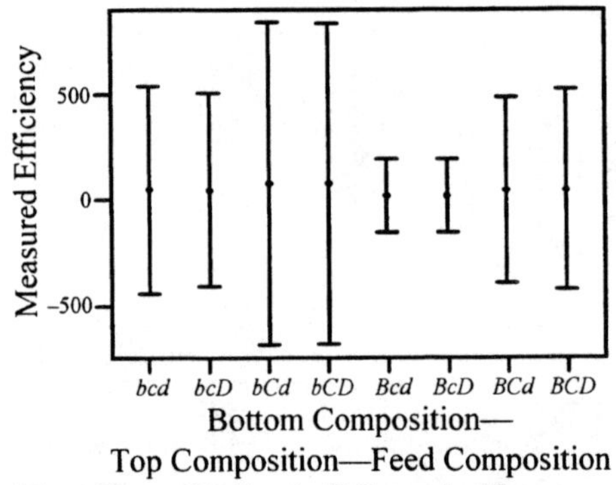

(g) The effects of *BC* and *ABC* are significant.

12. (a)

Factors	Main Effect
A	36.125
B	76.375
C	5.376
D	110.125
AB	9.625
AC	4.626
AD	3.876
BC	6.125
BD	2.377
CD	0.375
ABC	0.158
ABD	2.627
ACD	0.387
BCD	2.877
ABCD	5.876

(b) **Main Effects Plot—Data Means for Time**

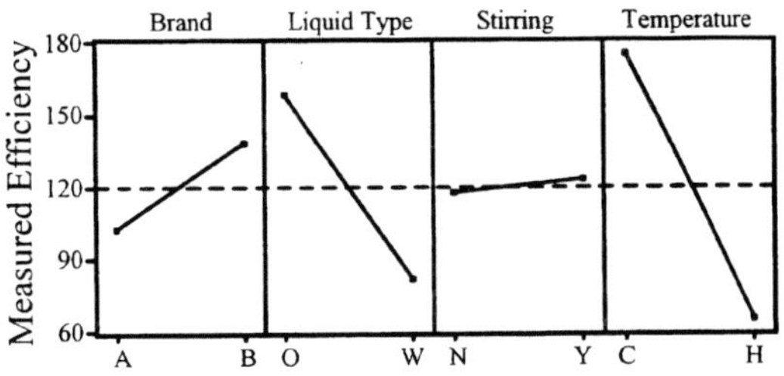

(c) **Interaction Plot—Data Means for Time**

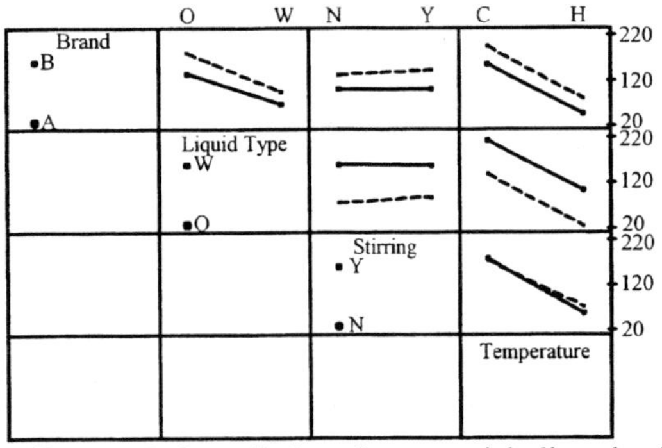

(d) **Normal Probability Plot for Main Effects and Interactions**

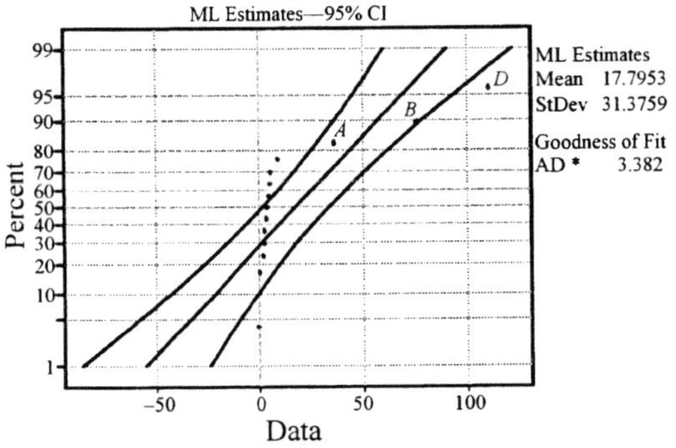

(e) Effects *A*, *B*, *D* are farthest from a straight line; that is zero on the *x*-axis. All other factor combinations can be considered as components of the random error.

(f)

Analysis of Variance for Time

Source	DF	SS	MS	F	P
Brand	1	5220	5220	46.32	0.000
Liquid t	1	23333	23333	207.03	0.000
Stirring	1	116	116	1.03	0.333
Temperat	1	48510	48510	430.44	0.000
Error	11	1240	113		
Total	15	78418			

The single factors A, B and D all cause a significant effect.

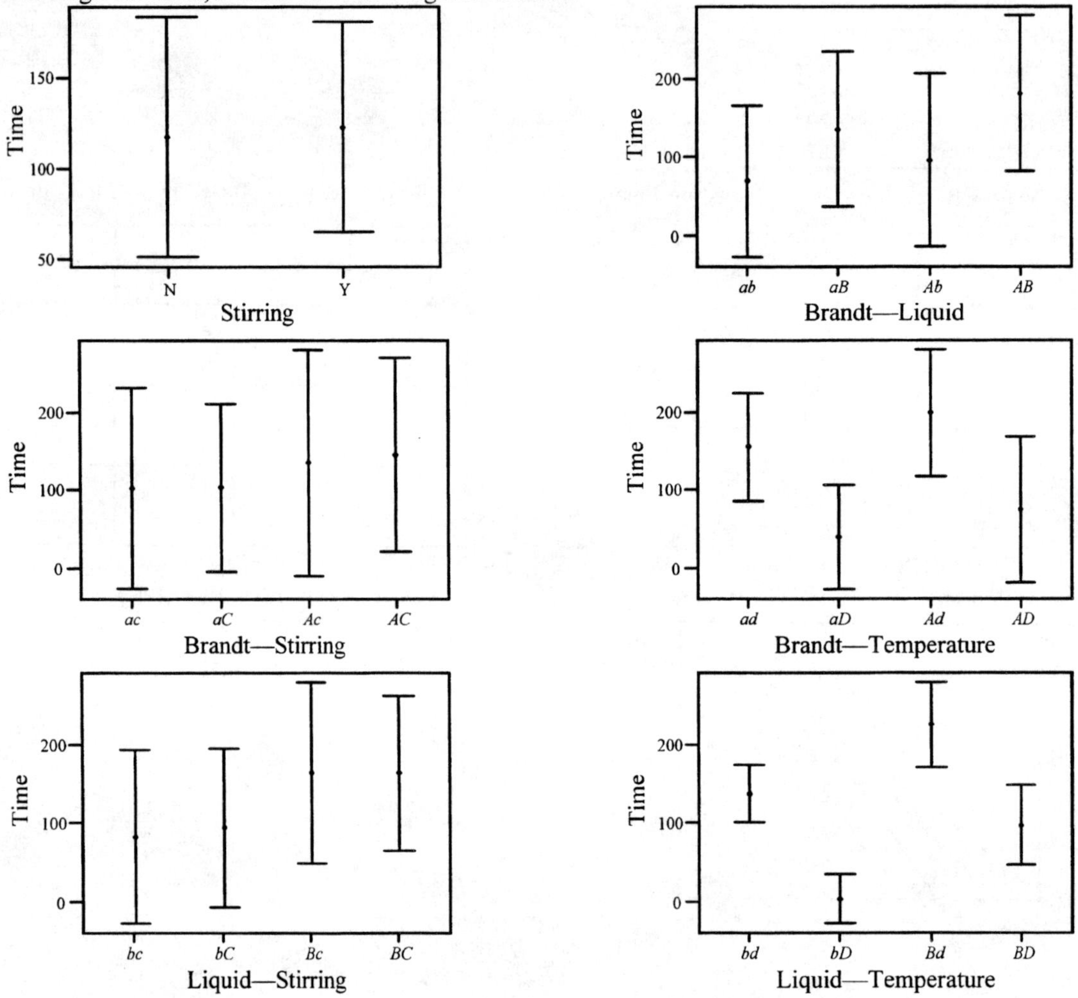

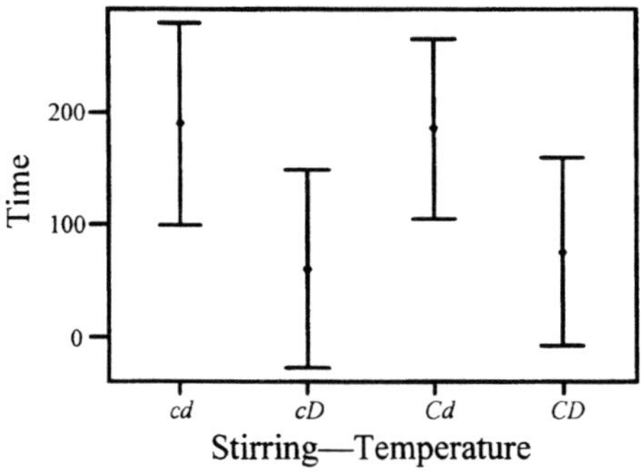

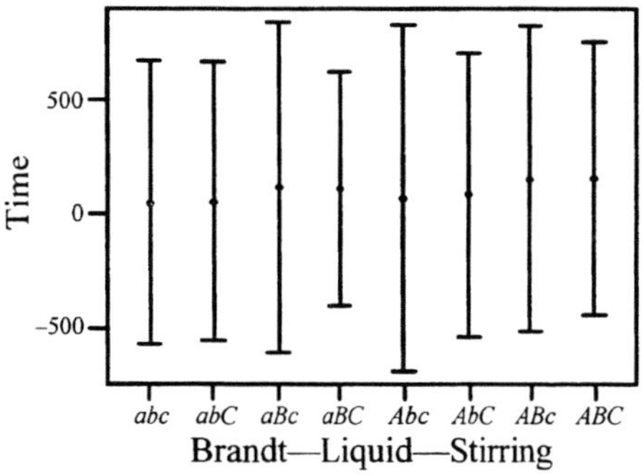

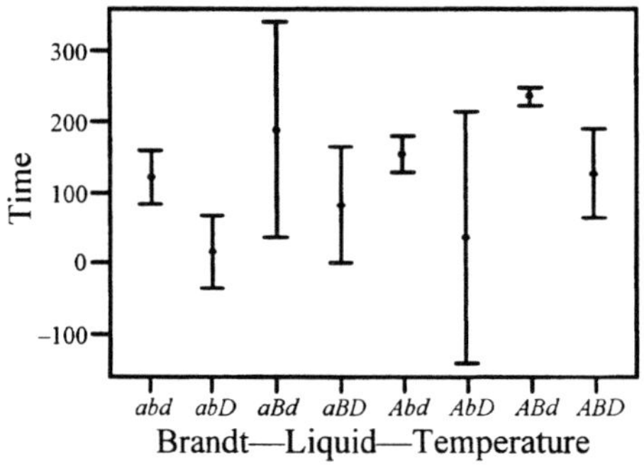

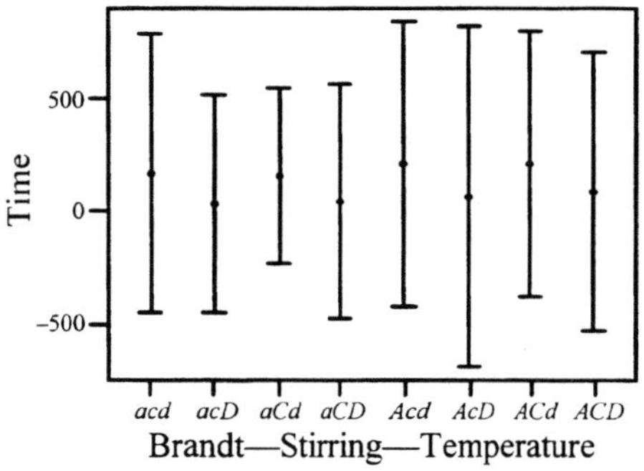

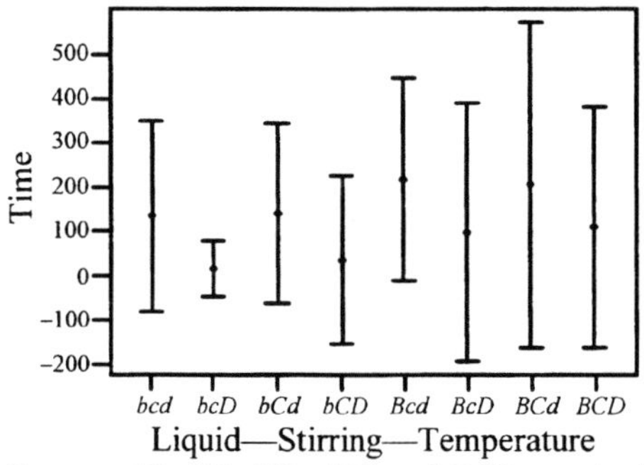

(g) Factors *AD*, *BD*, *CD*, *AB*D and *BCD* are significant.

13. (a)

Balls	C. D.	G.	A.G.	A. life	*A*	*B*	*C*	*D*	*AB* + *CD*	*AC* + *BD*	*AD* + *AD*
S	S	S	N	0.31	*a*	*b*	*c*	*d*	+	+	+
M	M	S	N	2.17	*A*	*B*	*c*	*d*	+	–	–
M	S	M	N	1.37	*A*	*b*	*C*	*d*	–	+	–
M	S	S	L	1.38	*A*	*b*	*c*	*D*	–	–	+
S	M	M	N	0.92	*a*	*B*	*C*	*d*	–	–	+
S	M	S	L	0.73	*a*	*B*	*c*	*D*	–	+	–
S	S	M	L	0.95	*a*	*b*	*C*	*D*	+	–	–
M	M	M	L	2.57	*A*	*B*	*C*	*D*	+	+	+

Factors	Main Effect
A	1.145
B	0.595
C	0.305
D	0.215
$AB + CD$	0.400
$AC + BD$	−0.110
$AD + BC$	−0.010

(b)

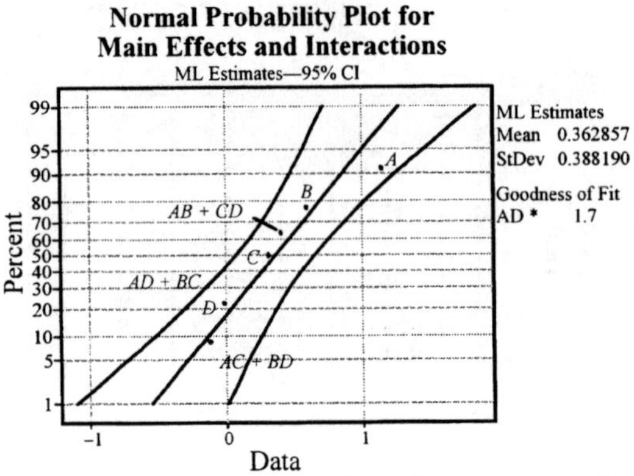

(c) Factors A and B cause significant effects.

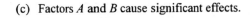

(d)

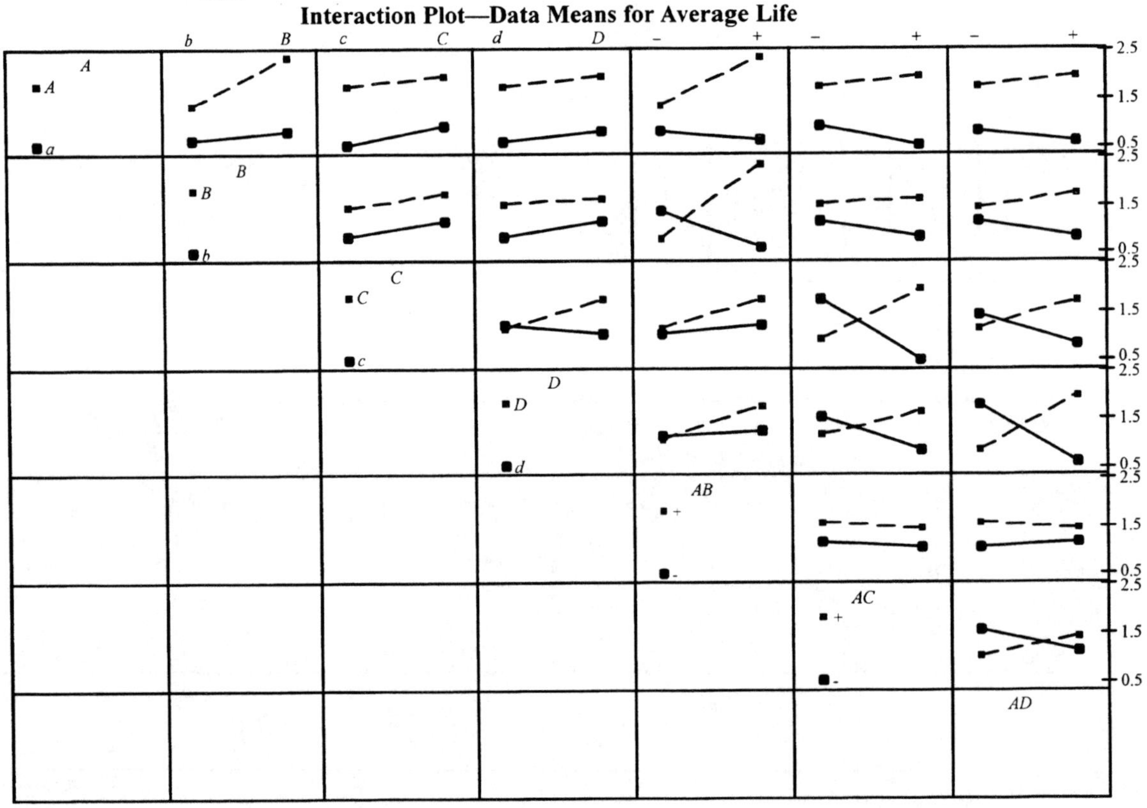

(e) Modified balls have an average life that is 1.14 higher than that of standard balls. A modified cage design resulted in and average life that is 0.60 higher than the standard cage design. There is no reason to suspect important interaction effects.

14. (a)

Cups	I.W.	O.W.	Rice	Time	*A*	*B*	*C*	*D*	*AB* + *CD*	*AC* + *BD*	*AD* + *AD*
1	2	0.5	S	26.4	*a*	*b*	*c*	*d*	+	+	+
2	3	0.5	S	28.9	*A*	*B*	*c*	*d*	+	–	–
2	2	1.0	S	28.4	*A*	*b*	*C*	*d*	–	+	–
2	2	0.5	L	27.1	*A*	*b*	*c*	*D*	–	–	+
1	3	1.0	S	30.1	*a*	*B*	*C*	*d*	–	–	+
1	3	0.5	L	28.6	*a*	*B*	*c*	*D*	–	+	–
1	2	1.0	L	27.9	*a*	*b*	*C*	*D*	+	–	–
2	3	1.0	L	31.5	*A*	*B*	*C*	*D*	+	+	+

Factors	Main Effect
A	0.725
B	2.325
C	1.725
D	0.325
AB + *CD*	0.125
AC + *BD*	0.225
AD + *BC*	0.325

(b)

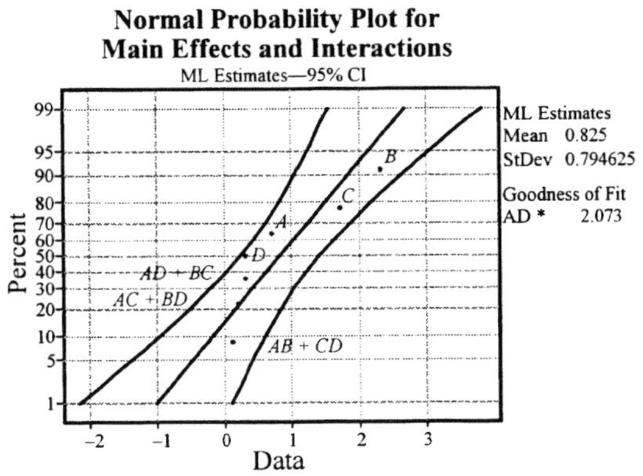

(c) All factors (*A*, *B*, *C*, *D*) and their combination (*AB* + *CD*, *AC* + *BD*, *AD* + *BC*) are important.

(d) **Interaction Plot—Data Means for Average Life**

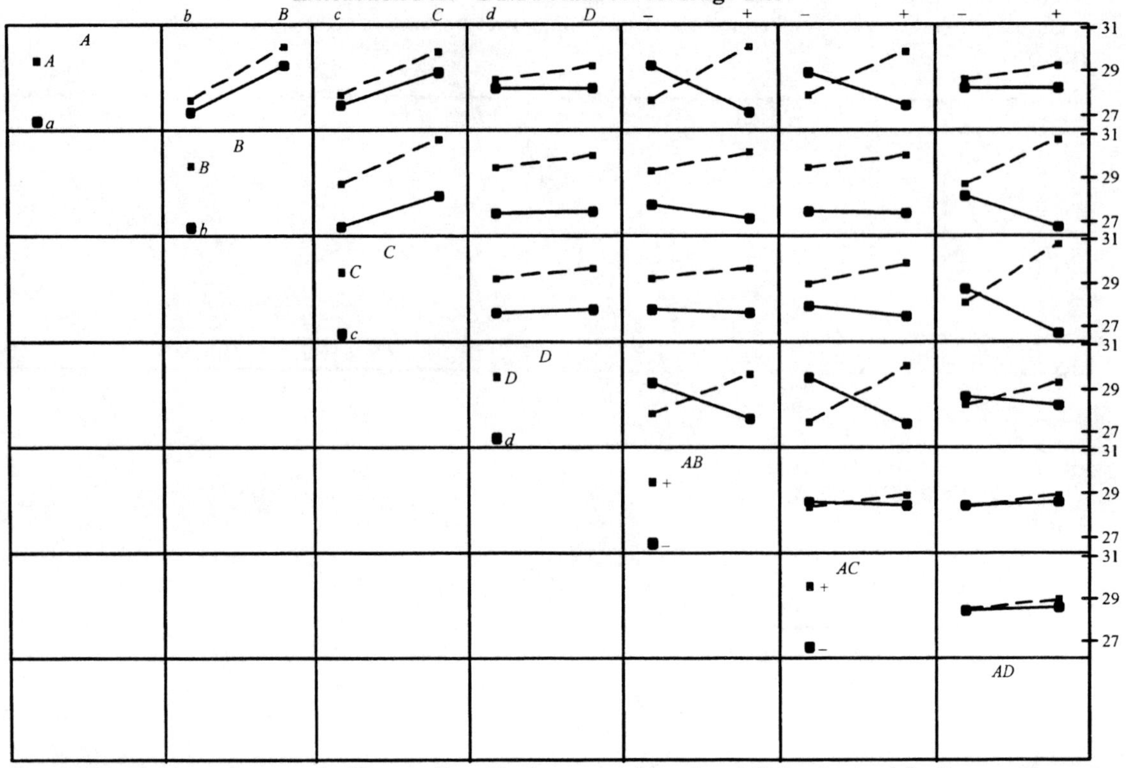

(e) Factors *B* and *C* have the most significant effect. The lowest cooking time will be obtained for 2 cups of inner water and 0.5 cups of outside water.

15. (a)

L.	P.	B.	R.	Score	*A*	*B*	*C*	*D*	*AB* + *CD*	*AC* + *BD*	*AD* + *AD*
75	0	0	N	89	*a*	*b*	*c*	*d*	+	+	+
100	5	0	N	87	*A*	*B*	*c*	*d*	+	–	–
100	0	2	N	71	*A*	*b*	*C*	*d*	–	+	–
100	0	0	Y	78	*A*	*b*	*c*	*D*	–	–	+
75	5	2	N	68	*a*	*B*	*C*	*d*	–	–	+
75	5	0	Y	76	*a*	*B*	*c*	*D*	–	+	–
75	0	2	Y	68	*a*	*b*	*C*	*D*	+	–	–
100	5	2	Y	67	*A*	*B*	*C*	*D*	+	+	+

Factors	Main effect
A	0.5
B	–2.0
C	–14.0
D	–6.5
AB + *CD*	4.5
AC + *BD*	0.5
AD + *BC*	0.0

(b)

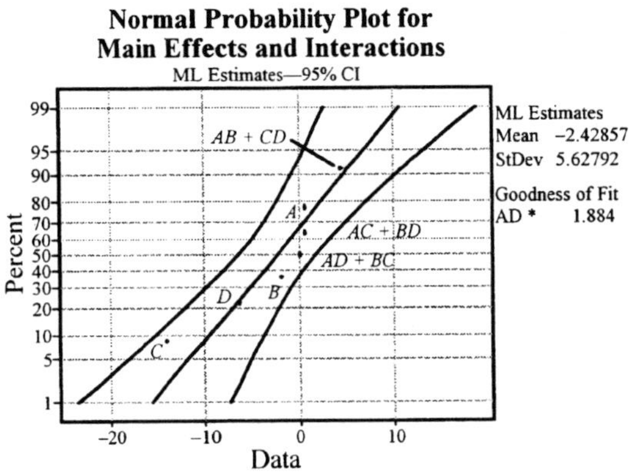

(c) Single factors (C, D and B) are significant. The combination factor $AB + CD$ is also significant.

(d)

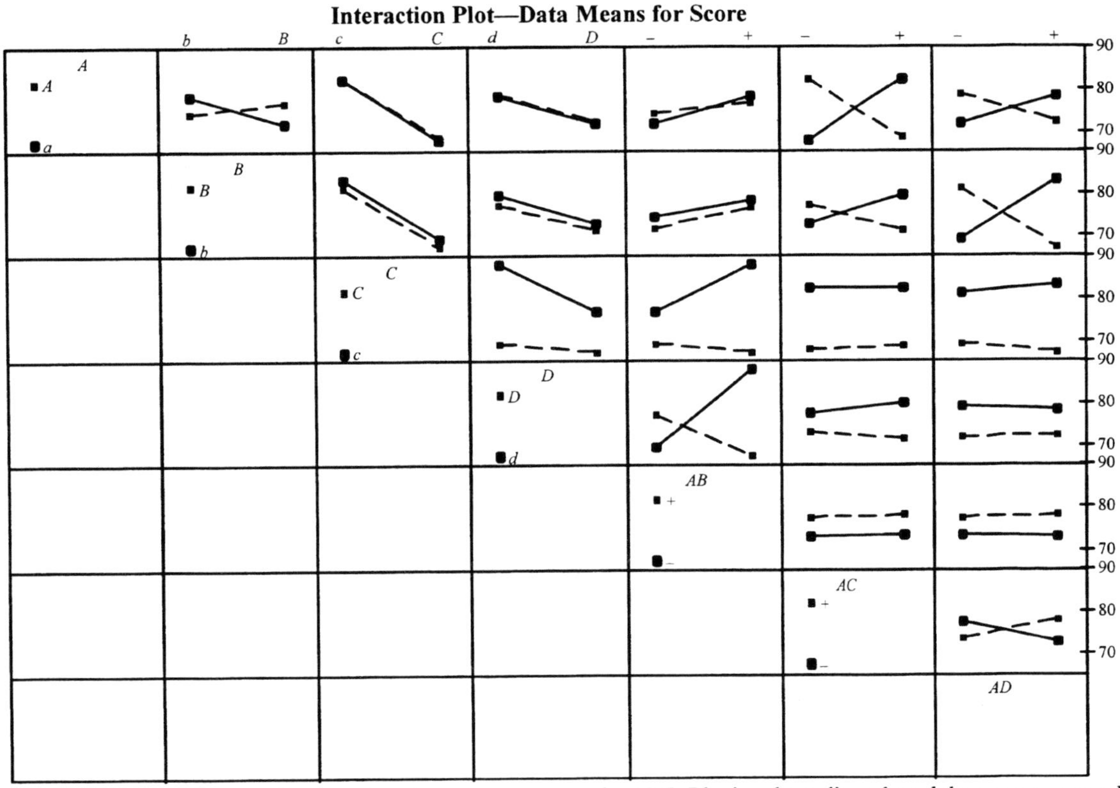

(e) Consumption of two cans of beer reduced the average score by 13.5. Playing the radio reduced the average score by 7. The interaction of lighting and practice time and/or beer consumption and radio playing seems important, but these two interactions cannot be separated by this fractional factorial design.

16. (a) **Fractional Factorial Fit: Amount Dissolved versus A; B; C; D; E**

Estimated Effects and Coefficients for Amount (coded units)

Term	Effect	Coef
Constant		54.96
A	-10.49	-5.24
B	51.91	25.96
C	19.34	9.67
D	10.41	5.21
E	-17.41	-8.71
A*B	-11.04	-5.52
A*C	21.04	10.52
A*D	-40.34	-20.17
A*E	-21.01	-10.51
B*C	11.59	5.79
B*D	7.71	3.86
B*E	-22.51	-11.26
C*D	-13.96	-6.98
C*E	-39.29	-19.64
D*E	16.54	8.27

(b)

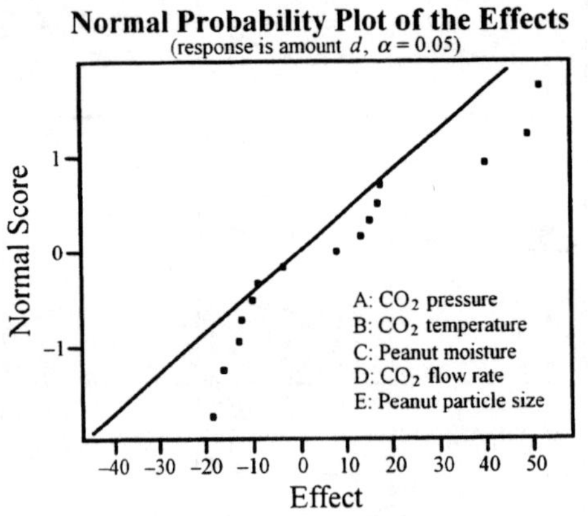

(c) All factors and their interactions are significant.

(d)

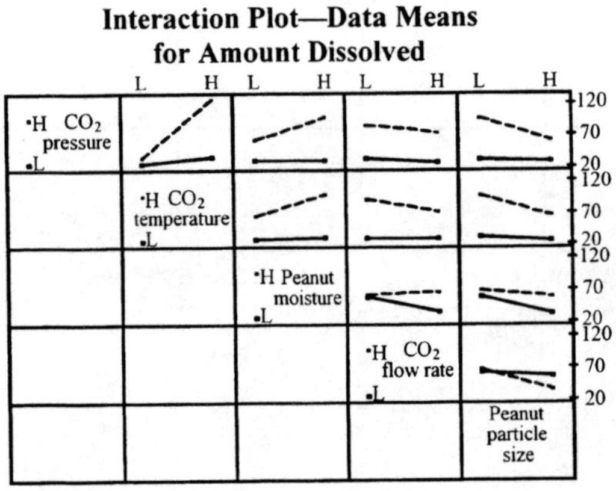

(e) There is a significant effect of all factors and their interactions.

(f) (a) **Fractional Factorial Fit: Amount Dissolved versus CO2 pressure; CO2 temperature; ...**

```
Estimated Effects and Coefficients for Amount (coded units)
Term                      Effect      Coef
Constant                            61.206
CO2 pres                  61.837    30.919
CO2 temp                  64.287    32.144
peanut m                   5.312     2.656
CO2 flow                   3.788     1.894
Peanut p                  -6.038    -3.019
CO2 pres*CO2 temp         52.613    26.306
CO2 pres*peanut m          4.688     2.344
CO2 pres*CO2 flow          9.263     4.631
CO2 pres*Peanut p         -3.613    -1.806
CO2 temp*peanut m          3.088     1.544
CO2 temp*CO2 flow          2.563     1.281
CO2 temp*Peanut p         -0.363    -0.181
peanut m*CO2 flow          1.137     0.569
peanut m*Peanut p         -4.437    -2.219
CO2 flow*Peanut p          0.237     0.119
```

(b) **Normal Probability Plot of the Effects**
(response is amount d, $\alpha = 0.05$)

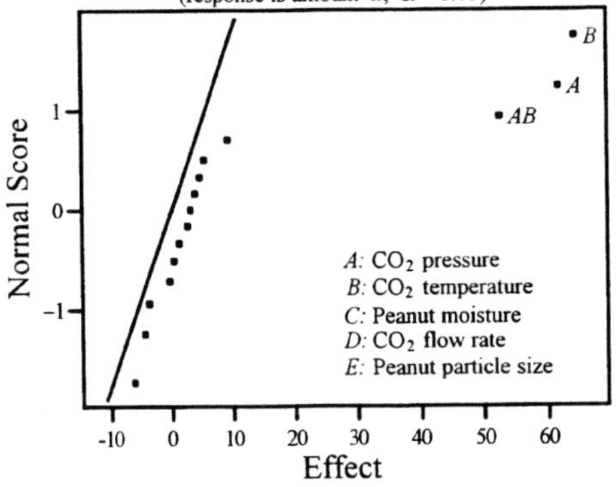

(c) Factors A, B and AB all have significant effects.

(d) **Interaction Plot—Data Means for Amount Dissolved**

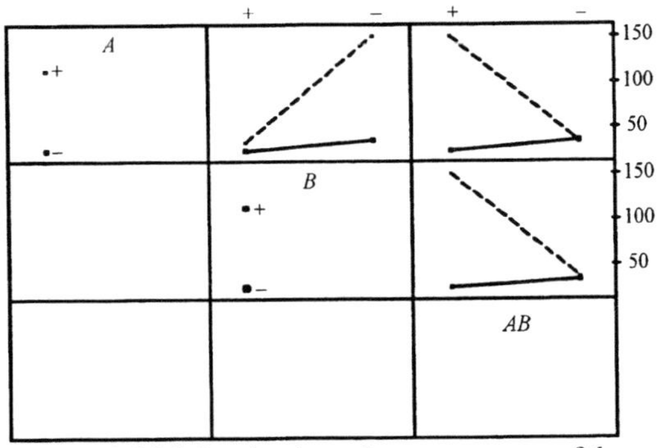

(e) There are important effects of factors A, B and AB. The highest responses occur at high values of CO_2 pressure and/or high values of CO_2 temperature.

(f) Correct initial data leads to the appearance of the significant factors.

(g) The combination of factors A and B produce a high response each time they occur together (*ab*—139.7, *abce*—141.4, *abcd*—172.6). Therefore, it is reasonable to expect a similarly large response for *abde*.

17. (a) **Fractional Factorial Fit: Yield of Oil versus CO2 Pressure; CO2 Temperature; ...**

```
Estimated Effects and Coefficients for Yield (coded units)
Term                       Effect        Coef
Constant                                54.25
CO2 pres                     7.50        3.75
CO2 temp                    19.75        9.87
peanut m                     1.25        0.63
CO2 flow                    -0.00       -0.00
Peanut p                   -44.50      -22.25
CO2 pres*CO2 temp            5.25        2.63
CO2 pres*peanut m            1.25        0.62
CO2 pres*CO2 flow           -4.00       -2.00
CO2 pres*Peanut p           -7.00       -3.50
CO2 temp*peanut m            3.00        1.50
CO2 temp*CO2 flow           -1.75       -0.88
CO2 temp*Peanut p           -0.25       -0.13
peanut m*CO2 flow            2.25        1.12
peanut m*Peanut p            6.25        3.13
CO2 flow*Peanut p           -3.50       -1.75
```

(b) **Normal Probability Plot of the Effects**

(response is yield of, $\alpha = 0.10$)

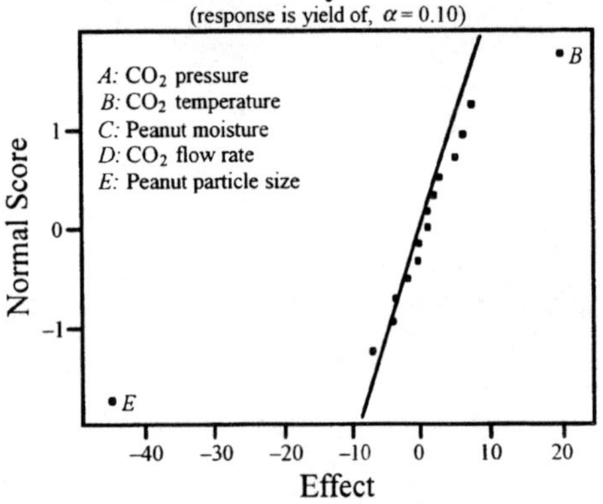

(c) Factors B and E appear significant.

(d) **Interaction Plot—Data Means for Yield of Oil**

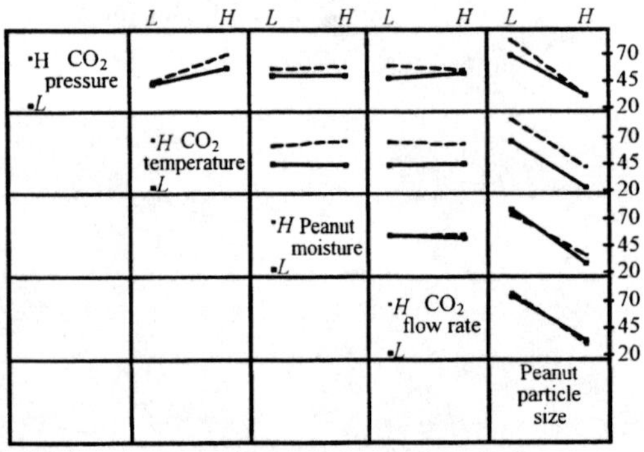

(e) Factors B and E are significant. The highest responses occur when the carbon dioxide pressure is high and the peanut particle size is low.

18. In the factorial design approach, variation in the parameter of interest is attributed to each of the factor components and to one overall error component. In the Taguchi approach factors are divided into controllable design parameters and uncontrollable noise factors related to the environment. Both methods utilize 23 factorial design and normal distribution assumptions.

19. (a)

Treatment	Signal-to-Noise Ratio
(1)	15.644
a	4.425
b	20.491
ab	15.317

(b) Treatment combination *b*, consisting of receiver R^2 and amplifier *B* provides the highest signal to noise ratio.

(c) Results are the same.

20. (a)

Fabric	Treatment	SN_S
C	*X*	–32.2
C	*Y*	–29.5
P	*X*	–33.5
P	*Y*	–29.7

(b) Higher SN_S is provided by Treatment *Y*. With respect to the fabric, there is no significant difference between cotton and polyester in the Taguchi approach.

(c) In the ANOVA in Problem 3, there was no significant interaction between the fabric and the treatment.

21. Note: With the data provided in file *photo* MINITAB crashes. It produces the following error message: * Error ** One or more response is zero or negative. "Larger is Better" signal to noise ratio can not be calculated; execution aborted.***

The simplest thing to do is to compute the signal-to-noise ratios without using the software with the appropriate formula.

See Table (larger is better) on Problem 4.

$$SN_L = -10\log_{10}\frac{\sum_{i=1}^{n}\left(\frac{1}{Y_i}\right)^2}{n}-0$$

22. (a)

Treatment	Signal-to-Noise Ratio
(1)	11.073
a	4.551
b	5.621
c	3.361
ab	9.850
ac	10.662
bc	2.370
abc	15.999

(b) Using the above signal-to-noise ratios, MINITAB may be used to analyze the data following the steps outlined on pages 554 and 555.

Normal Probability Plot for Main Effects and Interactions

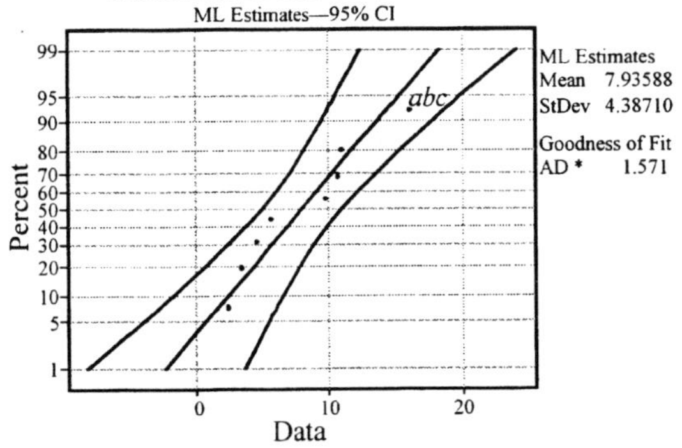

Interaction Plot—Data Means for Deviation from ?

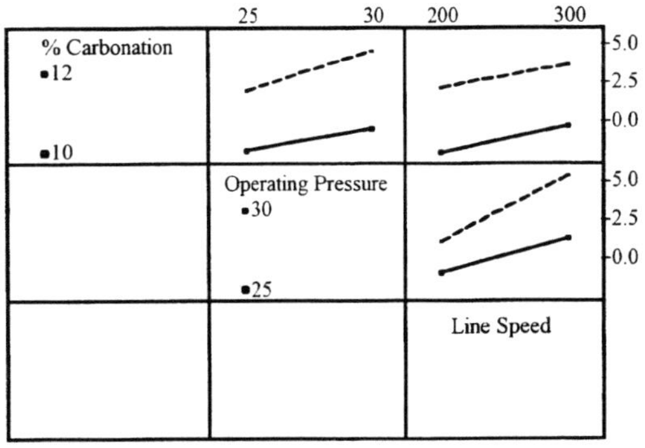

There are no significant interaction terms.

(c) Better factor combination is abc (10% carbonation, 25 operating pressure and 200 line speed). These levels should be used to reduce the deviation from the target.

(d) In terms of percent carbonation and operating pressure, Taguchi approach does not contradict ANOVA. Results for line speed differ, so it is necessary to verify initial assumptions of validity for both procedures.

23. (a)

Design	Weight	Size	SN_L
S	L	S	47.7
C	L	S	44.0
S	H	S	46.3
S	L	L	46.0
C	H	S	42.1
C	L	L	47.6
S	H	L	47.1
C	H	L	47.7

(b)–(c) There is no significant difference in SN_L values for various factor combinations. Worst combinations are CHS and CLS.

(d) The Taguchi approach does not contradict ANOVA, but it is less sensitive.

24. The one-way ANOVA model involves the levels of only *one* factor; thus, the total variation is partitioned into *two* components: the variation of this factor and the random variation. The two-way ANOVA model, on the other hand, involves the levels of *two* factors, say, A and B; thus, the total variation is partitioned into *four* components: factor A variation, factor B variation, interaction , and the random variation.

25. The randomized block design model deals with only *one* factor and matched items. The two-factor factorial design model evaluates the effects of *two* factors simultaneously.

26. Interaction in a factorial design is best explained by describing the lack of interaction. In other words, if there is no interaction between two factors A and B, then any difference in the response variable between the two levels of factor A would be the same at each level of factor B.

27. To determine the interaction between the levels of factors V_i and V_j , $V_i \neq V_j$, $V_i, V_J \in \{A, B, C\}$ it is necessary to calculate test statistic $F = \dfrac{MSV_iV_j}{\text{MSE}}$ and compare it with critical value $F_{cr} = F_U(\alpha, df_1 df_2)$, where $df_1 = (l_i - 1)(l_j - 1)$, $df_2 = ijk(n' - 1)$, l_i is the number of levels of factor V_i, and l_j is the number of levels of factor V_j. Decision rule: Reject H_0 if $F > F_{cr}$. To determine the interaction between all three factors it is necessary to consider test statistic $F = \dfrac{MSABC}{\text{MSE}}$ and compare it with $F_{cr} = F_U(\alpha, df_1 df_2)$, where $df_1 = (i-1)(j-1)(k-1)$, $df_2 = ilk(n' - 1)$, and i, j, k are numbers of levels of factors A, B, C, respectively. Decision rule: Reject H_0 if $F > F_{cr}$.

28. *Purpose*: Fractional Factorial Design is used for situations in which many factors need to be evaluated simultaneously. Fractional factorial design allows the consideration of more binary factors than the $\log_2 n$, where n is the number of observations.
Limitations: The number of observations must be $n = 2^m$, then one can consider $m+1$ (half-fractional) or $m+2$ (quarter fractional) designs.
Assumptions: In fractional factorial design, populations are assumed to be independent and normally distributed.

29. One-way design considers independent observations for various levels of only one factor. Two-way design deals with independent observations for various levels of two factors. In these cases the number of observations is not less than the number of all factor level combinations. Fractional factorial design considers binary factors only, but it is possible to analyze one or two more additional factors than for a standard factorial design.

30. In Resolution III factorial design, main effects are confounded with two-way interactions. In Resolution IV factorial design, main effects are not confounded with two-way interactions. In such designs, a two-way interaction is confounded with another two-way interaction. Finally, in Resolution V factorial design, each main effect and each two-factor interaction can be independently estimated without being confounded with any other main effect or interactions. In such designs, main effects or two-way interactions are confounded with three-way or higher-order interactions.

31. In a fractional design, some of the effects are confounded with each other; that is, one cannot estimate all of the effects separately. For example, if factor *A* is confounded with a three-way interaction *BCD*, then the estimated effect for *A* also includes any effect due to interaction *BCD*. Effects that are confounded are said to be aliased. The alias structure describes the confounding that occurs in a design.

32. The Taguchi philosophy is concerned with the following points:
(a) Minimizing the squared error around a target value.
(b) Making products robust against variations in environmental conditions using design parameters and noise factors.
(c) Making products less sensitive to unit-to-unit variation, using signal-to-noise ratios.

33. Inner arrays, or controllable factors should be the focus in the process improvement study. Outer arrays, or noise factors are environmental and represent conditions under which the product is expected to perform.

34. There are three types of signal-to-noise ratios: SN_T , SN_S, and SN_L . A high value of the proper signal-to-noise ratio indicates a high significance of the corresponding factor combinations. SN_T is centered around the target value; it should be used when the goal is to meet a specific target value. SN_S is used when the goal is to minimize the response, so it is appropriate in the cases when the quality characteristic being evaluated is such that a lower value indicates higher quality. SN_L is used when the aim is to maximize the response and so its use is appropriate when the quality characteristic being evaluated is such that a higher value indicates higher quality.

35. The Taguchi approach provides an advantage in quality engineering in that it leads to products that are robust against environmental variation and that are less sensitive to unit-to-unit variation. Some of the disadvantages to the Taguchi approach are summarized as follows: (1) Often fractional designs used with the Taguchi approach are Resolution III designs that contain a complicated confounding structure in which main effects are comfounded with simple two-factor interactions. Such designs may provide misleading results in circumstances when there is a lack of extensive experience with the process or when these designs are used without sufficient awareness of the design assumptions and limitations. (2) Implication that the separation of location and dispersion effects can always be accomplished merely by using a log transformation does not always seem right. The argument could be made that situations may exist in which a different transformation (or no transformation) is needed to obtain this separation. (3) The signal-to-noise ratio is often criticized over its complexity and inefficiency. Also, there are some problems with local and asymptotic properties of the SN estimators.

36. **Two-way ANOVA: Weight versus Type; Cooking Time**

Analysis of Variance for Weight

Source	DF	SS	MS	F	P
Type	1	528.1	528.1	24.14	0.008
Cooking time	1	5253.1	5253.1	240.14	0.000
Interaction	1	28.1	28.1	1.29	0.320
Error	4	87.5	21.9		
Total	7	5896.9			

(a) $H_0: \mu_A = \mu_I$, $H_1: \mu_A \neq \mu_B$
Decision rule: Reject H_0 if $F > 7.71$. Test statistic: $F = 24.14$. Decision: Because $F > 7.71$, reject H_0. The type of pasta is a significant factor.

(b) $H_0: \mu_4 = \mu_8$, $H_1: \mu_4 \neq \mu_8$
Decision rule: Reject H_0 if $F > 7.71$. Test statistic: $F = 240.14$. Decision: Because $F > 7.71$, reject H_0.
The cooking time is a significant factor.

(c) H_0: There is no interaction between the type of pasta and cooking time.
H_1: There is an interaction due to the type of pasta and cooking time.
Decision rule: Reject H_0 if $F > 7.71$. Test statistic: $F = 1.29$. Decision: Because $F < 7.71$, do not reject H_0. There is no significant interaction between the type of pasta and cooking time.

(d)

```
                         Individual 95% CI
Type         Mean      -------+---------+---------+---------+----
A            291.3                                (--------*--------)
I            275.0      (--------*--------)
                       -------+---------+---------+---------+----
                            273.0     280.0     287.0     294.0
```

```
                          Individual 95% CI
Cooking time   Mean      ----+---------+---------+---------+-------
4              257.5      (---*---)
8              308.8                                   (---*---)
                         ----+---------+---------+---------+-------
                         256.0     272.0     288.0     304.0
```

(e) The type of pasta and the cooking time are significant effects. There is no significant interaction between the type of pasta and cooking time. Lower weight corresponds to the Italian type of pasta and to 4 minutes cooking time.

(f) It will be reasonable to study various Italian pasta brands, cooking temperature, and components.

(g) Answers will vary.

(h) Answers will vary.

37. **Two-way ANOVA: Displacement versus Intensity; Location**

Analysis of Variance for Displace

Source	DF	SS	MS	F	P
Intensity	2	0.004744	0.002372	7.35	0.005
Location	2	0.259926	0.129963	402.60	0.000
Interaction	4	0.000242	0.000060	0.19	0.942
Error	18	0.005811	0.000323		
Total	26	0.270722			

(a) $H_0: \mu_{860} = \mu_{1041} = \mu_{1246}$, H_1: At least one of the means is different.
Decision rule: Reject H_0, if $F > 3.55$. Test statistic: $F = 7.35$. Decision: Because $F > 3.55$, reject H_0. The effect of the clamp actuation intensity is significant for the 0.05 significance level.

(b) $H_0: \mu_1 = \mu_2 = \mu_3$, H_1: At least of the means is different.
Decision rule: Reject H_0, if $F > 3.55$. Test statistic: $F = 412.60$. Decision: Because $F > 3.55$, reject H_0. The location is a significant factor.

(c) H_0: There is no interaction between the clamp actuation intensity and location.
H_1: There is an interaction between the clamp actuation intensity and location.
Decision rule: Reject H_0 if $F > 2.93$. Test statistic: $F = 0.19$. Decision: Because $F < 2.93$, do not reject H_0. There is no significant interaction between the clamp actuation intensity and location.

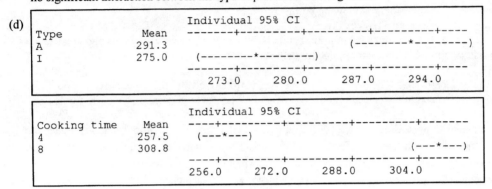

(d)

```
                              Individual 95% CI
Intensity        Mean   --------+---------+---------+---------+---
 890           0.1965    (-------*-------)
1041           0.2104             (-------*--------)
1246           0.2289                        (--------*-------)
                        --------+---------+---------+---------+---
                            0.1950    0.2100    0.2250    0.2400
```

```
                              Individual 95% CI
location         Mean   ---------+---------+---------+---------+--
1              0.1453    (-*-)
2              0.3506                                 (-*--)
3              0.1398   (-*-)
                        ---------+---------+---------+---------+--
                            0.1800    0.2400    0.3000    0.3600
```

(e) The clamp actuation intensity, and the location of the fixture are both significant factors at a 0.05 significance level. There is no significant interaction between the clamp actuation intensity and location. Placing the clamp at a location of 1 or 3 with an intensity of 890 gives the lowest displacements.

38. (a)

Estimated Effects and Coefficients for Spectrum (coded units)

Term	Effect	Coef
Constant		874.1
Color	-64.3	-32.1
Temperature	602.2	301.1
Light	498.3	249.1
Color*Temperature	-50.3	-25.1
Color*Light	-9.2	-4.6
Temperature*Light	-220.8	-110.4

(b)

Main Effects Plot—Data Means for Spectrometer

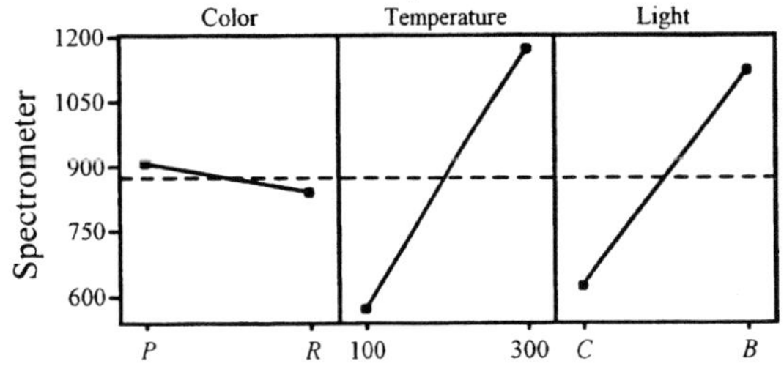

(c)

Interaction Plot—Data Means for Spectrometer

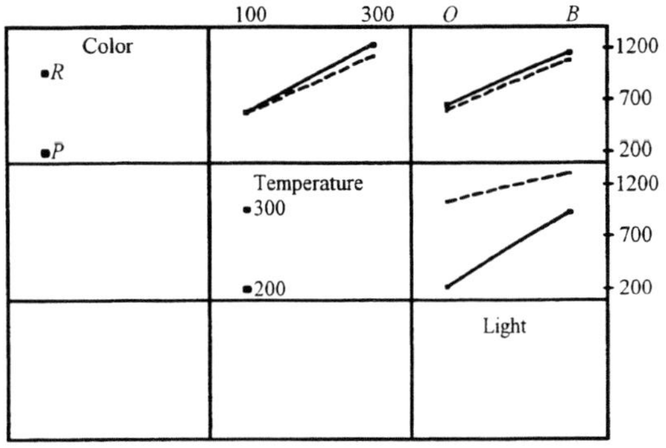

(d)

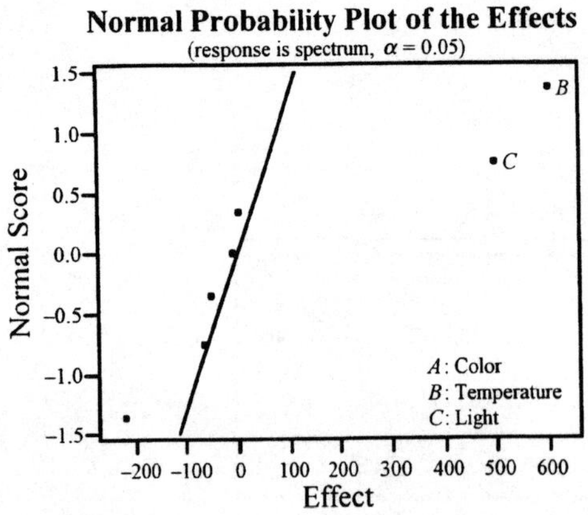

(e) Single factors B (Temperature) and C (Light) are significant.

(f) **Analysis of Variance for Spectrum**

Source	DF	SS	MS	F	P
Color	1	8256	8256	0.32	0.601
Temperat	1	725410	725410	28.26	0.006
Light	1	496506	496506	19.34	0.012
Error	4	102689	25672		
Total	7	1332861			

Factor B (temperature) is significant.

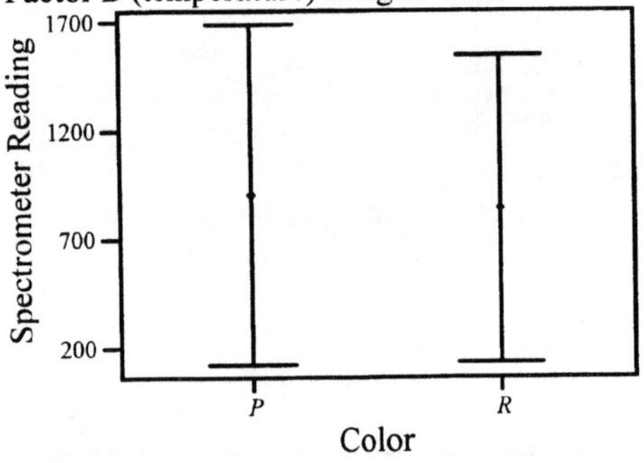

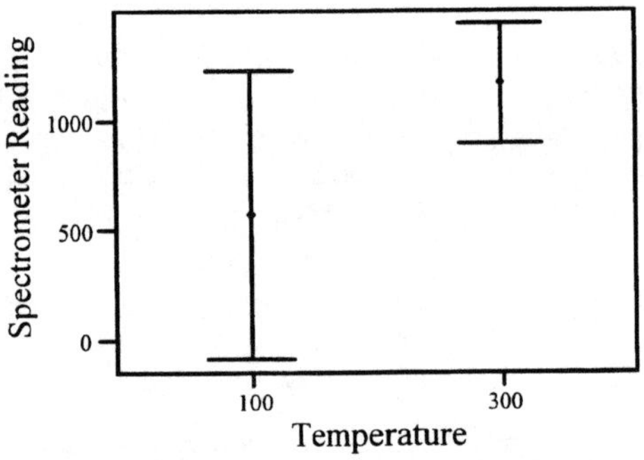

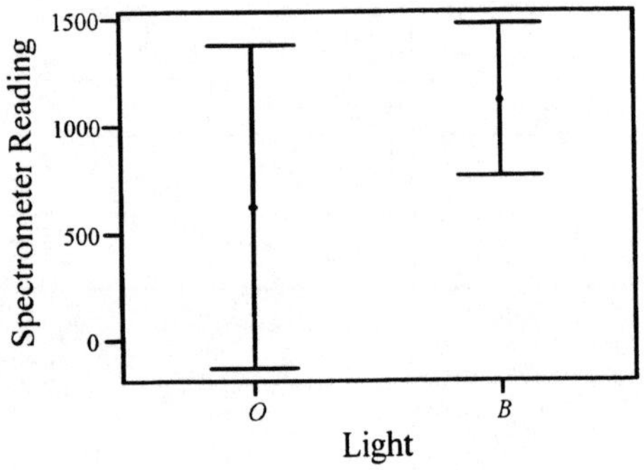

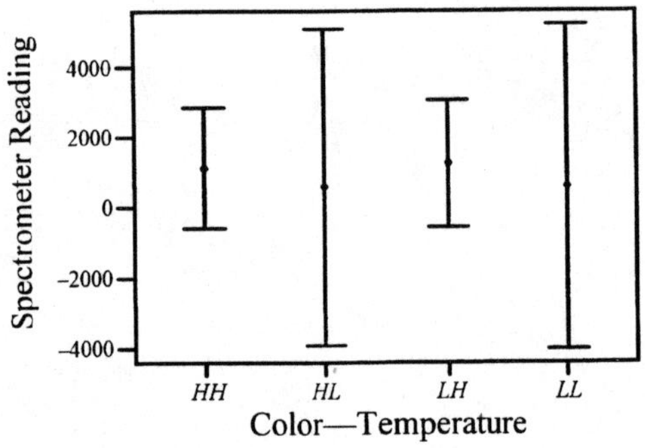

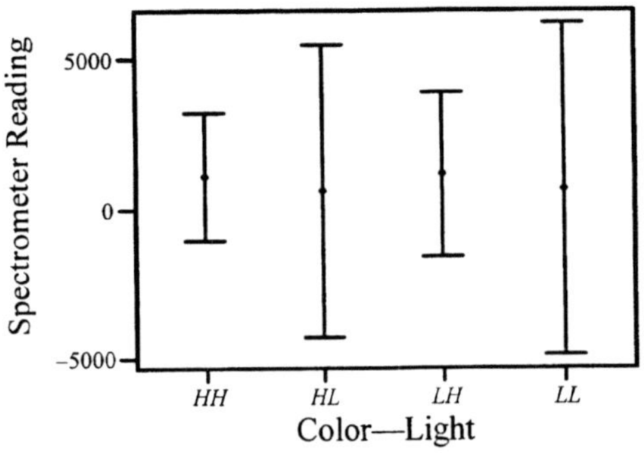

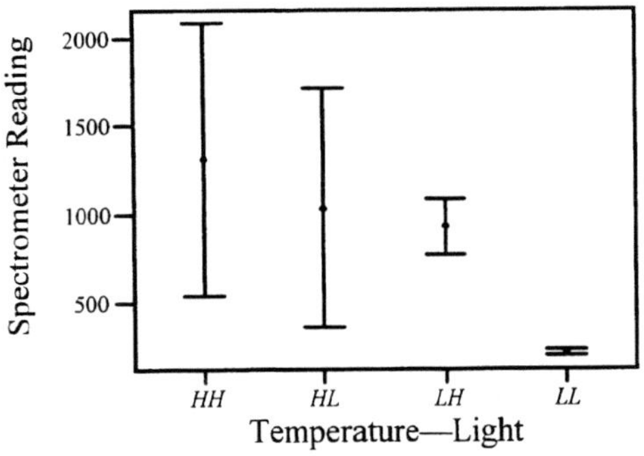

(g) Single factors B (temperature) and C (light) are significant.

(h) **Two-way ANOVA: Spectrometer Reading versus Temperature; Light**

```
Analysis of Variance for Spectrum
Source        DF        SS        MS        F        P
Temperature    1    725410    725410   215.20    0.000
Light          1    496506    496506   147.29    0.000
Interaction    1     97461     97461    28.91    0.006
Error          4     13484      3371
Total          7   1332861
```

```
                           Individual 95% CI
Temperature      Mean   ------+---------+---------+---------+-----
100               573    (---*---)
300              1175                                   (---*---)
                        ------+---------+---------+---------+-----
                             600       800      1000      1200
```

```
                           Individual 95% CI
Light            Mean   ------+---------+---------+---------+-----
O                 625   (----*----)
B                1123                                  (----*----)
                        ------+---------+---------+---------+-----
                             640       800       960      1120
```

Factors B (temperature) and C (light) are significant.

(i) Results of parts (e) and (g) are the same. The result of part (h) does not contradict the previous two.

39. **Penetration Rate**

Analysis of Variance for penetration.

Source	DF	SS	MS	F	P
Rake ang	1	94.58	94.58	5.23	0.052
Thrust	1	280.73	280.73	15.52	0.004
Speed	1	121.00	121.00	6.69	0.032
Rake ang*Thrust	1	55.95	55.95	3.09	0.117
Rake ang*Speed	1	0.78	0.78	0.04	0.840
Thrust*Speed	1	4.14	4.14	0.23	0.645
Rake ang*Thrust*Speed	1	6.76	6.76	0.37	0.558
Error	8	144.74	18.09		
Total	15	708.68			

(a) There is no significant effect due to rake angle for the 0.05 significance level.
(b) There is significant effect due to thrust for the 0.05 significance level.
(c) There is significant effect due to speed for the 0.05 significance level.
(d) There are no significant factor interactions.
(e) **Main Effects Plot—Data Means for Penetration**

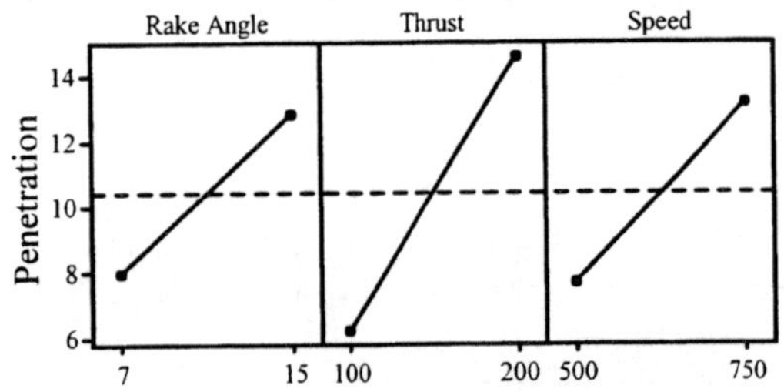

(f) **Interaction Plot—Data Means for Penetration**

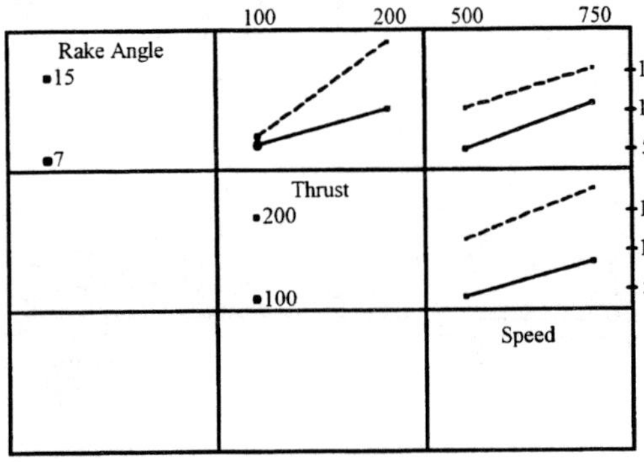

(g) **Estimated Effects and Coefficients for Penetration (coded units)**

Term	Effect	Coef	SE Coef	T	P
Constant		10.4075	1.063	9.79	0.000
Rake ang	4.8625	2.4313	1.063	2.29	0.052
Thrust	8.3775	4.1887	1.063	3.94	0.004
Speed	5.5000	2.7500	1.063	2.59	0.032
Rake ang*Thrust	3.7400	1.8700	1.063	1.76	0.117
Rake ang*Speed	-0.4425	-0.2212	1.063	-0.21	0.840
Thrust*Speed	1.0175	0.5088	1.063	0.48	0.645
Rake ang*Thrust*Speed	1.3000	0.6500	1.063	0.61	0.558

(h)

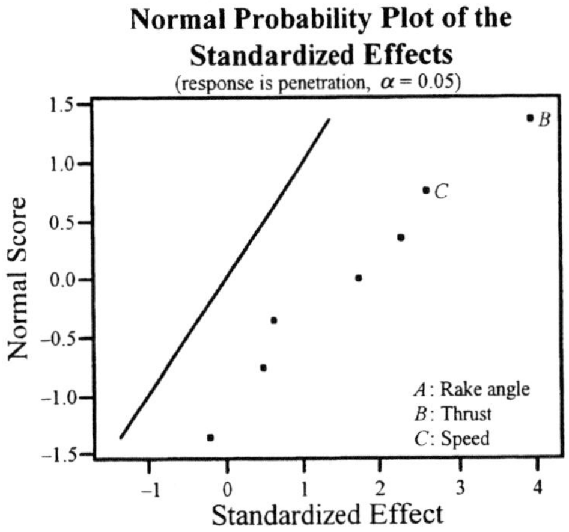

(i) There are significant effects due to all factors and interactions. Speed and thrust levels are most significant.

(j) The ANOVA results indicate that none of the interaction factors are significant and that there is no significant effect due to the rake angle. Both the ANOVA results and the probability table agree that the thrust and speed are the most significant factors. Therefore, there are no significant differences in the results of parts (a)–(d) and part (i). It is important to note that the significance level used affects whether an effect is found to be significant.

(k) **Analysis of Means**

Summary Table
Contents: number of nonmissing data cell mean

Rows: Rake ang	Columns: Speed 500	750	All
7	4	4	8
	5.005	10.948	7.976
15	4	4	8
	10.310	15.368	12.839
All	8	8	16
	7.658	13.158	10.408

Rows: Rake ang	Columns: Thrust 100	200	All
7	4	4	8
	5.658	10.295	7.976
15	4	4	8
	6.780	18.898	12.839
All	8	8	16
	6.219	14.596	10.408

Rows: Thrust	Columns: Speed 500	750	All
100	4	4	8
	3.978	8.460	6.219
200	4	4	8
	11.338	17.855	14.596
All	8	8	16
	7.658	13.157	10.407

The highest penetration rate corresponds to rake angle of 15, a thrust of 200 and a speed of 750.

(l)

Rake Angle	Thrust	Speed	SN_L
7	100	500	3.4
7	100	750	16.3
7	200	500	17.3
7	200	750	18.5
15	100	500	14.7
15	100	750	18.0
15	200	500	23.5
15	200	750	27.0

(m) The highest SN_L corresponds to a rank angle of 15°, 200 pounds of thrust, and a speed of 750 rpm; the same as in part (k).

(n) The best choice would be a rake angle of 15°, a thrust of 200 pounds and a speed of 750 rpm.

(o) Conclusions for parts (n) and (k) are the same.

Torque

Analysis of Variance for Torque

Source	DF	SS	MS	F	P
Rake ang	1	18.1	18.1	0.10	0.757
Thrust	1	6045.1	6045.1	34.29	0.000
Speed	1	315.1	315.1	1.79	0.218
Rake ang*Thrust	1	10.6	10.6	0.06	0.813
Rake ang*Speed	1	68.1	68.1	0.39	0.552
Thrust*Speed	1	217.6	217.6	1.23	0.299
Rake ang*Thrust*Speed	1	52.6	52.6	0.30	0.600
Error	8	1410.5	176.3		
Total	15	8137.4			

(a) There is no significant effect due to rake angle.

(b) There is a significant effect due to thrust.

(c) There is no significant effect due to speed.

(d) There are no significant factor interactions.

(e) **Main Effects Plot—Data Means for Torque**

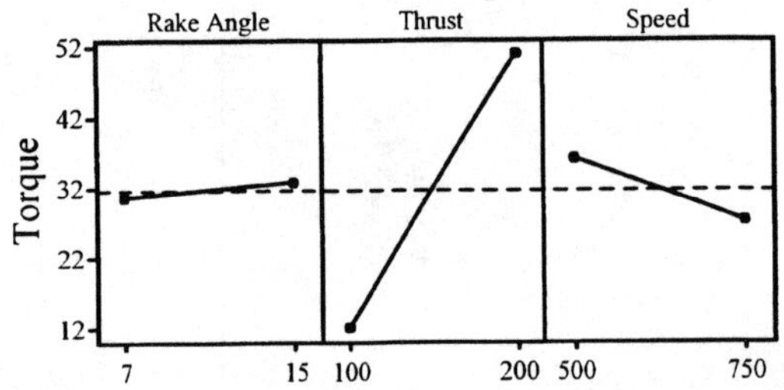

(f) **Interaction Plot—Data Means for Torque**

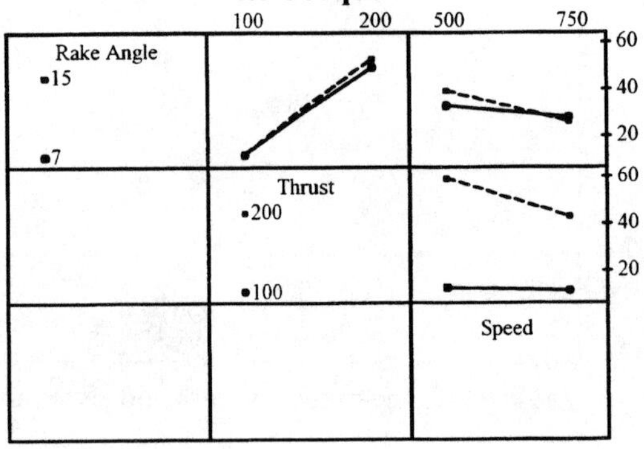

(g) **Estimated Effects and Coefficients for Torque (coded units)**

Term	Effect	Coef	SE Coef	T	P
Constant		31.688	3.320	9.55	0.000
Rake ang	2.125	1.062	3.320	0.32	0.757
Thrust	38.875	19.438	3.320	5.86	0.000
Speed	-8.875	-4.438	3.320	-1.34	0.218
Rake ang*Thrust	1.625	0.813	3.320	0.24	0.813
Rake ang*Speed	-4.125	-2.063	3.320	-0.62	0.552
Thrust*Speed	-7.375	-3.687	3.320	-1.11	0.299
Rake ang*Thrust*Speed	-3.625	-1.813	3.320	-0.55	0.600

(h)

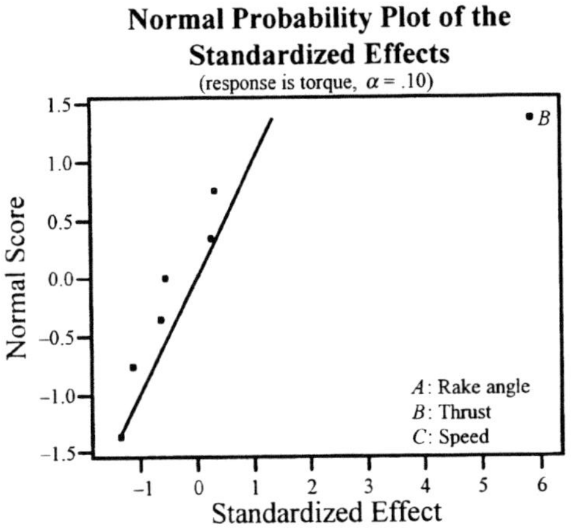

(i) There is a significant effect of factor B (Thrust).

(j) Results of parts (a)–(d) and part (i) are the same.

(k) The only significant factor is the thrust level, which should be set at 100 pounds.

(l)

Rake Angle	Thrust	Speed	SN_S
7	100	500	–21.9
7	100	750	–23.1
7	200	500	–34.7
7	200	750	–33.8
15	100	500	–23.5
15	100	750	–21.3
15	200	500	–36.4
15	200	750	–32.3

(m) Significantly higher SN_S values correspond to 100 thrust and 750 or 500 speed levels.

(n) It will be reasonable to recommend 15 (rake angle), 100 (thrust), and 750 (speed) levels.

(o) Results of parts (k)–(n) does not contradict each other.

40. (a)

Estimated Effects and Coefficients for Tenacity (coded units)

Term	Effect	Coef
Constant		24.4069
Side-to-	-0.6412	-0.3206
yarn typ	0.2062	0.1031
pick den	0.5713	0.2856
Air pres	-0.3812	-0.1906
Side-to-*yarn typ	0.0212	0.0106
Side-to-*pick den	0.4813	0.2406
Side-to-*Air pres	0.0587	0.0294
yarn typ*pick den	-1.1213	-0.5606
yarn typ*Air pres	-0.3937	-0.1969
pick den*Air pres	0.8913	0.4456
Side-to-*yarn typ*pick den	-0.1713	-0.0856
Side-to-*yarn typ*Air pres	0.1863	0.0931
Side-to-*pick den*Air pres	0.2162	0.1081
yarn typ*pick den*Air pres	-0.2562	-0.1281
Side-to-*yarn typ*pick den *Air pres	-0.0213	-0.0106

(b) **Main Effects Plot—Data Means for Air Pressure**

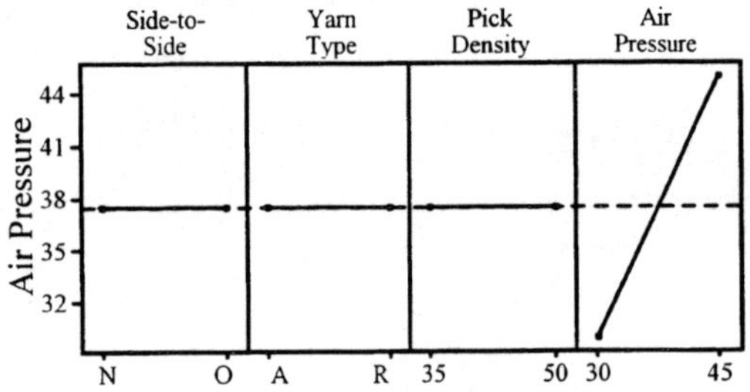

(c) **Interaction Plot—Data Means for Tenacity**

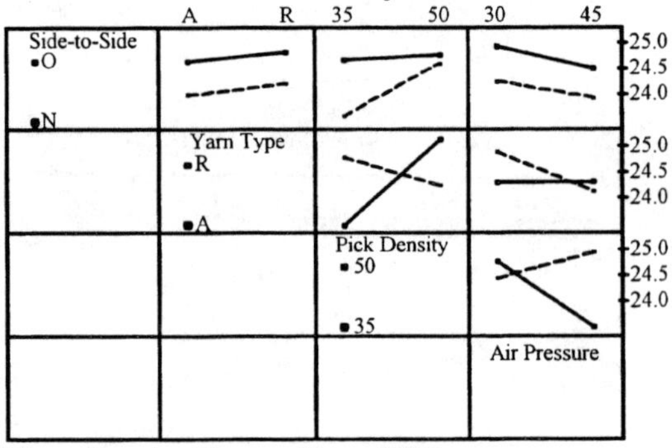

(d) **Normal Probability Plot of the Effects**
(response is tenacity, $\alpha = 0.05$)

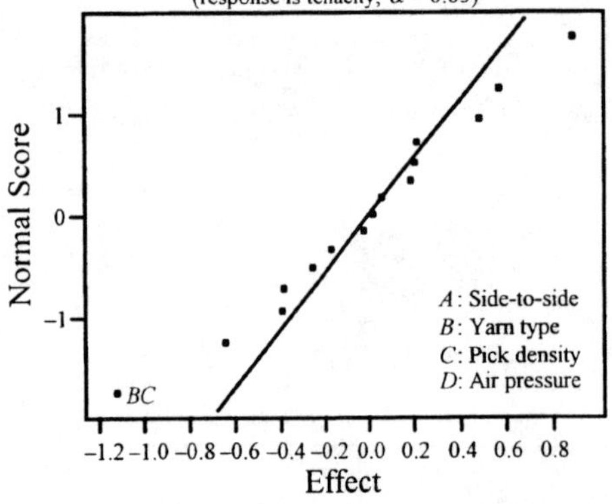

(e) There is a significant effect of *BC*.

(f) **Analysis of Variance for Tenacity**

Source	DF	SS	MS	F	P
Side-to-	1	1.6448	1.6448	1.73	0.216
yarn typ	1	0.1702	0.1702	0.18	0.681
pick den	1	1.3053	1.3053	1.37	0.266
Air pres	1	0.5814	0.5814	0.61	0.451
Error	11	10.4759	0.9524		
Total	15	14.1775			

There are no significant effects of the single factors.

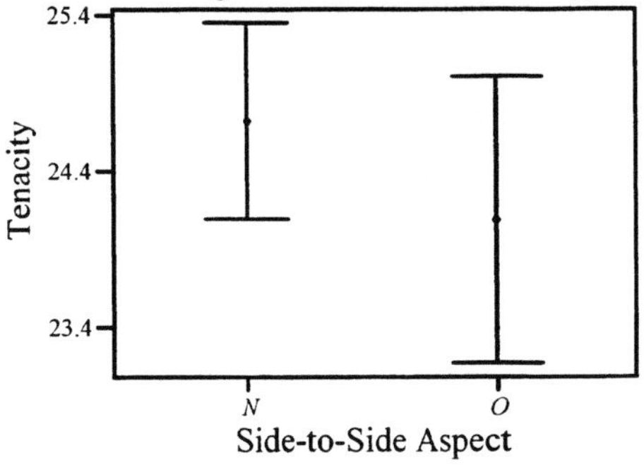

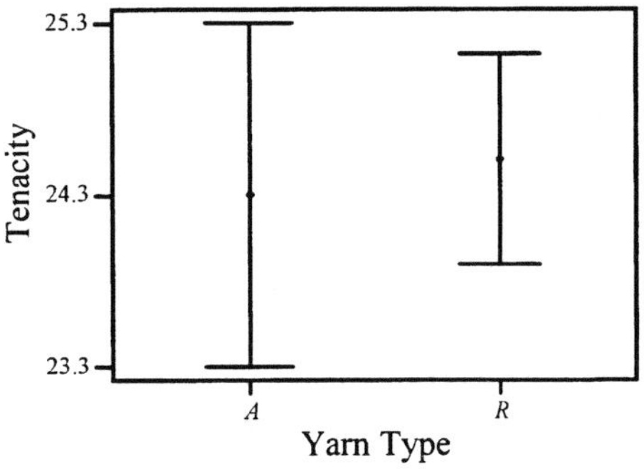

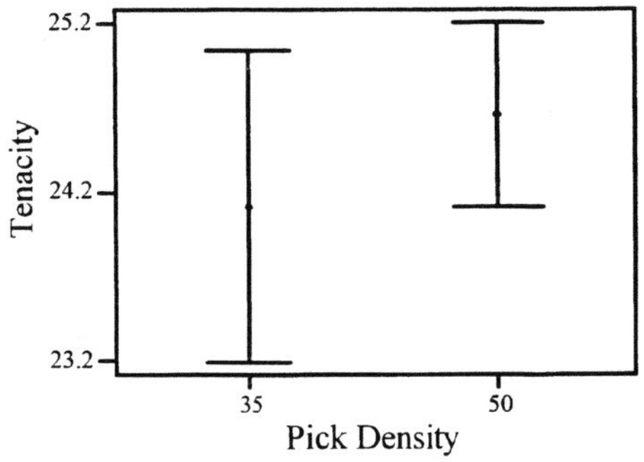

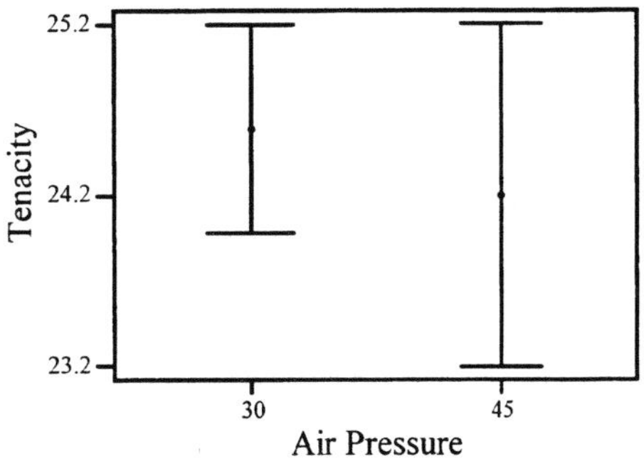

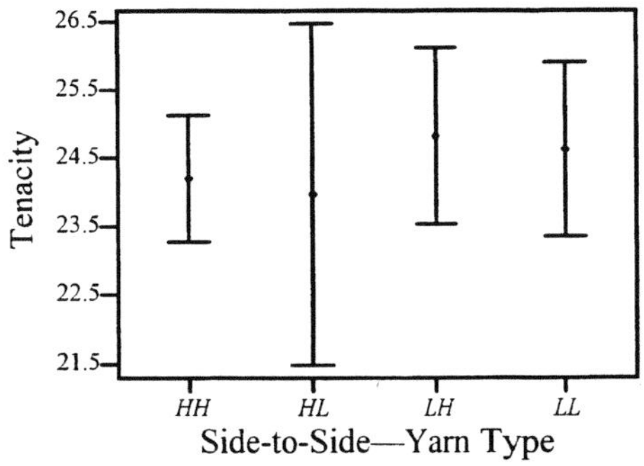

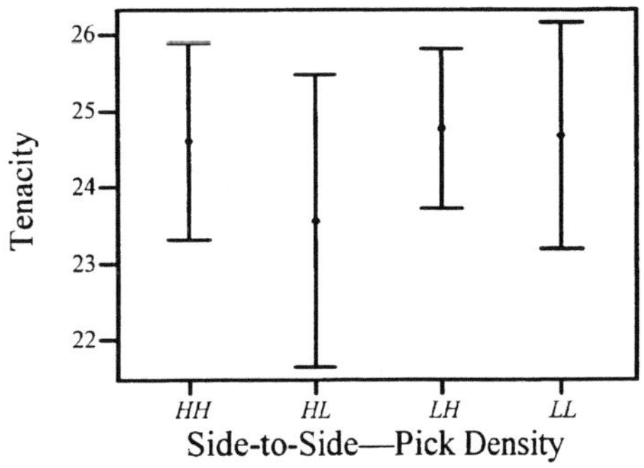

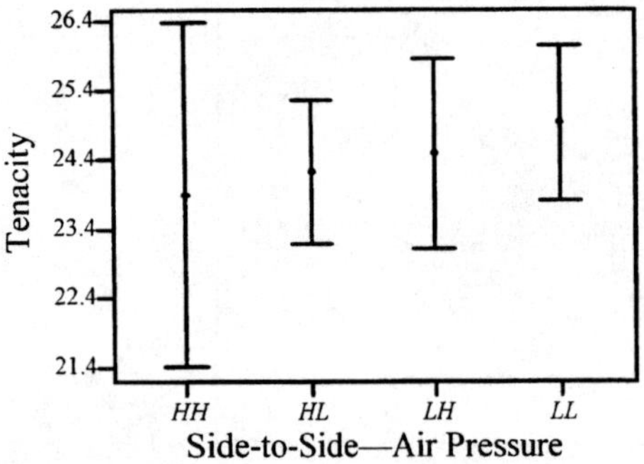

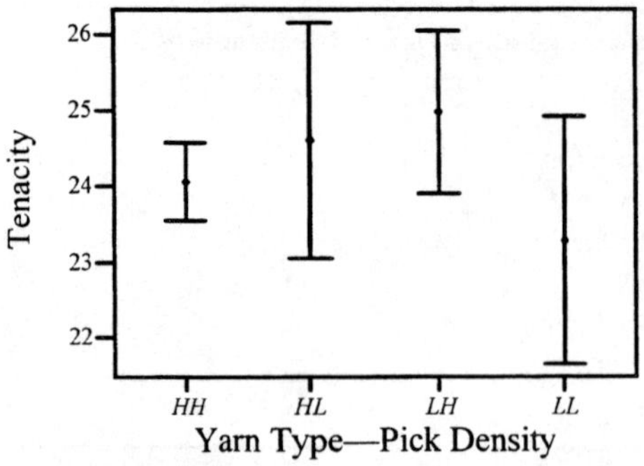

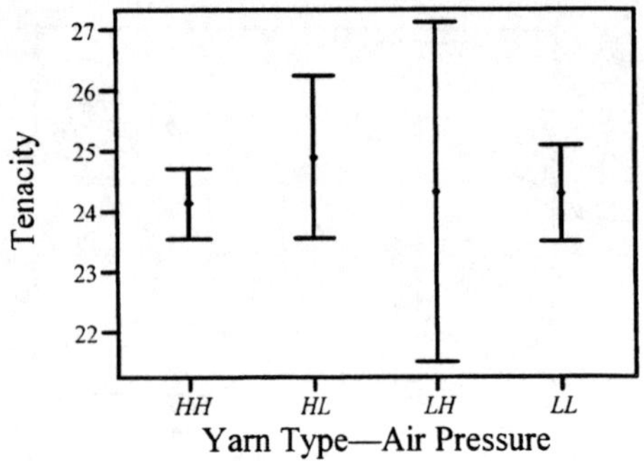

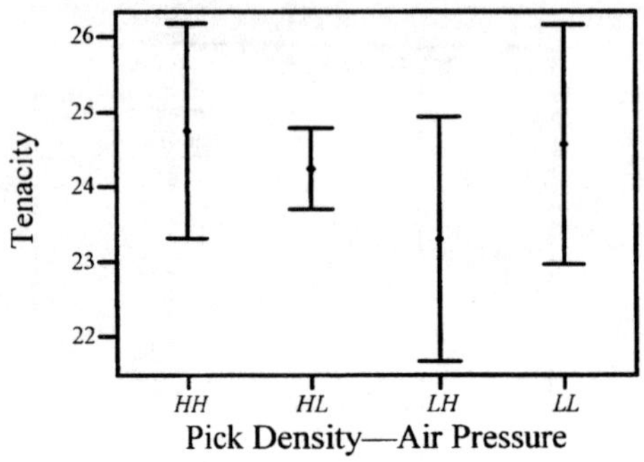

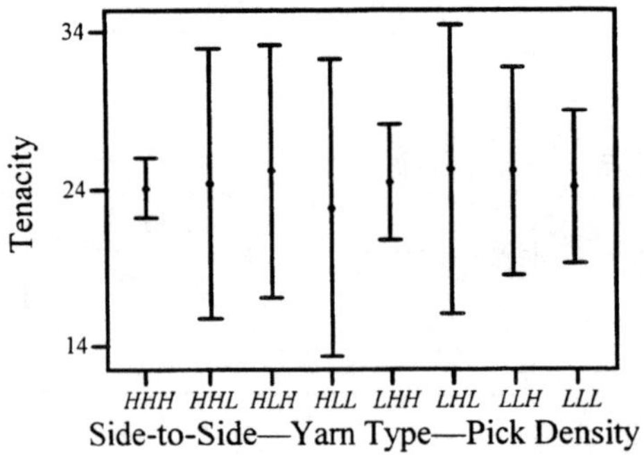

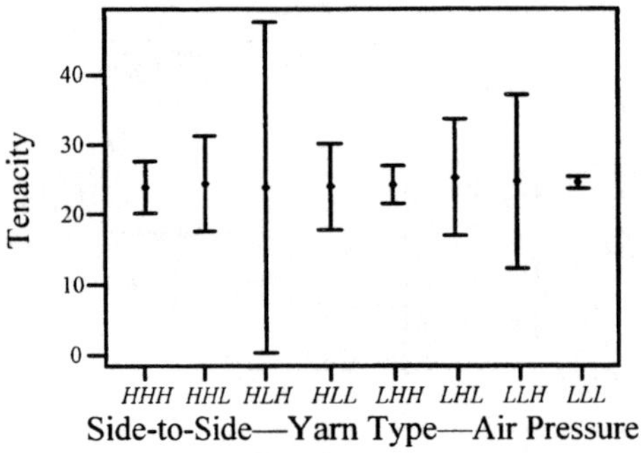

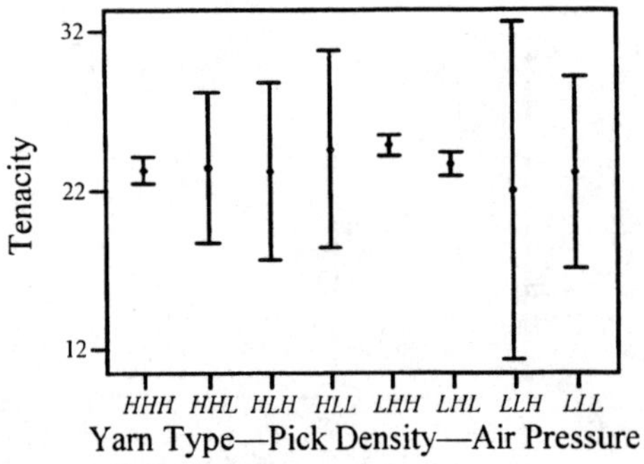

(g) There are significant effects of single factors A, C, D.

(h) (a)

Fractional Factorial Fit: Tenacity versus Side-to-Side; Yarn Type; ...

```
Estimated Effects and Coefficients for tenacity (coded units)
Term                     Effect      Coef
Constant                          24.3963
Side-to-                -0.8975   -0.4487
yarn typ                 0.4225    0.2112
pick den                 0.7575    0.3788
Air pres                -0.5525   -0.2763
Side-to-*yarn typ        0.9125    0.4562
Side-to-*pick den        0.0875    0.0438
Side-to-*Air pres       -1.0625   -0.5312
```

(b)

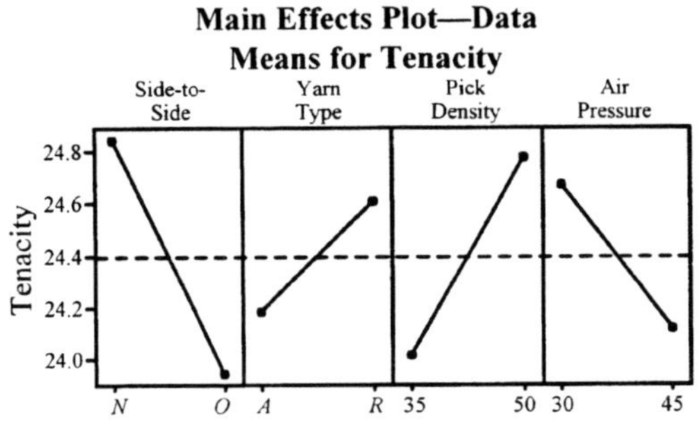

(c)

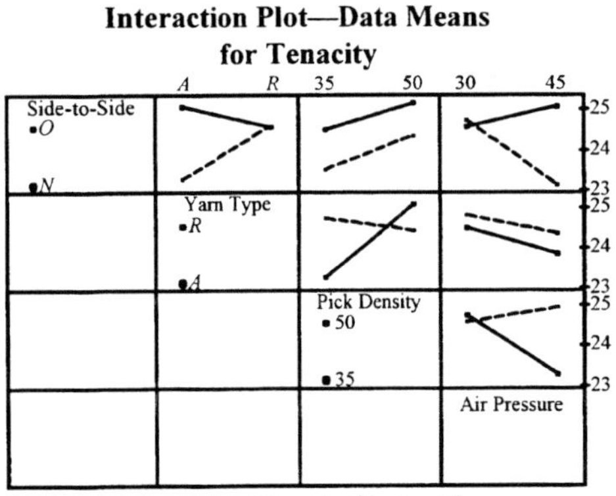

(d)

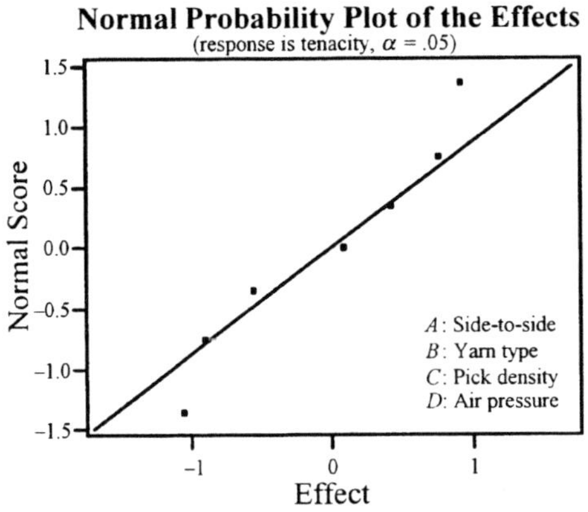

(e) There are two significant effects. They correspond to $AD + BC$ and $AB + CD$.

(f)

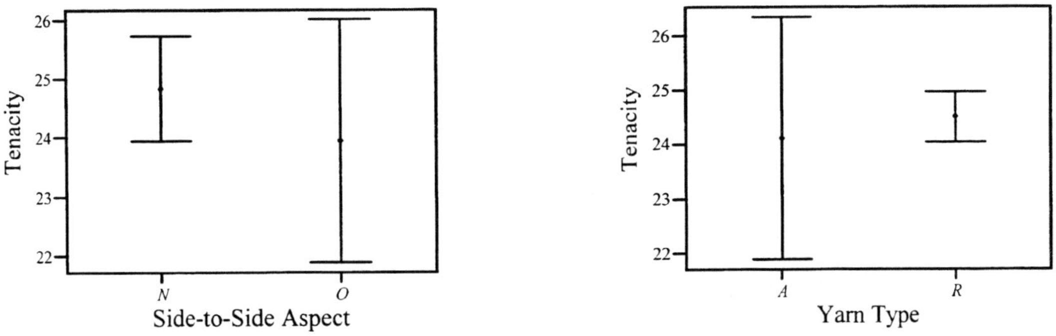

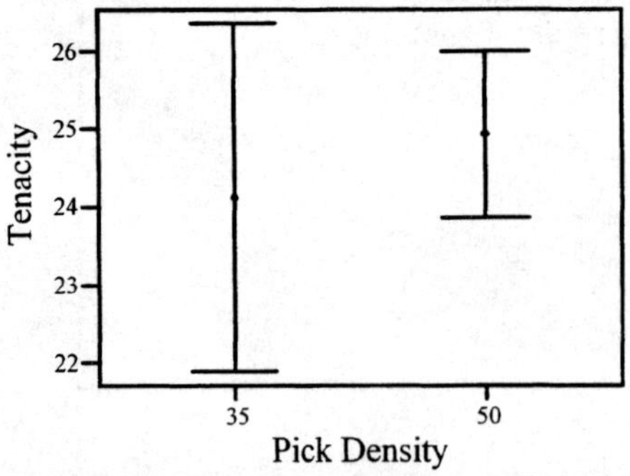

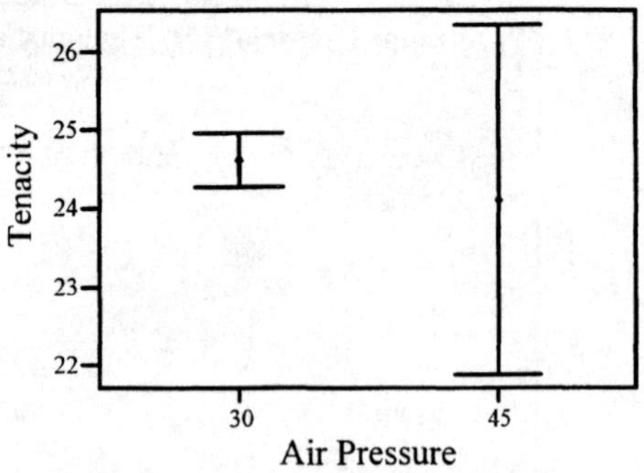

There is significant dependence on all single factors.

(i) There is no principal difference between results for parts (g) and (h). The half sample size fractional factorial sign is more efficient in this particular case.

41. Answers will vary. **42.** Answers will vary. **43.** Answers will vary.

chapter 12

Simple Linear Regression and Correlation

1. (a) The Y-intercept, b_0, indicates that when $X = 0$, the expected valued of Y is 2.
(b) The slope b_1 indicates that for a one unit increase in X the expected change in Y is 5 units.
(c) $\hat{Y} = 2 + 5 = 2 + 5(3) = 17$
(d) (1) yes (2) no (3) no (4) yes (5) no

2. (a) The Y-intercept, b_0, indicates that when $X = 0$, the expected valued of Y is 16.
(b) The slope b_1 indicates that for a one unit increase in X the expected change in Y is 0.6 units.
(c) $\hat{Y}(6) = 16 - 5 \times 6 = -14$
(d) (1) yes (2) no (3) no (4) yes (5) no

3. **Regression Analysis for Film**

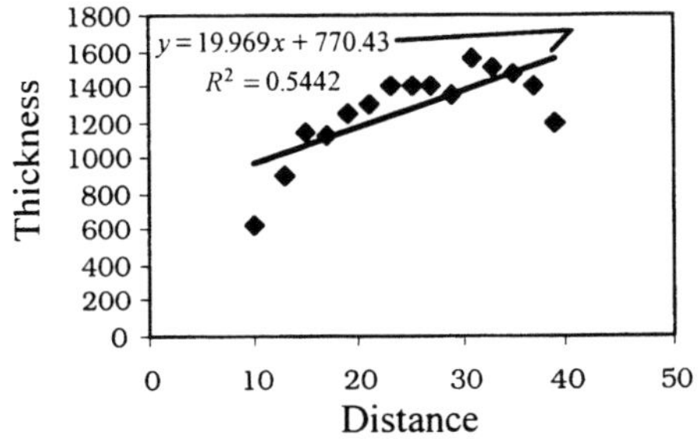

(a) Linear trend, Better result – logarithmic trend

Regression Analysis for Film

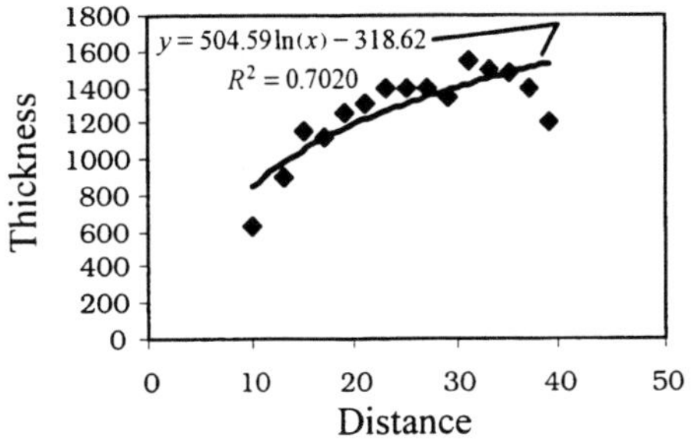

(b) Regression Analysis

Regression Statistics	
Multiple R	0.738
R^2	0.544
Adjusted R^2	0.509
Standard Error	171.794
Observations	15.000

ANOVA

	df	SS	MS	F	Significance F
Regression	1.000	458161.080	458161.080	15.524	0.002
Residual	13.000	383672.240	29513.249		
Total	14.000	841833.330			

	Coefficients	Standard Error	t Stat	p-value	Lower 95%	Upper 95%
Intercept	770.433	133.928	5.753	6.681×10^{-05}	481.099	1059.767
Distance	19.969	5.068	3.940	0.002	9.020	30.919

(c) The slope, b_1 represents the expected change in Y (19.969) per unit change in X.

(d) $\hat{Y}(20) = 770.43 + 19.969 \times 20 = 1169.81$

(e) (1) Regression Analysis

Regression Statistics	
Multiple R	0.853
R^2	0.728
Adjusted R^2	0.707
Standard Error	185.289
Observations	15.000

ANOVA

	df	SS	MS	F	Significance F
Regression	1.000	1192184.100	1192184.100	34.725	5.298×10^{-5}
Residual	13.000	446315.850	34331.989		
Total	14.000	1638500.000			

	Coefficients	Standard Error	t Stat	p-value	Lower 95%	Upper 95%
Intercept	531.835	144.4484	3.682	0.003	219.774	843.897
Distance	32.212	5.466	5.893	5.298×10^{-5}	20.403	44.022

(2) The slope (distance) by represents the expected change in Y (32.212) per unit change in X.

(3) $\hat{Y}(20) = 531.835 + 32.212 \times 20 = 1176.075$

4. (a) **Regression Analysis for Generator**

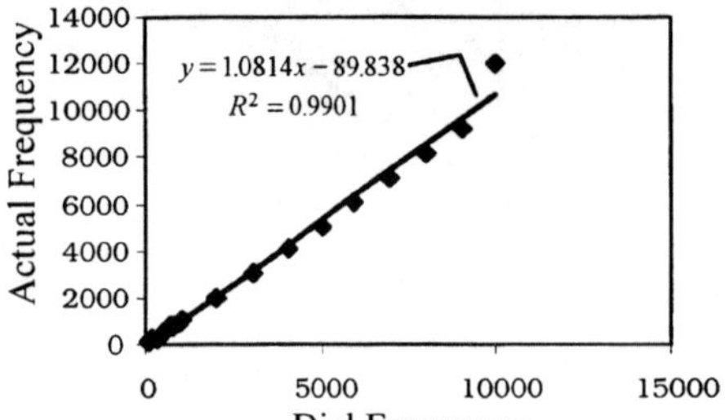

(b) Regression Analysis

Regression Statistics	
Multiple R	0.995
R^2	0.990
Adjusted R^2	0.989
Standard Error	373.167
Observations	19.000

ANOVA

	df	SS	MS	F	Significance F
Regression	1.000	235668542.400	235668542.400	1692.366	1.828×10^{-18}
Residual	17.000	2367315.600	139253.860		
Total	18.000	238035858.100			

	Coefficients	Standard Error	t Stat	p-value	Lower 95%	Upper 95%
Intercept	−89.838	118.768	−0.756	0.460	−340.417	160.740
Distance	1.081	0.026	41.138	1.828×10^{-18}	1.026	1.137

(c) The slope, b_1 represents the expected change in Y (1.081) per unit change in X.

(d) $\hat{Y}(5000) = -89.83 + 1.081 \times 5000 = 5317$

(e)

Confidence Interval Estimate	
X Value	5000.000
Confidence Level	95%
Sample Size	19.000
Degrees of Freedom	17.000
t Value	2.110
Sample Mean	3131.579
Sum of Squared Difference	201521052.630
Standard Error of the Estimate	373.167
h Statistic	0.070
Average Predicted Y $(\hat{Y})$	5317.214

For Average Predicted Y $(\hat{Y})$	
Interval Half Width	208.237
Confidence Interval Lower Limit	5108.978
Confidence Interval Upper Limit	5525.451

For Individual Response Y	
Interval Half Width	814.388
Prediction Interval Lower Limit	4502.826
Prediction Interval Upper Limit	6131.603

$P(4503 < Y(5000) < 6132) \approx 0.95$. There is no contradiction between the observed and predicted values.

5. (a) **Regression Analysis for Hardness**

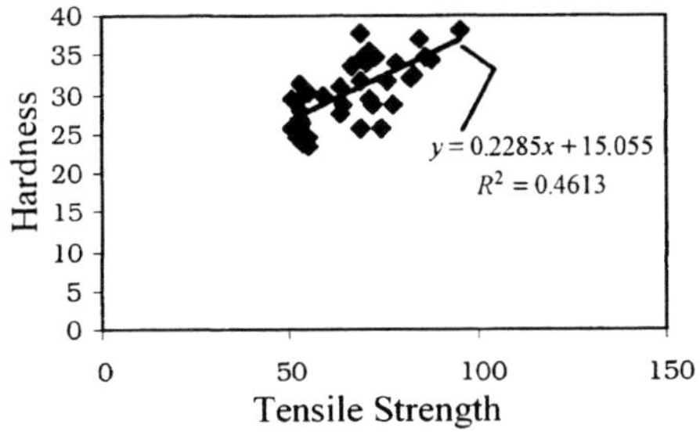

(b) Regression Analysis

Regression Statistics	
Multiple R	0.679
R^2	0.461
Adjusted R^2	0.445
Standard Error	3.048
Observations	35.000

ANOVA

	df	SS	MS	F	Significance F
Regression	1.000	262.560	262.560	28.258	7.265×10^{-6}
Residual	33.000	306.624	9.292		
Total	34.000	569.184			

	Coefficients	Standard Error	t Stat	p-value	Lower 95%	Upper 95%
Intercept	15.055	2.953	5.098	1.381×10^{-5}	9.047	21.062
Tensile Strength	0.228	0.043	5.316	7.265×10^{-6}	0.141	0.316

(c) The slope, b_1 represents the expected change in Y (0.22847) per unit change in X.

(d) $\hat{Y}(70) = 15.1 + 0.228 \times 70 = 31.0$

6. (a) **Regression Analysis for Orders**

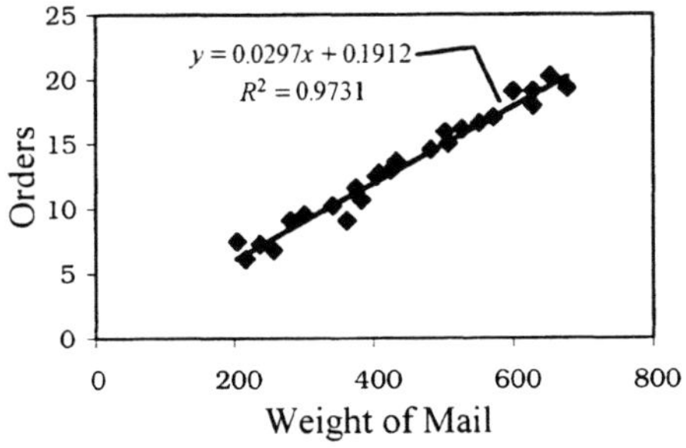

(b) Regression Analysis

Regression Statistics	
Multiple R	0.986
R^2	0.973
Adjusted R^2	0.972
Standard Error	0.726
Observations	25.000

ANOVA

	df	SS	MS	F	Significance F
Regression	1.000	437.644	437.644	830.820	1.482×10^{-19}
Residual	23.000	12.116	0.527		
Total	24.000	449.760			

	Coefficients	Standard Error	t Stat	p-value	Lower 95%	Upper 95%
Intercept	0.191	0.475	0.403	0.691	−0.791	1.173
Weight	0.030	0.001	28.824	1.482×10^{-19}	0.028	0.032

(c) The slope (weight) represents the expected change in Y (0.0297) per unit change in X.

(d) $\hat{Y}(500)=0.191+0.0297\times500=15.04$

7. (a) **Regression Analysis for Pumpkin**

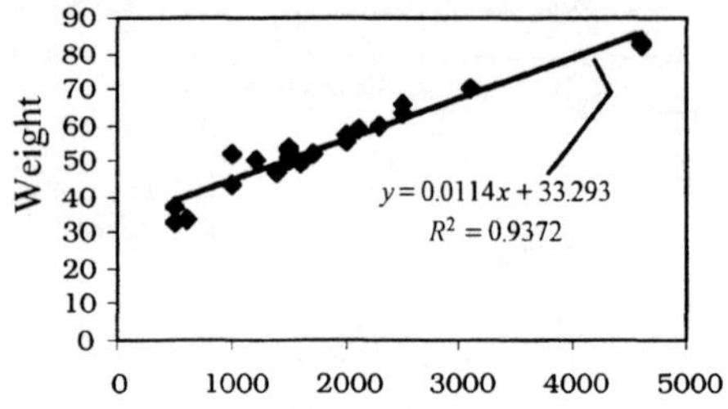

(b) Regression Analysis

Regression Statistics	
Multiple R	0.968
R^2	0.937
Adjusted R^2	0.934
Standard Error	3.260
Observations	23.000

ANOVA

	df	SS	MS	F	Significance F
Regression	1.000	3334.239	3334.239	313.650	4.203×10^{-14}
Residual	21.000	223.239	10.630		
Total	22.000	3557.478			

	Coefficients	Standard Error	t Stat	p-value	Lower 95%	Upper 95%
Intercept	33.293	1.372	24.272	7.566×10^{-17}	30.440	36.145
Circumference	0.011	0.001	17.710	4.203×10^{-14}	0.010	0.013

(c) The slope (circumference) represents the expected change in Y (0.0114) per unit change in X.

(d) $X=60$ does not fall within the range of X, so it is incorrect to use the regression equation for this prediction.

(e) Because circumference is such a strong predictor of weight, the farmer might want to sell the pumpkins on the basis of circumference.

8. (a) $\text{SST}=\text{SSR}+\text{SSE}=36+4=40$

(b) $r^2=\dfrac{\text{SSR}}{\text{SST}}=\dfrac{36}{40}=0.9$, 90% of the variation is explained by the independent variable in the regression model.

9. $\text{SST}=\text{SSR}+\text{SSE}$; $\text{SSR}=120$, $\text{SST}\geq0$, then $\text{SST}\geq120$ and $\text{SST}\neq110$.

10. (a) $\text{SST}=841833$, $\text{SSR}=458161$, $r^2=\dfrac{458161}{841833}=0.5442$. 54.42% of the variation is explained by the independent variable in the regression model.

(b) $S_{XY}=\sqrt{\dfrac{\text{SSE}}{n-2}}=\sqrt{\dfrac{3836721}{13}}=171.794$

(c) Due to a low r^2 and large standard error values, the linear regression is not adequate for processing description as well as for the predicting the thickness of the film.

11. (a) SST = 238035858, SSR = 235668542, $r^2 = \frac{235668542}{238035858} = 0.9900547$. 99% of the variation is explained by the independent variable in the regression model.

(b) $S_{XY} = \sqrt{\frac{\text{SSE}}{n-2}} = \sqrt{\frac{2367315}{17}} = 373.167$

(c) Based on the large r^2 value, one can conclude that the regression model is adequate for predicting the actual frequency of a generator.

12. (a) SSR = 262.560, SST = 569.184, $r^2 = \frac{262.560}{569.184} = 0.461$. 46.13% of the variation is explained by the independent variable in the regression model.

(b) $S_{XY} = \sqrt{\frac{\text{SSE}}{n-2}} = \sqrt{\frac{306.62394}{33}} = 3.048$

(c) Due to a low r^2 value, this model is not adequate for predicting the tensile strength of the die-cast aluminum.

13. (a) SSR = 437.64447, SST = 449.76, $r^2 = \frac{437.644}{449.76} = 0.973$. 97.3% of the variation is explained by the independent variable in the regression model.

(b) $S_{XY} = \sqrt{\frac{\text{SSE}}{n-2}} = \sqrt{\frac{12.115529}{23}} = 0.726$

(c) Based on the large r^2 value, one can conclude that the regression model is adequate for predicting the weight of the mail received.

14. (a) SSR = 3334.239, SST = 35557.478, $r^2 = \frac{3334.239}{3557.478} = 0.937$. 93.7% of the variation is explained by the independent variable in the regression model.

(b) $S_{XY} = \sqrt{\frac{\text{SSE}}{n-2}} = \sqrt{\frac{223.23911}{21}} = 3.260$

(c) Based on the large r^2 value one can conclude that the regression model is adequate for predicting the weight of a pumpkin.

15. A stratification pattern exists due to the decreasing variation in the data.

16. There is a cyclic pattern in the data. There are not enough data to conclude whether a stratification effect is present in the data set.

17. (a)–(b)

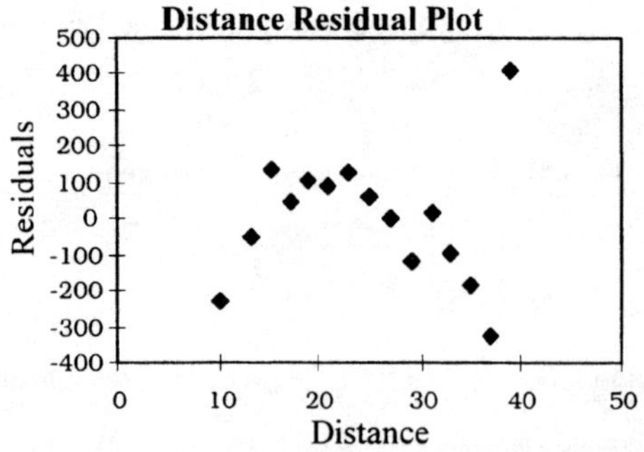

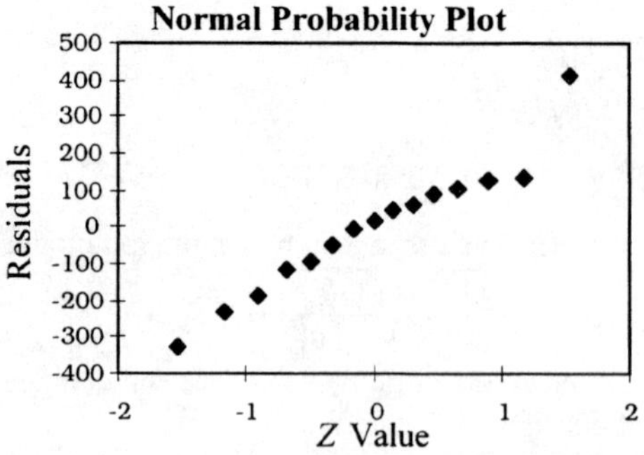

The homoscedasticity and independence assumptions both appear to be valid. The assumption of normality appears to be valid. Gaussian simple linear regression is adequate.

18. (a)–(b) There are doubts about the validity of the homoscedasticity assumption. The independence assumption appears to be valid.

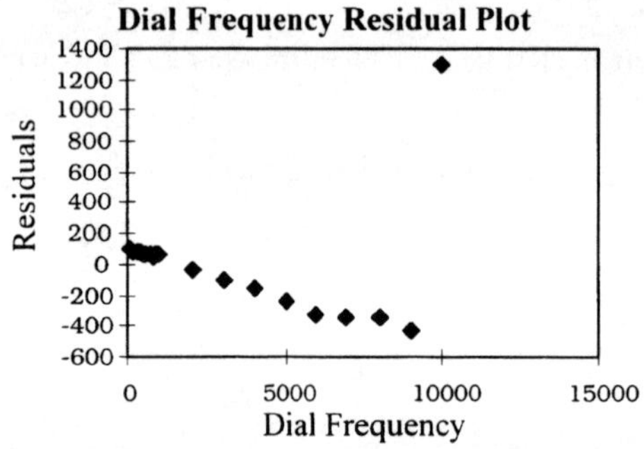

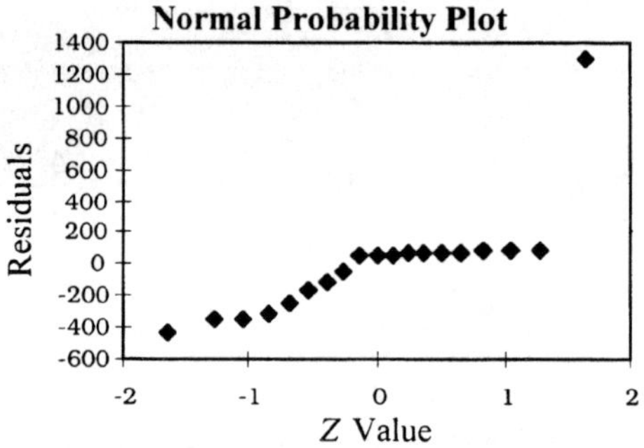

The assumption of normality is not valid. The Gaussian regression model is not adequate.

19. (a)–(b)

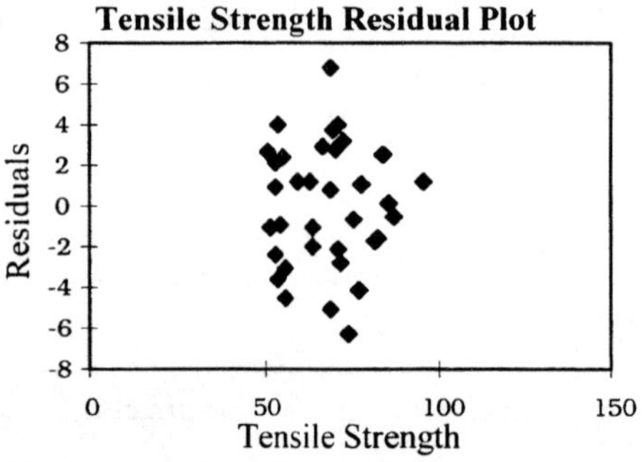

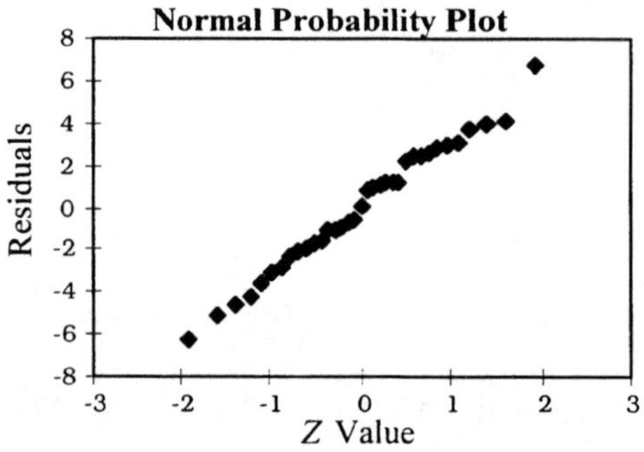

The homoscedasticity and independence assumptions both appear to be valid. The assumption of normality appears to be valid. The Gaussian simple linear regression is adequate.

20. (a)–(b)

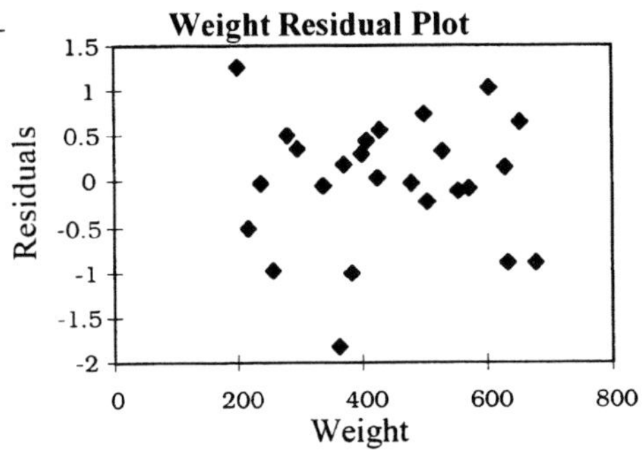

The homoscedasticity and independence assumptions both appear to be valid.

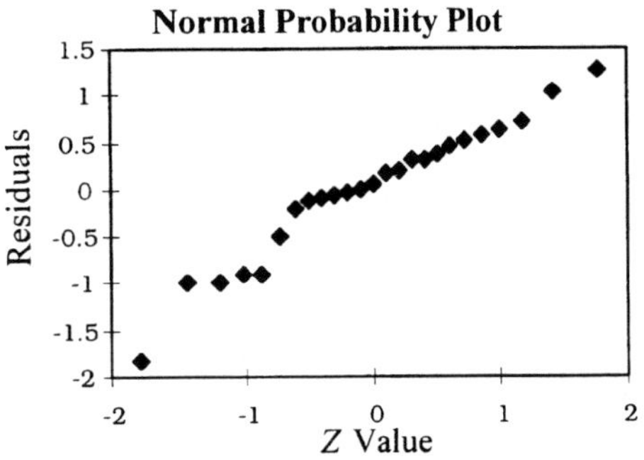

The assumption of normality appears to be valid. The Gaussian simple linear regression is adequate.

21. (a)–(b)

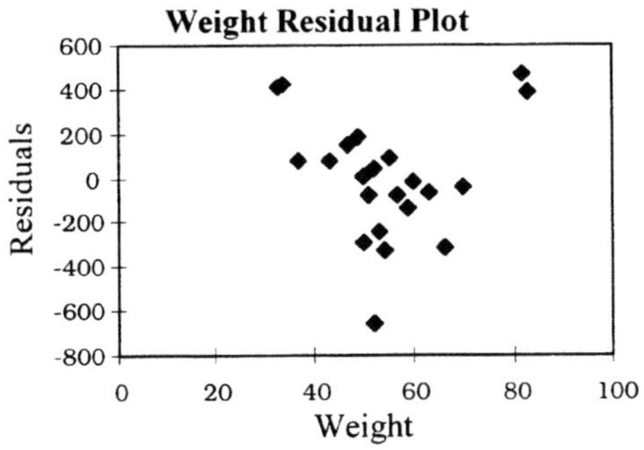

The homoscedasticity and independence assumptions both appear to be valid.

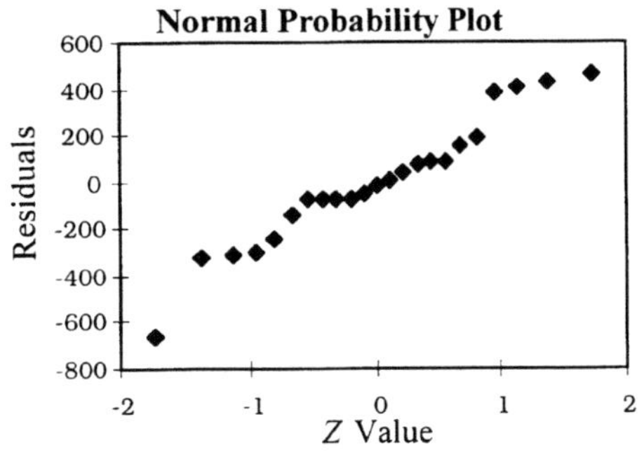

The assumption of normality appears to be valid. The Gaussian simple linear regression is adequate.

22. (a) $H_0: \beta_1 = 0$, $H_1: \beta_1 \neq 0$

Test statistic: $t = 5.753$, p-value is 6.68×10^{-5}. Decision: Because the p-value is less than 0.05, reject the null hypothesis. There is a significant linear relationship between X and Y.

(b) $b_1 \pm t_{n-2} S_{b_1} = 20.0 \pm t_{13} 5.07 = 20.0 \pm 2.1 \cdot 5.07 = 20.0 \pm 10.9$, $P(9.02 \leq \beta_1 \leq 30.9) \approx 0.95$. The confidence interval constructed above does not include zero, so the linear dependence of Y on X is significant.

23. (a) $H_0: \beta_1 = 0$, $H_1: \beta_1 \neq 0$

Test statistic: $t = 41.138$, p-value is 1.8×10^{-18}. Decision: Because the p-value is less than 0.05, reject the null hypothesis. There is a significant linear relationship between X and Y.

(b) $b_1 \pm t_{n-2} S_{b_1} = 1.081 \pm t_{17} 0.026 = 1.081 \pm 2.110 \cdot 0.026 = 1.081 \pm 0.055$, $P(1.026 \leq \beta_1 \leq 1.137) \approx 0.95$. The confidence interval constructed above does not include zero, so the linear dependence of Y on X is significant.

24. (a) $H_0: \beta_1 = 0$, $H_1: \beta_1 \neq 0$

Test statistic: $t = 5.316$, p-value is 7.265×10^{-6}. Decision: Because the p-value is less than 0.05, reject the null hypothesis. There is a significant linear relationship between X and Y.

(b) $b_1 \pm t_{n-2} S_{b_1} = 0.228 \pm t_{33} 0.043 = 0.228 \pm 2.035 \cdot 0.043 = 0.228 \pm 0.087$, $P(0.141 \leq \beta_1 \leq 0.316) \approx 0.95$. The confidence interval constructed above does not include zero, so the linear dependence of Y on X is significant.

25. (a) $H_0: \beta_1 = 0$, $H_1: \beta_1 \neq 0$

Test statistic: $t = 28.824$, p-value is 1.48×10^{-19}. Decision: Because the p-value is less than 0.05, reject the null hypothesis. There is a significant linear relationship between X and Y.

(b) $b_1 \pm t_{n-2} S_{b_1} = 0.030 \pm t_{23} 0.001 = 0.030 \pm 2.069 \cdot 0.001 = 0.030 \pm 0.002$, $P(0.028 \le \beta_1 \le 0.032) \approx 0.95$. The confidence interval constructed above does not include zero, so the linear dependence of Y on X is significant.

26. (a) $H_0: \beta_1 = 0$, $H_1: \beta_1 \neq 0$

Test statistic: $t = 17.710$, p-value is 4.2×10^{-14}. Decision: Because the p-value is less than 0.05, reject the null hypothesis. There is a significant linear relationship between X and Y.

(b) $b_1 \pm t_{n-2} S_{b_1} = 0.0114 \pm t_{21} 0.001 = 0.011 \pm 2.080 \cdot 0.001 = 0.011 \pm 0.001$, $P(0.01 \le \beta_1 \le 0.013) \approx 0.95$. The confidence interval constructed above does not include zero, so the linear dependence of Y on X is significant.

27. (a) $h = \frac{1}{n} + \frac{(X_0 - \overline{X})^2}{\sum_{i=1}^{n}(X_i - \overline{X})^2} = \frac{1}{20} + \frac{(2-2)^2}{20} = 0.05$. 95% confidence interval of the population average response:

$\hat{Y} \pm t_{18} S_{XY} \sqrt{h} = 11 \pm 2.100 \cdot 1 \cdot \sqrt{0.05} = 11 \pm 0.470$, $P(10.53 \le \mu_{XY} \le 11.470) \approx 0.95$

(b) 95% prediction interval of the individual response: $\hat{Y} \pm t_{18} S_{XY} \sqrt{1+h} = 11 \pm 2.101 \cdot 1 \cdot \sqrt{1.05} = 11 \pm 2.153$, $P(8.847 \le Y_i \le 13.153) \approx 0.95$

(c) $h = \frac{1}{n} + \frac{(X_0 - \overline{X})^2}{\sum_{i=1}^{n}(X_i - \overline{X})^2} = \frac{1}{20} + \frac{(4-2)^2}{20} = 0.25$. 95% confidence interval of the population average response:

$\hat{Y} \pm t_{18} S_{XY} \sqrt{h} = 17 \pm 2.101 \cdot 1 \cdot \sqrt{0.25} = 17 \pm 1.050$, $P(15.950 \le \mu_{XY} \le 18.050) \approx 0.95$

(d) 95% prediction interval of the individual response: $\hat{Y} \pm t_{18} S_{XY} \sqrt{1+h} = 17 \pm 2.101 \cdot 1 \cdot \sqrt{1.25} = 17 \pm 2.349$, $P(14.651 \le Y_i \le 19.349) \approx 0.95$

(e) The intervals for parts (c) and (d) are wider than parts (a) and (b) because point X is farther away from the central point, $\overline{X}$.

28. $\hat{Y}(X) = 770.43 + 2.0 \times X$, $S_{XY} = 172$, $\overline{X} = 24.9$, $n = 15$, $\sum_{i=1}^{n} X_i^2 = 10474$,

$$SSX = \sum_{i=1}^{n}(X_i - \overline{X})^2 = \sum_{i=1}^{n} X_i^2 - n\overline{X}^2 = 10474 - 15 \cdot 24.9^2 = 1149,\ h = \frac{1}{n} + \frac{(X_0 - \overline{X})^2}{\sum_{i=1}^{n}(X_i - \overline{X})^2} = \frac{1}{15} + \frac{(20-24.9)^2}{1149} = 0.087$$

(a) 95% confidence interval of the population average response: $\hat{Y} \pm t_{13} S_{XY} \sqrt{h} = 1176 \pm 2.16 \cdot 172 \cdot \sqrt{0.088} = 1176 \pm 119$, $P(1057.44 \le \mu_{XY} \le 1295) \approx 0.95$

(b) 95% prediction interval of the individual response: $\hat{Y} \pm t_{13} S_{XY} \sqrt{1+h} = 1176 \pm 2.16 \cdot 172 \cdot \sqrt{1.09} = 1176 \pm 418$, $P(759 \le Y_i \le 1594) \approx 0.95$

Confidence Interval Estimate	
X Value	20.000
Confidence Level	95%
Sample Size	15.000
Degrees of Freedom	13.000
t Value	2.160
Sample Mean	24.933
Sum of Squared Difference	1148.930
Standard Error of the Estimate	185.289
h Statistic	0.088
Average Predicted Y $(\hat{Y})$	1176.085

For Average Predicted Y $(\hat{Y})$	
Interval Half Width	118.644
Confidence Interval Lower Limit	1057.441
Confidence Interval Upper Limit	1294.729

For Individual Response Y	
Interval Half Width	417.505
Prediction Interval Lower Limit	758.580
Prediction Interval Upper Limit	1593.590

(c) The prediction interval is wider than the confidence interval because variations in the predicted individual values are wider than in the predicted average values.

29.

Confidence Interval Estimate	
X Value	3000.000
Confidence Level	95%
Sample Size	19.000
Degrees of Freedom	17.000
t Value	2.110
Sample Mean	3131.579
Sum of Squared Difference	201521052.630
Standard Error of the Estimate	373.167
h Statistic	0.053
Average Predicted Y $(\hat{Y})$	3154.393

For Average Predicted Y $(\hat{Y})$	
Interval Half Width	180.770
Confidence Interval Lower Limit	2973.623
Confidence Interval Upper Limit	3335.163

For Individual Response Y	
Interval Half Width	807.801
Prediction Interval Lower Limit	2346.592
Prediction Interval Upper Limit	3962.195

(a) 95% confidence interval of the population average response: $\hat{Y} \pm t_{17} S_{XY} \sqrt{h} = 3154 \pm 181$,
$P(2974 \le \mu_{XY} \le 3335) \approx 0.95$

(b) 95% prediction interval of the individual response: $\hat{Y} \pm t_{17} S_{XY} \sqrt{1+h} = 3154 \pm 808$, $P(2347 \le Y_i \le 3962) \approx 0.95$

(c) The prediction interval is wider than the confidence interval, because variations in the predicted individual values are wider than in the predicted average values.

30.

Confidence Interval Estimate	
X Value	70.000
Confidence Level	95%
Sample Size	35.000
Degrees of Freedom	33.000
t Value	2.035
Sample Mean	67.651
Sum of Squared Difference	5030.070
Standard Error of the Estimate	3.048
h Statistic	0.030
Average Predicted Y $(\hat{Y})$	31.047

For Average Predicted Y $(\hat{Y})$	
Interval Half Width	1.068
Confidence Interval Lower Limit	29.979
Confidence Interval Upper Limit	32.116

For Individual Response Y	
Interval Half Width	6.293
Prediction Interval Lower Limit	24.754
Prediction Interval Upper Limit	37.340

(a) 95% confidence interval of the population average response: $\hat{Y} \pm t_{33} S_{XY} \sqrt{h} = 31 \pm 1.07$, $P(30.0 \le \mu_{XY} \le 32.1) \approx 0.95$

(b) 95% prediction interval of the individual response: $\hat{Y} \pm t_{33} S_{XY} \sqrt{1+h} = 31.0 \pm 6.29$, $P(24.8 \le Y_i \le 37.3) \approx 0.95$

(c) The prediction interval is wider than confidence interval, because variations in the predicted individual values are wider than in the predicted average values.

31.

Confidence Interval Estimate	
X Value	500.000
Confidence Level	95%
Sample Size	25.000
Degrees of Freedom	23.000
t Value	2.069
Sample Mean	438.640
Sum of Squared Difference	496055.760
Standard Error of the Estimate	0.726
h Statistic	0.048
Average Predicted Y ($\hat{Y}$)	15.043

For Average Predicted Y ($\hat{Y}$)	
Interval Half Width	0.328
Confidence Interval Lower Limit	14.715
Confidence Interval Upper Limit	15.370

For Individual Response Y	
Interval Half Width	1.537
Prediction Interval Lower Limit	13.506
Prediction Interval Upper Limit	16.579

(a) 95% confidence interval of the population average response: $\hat{Y} \pm t_{23} S_{XY} \sqrt{h} = 15.0 \pm 0.328$, $P(14.7 \le \mu_{XY} \le 15.4) \approx 0.95$

(b) 95% prediction interval of the individual response: $\hat{Y} \pm t_{23} S_{XY} \sqrt{1+h} = 15.0 \pm 1.54$, $P(13.5 \le Y_i \le 16.6) \approx 0.95$

(c) The prediction interval is wider than the confidence interval, because variations in the predicted individual values are wider than in the predicted average values.

32. (a)– $X = 60$ does not fall within the range of X, so it is incorrect to use the regression equation for its prediction.
(c)

33. $r = +\sqrt{r^2} = +\sqrt{0.81} = 0.9$ **34.** $r = -\sqrt{r^2} = -\sqrt{0.49} = -0.7$ **35.** $r^2 = \dfrac{SSR}{SST} = 1$, $r < 0$, $r = -1$

36. $SST = SSR + SSE$, if $SSE = 0$, then $SST = SSR$ and $r^2 = 1$. Because $r > 0$, $r = 1$.

37. (a) $r = 0.543$

(b) $H_0: \rho = 0$, $H_1: \rho \ne 0$

Decision rule: Reject H_0 if $|t| > t_{14} = 2.1448$.

Test statistic: $t = \dfrac{r}{\sqrt{(1-r^2)/(n-2)}} = \dfrac{0.543}{\sqrt{0.705/14}} = 2.42$. Decision: Because $t > 2.14$, reject the null hypothesis.

There is a significant linear relationship between X and Y for the 0.05 significance level.

(c) Part (a) provides $r > 0$,and part (b) provides the significance of r. Therefore, there is a significant positive relationship between rainfall depth and runoff depth for the 0.05 significance level.

38. (a) $r = -0.352$

(b) $H_0: \rho = 0$, $H_1: \rho \ne 0$

Decision rule: Reject H_0 if $|t| > t_{21} = 2.080$. Test statistic: $t = \dfrac{r}{\sqrt{(1-r^2)/(n-2)}} = \dfrac{-0.352}{\sqrt{0.876/21}} = -1.72$. Decision:

Because $|t| < 2.080$, do not reject the null hypothesis. There is no significant linear relationship between X and Y for the 0.05 significance level.

39. (a) $r = 0.992$

(b) $H_0\!:\rho = 0,\ H_1\!:\rho \neq 0$

Decision rule: Reject H_0 if $|t| > t_9 = 2.26$. Test statistic: $t = \dfrac{r}{\sqrt{(1-r^2)/(n-2)}} = \dfrac{0.992}{\sqrt{0.0161/9}} = 23.4$. Decision:

Because $|t| > 2.26$, reject H_0. There is a significant linear relationship between *X* and *Y* for the 0.05 significance level.

(c) Because there is a large significant correlation between the non-destructive and the destructive methods, it is not appropriate to consider the initial samples as independent. The paired test is more appropriate than the *t* test for this application.

40. (a) $r = 0.7212$

(b) $H_0\!:\rho = 0,\ H_1\!:\rho \neq 0$

Decision rule: Reject H_0 if $|t| > t_{38} = 2.024$. Test statistic: $t = \dfrac{r}{\sqrt{(1-r^2)/(n-2)}} = \dfrac{0.721}{\sqrt{0.4780/38}} = 6.42$. Decision:

Because $|t| > 2.02$, reject H_0. There is a significant linear relationship between *X* and *Y* for the 0.05 significance level.

(c) Because there is a large significant correlation between the non-destructive and the destructive methods, it is not appropriate to consider the initial samples as independent. The paired test is more appropriate than the *t* test for this application.

41. (a) $r = 0.738$

(b) $H_0\!:\rho = 0,\ H_1\!:\rho \neq 0$

Decision rule: Reject H_0 if $|t| > t_{13} = 2.160$.

Test statistic: $t = \dfrac{r}{\sqrt{(1-r^2)/(n-2)}} = \dfrac{0.738}{\sqrt{0.456/13}} = 3.940$. Decision: Because $|t| > 2.160$, reject H_0.

There is a significant linear relationship between *X* and *Y* for the 0.05 significance level.

(c) Due to the linear dependence of $b_1 = \rho\sqrt{\dfrac{\text{SSX}}{\text{SSY}}}$, the two tests in problem 22 (a) and problem 41 (b) must give the same results for the same level.

42. (a) $r = 0.995$

(b) $H_0\!:\rho = 0,\ H_1\!:\rho \neq 0$

Decision rule: Reject H_0 if $|t| > t_{17} = 2.11$. Test statistic: $t = \dfrac{r}{\sqrt{(1-r^2)/(n-2)}} = \dfrac{0.995}{\sqrt{0.00998/17}} = 41.066$. Decision:

Because $|t| > 2.11$, reject H_0. There is evidence of a linear relationship between *X* and *Y* for the 0.05 significance level.

(c) Due to the linear dependence of $b_1 = \rho\sqrt{\dfrac{\text{SSX}}{\text{SSY}}}$, the two tests in problem 23 (a) and problem 42 (b) must give the same results for the same level.

43. (a) $r = 0.679$

(b) $H_0: \rho = 0,\ H_1: \rho \neq 0$

Decision rule: Reject H_0 if $|t| > t_{33} = 2.035$. Test statistic: $t = \dfrac{r}{\sqrt{(1-r^2)/(n-2)}} = \dfrac{0.679}{\sqrt{0.539/33}} = 5.32$. Decision:

Because $|t| > 2.03$, reject H_0. There is a significant linear relationship between X and Y for the 0.05 significance level.

(c) Due to the linear dependence $b_1 = \rho\sqrt{\dfrac{\text{SSX}}{\text{SSY}}}$ the two tests in problem 24 (a) and problem 43 (b) must give the same results for the same level .

44. (a) $r = 0.98$

(b) $H_0: \rho = 0,\ H_1: \rho \neq 0$

Decision rule: Reject H_0 if $|t| > t_{23} = 2.069$. Test statistic: $t = \dfrac{r}{\sqrt{(1-r^2)/(n-2)}} = \dfrac{0.986}{\sqrt{0.027/23}} = 28.78$. Decision:

Because $|t| > 2.069$, reject H_0. There is evidence of a linear relationship between X and Y for the 0.05 significance level.

(c) Due to the linear dependence of $b_1 = \rho\sqrt{\dfrac{\text{SSX}}{\text{SSY}}}$, the two tests in problem 25 (a) and problem 44 (b) must give the same results for the same level.

45. (a) $r = 0.9681$

(b) $H_0: \rho = 0,\ H_1: \rho \neq 0$

Decision rule: Reject H_0 if $|t| > t_{21} = 2.0796$. Test statistic: $t = \dfrac{r}{\sqrt{(1-r^2)/(n-2)}} = \dfrac{0.968}{\sqrt{0.063/21}} = 17.7$. Decision:

Because $|t| > 2.080$, reject H_0. There is evidence of a linear relationship between X and Y for the 0.05 significance level.

(c) Due to the linear dependence of $b_1 = \rho\sqrt{\dfrac{\text{SSX}}{\text{SSY}}}$, the two tests 12.26 (a) and 12.45 (b) must give the same results for the same level.

46. The Y intercept represents the average value of Y when $X = 0$. The slope of the line represents the expected change in Y per unit change in X.

47. The coefficient of determination measures the proportion of the variation that is explained by the independent variable in the regression model.

48. For the condition $\text{SSE} = 0$, all points must strictly satisfy the regression model (all residuals must be equal to 0).

49. $\text{SSR} = 0$ for all $\hat{Y}_i = \overline{Y}$, $1 \leq i \leq n$.

50. Residual analysis is helpful for testing the validity of the regression assumptions. It can also provide the regression model for further studies.

51. Assumptions of regression analysis:

(1) Normality of error. It is possible to check the validity of this assumption by constructing the residual normal probability plot.

(2) Homoscedasticity. It is possible to check this assumption visually using the scatterplot.
(3) Independence of error. It is possible to check this assumption visually using the scatterplot and the residual plot.

52. A confidence interval estimates an *average* response Y for a given X. A prediction interval estimates a possible *individual* response Y for a given X. This is why the prediction interval is wider than the confidence interval.

53. (a)

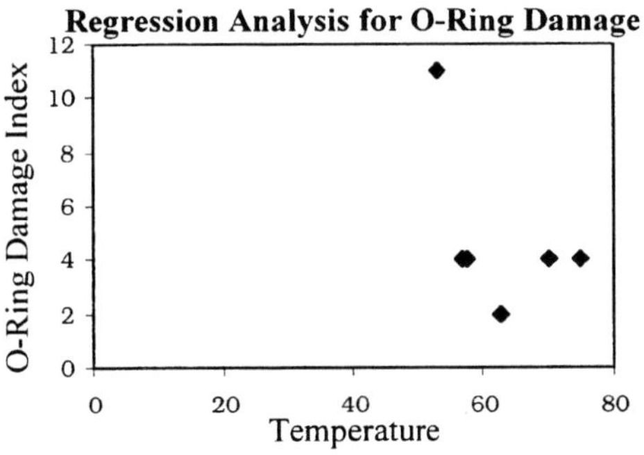

(b)

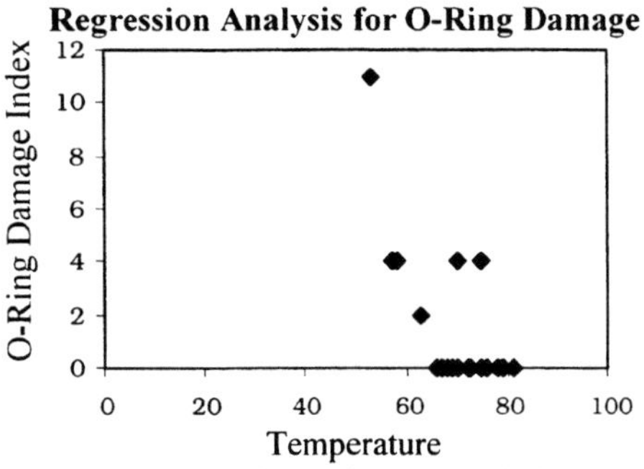

(1) Different samples provide different scatter diagrams. For example, part (a) shows that the study index is positive.
(2) The value $X = 31$ does not belong to the range of independent values.
(3) Regression Analysis

Regression Statistics	
Multiple R	0.641
R^2	0.411
Adjusted R^2	0.381
Standard Error	2.141
Observations	22.000

ANOVA

	df	SS	MS	F	Significance F
Regression	1.000	63.836	63.836	13.928	0.001
Residual	20.000	91.664	4.583		
Total	21.000	155.500			

	Coefficients	Standard Error	t Stat	p-value	Lower 95%	Upper 95%
Intercept	18.618	4.609	4.039	0.001	9.003	28.233
Distance	–0.247	0.066	–3.732	0.001	–0.385	–0.109

(c)

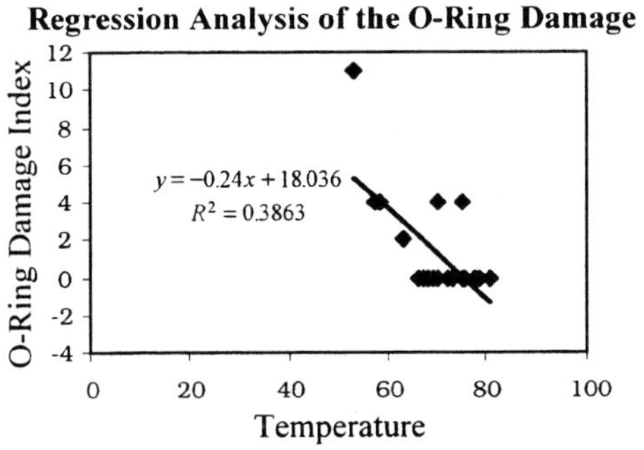

(d) The points are not concentrated around the regression line, so a simple linear model is not appropriate for this data set.

(e)

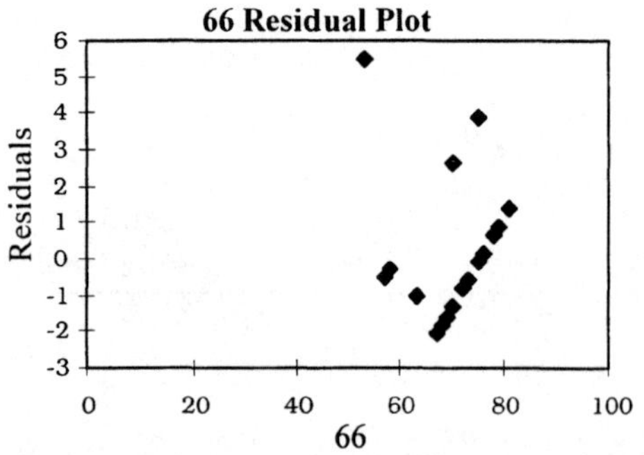

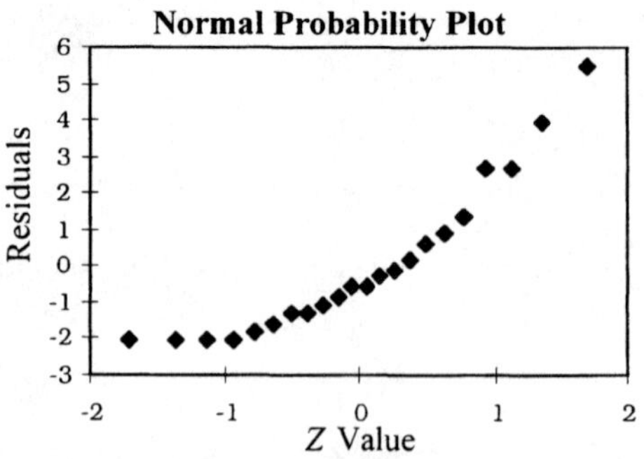

There is evidence of a residual tendency, so a simple linear regression model is not adequate to describe this data set.

54. (a)

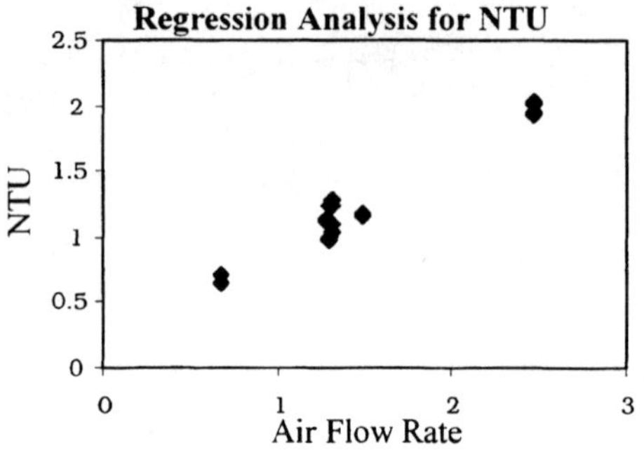

(b) Regression Analysis

Regression Statistics	
Multiple R	0.978
R^2	0.957
Adjusted R^2	0.954
Standard Error	0.091
Observations	18.000

ANOVA

	df	SS	MS	F	Significance F
Regression	1.000	2.937	2.937	356.861	2.302×10^{-12}
Residual	16.000	0.132	0.008		
Total	17.000	3.068			

	Coefficients	Standard Error	t Stat	p-value	Lower 95%	Upper 95%
Intercept	0.186	0.061	3.037	0.008	0.056	0.316
Air flow	0.721	0.038	18.891	2.302×10^{-12}	0.640	0.802

(c) $\hat{Y} = 0.186 + 0.721 \times X$

(d) The intercept, 0.18598, represents the average value of Y for $X = 0$. The slope, 0.72086, represents the expected change in Y per unit change in X.

(e)

Confidence Interval Estimate	
X Value	2.000
Confidence Level	95%
Sample Size	18.000
Degrees of Freedom	16.000
t Value	2.120
Sample Mean	1.504
Sum of Squared Difference	5.650
Standard Error of the Estimate	0.091
h Statistic	0.099
Average Predicted Y $(\hat{Y})$	1.628

For Average Predicted Y $(\hat{Y})$	
Interval Half Width	0.061
Confidence Interval Lower Limit	1.567
Confidence Interval Upper Limit	1.688

For Individual Response Y	
Interval Half Width	0.202
Prediction Interval Lower Limit	1.426
Prediction Interval Upper Limit	1.829

$\hat{Y}(2) = 1.63$, $P(1.43 < \hat{Y}(2) < 1.83) \approx 0.95$

(f) $X = 4.0$ does not fall within to the given range of X, so it is incorrect to use the regression equation for the prediction of X.

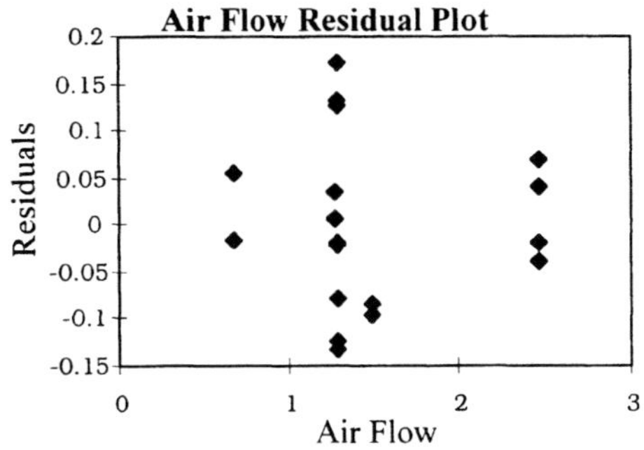

(g) $r^2 = 0.957$, 95.7% of the variation is explained by the independent variable in the regression model.

(h) $r = +\sqrt{r^2} = \sqrt{0.957} = 0.978$

(i) $S_{XY} = \sqrt{\dfrac{\text{SSE}}{n-2}} = 0.0907$

(j)

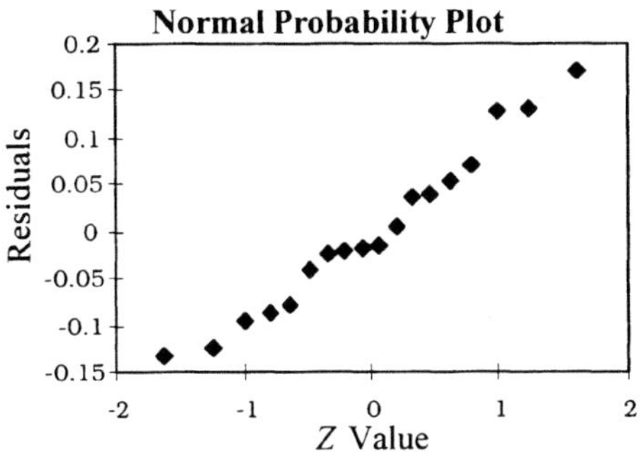

The normality of error and independence appears to be a valid assumption. Homoscedasticity does not appear to be valid. About half of all of the X values occur in the (1.29; 1.30) interval. Their responses are typical.

(k)

	Coefficients	Standard Error	*t* Stat	*p*-value	Lower 95%	Upper 95%
Intercept	0.186	0.061	3.037	0.008	0.056	0.316
Airflow	0.721	0.038	18.891	2.302×10^{-12}	0.640	0.802

The constructed simple linear regression is significant because the p-values are less than 0.05,

(l) See the plot for part (e). 95% confidence interval of the population average response: $\hat{Y} \pm t_{16} S_{XY} \sqrt{h} = 1.63 \pm 0.0605$, $P(1.57 \le \mu_{XY} \le 1.69) \approx 0.95$

(m) See the plot for part (e). 95% prediction interval of the individual response: $\hat{Y} \pm t_{16} S_{XY} \sqrt{1+h} = 1.63 \pm 0.202$, $P(1.426 \le Y_i \le 1.83) \approx 0.95$

(n) See the plot for part (b): $P(0.64 < \beta_1 < 0.80) \approx 0.95$

55. (a)

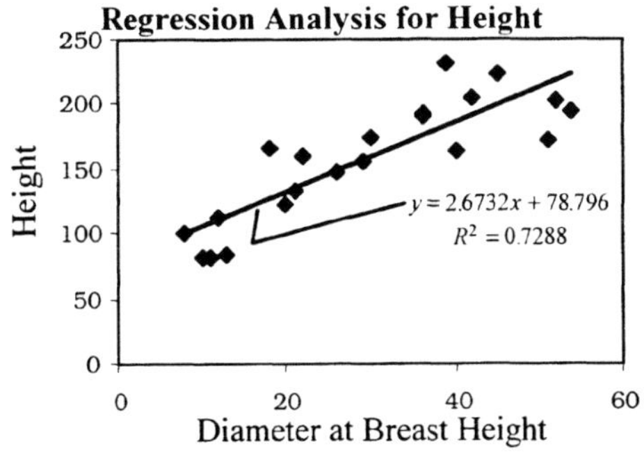

(b) Regression Analysis

Regression Statistics	
Multiple R	0.854
R^2	0.729
Adjusted R^2	0.715
Standard Error	24.749
Observations	21.000

ANOVA

	df	SS	MS	F	Significance F
Regression	1.000	31273.267	31273.267	51.059	8.598×10^{-7}
Residual	19.000	11637.400	612.495		
Total	20.000	42910.667			

	Coefficients	Standard Error	t Stat	p-value	Lower 95%	Upper 95%
Intercept	78.796	12.215	6.451	3.493×10^{-6}	53.230	104.362
Diameter at Breast Height	2.673	0.374	7.146	8.598×10^{-7}	1.890	3.456

(c) $\hat{Y} = 78.796 + 2.673\times X$

(d) The intercept, 78.80, represents the average value of Y for $X = 0$. The slope, 2.673, represents the expected change in Y per unit change in X.

(e) $\hat{Y}(30) = 78.80 + 2.67\times 30 = 158.99$

(f) $X = 4.0$ does not fall within to the range of X, so it is not appropriate to use the regression equation for the prediction of X.

(g) $r^2 = 0.729$, 72.88% of variation is explained by the independent variable in the regression model.

(h) $r = +\sqrt{r^2} = \sqrt{0.729} = 0.854$

(i) $S_{XY} = \sqrt{\dfrac{\text{SSE}}{n-2}} = 24.749$

(j) There is not any evidence of a pattern in the residuals.

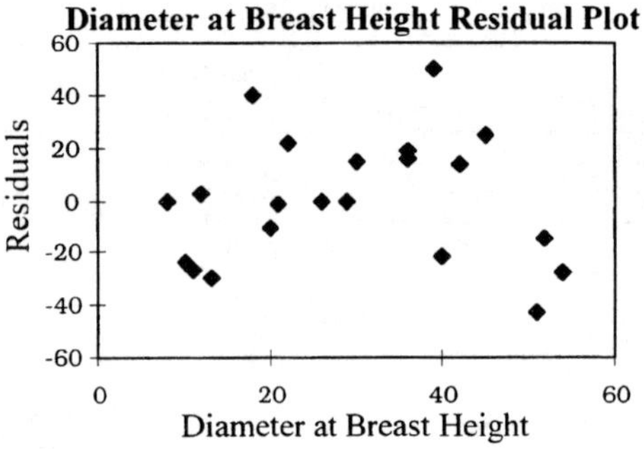

(k)

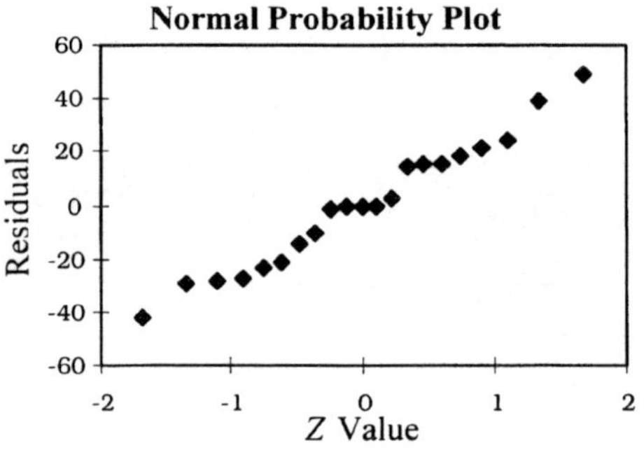

	Coefficients	Standard Error	t Stat	p-value	Lower 95%	Upper 95%
Intercept	78.796	12.215	6.451	3.493×10^{-6}	53.230	104.362
Diameter at Breast Height	2.673	0.374	7.146	8.598×10^{-7}	1.890	3.456

The constructed simple linear regression is significant, because the p-values are less than 0.05.

(l)

Confidence Interval Estimate	
X Value	30.000
Confidence Level	95%
Sample Size	2.000
Degrees of Freedom	1.000
t Value	2.093
Sample Mean	29.286
Sum of Squared Difference	4376.290
Standard Error of the Estimate	24.749
h Statistic	0.0477
Average Predicted Y $(\hat{Y})$	158.993

For Average Predicted Y $(\hat{Y})$	
Interval Half Width	11.317
Confidence Interval Lower Limit	147.675
Confidence Interval Upper Limit	170.310

For Individual Response Y	
Interval Half Width	53.021
Prediction Interval Lower Limit	105.971
Prediction Interval Upper Limit	212.014

95% confidence interval of the population average response: $\hat{Y} \pm t_{16} S_{XY} \sqrt{h} = 158.99 \pm 11.32$,
$P(147.68 \le \mu_{XY} \le 170.31) \approx 0.95$

(m) (See part (l)) 95% prediction interval for the individual response: $\hat{Y} \pm t_{16} S_{XY} \sqrt{h+1} = 158.99 \pm 53.02$,
$P(105.97 \le Y_i \le 212.01) \approx 0.95$

(n) (See part (b)) $P(1.89 < \beta_1 < 3.46) \approx 0.95$

(o) The height of the redwood can be successfully approximated by the linear dependence of height on the diameter at breast height. However, the definition of "diameter at breast height" is vague and would depend on the person making the measurement. A better parameter for the approximation would be "diameter at five feet above the ground".

56. (a)

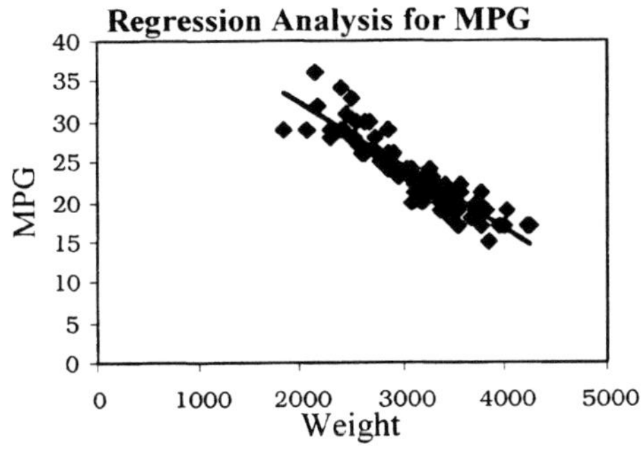

(b) Regression Analysis

Regression Statistics	
Multiple R	0.906
R^2	0.820
Adjusted R^2	0.818
Standard Error	1.935
Observations	89.000

ANOVA

	df	SS	MS	F	Significance F
Regression	1.000	1484.545	1484.545	396.354	3.772×10^{-34}
Residual	87.000	325.859	3.746		
Total	88.000	1810.404			

	Coefficients	Standard Error	t Stat	p-value	Lower 95%	Upper 95%
Intercept	47.885	1.252	38.240	3.477×10^{-56}	45.396	50.374
Diameter at Breast Height	–0.008	0.000	–19.909	3.772×10^{-34}	–0.009	–0.007

(c) $\hat{Y} = 47.89 - 0.0078 \times X$

(d) The intercept, 47.89, represents the average value of Y for $X = 0$. The slope, –0.0079, represents the expected change in Y per unit change in X.

(e) $\hat{Y}(2500) = 47.89 - 0.00785 \times 2500 = 28.25$

(f) $X = 6000$ does not fall within the range of X, so it is appropriate to use regression equation for the prediction of X.

(g) $r^2 = 0.82$, 82% of the variation is explained by the independent variable in the regression model.

(h) $r = -\sqrt{r^2} = -\sqrt{0.82} = -0.906$

(i) $S_{XY} = \sqrt{\frac{\text{SSE}}{n-2}} = 1.94$

(j)

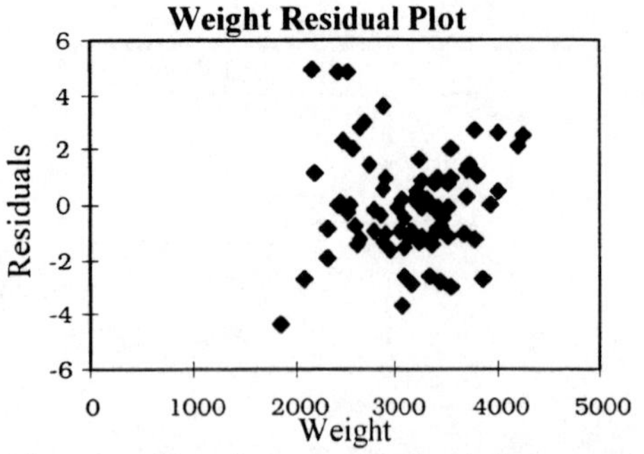

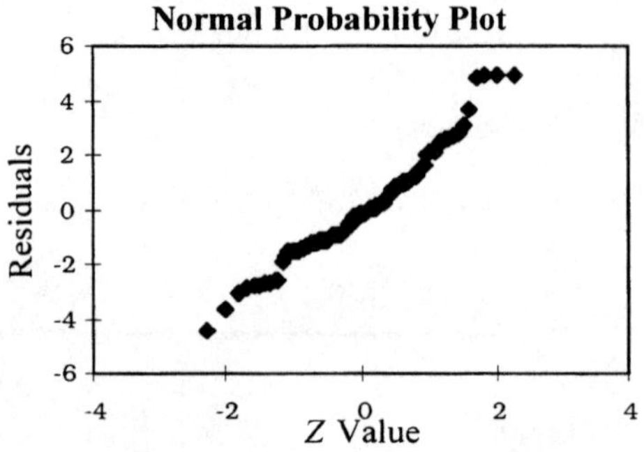

The normality of error and independence assumptions appear to be valid. The homoscedasticity assumption appears to be invalid.

(k)

	Coefficients	Standard Error	*t* Stat	*p*-value	Lower 95%	Upper 95%
Intercept	47.885	1.252	38.240	3.477×10^{-56}	45.396	50.374
Weight	–0.008	0.000	–19.909	3.772×10^{-34}	–0.009	–0.007

The constructed simple linear regression is significant, because the *p*-values are less than 0.05.

(l)

Confidence Interval Estimate	
X Value	2500.000
Confidence Level	95%
Sample Size	89.000
Degrees of Freedom	87.000
t Value	1.988
Sample Mean	3131.393
Sum of Squared Difference	24067827.240
Standard Error of the Estimate	1.935
h Statistic	0.0278
Average Predicted Y ($\hat{Y}$)	28.251

For Average Predicted Y ($\hat{Y}$)	
Interval Half Width	0.641
Confidence Interval Lower Limit	27.610
Confidence Interval Upper Limit	28.892

For Individual Response Y	
Interval Half Width	3.900
Prediction Interval Lower Limit	24.351
Prediction Interval Upper Limit	32.151

95% confidence interval of the population average response: $\hat{Y} \pm t_{87} S_{XY} \sqrt{h} = 28.251 \pm 0.64$,

$P(27.61 \le \mu_{XY} \le 28.89) \approx 0.95$

(n) (See part (l)) 95% prediction interval for the individual response: $\hat{Y} \pm t_{87} S_{XY} \sqrt{h+1} = 28.25 \pm 3.9$,

$P(24.35 \le Y_i \le 32.15) \approx 0.95$

(n) (See part (b)) 95% confidence interval estimate of the population slope: $P(-0.0086638 < \beta_1 < -0.00707) \approx 0.95$

57. (a) **Regression Analysis of the Serum Cholesterol**

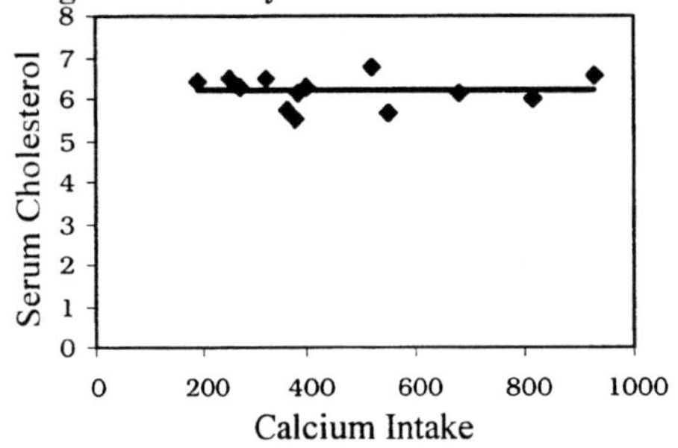

ANOVA

	df	SS	MS	F	Significance F
Regression	1.000	1.547×10^{-6}	1.547×10^{-6}	1.004×10^{-5}	0.998
Residual	11.000	1.695	0.154		
Total	12.000	1.695			

	Coefficients	Standard Error	t Stat	p-value	Lower 95%	Upper 95%
Intercept	6.185	0.260	23.742	8.430×10^{-11}	5.611	6.758
Diameter at Breast Height	-1.61×10^{-6}	0.001	−0.003	0.998	−0.001	0.001

(b) Regression Analysis

Regression Statistics	
Multiple R	0.001
R^2	9.126×10^{-7}
Adjusted R^2	−0.091
Standard Error	0.393
Observations	13.000

(c) $\hat{Y} = 6.1846 - 1.61\times10^{-6}\times X$

(d) The intercept, 6.1846, represents the average value of Y for $X = 0$. The slope, 1.61×10^{6}, represents the expected change in Y per unit change in X.

(e) $\hat{Y}(500) = 6.18 - 1.61\times10^{-6}\times500 = 6.18$

(f) $X = 1500$ does not fall within the range of X, so it is appropriate to use a regression equation for the prediction of X.

(g) $r^2 = 9.13\times10^{-7}$, 0.00009% of the variation is explained by the independent variable in the regression model.

(h) $r = -\sqrt{r^2} = -9.55\times10^{-4}$

(i) $S_{XY} = \sqrt{\dfrac{\text{SSE}}{n-2}} = 0.393$

(j) **Calcium Intake Residual Plot**

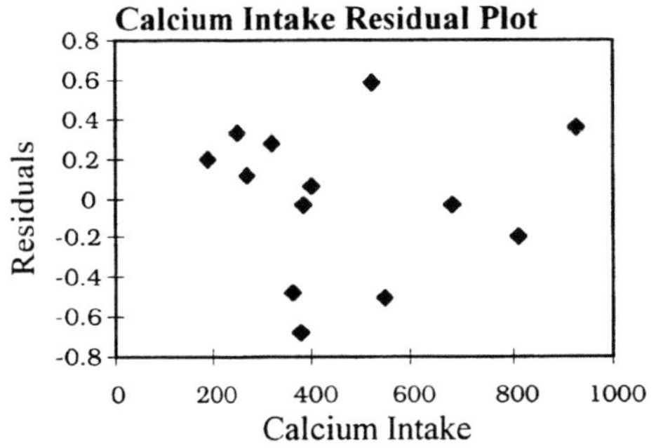

Normal Probability Plot

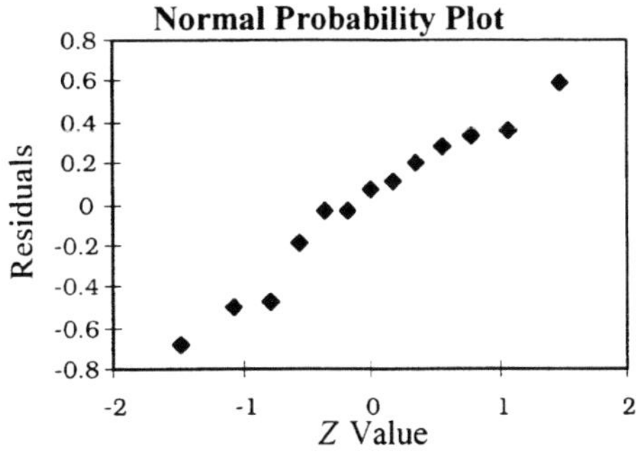

The normality of error and independence assumptions appear to be valid. The homoscedasticity assumption appears to be invalid.

(k)

	Coefficients	Standard Error	t Stat	p-value	Lower 95%	Upper 95%
Intercept	6.185	0.260	23.742	8.430×10^{-11}	5.611	6.758
Calcium Intake	-1.61×10^{-6}	0.001	−0.003	0.998	−0.001	0.001

The constructed simple linear regression is not significant because the slope p-values are greater than 0.05.

(l)

Confidence Interval Estimate	
X Value	500.000
Confidence Level	95%
Sample Size	13.000
Degrees of Freedom	11.000
t Value	2.201
Sample Mean	465.615
Sum of Squared Difference	596617.080
Standard Error of the Estimate	0.393
h Statistic	0.079
Average Predicted Y $(\hat{Y})$	6.184

For Average Predicted Y $(\hat{Y})$	
Interval Half Width	0.243
Confidence Interval Lower Limit	5.941
Confidence Interval Upper Limit	6.427

For Individual Response Y	
Interval Half Width	0.898
Prediction Interval Lower Limit	5.286
Prediction Interval Upper Limit	7.081

95% confidence interval of the population average response: $\hat{Y} \pm t_{11} S_{XY} \sqrt{h} = 6.1838 \pm 0.243$,
$P(5.94 \le \mu_{XY} \le 6.43) \approx 0.95$

(m) (See part (l)) 95% prediction interval of serum cholesterol: $P(5.286 \le Y_i \le 7.081) \approx 0.95$

(n) (See part (b)) 95% confidence interval estimate of the population slope: $P(-0.00112 < \beta_1 < 0.00112) \approx 0.95$. The simple linear regression model is not significant because the interval includes zero.

58.

Food	X (Fat)	Y (Cholesterol)	$(X-\bar{X})^2$	$(Y-\bar{Y})^2$	$(X-\bar{X})(Y-\bar{Y})$
Beef, ground extra lean	58	82	16	6.25	10
Beef, ground regular	66	87	16	6.25	10
	$\bar{X}$	$\bar{Y}$	SSX	SSY	SSXY
	62	84.5	32	12.5	20
		$r =$	1		

Food	X (Fat)	Y (Cholesterol)	$(X-\bar{X})^2$	$(Y-\bar{Y})^2$	$(X-\bar{X})(Y-\bar{Y})$
Beef, round	24	82	225	20.25	67.5
Beef, brisket	54	91	225	20.25	67.5
	$\bar{X}$	$\bar{Y}$	SSX	SSY	SSXY
	39	86.5	450	40.5	135
		$r =$	1		

Food	X (Fat)	Y (Cholesterol)	$(X-\bar{X})^2$	$(Y-\bar{Y})^2$	$(X-\bar{X})(Y-\bar{Y})$
Flank steak	51	71	42.25	81	–58.5
Lamb leg roast	38	89	42.25	81	–58.5
	$\bar{X}$	$\bar{Y}$	SSX	SSY	SSXY
	44.5	80	84.5	162	–117
		$r =$	–1		

Food	X (Fat)	Y (Cholesterol)	$(X-\bar{X})^2$	$(Y-\bar{Y})^2$	$(X-\bar{X})(Y-\bar{Y})$
Lamb loin chop broiled	42	94	9	37636	–582
Liver, fried	36	482	9	37636	–582
	$\bar{X}$	$\bar{Y}$	SSX	SSY	SSXY
	39	288	18	75272	–1164
		$r =$	–1		

Food	X (Fat)	Y (Cholesterol)	$(X-\overline{X})^2$	$(Y-\overline{Y})^2$	$(X-\overline{X})(Y-\overline{Y})$
Spare ribs	67	121	158.25	9	–37.5
Veal cutlet, fried	42	127	156.25	9	–37.5
	$\overline{X}$	$\overline{Y}$	**SSX**	**SSY**	**SSXY**
	54.5	124	312.5	18	–75
		$r =$	–1		

Food	X (Fat)	Y (Cholesterol)	$(X-\overline{X})^2$	$(Y-\overline{Y})^2$	$(X-\overline{X})(Y-\overline{Y})$
Veal rib roast	26	131	0.25	462.25	–10.75
Chicken, with skin, roasted	27	88	0.25	462.25	–10.75
	$\overline{X}$	$\overline{Y}$	**SSX**	**SSY**	**SSXY**
	26.5	109.5	0.5	924.5	–21.5
		$r =$	–1		

Food	X (Fat)	Y (Cholesterol)	$(X-\overline{X})^2$	$(Y-\overline{Y})^2$	$(X-\overline{X})(Y-\overline{Y})$
Chicken, no skin, roast	37	89	90.25	100	95
Turkey, light meat, no skin	18	69	90.25	100	95
	$\overline{X}$	$\overline{Y}$	**SSX**	**SSY**	**SSXY**
	27.5	79	180.5	200	190
		$r =$	1		

Food	X (Fat)	Y (Cholesterol)	$(X-\overline{X})^2$	$(Y-\overline{Y})^2$	$(X-\overline{X})(Y-\overline{Y})$
Clams	6	39	1	306.25	17.5
Cod	8	74	1	306.25	17.5
	$\overline{X}$	$\overline{Y}$	**SSX**	**SSY**	**SSXY**
	7	56.5	2	512.5	35
		$r =$	1		

Food	X (Fat)	Y (Cholesterol)	$(X-\overline{X})^2$	$(Y-\overline{Y})^2$	$(X-\overline{X})(Y-\overline{Y})$
Flounder	12	54	1056.25	529	747.5
Mackeral	77	100	1056.25	529	747.5
	$\overline{X}$	$\overline{Y}$	**SSX**	**SSY**	**SSXY**
	44.5	77	2112.5	1058	1495
		$r =$	1		

Food	X (Fat)	Y (Cholesterol)	$(X-\overline{X})^2$	$(Y-\overline{Y})^2$	$(X-\overline{X})(Y-\overline{Y})$
Ocean perch	13	53	30.25	400	110
Salmon	24	93	30.25	400	110
	$\overline{X}$	$\overline{Y}$	**SSX**	**SSY**	**SSXY**
	18.5	73	60.5	800	220
		$r =$	1		

Food	X (Fat)	Y (Cholesterol)	$(X-\bar{X})^2$	$(Y-\bar{Y})^2$	$(X-\bar{X})(Y-\bar{Y})$
Scallops	23	56	0.25	2500	25
Shrimp	24	156	0.25	2500	25
	$\bar{X}$	$\bar{Y}$	SSX	SSY	SSXY
	23.5	106	0.5	5000	50
		$r =$	1		

59. (a)

Correlations	
pH	–0.271
Conductivity	0.204
TAMP	–0.173
TOC	0.185

(b) $H_0: \rho = 0$, $H_1: \rho \neq 0$

Decision rule: Reject H_0 if $|t| > t_{10} = 2.2281$. Test statistic: $t = \dfrac{r}{\sqrt{(1-r^2)/(n-2)}}$.

Correlation	Test statistic	Decision
PH	–0.891	Do not reject H_0
Conductivity	0.661	Do not reject H_0
TAMP	–0.556	Do not reject H_0
TOC	0.595	Do not reject H_0

There are no significant correlations for 0.05 significance level.

60. (a)

Correlation	
HC–CO	0.901
HC–NO	–0.559
CO–NO	–0.686

(b) $H_0: \rho = 0$, $H_1: \rho \neq 0$

Decision rule: Reject H_0 if $|t| > t_{44} = 2.02$. Test statistic: $t = \dfrac{r}{\sqrt{(1-r^2)/(n-2)}}$.

Correlation	Test statistic	Decision
HC–CO	13.741	Reject H_0
HC–NO	–4.470	Reject H_0
CO–NO	–6.256	Reject H_0

All of the correlations are significant for the 0.05 significance level.

chapter 13

Multiple Regression

1. (a) When the effect of X_2 is held constant, the response variable Y is expected to increase on average by 5 units for each additional unit of X_1. When the effect of X_1 is held constant, the response variable Y is expected to increase on average by 3 units for each additional unit of X_2.
   (b) The Y-intercept, 10, represents the portion of the measurement of Y that is not affected by the factors measured by X_1 and X_2.
   (c) The computed coefficient of multiple determination means that 60% of the variation can be explained by the variations in the X_1 and X_2.

2. (a) $\hat{Y}_i = -0.027 + 0.791 \times X_{1i} + 0.605 \times X_{2i}$
   (b) Slope 0.791 represents the expected change in Y per unit change in X_1. Slope 0.605 represents the expected change in Y per unit change in X_2.
   (c) $R^2_{Y.12} = \dfrac{\text{SSR}}{\text{SST}} = \dfrac{12.612}{13.385} = 0.942$, 94.2% of the variation can be explained by the variations in X_1 and X_2.
   (d) $R^2_{adj} = 1 - \left[(1 - r^2_{Y,12})\dfrac{n-1}{n-p-1}\right] = 1 - \left[(1 - 0.942)\dfrac{14}{12}\right] = 1 - 0.067 = 0.933$

3. Regression Analysis

Regression Statistics	
Multiple R	0.906
R^2	0.821
Adjusted R^2	0.816
Standard Error	1.944
Observations	89.000

ANOVA

	df	SS	MS	F	Significance F
Regression	2.000	1485.519	742.760	196.615	8.318×10^{-33}
Residual	86.000	324.885	3.778		
Total	88.000	1810.405			

	Coefficients	Standard Error	t Stat	p-value	Lower 95%	Upper 95%
Intercept	50.018	4.384	11.408	6.757×10^{-19}	41.302	58.734
Weight	−0.007	0.001	−7.895	8.611×10^{-12}	−0.009	−0.006
Length	−0.019	0.037	−0.508	0.613	−0.092	0.055

   (a) $\hat{Y}_i = 50.01886 - 0.00741 \times X_{1i} - 0.018776 \times X_{2i}$, Gas mileage $= 50.01886 - 0.007421 \times$ Weight $- 0.018776 \times$ Length
   (b) Slope −0.007421 represents the expected change in gas mileage per unit change in weight. Slope −0.018776 represents the expected change in gas mileage per unit change in length.

(c) $\widehat{Y}_i = 50.019 - 0.00742 \times 3000 - 0.0188 \times 195 = 24.095$

(d) $R^2_{Y.12} = 0.821$, 82.1% of the variation can be explained by the variations in the X_1 and X_2.

4. Regression Analysis

Regression Statistics	
Multiple R	0.854
R^2	0.729
Adjusted R^2	0.699
Standard Error	8.113
Observations	21.000

ANOVA

	df	SS	MS	F	Significance F
Regression	2.000	3191.622	1595.811	24.247	7.805×10^{-6}
Residual	18.000	1184.664	65.815		
Total	20.000	4376.286			

	Coefficients	Standard Error	t Stat	p-value	Lower 95%	Upper 95%
Intercept	−13.518	6.403	−2.111	0.049	−26.970	−0.067
Height	0.265	0.057	4.645	0.000	0.145	0.385
Bark Thickness	0.526	2.885	0.182	0.857	−5.535	6.587

(a) $\widehat{Y}_i = -13.518 + 0.265 \times X_{1i} + 0.526 \times X_{2i}$,
Redwood height $= -13.518 + 0.265 \times$ Diameter at breast height $+ 0.526 \times$ Bark thickness

(b) Slope 0.265 represents the expected change in redwood height per unit diameter at breast height. Slope 0.526 represents the expected change in redwood height per unit change in bark thickness.

(c) $R^2_{Y.12} = 0.729$, 72.9% of the variation can be explained by the variations in the diameter at breast height and bark thickness.

(d) $R^2_{Y.12} = 0.729$, 72.9% of the variation can be explained by the variations in X_1 and X_2.

5. Regression Analysis

Regression Statistics	
Multiple R	0.791
R^2	0.625
Adjusted R^2	0.518
Standard Error	0.032
Observations	10.000

ANOVA

	df	SS	MS	F	Significance F
Regression	2.000	0.012	0.006	5.844	0.032
Residual	7.000	0.007	0.001		
Total	9.000	0.020			

	Coefficients	Standard Error	*t* Stat	*p*-value	Lower 95%	Upper 95%
Intercept	1.590	0.362	4.395	0.003	0.735	2.446
Lamp Output	–0.024	0.010	–2.320	0.053	–0.048	0.001
Lamp Temperature	–0.002	0.003	–0.640	0.542	–0.011	0.006

(a) $\hat{Y}_i = 1.5900851 - 0.02368 \times X_{1i} - 0.002239 \times X_{2i}$,
$BEF = 1.5900851 - 0.02368 \times \text{Lamp Output} - 0.002239 \times \text{Lamp Temperature}$

(b) Holding constant the lamp temperature, for each increase of light output by one foot candle, the average *BEF* is predicted to decrease by 0.0237 foot candle. Holding constant the light output, for each increase in lamp temperature of one degree Celsius, the average *BEF* is predicted to decrease by 0.002 footcandle.

(c) $\hat{Y}_i = 1.5900851 - 0.0237 \times 40 - 0.00224 \times 40 = 0.5533251$

(d) $R^2_{Y.12} = 0.625$, 62.5% of the variation can be explained by the variations in X_1 and X_2.

6. Regression Analysis

Regression Statistics	
Multiple R	0.417
R^2	0.174
Adjusted R^2	0.129
Standard Error	0.526
Observations	40.000

ANOVA

	df	SS	MS	*F*	Significance *F*
Regression	2.000	2.156	1.078	3.899	0.029
Residual	37.000	10.228	0.276		
Total	39.000	12.384			

	Coefficients	Standard Error	*t* Stat	*p*-value	Lower 95%	Upper 95%
Intercept	–0.286	3.594	–0.079	0.937	–7.567	6.996
Soil Radiation	0.000	0.000	2.791	0.008	9.801×10^{-5}	0.001
Soil Temperature	0.013	0.052	0.250	0.804	–0.093	0.119

(a) $\hat{Y}_i = -0.285536 + 0.000 \times X_{1i} + 0.0003576 \times X_{2i}$,
$\text{Radon concentration} = -0.285536 + 0.0003576 \times \text{Solar radiation} + 0.0130288 \times \text{Soil temperature}$

(b) Holding constant the soil temperature, for each increase of solar radiation, the average radon concentration is predicted to increase by 0.000358. Holding constant the solar radiation, for each increase in soil temperature, the average radon concentration is predicted to increase by 0.0130.

(c) $\hat{Y}_i = -0.286 + 0.001 \times 100 + 0.013 \times 71 = 0.675$

(d) $R^2_{Y.12} = 0.1741$, Only 17.4% of the variation can be explained by the variations in X_1 and X_2.

7.

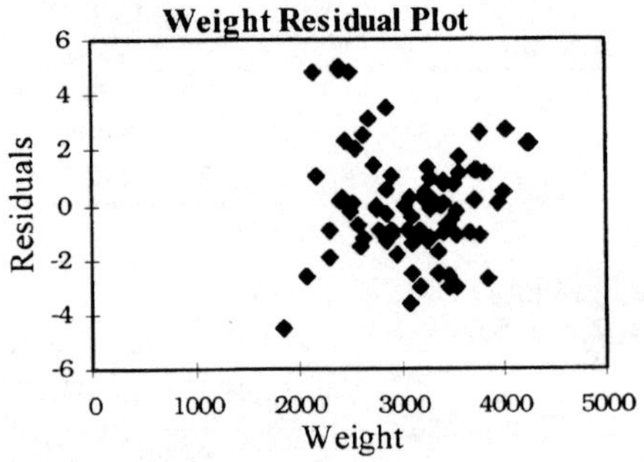

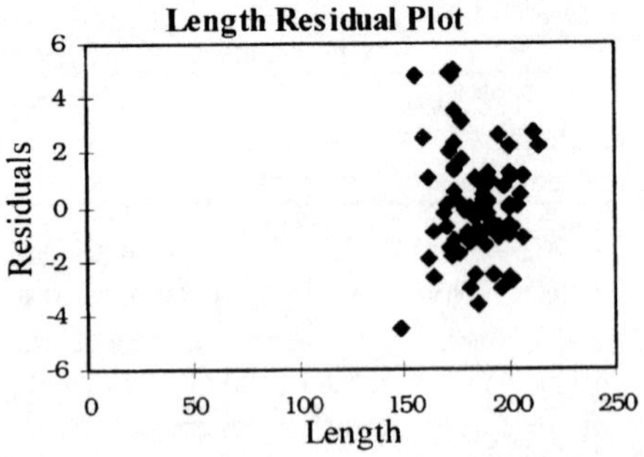

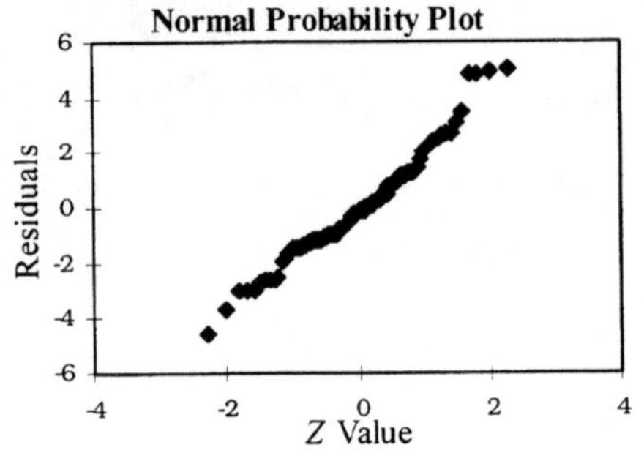

The multiple linear regression model appears to be adequate.

8.

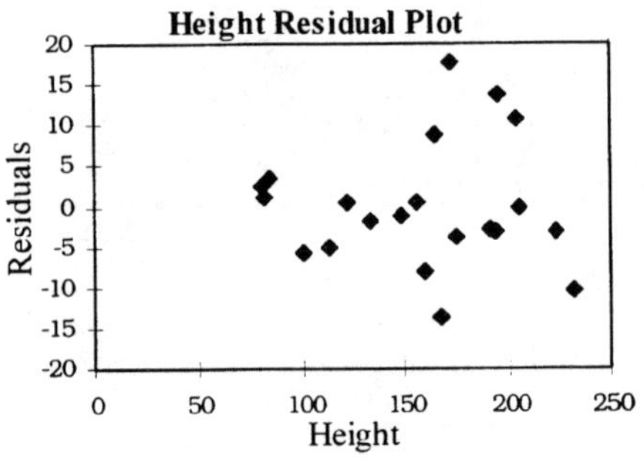

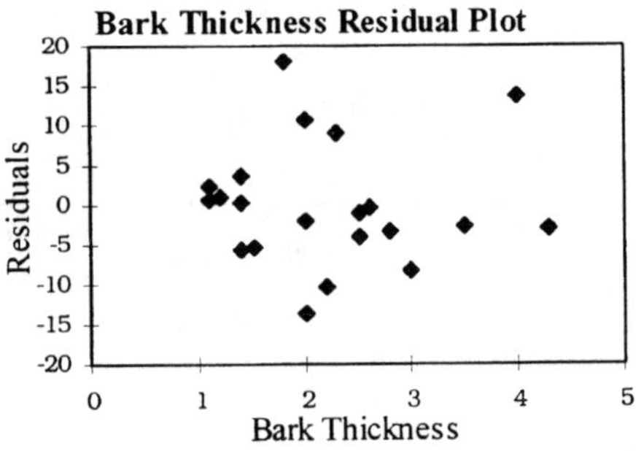

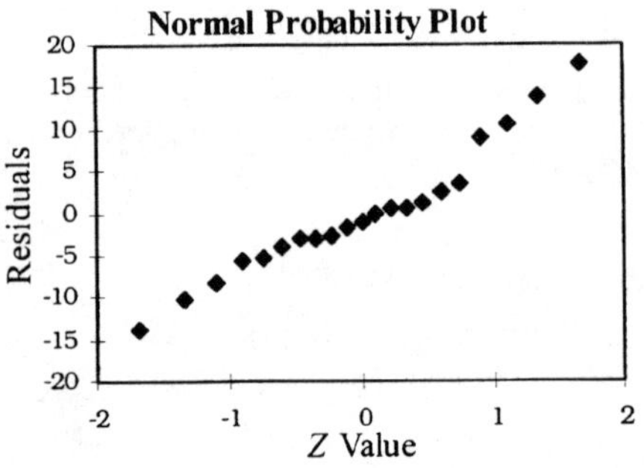

The multiple linear regression model appears to be adequate.

9.

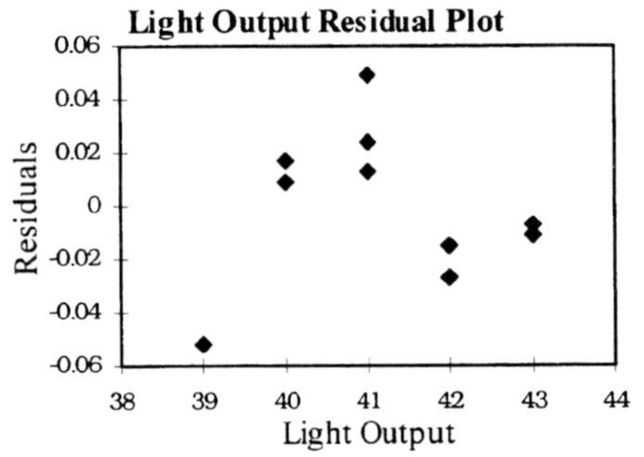

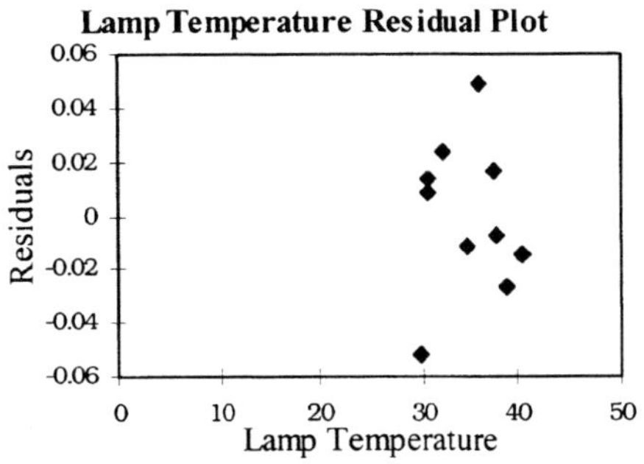

The linear dependence of Y on X_1 is not adequate.

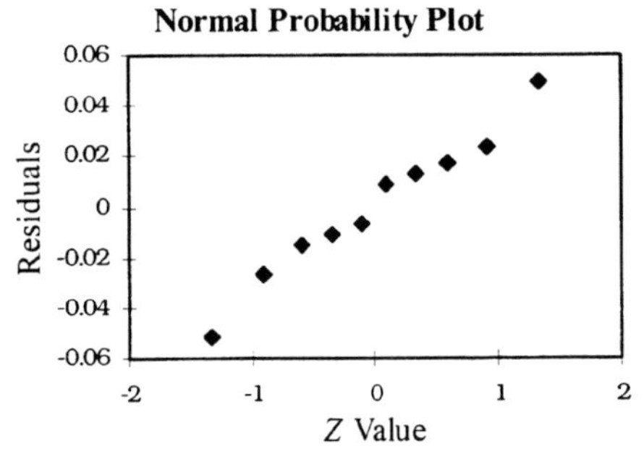

There are some doubts about the validity of the multiple linear regression model.

10.

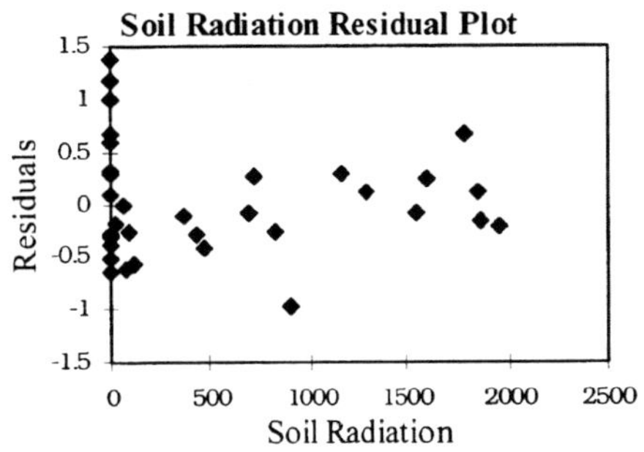

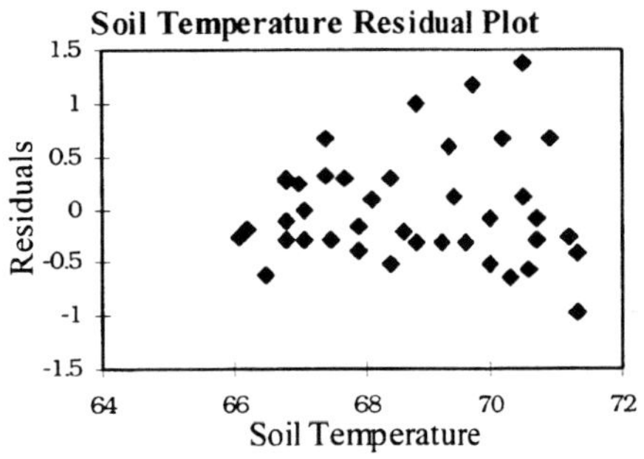

There are some doubts about the validity of the multiple linear regression model.

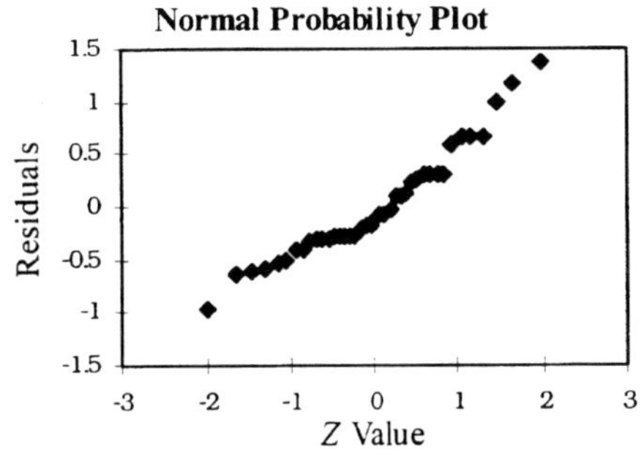

11. (a) $\text{MSR} = \dfrac{\text{SSR}}{p} = \dfrac{60}{2} = 30$, $\text{MSR} = \dfrac{\text{SSR}}{n-p-1} = \dfrac{120}{18} = 6.67$

(b) $F = \frac{\text{MSR}}{\text{MSE}} = \frac{30}{6.(6)} = 4.5$

(c) $H_0{:}\beta_1 = \beta_2 = 0$, $H_1{:}\beta_1^2 + \beta_2^2 > 0$

Decision rule: Reject H_0 if $F > 3.555$. Test statistic: $F = 4.5$. Decision: Because $F > 3.555$, reject H_0. There is a significant linear relationship between Y and X_1, X_2 for the 0.05 significance level.

12. (a) $H_0{:}\beta_1 = \beta_2 = 0$, $H_1{:}\beta_1^2 + \beta_2^2 > 0$

Decision rule: Reject H_0 if $F > 3.89$. Test statistic: $F = 97.69$. Decision: Because $F > 3.89$, reject H_0. There is a significant linear relationship between long-term impact and the two explanatory variables for the 0.05 significance level.

(b) The *p*-value of 0.0001 is the probability of obtaining an *F* statistic of 97.69 or larger when H_0 is true.

(c) The multiple regression model is significant, so there is a significant dependence between Y, X_1, and X_2. For a more precise investigation, it is necessary to construct interval estimators for β_1 and β_2.

13. (a) $H_0{:}\beta_1 = \beta_2 = 0$, $H_1{:}\beta_1^2 + \beta_2^2 > 0$

Decision rule: Reject H_0 if $F > 3.103$. Test statistic: $F = 196.6$. Decision: Because $F > 3.103$, reject H_0. There is a significant linear relationship between MPG and the two explanatory variables for the 0.05 significance level.

(b) The *p*-value of 8.31×10^{-33} is the probability of obtaining an *F* statistic of 196.6 or larger when H_0 is true.

(c) The multiple regression model is significant, so there is a significant dependence between Y, X_1, and X_2. For a more precise investigation, it is necessary to construct interval estimators for β_1 and β_2.

14. (a) $H_0{:}\beta_1 = \beta_2 = 0$, $H_1{:}\beta_1^2 + \beta_2^2 > 0$

Decision rule: Reject H_0 if $F > 3.55$. Test statistic: $F = 24.247$. Decision: Because $F > 3.55$, reject H_0. There is a significant linear relationship between the height of the redwood trees and the two explanatory variables for the 0.05 significance level.

(b) The *p*-value of 7.8×10^{-6} is the probability of obtaining an *F* statistic of 24.247 or larger when H_0 is true.

(c) The multiple regression model is significant, so there is a significant dependence between Y and X_1, X_2. For a more precise investigation, it is necessary to construct interval estimators for β_1 and β_2.

15. (a) $H_0{:}\beta_1 = \beta_2 = 0$, $H_1{:}\beta_1^2 + \beta_2^2 > 0$

Decision rule: Reject H_0 if $F > 4.737$. Test statistic: $F = 5.844$. Decision: Because $F > 4.737$, reject H_0. There is a significant linear relationship between the height of the redwood trees and the two explanatory variables for the 0.05 significance level.

(b) The *p*-value of 0.032 is the probability of obtaining an *F* statistic of 5.844 or larger when H_0 is true.

(c) The multiple regression model is significant, so there is a significant dependence between Y, X_1, and X_2. For a more precise investigation, it is necessary to construct interval estimators for β_1 and β_2.

16. (a) $H_0{:}\beta_1 = \beta_2 = 0$, $H_1{:}\beta_1^2 + \beta_2^2 > 0$

Decision rule: Reject H_0 if $F > 3.252$. Test statistic: $F = 3.899$. Decision: Because $F > 3.252$, reject H_0. There is a significant linear relationship between the height of the redwood trees and the two explanatory variables for the 0.05 significance level.

(b) The *p*-value of 0.029 is the probability of obtaining an *F* statistic of 3.899 or larger when H_0 is true.

(c) The multiple regression model is significant, so there is a significant dependence between Y, X_1, and X_2. For a more precise investigation, it is necessary to construct interval estimators for β_1 and β_2.

17. (a) $b_1 \pm t_{n-p-1}S_{b_1} = 0.791 \pm 2.179 \times 0.063 = 0.791 \pm 0.137$, $P(0.654 \le \beta_1 \le 0.928) \approx 0.95$. The confidence interval does not contain a zero, so there is a significant linear dependence of Y on X_1 for the $1-0.95=0.05$ significance level.

(b) $H_0'\text{:}\ \beta_1 = 0$, $H_1'\text{:}\ \beta_1 \neq 0$

Decision rule: Reject H_0' if $|t| > 2.179$. Test statistic: $t = \dfrac{b_1}{S_{b_1}} = \dfrac{0.79116}{0.063295} = 12.568$. Decision: Because $t > 2.1788$, reject H_0'. There is a significant linear dependence of Y on X_1 in the model already containing X_2 for the 0.05 significance level.

$H_0''\text{:}\ \beta_2 = 0$, $H_1''\text{:}\ \beta_2 \neq 0$

Decision rule: Reject H_0'' if $|t| > 2.179$. Test statistic: $t = \dfrac{b_2}{S_{b_2}} = \dfrac{0.60484}{0.07174} = 8.431$. Decision: Because $t > 2.1788$, reject H_0''. There is a significant linear dependence of Y on X_2 in the model already containing X_1 for the 0.05 significance level.

18. (a) $b_1 \pm t_{n-p-1}S_{b_1} = -0.00742 \pm 1.9879 \times 0.00094 = -0.00742 \pm 0.00187$, $P(-0.009 \le \beta_1 \le -0.006) \approx 0.95$. The confidence interval does not contain zero, so there is a significant linear dependence of Y on X_1 for the $1-0.95=0.05$ significance level.

$b_2 \pm t_{n-p-1}S_{b_2} = -0.019 \pm 1.988 \times 0.037 = -0.019 \pm 0.074$, $P(-0.092 \le \beta_1 \le 0.055) \approx 0.95$. The confidence interval contains zero, so there is no significant linear dependence of Y on X_2 for the $1-0.95=0.05$ significance level.

(b) $H_0'\text{:}\ \beta_1 = 0$, $H_1'\text{:}\ \beta_1 \neq 0$

Decision rule: Reject H_0' if $|t| > 1.988$. Test statistic: $t = \dfrac{b_1}{S_{b_1}} = -7.895$. Decision: Because $|t| > 1.988$, reject H_0'. There is a significant linear dependence of Y on X_1 in the model already containing X_2 for the 0.05 significance level.

$H_0''\text{:}\ \beta_2 = 0$, $H_1''\text{:}\ \beta_2 \neq 0$

Decision rule: Reject H_0'' if $|t| > 1.988$. Test statistic: $t = \dfrac{b_2}{S_{b_2}} = -0.508$. Decision: Because $|t| < 1.988$, do not reject H_0''. There is no significant linear dependence of Y on X_2 in the model already containing X_1 for the 0.05 significance level. There is a significant linear dependence of Y only on the variable X_1 for the 0.05 significance level.

19. (a) $b_1 \pm t_{n-p-1}S_{b_1} = 0.265063 \pm 2.1009 \times 0.0570665 = 0.265063 \pm 0.119891$, $P(0.14517 \le \beta_1 \le 0.385) \approx 0.95$. The confidence interval does not contain zero, so there is a significant linear dependence of Y on X_1 for the $1-0.95=0.05$ significance level.

$b_2 \pm t_{n-p-1}S_{b_2} = 0.525899 \pm 2.1009 \times 2.8847485 = 0.525899 \pm 6.060568$, $P(-5.5347 \le \beta_2 \le 6.5865) \approx 0.95$. The confidence interval contains zero, so there is no significant linear dependence of Y on X_2 for the $1-0.95=0.05$ significance level.

(b) $H_0': \beta_1 = 0$, $H_1': \beta_1 \neq 0$

Decision rule: Reject H_0' if $|t| > 2.101$. Test statistic: $t = \dfrac{b_1}{S_{b_1}} = 4.645$. Decision: Because $|t| > 2.101$, reject H_0'.

There is a significant linear dependence of Y on X_1 in the model already containing X_2 for the 0.05 significance level.

$H_0'': \beta_2 = 0$, $H_1'': \beta_2 \neq 0$

Decision rule: Reject H_0'' if $|t| > 2.101$. Test statistic: $t = \dfrac{b_2}{S_{b_2}} = 0.182$. Decision: Because $|t| < 2.101$, do not reject H_0''. There is no significant linear dependence of Y on X_2 in the model already containing X_1 for the 0.05 significance level. There is a significant linear dependence of Y only on the variable X_1 for the 0.05 significance level.

20. (a) $b_1 \pm t_{n-p-1} S_{b_1} = -0.0237 \pm 2.3646 \times 0.0102 = -0.02368 \pm 0.02449$, $P(-0.0449 \leq \beta_1 \leq 0.000452) \approx 0.95$. The confidence interval contains zero, so there is no significant linear dependence of Y on X_1 for the $1 - 0.95 = 0.05$ significance level.

$b_2 \pm t_{n-p-1} S_{b_2} = -0.002226 \pm 2.3646 \times 0.003496 = -0.00224 \pm 0.00807$, $P(-0.01105 \leq \beta_2 \leq 0.006) \approx 0.95$. The confidence interval contains zero, so there is no significant linear dependence of Y on X_2 for the $1 - 0.95 = 0.05$ significance level.

(b) $H_0': \beta_1 = 0$, $H_1': \beta_1 \neq 0$

Decision rule: Reject H_0' if $|t| > 2.365$. Test statistic: $t = \dfrac{b_1}{S_{b_1}} = -2.32$. Decision: Because $|t| < 2.365$, do not reject H_0'. There is no significant linear dependence of Y on X_1 in the model already containing X_2 for the 0.05 significance level.

$H_0'': \beta_2 = 0$, $H_1'': \beta_2 \neq 0$

Decision rule: Reject H_0'' if $|t| > 2.365$. Test statistic: $t = \dfrac{b_2}{S_{b_2}} = -0.64$. Decision: Because $|t| > 2.365$, do not reject H_0''. There is no significant linear dependence of Y on X_2 in the model already containing X_1 for the 0.05 significance level. There is no significant linear dependence of Y on the variables X_1 and X_2 for the 0.05 significance level.

21. (a) $b_1 \pm t_{n-p-1} S_{b_1} = 0.000358 \pm 2.0262 \times 0.000128 = 0.000358 \pm 0.000260$, $P(0.00098 \leq \beta_1 \leq 0.0006173) \approx 0.95$. The confidence interval does not contain zero, so there is a significant linear dependence of Y on X_1 for the $1 - 0.95 = 0.05$ significance level.

$b_2 \pm t_{n-p-1} S_{b_2} = 0.013 \pm 2.026 \times 0.052 = 0.013 \pm 0.106$, $P(-0.093 \leq \beta_2 \leq 0.119) \approx 0.95$. The confidence interval contains zero, so there is no significant linear dependence of Y on X_2 for the $1 - 0.95 = 0.05$ significance level.

(b) $H_0': \beta_1 = 0$, $H_1': \beta_1 \neq 0$

Decision rule: Reject H_0' if $|t| > 2.026$. Test statistic: $t = \dfrac{b_1}{S_{b_1}} = 2.79$. Decision: Because $|t| > 2.026$, reject H_0'.

There is a significant linear dependence of Y on X_1 in the model already containing X_2 for the 0.05 significance level.

$H_0'': \beta_2 = 0$, $H_1'': \beta_2 \neq 0$

Decision rule: Reject H_0'' if $|t| > 2.026$. Test statistic: $t = \frac{b_2}{S_{b_2}} = 0.2495$. Decision: Because $|t| < 2.026$, do not reject H_0''. There is no significant linear dependence of Y on X_2 in the model already containing X_1 for the 0.05 significance level. There is a significant linear dependence of Y only on the variables X_1 for the 0.05 significance level.

22. (a) H_0': Variable X_1 does not significantly improve the model once the variable X_2 has been included.

H_1': Variable X_1 significantly improves the model once the variable X_2 has been included.

Decision rule: Reject H_0' if $F > 4.41$. Test statistic:

$F = \frac{\text{SSR}(X_1|X_2)}{\text{MSE}} = \frac{\text{SSR}(X_1 \text{ and } X_2) - \text{SSR}(X_2)}{\text{MSE}} = \frac{60-25}{120} \cdot 18 = 5.25$. Decision: Because $F > 4.41$, reject H_0'.

Variable X_1 significantly improves the model once the variable X_2 has been included.

H_0'': Variable X_2 does not significantly improve the model once the variable X_1 has been included.

H_1'': Variable X_2 significantly improves the model once the variable X_1 has been included.

Decision rule: Reject H_0'' if $F > 4.41$. Test statistic:

$F = \frac{\text{SSR}(X_2|X_1)}{\text{MSE}} = \frac{\text{SSR}(X_1 \text{ and } X_2) - \text{SSR}(X_1)}{\text{MSE}} = \frac{60-45}{120} \cdot 18 = 2.25$. Decision: Because $F < 4.41$, do not reject H_0''. Variable X_2 does not significantly improve the model once the variable X_1 has been included.

(b) $R^2_{Y1.2} = \frac{\text{SSR}(X_1|X_2)}{\text{SST} - \text{SSR}(X_1 \text{ and } X_2) + \text{SSR}(X_1|X_2)} = \frac{45}{180-60+45} = \frac{45}{165} = 0.273$, 27.3% of the variation in Y can be explained by the variation of X_1.

$R^2_{Y2.1} = \frac{\text{SSR}(X_2|X_1)}{\text{SST} - \text{SSR}(X_1 \text{ and } X_2) + \text{SSR}(X_2|X_1)} = \frac{25}{180-60+25} = \frac{25}{145} = 0.172$, 17.2% of the variation in Y can be explained by the variation of X_2.

23. Summary Output: All but Weight

Regression Statistics	
Multiple R	0.831
R^2	0.690
Adjusted R^2	0.687
Standard Error	2.538
Observations	89.000

ANOVA

	df	SS	MS	F	Significance F
Regression	1.000	1250.034	1250.034	194.074	7.16×10^{-24}
Residual	87.000	560.370	6.441		
Total	88.000	1810.404			

	Coefficients	Standard Error	t Stat	p-value	Lower 95%	Upper 95%
Intercept	75.961	3.790	20.0411	2.35×10^{-34}	68.428	83.495
Length	–0.284	0.020	–13.931	7.16×10^{-24}	–0.324	–0.243

Summary Output: All but Length

Regression Statistics	
Multiple R	0.906
R^2	0.820
Adjusted R^2	0.818
Standard Error	1.935
Observations	89.000

ANOVA

	df	SS	MS	F	Significance F
Regression	1.000	1484.545	1484.545	396.354	3.77×10^{-34}
Residual	87.000	325.859	3.746		
Total	88.000	1810.404			

	Coefficients	Standard Error	t Stat	p-value	Lower 95%	Upper 95%
Intercept	47.885	1.252	38.240	3.48×10^{-56}	45.396	50.374
Weight	–0.008	0.000	–19.909	3.77×10^{-34}	–0.009	–0.007

Regression Analysis

Coefficients of Partial Determination			
$SSR(X_1, X_2)$	1485.519		
SST	1810.404		
$SSR(X_2)$	1250.034	$SSR(X_1\|X_2)$	235.485
$SSR(X_1)$	1484.545	$SSR(X_2\|X_1)$	0.974
$R^2_{Y1.2}$	0.420		
$R^2_{Y2.1}$	0.003		

(a) H_0': Variable X_1 does not significantly improve the model once the variable X_2 has been included.
H_1': Variable X_1 significantly improves the model once the variable X_2 has been included.
Decision rule: Reject H_0' if $F > 3.952$. Test statistic: $F = \frac{SSR(X_1|X_2)}{MSE} = \frac{235.485}{3.778} = 62.33$. Decision: Because $F > 3.952$, reject H_0'. Variable X_1 significantly improves the model once the variable X_2 has been included.
H_0'': Variable X_2 does not significantly improve the model once the variable X_1 has been included.
H_1'': Variable X_2 significantly improves the model once the variable X_1 has been included.
Decision rule: Reject H_0'' if $F > 3.952$. Test statistic: $F = \frac{SSR(X_2|X_1)}{MSE} = \frac{0.974}{3.778} = 0.258$. Decision: Because $F < 3.952$, do not reject H_0''. Variable X_2 does not significantly improve the model once the variable X_1 has been included. Appropriate regression model is $\hat{Y}_i = \beta_0 + \beta_1 X_{1i} + \varepsilon_i$.

(b) $R^2_{Y1.2} = \frac{SSR(X_1|X_2)}{SST - SSR(X_1 \text{ and } X_2) + SSR(X_1|X_2)} = 0.420$, 42.0% of the variation in Y can be explained by the variation of X_1.

$R^2_{Y2.1} = \frac{SSR(X_2|X_1)}{SST - SSR(X_1 \text{ and } X_2) + SSR(X_2|X_1)} = 0.003$, 0.3% of the variation in Y can be explained by the variation of X_2.

24. Summary Output: All but Height

Regression Statistics	
Multiple R	0.636
R^2	0.405
Adjusted R^2	0.374
Standard Error	11.708
Observations	21.000

ANOVA

	df	SS	MS	F	Significance F
Regression	1.000	1771.716	1771.716	12.924	0.002
Residual	19.000	2604.570	137.083		
Total	20.000	4376.286			

	Coefficients	Standard Error	t Stat	p-value	Lower 95%	Upper 95%
Intercept	6.492	6.836	0.950	0.354	–7.815	20.800
Bark Thickness	10.272	2.857	3.595	0.002	4.292	16.252

Summary Output: All but Bark Thickness

Regression Statistics	
Multiple R	0.854
R^2	0.729
Adjusted R^2	0.715
Standard Error	7.904
Observations	21.000

ANOVA

	df	SS	MS	F	Significance F
Regression	1.000	3189.434	3189.434	51.059	8.6×10^{-7}
Residual	19.000	1186.851	62.466		
Total	20.000	4376.286			

	Coefficients	Standard Error	t Stat	p-value	Lower 95%	Upper 95%
Intercept	–13.540	6.237	–2.171	0.043	–26.593	–0.487
Height	0.273	0.0381	7.146	8.6×10^{-7}	0.193	0.352

Regression Analysis

Coefficients of Partial Determination			
$SSR(X_1, X_2)$	3191.622		
SST	4376.286		
$SSR(X_2)$	1771.716	$SSR(X_1\vert X_2)$	1419.906
$SSR(X_1)$	3189.434	$SSR(X_2\vert X_1)$	2.187
$R^2_{Y1.2}$	0.545		
$R^2_{Y2.1}$	0.002		

(a) H_0' : Variable X_1 does not significantly improve the model once the variable X_2 has been included.

H_1' : Variable X_1 significantly improves the model once the variable X_2 has been included.

Decision rule: Reject H_0' if $F > 4.41$. Test statistic: $F = \frac{\text{SSR}(X_1|X_2)}{\text{MSE}} = \frac{1419.906}{65.815} = 21.574$. Decision: Because $F > 4.41$, reject H_0'. Variable X_1 significantly improves the model once the variable X_2 has been included.

H_0'' : Variable X_2 does not significantly improve the model once the variable X_1 has been included.

H_1'' : Variable X_2 significantly improves the model once the variable X_1 has been included.

Decision rule: Reject H_0'' if $F > 4.41$. Test statistic: $F = \frac{\text{SSR}(X_2|X_1)}{\text{MSE}} = \frac{2.187}{65.815} = 0.033$. Decision: Because $F < 4.41$, do not reject H_0''. Variable X_2 does not significantly improve the model once the variable X_1 has been included. Appropriate regression model is $\widehat{Y}_i = \beta_0 + \beta_1 X_{1i} + \varepsilon_i$.

(b) $R^2_{Y1.2} = \frac{\text{SSR}(X_1|X_2)}{\text{SST} - \text{SSR}(X_1 \text{ and } X_2) + \text{SSR}(X_1|X_2)} = 0.545$, 54.5% of the variation in Y can be explained by the variation of X_1.

$R^2_{Y2.1} = \frac{\text{SSR}(X_2|X_1)}{\text{SST} - \text{SSR}(X_1 \text{ and } X_2) + \text{SSR}(X_2|X_1)} = 0.002$, 0.2% of the variation in Y can be explained by the variation of X_2.

25. Summary Output: All but Light Output

Regression Statistics	
Multiple R	0.581
R^2	0.337
Adjusted R^2	0.254
Standard Error	0.040
Observations	10.000

ANOVA

	df	SS	MS	F	Significance F
Regression	1.000	0.007	0.007	4.072	0.0783
Residual	8.000	0.013	0.002		
Total	9.000	0.020			

	Coefficients	Standard Error	t Stat	p-value	Lower 95%	Upper 95%
Intercept	0.782	0.122	6.387	0.000	0.500	1.065
Lamp Temperature	–0.007	0.003	–2.018	0.078	–0.015	0.001

Summary Output: All but Lamp Temperature

Regression Statistics	
Multiple R	0.777
R^2	0.603
Adjusted R^2	0.554
Standard Error	0.031
Observations	10.000

ANOVA

	df	SS	MS	F	Significance F
Regression	1.000	0.012	0.012	12.175	0.008
Residual	8.000	0.008	0.001		
Total	9.000	0.020			

	Coefficients	Standard Error	*t* Stat	*p*-value	Lower 95%	Upper 95%
Intercept	1.672	0.326	5.135	0.001	0.921	2.423
Light Output	–0.028	0.008	–3.489	0.008	–0.046	–0.009

Regression Analysis

Coefficients of Partial Determination			
$SSR(X_1, X_2)$	0.012		
SST	0.020		
$SSR(X_2)$	0.007	$SSR(X_1 \mid X_2)$	0.006
$SSR(X_1)$	0.012	$SSR(X_2 \mid X_1)$	0.000
$R^2_{Y1.2}$	0.435		
$R^2_{Y2.1}$	0.055		

(a) H_0': Variable X_1 does not significantly improve the model once the variable X_2 has been included.

H_1': Variable X_1 significantly improves the model once the variable X_2 has been included.

Decision rule: Reject H_0' if $F > 5.59$. Test statistic: $F = \frac{SSR(X_1 \mid X_2)}{MSE} = \frac{0.006}{0.001} = 5.383$. Decision: Because $F < 5.59$, do not reject H_0'. Variable X_1 does not significantly improve the model once the variable X_2 has been included for the 0.05 significance level.

H_0'': Variable X_2 does not significantly improve the model once the variable X_1 has been included.

H_1'': Variable X_2 significantly improves the model once the variable X_1 has been included.

Decision rule: Reject H_0'' if $F > 5.59$. Test statistic: $F = \frac{SSR(X_2 \mid X_1)}{MSE} = \frac{0.000}{0.001} = 0.41$. Decision: Because $F < 5.59$, do not reject H_0''. Variable X_2 does not significantly improve the model once the variable X_1 has been included. An appropriate regression model will not include linear terms on X_1 and X_2.

(b) $R^2_{Y1.2} = \frac{SSR(X_1 \mid X_2)}{SST - SSR(X_1 \text{ and } X_2) + SSR(X_1 \mid X_2)} = 0.435$, 43.5% of the variation in Y can be explained by the variation of X_1.

$R^2_{Y2.1} = \frac{SSR(X_2 \mid X_1)}{SST - SSR(X_1 \text{ and } X_2) + SSR(X_2 \mid X_1)} = 0.055$, 5.5% of the variation in Y can be explained by the variation of X_2.

26. Summary Output: All but Soil Radiation

Regression Statistics	
Multiple R	0.014
R^2	0.000
Adjusted R^2	–0.026
Standard Error	0.571
Observations	40.000

ANOVA

	df	SS	MS	*F*	Significance *F*
Regression	1.000	0.002	0.002	0.007	0.932
Residual	38.000	12.382	0.326		
Total	39.000	12.384			

	Coefficients	Standard Error	*t* Stat	*p*-value	Lower 95%	Upper 95%
Intercept	0.435	3.892	0.112	0.911	–7.442	8.313
Soil Temperature	0.005	0.057	0.086	0.932	–0.110	0.119

Summary Output: All but Soil Temperature

Regression Statistics	
Multiple R	0.416
R^2	0.173
Adjusted R^2	0.151
Standard Error	0.519
Observations	40.000

ANOVA

	df	SS	MS	F	Significance F
Regression	1.000	2.139	2.139	7.932	0.008
Residual	38.000	10.245	0.270		
Total	39.000	12.384			

	Coefficients	Standard Error	*t* Stat	*p*-value	Lower 95%	Upper 95%
Intercept	0.611	0.100	6.128	3.79×10^{-7}	0.409	0.813
Soil Radiation	0.000	0.000	2.816	0.008	0.000	0.001

Regression Analysis

Coefficients of Partial Determination			
$SSR(X_1, X_2)$	2.156		
SST	12.384		
$SSR(X_2)$	0.002	$SSR(X_1\|X_2)$	2.153
$SSR(X_1)$	2.139	$SSR(X_2\|X_1)$	0.017
$R^2_{Y1.2}$	0.174		
$R^2_{Y2.1}$	0.002		

(a) H_0': Variable X_1 does not significantly improve the model once the variable X_2 has been included.
H_1': Variable X_1 significantly improves the model once the variable X_2 has been included.
Decision rule: Reject H_0' if $F > 4.105$. Test statistic: $F = \frac{SSR(X_1|X_2)}{MSE} = \frac{2.153}{0.276} = 8.738$. Decision: Because $F > 4.105$, reject H_0'. Variable X_1 significantly improves the model once the variable X_2 has been included.
H_0'': Variable X_2 does not significantly improve the model once the variable X_1 has been included.
H_1'': Variable X_2 significantly improves the model once the variable X_1 has been included.
Decision rule: Reject H_0'' if $F > 4.105$. Test statistic: $F = \frac{SSR(X_2|X_1)}{MSE} = \frac{0.017}{0.276} = 0.062$. Decision: Because $F < 4.105$, do not reject H_0''. Variable X_2 does not significantly improve the model once the variable X_1 has been included. Appropriate regression model is $\hat{Y}_i = \beta_0 + \beta_1 X_{1_i} + \varepsilon_i$.

(b) $R^2_{Y1.2} = \frac{SSR(X_1|X_2)}{SST - SSR(X_1 \text{ and } X_2) + SSR(X_1|X_2)} = 0.174$, 17.4% of the variation in Y can be explained by the variation of X_1.

$R^2_{Y2.1} = \dfrac{\text{SSR}(X_2|X_1)}{\text{SST} - \text{SSR}(X_1 \text{ and } X_2) + \text{SSR}(X_2|X_1)} = 0.002$, 0.2% of the variation in Y can be explained by the variation of X_2.

27. (a)

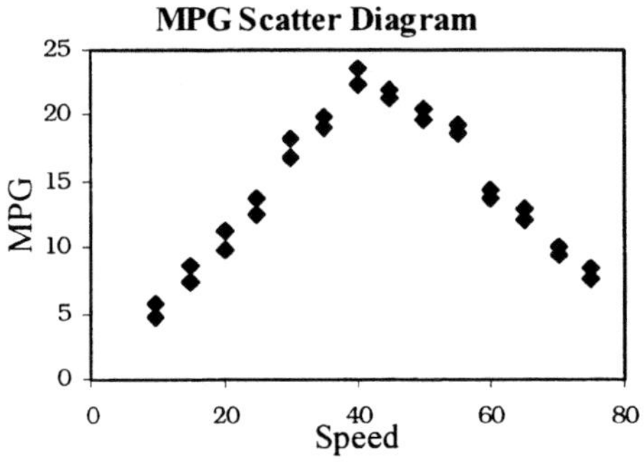

(b) Regression Analysis

Regression Statistics	
Multiple R	0.959
R^2	0.919
Adjusted R^2	0.912
Standard Error	1.663
Observations	28.000

ANOVA

	df	SS	MS	F	Significance F
Regression	2.000	782.825	391.412	141.460	2.338×10^{-14}
Residual	25.000	69.174	2.767		
Total	27.000	851.999			

	Coefficients	Standard Error	t Stat	p-value	Lower 95%	Upper 95%
Intercept	–7.556	1.424	–5.305	1.694×10^{-5}	–10.489	–4.623
Speed	1.272	0.076	16.792	3.992×10^{-15}	1.116	1.428
Speed^2	–0.015	0.001	–16.633	4.973×10^{-15}	–0.016	–0.013

$\hat{Y}_i = -7.556 + 1.272 \times X_i - 0.015 \times X_i^2$

(c) $\hat{Y}_i = -7.556 + 1.272 \times 55 - 0.015 \times 55^2 = 18.509$

(d) $H_0: \beta_1 = \beta_2 = 0$, $H_1: \beta_1^2 + \beta_2^2 > 0$

Decision rule: Reject H_0 if $F > 4.29$. Test statistic: $F = \dfrac{\text{MSR}}{\text{MSE}} = \dfrac{391.412}{2.767} = 141.460$. Decision: Because $F > 4.29$, reject H_0. Curvilinear relationship between mileage and speed is significant.

(e) $R^2_{Y.12} = \dfrac{\text{SSR}}{\text{SST}} = \dfrac{782.825}{851.999} = 0.919$, 91.9% of the variation in Y can be explained by the constructed curvilinear relationship.

(f) $R^2_{adj} = 1 - \left[(1 - R^2_{Y.12})\dfrac{(n-1)}{(n-p-1)}\right] = 1 - \left[(1 - 0.919)\dfrac{27}{25}\right] = 0.912$

(g)

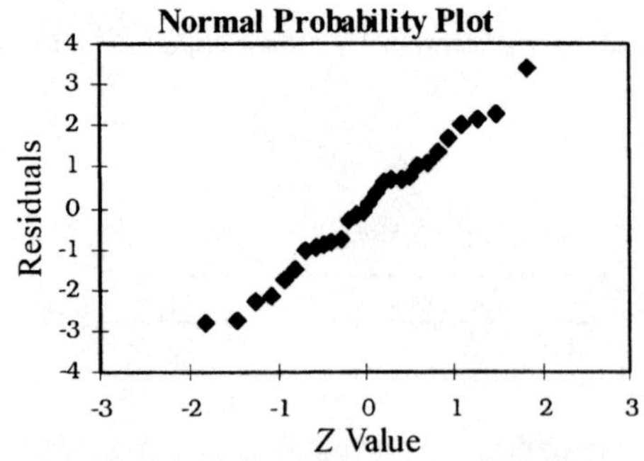

The constructed curvilinear regression seems to be adequate.

(h) H_0 : Including the curvilinear effect does not significantly improve the model ($\beta_2 = 0$).

H_1 : Including the curvilinear effect significantly improves the model ($\beta_2 \neq 0$).

Decision rule: Reject H_0 if $|t| > 2.060$. Test statistic: $t = \frac{b_2}{S_{b_2}} = \frac{-0.015}{0.001} = -16.63$. Decision: Because $t > 2.060$, reject H_0 . The curvilinear model is better than simple linear one.

28. (a)

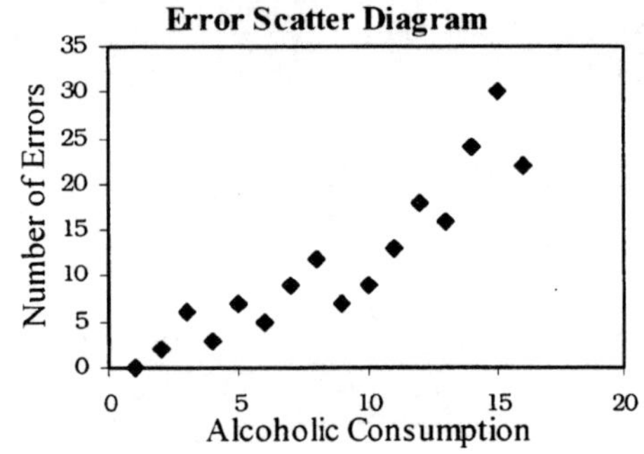

(b) Regression Analysis

Regression Statistics	
Multiple R	0.955
R^2	0.912
Adjusted R^2	0.898
Standard Error	2.641
Observations	15.000

ANOVA

	df	SS	MS	F	Significance F
Regression	2.000	870.724	435.362	62.435	4542×10^{-7}
Residual	12.000	83.676	6.973		
Total	14.000	954.400			

	Coefficients	Standard Error	t Stat	p–value	Lower 95%	Upper 95%
Intercept	4.181	1.435	2.914	0.013	1.055	7.307
Consumption	0.438	1.700	0.258	0.801	–3.265	4.141
Consumption^2	1.190	0.407	2.922	0.013	0.303	2.078

$\hat{Y}_i = 4.181 + 0.438 \times X_i + 1.190 \times X_i^2$

(c) $\hat{Y}_i = 4.181 + 0.438 \times 2.5 + 1.190 \times 2.5^2 = 12.717$

(d) $H_0{:}\beta_1 = \beta_2 = 0$, $H_1{:}\beta_1^2 + \beta_2^2 > 0$

Decision rule: Reject H_0 if $F > 3.89$. Test statistic: $F = \frac{\text{MSR}}{\text{MSE}} = \frac{435.362}{6.973} = 62.435$. Decision: Because $F > 3.89$, reject H_0 . The curvilinear relationship between mileage and speed is significant

(e) $R^2_{Y.12} = \frac{\text{SSR}}{\text{SST}} = \frac{870.728}{954.4} = 0.912$, 91.2% of the variation in Y can be explained by the constructed curvilinear relationship.

(f) $R^2_{adj} = 1 - \left[(1 - R^2_{Y.12}) \frac{(n-1)}{(n-p-1)} \right] = 0.898$

(g)

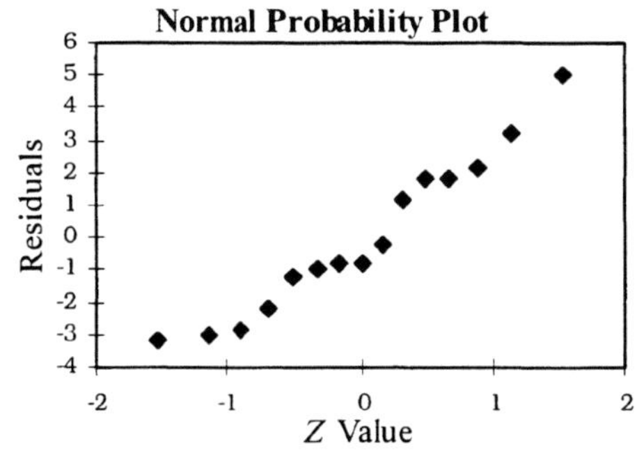

The constructed curvilinear regression seems to be adequate.

(h) H_0 : Including the curvilinear effect does not significantly improve the model ($\beta_2 = 0$).

H_1 : Including the curvilinear effect significantly improves the model ($\beta_2 \neq 0$).

Decision rule: Reject H_0 if $|t| > 2.179$. Test statistic: $t = \frac{b_2}{S_{b_2}} = \frac{1.190}{0.407} = 2.923$. Decision: Because $t > 2.179$, reject H_0 . The curvilinear model is better than the simple linear model.

29. (a)

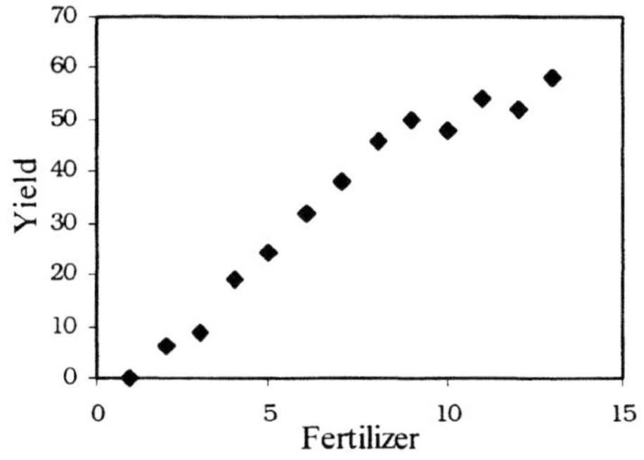

(b) Regression Analysis

Regression Statistics	
Multiple R	0.986
R^2	0.972
Adjusted R^2	0.966
Standard Error	3.328
Observations	12.000

ANOVA

	df	SS	MS	F	Significance F
Regression	2.000	3484.981	1742.490	157.319	9.973×10^{-8}
Residual	9.000	99.686	11.076		
Total	11.000	3584.667			

	Coefficients	Standard Error	t Stat	p-value	Lower 95%	Upper 95%
Intercept	6.643	2.133	3.115	0.012	1.818	11.468
Fertilizer	0.895	0.100	8.922	9.166×10^{-6}	0.668	1.122
Fertilizer^2	–0.004	0.001	–4.265	0.002	–0.006	–0.002

$\hat{Y}_i = 6.643 + 0.895 \times X_i - 0.004 \times X_i^2$

(c) $\hat{Y}_i = 6.643 + 0.895 \times 70 - 0.004 \times 70^2 = 49.169$

(d) $H_0: \beta_1 = \beta_2 = 0$, $H_1: \beta_1^2 + \beta_2^2 > 0$

Decision rule: Reject H_0 if $F > 4.26$. Test statistic: $F = \frac{\text{MSR}}{\text{MSE}} = \frac{1742.490}{11.076} = 157.318$. Decision: Because $F > 4.26$, reject H_0. The curvilinear relationship between mileage and speed is significant.

(e) The p-value in part (d) is 9.97×10^{-8}. This is the probability of obtaining $F \geq 157.318$ when H_0 is true.

(f) $R^2_{Y.12} = \frac{\text{SSR}}{\text{SST}} = \frac{3484.981}{3584.667} = 0.972$, 97.2% of the variation in Y can be explained by the constructed curvilinear relationship.

(g) $R^2_{adj} = 1 - \left[(1 - R^2_{Y.12})\frac{(n-1)}{(n-p-1)}\right] = 0.966$

(h) H_0: Including the curvilinear effect does not significantly improve the model ($\beta_2 = 0$).
H_1: Including the curvilinear effect significantly improves the model ($\beta_2 \neq 0$).

Decision rule: Reject H_0 if $|t| > 2.262$. Test statistic: $t = \frac{b_2}{S_{b_2}} = \frac{-0.004}{0.001} = -4.265$. Decision: Because $|t| > 2.262$, reject H_0. The curvilinear model is better than the simple linear model.

(i) The p-value in part (h) is 0.002. This is a probability of obtaining $|t| \geq 4.265$ when H_0 is true.

(j)

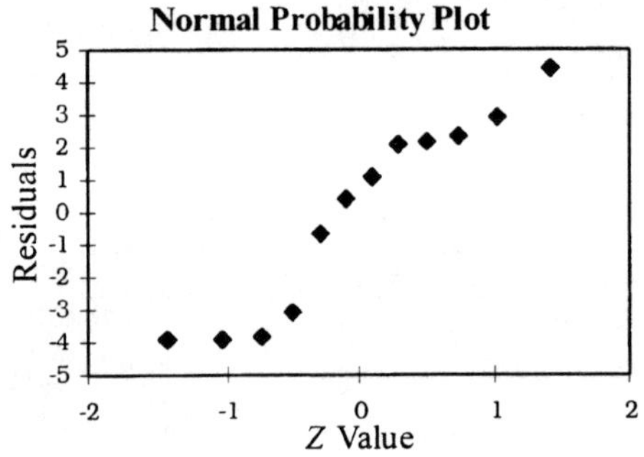

The constructed curvilinear regression does not appear to be adequate.

30. (a)

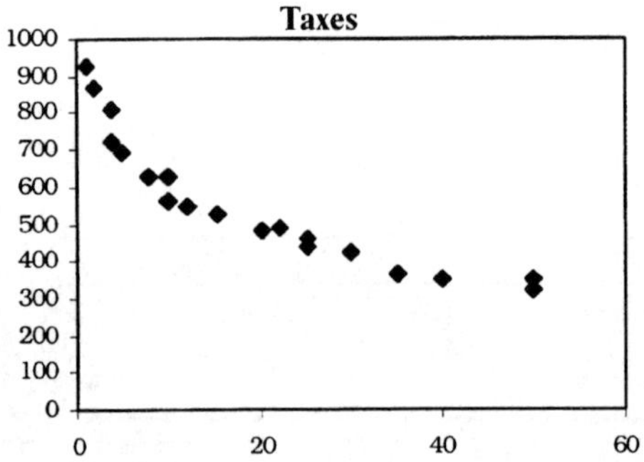

(b) Regression Analysis

Regression Statistics	
Multiple R	0.967
R^2	0.936
Adjusted R^2	0.927
Standard Error	48.408
Observations	19.000

ANOVA

	df	SS	MS	F	Significance F
Regression	2.000	544220.940	272110.470	116.123	2.978×10^{-10}
Residual	16.000	37492.736	2343.296		
Total	18.000	581713.680			

	Coefficients	**Standard Error**	***t* Stat**	***p*–value**	**Lower 95%**	**Upper 95%**
Intercept	857.588	25.189	34.046	2.334×10^{-16}	804.189	910.988
Age	–24.722	2.624	–9.422	6.244×10^{-8}	–30.284	–19.160
Age^2	0.294	0.051	5.731	3.092×10^{-5}	0.185	0.402

$\hat{Y}_i = 857.588 - 24.722\times X_i + 0.294\times X_i^2$

(c) $\hat{Y}_i = 857.588 - 24.722\times 20 + 0.294\times 20^2 = 480.563$

(d)

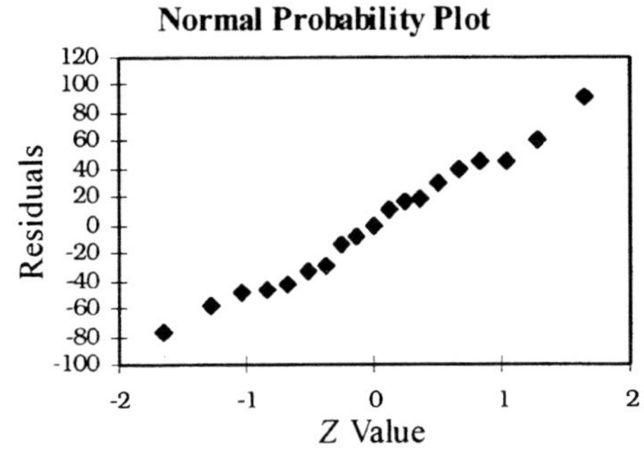

The constructed curvilinear regression seems to be adequate.

(e) $H_0\!: \beta_1 = \beta_2 = 0$, $H_1\!: \beta_1^2 + \beta_2^2 > 0$

Decision rule: Reject H_0 if $F > 3.63$. Test statistic: $F = \dfrac{\text{MSR}}{\text{MSE}} = \dfrac{272110.47}{2343.3} = 116.123$. Decision: Because $F > 3.63$, reject H_0. The curvilinear relationship between age and county taxes is significant.

(f) The *p*-value in part (d) is 2.978×10^{-10}. This is the probability of obtaining $F \ge 116.123$ when H_0 is true.

(g) H_0 : Including the curvilinear effect does not significantly improve the model ($\beta_2 = 0$).

H_1 : Including the curvilinear effect significantly improves the model ($\beta_2 \ne 0$).

Decision rule: Reject H_0 if $|t| > 2.120$. Test statistic: $t = \dfrac{b_2}{S_{b_2}} = \dfrac{0.294}{0.051} = 5.73$. Decision: Because $t > 2.120$, reject H_0. The curvilinear model is better than the simple linear model.

(h) The *p*-value in part (g) is 3.092×10^{-5}. This is the probability of obtaining $|t| \ge 5.73$ when H_0 is true.

(i) $R^2_{Y.12} = \dfrac{\text{SSR}}{\text{SST}} = \dfrac{544220.94}{581713.68} = 0.936$, 93.6% of the variation in Y can be explained by the constructed curvilinear relationship.

(j) $R^2_{adj} = 1 - \left[(1 - R^2_{Y.12})\dfrac{(n-1)}{(n-p-1)}\right] = 0.928$

31. (a) First, develop a multiple regression model using X_1 as the variable for the SAT score and X_2 as a dummy variable ($X_2 = 1$ if a student received a grade of B or higher in the introductory statistics course and $X_2 = 0$ otherwise). If we claim (say, using PHStat) that each of the two variables is making a significant contribution to the model, we still need to do one more test before we can use this model: We need to verify that the slope of the total SAT score and the grade-point average must be the same for both levels of the variable X_2. A hypothesis of equal slopes of the X_1 variable with grade-point average should be evaluated (say, using PHStat) by defining an interaction term $X_1 \times X_2$ and then testing whether this new term makes a significant contribution to the original regression model (that contains X_1 and X_2 terms only).

(b) If a student received a grade of B or better, in the introductory statistics course, the student would be expected to have a grade-point average in computer science that is 0.30 higher than a student who had the same SAT score, but did not get a grade of B or better in the introductory statistical course.

32. Regression Analysis

Regression Statistics	
Multiple R	0.908
R^2	0.825
Adjusted R^2	0.821
Standard Error	1.920
Observations	89.000

ANOVA

	df	SS	MS	F	Significance F
Regression	2.000	1493.472	746.736	202.628	2.865×10^{-33}
Residual	86.000	316.932	3.685		
Total	88.000	1810.405			

	Coefficients	Standard Error	t Stat	p–value	Lower 95%	Upper 95%
Intercept	49.813	1.754	28.401	1.816×10^{-45}	46.326	53.299
Weight	–0.008	0.000	–17.944	8.118×10^{-31}	–0.009	–0.007
Type of Drive	–0.944	0.606	–1.556	0.123	–2.149	0.262

(a) $\hat{Y}_i = 49.813 - 0.008 \times X_{1i} - 0.944 \times X_{2i}$

(b) The slope equal to –0.008 represents the expected change in Y per unit change in X_1 (weight). The slope equal to –0.944 represents the expected change in Y per unit change in X_2 (from rear wheel drive to front wheel drive).

(c) $\hat{Y}_i = 49.813 - 0.008 \times 2500 - 0.944 \times 1 = 28.306$

(d) Due to the very small p-value 8×10^{-31} there is significant dependence of Y on X_1 (weight). With respect to the second variable, it has a big p-value, 0.1234, so there is no significant dependence of Y on X_2 (type of drive).

(e) $R^2_{Y.12} = 0.825$, 82.5% of the variation can be explained by the variations in the X_1 and X_2

(f) $R^2_{adj} = 0.821$

(g)

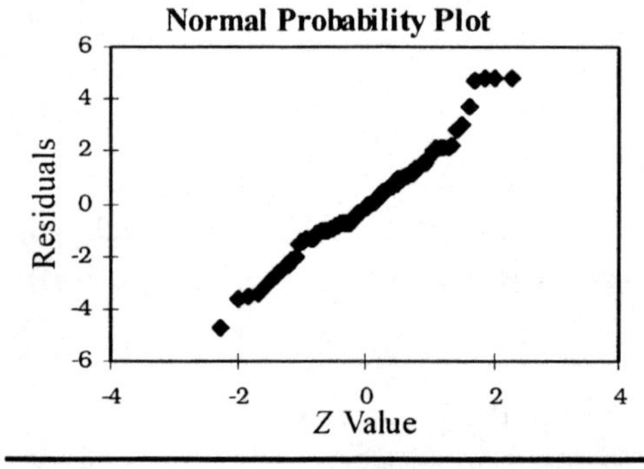

The developed regression model seems to be adequate.

(h)

	Coefficients	Standard Error	t Stat	p–value	Lower 95%	Upper 95%
Intercept	49.813	1.754	28.401	1.816×10^{-45}	46.326	53.299
Weight	–0.008	0.000	–17.944	8.118×10^{-31}	–0.009	–0.007
Type of Drive	–0.944	0.606	–1.556	0.123	–2.149	0.262

There is a significant dependence of Y only on the X_1. It is appropriate use the simple regression model developed and analyzed in Chapter 12, Problem 56 for this problem.

(i) $P(-0.009 \le \beta_1 \le -0.007) \approx 0.95$. The confidence interval does not contain zero, so there is a significant linear dependence of Y on X_1 for the $1-0.95 = 0.05$ significance level.

$P(-2.149 \le \beta_2 \le 0.262) \approx 0.95$ The confidence interval contains zero, so there is no significant linear dependence of Y on X_2 for the $1-0.95 = 0.05$ significance level.

(j) Regression Analysis

Coefficients of Partial Determination			
$SSR(X_1, X_2)$	1493.472		
SST	1810.404		
$SSR(X_2)$	306.891	$SSR(X_1 \vert X_2)$	1186.581
$SSR(X_1)$	1484.545	$SSR(X_2 \vert X_1)$	8.927
$R^2_{Y1.2}$	0.789		
$R^2_{Y2.1}$	0.027		

$R^2_{Y1.2} = \dfrac{SSR(X_1|X_2)}{SST - SSR(X_1 \text{ and } X_2) + SSR(X_1|X_2)} = 0.789$, 78.9% of the variation in Y can be explained by the variation of X_1.

$R^2_{Y2.1} = \dfrac{SSR(X_2|X_1)}{SST - SSR(X_1 \text{ and } X_2) + SSR(X_2|X_1)} = 0.027$, 2.7% of the variation in Y can be explained by the variation of X_2.

(k) The slope of the weight of an automobile with the MPG is the same for various wheel drives.

(l) Regression Analysis

Regression Statistics	
Multiple R	0.919
R^2	0.844
Adjusted R^2	0.839
Standard Error	1.823
Observations	89.000

ANOVA

	df	SS	MS	F	Significance F
Regression	3.000	1528.038	509.346	153.327	3.457×10^{-34}
Residual	85.000	282.367	3.322		
Total	88.000	1810.405			

	Coefficients	Standard Error	t Stat	p-value	Lower 95%	Upper 95%
Intercept	32.085	5.742	5.587	2.722×10^{-7}	20.667	43.503
Weight	–0.003	0.002	–2.203	0.030	–0.007	–0.000
Type of Drive	18.014	5.905	3.051	0.003	6.273	29.755
WeightxType of Drive	–0.005	0.002	–3.226	0.002	–0.008	–0.002

$H_0\!: \beta_3 = 0$, $H_1\!: \beta_3 \ne 0$, $P(-0.008 \le \beta_3 \le -0.002) \approx 0.95$. Zero does not belong to this interval, so reject H_0 for 0.05 level. There is a significant interaction between the weight and type of drive.

(m) The model $\widehat{Y}_i = \beta_0 + \beta_1 \times X_{1i} + \beta_2 \times X_{2i} + \beta_3 \times X_{1i} \times X_{2i}$ is the most appropriate.

33. Regression Analysis

Regression Statistics	
Multiple R	0.981
R^2	0.962
Adjusted R^2	0.951
Standard Error	0.010
Observations	10.000

ANOVA

	df	SS	MS	F	Significance F
Regression	2.000	0.019	0.009	88.559	1.071×10^{-5}
Residual	7.000	0.001	0.000		
Total	9.000	0.020			

	Coefficients	Standard Error	t Stat	p–value	Lower 95%	Upper 95%
Intercept	0.399	0.048	8.388	6.728×10^{-5}	0.286	0.511
Lamp Temperature	0.002	0.001	1.794	0.116	–0.001	0.005
Type	0.099	0.009	10.724	1.347×10^{-5}	0.078	0.121

(a) $\widehat{Y}_i = 0.399 + 0.002 \times X_{1i} + 0.099 \times X_{2i}$

(b) The slope equal to 0.002 represents the expected change in Y per unit change in X_1 (lamp temperature). The slope equal to 0.099 represents the expected change in Y per unit change in X_2 (type of ballast).

(c) $\widehat{Y}_i = 0.399 + 0.002 \times 40 + 0.099 \times 0 = 0.488$

(d) Due to the very small p-value 1.347×10^{-5} there is significant dependence of Y on X_2 (type of ballast). With respect to the first variable, it has a big p-value, 0.116, so there is no significant dependence of Y on X_1 (lamp temperature).

(e) $R^2_{Y.12} = 0.962$, 96.2% of the variation can be explained by the variations in the X_1 and X_2.

(f) $R^2_{adj} = 0.951$

(g)

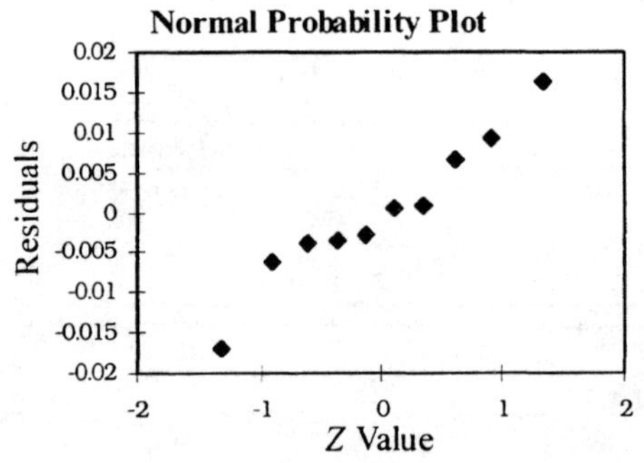

There are some doubts about the validity of the multiple linear regression model.

(h)

	Coefficients	Standard Error	t Stat	p–value	Lower 95%	Upper 95%
Intercept	0.399	0.048	8.388	6.728×10^{-5}	0.286	0.511
Lamp Temperature	0.002	0.001	1.794	0.116	–0.001	0.005
Type	0.099	0.009	10.724	1.347×10^{-5}	0.078	0.121

There is a significant dependence of Y on X_2. Model $\widehat{Y}_i = \beta_0 + \beta_2 \times X_{2i} + \varepsilon_i$ should be used.

(i) $P(-0.001 \le \beta_1 \le 0.002) \approx 0.95$. The confidence interval contains zero, so there is no significant linear dependence of Y on X_1 for the $1-0.95=0.05$ significance level.

$P(0.078 \le \beta_2 \le 0.121) \approx 0.95$

The confidence interval does not contain zero, so there is a significant linear dependence of Y on X_2 for the $1-0.95=0.05$ significance level.

(j) Regression Analysis

Coefficients of Partial Determination			
SSR(X_1, X_2)	0.019		
SST	0.020		
SSR(X_2)	0.019	SSR($X_1 \mid X_2$)	0.000
SSR(X_1)	0.007	SSR($X_2 \mid X_1$)	0.012
$R^2_{Y1.2}$	0.315		
$R^2_{Y2.1}$	0.943		

$R^2_{Y1.2} = \dfrac{\text{SSR}(X_1 \mid X_2)}{\text{SST} - \text{SSR}(X_1 \text{ and } X_2) + \text{SSR}(X_1 \mid X_2)} = 0.315$, 3.15% of the variation in Y can be explained by the variation of X_1.

$R^2_{Y2.1} = \dfrac{SSR(X_2 \mid X_1)}{SST - SSR(X_1 \text{ and } X_2) + SSR(X_2 \mid X_1)} = 0.943$, 94.3% of the variation in Y can be explained by the variation in X_2.

(k) The slope of the temperature of the lamp with the ballast efficiency factor is the same for various types of ballast.

(l) Regression Analysis

Regression Statistics	
Multiple R	0.982
R^2	0.964
Adjusted R^2	0.946
Standard Error	0.011
Observations	10.000

ANOVA

	df	SS	MS	F	Significance F
Regression	3.000	0.019	0.006	53.348	0.000
Residual	6.000	0.001	0.000		
Total	9.000	0.020			

	Coefficients	Standard Error	t Stat	p-value	Lower 95%	Upper 95%
Intercept	0.447	0.099	4.501	0.004	0.204	0.690
Lamp Temperature	0.001	0.003	0.372	0.723	–0.005	0.007
Type	0.038	0.111	0.338	0.747	–0.234	0.310
Lamp Temperature×Type	0.002	0.003	0.559	0.596	–0.006	0.009

$H_0{:}\beta_3 = 0$, $H_1{:}\beta_3 \ne 0$, $P(-0.006 \le \beta_3 \le 0.009) \approx 0.95$. Zero belongs to this interval, so do not reject H_0 for the 0.05 significance level. There is no significant interaction between the lamp temperature and the type of ballast.

(m) Model $\widehat{Y}_i = \beta_0 + \beta_2 \times X_{2i} + \varepsilon_i$ is appropriate.

34. Regression Analysis

Regression Statistics	
Multiple R	0.891
R^2	0.793
Adjusted R^2	0.788
Standard Error	2.715
Observations	80.000

ANOVA

	df	SS	MS	F	Significance F
Regression	2.000	2176.002	1088.001	147.559	4.557×10^{-27}
Residual	77.000	567.748	7.373		
Total	79.000	2743.750			

	Coefficients	Standard Error	t Stat	p–value	Lower 95%	Upper 95%
Intercept	−3.467	3.083	−1.124	0.264	−9.607	2.673
Average Total SAT	0.016	0.003	5.792	1.437×10^{-7}	0.011	0.022
Type of School	8.128	0.717	11.337	4.375×10^{-18}	6.701	9.556

(a) $\hat{Y}_i = -3.467 + 0.016 \times X_{i1} + 0.813 \times X_{2i}$

(b) The slope equal to 0.016 represents the expected change in Y per unit change in X_1 (average total of SAT). The slope equal to 0.813 represents the expected change in Y per unit change in X_2 (type of school).

(c) $\hat{Y}_i = -3.467 + 0.013 \times 1000 + 0.813 \times 0 = 9.613$

(d)

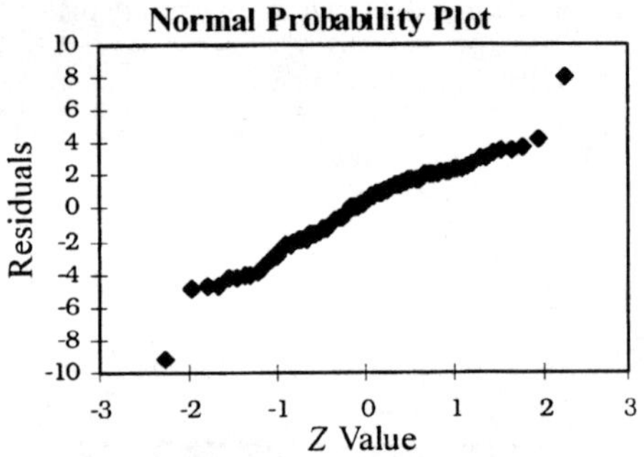

The developed regression model seems to be adequate.

(e) Due to the very small p-values (1.436×10^{-7} and 4.375×10^{-18}) there is a significant dependence of Y on X_1 (average total SAT) and X_2 (type of school).

(f)-
(g)

	Coefficients	Standard Error	t Stat	p–value	Lower 95%	Upper 95%
Intercept	−3.467	3.083	−1.124	0.264	−9.607	2.673
Average Total SAT	0.016	0.003	5.792	1.437×10^{-7}	0.011	0.022
Type of School	8.128	0.717	11.337	4.375×10^{-18}	6.701	9.556

There is a significant dependence of Y on X_1 and X_2. Model $\hat{Y}_i = \beta_0 + \beta_1 \times X_{1i} + \beta_2 \times X_{2i} + \varepsilon_i$ should be used.

(h) $R^2 = 0.793$, 79.3% of the variation in Y can be explained by the developed regression.

(i) $R^2_{adj} = 0.788$

(j) Regression Analysis

Coefficients of Partial Determination			
SSR(X_1, X_2)	2176.002		
SST	2743.750		
SSR(X_2)	1928.628	SSR($X_1 \vert X_2$)	247.374
SSR(X_1)	1228.376	SSR($X_2 \vert X_1$)	947.626
$R^2_{Y1.2}$	0.303		
$R^2_{Y2.1}$	0.625		

$R^2_{Y1.2} = \dfrac{\text{SSR}(X_1|X_2)}{\text{SST} - \text{SSR}(X_1 \text{ and } X_2) + \text{SSR}(X_1|X_2)} = 0.304$, 30.4% of the variation in Y can be explained by the variation of X_1.

$R^2_{Y2.1} = \dfrac{\text{SSR}(X_2|X_1)}{\text{SST} - \text{SSR}(X_1 \text{ and } X_2) + \text{SSR}(X_2|X_1)} = 0.625$, 62.5% of the variation in Y can be explained by the variation of X_2.

(k) The slope of the total SAT scores and the annual total cost is the same for the various types of schools.

(l) Regression Analysis

Regression Statistics	
Multiple R	0.895
R^2	0.801
Adjusted R^2	0.793
Standard Error	2.680
Observations	80.000

ANOVA

	df	SS	MS	F	Significance F
Regression	3.000	2197.827	732.609	101.989	1.425×10^{-26}
Residual	76.000	545.923	7.183		
Total	79.000	2743.750			

	Coefficients	Standard Error	t Stat	p-value	Lower 95%	Upper 95%
Intercept	7.684	9.208	0.834	0.407	–10.656	26.024
Average Total SAT	0.002	0.008	0.283	0.778	–0.014	0.019
Type of School	–0.427	0.715	–0.598	0.552	–1.852	0.997
SAT×Type	0.001	0.001	1.743	0.085	–0.000	0.002

$H_0: \beta_3 = 0$, $H_1: \beta_3 \neq 0$, $P(-0.000 \leq \beta_3 \leq 0.002) \approx 0.95$. Zero belongs to this interval, so do not reject H_0 for the 0.05 significance level. There is no significant interaction between the average total SAT scores and the type of school.

(m) Model $\hat{Y}_i = \beta_0 + \beta_1 \times X_{1i} + \beta_2 \times X_{2i} + \varepsilon_i$ is adequate.

35. Regression Analysis

Regression Statistics	
Multiple R	0.711
R^2	0.506
Adjusted R^2	0.341
Standard Error	96.656
Observations	9.000

ANOVA

	df	SS	MS	F	Significance F
Regression	2.000	57339.379	28669.689	3.069	0.121
Residual	6.000	56054.177	9342.363		
Total	8.000	113393.560			

	Coefficients	Standard Error	*t* Stat	*p*–value	Lower 95%	Upper 95%
Intercept	–572.097	405.388	–1.411	0.208	–1564.046	419.852
Diastolic	10.952	6.098	1.796	0.123	–3.970	25.875
Gender	–3.253	90.701	–0.036	0.973	–225.190	218.684

(a) $\hat{Y}_i = -572.097 + 10.952 \times X_{1i} - 3.253 \times X_{2i}$

(b) The slope equal to 10.952 represents the expected change in Y per unit change in X_1 (diastolic blood pressure). The slope equal to 3.25 represents the expected change in Y per unit change in X_2 (gender).

(c) $\hat{Y}_i = -572.097 + 10.952 \times 80 - 3.253 \times 0 = 304.081$

(d) $F = 3.069$. Because $F < 5.14$, do not reject H_0. There is no significant dependence Y on single variables X_1 and X_2. (This is also indicated by the large *p*-values: 0.123 and 0.973). Note: If gender is deleted from the model, the relationship of diastolic blood pressure and recovery is significant.

(e) $R^2_{Y.12} = 0.506$, 50.6% of the variation can be explained by the variations in the X_1 and X_2.

(f) $R^2_{adj} = 0.311$

(g) 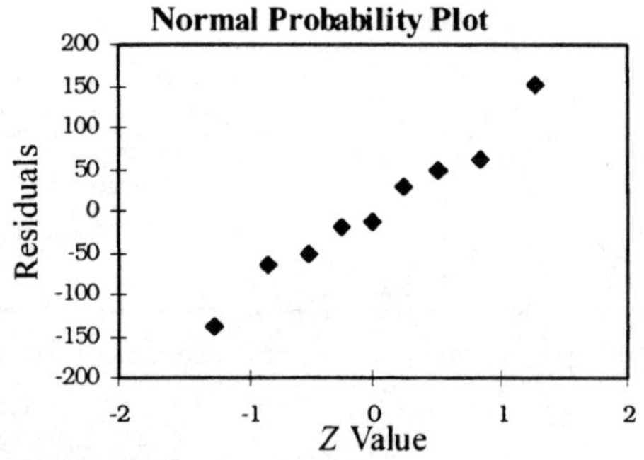

There are some doubts about the validity of the multiple linear regression model.

(h) ANOVA

	df	SS	MS	F	Significance F
Regression	2.000	57339.379	28669.689	3.069	0.121
Residual	6.000	56054.177	9342.363		
Total	8.000	113393.560			

	Coefficients	Standard Error	*t* Stat	*p*–value	Lower 95%	Upper 95%
Intercept	–572.097	405.388	–1.411	0.208	–1564.046	419.852
Diastolic	10.952	6.098	1.796	0.123	–3.970	25.875
Gender	–3.253	90.701	–0.036	0.973	–225.190	218.684

There is no significant dependence Y on single variables X_1 and X_2 Note: If gender is delete from the model, the relationship of diastolic blood pressure and recovery is significant.

(i) $P(-3.970 \le \beta_1 \le 25.875) \approx 0.95$. The confidence interval contains zero, so there is no significant linear dependence of Y on X_1 for the $1-0.95=0.05$ significance level.

$P(-225.190 \le \beta_2 \le 218.684) \approx 0.95$.

The confidence interval contains zero, so there is no significant linear dependence of Y on X_2 for the $1-0.95=0.05$ significance level.

(j) Regression Analysis

Coefficients of Partial Determination			
$\text{SSR}(X_1, X_2)$	57339.379		
SST	113393.556		
$\text{SSR}(X_2)$	27207.606	$\text{SSR}(X_1 \| X_2)$	30131.773
$\text{SSR}(X_1)$	57327.360	$\text{SSR}(X_2 \| X_1)$	12.019
$R^2_{Y1.2}$	0.350		
$R^2_{Y2.1}$	0.000		

$R^2_{Y1.2} = \dfrac{\text{SSR}(X_1|X_2)}{\text{SST} - \text{SSR}(X_1 \text{ and } X_2) + \text{SSR}(X_1|X_2)} = 0.350$, 35.0% of the variation in Y can be explained by the variation of X_1.

$R^2_{Y2.1} = \dfrac{\text{SSR}(X_2|X_1)}{\text{SST} - \text{SSR}(X_1 \text{ and } X_2) + \text{SSR}(X_2|X_1)} = 0.000$, 0.00% of the variation in Y can be explained by the variation in X_2.

(k) The slope of the diastolic blood pressure and recovery time is the same for female and male gender.

(l) Regression Analysis

Regression Statistics	
Multiple *R*	0.757
R^2	0.572
Adjusted R^2	0.316
Standard Error	98.471
Observations	9.000

ANOVA

	df	SS	MS	*F*	Significance *F*
Regression	3.000	64911.192	21637.064	2.231	0.203
Residual	5.000	48482.363	9696.473		
Total	8.000	113393.560			

	Coefficients	Standard Error	*t* Stat	*p*-value	Lower 95%	Upper 95%
Intercept	47.625	813.87363	0.0585165	0.9556039	–2044.500	2139.7504
Diastolic	1.5625	12.308834	0.1269414	0.9039338	–30.07831	33.203312
Gender	–868.2318	983.19322	–0.883073	0.4176262	–3395.606	1659.1427
Diastolic×Gender	12.599893	14.258499	0.8836760	0.4173302	–24.05268	49.252471

$H_0: \beta_3 = 0$, $H_1: \beta_3 \neq 0$, $P(-24.1 \le \beta_3 \le 49.3) \approx 0.95$. Zero belongs to this interval, so do not reject H_0 for the 0.05 significance level. There is no significant interaction between the lamp temperature and the type of ballast.

(m) Since the interaction term is not significant, and gender does not have any effect, a model that includes only diastolic blood pressure in predicting recovery time should be investigated.

36. Regression Analysis

Regression Statistics	
Multiple R	0.994
R^2	0.988
Adjusted R^2	0.985
Standard Error	15.749
Observations	15.000

ANOVA

	df	SS	MS	F	Significance F
Regression	3.000	233406.910	77802.303	313.682	6.215×10^{-11}
Residual	11.000	2728.320	248.029		
Total	14.000	236135.230			

	Coefficients	Standard Error	*t* Stat	*p*–value	Lower 95%	Upper 95%
Intercept	592.5401	14.337	41.329	2.023×10^{-13}	560.985	624.096
Temp(F)	–5.525	0.204	–27.027	2.072×10^{-11}	–5.975	–5.075
Insulation	–21.376	1.448	–14.762	1.348×10^{-8}	–24.563	–18.189
Ranch	–38.973	8.358	–4.663	0.001	–57.369	–20.576

(a) $\hat{Y}_i = 592.54012 - 5.5251009 \times X_{1i} - 21.37613 \times X_{2i} - 38.97267 \times X_{3i}$

(b) Slope –5.5251009 represents the expected change in Y per unit change in X_1 (atmospheric temperature). Slope –21.37613 represents the expected change in Y per unit change in X_2 (the amount of attic insulation). Slope –38.97267 represents the expected change in Y for ranch-style house.

(c) $\hat{Y} = 592.54012 - 5.5251009 \times 30 - 21.37613 \times 6 - 38.97267 \times 1 = 259.55764$

(d) As all p-values are less than 0.05, there is significant dependence between Y and all variables X_1, X_2, X_3.

(e) $r^2_{Y.123} = 0.9884$, 98.84% of the variation can be explained by the variations in the X_1, X_2 and X_3.

(f) $r^2_{adj} = 0.9853$

(g)

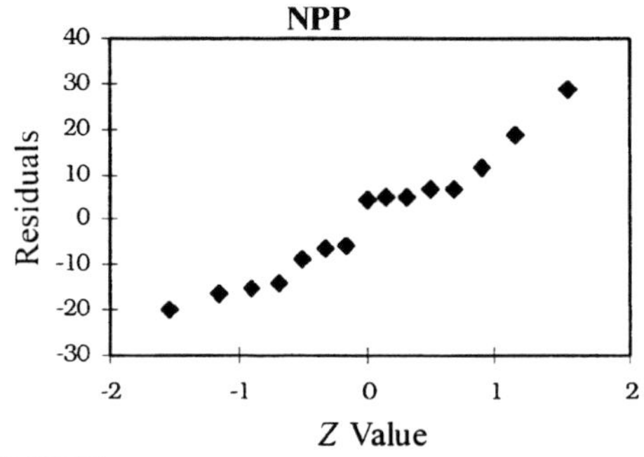

There are some doubts about the validity of the multiple linear regression model.

(h) ANOVA

	df	SS	MS	F	Significance F
Regression	3.000	233406.910	77802.303	313.682	6.215×10^{-11}
Residual	11.000	2728.320	248.029		
Total	14.000	236135.230			

	Coefficients	Standard Error	t Stat	p–value	Lower 95%	Upper 95%
Intercept	592.540	14.337	41.329	2.023×10^{-13}	560.985	624.096
Temp(F)	–5.525	0.204	–27.027	2.072×10^{-11}	–5.975	-5.075
Insulation	–21.376	1.448	–14.762	1.348×10^{-8}	–24.563	–18.189
Ranch	–38.973	8.358	–4.663	0.001	–57.369	–20.576

There is significant dependence of Y on X_1, X_2 and X_3. The multiple regression model is

$\hat{Y}_i = 592.54012 - 5.5251009\times X_{1i} - 21.37613\times X_{2i} - 38.97267\times X_{3i}$

(i) $P(-5.975051 \le \beta_1 \le -5.075151) \approx 0.95$. Confidence interval does not contain zero, so there is significant linear dependence for Y on X1 for 1 – 0.95 = 0.05 level.
$P(-24.5632 \le \beta_2 \le -18.18906) \approx 0.95$. Confidence interval does not contain zero, so there is significant linear dependence for Y on X2 for 1 – 0.95 = 0.05 level.
$P(-57.36947 \le \beta_3 \le -20.57586) \approx 0.95$. Confidence interval does not contain zero, so there is significant linear dependence for Y on X3 for 1 – 0.95 = 0.05 level.

(j) Regression Analysis

Coefficients of Partial Determination			
$SSR(X_1, X_2, X_3)$	233406.909		
SST	236135.229		
$SSR(X_2, X_3)$	52235.957		
$SSR(X_1, X_3)$	179354.881	$SSR(X_1\|X_2, X_3)$	181170.952
$SSR(X_1, X_2)$	228014.626	$SSR(X_2\|X_1, X_3)$	54052.028
$R^2_{Y1.23}$	0.985	$SSR(X_3\|X_1, X_2)$	5392.283
$R^2_{Y2.13}$	0.952		
$R^2_{Y3.12}$	0.664		

$r^2_{Y1.23} = 0.9852$, 98.52% of the variation in Y can be explained by the variation of X_1
$r^2_{Y2.13} = 0.9519$, 95.19% of the variation in Y can be explained by the variation of X_2
$r^2_{Y3.12} = 0.664$, 66.4% of the variation in Y can be explained by the variation of X_3

(k) The slope of the monthly heating oil usage is the same for ranch-stylehouses.

(l) Regression Analysis

Regression Statistics	
Multiple R	0.9966791
R^2	0.9933692
Adjusted R^2	0.9867384
Standard Error	14.955973
Observations	15

ANOVA

	df	SS	MS	F	Significance F
Regression	7	234569.46	33509.923	149.81114	4.365×10^{-7}
Residual	7	1565.7678	223.68112		
Total	14	236135.23			

	Coefficients	Standard Error	t Stat	p-value	Lower 95%	Upper 95%
Intercept	653.82318	35.212672	18.567838	3.26×10^{-7}	570.5585	737.08786
Temp(F)	−7.257971	1.0211263	−7.107809	0.0001923	−9.672549	−4.843392
Insulation	−29.42042	4.8065059	−6.120959	0.000481	−40.786	−18.05485
Ranch	−106.3888	52.849871	−2.0130389	0.0839884	−231.35884	18.581154
Temp*Ins	0.2135956	0.12571	1.6991135	0.1331003	−0.0836612	0.5108523
Temp*Ranch	1.306389	1.3506208	0.9672507	0.3656407	−1.887319	4.5000974
Ins*Ranch	8.0581928	7.0307478	1.1461359	0.289404	−8.566872	24.683258
Temp*Ins*Ranch	−0.095885	0.1868885	−0.51306	0.6237	−0.537806	0.3460357

There are no any significant interaction terms in the multiple regression models (zero belongs to the correspondence confidence intervals).

(m) Model $\hat{Y}_i = 592.54012 - 5.5251009\times X_{1i} - 21.37613\times X_{2i} - 38.97267\times X_{3i}$ is appropriate.

37. Regression Analysis

Regression Statistics	
Multiple R	0.2565
R^2	0.0658
Adjusted R^2	0.0299
Standard Error	5.5327
Observations	28.000

ANOVA

	df	SS	MS	F	Significance F
Regression	1.000	56.098	56.098	1.833	0.187
Residual	26.000	795.900	30.612		
Total	27.000	851.999			

	Coefficients	Standard Error	t Stat	p-value	Lower 95%	Upper 95%
Intercept	9.036	4.103	2.202	0.037	0.602	17.470
SQRT(Speed)	0.852	0.629	1.354	0.187	−0.442	2.146

(a) $\hat{Y}_i = 9.036 + 0.852\times\sqrt{X_i}$

(b) $\hat{Y} = 9.036 + 0.852\times\sqrt{55} = 15.355$

(c)

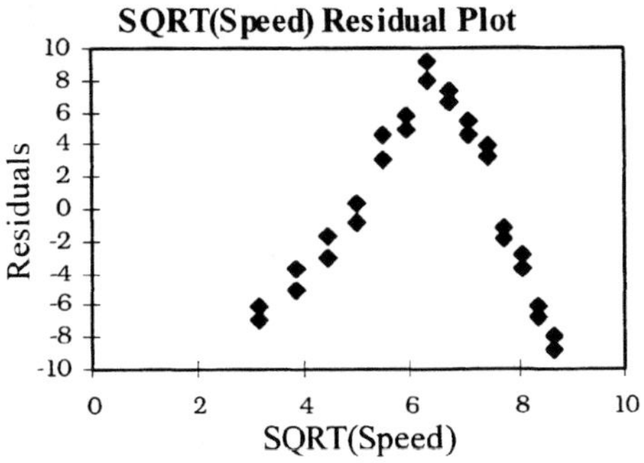

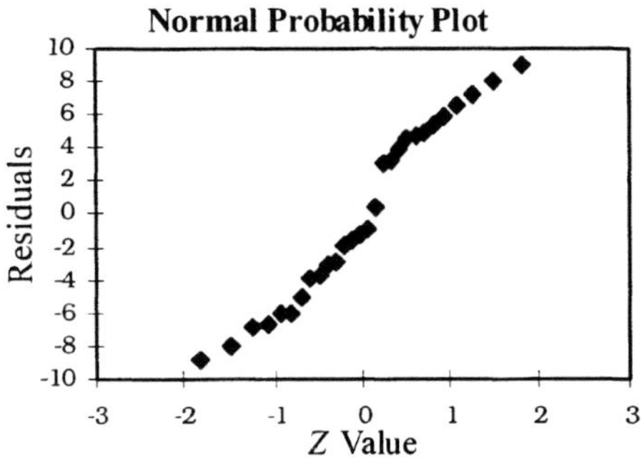

The developed regression model is not adequate.

(d) $H_0: \beta_1 = 0$, $H_1: \beta_1 \neq 0$

Decision rule: Reject H_0 if $|t| > 2.056$. Test statistic: t=1.3537. Decision: Because $|t| > 2.056$, do not reject H_0. There is no significant dependence of Y on $\sqrt{X}$ for the 0.05 significance level.

(e) $R^2 = 0.066$, 6.6% of the variation can be explained by the variation in the $\sqrt{X}$.

(f) $R^2_{adj} = 0.030$

(g) The curvilinear model $\hat{Y}_i = -7.556 + 1.272 \times X_i - 0.015 \times X_i^2$ is better than the square root model. It is significant, adequate and has a large r^2.

38. Regression Analysis

Regression Statistics	
Multiple R	0.212
R^2	0.045
Adjusted R^2	0.008
Standard Error	0.440
Observations	28.000

ANOVA

	df	SS	MS	F	Significance F
Regression	1.000	0.236	0.236	1.218	0.280
Residual	26.000	5.041	0.194		
Total	27.000	5.277			

	Coefficients	Standard Error	t Stat	p-value	Lower 95%	Upper 95%
Intercept	2.388	0.194	12.298	2.43×10^{-12}	1.989	2.787
Speed	0.005	0.004	1.104	0.280	–0.004	0.013

(a) $\ln \hat{Y}_i = 2.388 + 0.005 \times X_i$

(b) $\hat{Y} = \exp(2.388 + 0.005 \times 55) = 13.996$

(c)

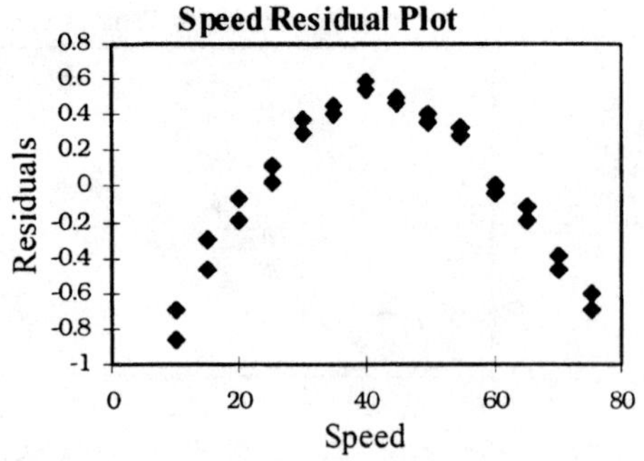

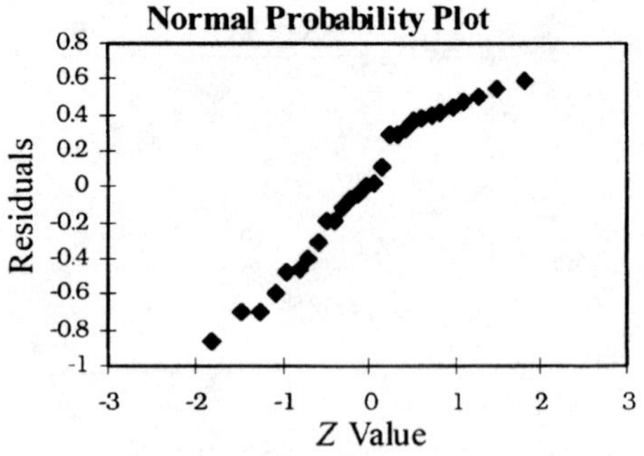

The developed regression model is not adequate.

(d) $H_0: \beta_1 = 0$, $H_1: \beta_1 \neq 0$

Due to the large p-value $0.280 > 0.05$ one must not reject H_0. There is no significant dependence in $\ln Y$ on X.

(e) $R^2 = 0.045$, 4.5% of the variation in $\ln Y$ can be explained by the variation in X.

(f) $R^2_{adj} = 0.008$

(g)

Problem	Model	R^2	Significance	Adequacy
27	$\widehat{Y}_i = -7.556 + 1.272 \times X_i - 0.015 \times X_i^2$	0.919	Yes	Yes
37	$\widehat{Y}_i = 9.036 + 0.852 \times \sqrt{X_i}$	0.066	No	No
38	$\ln \widehat{Y}_i = 2.388 + 0.005 \times X_i$	0.045	No	No

Curvilinear model $\widehat{Y}_i = -7.556 + 1.272 \times X_i - 0.015 \times X_i^2$ is better. It is significant, adequate and has a large r^2.

39. Regression Analysis

Regression Statistics	
Multiple R	0.888
R^2	0.789
Adjusted R^2	0.768
Standard Error	0.359
Observations	12.000

ANOVA

	df	SS	MS	F	Significance F
Regression	1.000	4.815	4.815	37.318	0.000
Residual	10.000	1.290	0.129		
Total	11.000	6.105			

	Coefficients	Standard Error	t Stat	p-value	Lower 95%	Upper 95%
Intercept	2.475	0.184	13.463	9.832×10^{-8}	2.065	2.885
Fertilizer	0.019	0.003	6.109	0.000	0.012	0.025

(a) $\ln \widehat{Y}_i = 2.475 + 0.019 \times X_i$

(b) $\widehat{Y} = \exp(2.475 + 0.019 \times 55) = 32.868$

(c)

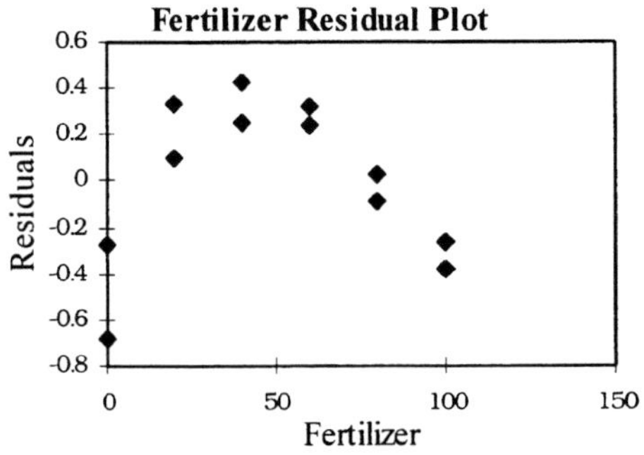

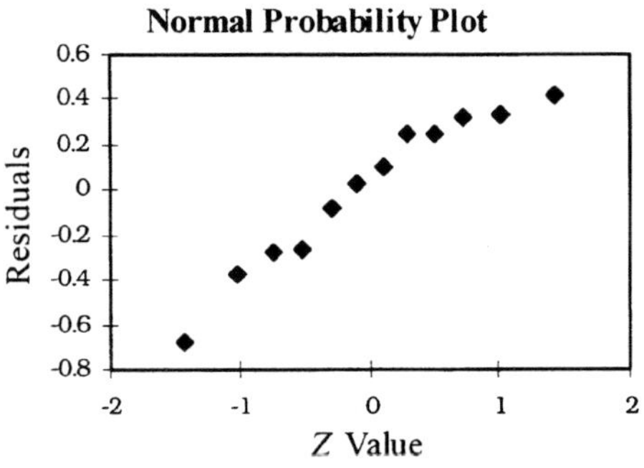

The developed regression model is not adequate

(d) $H_0\!:\beta_1 = 0$, $H_1\!:\beta_1 \neq 0$

Due to the small p-value $0.000 < 0.05$, one must reject H_0. There is significant dependence $\ln Y$ on X.

(e) $R^2 = 0.789$, 78.9% of the variation in $\ln Y$ can be explained by the variation in X.

(f) $R^2_{adj} = 0.768$

(g) The curvilinear regression model $\hat{Y}_i = 6.643 + 0.895 \times X_i - 0.004 \times X_i^2$ is significant and it has a greater r^2, so it is preferable.

40. Regression Analysis

Regression Statistics	
Multiple R	0.971
R^2	0.943
Adjusted R^2	0.937
Standard Error	4.522
Observations	12.000

ANOVA

	df	SS	MS	F	Significance F
Regression	1.000	3380.191	3380.191	165.310	1523×10^{-7}
Residual	10.000	204.476	20.448		
Total	11.000	3584.667			

	Coefficients	Standard Error	t Stat	p-value	Lower 95%	Upper 95%
Intercept	4.666	2.788	1.674	0.1251	−1.545	10.877
SQRT(Fertilizer)	5.069	0.394	12.857	1523×10^{-7}	4.190	5.947

(a) $\hat{Y}_i = 4.666 + 5.069 \times \sqrt{X_i}$

(b) $\hat{Y} = 4.666 + 5.069 \times \sqrt{55} = 42.255$

(c)

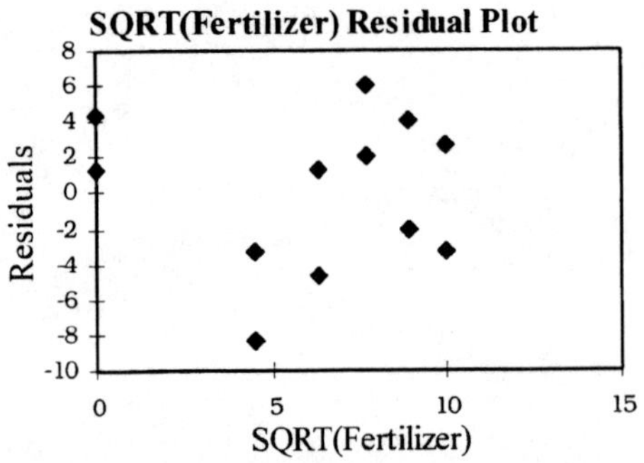

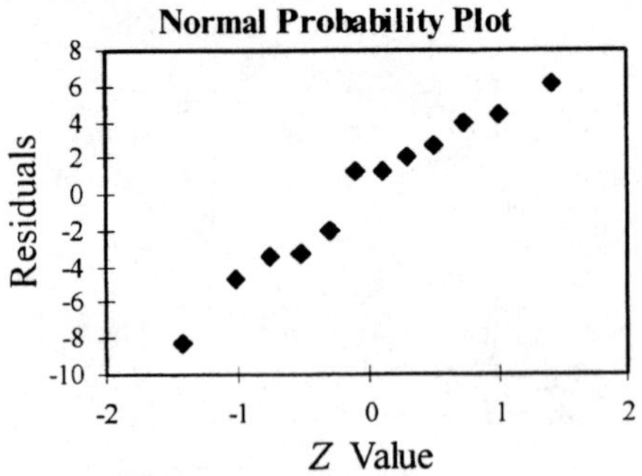

The developed regression model is not adequate

(d) $H_0: \beta_1 = 0$, $H_1: \beta_1 \neq 0$

Due to the small p-value $1.523 \times 10^{-7} < 0.05$ one must reject H_0. There is a significant dependence of Y on $\sqrt{X}$.

(e) $R^2 = 0.943$, 94.3% of the variation in Y can be explained by the variation in the $\sqrt{X}$.

(f) $R^2_{adj} = 0.937$

(g)

Problem	Model	R^2	Significance	Adequacy
29	$\hat{Y}_i = 6.643 + 0.895 \times X_i - 0.004 \times X_i^2$	0.9722	Yes	?
39	$\ln \hat{Y}_i = 2.388 + 0.005 \times X_i$	0.7887	Yes	?
40	$\hat{Y}_i = 4.666 + 5.069 \times \sqrt{X_i}$	0.943	Yes	?

All models are significant and there exists the same doubts about adequacy for each model. Based on coefficients of determination, the quadratic regression of Problem 29 should be used.

41. Summary Output: Length and all other X

Regression Statistics	
Multiple R	0.907
R^2	0.822
Adjusted R^2	0.820
Standard Error	221.697
Observations	89.000
VIF	5.629

$VIF_1 = VIF_2 = \dfrac{1}{1-R^2} = \dfrac{1}{1-0.822} = 5.629 < 10$. There is no reason to suspect the existence of collinearity.

42. Summary Output: Bark Thickness and all other X

Regression Statistics	
Multiple R	0.727
R^2	0.529
Adjusted R^2	0.504
Standard Error	32.614
Observations	21.000
VIF	2.123

$VIF_1 = VIF_2 = \dfrac{1}{1-R^2} = 2.123 < 10$. There is no reason to suspect the existence of collinearity.

43. Summary Output: Lamp Temperature and all other X

Regression Statistics	
Multiple R	0.594
R^2	0.353
Adjusted R^2	0.272
Standard Error	1.123
Observations	10.000
VIF	1.546

$VIF_1 = VIF_2 = \dfrac{1}{1-R^2} = 1.546 < 10$. There is no reason to suspect the existence of collinearity.

44. Summary Output: Soil Temperature and all other X

Regression Statistics	
Multiple R	0.056
R^2	0.003
Adjusted R^2	–0.023
Standard Error	665.618
Observations	40.000
VIF	1.003

$VIF_1 = VIF_2 = \dfrac{1}{1-R^2} = 1.003 < 10$. There is no reason to suspect the existence of collinearity.

45.

Model	Variables	$P+1$	C_p
M_1	A, B	3	4.6
M_2	A, C	3	2.4
M_3	A, B, C	4	2.7

(a) For the model that includes independent variables A and B, the values of C_p exceeds 3, the number of parameters, so this model does not meet the criterion for consideration. For the model that includes independent variables A and C, the value of C_p is less than or equal to 3, the number of parameters, so this model does meet the criterion for future consideration. For the model that includes independent variables A, B, and C the value of C_p is less than or equal to 4, the number of parameters so this model does not meet the criterion for future consideration.

(b) The inclusion of variable C in the model appears to improve the model's ability to explain variation in the dependent variable sufficiently to justify the inclusion of variable C in a model that contains only the variables A and B.

46. Stepwise Analysis: Table of Results for General Stepwise, Weight entered.

	df	SS	MS	F	Significance F
Regression	1.000	1484.545	1484.545	396.354	3.772×10^{34}
Residual	87.000	325.859	3.746		
Total	88.000	1810.404			

	Coefficients	Standard Error	t Stat	p–value	Lower 95%	Upper 95%
Intercept	47.885	1.252	38.240	3.477×10^{-56}	45.396	50.374
Weight	–0.008	0.000	–19.909	3.772×10^{-34}	–0.009	–0.007

No other variables can be entered into the model. Stepwise ends.

The developed regression model is: MPG = 47.885 − 0.008 × Weight

Best Subsets Analysis	
R^2T	0.827
$1-R^2T$	0.173
n	89.000
T	5.000
$n-T$	84.000

	C_p	$p+1$	R^2	Adj. R^2	Std. Error	Consider This Model?
X_1	2.219	2.000	0.820	0.818	1.935	No
X_1X_2	3.614	3.000	0.821	0.817	1.940	No
$X_1X_2X_3$	5.585	4.000	0.821	0.815	1.951	No
$X_1X_2X_3X_4$	5.000	5.000	0.827	0.818	1.933	Yes
$X_1X_2X_4$	3.246	4.000	0.826	0.820	1.924	Yes
X_1X_3	3.958	3.000	0.821	0.816	1.944	No
$X_1X_3X_4$	3.826	4.000	0.825	0.819	1.931	Yes
X_1X_4	1.829	3.000	0.825	0.821	1.920	Yes
X_2	94.865	2.000	0.629	0.625	2.779	No
X_2X_3	58.322	3.000	0.708	0.702	2.478	No
$X_2X_3X_4$	55.575	4.000	0.718	0.708	2.450	No
X_2X_4	94.582	3.000	0.634	0.625	2.778	No
X_3	64.987	2.000	0.690	0.687	2.538	No
X_3X_4	58.027	3.000	0.709	0.702	2.475	No
X_4	317.426	2.000	0.170	0.160	4.157	No

Adjusted r^2 criterion: r^2 reaches a maximum value of 0.821 for X_1X_4 model (weight and type of drive). C_p criterion: $p+1 \geq C_p$ for $X_1X_2X_3X_4$, $X_1X_2X_4$, $X_1X_3X_4$ and X_1X_4 models. Common subset is X_1X_4 (weight and type of drive). It is necessary to test the significance of including X_2 (width) and/or X_3 (length).

$X_1X_2X_4$ model: Regression Analysis

Regression Statistics	
Multiple R	0.909
R^2	0.826
Adjusted R^2	0.820
Standard Error	1.924
Observations	89.000

ANOVA

	df	SS	MS	F	Significance F
Regression	3.000	1495.650	498.550	134.634	3.454×10^{-32}
Residual	85.000	314.755	3.703		
Total	88.000	1810.405			

	Coefficients	Standard Error	*t* Stat	*p*-value	Lower 95%	Upper 95%
Intercept	54.530	6.398	8.523	4.991×10^{-13}	41.809	67.251
Width	–0.090	0.117	–0.767	0.445	–0.323	0.143
Type of Drive	–0.940	0.608	–1.546	0.126	–2.148	0.269
Weight	–0.008	0.001	–9.704	2.031×10^{-15}	–0.009	–0.006

Including X_2 (width) into X_1X_4 model is not significant.

$X_1X_3X_4$ model: Regression Analysis

Regression Statistics	
Multiple *R*	0.908
R^2	0.825
Adjusted R^2	0.819
Standard Error	1.931
Observations	89.000

ANOVA

	df	SS	MS	*F*	Significance *F*
Regression	3.000	1493.483	497.828	133.520	4.62×10^{-32}
Residual	85.000	316.921	3.728		
Total	88.000	1810.405			

	Coefficients	Standard Error	*t* Stat	*p*-value	Lower 95%	Upper 95%
Intercept	49.595	4.365	11.361	9.862×10^{-19}	40.916	58.275
Length	0.002	0.039	0.054	0.957	–0.076	0.081
Type of Drive	–0.957	0.655	–1.462	0.148	–2.258	0.345
Weight	–0.008	0.001	–7.504	5.568×10^{-11}	–0.010	–0.006

Including of the X_3 (length) into X_1X_4 model is not significant

$X_1X_2X_3X_4$ model: Regression Analysis

Regression Statistics	
Multiple *R*	0.909
R^2	0.827
Adjusted R^2	0.818
Standard Error	1.933
Observations	89.000

ANOVA

	df	SS	MS	*F*	Significance *F*
Regression	4.000	1496.570	374.143	100.142	3.870×10^{-31}
Residual	84.000	313.834	3.736		
Total	88.000	1810.405			

	Coefficients	Standard Error	t Stat	p–value	Lower 95%	Upper 95%
Intercept	53.991	6.518	8.284	1.638×10^{-12}	41.029	66.952
Weight	–0.008	0.001	–7.251	1.872×10^{-10}	–0.010	–0.006
Width	–0.123	0.135	–0.909	0.366	–0.392	0.146
Length	0.023	0.045	0.496	0.621	–0.068	0.113
Type of Drive	–1.074	0.668	–1.608	0.112	–2.402	0.254

Including the X_2X_3 (width and length) into X_1X_4 (weight and type of drive) model is not significant. The best subset approach result is the X_1X_4 model. We now compare the stepwise regression and best subset approach results.

X_4 model: Regression Analysis

Regression Statistics	
Multiple R	0.906
R^2	0.820
Adjusted R^2	0.818
Standard Error	1.935
Observations	89.000

ANOVA

	df	SS	MS	F	Significance F
Regression	1.000	1484.545	1484.545	396.354	3.772×10^{-34}
Residual	87.000	325.859	3.746		
Total	88.000	1810.405			

	Coefficients	Standard Error	t Stat	p–value	Lower 95%	Upper 95%
Intercept	47.885	1.252	38.240	3.477×10^{-56}	45.396	50.374
Weight	–0.008	0.000	–19.909	3.772×10^{-34}	–0.009	–0.007

X_1X_4 model: Regression Analysis

Regression Statistics	
Multiple R	0.908
R^2	0.825
Adjusted R^2	0.821
Standard Error	1.920
Observations	89.000

ANOVA

	df	SS	MS	F	Significance F
Regression	2.000	1493.472	746.736	202.628	2.865×10^{-33}
Residual	86.000	316.932	3.685		
Total	88.000	1810.405			

	Coefficients	Standard Error	t Stat	p–value	Lower 95%	Upper 95%
Intercept	49.813	1.754	28.401	1.816×10^{-45}	46.326	53.299
Type of Drive	–0.944	0.606	–1.556	0.123	–2.149	0.262
Weight	–0.008	0.000	–17.944	8.118×10^{-31}	–0.009	–0.007

Involving a drive type into the simple linear regression model $MPG = 47.885 - 0.008 \times \text{Weight}$ is not significant. Residual analysis for a model $MPG = 47.885 - 0.008 \times \text{Weight}$.

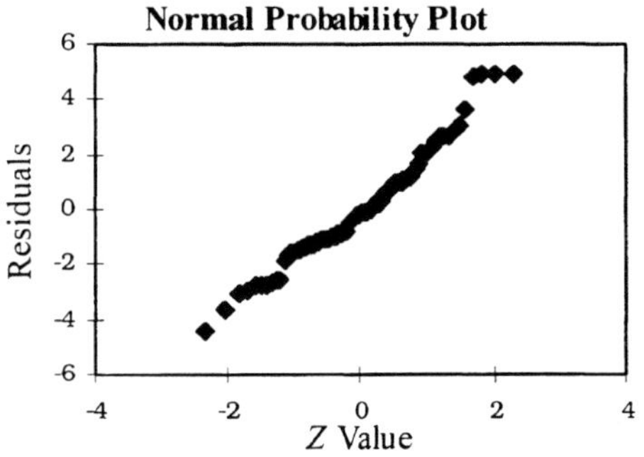

The developed regression model to predict gasoline mileage is: $MPG = 47.885 - 0.008 \times \text{Weight}$

47. Stepwise Analysis: Table of Results for General Stepwise, Diastolic entered.

	df	SS	MS	*F*	Significance *F*
Regression	1.000	57327.360	57327.360	7.157	0.032
Residual	7.000	56066.195	8009.456		
Total	8.000	113393.556			

	Coefficients	Standard Error	*t* Stat	*p*-value	Lower 95%	Upper 95%
Intercept	–562.926	291.270	–1.933	0.095	–1251.668	125.817
Diastolic	10.799	4.037	2.675	0.032	1.254	20.344

No other variables can be entered into the model. Stepwise ends.
The developed regression model is: $\text{Recovery time} = -562.926 + 10.799 \times \text{Diastolic}$

Best Subsets Analysis	
R^2T	0.510
$1 - R^2T$	0.490
n	9.000
T	5.000
$n - T$	4.000

	C_p	$p+1$	R^2	Adj. R^2	Std. Error	Consider This Model?
X_1	2.028	2.000	0.138	0.015	118.158	No
X_1X_2	2.994	3.000	0.265	0.020	117.860	Yes
$X_1X_2X_3$	4.393	4.000	0.339	−0.058	122.460	No
$X_1X_2X_3X_4$	5.000	5.000	0.510	0.019	117.918	Yes
$X_1X_2X_4$	3.016	4.000	0.508	0.212	105.677	Yes
X_1X_3	2.625	3.000	0.310	0.080	114.175	Yes
$X_1X_3X_4$	3.000	4.000	0.510	0.215	105.469	Yes
X_1X_4	1.016	3.000	0.508	0.343	96.472	Yes
X_2	1.198	2.000	0.240	0.131	110.961	Yes
X_2X_3	2.975	3.000	0.267	0.023	117.674	Yes
$X_2X_3X_4$	3.031	4.000	0.506	0.209	105.881	Yes
X_2X_4	1.031	3.000	0.506	0.341	96.656	Yes
X_3	2.353	2.000	0.098	−0.030	120.856	No
X_3X_4	1.032	3.000	0.506	0.341	96.666	Yes
X_4	−0.968	2.000	0.506	0.435	89.496	Yes

Adjusted r^2 criterion: r^2 reaches a maximum value of 0.4349269 for X_4 model (diastolic). C_p criterion: $p+1 \geq C_p$ for all models except X_1, X_3 and $X_1X_2X_3$.

Summary Output: X_2

Regression Statistics	
Multiple R	0.490
R^2	0.240
Adjusted R^2	0.131
Standard Error	110.961
Observations	9.000

ANOVA

	df	SS	MS	F	Significance F
Regression	1.000	27207.610	27207.610	2.210	0.181
Residual	7.000	86185.950	12312.280		
Total	8.000	113393.600			

	Coefficients	Standard Error	t Stat	p–value	Lower 95%	Upper 95%
Intercept	150.750	55.480	2.717	0.030	19.560	281.940
Gender	110.650	74.435	1.487	0.181	−65.360	286.660

Simple linear regression of the recovery time on gender is not significant.

Summary Output: X_4

Regression Statistics	
Multiple R	0.711
R^2	0.506
Adjusted R^2	0.435
Standard Error	89.496
Observations	9.000

ANOVA

	df	SS	MS	F	Significance F
Regression	1.000	57327.360	57327.360	7.157	0.032
Residual	7.000	56066.200	8009.456		
Total	8.000	113393.600			

	Coefficients	Standard Error	t Stat	p–value	Lower 95%	Upper 95%
Intercept	–562.926	291.270	–1.933	0.095	–1251.670	125.817
Diastolic	10.799	4.037	2.675	0.032	1.254	20.344

For a 0.05 significance level simple linear regression of the recovery time on diastolic is significant.

Summary Output: X_1X_2

Regression Statistics	
Multiple R	0.515
R^2	0.265
Adjusted R^2	0.0200
Standard Error	117.860
Observations	9.000

ANOVA

	df	SS	MS	F	Significance F
Regression	2.000	30047.810	15023.910	1.082	0.397
Residual	6.000	83345.740	13890.960		
Total	8.000	113393.600			

	Coefficients	Standard Error	t Stat	p–value	Lower 95%	Upper 95%
Intercept	–288.016	972.128	–0.296	0.777	–2666.730	2090.698
Age	21.403	47.334	0.452	0.667	–94.418	137.225
Gender	91.387	89.809	1.018	0.348	–128.369	311.143

The multiple regression of the recovery time on age and gender is not significant.

Summary Output: X_1X_3

Regression Statistics	
Multiple R	0.557
R^2	0.310
Adjusted R^2	0.080
Standard Error	114.175
Observations	9.000

ANOVA

	df	SS	MS	F	Significance F
Regression	2.000	35177.390	17588.700	1.349	0.328
Residual	6.000	78216.160	13036.030		
Total	8.000	113393.600			

	Coefficients	Standard Error	t Stat	p–value	Lower 95%	Upper 95%
Intercept	–1925.910	1302.449	–1.479	0.190	–5112.890	1261.073
Age	56.452	41.581	1.358	0.223	–45.293	158.197
Systolic	8.135	6.649	1.223	0.267	–8.135	24.404

The multiple regression of the recovery time on age and systolic is not significant.

Summary Output: X_1X_4

Regression Statistics	
Multiple R	0.712
R^2	0.508
Adjusted R^2	0.343
Standard Error	96.472
Observations	9.000

ANOVA

	df	SS	MS	F	Significance F
Regression	2.000	57552.820	28776.410	3.092	0.119
Residual	6.000	55840.740	9306.790		
Total	8.000	113393.600			

	Coefficients	Standard Error	t Stat	p–value	Lower 95%	Upper 95%
Intercept	–460.855	727.084	–0.634	0.550	–2239.970	1318.257
Age	–6.483	41.656	–0.156	0.881	–108.412	95.445
Diastolic	11.274	5.314	2.122	0.078	–1.729	24.277

The multiple regression of the recovery time on age and diastolic is not significant.

Summary Output: X_2X_3

Regression Statistics	
Multiple R	0.517
R^2	0.267
Adjusted R^2	0.023
Standard Error	117.674
Observations	9.000

ANOVA

	df	SS	MS	F	Significance F
Regression	2.000	30310.300	15155.150	1.094	0.393
Residual	6.000	83083.260	13847.210		
Total	8.000	113393.600			

	Coefficients	Standard Error	*t* Stat	*p*–value	Lower 95%	Upper 95%
Intercept	–231.519	809.711	–0.286	0.785	–2212.810	1749.774
Gender	98.019	83.327	1.176	0.284	–105.875	301.912
Systolic	3.324	7.022	0.473	0.653	–13.859	20.507

The multiple regression of the recovery time on gender and systolic is not significant.
Summary Output: X_2X_4

Regression Statistics	
Multiple *R*	0.711
R^2	0.506
Adjusted R^2	0.341
Standard Error	96.656
Observations	9.000

ANOVA

	df	SS	MS	*F*	Significance *F*
Regression	2.000	57339.380	28669.690	3.068	0.121
Residual	6.000	56054.180	9342.363		
Total	8.000	113393.600			

	Coefficients	Standard Error	*t* Stat	*p*–value	Lower 95%	Upper 95%
Intercept	–572.097	405.388	–1.411	0.208	–1564.050	419.852
Gender	–3.253	90.701	–0.036	0.973	–225.190	218.684
Diastolic	10.952	6.098	1.796	0.123	–3.970	25.875

The multiple regression of the recovery time on gender and diastolic is not significant.
Summary Output: X_3X_4

Regression Statistics	
Multiple *R*	0.711
R^2	0.506
Adjusted R^2	0.341
Standard Error	96.666
Observations	9.000

ANOVA

	df	SS	MS	*F*	Significance *F*
Regression	2.000	57328.110	28664.050	3.068	0.121
Residual	6.000	56065.450	9344.241		
Total	8.000	113393.600			

	Coefficients	Standard Error	*t* Stat	*p*–value	Lower 95%	Upper 95%
Intercept	–557.926	641.600	–0.870	0.418	–2127.870	1012.014
Systolic	–0.055	6.100	–0.009	0.993	–14.980	14.871
Diastolic	10.819	4.867	2.223	0.068	–1.089	22.727

The multiple regression of the recovery time on systolic and diastolic is not significant.

Summary Output: $X_1X_2X_4$

Regression Statistics	
Multiple R	0.712
R^2	0.508
Adjusted R^2	0.212
Standard Error	105.677
Observations	9.000

ANOVA

	df	SS	MS	F	Significance F
Regression	3.000	57555.410	19185.140	1.718	0.278
Residual	5.000	55838.150	11167.630		
Total	8.000	113393.600			

	Coefficients	Standard Error	t Stat	p–value	Lower 95%	Upper 95%
Intercept	–466.518	879.031	–0.531	0.618	–2726.130	1793.098
Age	–6.396	45.989	–0.139	0.895	–124.614	111.822
Gender	–1.522	99.944	–0.015	0.988	–258.437	255.393
Diastolic	11.339	7.225	1.569	0.177	–7.233	29.912

The multiple regression of the recovery time on age, gender and diastolic is not significant.

Summary Output: $X_1X_3X_4$

Regression Statistics	
Multiple R	0.714
R^2	0.510
Adjusted R^2	0.215
Standard Error	105.469
Observations	9.000

ANOVA

	df	SS	MS	F	Significance F
Regression	3.000	57774.630	19258.210	1.731	0.276
Residual	5.000	55618.920	11123.780		
Total	8.000	113393.600			

	Coefficients	Standard Error	t Stat	p–value	Lower 95%	Upper 95%
Intercept	–251.612	1681.510	–0.150	0.887	–4574.060	4070.840
Age	–12.361	61.695	–0.200	0.849	–170.953	146.232
Systolic	–1.273	9.016	–0.141	0.893	–24.450	21.903
Diastolic	12.156	8.529	1.4253	0.213	–9.768	34.079

The multiple regression of the recovery time on age, systolic and diastolic is not significant.

Summary Output: $X_2X_3X_4$

Regression Statistics	
Multiple R	0.711
R^2	0.506
Adjusted R^2	0.209
Standard Error	105.880
Observations	9.000

ANOVA

	df	SS	MS	F	Significance F
Regression	3.000	57340.040	19113.350	1.705	0.281
Residual	5.000	56053.520	11210.700		
Total	8.000	113393.600			

	Coefficients	Standard Error	t Stat	p–value	Lower 95%	Upper 95%
Intercept	–567.365	759.988	–0.746	0.489	–2520.970	1386.242
Gender	–3.242	99.368	–0.033	0.975	–258.676	252.192
Systolic	–0.051	6.682	–0.008	0.994	–17.228	17.125
Diastolic	10.970	7.065	1.553	0.181	–7.191	29.130

The multiple regression of the recovery time on gender, systolic and diastolic is not significant.
Summary Output: $X_1X_2X_3X_4$

Regression Statistics	
Multiple R	0.714
R^2	0.510
Adjusted R^2	0.019
Standard Error	117.918
Observations	9.000

ANOVA

	df	SS	MS	F	Significance F
Regression	4.000	57774.800	14443.700	1.039	0.486
Residual	4.000	55618.750	13904.690		
Total	8.000	113393.600			

	Coefficients	Standard Error	t Stat	p–value	Lower 95%	Upper 95%
Intercept	–249.379	1987.529	–0.125	0.906	–5767.660	5268.898
Age	–12.405	70.155	–0.177	0.868	–207.187	182.377
Gender	0.390	112.555	0.003	0.997	–312.114	312.893
Systolic	–1.278	10.174	–0.126	0.906	–29.525	26.9688
Diastolic	12.142	10.290	1.180	0.303	–16.426	40.7110

The multiple regression of the recovery time on age, gender, systolic and diastolic is not significant. There is only one significant regression model , X_4. Residual analysis:

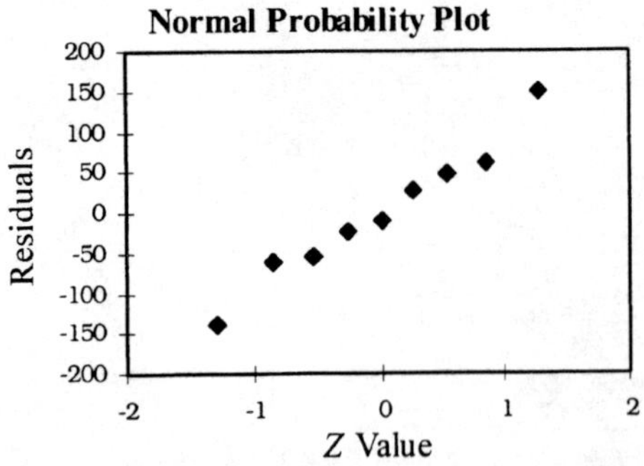

The developed regression model is:
Recovery time = $-562.926 + 10.799 \times$ Diastolic

48. Stepwise Analysis: Table of Results for General Stepwise, COD entered.

	df	SS	MS	*F*	Significance *F*
Regression	1.000	782273.430	782273.430	19.428	0.000
Residual	33.000	1328774.400	40265.892		
Total	34.000	2111047.900			

	Coefficients	Standard Error	*t* Stat	*p*–value	Lower 95%	Upper 95%
Intercept	1322.903	90.126	14.678	5.038×10^{-16}	1139.542	1506.265
COD	3.525	0.800	4.408	0.000	1.898	5.152

Conductivity entered.

	df	SS	MS	*F*	Significance *F*
Regression	2.000	949959.380	474979.690	13.091	7.013×10^{-5}
Residual	32.000	1161088.500	36284.016		
Total	34.000	2111047.900			

	Coefficients	Standard Error	*t* Stat	*p*–value	Lower 95%	Upper 95%
Intercept	876.229	224.703	3.900	0.000	418.525	1333.933
COD	2.542	0.886	2.867	0.007	0.736	4.347
Conductivity	0.229	0.106	2.150	0.039	0.012	0.445

No other variables can be entered into the model. Stepwise ends.
Developed regression model is: TDS = $876.229 + 2.542 \times COD + 0.229 \times$ Conductivity

Best Subsets Analysis	
R^2T	0.470
$1 - R^2T$	0.530
n	35.000
T	4.000
$n - T$	31.000

	C_p	$p+1$	R^2	Adj. R^2	Std. Error	Consider This Model?
X_1	27.417	2.000	0.001	–0.030	252.843	No
X_1X_2	10.600	3.000	0.323	0.280	211.403	No
$X_1X_2X_3$	4.000	4.000	0.470	0.418	190.038	Yes
X_1X_3	7.109	3.000	0.382	0.344	201.870	No
X_2	9.411	2.000	0.309	0.288	210.295	No
X_2X_3	3.150	3.000	0.450	0.416	190.484	No
X_3	5.794	2.000	0.371	0.351	200.664	No

Adjusted R^2 criterion: R^2 reaches a maximum value of 0.418 for $X_1X_2X_3$ model. C_p criterion: $p+1 \geq C_p$ only for $X_1X_2X_3$ model.

Summary Output: $X_1X_2X_3$

Regression Statistics	
Multiple R	0.685
R^2	0.470
Adjusted R^2	0.418
Standard Error	190.038
Observations	35.000

ANOVA

	df	SS	MS	F	Significance F
Regression	3.000	991504.900	330501.600	9.152	0.000
Residual	31.000	1119543.000	36114.290		
Total	34.000	2111048.000			

	Coefficients	Standard Error	t Stat	p–value	Lower 95%	Upper 95%
Intercept	1796.256	886.594	2.026	0.051	–11.966	3604.478
pH	–142.190	132.571	–1.073	0.292	–412.570	128.190
Conductivity	0.241	0.107	2.260	0.031	0.024	0.459
COD	2.598	0.886	2.933	0.006	0.791	4.405

There is no significant dependence of the TDS on pH in this model for the 0.05 significance level.

Summary Output: X_2X_3

Regression Statistics	
Multiple R	0.671
R^2	0.450
Adjusted R^2	0.416
Standard Error	190.484
Observations	35.000

ANOVA

	df	SS	MS	F	Significance F
Regression	2.000	949959.400	474979.700	13.091	7.01×10^{-5}
Residual	32.000	1161089.000	36284.020		
Total	34.000	2111048.000			

	Coefficients	Standard Error	*t* Stat	*p*–value	Lower 95%	Upper 95%
Intercept	876.229	224.703	3.900	0.000	418.526	1333.933
Conductivity	0.229	0.106	2.150	0.039	0.012	0.445
COD	2.542	0.886	2.867	0.007	0.736	4.347

This is a significant regression of TDS on Conductivity and COD; the same as is noted in the stepwise procedure.

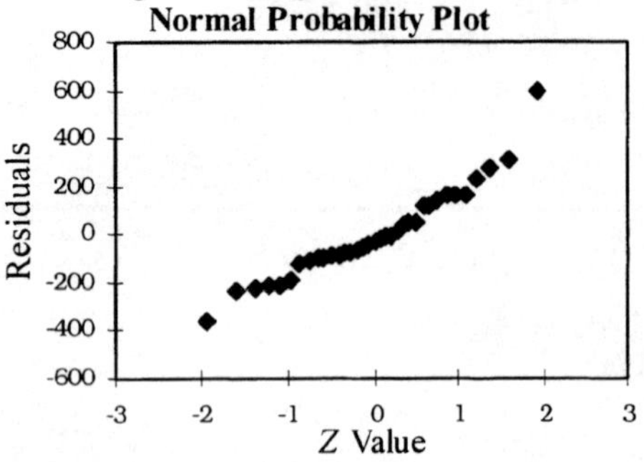

The developed regression model is:

$$\text{TDS} = 876.229 + 2.542 \times \text{COD} + 0.229 \times \text{Conductivity}$$

49. Type of school: 5 for public, 15 for private.
Stepwise Analysis: Table of Results for General Stepwise, Type of School entered.

	df	SS	MS	*F*	Significance *F*
Regression	1.000	1928.628	1928.628	184.553	2.958×10^{-22}
Residual	78.000	815.122	10.450		
Total	79.000	2743.750			

	Coefficients	Standard Error	*t* Stat	*p*–value	Lower 95%	Upper 95%
Intercept	14.160	0.590	23.992	9.46×10^{-38}	12.985	15.335
Type of School	10.142	0.747	13.585	2.958×10^{-22}	8.656	11.628

Average Total SAT entered.

	df	SS	MS	*F*	Significance *F*
Regression	2.000	2176.002	1088.001	147.559	4557×10^{-27}
Residual	77.000	567.748	7.373		
Total	79.000	2743.750			

	Coefficients	Standard Error	*t* Stat	*p*–value	Lower 95%	Upper 95%
Intercept	–3.467	3.083	–1.124	0.264	–9.607	2.673
Type of School	8.128	0.717	11.337	4.37×10^{-18}	6.701	9.556
Average Total SAT	0.016	0.003	5.792	1.436×10^{-7}	0.011	0.022

Room and Board entered.

	df	SS	MS	*F*	Significance *F*
Regression	3.000	2276.455	758.818	123.413	3.931×10^{-29}
Residual	76.000	467.295	6.149		
Total	79.000	2743.750			

	Coefficients	Standard Error	*t* Stat	*p*–value	Lower 95%	Upper 95%
Intercept	–9.615	3.200	–3.004	0.004	–15.989	–3.241
Type of School	5.912	0.854	6.922	1.233×10^{-9}	4.211	7.613
Average Total SAT	0.017	0.003	6.578	5.406×10^{-9}	0.012	0.022
Room and Board	1.200	0.297	4.042	0.000	0.609	1.791

TOEFL Score entered.

	df	SS	MS	*F*	Significance *F*
Regression	4.000	2342.712	585.678	109.530	1.586×10^{-30}
Residual	75.000	401.038	5.347		
Total	79.000	2743.750			

	Coefficients	Standard Error	*t* Stat	*p*–value	Lower 95%	Upper 95%
Intercept	–7.786	3.029	–2.570	0.012	–13.820	–1.751
Type of School	6.096	0.798	7.637	5.836×10^{-11}	4.506	7.686
Average Total SAT	0.014	0.003	5.397	7.612×10^{-7}	0.009	0.019
Room and Board	1.134	0.277	4.086	0.000	0.581	1.686
TOEFL Score	2.519	0.716	3.520	0.001	1.093	3.945

Developed regression model is:

$$\text{Annual total cost} = -7.786 + 6.096\times\text{Type of School} + 0.014\times\text{Average Total SAT} + 1.134 \times\text{Room and Board} + 2.512\times\text{TOEFL Score}$$

Best Subsets Analysis	
R^2T	0.854
$1-R^2T$	0.146
n	80.000
T	5.000
$n-T$	75.000

	C_p	$p+1$	R^2	Adj. R^2	Std. Error	Consider This Model?
X_1	207.397	2.000	0.448	0.441	4.408	No
X_1X_2	68.480	3.000	0.722	0.715	3.146	No
$X_1X_2X_3$	15.391	4.000	0.830	0.823	2.480	No
$X_1X_2X_3X_4$	5.000	5.000	0.854	0.846	2.312	Yes
$X_1X_2X_4$	61.325	4.000	0.740	0.730	3.063	No
X_1X_3	32.177	3.000	0.793	0.788	2.715	No
$X_1X_3X_4$	19.698	4.000	0.821	0.814	2.540	No
X_1X_4	197.707	3.000	0.470	0.457	4.344	No
X_2	189.124	2.000	0.483	0.477	4.263	No
X_2X_3	63.153	3.000	0.733	0.726	3.086	No
$X_2X_3X_4$	32.132	4.000	0.797	0.789	2.707	No
X_2X_4	145.979	3.000	0.571	0.560	3.908	No
X_3	76.440	2.000	0.703	0.699	3.233	No
X_3X_4	43.546	3.000	0.771	0.765	2.857	No
X_4	359.373	2.000	0.152	0.141	5.463	No

Adjusted R^2 criterion: R^2 reaches a maximum value of 0.846 for the $X_1X_2X_3X_4$ model. C_p criterion: $p+1 \geq C_p$ only for $X_1X_2X_3X_4$ model.

Summary Output: $X_1X_2X_3X_4$

Regression Statistics	
Multiple R	0.924
R^2	0.854
Adjusted R^2	0.846
Standard Error	2.312
Observations	80.000

ANOVA

	df	SS	MS	F	Significance F
Regression	4.000	2342.712	585.678	109.530	1.59×10^{-30}
Residual	75.000	401.038	5.347		
Total	79.000	2743.750			

	Coefficients	Standard Error	t Stat	p-value	Lower 95%	Upper 95%
Intercept	−7.786	3.029	−2.570	0.012	−13.820	−1.751
Average Total SAT	0.014	0.003	5.397	7.61×10^{-7}	0.009	0.019
Room and Board	1.134	0.277	4.086	0.000	0.581	1.686
Type of School	6.096	0.798	7.637	5.84×10^{-11}	4.506	7.686
TOEFL Score	2.519	0.716	3.520	0.001	1.093	3.945

The only significant model is the regression of the annual total cost on all other parameters. The same was found in the stepwise procedure.

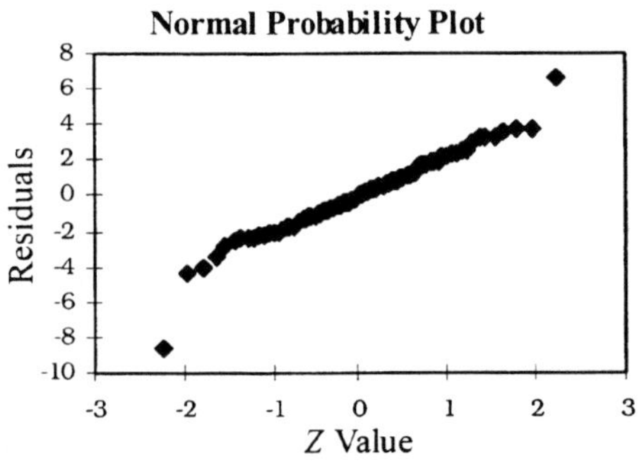

The developed regression model is:

Annual total cost $= -7.786 + 6.096 \times$ Type of School $+0.014 \times$ Average Total SAT $+ 1.134 \times$Room and Board $+ 2.512 \times$TOEFL Score

50. In the multiple regression model $Y_i = \beta_0 + \sum_{k=1}^{p} \beta_k X_{li} + \varepsilon_i$. Coefficient β_k is a slope of Y with variable X_k holding all other variables X_m constant.

51. Testing of the entire model's significance means testing of the hypothesis that *Y* depends on *X*'s at least in one term. The *F* test is used for testing of this hypothesis. Testing of the significant contribution of the particular variable X_k means testing of the hypothesis $H_0: \beta_k = 0$ versus $H_1: \beta_k \neq 0$. The *t* test is appropriate for this problem.

52. The coefficients of partial determination measure the proportion of the variation in the dependent variable that is explained by each explanatory variable while holding constant all other explanatory variables. The coefficient of multiple determination measures the proportion of variation in the dependent variable that is explained by variation in the explanatory variables.

53. Dummy variables are used in shift regression models. The use of dummy variables permits us to consider categorical explanatory variables as part of the regression model. If a given categorical explanatory variable has two categories, then the corresponding binary dummy variable indicates that it belongs to one fixed category.

54. It is necessary to include the interaction term into the regression model. If this term makes no significant contribution to a regression model that contains single variables, then one can assume that the slope of an independent variable with the response variable is the same for each level of the dummy variable.

55. It makes it possible to study the common linear regression model $f(Y_i) = \beta_0 + \sum_{k=1}^{p} \beta_k g(X_{ki}) + \varepsilon_i$, where the values ε_i are independent identically distributed gaussian random values.

56. For measuring collinearity it is possible to use the variance inflationary factor (VIF) for each explanatory variable. If a set of explanatory variables is uncorrelated, then the VIF will be equal to 1. If the set is highly intercorrelated, then the VIF might even exceed 10.

57. Dummy variables are used in shift regression models. The use of dummy variables is the mechanism that permits us to consider categorical explanatory variables as part of the regression model.

58. Slopes of all explanatory variables with the dependent variable must be the same for various levels of categorical variable.

59. *The Stepwise regression* procedure attempts to find the "best" regression model without examining all possible regressions. Once a best model has been found, residual analysis is utilized to evaluate the aptness of the model. (At each step of the model–building process, variables are either added to or deleted from the regression model. The stepwise procedure terminates with the selection of a best-fitting model, when no variables can be added to or deleted from the last model fitted.) *The best subset approach* evaluates either all possible regression models for a given set of independent variables or at least the best subset of models for a given number of independent variables. (In this procedure, the entire set of multiple regression models is divided into two parts and the "best" models are marked for further studying.)

60. One should determine a common subset of variables for all "best" models and then test whether the contribution of the additional variables is significant. If two models have the same quality of regression characteristics, one must choose a model with fewer independent variables.

61. Regression Analysis

Regression Statistics	
Multiple R	0.785
R^2	0.616
Adjusted R^2	0.571
Standard Error	122.144
Observations	20.000

ANOVA

	df	**SS**	**MS**	***F***	**Significance *F***
Regression	2.000	406962.030	203481.020	13.639	0.000
Residual	17.000	253626.520	14919.207		
Total	19.000	660588.550			

	Coefficients	**Standard Error**	***t* Stat**	***p*–value**	**Lower 95%**	**Upper 95%**
Intercept	–1806.474	934.749	–1.933	0.070	–3778.625	165.678
Thickness	7.921	3.658	2.165	0.045	0.202	15.639
Hardness	2.738	0.582	4.708	0.000	1.511	3.965

(a) $\hat{Y}_i = -1806.474 + 7.921 \times X_{1i} + 2.738 \times X_{2i}$

(b) The slope 7.921 represents the expected change in Y per unit change in X_1. The slope 2.738 represents the expected change in Y per unit change in X_2.

(c) $\hat{Y} = -1806.474 + 7.921 \times 275 + 2.738 \times 350 = 1330$

(d)

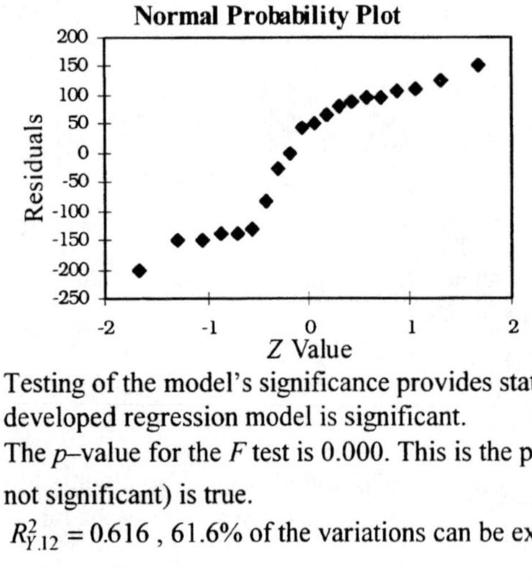

There are some doubts about the validity of the multiple linear regression model.

(e) Testing of the model's significance provides statistic $F = 13.639$, its significance level is $0.000 < 0.05$, so the developed regression model is significant.

(*f*) The *p*–value for the *F* test is 0.000. This is the probability of obtaining $F \geq 13.639$ when H_0 (regression model is not significant) is true.

(g) $R^2_{Y.12} = 0.616$, 61.6% of the variations can be explained by the variations in the X_1 and X_2.

(h) $R^2_{adj} = 0.571$

(i)

	Coefficients	Standard Error	*t* Stat	*p*–value	Lower 95%	Upper 95%
Intercept	–1806.474	934.749	–1.933	0.070	–3778.625	165.678
Thickness	7.921	3.658	2.165	0.045	0.202	15.639
Hardness	2.738	0.582	4.708	0.000	1.511	3.965

$P(0.202 \le \beta_1 \le 15.639) \approx 0.95$. The confidence interval does not contain zero, so there is a significant linear dependence of *Y* on X_1 for the $1-0.95=0.05$ significance level.

$P(1.511 \le \beta_2 \le 3.965) \approx 0.95$. The confidence interval does not contain zero, so there is significant linear dependence of *Y* on X_2 for the $1-0.95=0.05$ significance level.

(j) *p*-value 0.045 is a probability of obtaining $|t| \ge 2.165$ when H_0 (there is no significant linear dependence of *Y* on X_1) is true.

p-value 0.000 is a probability of obtaining $|t| \ge 4.708$ when H_0 (there is no significant linear dependence of *Y* on X_2) is true.

(k) $P(0.202 \le \beta_1 \le 15.639) \approx 0.95$, $P(1.511 \le \beta_2 \le 3.965) \approx 0.95$

(l) Regression Analysis

Coefficients of Partial Determination			
SSR(X_1, X_2)	406962.031		
SST	660588.550		
SSR(X_2)	337028.451	SSR(X_1|X_2)	69933.580
SSR(X_1)	76220.431	SSR(X_2|X_1)	330741.601
$R^2_{Y1.2}$	0.216		
$R^2_{Y2.1}$	0.566		

$R^2_{Y1.2} = \dfrac{\text{SSR}(X_1|X_2)}{\text{SST}-\text{SSR}(X_1 \text{ and } X_2)+\text{SSR}(X_1|X_2)} = 0.216$, 21.6% of the variation in *Y* can be explained by the variation of X_1. $R^2_{Y2.1} = \dfrac{\text{SSR}(X_2|X_1)}{\text{SST}-\text{SSR}(X_1 \text{ and } X_2)+\text{SSR}(X_2|X_1)} = 0.566$, 56.6% of the variation in *Y* can be explained by the variation of X_2.

62. Regression Analysis

Regression Statistics	
Multiple *R*	0.804
R^2	0.646
Adjusted R^2	0.592
Standard Error	94.483
Observations	16.000

ANOVA

	df	SS	MS	*F*	Significance *F*
Regression	2.000	211905.000	105952.500	11.869	0.001
Residual	13.000	116050.750	8926.981		
Total	15.000	327955.750			

	Coefficients	Standard Error	*t* Stat	*p*–value	Lower 95%	Upper 95%
Intercept	431.625	102.960	4.192	0.001	209.193	654.056
Calcium	0.912	0.189	4.826	0.000	0.504	1.320
Boron	–6.300	9.448	–0.667	0.517	–26.712	14.112

(a) $\hat{Y}_i = 431.625 + 0.912 \times X_{1i} - 6.3 \times X_{2i}$

(b) The slope equal to 0.912 represents the expected change in Y per unit change in X_1. The slope equal to –6.3 represents the expected change in Y per unit change in X_2.

(c) $\hat{Y} = 431.625 + 0.912 \times 250 - 6.3 \times 10 = 596.625$

(d)

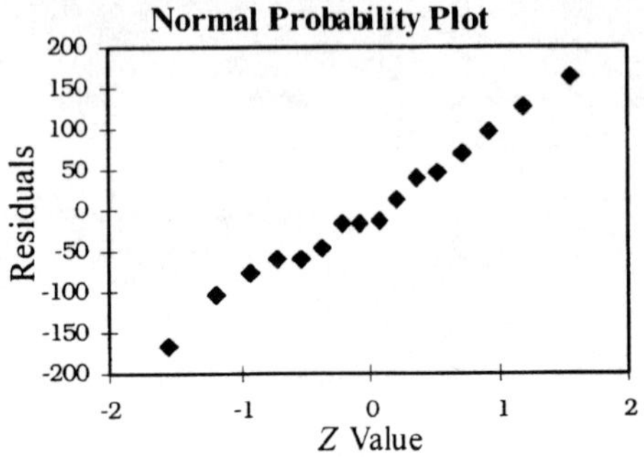

The multiple linear regression model appears to be adequate.

(e) Testing of the model's significance provides statistic $F = 11.869$, its significance level is $0.001 < 0.05$, so the developed regression model is significant.

(*f*) the *p*-value for the *F* test is 0.001. This is the probability of obtaining $F \geq 11.869$ when H_0 is true.

(g) $R^2_{Y.12} = 0.646$, 64.6% of the variation can be explained by the variations in the X_1 and X_2.

(h) $R^2_{adj} = 0.592$

(i)

	Coefficients	Standard Error	*t* Stat	*p*–value	Lower 95%	Upper 95%
Intercept	431.625	102.960	4.192	0.001	209.193	654.056
Calcium	0.912	0.189	4.826	0.000	0.504	1.320
Boron	–6.300	9.448	–0.667	0.517	–26.712	14.112

$P(0.504 \leq \beta_1 \leq 1.320) \approx 0.95$. The confidence interval does not contain zero, so there is a significant linear dependence of *Y* on X_1 for the $1 - 0.95 = 0.05$ significance level.

$P(-26.712 \leq \beta_2 \leq 14.112) \approx 0.95$. The confidence interval contains zero, so there is no significant linear dependence of *Y* on X_2 for the $1 - 0.95 = 0.05$ significance level.

(j) The *p*-value 0.000 is the probability of obtaining $|t| \geq 4.826$ when H_0 (there is no significant linear dependence of *Y* on X_1) is true. The *p*-value 0.517 is a probability of obtaining $|t| \geq 0.667$ when H_0 (there is no significant linear dependence of *Y* on X_2) is true.

(k) $P(0.504 \leq \beta_1 \leq 1.320) \approx 0.95$, $P(-26.712 \leq \beta_2 \leq 14.112) \approx 0.95$

(l) Regression Analysis

Coefficients of Partial Determination			
SSR(X_1, X_2)	211905.000		
SST	327955.750		
SSR(X_2)	3969.000	SSR($X_1 \mid X_2$)	207936.000
SSR(X_1)	207936.000	SSR($X_2 \mid X_1$)	3969.000
$R^2_{Y1.2}$	0.642		
$R^2_{Y2.1}$	0.033		

$R^2_{Y1.2} = \dfrac{\text{SSR}(X_1|X_2)}{\text{SST} - \text{SSR}(X_1 \text{ and } X_2) + \text{SSR}(X_1|X_2)} = 0.642$, 64.2% of the variation in Y can be explained by the variation of X_1. $R^2_{Y2.1} = \dfrac{\text{SSR}(X_2|X_1)}{\text{SST} - \text{SSR}(X_1 \text{ and } X_2) + \text{SSR}(X_2|X_1)} = 0.033$, 3.3% of the variation in Y can be explained by the variation of X_2.

63. Stepwise Analysis: Table of Results for General Stepwise, SiO_2 entered.

	df	SS	MS	*F*	Significance *F*
Regression	1.000	4774289.700	4774289.700	76.241	5.315×10^{-15}
Residual	146.000	9142718.800	62621.362		
Total	147.000	13917008.000			

	Coefficients	Standard Error	*t* Stat	*p*-value	Lower 95%	Upper 95%
Intercept	119.478	24.182	4.941	2.106×10^{-6}	71.685	167.271
SiO_2	42.880	4.911	8.732	$5.315 \times 10^{-1}5$	33.174	52.585

Type entered.

	df	SS	MS	*F*	Significance *F*
Regression	2.000	6151597.300	3075798.700	57.433	4.264×10^{-19}
Residual	145.000	7765411.200	53554.560		
Total	147.000	13917009.000			

	Coefficients	Standard Error	*t* Stat	*p*-value	Lower 95%	Upper 95%
Intercept	76.215	23.935	3.184	0.002	28.907	123.522
SiO_2	30.982	5.112	6.061	1.113×10^{-8}	20.878	41.085
Type	233.242	45.993	5.071	1.189×10^{-6}	142.339	324.145

No other variables can be entered into the model. Stepwise ends. The developed regression model is:
$\text{ANC} = 76.215 + 30.981 \times SiO_2 + 233.242 \times \text{Type}$

Best Subsets Analysis	
R^2T	0.449
$1 - R^2T$	0.551
n	148.000
T	4.000
$n - T$	144.000

	C_p	$p+1$	R^2	Adj. R^2	Std. Error	Consider This Model?
X_1	38.880	2.000	0.301	0.296	258.191	No
X_1X_2	3.914	3.000	0.442	0.434	231.419	No
$X_1X_2X_3$	4.000	4.000	0.449	0.438	230.693	Yes
X_1X_3	40.078	3.000	0.304	0.294	258.511	No
X_2	27.794	2.000	0.343	0.339	250.243	No
X_2X_3	23.437	3.000	0.367	0.359	246.414	No
X_3	109.535	2.000	0.030	0.024	304.003	No

The higher adjusted R^2 corresponds to the $X_1X_2X_3$ model. This is the only model with $C_p \le p+1$.

Summary Output: $X_1X_2X_3$

Regression Statistics	
Multiple R	0.670
R^2	0.449
Adjusted R^2	0.438
Standard Error	230.693
Observations	148.000

ANOVA

	df	SS	MS	F	Significance F
Regression	3.000	6253440.000	2084480.000	39.168	1.440×10^{-18}
Residual	144.000	7663569.000	53219.230		
Total	147.000	13917009.000			

	Coefficients	Standard Error	t Stat	p-value	Lower 95%	Upper 95%
Intercept	74.435	23.895	3.115	0.002	27.205	121.665
Type	218.180	47.124	4.630	8.100×10^{-6}	125.037	311.324
SiO_2	31.544	5.112	6.171	6.530×10^{-9}	21.440	41.648
Lake Area	0.0455	0.033	1.383	0.169	−0.020	0.110

$X_1X_2X_3$ model does not significantly depend on X_3 (Lake Area), so it will be reasonable to delete this variable from the model.

Summary Output: X_1X_2

Regression Statistics	
Multiple R	0.665
R^2	0.4420
Adjusted R^2	0.434
Standard Error	231.419
Observations	148.000

ANOVA

	df	SS	MS	F	Significance F
Regression	2.000	6151597.000	3075799.000	57.433	4.26×10^{-19}
Residual	145.000	7765411.000	53554.560		
Total	147.000	13917009.000			

	Coefficients	Standard Error	t Stat	p–value	Lower 95%	Upper 95%
Intercept	76.215	23.935	3.184	0.002	28.907	123.522
Type	233.242	45.993	5.071	1.190×10^{-6}	142.339	324.145
SiO_2	30.982	5.112	6.061	1.110×10^{-8}	20.878	41.085

This model is significant and depends on all explanatory variables.

Normal Probability Plot

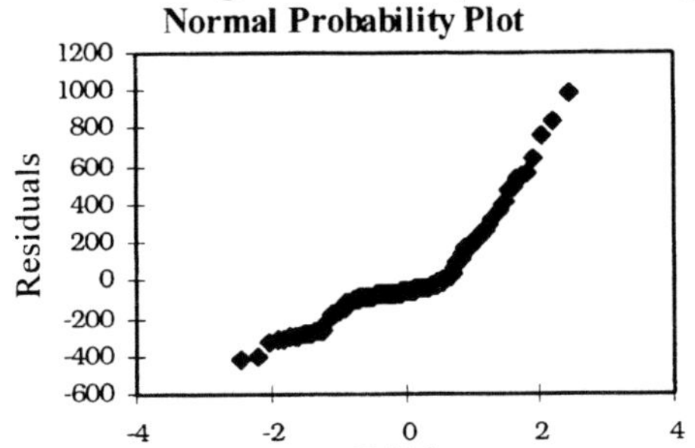

Residual analysis: There are some doubts about the adequacy of the developed regression. Let us include interaction X_1X_2 term into the regression equation.

Regression Analysis

Regression Statistics	
Multiple R	0.665
R^2	0.442
Adjusted R^2	0.431
Standard Error	232.186
Observations	148.000

ANOVA

	df	SS	MS	F	Significance F
Regression	3.000	6153918.400	2051306.100	38.050	3.606×10^{-18}
Residual	144.000	7763090.100	53910.348		
Total	147.000	13917009.000			

	Coefficients	Standard Error	t Stat	p–value	Lower 95%	Upper 95%
Intercept	74.417	25.529	2.915	0.004	23.958	124.877
Type	239.393	54.847	4.365	2.414×10^{-5}	130.984	347.802
SiO_2	32.388	8.500	3.810	0.000	15.587	49.189
Type $\times SiC_2$	–2.212	10.659	–0.207	0.836	–23.280	18.856

Due to the very large p–value 0.836 term X_1X_2 does not provide a significant effect on Y. The developed regression model is: $\text{ANC} = 76.215 + 30.981\times \text{SiO}_2 + 233.242\times \text{Type}$

64. Stepwise Analysis: Table of Results for General Stepwise, Air flow entered.

	df	SS	MS	F	Significance F
Regression	1.000	2.937	2.937	356.861	2.302×10^{-12}
Residual	16.000	0.132	0.008		
Total	17.000	3.068			

	Coefficients	Standard Error	t Stat	p–value	Lower 95%	Upper 95%
Intercept	0.186	0.061	3.037	0.008	0.056	0.316
Air flow	0.721	0.038	18.891	2.302×10^{-12}	0.640	0.802

No other variables could be entered into the model. Stepwise ends.
Developed regression model is $NTU = 0.1859851 + 0.72086 \times \text{Air Flow}$

Best Subsets Analysis	
R^2T	0.965
$1-R^2T$	0.035
n	18.000
T	5.000
$n-T$	13.000

	C_p	$p+1$	R^2	Adj. R^2	Std. Error	Consider This Model?
X_1	2.0000	2.000	0.957	0.954	0.091	No
X_1X_2	1.748	3.000	0.963	0.958	0.087	Yes
$X_1X_2X_3$	3.298	4.000	0.964	0.957	0.088	Yes
$X_1X_2X_3X_4$	5.000	5.000	0.965	0.954	0.091	Yes
$X_1X_2X_4$	3.460	4.000	0.964	0.956	0.089	Yes
X_1X_3	3.878	3.000	0.957	0.952	0.093	No
$X_1X_3X_4$	5.860	4.000	0.957	0.948	0.097	No
X_1X_4	3.978	3.000	0.957	0.951	0.094	No
X_2	268.616	2.000	0.242	0.195	0.381	No
X_2X_3	269.467	3.000	0.245	0.144	0.393	No
$X_2X_3X_4$	188.119	4.000	0.469	0.355	0.341	No
X_2X_4	186.478	3.000	0.468	0.397	0.330	No
X_3	345.846	2.000	0.035	–0.025	0.430	No
X_3X_4	202.648	3.000	0.424	0.348	0.343	No
X_4	203.025	2.000	0.418	0.382	0.334	No

Higher adjusted r^2 corresponds to the X_1X_2 model.

There are 4 models with $C_p \le p+1$: X_1X_2, $X_1X_2X_3$, $X_1X_2X_4$, and $X_1X_2X_3X_4$.

Common subset is X_1X_2. Let us test the significance of X_3 and X_4 variables in the laes three models.

Summary Output: $X_1X_2X_3$

Regression Statistics	
Multiple R	0.982
R^2	0.964
Adjusted R^2	0.957
Standard Error	0.088
Observations	18.000

ANOVA

	df	SS	MS	F	Significance F
Regression	3.000	2.959	0.986	126.186	2.27×10^{-10}
Residual	14.000	0.109	0.008		
Total	17.000	3.068			

	Coefficients	Standard Error	t Stat	p–value	Lower 95%	Upper 95%
Intercept	0.129	0.090	1.437	0.173	–0.064	0.322
Air flow	0.697	0.041	16.803	1.12×10^{-10}	0.608	0.785
Water flow	0.022	0.014	1.648	0.122	–0.007	0.051
Recirc. Water flow	–0.002	0.002	–0.689	0.502	–0.007	0.003

Variables X_2 and X_3 in this model are not significant.

Summary Output: $X_1X_2X_4$

Regression Statistics	
Multiple R	0.982
R^2	0.964
Adjusted R^2	0.956
Standard Error	0.089
Observations	18.000

ANOVA

	df	SS	MS	F	Significance F
Regression	3.000	2.958	0.986	124.605	2.47×10^{-10}
Residual	14.000	0.111	0.008		
Total	17.000	3.068			

	Coefficients	Standard Error	t Stat	p–value	Lower 95%	Upper 95%
Intercept	0.110	0.082	1.330	0.205	–0.067	0.287
Air flow	0.710	0.051	13.872	1.42×10^{-9}	0.600	0.820
Water flow	0.022	0.014	1.618	0.128	–0.007	0.052
Orifice Diameter	–0.025	0.045	–0.547	0.593	–0.122	0.073

Variables X_2 and X_4 in this model are not significant.

Summary Output: $X_1X_2X_3X_4$

Regression Statistics	
Multiple R	0.982
R^2	0.965
Adjusted R^2	0.954
Standard Error	0.091
Observations	18.000

ANOVA

	df	SS	MS	F	Significance F
Regression	4.000	2.961	0.740	89.966	2.44×10^{-9}
Residual	13.000	0.107	0.008		
Total	17.000	3.068			

	Coefficients	Standard Error	t Stat	p–value	Lower 95%	Upper 95%
Intercept	0.137	0.093	1.469	0.166	–0.065	0.339
Air Flow	0.713	0.052	13.606	4.57×10^{-9}	0.600	0.826
Water Flow	0.024	0.014	1.691	0.115	–0.007	0.055
Recirc. Water Flow	–0.002	0.002	–0.678	0.509	–0.007	0.004
Orifice Diameter	–0.025	0.046	–0.546	0.595	–0.125	0.075

Variables X_2, X_3 and X_4 in this model are not significant.

Let us test the common set model X_1X_2.

Summary Output: X_1X_2

Regression Statistics	
Multiple R	0.981
R^2	0.963
Adjusted R^2	0.958
Standard Error	0.087
Observations	18.000

ANOVA

	df	SS	MS	F	Significance F
Regression	2.000	2.955	1.478	195.906	1.78×10^{-11}
Residual	15.000	0.113	0.008		
Total	17.000	3.068			

	Coefficients	Standard Error	t Stat	p–value	Lower 95%	Upper 95%
Intercept	0.102	0.079	1.286	0.218	–0.067	0.271
Air Flow	0.693	0.040	17.127	2.94×10^{-11}	0.607	0.780
Water Flow	0.020	0.013	1.567	0.138	–0.007	0.048

Variables X_2, X_3 and X_4 in this model are not significant.

There is only one significant variable in the models X_1X_2, $X_1X_2X_3$, $X_1X_2X_4$, and $X_1X_2X_3X_4$. This is the variable X_1.

Let us develop and study a simple regression Y on X_1.

Regression Analysis

Regression Statistics	
Multiple R	0.978
R^2	0.957
Adjusted R^2	0.954
Standard Error	0.091
Observations	18

ANOVA

	df	**SS**	**MS**	***F***	**Significance *F***
Regression	1.000	2.937	2.937	356.861	2.302×10^{-12}
Residual	16.000	0.132	0.008		
Total	17.000	3.068			

	Coefficients	**Standard Error**	***t* Stat**	***p*–value**	**Lower 95%**	**Upper 95%**
Intercept	0.186	0.061	3.037	0.008	0.056	0.316
Air flow	0.721	0.038	18.891	2.302×10^{-12}	0.640	0.802

This model is significant.

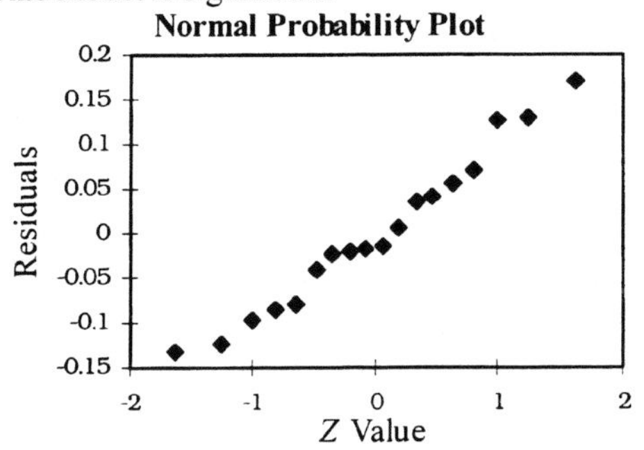

Simple regression model seems to be adequate.
Developed regression model is
$NTU = 0.1859851 + 0.72086 \times \text{Air Flow}$

65. Stepwise Analysis: Table of Results for General Stepwise, Soil radiation entered.

	df	**SS**	**MS**	***F***	**Significance *F***
Regression	1.000	2.139	2.139	7.932	0.008
Residual	38.000	10.245	0.270		
Total	39.000	12.384			

	Coefficients	**Standard Error**	***t* Stat**	***p*–value**	**Lower 95%**	**Upper 95%**
Intercept	0.611	0.100	6.128	3.794×10^{-7}	0.409	0.813
Soil Radiation	0.000	0.000	2.816	0.008	0.000	0.001

No other variables can be entered into the model. Stepwise ends.The developed regression model is:
Radon concentration $= 0.641 + 0.000 \times$ Soil radiation

Best Subsets Analysis	
R^2T	0.498
$1-R^2T$	0.502
n	40.000
T	8.000
$n-T$	32.000

	C_p	$p+1$	R^2	Adj. R^2	Std. Error	Consider This Model?
X_1	16.739	2.000	0.173	0.151	0.519	No
X_1X_2	18.651	3.000	0.174	0.129	0.526	No
$X_1X_2X_3$	15.427	4.000	0.256	0.194	0.506	No
$X_1X_2X_3X_4$	4.970	5.000	0.451	0.389	0.441	Yes
$X_1X_2X_3X_4X_5$	6.808	6.000	0.454	0.374	0.450	No
$X_1X_2X_3X_4X_5X_6$	8.803	7.000	0.454	0.355	0.453	No
$X_1X_2X_3X_4X_5X_6X_7$	8.000	8.000	0.498	0.388	0.441	Yes
$X_1X_2X_3X_4X_5X_7$	6.004	7.000	0.498	0.407	0.434	Yes
$X_1X_2X_3X_4X_6$	6.886	6.000	0.452	0.372	0.446	No
$X_1X_2X_3X_4X_6X_7$	6.679	7.000	0.487	0.394	0.439	Yes
$X_1X_2X_3X_4X_7$	5.476	6.000	0.475	0.398	0.437	Yes
$X_1X_2X_3X_5$	17.179	5.000	0.260	0.175	0.512	No
$X_1X_2X_3X_5X_6$	19.133	6.000	0.261	0.152	0.519	No
$X_1X_2X_3X_5X_6X_7$	20.982	7.000	0.263	0.129	0.526	No
$X_1X_2X_3X_5X_7$	19.030	6.000	0.262	0.154	0.518	No
$X_1X_2X_3X_6$	17.348	5.000	0.257	0.172	0.513	No
$X_1X_2X_3X_6X_7$	19.301	6.000	0.258	0.149	0.520	No
$X_1X_2X_3X_7$	17.420	5.000	0.256	0.171	0.513	No
$X_1X_2X_4$	5.261	4.000	0.416	0.367	0.448	No
$X_1X_2X_4X_5$	6.898	5.000	0.421	0.355	0.453	No
$X_1X_2X_4X_5X_6$	6.897	6.000	0.453	0.372	0.447	No
$X_1X_2X_4X_5X_6X_7$	6.408	7.000	0.492	0.399	0.437	Yes
$X_1X_2X_4X_5X_7$	8.892	6.000	0.421	0.336	0.459	No
$X_1X_2X_4X_6$	4.903	5.000	0.452	0.390	0.440	Yes
$X_1X_2X_4X_6X_7$	4.680	6.000	0.487	0.412	0.432	Yes
$X_1X_2X_4X_7$	7.149	5.000	0.417	0.351	0.454	No
$X_1X_2X_5$	19.983	4.000	0.185	0.117	0.530	No
$X_1X_2X_5X_6$	17.460	5.000	0.256	0.170	0.513	No
$X_1X_2X_5X_6X_7$	19.394	6.000	0.257	0.147	0.520	No
$X_1X_2X_5X_7$	19.793	5.000	0.219	0.130	0.526	No
$X_1X_2X_6$	15.460	4.000	0.256	0.193	0.506	No
$X_1X_2X_6X_7$	17.402	5.000	0.256	0.171	0.513	No

(continued)	C_p	$p+1$	R^2	Adj. R^2	Std. Error	Consider This Model?
$X_1X_2X_7$	17.804	4.000	0.219	0.154	0.518	No
X_1X_3	16.819	3.000	0.203	0.160	0.517	No
$X_1X_3X_4$	17.360	4.000	0.226	0.161	0.516	No
$X_1X_3X_4X_5$	19.346	5.000	0.226	0.137	0.523	No
$X_1X_3X_4X_5X_6$	21.323	6.000	0.226	0.113	0.531	No
$X_1X_3X_4X_5X_6X_7$	22.979	7.000	0.232	0.092	0.537	No
$X_1X_3X_4X_5X_7$	21.002	6.000	0.231	0.118	0.529	No
$X_1X_3X_4X_6$	19.360	5.000	0.226	0.137	0.523	No
$X_1X_3X_4X_6X_7$	21.113	6.000	0.230	0.116	0.530	No
$X_1X_3X_4X_7$	19.155	5.000	0.229	0.141	0.522	No
$X_1X_3X_5$	18.756	4.000	0.204	0.137	0.523	No
$X_1X_3X_5X_6$	20.718	5.000	0.204	0.113	0.531	No
$X_1X_3X_5X_6X_7$	22.616	6.000	0.206	0.089	0.538	No
$X_1X_3X_5X_7$	20.656	5.000	0.205	0.115	0.530	No
$X_1X_3X_6$	18.811	4.000	0.203	0.137	0.524	No
$X_1X_3X_6X_7$	20.770	5.000	0.204	0.113	0.531	No
$X_1X_3X_7$	18.798	4.000	0.203	0.137	0.524	No
X_1X_4	15.396	3.000	0.225	0.183	0.509	No
$X_1X_4X_5$	17.374	4.000	0.225	0.161	0.516	No
$X_1X_4X_5X_6$	19.354	5.000	0.226	0.137	0.523	No
$X_1X_4X_5X_6X_7$	21.058	6.000	0.23	0.117	0.529	No
$X_1X_4X_5X_7$	19.310	5.000	0.226	0.138	0.523	No
$X_1X_4X_6$	17.361	4.000	0.226	0.161	0.516	No
$X_1X_4X_6X_7$	19.113	5.000	0.230	0.142	0.522	No
$X_1X_4X_7$	17.371	4.000	0.226	0.161	0.516	No
X_1X_5	18.275	3.000	0.180	0.136	0.524	No
$X_1X_5X_6$	18.836	4.000	0.203	0.136	0.524	No
$X_1X_5X_6X_7$	20.779	5.000	0.203	0.112	0.531	No
$X_1X_5X_7$	19.464	4.000	0.193	0.125	0.527	No
X_1X_6	16.839	3.000	0.203	0.159	0.517	No
$X_1X_6X_7$	18.792	4.000	0.203	0.137	0.524	No
X_1X_7	17.478	3.000	0.192	0.149	0.520	No
X_2	27.736	2.000	0.000	–0.026	0.571	No
X_2X_3	22.458	3.000	0.114	0.066	0.544	No
$X_2X_3X_4$	18.558	4.000	0.207	0.141	0.522	No
$X_2X_3X_4X_5$	19.508	5.000	0.223	0.135	0.524	No
$X_2X_3X_4X_5X_6$	20.883	6.000	0.233	0.120	0.528	No

(continued)	C_p	$p+1$	R^2	Adj. R^2	Std. Error	Consider This Model?
$X_2X_3X_4X_5X_6X_7$	10.157	7.000	0.433	0.330	0.461	No
$X_2X_3X_4X_5X_7$	8.2537	6.000	0.431	0.348	0.455	No
$X_2X_3X_4X_6$	18.887	5.000	0.233	0.145	0.521	No
$X_2X_3X_4X_6X_7$	9.339	6.000	0.414	0.328	0.462	No
$X_2X_3X_4X_7$	11.497	5.000	0.349	0.275	0.480	No
$X_2X_3X_5$	23.523	4.000	0.129	0.056	0.547	No
$X_2X_3X_5X_6$	25.271	5.000	0.133	0.034	0.554	No
$X_2X_3X_5X_6X_7$	22.807	6.000	0.203	0.086	0.539	No
$X_2X_3X_5X_7$	20.826	5.000	0.203	0.112	0.531	No
$X_2X_3X_6$	23.292	4.000	0.133	0.060	0.546	No
$X_2X_3X_6X_7$	21.478	5.000	0.192	0.100	0.535	No
$X_2X_3X_7$	21.443	4.000	0.162	0.092	0.537	No
X_2X_4	27.763	3.000	0.031	–0.021	0.569	No
$X_2X_4X_5$	28.710	4.000	0.048	–0.032	0.572	No
$X_2X_4X_5X_6$	20.111	5.000	0.214	0.124	0.527	No
$X_2X_4X_5X_6X_7$	8.253	6.000	0.431	0.348	0.455	No
$X_2X_4X_5X_7$	11.570	5.000	0.348	0.273	0.480	No
$X_2X_4X_6$	20.231	4.000	0.181	0.112	0.531	No
$X_2X_4X_6X_7$	8.525	5.000	0.396	0.327	0.462	No
$X_2X_4X_7$	12.098	4.000	0.308	0.251	0.488	No
X_2X_5	28.517	3.000	0.019	–0.034	0.573	No
$X_2X_5X_6$	23.646	4.000	0.127	0.054	0.548	No
$X_2X_5X_6X_7$	20.914	5.000	0.201	0.110	0.532	No
$X_2X_5X_7$	21.928	4.000	0.154	0.084	0.539	No
X_2X_6	22.912	3.000	0.107	0.059	0.547	No
$X_2X_6X_7$	19.912	4.000	0.186	0.118	0.529	No
X_2X_7	21.139	3.000	0.135	0.088	0.538	No
X_3	20.606	2.000	0.112	0.089	0.538	No
X_3X_4	18.711	3.000	0.173	0.128	0.526	No
$X_3X_4X_5$	20.315	4.000	0.179	0.111	0.531	No
$X_3X_4X_5X_6$	22.160	5.000	0.182	0.088	0.538	No
$X_3X_4X_5X_6X_7$	21.412	6.000	0.225	0.111	0.531	No
$X_3X_4X_5X_7$	19.413	5.000	0.225	0.136	0.524	No
$X_3X_4X_6$	20.160	4.000	0.182	0.114	0.531	No
$X_3X_4X_6X_7$	19.651	5.000	0.221	0.132	0.525	No
$X_3X_4X_7$	18.171	4.000	0.2123	0.147	0.520	No
X_3X_5	21.526	3.000	0.129	0.082	0.540	No

(continued)	C_p	$p+1$	R^2	Adj. R^2	Std. Error	Consider This Model?
$X_3X_5X_6$	23.273	4.000	0.133	0.061	0.546	No
$X_3X_5X_6X_7$	22.029	5.000	0.184	0.091	0.537	No
$X_3X_5X_7$	20.030	4.000	0.184	0.116	0.530	No
X_3X_6	21.294	3.000	0.133	0.086	0.539	No
$X_3X_6X_7$	20.433	4.000	0.177	0.109	0.532	No
X_3X_7	19.641	3.000	0.159	0.113	0.531	No
X_4	26.171	2.000	0.025	–0.001	0.564	No
X_4X_5	26.799	3.000	0.046	–0.005	0.565	No
$X_4X_5X_6$	20.557	4.000	0.176	0.107	0.533	No
$X_4X_5X_6X_7$	19.448	5.000	0.224	0.136	0.524	No
$X_4X_5X_7$	17.928	4.000	0.217	0.152	0.519	No
X_4X_6	19.565	3.000	0.160	0.114	0.530	No
$X_4X_6X_7$	17.820	4.000	0.218	0.153	0.519	No
X_4X_7	16.484	3.000	0.208	0.165	0.515	No
X_5	26.726	2.000	0.016	–0.010	0.566	No
X_5X_6	21.651	3.000	0.127	0.080	0.541	No
$X_5X_6X_7$	20.099	4.000	0.183	0.115	0.530	No
X_5X_7	19.955	3.000	0.154	0.108	0.532	No
X_6	21.107	2.000	0.104	0.081	0.540	No
X_6X_7	18.685	3.000	0.174	0.129	0.526	No
X_7	19.177	2.000	0.134	0.112	0.531	No

List of best models: $X_1X_2X_3X_4$, $X_1X_2X_3X_4X_5X_6X_7$, $X_1X_2X_3X_4X_5X_7$, $X_1X_2X_3X_4X_6X_7$, $X_1X_2X_3X_4X_7$, $X_1X_2X_4X_5X_6X_7$, $X_1X_2X_4X_6$, $X_1X_2X_4X_6X_7$

Common subset is $X_1X_2X_4$. This will be a base model (BM).

Model	Including to the BM	p-value	Significantly Different From BM
$X_1X_2X_3X_4$	X_3	0.139	No
$X_1X_2X_3X_4X_5X_6X_7$	X_3	0.528	No
	X_5	0.416	No
	X_6	0.951	No
	X_7	0.104	No
$X_1X_2X_3X_4X_5X_7$	X_3	0.032	Yes
	X_5	0.227	No
	X_7	0.098	No
$X_1X_2X_3X_4X_6X_7$	X_3	0.976	No
	X_6	0.376	No
	X_7	0.145	No
$X_1X_2X_3X_4X_7$	X_3	0.062	No
	X_7	0.226	No
$X_1X_2X_4X_5X_6X_7$	X_5	0.602	No
	X_6	0.040	Yes
	X_7	0.121	No
$X_1X_2X_4X_6$	X_6	0.133	No
$X_1X_2X_4X_6X_7$	X_6	0.038	Yes
	X_7	0.138	No

Including X_3 to the BM provides a model that does not significantly differ from BM. The same is true for including X_6.

Summary Output: $X_1X_2X_4$

Regression Statistics	
Multiple R	0.645
R^2	0.416
Adjusted R^2	0.367
Standard Error	0.448
Observations	40.000

ANOVA

	df	SS	MS	F	Significance F
Regression	3.000	5.146	1.715	8.531	0.000
Residual	36.000	7.238	0.201		
Total	39.000	12.384			

	Coefficients	Standard Error	t Stat	p-value	Lower 95%	Upper 95%
Intercept	−18.201	5.566	−3.270	0.002	−29.489	−6.913
Soil radiation	0.001	0.000	4.866	2.26×10^{-5}	0.001	0.002
Soil temperature	0.287	0.084	3.424	0.002	0.117	0.458
Wind speed	−0.408	0.106	−3.856	0.000	−0.622	−0.193

Residual analysis:

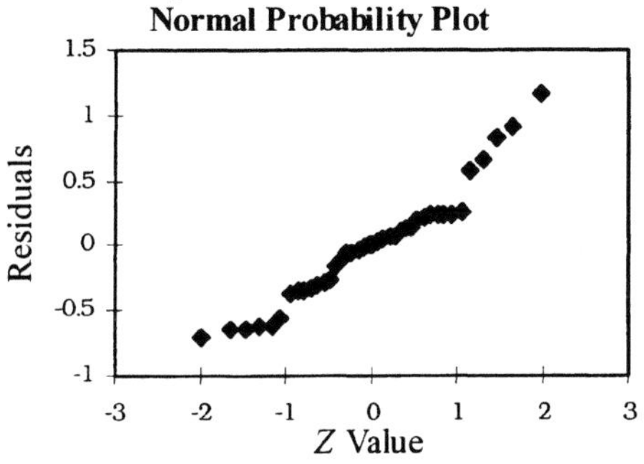

The developed regression model is:
Radon concentration = $-18.201 + 0.001 \times$ Soil radiation $+0.288 \times$ Soil temperature $- 0.408 \times$ Wind speed

66. There are more than 7 variables in algae.xls file, so PHStat cannot analyze this data.
Below is MINITAB's solution:

Stepwise Regression: Algal growth versus Water veloci; Volume rate ; ...

```
Alpha-to-Enter: 0.15 Alpha-to-Remove: 0.15
Response is Algal gr on 14 predictors, with N= 66
```

Step	1	2	3	4
Constant	50.16	27.48	52.25	66.14
Dissolve	-4.0	-17.1	-19.1	-20.1
T-Value	-3.31	-3.42	-3.80	-4.00
P-Value	0.002	0.001	0.000	0.000
Saturati		1.55	1.65	1.70
T-Value		2.70	2.92	3.03
P-Value		0.009	0.005	0.004
TDS			-41	-58
T-Value			-1.80	-2.28
P-Value			0.076	0.026
S	17.2	16.4	16.1	15.9
R-Sq	14.60	23.46	27.27	29.76
R-Sq(adj)	13.27	21.03	23.75	25.15
C-p	8.7	3.4	2.2	2.2
PRESS	19852.9	18124.4	18249.8	18180.4
R-Sq(pred)	10.12	17.95	17.38	17.69

Developed regression model is:
Algal growth = $66.14 - 20.1 \times$ Dissolved Oxygen $+ 1.70 \times$ Saturation of Oxygen $- 58 \times TDS - 0.61 \times$ Leaves

Best Subsets Regression: Algal growth versus Water veloci; Volume rate ; ...

```
Response is Algal gr
                                    W V R       P D S
                                    a o a A N N h i a
                                    t l i m i i o s t     L
                                    e u n m t t s s u   e R S L
                                    r m f o r r p o r   a o t i
                                      e a n i a h l a T v o e g
                                    v   l i t t a v t D e t m h
Vars  R-Sq  R-Sq(adj)   C-p       S e r l a e e t e i S s s s t
   1  14.6       13.3   8.7  17.168               X
   1   9.2        7.8  13.2  17.702                 X
   2  23.5       21.0   3.4  16.382               X X
   2  18.5       15.9   7.5  16.905               X         X
   3  27.3       23.8   2.2  16.097               X X X
   3  25.2       21.5   4.0  16.328               X X       X
   4  29.8       25.1   2.2  15.949               X X X X
   4  29.1       24.5   2.7  16.018               X X X     X
   5  31.8       26.1   2.5  15.847               X X X X   X
   5  30.6       24.8   3.5  15.986               X X X X X
   6  33.4       26.6   3.2  15.795 X             X X X X   X
   6  32.9       26.0   3.6  15.853               X X X X X X
   7  34.9       27.0   3.9  15.746 X             X X X X X X
   7  34.5       26.6   4.3  15.797 X X           X X X X   X
   8  36.2       27.3   4.8  15.723 X X     X     X X X X   X
   8  35.8       26.8   5.1  15.767 X X     X X   X X X     X
   9  37.7       27.7   5.6  15.679 X X     X     X X X X X X
   9  37.2       27.1   6.0  15.739 X X     X X   X X X X   X
  10  38.1       26.9   7.3  15.766 X X     X X   X X X X X X
  10  37.9       26.6   7.4  15.794 X X X   X     X X X X X X
  11  38.2       25.6   9.2  15.901 X X X   X X   X X X X X X
  11  38.2       25.6   9.2  15.903 X X     X X X X X X X X X
  12  38.3       24.3  11.1  16.039 X X X   X X X X X X X X X
  12  38.2       24.3  11.1  16.043 X X   X X X X X X X X X X
  13  38.4       23.0  13.0  16.176 X X X X X X X X X X X X X
  13  38.3       22.9  13.1  16.190 X X X   X X X X X X X X X X
  14  38.4       21.5  15.0  16.333 X X X X X X X X X X X X X X
```

Based on R^2 and adjusted R^2, the best multiple regression model must include Dissolve, Saturation, TDS and Leaves variables. This is the same result as found in the stepwise regression procedure.

67. There are more than 7 variables in univ&col.xls file, so PHStat cannot analyze this data.
Below is MINITAB's solution:

Stepwise Regression: Average indebted versus Type of term; Location; ...

```
Alpha-to-Enter: 0.15  Alpha-to-Remove: 0.15
Response is Average  on  7 predictors, with N= 80
```

```
    Step            1        2
Constant        6.869   13.239
```

```
Annual t        0.306    0.409
T-Value          4.14     4.15
P-Value         0.000    0.000
```

```
Average              -0.0072
T-Value                -1.56
P-Value                0.122
```

```
Average              -0.0072
T-Value                -1.56
P-Value                0.122
```

```
S               3.88      3.84
R-Sq           17.98     20.50
R-Sq(adj)      16.93     18.44
C-p             -0.1      -0.5
PRESS        1227.43   1248.15
R-Sq(pred)     14.12     12.67
```

Developed regression model is:
Average indebtedness at graduation = 13.239 + 0.409 × Annual total cost − 0.007 × Average total SAT

Best Subsets Regression: Average inde versus Type of term; Location; ...

```
Response is Average

                                                             L       T R A
                                                           T o T A O o n
                                                           y c y v E o n
                                                           p a p e F m u
                                                           e t e r L   a
                                                             i   a 5 a l
                                                           o o o g 5 n
Vars   R-Sq    R-Sq(adj)      C-p         S                f n f e 0 d t
   1   18.0         16.9     -0.1    3.8766                            X
   1   16.3         15.3      1.4    3.9152                    X
   2   20.5         18.4     -0.5    3.8412                      X     X
   2   18.8         16.7      1.1    3.8826                    X       X
   3   21.0         17.9      1.1    3.8548                      X X   X
   3   20.9         17.7      1.2    3.8575                    X X     X
   4   21.7         17.6      2.4    3.8619                    X X X   X
   4   21.3         17.1      2.8    3.8737                X     X X   X
   5   22.0         16.7      4.2    3.8824                X   X X X   X
   5   21.8         16.5      4.3    3.8857                    X X X X X
   6   22.1         15.7      6.0    3.9049                X   X X X X X
   6   22.0         15.6      6.1    3.9065                X X X X X   X
   7   22.2         14.6      8.0    3.9307                X X X X X X X
```

Based on the R^2 and adjusted R^2, the best multiple regression model must include the Average total SAT and Annual total variables. This is the same result as found in the stepwise regression procedure.